An Illustrated Dictionary of Ceramics

GEORGE SAVAGE
HAROLD NEWMAN

An Illustrated Dictionary of Ceramics

defining 3,054 terms relating to wares, materials, processes, styles, patterns, and shapes from antiquity to the present day

with an introductory list of the principal European factories and their marks, compiled by JOHN CUSHION, formerly of the Department of Ceramics, Victoria and Albert Museum, London

604 illustrations

For Wendy

First published in paperback in the United States of America in 1985 by Thames & Hudson Inc., 500 Fifth Avenue, New York, New York 10110
Reprinted 2000

Library of Congress Catalog Card Number 85-51073
ISBN 0-500-27380-4

Printed and bound in Singapore by C.S. Graphics

Preface

This book is primarily a dictionary of terms – nouns, verbs, adjectives, and descriptive names and phrases – encountered in the world of ceramics. Some so-called dictionaries of pottery and porcelain, although useful and excellent in themselves, are in fact encyclopaedias, being in reality treatises arranged in alphabetical order rather than in any historical or geographical sequence, and include lengthy historical and biographical material. This dictionary, on the other hand, deals with potting, painting, and pieces, rather than with potteries, places, and people, but includes an introductory section, by Mr John Cushion of the Victoria and Albert Museum, serving as a reference list of many of the European factories, modellers, decorators, etc., mentioned in the definitions; this list affords the necessary background information on locations, historical dates, and personalities, together with the main factory-marks found on ceramic wares.

Often, in fact too often, certain terms are used loosely and interchangeably by writers on ceramic subjects (as well as on other branches of the arts); examples are 'amorino' and 'putto', 'cover' and 'lid', and such deceptively simple terms as 'rim' and 'edge'. We have tried to break new ground in defining some terms, occasionally without the supporting authority of the standard dictionaries, and have drawn distinctions which seem helpful and valid in the context of ceramics. If the definitions in this dictionary win the acceptance and support of writers, museum experts, dealers, auction houses, and especially collectors, they will become the basis for a greater degree of precision and mutual understanding. The hope that this would result was a major motivating force in the writing of this dictionary.

In planning the dictionary, it was necessary, after deciding on the type of terms to be defined, to consider the range of coverage – whether to seek to offer an exhaustive dictionary with all the esoteric terms that a specialist might wish to look up, or a limited glossary useful to the neophyte collector. The former course would have led to a vast field extending to the farthest reaches of time and geography, which would have rendered a single volume both unwieldy and far too cluttered for most interested persons. The latter course would have largely duplicated the many glossaries already in existence, either at the end of general treatises or in small handbooks for beginners. We have chosen a middle course, aiming for a reasonably comprehensive dictionary with enough basic terms to meet the needs of those just entering the field, and also – for collectors generally – a wide range of specialized terms rarely defined elsewhere.

Among the terms included here and not generally listed elsewhere are the names of various forms of vase, coffee-cup, handle, spout, finial, etc., which are sufficiently important to have recognized designations; of outstanding dinner-services (with a brief description of the decoration); of the better-known Robert Hancock engravings found on English transfer-printed porcelain; of significant porcelain and pottery figures and groups; and of many of the established glazes and ground patterns. Geographically, the terms defined range from English and Continental (and some American) wares to those of the Middle East and of China, Japan, and other countries in the Far East. The time span extends from the pottery of antiquity to contemporary wares. Particular attention has been given to terms relating to the making and decorating of ceramic ware, as well as the materials and tools employed.

It may seem at first glance a supererogation to define such common objects as a plate, bowl, jug, or handle, but it will soon be seen that this approach not only leads to an exactitude in terminology often ignored in practice, but provides pegs on which to hang cross-references to various specific types of such objects. Indeed, the maximum usefulness of this book lies in its extensive use of cross-references (which are printed in small capitals). By this method, each definition could be confined to essentials and duplication avoided, and a cue could be given for finding related subjects, whether a term more basic than the word defined, or some specific example, e.g. a glaze, process, style of decoration, or type of object.

In preparing a book of this type and scope, it is normal, indeed inevitable, to draw on the writings and knowledge of predecessors and contemporaries, whether they be the authors of previous dictionaries or encyclopaedias, of treatises on certain factories or countries, or of magazine articles. However, to mention any sources, even by way of a brief bibliography, would over-emphasize those named and be unjust to the many others inevitably omitted. We express here our appreciation to them all, albeit in some cases we have had to modify some authors' views, in a few cases even to disagree.

We wish also to express our thanks to the various museums, antique dealers, and private collectors, and especially to Sotheby's and Christie's, for their generous co-operation and assistance in making available photographs for use as illustrations. Among the museums that were especially helpful with furnishing photographs were: in London, the Victoria and Albert Museum, the British Museum, the Wallace Collection, the Percival David Foundation of Chinese Art, and the Wellcome Museum; in Stoke-on-Trent, the City Museum and Art Gallery; in the United States, the William Rockhill Nelson Gallery of Art in Kansas City, Mo., the Smithsonian Institution (National Museum of History and Technology) in Washington, D.C., the Wadsworth Atheneum in Hartford, Conn., and the Buten Museum of Wedgwood in Merion, Pa. Substantial assistance was also received from the Worcester Royal Porcelain Company and Josiah Wedgwood & Sons Ltd. The source of each illustration is shown in the caption.

In concluding this Preface to a dictionary for the use of collectors of ceramics, it seems appropriate to offer a definition of the word 'collector'. None could be more felicitous than that given by Thomas Greg, whose superb collection of English pottery was given by him to the City Art Gallery, Manchester:

'No collector who is worthy of the name amasses a number of objects, be they pieces of old silver, old pottery, coins or postage stamps, simply for the selfish pleasure of looking at them or gloating over the fact that amongst his gallimaufry of specimens he possesses one or more than his less-favoured competitor has been able to attain. He opens to himself and others new fields of knowledge; his newly awakened sense of wonder reveals his own depth of ignorance and as he endeavours to remedy it, he sees the horizon widen out before him; he is filled with the zeal of a missionary and he wishes to share his new possession with others whose eyes are temporarily shut and their ears closed.'

GEORGE SAVAGE
HAROLD NEWMAN

1973

The idea for a comprehensive dictionary of ceramic terms, as distinguished from the many extant encyclopaedias of people and places, was conceived by Harold Newman, who compiled the list of some 3,000 entries, drafted many of the definitions, gathered most of the illustrations, and developed the format and style of the book. Many entries have been written by me, especially those relating to the Far East, and all have been edited and checked for accuracy by me.

G.S.

Principal European Factories and their Marks

This list, compiled by JOHN CUSHION, formerly of the Department of Ceramics, Victoria and Albert Museum, London, includes principal factories in each country. The major producing countries are subdivided as appropriate into sections on porcelain and types of pottery, the factories being listed under individual place-names or regional names, e.g. Staffordshire. Words and phrases printed in small capitals refer to entries in the dictionary.

Factory and proprietor(s)	*Products, styles, and personalities*	*Marks*
AUSTRIA		
Vienna, *c.* 1719–1864		
C. I. du Paquier, *c.* 1719–44. State factory from 1744; Konrad von Sorgenthal, director 1784–1805; Matthias Niedermeyer, director 1805–64.	Hard-paste porcelain. Tableware of first period in extreme baroque style. Many pieces decorated by HAUSMALER. From 1744 rococo styles in the manner of Meissen (cf. *Germany* below). In the Sorgenthal period lavish and meticulously painted decoration covering the entire surface; revived in mid-19th century. Biscuit figures.	first used in 1744; often copied by late 19th-century imitators.
BELGIUM		
Tournai, 1750–late 19th century		
François-Joseph Peterinck and family successors, under royal patronage, 1751–1885.	Wares and figures of soft-paste porcelain, similar to those of Worcester, Derby, Meissen, and Sèvres; sometimes decorated at The Hague. In the 19th century mostly earthenware.	in various colours.
Henri de Bettignies, *c.* 1817–50.	Reproductions of Sèvres, Worcester, and Chelsea wares.	
Brussels		
J.S. Vaume (at Schaerbeek), 1786–90.	Hard-paste porcelain. Popular Paris styles.	B
Chrétien Kuhne (at Etterbeek), 1787–1803.	Hard-paste porcelain. French-style tablewares. Figures in biscuit or glazed porcelain.	
DENMARK		
Copenhagen		
L. Fournier, at invitation of Frederick V, 1759–65.	Soft-paste porcelain. Tablewares with a slight yellowish tinge and a dull glaze.	F5
F.H. Müller, 1771–present. Factory taken over by Frederick V in 1779 and subsequently known as the Royal Copenhagen Manufactory.	Hard-paste porcelain with a cold-grey body. Early wares similar to those of Fürstenberg (cf. *Germany* below); later wares in NEO-CLASSICAL STYLES.	from 1775 on.
ENGLAND		
	PORCELAIN	
Chelsea (London), *c.* 1745–84		
Charles Gouyn, jeweller, *c.* 1745–49; Nicholas Sprimont (1716–71), silversmith and manager, later proprietor, *c.* 1745–70; William Duesbury I, 1770–84. (Chelsea-Derby period; cf. Derby below.)	Soft-paste porcelain. Tableware and figures in Meissen style. Later wares in the style of Sèvres. Services for royal presentation and other costly and decorative wares. All figures slip-cast. Joseph Willems, modeller; Jeffryes Hamett O'Neale and John Donaldson, painters.	 incised. 1745–50, in underglaze blue; 1750–51, raised on a medallion; 1752–56, red; 1756 and after, gold.
Chelsea ('Girl-in-a-Swing' factory), *c.* 1749–54		
Probably under the direction of Charles Gouyn.	Soft-paste porcelain of a very glassy type. Few useful wares or figures, many TOYS.	
Bow (nr London), *c.* 1747–76		
Edward Heylyn and Thomas Frye, first patentees of a porcelain body in England, 5 April 1745.	Soft-paste porcelain including bone-ash. Many tablewares decorated in underglaze blue. Figures made by press-moulding. Later enamelled wares in Sèvres styles.	in red enamel. A on figures, underglaze blue.

Factory and proprietor(s)	*Products, styles, and personalities*	*Marks*
Lowestoft (Suffolk), *c.* 1757–1802 Four partners including Robert Browne, the chemist.	Soft-paste porcelain including bone-ash. Decorated only in underglaze blue until *c.* 1770, after which enamel colours were also used. Only a few figures made.	3 5 numbers 1 to 17 in underglaze blue; crossed swords of Meissen and crescent of Worcester also copied.
Bristol (Gloucestershire) Lund's Bristol factory, *c.* 1748–52; Benjamin Lund and William Miller. Factory taken over by Worcester (q.v.) partnership in 1752.	Soaprock porcelain. Small tablewares decorated in underglaze blue or enamel colours. Few figures.	'BRISTOLL' moulded in relief.
Champion's factory: see under Plymouth below.		
Worcester (Worcestershire), 1751–present Founded by Dr John Wall and other partners. Dr Wall period, or First period, 1751–76; Davis and Flight period, 1776–93; Flight & Barr, 1793–1807; Barr, Flight & Barr, 1807–13; Flight, Barr & Barr, 1813–40; Chamberlain's, 1840–52; Kerr & Binns, 1852–62; Worcester Royal Porcelain Co., 1862–present.	Soaprock porcelain of Bristol (q.v.) type until the the adoption of bone-china in the 19th century. Many useful wares in blue and white, and polychrome enamels; much use of transfer prints. Very few figures. Many useful wares of the Davis and Flight period more certainly identifiable following recent excavations at Worcester and Caughley (see below). Modern wares include DOUGHTY BIRDS.	in underglaze blue.  in underglaze blue, usually on pieces with oriental decoration. on transfer-printed wares. usually in blue.
Chamberlain's factory, *c.* 1786–1840 Robert Chamberlain left earlier Worcester factory to found his own decorating firm; became manufacturer from *c.* 1791. Took over Flight, Barr & Barr, 1840.	Good, well-decorated tablewares in soaprock porcelain; later in highly decorated bone-china.	
Derby, *c.* 1750–1848 André Planché, *c.* 1750–56.	Soft-paste porcelain. Rare figures made prior to establishment of the Duesbury factory.	
William Duesbury I, 1756–86.	Soft-paste porcelain. Many wares in imitation of Meissen, especially figures; early figures have a very blued glaze.	from *c.* 1784, incised, in blue, purple or, most commonly, red.
(Chelsea-Derby period, 1770–84, with both factories under the management of Duesbury.)	Fine tablewares, many in neo-classical styles.	usually in gold.
William Duesbury II and Michael Kean, 1786–97. Michael Kean, 1797–1811. Robert Bloor, *c.* 1811–45. Thomas Clarke, 1845–48.	William Billingsley, flower painter and gilder, 1774–96.	 printed in red.
Pinxton (Derbyshire), 1796–1813 John Coke and William Billingsley, 1796–99. John Cutts, *c.* 1803–13.	Soft-paste porcelain. Many tablewares of distinctive and tasteful shapes. Decoration of scenic panels or flowers.	
Longton Hall (Staffordshire), 1749–60 W. Jenkinson, proprietor 1749–53; W. Littler, 1749–60.	Soft-paste porcelain of a glassy type; shows a distinct relationship to Staffordshire pottery. Figures show little feeling for rococo styles.	 in blue.

Factory and proprietor(s)	*Products, styles, and personalities*	*Marks*
Liverpool (Lancashire) There were many manufacturers in the area, the best known being:		
Richard Chaffers, 1756–65, succeeded by his former partner Philip Christian, 1766–76.	Soaprock porcelain similar to that of Worcester and Caughley. Underglaze-blue wares decorated in Worcester styles.	
Pennington brothers, 1769–99.	Soft-paste porcelain including bone-ash. Many wares with enamel decoration.	
Samuel Gilbody, 1754–61.	Soft-paste porcelain. Recent excavations have shown that Gilbody also made figures.	
William Reid, 1755–61.	Soft-paste porcelain containing bone-ash, and soaprock porcelain.	
Caughley (Shropshire), *c.* 1772–99 Thomas Turner, proprietor. Factory taken over in 1799 by John Rose of Coalport, who finally closed the Caughley works, *c.* 1812.	Soaprock porcelain similar to that of Worcester (see above). Good-quality tablewares, mostly in blue and white, with occasional gilt decoration. Some finely applied decoration added by the Worcester firm of Chamberlain.	Salopian either impressed or in blue.
Swansea and **Nantgarw** (South Wales), 1813–22 William Billingsley at Nantgarw 1813–14 and 1817–19, at Swansea 1815–16; T. & J. Bevington leased Swansea 1817–*c.* 1826; Nantgarw closed 1822.	Fine soft-paste porcelain of a glassy type, but costly and wasteful. Products consisted mainly of tea-services, vases, and plates; many wares decorated in London.	NANT-GARW C.W. impressed. SWANSEA impressed, printed, or written in red.
Rockingham (Swinton, Yorkshire), 1826–42 Brameld & Co. (earthenware made here from the middle of the 18th century).	Fine-quality bone-china. Services, plates, and figures. Wares often unmarked except for a single piece of a service. There is no evidence to suggest that cottages or 'shaggy' poodles were made.	printed in red, 1826–30, in purple, 1830–42.
Plymouth (Devon), 1768–70, moving to Bristol, 1770–81 William Cookworthy; Richard Champion, former manager, took over as proprietor in 1774 at Bristol. See New Hall below.	Hard-paste porcelain. Early wares decorated in underglaze blue; later wares in Sèvres styles. Figures made at both factories, many from moulds previously used at Longton Hall (Staffordshire).	in underglaze blue or enamel colours.
New Hall (Staffordshire), 1781–1835 Group of partners, who purchased the remaining rights to the hard-paste porcelain patent of Richard Champion of Bristol (see above).	Hard-paste porcelain, 1781–1812; bone-china 1812–35. Early decoration in blue-and-white and 'cottage' styles (see COTTAGE BRISTOL); some transfer printing.	 printed in enamel.

EARTHENWARE AND STONEWARE

Staffordshire

Factory and proprietor(s)	*Products, styles, and personalities*	*Marks*
Wedgwood, 1759–present Josiah Wedgwood (1730–95), Burslem, nr Stoke-on-Trent, 1759–69; Etruria factory, 1769–1940, with Thomas Bentley as partner until 1780, followed by Josiah Wedgwood II (1769–1843) and successors. Factory moved to Barlaston, nr Stoke-on-Trent, 1940.	All types of saltglazed stoneware, lead-glazed earthenware, black basaltes, jasper ware; bone-china made 1812–22 and 1878–present. Wares rarely unmarked after 1772.	Wedgwood WEDGWOOD impressed; red enamel on bone-china.

Factory and proprietor(s)	*Products, styles, and personalities*	*Marks*
Thomas Whieldon, Fenton Vivien, nr Stoke-on-Trent, 1740–80 In partnership with Josiah Wedgwood 1754–59.	Saltglazed stoneware, including SCRATCH BLUE decoration, agate ware (stoneware and earthenware), and earthenware with variegated coloured glazes.	
Wood family, Burslem nr Stoke-on-Trent Ralph Wood I (1715–72) and his son Ralph Wood II (1745–95), Hill Top factory, mid-18th century–*c.* 1801.	Chiefly earthenware figures of fine quality, some probably modelled by Jean Voyez, decorated with coloured glazes; also sauce-boats, etc.	Ra WOOD impressed or incised.
Enoch Wood (1759–1840), established at Fountain Place, 1783; subsequently Enoch Wood & Co., 1783–90; Wood & Caldwell, 1790–1818; Enoch Wood & Sons, 1818–46.	All kinds of pottery in contemporary production, including creamware, basaltes, jasper, blue-printed pearlware, perhaps porcelain. Many enamel-painted figures of good quality.	 impressed.
Spode, Stoke-on-Trent, 1770–present Josiah Spode (1733–97); Josiah Spode II (1754–1827); Josiah Spode III (d. 1829); W.T. Copeland, previously manager of London showroom, and Thomas Garrett, 1833–47 (Copeland & Garrett); W.T. Copeland, 1847–68, and family successors; Spode Ltd, 1970–	Fine-quality earthenwares, stoneware, stone-china, and bone-china. Earthenware decorated with underglaze-blue prints. Copeland's are credited with the introduction of PARIAN PORCELAIN, *c.* 1846.	 printed in black or blue. COPELAND printed, *c.* 1847–51.
Minton, Stoke-on-Trent, 1793–present Thomas Minton (1765–1836), 1793–96; Minton & Poulson, 1796–1803; Minton, Poulson & Pownall, 1803–09; Thomas Minton, 1809–17; Thomas Minton & Sons, 1817–23; Thomas Minton & Co., 1823–36; Minton & Boyle, 1836–41; Herbert Minton & Co., 1841–73; Mintons, 1873–83; Mintons Ltd, 1883–1968; Minton Ltd, 1968–	Good-quality earthenwares and bone-china, and Parian porcelain by well-known modellers. PÂTE-SUR-PÂTE by Marc-Louis Solon.	M 780 in blue enamel, *c.* 1800–39.  printed, *c.* 1822–36
Yorkshire		
Leeds The Old Pottery, 1760–1878. Several proprietors including: Humble, Greens & Co. (1770–75); Humble, Hartley, Greens & Co. (1775–80); . Hartley, Greens & Co. (1781–1820).	Creamware with glassy, clear yellow glaze. Many wares feature pierced decoration. Twisted handles with leaf and flower terminals. Tablewares, centrepieces, and figures. Transfer-printed decoration and enamel flower painting. Black basaltes, red stoneware, and saltglazed stoneware.	LEEDS POTTERY L. P. usually impressed.
Slee's Modern Pottery, founded 1888.	Creamware using the old moulds. Black basaltes, silver lustre reliefs.	

FRANCE

PORCELAIN

Rouen (Normandy), 1673–*c.* 1700 Louis Poterat (1641–96) (see also § FAIENCE below).	Soft-paste porcelain of a very rare type, difficult to identify with certainty.	

Factory and proprietor(s)	*Products, styles, and personalities*	*Marks*
Saint-Cloud (Seine-et-Oise), *c.* 1690–1766 Pierre Chicaneau, his widow, and Henri-Charles Trou.	Soft-paste porcelain. Tablewares, thickly potted with either applied decoration (e.g. prunus), or underglaze-blue or enamel colours. Many beautiful snuff-boxes.	S.C T used separately or, occasionally, together.
Chantilly (Oise), 1725–*c.* 1800 Ciquaire Cirou, under the patronage of Louis-Henri de Bourbon, Prince de Condé.	Soft-paste porcelain. The glaze was often opacified with tin oxide to suggest oriental porcelain. Many early wares decorated in Kakiemon style.	in blue or red.
Limoges (Haute-Vienne) Grellet, Massié and Fourneira, 1771–84. Factory under the direction of the king, 1784–96.	Hard-paste porcelain decorated in a similar fashion to the wares of Paris and Sèvres.	CD CD incised or in enamel.
Baignol, 1797–1854.		
Joubert and Monnerie, 1795–1808; Alluard, and family successors, 1808–*c.* 1878.		
Numerous other factories started in the 19th century; production continues today.	The productions, when marked, bear the name of the place or maker.	
Lunéville (Meurthe-et-Moselle), *c.* 1755–19th century Paul-Louis Cyfflé, 1755–77 (factory sold in 1780). See also § FAIENCE below.	Biscuit figures, and groups of hard-paste porcelain and TERRE DE PIPE.	CYFFLE A LUNEVILLE impressed.
Mennecy (Île-de-France), 1734–1806 François Barbin, under the patronage of Louis-François de Neufville, duc de Villeroy.	Soft-paste porcelain. Tablewares of simple form with Meissen-type flower painting of great beauty. Snuff-boxes, scent-bottles, and knife-handles. Figures, either white glazed or enamelled.	D.V in blue, red, black, or incised.
Vincennes and **Sèvres,** 1738–present Orry de Fulvy, 1738–45; Charles Adam company, 1745–53; Éloi Brichard company, 1753–59; factory purchased by Louis XV, 1759. (Started at Vincennes, the factory moved to Sèvres in 1756; from 1753 it was under the patronage of Louis XV and Mme de Pompadour.)	Soft-paste porcelain of outstanding quality. Early styles of decoration after Meissen (until *c.* 1753, when the rococo style became the rule). Noted for exceptionally fine painting, also for well-modelled biscuit figures by Étienne-Maurice Falconet. Soft-paste gradually gave way to hard-paste porcelain, and was finally abandoned *c.* 1804.	B in blue enamel; 'B' is date-letter for 1754.
PARIS		
Rue Clignancourt, 1771–98 Pierre Deruelle, under the patronage of Monsieur le Comte de Provence.	Hard-paste porcelain of good quality.	in underglaze blue.
Rue Thiroux, 1775–1870 André-Marie Lebœuf, under the patronage of Marie-Antoinette.	Hard-paste porcelain tablewares.	A in underglaze blue.
Rue de Bondy, 1780–1817 Dihl et Guérhard, under the patronage of the Duc d'Angoulême.	Hard-paste porcelain, often decorated with ANGOULÊME SPRIG.	GA in gold.
Fontainebleau (nr Paris), 1830–62 Jacob Petit.	Hard-paste porcelain. Useful wares and figures in extravagant revived rococo styles.	JP in underglaze blue.

Factory and proprietor(s)	*Products, styles, and personalities*	*Marks*
Niderviller (Moselle), 1765–19th century Baron Jean-Louis de Beyerlé, 1765–70; Comte de Custine, 1770–93.	Hard-paste porcelain. Vases, clock-cases, and large tablewares in German rococo taste (as seen in Strasbourg faience).	1770–93, Custine, in blue.

FAIENCE

Factory and proprietor(s)	*Products, styles, and personalities*	*Marks*
Rouen (Normandy), 1526–*c.* 1800 Edmé Poterat (1612–87); Louis Poterat (1641–96).	Large chargers painted in high-temperature blue, with LAMBREQUIN and STYLE RAYONNANT decorations.	
Many other small factories in the 18th century.		
Moustiers (Basses-Alpes), late 17th–late 19th century Pierre Clerissy I and successors, 1679–1783; Joseph Fouqué, 1783–1800.	Dishes painted in blue after well-known engravings.	X
Jean-Baptiste Laugier and Joseph Olérys, 1739–*c.* 1790.	Wares decorated with BÉRAIN MOTIFS, painted in green, yellow, and purple high-temperature colours.	
Nevers (Nièvre), late 16th century–present Various Italian potters, e.g.: the Gambin family (Scipio, Giulio, Laurent); G. Gambin & Conrade, 1588–17th century. Pierre Custode, 1632–late 17th century. Numerous other manufacturers, at least twelve being in operation in the period 1743–54.	Early wares in the Italian style. Large dishes of 17th-century date painted with bold flower and figure subjects. Opaque white and yellow over a deep-blue (BLEU PERSAN) glaze in the second half of the 17th century, together with Delft styles in blue and manganese. From *c.* 1750 plates, bottles, and jugs with painted decoration (saints, emblems, woodcuts) in the revolutionary period FAIENCE PATRIOTIQUE, much faked today.	deconrade A Nevers 3: Custodeff
Lunéville (Meurthe-et-Moselle), 1731–19th century Jacques Chambrette, 1731–58; Gabriel Chambrette & Charles Loyal, 1758–88; Keller & Cuny and Keller & Guérin, 1788–19th century.	Wares in the style of Niderviller, Strasbourg and Sceaux. Large figures of dogs or lions. Cream-coloured wares in the English style.	K G Luneville
Marseilles (Bouches-du-Rhône), late 17th–late 19th century Joseph Fauchier and son, 1710–89.	Figures, fountains, wall-cisterns, holy-water stoups, and plaques, painted in both low- and high-temperature colours.	F
Veuve (widow) Perrin, *c.* 1748–*c.* 1795.	Fine tablewares decorated in enamel colours with flowers, fish, fruit, vegetables, insects, *chinoiseries*, etc.	VP
Joseph Gaspard Robert, *c.* 1750–1800.	Good tablewares, often with gilt borders and green and black enamel flower or *chinoiserie* painting.	R
Strasbourg (Alsace), 1721–81 Charles-François Hannong (1669–1739); Paul-Antoine Hannong, proprietor 1732–60; Joseph Hannong, proprietor 1760–80.	Early wares painted in high-temperature colours. In 1750 enamel colours were used on useful wares of rococo style. A rich purple-red was a predominant colour characteristic of many later wares.	PH in blue. H in blue.

Factory and proprietor(s)	*Products, styles, and personalities*	*Marks*
GERMANY		
	PORCELAIN	
Meissen (nr Dresden), 1710–present Factory founded in 1710 under the patronage of Augustus II (the Strong), Elector of Saxony and King of Poland, after experimental work from *c.* 1694 by E.W. von Tschirnhausen (d. 1708) and, from 1704, J.F. Böttger (d. 1719). Augustus undertook personal direction from 1731 until his death in 1733 when he was succeeded by his son, Augustus III, and the factory directed by Count Heinrich von Brühl until his death in 1763. Following the First period, 1710–56, and the Seven Years War, work resumed in 1763, the ensuing period, 1763–74, being known as the *Akademische Periode* (Academic, or dot period). Other important directors were Count Camillo Marcolini, 1774–1814, and Heinrich Gottlob Kühn, 1833–70. The period 1870–90 is known as the *Neuzeit* (New Period), and 1890–1910 as the *Jugendstil* period.	From *c.* 1709 BÖTTGER RED STONEWARE (until *c.* 1730). Hard-paste porcelain from 1710 onwards. First period: baroque and rococo styles; tablewares decorated with *chinoiseries*, landscapes, harbour scenes, Watteau subjects, *indianische* and *deutsche Blumen*. Principal decorator J.G. Höroldt (1696–1775), with C.F. Herold, J.G. Heintze, A.F. von Löwenfinck and others (the *Malerische Periode*). Early large figures, and later small figures, for table decoration. Principal modeller J.J. Kändler (1706–75), with J.F. Eberlein, P. Reinicke, F.E. Meyer and others (the *Plastische Periode*). In the *Akademische Periode* and the Marcolini period, neo-classical styles; in the Kühn period, revived rococo style; from the *Neuzeit* onwards, contemporary figures and groups.	in underglaze blue; monogram of Augustus II and III. in underglaze blue; adopted 1723.  the Academic (or dot) period, 1763–74.  the Marcolini period. The crossed swords and 'AR' marks have often been imitated.
Höchst (nr Frankfurt-on-Main), 1750–96 Johann Benckgraff and Johann Jakob Ringler (moulds later used at Damm, Bonn, and Passau).	Coarse hard-paste porcelain with milky-white glaze. Meissen-type tablewares, Commedia dell'Arte figures, pastoral and *chinoiserie* groups.	 incised, impressed, in blue or colours.
Fürstenberg (Brunswick), *c.* 1753–present Duke Karl I of Brunswick.	Hard-paste porcelain. Vases and tablewares with high-relief decoration. Figures, including satirical groups.	in underglaze blue.
Berlin Wilhelm Kaspar Wegely, 1751–57.	Hard-paste porcelain. Small figures of children.	 in underglaze blue.
Johann Ernst Gotzkowsky, 1761–63; purchased by Frederick the Great, 1763, and thereafter called the Königliche Porzellanmanufaktur (since 1918 Staatliche Porzellanmanufaktur).	Hard-paste porcelain; useful wares decorated with good landscapes, flowers, or battle-scenes. After 1763 large services and tablewares; figures, some biscuit; painted plaques and lithophanes.	 1761–63. 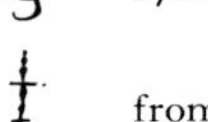 from *c.* 1765. K.P.M. in general use, *c.* 1832.
Nymphenburg (Bavaria), 1753–present Prince Max III Joseph of Bavaria.	Hard-paste porcelain. Rococo-style tablewares and outstanding figures by Franz Anton Bustelli and animal groups by Dominicus Auliczek.	 impressed.
Frankenthal (Palatinate), 1755–1800 Paul-Antoine Hannong, 1755–62; factory bought in 1762 by the Elector Karl Theodor; managed by Simon Feilner, 1775–97.	Hard-paste porcelain. Tablewares in high rococo style of Strasbourg and Sèvres. Figures by Johann Wilhelm Lanz. Groups by Konrad Linck.	 in underglaze blue; from 1762.
Ludwigsburg (Württemberg), 1758–1824 Duke Karl Eugen of Württemberg; managed by Johann Jakob Ringler, 1759–*c.* 1802.	Hard-paste porcelain of a smoky tone. Many figures associated with ballet. VENETIAN FAIR GROUPS by Jean-Jacob Louis.	 in underglaze blue.

Factory and proprietor(s)	*Products, styles, and personalities*	*Marks*
Keltersbach (Hesse-Darmstadt), 1761–68; 1789–92 Landgrave Ludwig VIII of Hesse-Darmstadt and C. D. Busch.	Hard-paste porcelain. Great variety of figures by Carl Vogelmann, and many TOYS.	HD. in underglaze blue.
Ottweiler (Rhineland), 1764–94 Prince Wilhelm Heinrich of Nassau-Saarbrücken.	Hard-paste porcelain. Tablewares in popular rococo styles.	.N S. in underglaze blue.
Fulda (Hesse) Heinrich VIII, Prince-Bishop of Fulda. Nikolaus Paul. (See also § FAIENCE below.)	Hard-paste porcelain. Tablewares of elegant rococo form with Meissen-style painting. Commedia dell'Arte figures after Callot.	FF in underglaze blue.

FAIENCE

Factory and proprietor(s)	*Products, styles, and personalities*	*Marks*
Hanau (Hesse), 1661–1806 Several proprietors.	Wares similar to those of Delft, but without KWAART. *Enghalskrüge* with rope handles. Chinese and European decoration in the Dutch manner.	HVX S 41 in blue.
Frankfurt-on-Main, 1662–1772 Several proprietors.	Early wares with Chinese subjects similar to Delft; KWAART used. Also biblical and figure subjects. *Enghalskrüge*. Factory supplied white wares to HAUSMALER.	F in blue.
Nuremberg, *c.* 1530–*c.* 1840 Centre for production from the 16th century. Factory established 1712.	Some rare early wares influenced by Italian maiolica. Fine 18th-century wares (dishes, tankards, *Enghalskrüge*) in blue and other high-temperature colours. Decoration in form of landscapes, armorial bearings, figure subjects, but rarely Chinese. White wares sold to HAUSMALER.	NB K:
Bayreuth, *c.* 1713–1852 Margrave of Brandenburg-Kulmbach and other proprietors.	Early wares in misty blue. Fine examples of baroque armorial painting. Excellent painting in individual styles by several hands. White wares supplied to HAUSMALER.	B.K. c.
Ansbach (Bavaria), 1708–1807 Margrave Friedrich Wilhelm of Brandenburg and other proprietors.	Early wares in blue influenced by Hanau and Delft. Rouen influence in the 1770s. *Enghalskrüge*, imitations of brocaded Imari and *famille verte* porcelain, armorial bearings.	on: 5
Fulda, 1741–58 Amadeus von Buseck, Prince-Bishop of Fulda, with the aid of A. F. von Löwenfinck and Johann Philipp Schick.	FAYENCE PORZELLAN based on Chinese *famille verte*. Rare specimens of *chinoiserie* flowers painted by Löwenfinck. Fine-quality wares. Porcelain also made.	FD. BK.
Höchst, *c.* 1746–58 Adam Friedrich von Löwenfinck; Johann Christoph Göltz, and Johann Felician Clarus.	Fine quality FAYENCE PORZELLAN wares of all kinds in rococo style, mostly painted by Johann Zeschinger and the brothers Hess. Small tureens in Strasbourg style. Figures and groups of birds.	AL

Factory and proprietor(s)	*Products, styles, and personalities*	*Marks*
HOLLAND		
	PORCELAIN	
Weesp, 1759–71 Count van Grunsveldt-Diepenbroik.	Hard-paste porcelain. Tablewares of high quality, decorated with landscapes, birds or flowers in German fashion.	in underglaze blue.
Factory transferred to Oude Loosdrecht, 1771–84; Johannes de Mol.	Hard-paste porcelain tablewares, usually decorated with landscapes in brown, black or purple monochrome.	M.O.L * in underglaze blue or colours.
Factory again transferred to Amstel, 1784–1820, F. Daüber. (From 1809 at Nieuwer Amstel.)	Hard-paste porcelain. Wares similar to those of Oude Loosdrecht until *c.* 1800, after which the popular Parisian Empire styles were adopted.	
The Hague A. Lyncker, 1776–90.	Hard-paste porcelain, especially tea-services in neo-classical styles.	 in blue, often overglaze on Tournai wares decorated here.
	DELFTWARE (tin-glazed earthware)	
Delft Centre of manufacture from the beginning of the 17th century to the present day. Many factories, most of which were located in disused breweries.	At first principally copies of late Ming CHINESE EXPORT PORCELAIN in blue and white, usually with a transparent overglaze (KWAART); also tiles, plates, and vases with Dutch subjects, often based on contemporary painting. Polychrome wares in Chinese and Japanese styles; black-ground vases; profusely gilded vases (DELFT DORÉE); CACHEMIRE decoration. Enamel colours from the early 18th century. Many figures and moulded wares including cow-creamers, violins, etc.	 in blue; the much imitated mark of Adriaenus & Pieter Kocks.
HUNGARY		
Herend, 1838–present Moritz Fischer (d. 1880); factory now state-owned.	Hard-paste porcelain. Good imitations of Meissen, Sèvres, and Chinese wares. Wares were popular with many royal houses, especially for purposes of presentation.	 in blue enamel.
ITALY		
	PORCELAIN	
Florence, 1575 Grand Duke Francesco I de' Medici.	Soft-paste MEDICI PORCELAIN.	F in underglaze blue.
Venice Giuseppe and Francesco Vezzi, 1720–27.	Hard-paste porcelain, after the more popular useful wares of Meissen and Vienna.	Ven:a in underglaze blue, red, blue, or gilt.
Geminiano Cozzi, 1765–1812.	Soft-paste porcelain of poor quality. Useful wares, often influenced by Sèvres. Later figures in neo-classical styles.	in red or gilt.
Nove (nr Bassano), 1728–1835 Pasquale Antonibon, retired 1773; Francesco Parolin, 1781–1802; Giovanni Baroni, 1802–25 (see also § CREAMWARE below).	Soft-paste porcelain similar to that of Cozzi (Venice). Useful wares, figures.	Nove * in red and gold.

Factory and proprietor(s)	*Products, styles, and personalities*	*Marks*
Vinovo (nr Turin), 1776–1820 G.V. Brodel and Dr Gioanetti.	Hard-paste porcelain of a creamy colour, with a glassy glaze. Tablewares in the style of Strasbourg faience. Figures similar to those of Frankenthal and Lunéville.	+ V D G in underglaze blue, incised, in colour or gilt.
Doccia (nr Florence), 1735–present Carlo Ginori and family successors.	Hard-paste porcelain with a greyish tint, but sometimes covered with an opaque tin-glaze. Baroque-style tablewares decorated in underglaze blue or enamel colours. Commedia dell'Arte and other figures.	in blue, red, or gold; also impressed.
Capodimonte (nr Naples), 1743–59 Charles of Bourbon. Factory continued at Buen Retiro (nr Madrid), 1760–1812; see *Spain*.	Fine-quality soft-paste porcelain. Tea-services, toys, snuff-boxes.	impressed, in gold or blue.
Naples, 1771–1806 Ferdinand IV, son of Charles III. (See also § CREAMWARE below.)	Soft-paste porcelain, tablewares and figures.	in red, blue, or purple.

MAIOLICA

Various centres rather than individual factories:		
Orvieto (Umbria), *c.* 1400–present.	Peasant-type forms.	
Florence (Tuscany), mid-15th century–present.	Large drug-jars.	
Faenza (Emilia), late 14th century–present.	Drug-jars, vases, dishes, etc.	
Caffaggiolo (nr Florence), *c.* 1506–*c.* 1600.	Wares for the Medicis.	
Siena (Tuscany), mid-13th century.	Dishes and tiles.	
Deruta (Umbria), late 15th century.	Brownish-yellow lustre ware, similar to GOLDEN POTTERY of Spain.	
Gubbio (Urbino), early 16th century.	Ruby-lustre ware.	
Castel Durante (Urbino), 16th century.	Notable painting by Nicola Pellipario.	
Urbino (capital of the duchy), 16th century.	Wares decorated with grotesques and arabesques, also ISTORIATO.	

CREAMWARE

Nove (nr Bassano), 1780–present day G.M. Baccin (formerly manager of the Nove porcelain factory); G.B. Viero. (Factory leased by G. & P. Baroni 1802–24.)	Fine-quality tablewares, decorated in rococo style, figures and groups.	G.M. B.*
Naples Giustiniani factory, 1760–late 19th century (Nicola Giustiniani, his son Biagio, and grandsons Antonio and Salvatore).	Good-quality wares; decoration in Pompeian and Etruscan styles.	GIUSTINIANI impressed.
C. & G. Del Vecchio, late 18th century–present.	Tableware decorated with Etruscan patterns and named views, silver lustre ware, figures, and groups.	del Vecchio N impressed.
Este (nr Padua), 1782– ? G.P. Varion; Giovanni Francini.	Creamware in the English manner.	GF impressed.

Factory and proprietor(s)	*Products, styles, and personalities*	*Marks*
Treviso (Venezia), potteries from *c.* 1500 G. Rossi di Stefano, 1766–71; G.M. Ruberti, 1771–77.	Good-quality ware in rococo style.	
G & A. Fontebasso, late 18th–19th century.	A type of soft-paste porcelain. Creamware similar to Este wares.	G.A.F.F Treviso
RUSSIA		
Moscow, 1765–present Francis Gardner; F.X. Hattenberger; Kusnetsoff family, 1891– ?	Good-quality hard-paste porcelain. Russian peasant-type figures, etc. Bright colours employed, especially a mat blue.	ГАРДНЕРЪ early 19th century, impressed.
Gorbunovo (nr Moscow) Founded by Charles Milly; A. Popoff, proprietor *c.* 1806–72.	Good-quality porcelain; productions similar to those of F. Gardner.	АП early 19th century.
St Petersburg (late Petrograd, now Leningrad), 1744–present Imperial Porcelain factory, founded by Empress Elizabeth; C.K. Hunger; Dimitri Vinogradoff. Now a state factory.	Good-quality porcelain, influenced by Meissen, Sèvres, and Vienna, in rococo and neo-classical styles.	1762–96, under Catherine II.
SPAIN		
Buen Retiro (nr Madrid), 1760–1812 Factory transferred from Capodimonte (see under Italy § PORCELAIN).	High-quality soft-paste porcelain wares with distinct Spanish style of modelling and decoration.	1760–1804, in blue and gold, as for Capodimonte M[D] Madrid mark, in red enamel, 1804–08.
SWEDEN		
Marieberg (nr Stockholm) J.E.L. Ehrenreich, 1760–66; P. Berthevin, 1766–69, manager; H. Sten, 1769–*c.* 1782, manager and director; Nordenstolpe and Schirmer, proprietors *c.* 1782–88.	Factory originally made faience; from 1766 soft-paste porcelain wares similar to those of Mennecy, and hard-paste porcelain from *c.* 1777.	in blue, red, or incised.
SWITZERLAND		
Zurich, 1763–90 Adam Spengler, director.	Soft-paste porcelain was superseded *c.* 1765 by hard-paste. Good-quality tablewares in German taste, and figures in contemporary costume. Faience wares were made from 1790.	Z in blue.
Nyon Jean-Jacques Dortu and Ferdinand Müller, 1781–86; J.G. Zinkernagel and others, 1786–1813.	Hard-paste porcelain after expensive Paris fashions. Wares were often imitated during the late 19th century.	in underglaze blue.
Lenzburg M. Hünerwadel: A.H. and H.C. Klug, 1762–67.	Tablewares decorated with hunting scenes, flowers, fruit, and coats of arms.	L2
H.J. Frey, 1745–1817.	Tablewares in the Strasbourg style. Fine-quality rococo faience stoves decorated in enamel colours.	

Dictionary of Ceramics

Alphabetization of entries in the dictionary is by the operative letter or word; thus 'C-scroll' precedes 'Caddy', and 'Press-mould' precedes 'Pressing'. Illustrations will as a rule be found on the same page as the relevant entry or on the facing page, though a few appear on adjacent pages due to considerations of space.

Cross-references to related subjects are indicated by the use of small capitals within entries.

A

A-marked porcelain. A rare 18th-century porcelain of excellent quality from an unidentified factory, so called from the mark, a capital A, either in blue or incised. This ware was formerly believed to have been made in Italy but more recent opinion is inclined to regard it as coming either from a little-known factory at Vauxhall (London) or from one in Scotland sponsored by the Duke of Argyll.

A.R. jug. A type of commemorative jug made of saltglazed stoneware, globular in shape, with a relief medallion bearing the initials A.R. for 'Anne Regina'. They were made of WESTERWALD WARE at Grenzhausen, Germany, for export to England during the reign of Queen Anne (1702–14). *See* C.R. JUG; G.R. JUG; W.R. JUG.

Acanthus. A southern European plant, the spiked leaf of which has been used as a decorative motif since very early times; on ceramic ware it was used as painted or relief decoration. In Greek and Byzantine forms it was stylized (as on capitals of the Corinthian order); in Roman and Renaissance decoration it was used naturalistically. In profile it is termed an 'acanthus scroll'.

Acanthus. Flower-pot with relief decoration; marbled ware, *c.* 1785. Courtesy, Wedgwood.

Accouchement bowl. (1) A covered bowl having attached on one side of the interior a pierced semi-circular well. These bowls were made in porcelain and pottery in the 17th and 18th centuries, especially in Hamburg and Frankfurt, and in Sweden. Soup was poured in through the strainer which collected the solids while the broth passed into the bowl. Similar pieces made in England were termed 'broth-bowls' or 'posset-bowls'. (2) A bowl, usually of maiolica, with an accouchement scene as painted decoration, is sometimes so designated.

Accouchement cup. A covered cup with two handles and a saucer made by 18th-century Continental porcelain factories. Such cups were presented, filled with sweetmeats, to a woman during confinement.

Accouchement bowl. Berlin faience, 18th century. National Museum, Stockholm.

Adam and Eve. Decoration on charger, Lambeth delftware, *c.* 1690–1700. Burnap Collection, William Rockhill Nelson Gallery of Art, Kansas City, Mo.

Accouchement set. *See* VASO PUERPERALE.

Acetabulum (Latin). A small cup of Roman pottery used as a measure and for serving vinegar. *See* OXYBAPHON.

Acid gilding. Usually a decorative border process by which a design or ground is etched on porcelain with hydrofluoric acid, and gold applied overall; after being burnished the polished raised areas contrast with the still mat etched areas. It was introduced in England by Minton, *c.* 1873. *See* GILDING.

Acoustic jar. A jar of slightly globular, but predominantly cylindrical shape, placed near the tops of walls, or on (or near) the floor, of some medieval churches to increase the resonance of the edifice. They are found in many parts of England.

Adam and Eve. A decorative subject which occurs fairly frequently on English earthenware of the 17th century, especially on English delftware and large Staffordshire slipware dishes. There are many variations of the motif, but usually the figures are on either side of the Tree of Life, around which is entwined the Serpent. Some versions, *c.* 1680, have at each side of the decoration stylized trees and bushes, referred to as 'side bushes'.

Adam style. The English version of the NEO-CLASSICAL STYLE introduced soon after 1760 by Robert Adam and his brothers. The repertory of ornament is similar in many ways to the French version, with festoons, medallions, and urns commonly employed for decorative purposes. It had small effect on English porcelain of the period, where the primary inspiration was French, but the products of Wedgwood (creamware, black basaltes, and jasper) were much influenced by it. Wedgwood also supplied jasper plaques for insetting into furniture in this style, and as decoration for such architectural features as chimneypieces. The prevailing Adam colour-scheme was repeated in the colours employed as background to Wedgwood's white applied-jasper reliefs.

Adobe (Spanish). Sun-baked bricks introduced into Spain by the Moors, and taken by the Spaniards to Mexico and South America. Straw was worked into the clay to assist cohesion, and it was then hardened by pressure.

Aerograph. An atomizer used from *c.* 1890 to apply ground colours to pottery and porcelain of cheap quality instead of the process of GROUND-LAYING. Atomizers are also employed today to apply glazes.

Affenkapelle. Porcelain figures from the Meissen monkey band. Morgan Collection, Wadsworth Atheneum, Hartford, Conn.

Aesop. A porcelain figure of the fabulist (fl. 560 BC) represented as a Negro, made at Chelsea in the red-anchor period, *c.* 1753. *See* FABLES, AESOP'S.

Affenkapelle (German). Literally, monkey band. This subject, first modelled *c.* 1750 by J. J. Kändler and Peter Reinicke at Meissen, was erroneously said to have been intended as a satire on the Dresden Court orchestra, but was actually derived from the SINGERIES of Watteau and Christoph Huet in France. The series consists of over 20 different figures including (in addition to the music-stand) a conductor, flautist, violinist, 'cellist, trumpeter, horn player, piper, side-drummer, kettle-drummer, bassoonist, cymbalist, oboe player, harpsichord player, bugler, French-horn player, songstress, recorder player, drummer with a drum suspended from a wrist-strap, drummer with twin drums on his back, triangle player, female hurdy-gurdy player, and organist. The series was copied partially at Chelsea, where the

1756 Catalogue lists five of the figures. They were also reproduced at Fürstenberg, Vienna, Paris, and other Continental factories, and at Derby. Many reproductions were made in the 19th century. *See* DOG ORCHESTRA.

Aesop. Porcelain figure, Chelsea, *c*. 1753. Fitzwilliam Museum, Cambridge.

Aftaba, sometimes ***aftabeh*** (Persian). A type of vessel for containing water to wash the hands. Adapted from a metal prototype, the *aftaba* has an ovoid shape, a long slender neck, a loop handle, and a long, curved spout. Vessels of this form were made in China during the Ming dynasty.

Agate ware. Pottery made in imitation of agate stone by combining differently coloured clays in the body, or by blending differently coloured surface slips. *See* SOLID AGATE WARE; SURFACE AGATE WARE; SPECKLED AGATE WARE; MARBLED WARE; VARIEGATED WARE.

Age-crack. *See* FIRE-CRACK.

Aiguière (French). A type of EWER, usually one with a globular body resting on a stemmed base, with a tall, slender neck and a loop handle, the latter sometimes in the form of a figure. Those of Rouen and Nevers faience are particularly notable.

Aiguière handle. A handle ornately modelled in the form of a reclining figure, or sometimes a serpent.

Air, À l' (French). A term applied to ceramic objects through which air passes freely, such as reticulated and pierced basketwork patterns. *See* OZIER.

Akaji kinga (Japanese). A style of decoration on certain Japanese KUTANI PORCELAIN known as HACHIROEMON KUTANI, with gold designs on red.

Alabastron (Greek), sometimes ***alabastrum.*** A small bottle or flask of Greek pottery for holding ointment, perfume, or oil. It is elongated in form, almost cylindrical, and rounded at the bottom. It has either no handles, or one small handle at the side. The mouth is a flat disk with a small central aperture. The *alabastron* was sometimes made in the form of a figure. Some were made to be suspended from the wrist by a string, but most were intended to stand on a small metal tripod. They range in height from about 1 in. to 15 in. *See* BOMBYLIOS.

Alabastron. Red earthenware covered with white slip, and having incised decoration painted in black and red; ht $3\frac{1}{8}$ in. Corinthian, 6th century BC. Victoria and Albert Museum, London.

Albarello (Italian of Arabic origin). A drug-jar for holding solid or viscous substances, but seldom liquids (*see* WET-DRUG JAR). The *albarello* is more or less cylindrical in shape, but slightly waisted. It has a low foot, a shoulder, and a short neck. A flange around the rim of the grooved neck permits a parchment cover to be fastened with string. The waisted form is to facilitate removal from a shelf of similar jars standing side by side. Occasionally the *albarello* has single or double side handles of loop form. This type of jar originated about the 12th century in the Near East and it was fairly common in 15th-century Spain among Moorish potters. *Albarelli* were imported into Italy, where they were copied almost at once, the earliest perhaps being from the first half of the 15th century. They were popular among Italian maiolica potters during the 15th and 16th centuries, and in other varieties of European faience from the early years of the 17th century, first occurring in England late in the second half of the 16th century. Decoration includes armorial bearings, portraits, and the name (often abbreviated) of the contents, sometimes in relief or in the SGRAFFITO technique. Inscriptions are often in Latin. Apart from drugs, the *albarello* was also used to contain pigments,

Albarello. Faience albarello, Nîmes, France, late 16th century. Victoria and Albert Museum, London.

scents, cosmetics, and sweetmeats; although in modern times *albarelli* are sometimes used as flower-vases there is no reason to suppose they were ever intended for this purpose. *See* PHARMACY WARE.

Alcarazza (Italian of Arabic origin). A vessel of porous pottery used for cooling water. It is comparable to the Spanish BÚCARO, the body of which is less porous. Similar vessels were made in Egypt (and there called a *bardach*), in Portugal (called an *alcaradza*), and in the East, especially in tropical and sub-tropical climates. The French term is *hydro-cérame*.

Alcora ware. Tin-enamelled pottery (faience) made at Alcora (Valencia, Spain) at a factory founded in 1727 by Don Bonaventura Pedro de Alcántara, Count of Aranda, which was started with the assistance of French workmen from Moustiers. The ware is often decorated in the Moustiers style, especially with BÉRAIN MOTIFS; the body is reddish in colour. Later the factory made creamware (*faïence fine*) in the manner of Wedgwood.

Alhambra Vase. A large pyriform Moorish vase, *c.* 1400, found at the Alhambra (Granada, Spain). It is over four feet in height, with decoration in blue and lustre, and with two large, vertical, wing-shaped handles. It seems to have been made either in Seville or Málaga, and is one of the earliest known examples of HISPANO-MORESQUE WARE. Other versions have since been made, inspired by the early example.

Alicatado (Spanish of Arabic origin). A 14th-century panel of Spanish tile mosaic.

Alkaline glaze. A glaze of soda-glass, principally to be found on Near Eastern pottery of the 12th and 13th centuries. Soda-glass, the type generally found along the Mediterranean littoral, was fluxed with the ashes of seaweed.

Allegorical subject. A subject which symbolizes another because of its analogous content. The fashion for allegory in ceramic ware was particularly to be seen during the 18th century, when many figures were made symbolizing a wide variety of subjects, especially by virtue of the objects carried by them or otherwise accompanying them. Thus, in The Four Seasons, a figure with a bunch of grapes symbolized Autumn. Sets symbolized such diverse concepts as The Four Elements and Liberty and Matrimony, and people of culture were expected to be able to recognize the allegorical content.

Alms bowl. Same as BEGGING BOWL.

Allegorical subjects. Porcelain groups: Science, Commerce and Art. Chelsea-Derby, *c.* 1773. Victoria and Albert Museum, London.

Altar cup. A name sometimes erroneously applied to white porcelain stem-cups of Chinese porcelain made in the Ming dynasty.

Altar ware. Vessels, statues, burettes, vases, candlesticks, and other objects of pottery or porcelain made for ecclesiastical use or decoration, and especially those intended for use on the altar. Wares of this kind were produced in most European factories in the 17th and 18th centuries.

Altbrandensteinmuster (German). Literally, old Brandenstein pattern. A moulded basketwork border pattern introduced by J. G. Höroldt at Meissen in 1740. It has panels divided into sets of three, one narrow and plain, one narrow with dotted squares, and one wide with circumferential moulding crossed by ribs which are a small segment of a spiral. These ribs encroach on the well of the plate. *See* ORDINAIR-OZIER; ALTOZIERRAND; NEUOZIERRAND; NEUBRANDENSTEINMUSTER.

Altozierrand (German). Literally, old osier border. A moulded basketwork border pattern similar to the ORDINAIR-OZIER, but more stylized and also divided by radial ribs. It was developed by J. G. Höroldt at Meissen in the 1730s. *See* ALTBRANDENSTEINMUSTER; NEUBRANDENSTEINMUSTER; NEUOZIERRAND.

Alva bottle, d'. *See* BELLARMINE.

Amalgam. Gold or silver alloyed with mercury. Mercury is a metal, liquid at ordinary temperatures but which vaporizes at 360°C. When powdered gold is mixed with mercury the two metals combine to form a stiff paste known as an amalgam. This can be painted on to a porcelain surface, and when fired to a point where the mercury vaporizes, it will leave the gold behind attached to the glaze. This is the classic method of gilding metals, known as fire-gilding, and it is also the technique of MERCURIC GILDING on ceramic ware. The technique is simple but highly dangerous, due to the poisonous nature of the fumes emitted during firing.

Amatori (Italian). Portrait ware, usually dishes and deep saucers, upon which was painted the portrait of a young woman with the word *bella* or some laudatory phrase, together with her name. Of Italian maiolica, some were painted by Nicola Pellipario at Castel Durante early in the 16th century. They were usually used as gifts from a man to his beloved. Sometimes called *coppa amatoria*. *See* FRUTTIERA.

Amatori. Maiolica dish inscribed 'Bella Diamante', Pesaro or Castel Durante, 1534. Wallace Collection, London.

Amatory trophies. *See* TROPHIES.

American porcelain. Porcelain made by a number of factories in the United States during the 18th, 19th, and 20th centuries, principally in New Jersey, New York, Ohio, Pennsylvania, and Vermont. Porcelain was first made in very limited quantity at Savannah, Georgia, in the 1730s by Andrew Duché who had experimented with UNAKER; a few specimens probably attributable to him survive. In 1766 a small factory is said to have been started in Savannah by John Bartlam. The real beginning of American porcelain was the factory of Bonnin and Morris, established in Philadelphia, Pa, *c.* 1769; it made, until it closed in 1772, attractive, though heavily potted, ware with underglaze blue related to that made at Bow and other English factories. A few early-19th-century pieces have been attributed to Dr Henry Mead's factory (in New York or New Jersey), to Abraham Miller in Philadelphia, and to the Jersey Porcelain and Earthenware Co. started in 1825 in Jersey City, N.J., and taken over *c.* 1829 by

David Henderson and renamed in 1833 the American Pottery Manufacturing Co. The first high-quality porcelain was made from 1826 until 1838 at Philadelphia by William Ellis Tucker, with various partners, including Dr Joseph Hemphill. After 1840 the revived rococo style became popular and was featured from 1847 by Christopher W. Fenton, who in 1849 started the United States Pottery Co. at Bennington, Vt; until 1858 it made principally FLINT ENAMEL WARE, SCRODLED WARE, and a type of BELLEEK PORCELAIN as well as white PARIAN PORCELAIN figures and such pieces as the CORN PITCHER that reflected the American influence on design (*see* BENNINGTON WARE). Charles Cartlidge & Co., Greenpoint, N.Y., made a great variety of wares from 1848 until 1856; the factory was reopened by William Boch in 1857 and was operated by the Union Porcelain Works from 1861 for many years, employing as modeller the sculptor Karl Müller. Trenton, N.J., also became a ceramic centre with the factory of Ott and Brewer, 1863–93, and the Ceramic Art Co. (known from 1906 as Lenox, Inc.) which was started in 1889 by William Scott Lenox and is still making high-quality porcelain tableware. Another centre was East Liverpool, Ohio, where Knowles, Taylor, and Knowles became well regarded for its type of BELLEEK PORCELAIN called there 'Lotus Ware'. In the 20th century Edward Marshall Boehm established in 1949 his studio pottery in New Jersey (*see* BOEHM BIRDS), and the prolific Cybis Porcelain Co. was founded in 1939 at Trenton, N.J., by Boleslaw Cybis and his wife, making a wide variety of wares, especially figures.

American pottery. Earthenware made by a considerable number of factories in the United States from Colonial days until the early part of the 20th century. The early pottery made by the Colonists employed techniques already established in their home countries, so far as local clay and material permitted. It is difficult to establish the early history with any kind of certainty, but the first earthenware of which a record survives was made near Burlington, N.J., by Dr Daniel Cox, *c.* 1685; the nature of the production is disputed, but it is said to have been similar to English delftware. PENNSYLVANIA DUTCH WARE was made from 1683. By 1735 there was a pottery in New York, started by John Remmy, which continued under his descendants until *c.* 1820; the New York Historical Society has a saltglazed stoneware pitcher dated 1798 that is attributed to this factory. Generally the wares made during the 18th century include white and grey stoneware, red stoneware, white ware of a CREAMWARE type, SGRAFFITO ware, and trailed slipware. The American Pottery Manufacturing Co., at Jersey City, N.J., made mainly earthenware after being taken over by David Henderson, *c.* 1829, producing some transfer-printed ware and relief-decorated pieces modelled by Daniel Greatbach (*see* HOUND-HANDLE PITCHER); in 1840 its name was changed to the American Pottery Co., in 1845 new owners changed the name to Jersey City Pottery Co., and there were successive owners until the factory finally closed in 1892.

During the early decades of the 19th century a factory at Bennington, Vt, started by Captain John Norton in 1794, made mainly useful wares of stoneware, redware, and a type of creamware, as well as a ware with the so-called Rockingham brown glaze (*see* ROCKINGHAM WARE); after 1823 the factory passed to various descendants and successors. In 1849 another factory, called the United States Pottery Co., was established in Bennington by Christopher W. Fenton, which continued until 1858. Abraham Miller made in Philadelphia, Pa, from 1824 until 1858, silver-lustre ware and also a type of ROCKINGHAM WARE. Much pottery was also made at several factories in East Liverpool, Ohio, from *c.* 1840, especially stoneware, creamware, and

Amphora. Decorated in the black-figure style by the Amasis painter, *c.* 540 BC. Antikenmuseum, Basle.

Rockingham ware. Other factories with a considerable output were at Trenton, N.J., from *c.* 1852, and at Baltimore, Md, from *c.* 1846. From 1880 until 1913 the best ornamental pottery made in the United States came from Cincinnati, Ohio. *See* ROOKWOOD POTTERY; TIFFANY POTTERY.

American views. Earthenware decorated with transfer-printing which depicts well-known American statesmen, scenes, emblems, and incidents. It was popular in the early years of the 19th century. Ware of this kind was made in Staffordshire, and one maker, Rogers, used the American eagle as a mark. *See* ANGLO-AMERICAN POTTERY.

Ammonite scroll. A border pattern of flat spiral curves somewhat resembling the curves of the shell of the fossil ammonite. Actually it is a degenerate version of the Chinese ROCK OF AGES BORDER found on Isnik pottery made in the early years of the 16th century.

Ammonite scroll. Decoration alternating with dollar pattern on Isnik pottery plate, late 16th century. Victoria and Albert Museum, London.

Amol ware. A type of Persian pottery with sgraffito decoration in which free engraving is contrasted with careful painting in green and brown. Painted spots and stripes were combined with engraving to form detached and asymmetrical decoration. The ware came from Amol, north-east of Teheran, during the 13th century.

Amorino (Italian). A winged infant Cupid employed as painted or modelled decoration, especially on Italian, French and German wares. Roman in origin, *amorini* (and *putti*) are to be found in the 1st-century frescoes in the House of the Vettii at Pompeii. They were popular in the art of the Renaissance as a decorative motif. The best of the 18th-century figure versions were based on the work of the Flemish sculptor living in Italy, François Duquesnoy, known as Il Fiammingo (the Fleming). Notable examples of *amorini* (and *putti*) in allegorical guises may be found in the porcelain of Meissen, Berlin, and Nymphenburg. *See* PUTTO; OVIDIAN GODS.

Amour, L'. A decorative subject frequently used on English porcelain in transfer-printed form. It depicts a gallant kissing the hand of a lady on a garden-seat, sometimes with a maid standing behind the seat, and sometimes with a dog and a garden-roller in the foreground. It was engraved by Robert Hancock from a design by C.N. Cochin *fils*, *c.* 1745. L'Amour was used at Bow and Worcester. *See* HANCOCK ENGRAVINGS.

L'Amour. Transfer-printed decoration on a Worcester coffee-pot, *c.* 1760.

Amphora. A large ovoid jar of Greek or Roman pottery, characterized by two vertical loop handles, the ends being attached at the shoulder and just below the rim of the mouth. There are two basic shapes: the 'neck amphora', in which the neck meets the body at an angle (*see* STAMNOS): and the more familiar 'continuous-curve amphora', in which neck and body merge in an unbroken curve. The amphora had two purposes: (1) for storing oil, wine, and other liquids, this type being generally undecorated and sometimes tapering to a point at the bottom to be inserted either into a stand or into soft earth, and sometimes referred to as a DIOTA; (2) for ornaments or as prizes, these being decorated and having a small circular base (*see* PANATHENAIC AMPHORA). In the case of the storage type, those made without a cover were sealed by stopping the mouth with wood or earth which was smeared with pitch or clay. On some the name of the contents was painted on, together with a date. *See* PELIKE.

A vessel of the same shape was made in the Rhineland and in Iberia for storing and transporting wine.

Ampulla (Latin). A type of vase of Roman pottery similar in purpose to the AMPHORA but smaller in size. The name is a diminutive of the latter term. The body of the *ampulla* is globular, with two handles. The vessel was used for pouring ointments and for serving drinks. The type sometimes called an *ampulla olearia* is squat; others are taller, with a longer, slender neck.

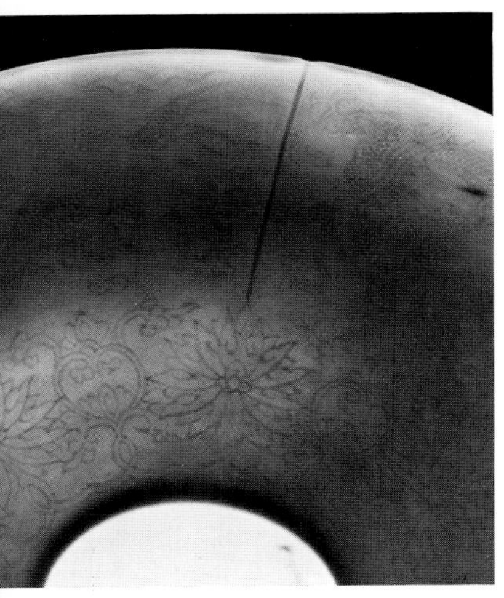

An hua. Detail of bowl showing decoration viewed by transmitted light; Ming dynasty, reign of Yung-lo (1403–24). Victoria and Albert Museum, London.

An hua (Chinese). Literally, secret decoration. The design was lightly incised into the body with a needle-point before glazing, and can be seen when the piece is held to the light. A similar effect was obtained by painting the design in white slip on a white body before glazing. The techniques were used on Chinese porcelain (usually EGGSHELL) from the reign of Yung-lo (1403–24), of the Ming dynasty, and again during the reign of Yung Chêng (1723–35), of the Ch'ing dynasty.

Angerstein service. A dinner-service of 98 pieces made at Coalport (England), *c.* 1805, for John Julius Angerstein, a banker whose collection of paintings formed the nucleus of the National Gallery, London. Each piece is decorated with a different black silhouette of children. *See* SILHOUETTE WARE.

Anglo-American pottery. Creamware or pearlware made in England for the American market between 1790 and 1840, and decorated with AMERICAN VIEWS, usually in blue.

Angoulême sprig. A sprig of cornflower used in sprays or as a repeating pattern on porcelain made at the factory of Dihl et Guérhard in the rue de Bondy, Paris, which was under the protection of the Duc d'Angoulême (1775–1844). Known in France as *barbeaux* (cornflowers), this decorative motif is said to have been designed by Hettlinger at Sèvres in 1782 to please Marie-Antoinette, and it was later taken up by other Paris factories, including that of André-Marie Lebœuf in the rue Thiroux which was under her protection. (*See* PORCELAINE DE LA REINE.) It was also used on English porcelain by Derby and others, and occurs occasionally on creamware made by Wedgwood and Enoch Wood. *See* CHANTILLY SPRAYS.

Animal figures. Popular figures and figure groups, made by many factories in porcelain and pottery, include CATS, DOGS, cows, sheep, GOATS, squirrels, BIRDS, as well as elephants, TIGERS, and other wild animals. Chinese tomb-figures of CAMELS and HORSES are especially notable. *See* also AFFENKAPELLE; DOG ORCHESTRA; FABULOUS ANIMALS.

Angoulême sprig. Cabaret, soft-paste porcelain with polychrome decoration, Sèvres, 1782. Courtesy, Antique Porcelain Co., London.

Angerstein service. Pieces from the service, Coalport, *c.* 1805. Courtesy, Christie's.

Annamese ware. Porcelain made in Annam in the 14th century and decorated somewhat in the Chinese manner in a greyish underglaze blue. The body is usually coarse and without refinement. Brownish celadons are ascribed to the same source. The glaze varies in thickness, and the thicker varieties are inclined to run into drops. *See* SAWANKHALOK WARE.

Annona pattern. Decoration on Chinese porcelain plates and platters made for export late in the 18th century. It depicts the flowers and leaves of the annona or custard-apple painted in vivid colours.

Antefix. (1) An ornament placed at the end of eaves to conceal the joint-tiles of the roof, or on a cornice to permit the escape of water through a pierced hole. Antefixes were made of terracotta in the form of masks by the Greeks and Romans. (2) The word is sometimes used to refer to a TERMINAL.

Anthemion. A decoration, painted or in low relief, which is a stylized form of the honeysuckle, being in floral or foliated patterns – sometimes in a radiating cluster. It somewhat resembles the PALMETTE.

Ao Kutani (Japanese). KUTANI PORCELAIN made in the 17th century decorated in a palette in which a fine green predominated. Specimens are rare. It is sometimes called 'green Kutani'.

Apostle jar. A type of faience drug-jar made at Winterthur (Switzerland), with painted decoration of the Twelve Apostles. The same subject is found in relief decoration on RHENISH STONEWARE.

Apostle tankard. A tankard decorated in relief with an encircling frieze of the Twelve Apostles, each named and accompanied by his attribute. They were made in Franconia (Germany), *c.* 1540, and by Charles Meigh in England, *c.* 1845.

Apple-green. A ground colour introduced at Sèvres in 1757 and later much used elsewhere. Sometimes called 'pea-green' when it is employed at Worcester from *c.* 1769. A somewhat similar colour sometimes occurs on 18th-century Chinese porcelain. The colour was also called *vert pomme* or *vert jaune* at Sèvres. *See* CHROME-GREEN.

Apple teapot. A teapot in the form of an apple, with CRABSTOCK spout and handle, and with applied leaves on the body and cover. They were made of earthenware, with a mottled coloured glaze, by William Greatbatch for Wedgwood, *c.* 1755–60 *See* PEAR TEAPOT.

Applied. Attached as an ornament by SPRIGGING. The French term is *appliqué*.

Arbour group. Porcelain group on a rococo base, Höchst, *c.* 1755. Cecil Higgins Museum, Bedford.

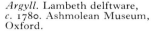

Apulian ware. *See* EGNATIAN WARE.

Aquamanile. A type of pottery EWER used in Roman times for washing the hands at table. Some were in the form of a figure or an animal; others were a horizontal cylinder with a spout in the form of an animal's head, and a bail handle. The *aquamanile* continued to be made, sometimes in pottery, sometimes in bronze, until the 17th century.

Arabesque. (1) In Islamic art, a flat decoration of intricate, interlaced lines and bands and abstract ornament adapted largely from Roman sources. As a popular Moorish decoration its Spanish form excluded close representations of animal forms, these coming from Christian potters. The strapwork of arabesques of this kind later influenced northern baroque ornament, and in 19th-century England such designs were often termed 'Moresques'. (2) In Renaissance and later European art, an ornament with flowing, curved lines and fanciful intertwining of leaves, scrolls, and animal forms. Ornament of this kind was popular during the NEO-CLASSICAL period, after *c.* 1760 and until *c.* 1790. The term is sometimes mistakenly applied to GROTESQUES. Arabesques on pottery are principally to be found on Italian maiolica. The Italian term is *arabesco* (pl. *arabeschi*).

Arbour group. A group depicting two or more figures under an arbour of trees and foliage. They were made by John Astbury, *c.* 1740–50, of English SALTGLAZED STONEWARE, and possibly by William Littler. An example is known in Longton Hall porcelain. Others are known of WHIELDON WARE, and the latest example to be recorded occurs in the porcelain of Grainger & Co., Worcester, early in the 19th century. Comparable, but not similar, groups were made at some of the German factories, such as Frankenthal, Ludwigsburg and Nymphenburg. The German term is *Läubengruppe*. *See* BOCAGE.

Arbre d'amour (French). Literally, tree of love. A satirical decorative subject used on faience bowls made at Nevers (France). It depicts several women around a tree trying to ensnare men who seek to escape in its branches.

Arcaded decoration. A decorative pattern in the form of a series of connected or interlocking arches supported by columns. The arches were round-headed during the Renaissance, and pointed during the Gothic period and the Gothic Revival.

Arcanist. A workman purporting to have secret knowledge about the making of faience or porcelain in the 18th century. Many were impostors, but some were recognized and competent, and played a very important part in establishing new factories in Germany.

Architectural elements. Porcelain replicas of architectural features, such as pilasters, Corinthian columns, tribunes, pedestals, etc. They were made principally at Meissen, and examples are known from Berlin, Frankenthal, and Capodimonte. Heights of individual pieces range from 2 to 15 inches.

Architectural pottery. Wares (apart from bricks and roof tiles) used in the construction and decoration of buildings, such as fireplaces, fountains, stoves, decorative tiles, and ridge tiles.

Argil. A type of potter's clay; when from Wales, it was sometimes called 'Cambria clay'.

Argyll. Lambeth delftware, *c.* 1780. Ashmolean Museum, Oxford.

Argyll. Sometimes (incorrectly) 'argyle'. A gravy-warmer with a handle and spout, similar in shape to a covered coffee-pot. The gravy is kept warm by hot water which is contained in a separate compartment created by a double wall, a false bottom or a central vertical tube. This peculiarly English utensil, said to have been invented by the third Duke of Argyll and originally of silver, *c.* 1750, was made in the last two forms above-mentioned of English delftware, of creamware (by Wedgwood and at Leeds, *c.* 1770–90), and of stoneware.

Arhat (Japanese). A Buddhist disciple. *See* LOHAN.

Arita porcelain. The product of the Arita kilns (Hizen province, Japan). The polychrome ware decorated by Sakaida Kakiemon was made here, as well as those wares categorized as IMARI – so called from the port of shipment at Imari not far away. Porcelain, using the natural mixture of porcelain clay and feldspathic rock found locally, was produced in kilns established at Arita early in the 17th century. The wares decorated by and in the manner of Kakiemon arrived in Europe *c.* 1680, imported by the Dutch, and soon acquired a greater esteem than the Chinese wares then being imported. Shapes and decoration greatly influenced the early European porcelain factories, especially Meissen and Chantilly, and octagonal dishes and bowls, as well as octagonal-, hexagonal-, and square-section vases made by European factories were based on Arita styles. The asymmetrical nature of Arita decoration played a part, which may have been considerable, in inspiring the same feature in the ROCOCO STYLE.

Armenian bole. A variety of clay coloured bright red by iron oxide. It is found in Armenia and Tuscany. It was especially used as a pigment on polychrome ISNIK POTTERY made from *c.* 1580. It stands up from the surface of the vessel in slight relief. *See* ARMENIAN RED; KÜTAHYA WARE; FAN-HUNG.

Armenian red. A brilliant red colour derived from Armenian bole and characteristic of ISNIK POTTERY. Also called 'tomato-red' and 'sealing-wax red'.

Armillaire cup. A style of teacup, wide and shallow, with a stemmed foot and a small loop handle; the lower half of the cup is reeded. It was introduced at Sèvres, *c.* 1830.

Armorial ware. Ceramic ware decorated with heraldic arms and crests, either painted or transfer-printed. Porcelain so decorated was made in China during the Ch'ing dynasty for export to Europe, principally during the 18th century. Engravings, sketches, and bookplates were sent to the Canton enamelling shops to serve as a guide. Armorial ware was made in Europe from the 16th century and in England after 1750 at Worcester, Plymouth, and Bristol, and in creamware by Wedgwood and at Leeds. Sometimes called 'heraldic ware'. The German term is *Wappengeschirr*. *See* ROYAL ARMORIAL WARE.

Arretine ware. Samian ware made at Arretium (Arezzo), Italy. A general term for such ware was TERRA SIGILLATA.

Arrosoir (French). A watering-pail; it was frequently made of porcelain.

Arrow vase. A globular Chinese vase with a long cylindrical neck and two small tubular loops attached on either side of the upper part of the neck. Vases of this kind were used in a competitive game in which arrows were thrown with the object of getting them either into the vase itself, or, better still, into one of the loops.

Architectural elements. Pilasters, columns and bases, ht 3½–14½ in., porcelain, Meissen and Berlin, *c.* 1745–60. Courtesy, Christie's.

Armorial ware. Chinese plate painted at Canton with a European coat of arms; reign of Ch'ien Lung (1736–96). Victoria and Albert Museum, London.

Arrow vase. Tz'ŭ Chou yao, decorated with white and brown slip covered with a clear glaze. Ming dynasty, 16th century; 15½ in. Victoria and Albert Museum, London.

Art Nouveau. A style of decoration introduced in England *c.* 1890, mainly as a product of the movement started by William Morris and the Pre-Raphaelites, which spread to the Continent and America. It came to an end with the outbreak of World War I. Applicable to all the decorative arts, it was adapted to the decoration of ceramics by Doulton's and others. It occurs on pottery mainly as floral motifs with elaborately twining tendrils. The German term is *Jugendstil*. *See* JEU DE L'ÉCHARPE.

Artemisia leaf. A decorative motif on Chinese porcelain. It is one of the EIGHT PRECIOUS THINGS. The Chinese term is *ai-yeh*. It is often found as an underglaze blue mark on porcelain of the reign of K'ang Hsi (1662–1722).

Articulated. Having movable parts, as the head and hands on certain oriental figures. *See* PAGOD.

Artificial porcelain. The same as SOFT-PASTE PORCELAIN, known in France as *pâte tendre*. Alternative terms are 'frit porcelain' (England) and *porcelaine de France* (France). Porcelain of this kind is made with powdered glass as a substitute for the feldspathic rock of true porcelain. Its translucency is variable in intensity and colour, and it can be cut by a file drawn firmly across an unglazed part. Artificial porcelain was first made in Italy at the end of the 16th century (MEDICI PORCELAIN), but the manufacture fell into disuse and was not revived until the second half of the 17th century in France. The first English factory to make soft-paste porcelain, based on that already being made in France, was Chelsea, starting *c.* 1743. There are a number of variations, particularly BONE-ASH porcelain. *See* SOAPROCK PORCELAIN; FRIT.

Aryballos. Corinthian, 600–575 BC; ht 2½ in. Victoria and Albert Museum, London.

Aryballos, sometimes *aryballas* (Greek). A small flask or bottle of ancient pottery, used for holding oil for the bath. It had a globular body, a short, thin neck, a flat disk mouth with a small orifice, and a handle (occasionally two) from the shoulder to the disk of the mouth. Usually a thong was tied to the handle, to be looped over the user's wrist. Some examples were made in anthropomorphic, zoomorphic, or mythological form, the last being represented by flasks in the form of Odyssean sirens and sometimes called SIREN VASES. They range in height from 1 inch to 8 inches or more.

Ash. Various ashes have been used as a FLUX and added to ceramic bodies and glazes; *see* BONE-ASH; FERN-ASH; SEA-WEED, ASHES OF.

Ashes of roses. A greyish-blue red employed on some Chinese porcelain of the reign of K'ang Hsi (1662–1722).

Askos. Cyprus, 5th century BC. British Museum, London.

Askos (Greek). A small pottery vessel, ranging in size from 3 inches to 8 inches, used in ancient Greece for pouring oil into lamps. It is in the form of a low bowl or jug with an overhead arched handle, at one end of which is a spout. It was so called from the fact that some examples were said to have been made in the shape of a wine-skin or leather bottle (*askos*); a few are in the form of an animal, bird, or lobster claw.

Asparagus butter bowl. A small, shallow, cup-like bowl about 2¼ inches in diameter, with one flat lateral handle. It was intended for individual use. The form is similar to that of the GODET of food-warmers in English delftware. *See* BLEEDING BOWL.

Asparagus butter dish. An oval dish in the centre of which is an affixed butter-dish; made by Wedgwood.

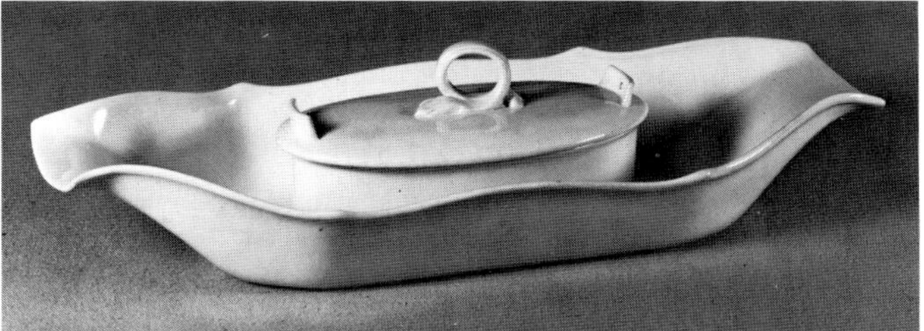

Asparagus butter-dish. Creamware, with attached butter-dish, Wedgwood, late 18th century. Victoria and Albert Museum, London.

Asparagus plate. A circular plate sloping downwards towards the centre (to which the asparagus stalks are pointed) and having a small well on one side near the rim for melted butter. They were made of creamware in Italy.

Asparagus shell. A small, flat receptacle, about three inches long, with low vertical sides and open at both ends. It is not quite rectangular, but tapers towards one end, so that about ten may be fitted into a circular arrangement to form a complete set. In the *Leeds Pattern Books* they are called an 'asparagus shell', although they are sometimes erroneously thought to serve as a KNIFE-REST. They were made at a number of English factories, including Spode and (in porcelain) Caughley and Derby.

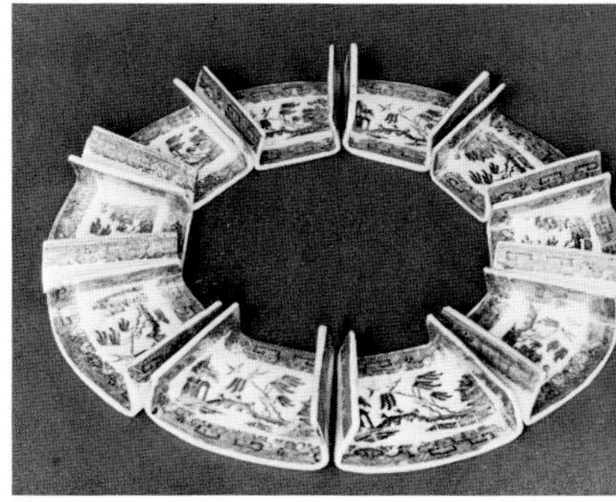

Asparagus shells. Transfer-printed with the willow pattern in underglaze blue; each 3¼ in. Spode, *c.* 1870–1900. David Drakard Collection.

Asparagus tureen. A covered tureen for the serving of asparagus, naturalistically modelled and coloured as a bundle of asparagus, which is often tied with two simulated raffia ribbons. One partially detached stalk forms the handle to the cover. Made at Chelsea and elsewhere during the middle of the 18th century.

Astbury ware. English pottery of a type associated with John Astbury in Staffordshire, *c.* 1730. It has a red-brown body decorated with stamped relief decoration in white clay, the whole being covered with a lead glaze. The term also refers to small figures, *c.* 1740–45, in similar clays to those used for the vessels, often combining differently coloured clays in the decoration. No marks are to be found on John Astbury's wares; an impressed mark 'Astbury' was used on the later wares, *c.* 1780–1800, of a son, Thomas Astbury.

Astbury-Whieldon figures. English figures made *c.* 1750–55 in the manner of John Astbury and Thomas Whieldon (*see* WHIEL-

Astbury ware. Typical figures, *c.* 1740–45. City Museums, Stoke-on-Trent.

Astbury-Whieldon figure. Mounted soldier, polychrome lead-glazed earthenware, *c.* 1750–55. Burnap Collection, William Rockhill Nelson Gallery of Art, Kansas City, Mo.

Aster pattern. Porcelain plate with underglaze decoration; reign of K'ang Hsi (1662–1722). Victoria and Albert Museum, London.

DON WARE) in clays of different colours with an added lead glaze coloured with metallic oxides. The figures are often amusing and, despite technical imperfections, are valued for their great charm. The term arises from the combination of Astbury and Whieldon techniques in the same piece. *See* ARBOUR GROUPS.

Aster pattern. A pattern of stylized asters on some Chinese underglaze blue porcelain of the reign of Wan Li (1579–1613). The pattern was very popular and was repeated, often with variations, on delftware and porcelain, e.g. the BLAUBLÜMCHENMUSTER. *See* ZWIEBELMUSTER; ROYAL LILY PATTERN.

Atlantes. Draped male figures representing Atlas who bore the vault of heaven (often erroneously stated to be the world) on his shoulders, and serving in place of a column to support an entablature. They were employed to decorate ceramic ware in relief or painted form. *See* TELAMON; CARYATID; CANEPHOROS; GUÉRIDON.

Ato Shonsui (Japanese). *See* SHONSUITEI.

Aubergine. A purple high-temperature or faience colour resembling the skin of a ripe eggplant or aubergine, introduced at Sèvres after 1770 as a porcelain glaze, and also used as an enamel in painted decoration at Meissen and elsewhere. Derived from manganese oxide, it varies in shade but usually comes close to the colour yielded by permanganate of potash crystals when dissolved in water. Also called 'bishop's purple' or '*violet d'évêque*'.

Augustus Rex ware. Ware, usually vases, made to the special order of Augustus the Strong, Elector of Saxony and King of Poland, and his son Augustus III, patrons of the Meissen porcelain factory. These often bear the royal monogram 'AR', usually on the base. Original specimens with this monogram, dating from the first half of the 18th century, are exceedingly rare. They should not be confused with a large group of wares, made *c.* 1870 and painted by Helena Wolfsohn, which bear the same monogram on the base and are often known to provincial auctioneers as CROWN DRESDEN.

Ausschuss Porzellan (German). Literally, reject porcelain. The lowest of the three categories into which Meissen porcelain was normally placed by the inspectors of finished ware, the other two being 'GUT' and 'MITTEL' (good and medium) quality. After 1760 defective ware was defaced by a cancellation mark incised with an engraver's wheel across the factory mark. Ware of this kind was sometimes sold to HAUSMALER, such as Ferner. Most of it is of little value in comparison with factory wares. Also called *Brack.*

Aventurine glaze. A glaze so called from its resemblance to the natural stone of this name. Aventurine glaze has copper particles suspended in it which resemble gold. Glass of this kind was first made by the Venetians, and the stone was imitated by the Japanese in lacquer with which they covered some late varieties of ceramic ware, the surface being dusted with gold powder. *See* TIGER'S-EYE GLAZE.

Aztec pottery. *See* CENTRAL AMERICAN POTTERY.

Azulejo (Spanish). A tile. The term is both Spanish and Portuguese, and is thought to be derived from the fact that the decoration was often in blue (*azul*).

B

B-shaped handle. A handle in the form of a capital letter B – a double loop, with the curves outward, such as that frequently seen on a TYG.

Baby-feeder. A small vessel in the shape of a teapot, with a long, curved nipple spout. They were made by Wedgwood *c.* 1810, but unmarked examples in creamware or stoneware of an earlier date, perhaps *c.* 1770, also occur. *See* BUBBY-POT; FEEDING POT.

Bacchante jug. A porcelain jug decorated with the head of a bacchante; made at Derby. *See* TOBY JUG.

Bacchus jug. A polychrome moulded jug decorated with coloured glazes in the form of a grotesque, semi-nude male figure, sometimes thought to be a caricature of George III, who is seated on an upturned barrel and surrounded by fruit. On the reverse is a satyr who helps to support a cornucopia from which a dolphin is emerging. This jug was first made by Ralph Wood I, possibly from a model by Jean Voyez, *c.* 1780. Later variations include a small dog at the man's side, and a small figure of a woman between his feet.

Bacchus jug. A version by Felix Pratt, Staffordshire, *c.* 1810. Courtesy, David Newbon Ltd, London.

Bacile (Italian). A plate of MEZZA-MAIOLICA, over 16 inches in diameter and sometimes decorated with painted portraits and the addition of lustre. The *giretto* (FOOT-RING) is usually pierced with two holes for suspension on a wall by string. They often had a deep well (*cavetto*). Many specimens made until the end of the 15th century come from Pesaro. *See* PIATTO DA POMPA.

Bacino (Italian). (1) A coloured MAIOLICA plate affixed to the font of some churches as decoration; of Moorish-Spanish or Italian origin. (2) The term is also used more generally to mean a BASIN. *See* BACILE; TONDINO; PIATTO DA POMPA; SCODELLA.

Back-stamp. A modern term sometimes applied to any mark (factory mark, painter's mark, decorator's mark, etc.) placed on the underside of any ceramic object, including marks made by incising, transfer-printing, hand-painting, etc., but strictly applicable only to such a mark made with a rubber stamp.

Bagyne cup. A bowl similar in form to the French ÉCUELLE, small and shallow, with two flat horizontal handles flush with the rim. Perhaps a BLEEDING-BOWL. Examples occur both in ARITA PORCELAIN and CHINESE EXPORT PORCELAIN, usually decorated in blue.

Bail-handle. Porcelain teapot, Coalport, *c.* 1820. Victoria and Albert Museum, London.

Bail-handle. An arched overhead handle rising over the cover of a vessel, either fixed or swivelling. A handgrip of wood or porcelain was sometimes provided. A fixed bail handle was often provided on late 17th-century Chinese spouted wine-pots.

Bain-marie (French). A double boiler. They sometimes formed part of a VEILLEUSE. *See* LINER; FOOD-WARMER.

Baldachin. A canopy raised on four poles. Used as a motif on 18th-century French faience decorated with designs after Jean Bérain *père*.

Baluster. Porcelain vase of baluster shape, Worcester (Dr Wall period). Courtesy, Christie's.

Bamboo ware. Teapot, enamel on biscuit; reign of K'ang Hsi (1662–1722). Victoria and Albert Museum, London.

Ball clay. A type of potter's clay found in England in Devon and Dorset, so called because the clay was cut into balls weighing about 30 lb. Unfired they are usually grey, blue, or a colour closely approaching black, but after firing the colour of the clay is white or almost so. Deposits of similar clay also occur in the United States and on the Continent. Sometimes called blue clay.

Ballot box. A BARM POT or SALT-KIT. Pots of this kind may have been employed as ballot boxes, but they were not made for this purpose.

Baluster. A shape, usually that of a vase, similar to that of the upright supports in a balustrade, with the upper and lower parts cylindrical or slightly flaring; it differs from a PEAR-SHAPED object in being less bulbous.

Baluster jug. *See* TRICHTENBECHER.

Bamboo ware. Chinese ware moulded and painted to simulate bamboo. Similar ware was introduced by Wedgwood, *c.* 1770. *See* CANEWARE.

Banded creamware. A type of MOCHA WARE with horizontal bands of various colours. It was originally produced in Staffordshire, and later in France.

Banded hedge. A decorative subject, originally on porcelain decorated by Kakiemon, depicting a hedgerow, sometimes with a squirrel and flying birds. It was copied in the 18th century at Meissen, Chelsea, Chantilly, and elsewhere. The French term is *haie fleurie*. *See* SQUIRREL, GOURD VINE AND BANDED HEDGE; DÉCOR CORÉEN; JABBERWOCKY PATTERN.

Banded spout. A type of spout, occurring mainly on WET-DRUG JARS, which has a reinforcing band around it, with the ends attached to the neck of the jar.

Banko ware. A type of Japanese pottery named after a well-known potter, *c.* 1736–95. Wares made by him include the RAKU and SATSUMA types, and decorations derived from Ming dynasty green-and-red porcelain. His work was copied in Japan in the 19th century.

Barbeaux (French). *See* ANGOULÊME SPRIG.

Barbed rim. A rim with sharp oblique points.

Barberini handle. A curved handle of the form found on the PORTLAND (BARBERINI) VASE.

Barberini Vase. *See* PORTLAND (BARBERINI) VASE.

Barber's bowl. A large, deep, wide-rimmed circular dish, characterized by an indentation in the rim which is a segment of a circle so that the bowl could be fitted snugly under the chin of the person being shaved. Examples in creamware from Leeds have a small well for soap, and opposite the indentation are two small pierced holes for a cord by which to suspend the bowl around the user's neck. Barber's bowls were sometimes decorated with the painted symbols of the barber's trade, and occasionally have jocular inscriptions, such as one (in French) on a faience basin of this kind: 'Here tomorrow one is shaved for nothing'. They are common in Continental faience, but also were made in Japanese porcelain, *c.* 1730. Also called a shaving bowl or MAMBRINO'S HELMET.

It has been said traditionally that a barber's bowl was also used as a BLEEDING BOWL before 1744 (perhaps based on the dual role of barber-surgeons and on the appearance of a lancet in the decoration of some barber's bowls), but this seems generally unlikely.

Barber's bowl. Creamware, Leeds, *c.* 1775–80. Courtesy, A.F. Allbrook, London.

Barbotine (French). Liquid slip. It was often laid on the ware by trailing.

Bargee teapot. The same as NARROW-BOAT TEAPOT.

Barlow ware. Stoneware made at Doulton's factory at Lambeth, *c.* 1870–1906, and decorated by three members of the Barlow family, of whom the best known are Hannah and Florence. Hannah specialized in incised animal decoration.

Barm pot. A pot for storing barm (a froth that forms on fermenting malt-liquors, used to leaven bread). Sometimes known as a BALLOT BOX. It is often confused with the SALT-KIT.

Baroque. A style in art which emerged shortly before 1600, of which the principal exponent was Giovanni Lorenzo Bernini. It remained current in Europe until the rise of the ROCOCO style, *c.* 1730. It was a development of the RENAISSANCE style, and is characterized by lively, curved, and exuberant forms, by vigorous movement in figures, and by ornament based on classical sources which is symmetrical, as distinct from the asymmetry of the following rococo. The 17th-century baroque style is to be seen in maiolica and faience of the more ambitious kinds, but it is best exemplified by the 18th-century porcelain of Meissen and the figures of J. J. Kändler, especially those modelled before 1740.

Bartmannkrug (German). Literally, bearded man jug. A jug having the mask of a bearded man ornamenting the space immediately below the neck, of which one variety is termed in England a BELLARMINE.

Basal ring. Same as FOOT-RING.

Basalt. The modern spelling of basaltes, the name given by Josiah Wedgwood to his black stoneware. *See* BLACK BASALTES.

Basaltes. The name given by Josiah Wedgwood to his black stoneware. *See* BLACK BASALTES.

Base. The bottom part of, or support for, a vessel or a figure; bases occur in many styles, and the style often helps in dating the complete piece. *See* PEDESTAL; PLINTH; SOCLE; KICK-IN BASE.

Basin. A concave ceramic vessel of a size sufficient to hold water for washing or for mixing food. The French term is *cuvette. See* BOWL; BASON; BACINO.

Basket ware (2). Creamware chestnut basket, Leeds, *c.* 1780. Courtesy, Jellinek & Sampson, London.

Basket dish. A ceramic dish modelled to imitate interwoven wickerwork such as is employed in the making of baskets. *See* OZIER.

Basket ware. (1) Pieces with relief decoration in the form of basket- or wicker-work. Examples were made in England of salt-glazed stoneware, *c.* 1760–80, e.g. by Baddeley of Shelton. *See* OZIER. (2) Pieces made, from the 18th century, of interlacing strips of clay imitating basket-weaving. (3) Primitive pottery made by smearing the inside of a wicker basket with clay, followed by firing. The wickerwork burned away, leaving its simulacrum on the exterior of the pot thus made.

Battle scene. Porcelain plate decorated by F. F. Mayer of Pressnitz, *c.* 1750. British Museum, London.

Bason. An older variant spelling of basin. A small bowl of several sizes holding up to a pint of liquid. It was often part of a TEA-SERVICE, used to hold either sugar or the dregs from the cups (*see* SLOP-BOWL). Bowls for other purposes held up to a quart.

Bas-relief. The French term for LOW RELIEF. *See* HIGH RELIEF; MEDIUM RELIEF.

Basse-taille (French). A type of decoration utilizing enamel on a metal base, in which the design is first chased, engraved, or stamped on the surface, and then covered with transparent enamel. By extension, decoration on porcelain using a similar technique, or by using foil as a background under an enamel or glaze and simulating the design on metal. Examples were made in and near Limoges in the second half of the 19th century. *See* ÉMAIL OMBRANT; CHAMPLEVÉ; CLOISONNÉ; PLIQUE-À-JOUR.

Basso rilievo. The Italian term for LOW RELIEF. The Italian porcelain factory of Doccia, near Florence, devised a low-relief decoration of figures to ornament porcelain vessels, vases, etc., which is often erroneously attributed to the Capodimonte (Naples) factory. This type of decoration was later reproduced at Naples and in Germany.

Basso rilievo istoriato (Italian). Figure subjects in low relief used as decoration on maiolica, and on porcelain at Doccia.

Bat. (1) A slab of soft clay, usually round, and flattened by a spreader, used in the first stage of making a plate or saucer (*see* JIGGER) or hollow ware (*see* JOLLY). (2) A slab of glue or gelatine used in the process of BAT-PRINTING. (3) The flying mammal employed as a decorative symbol on Chinese and Japanese porcelain, symbolizing happiness. *See* FU; KOMORI.

Bat-printing. A development, *c.* 1774, in the field of transfer-printing in which bats of soft glue or gelatine were substituted for the paper normally used, and by means of which the picture was transferred from the engraved plate to the glaze. Engravings employed in this way were usually stippled in the technique of the engraver Francesco Bartolozzi (1727–1815), who worked in England, *c.* 1764–1802. Bat-printing was very commonly used in the early decades of the 19th century by a number of Staffordshire factories.

Bear-jug. Glazed earthenware jug, Staffordshire, 18th century. Courtesy, Jellinek & Sampson, London.

Batavian ware. (1) A type of Chinese porcelain named after Batavia, the Dutch trading port in Java, from which ware was shipped to Europe during the first half of the 18th century by the Dutch East India Company. It has a lustrous brown ground with fan-shaped white reserves painted in FAMILLE ROSE colours or underglaze blue; the brown colour is termed 'café au lait' or 'dead-leaf brown'. It was imitated at Meissen, the brown ground being devised by the kilnmaster, Samuel Stölzel. (2) A type of pearlware made at Leeds, dipped into a dark brown slip, the reserves decorated with underglaze or enamel painting, or with transfer-prints.

Batter-jug. A stoneware jug, ovoid in shape with two loop handles and a tubular spout, for pouring batter mixture.

Battle for the breeches. A pottery group modelled in Staffordshire by Obadiah Sherratt, *c.* 1808; it depicts a husband resisting his wife's attempt to take possession of his breeches, which symbolize matrimonial supremacy. The subject was also used as a decoration on English slipware and on SPILL-VASES.

Battle scenes. Decoration on porcelain depicting battles, camp scenes and cavalry skirmishes. It was popular at Meissen from *c.* 1740, and was the speciality of Johann Balthasar Bormann (later at Berlin). It also occurs on the porcelain of Frankenthal, Vienna, and Sèvres. The German term is *Schlachtenszenen.*

Bauerntanzkrug (German). Same as PEASANT-DANCE JUG.

Bayreuth ware. A red-bodied ware made at Bayreuth (Germany) in competition with Meissen RED STONEWARE. It was usually covered with a brown glaze and some important examples have *chinoiseries* in silver silhouette.

Bead and gadroon. A border pattern of relief decoration, consisting of a row of beads in pairs, each pair being separated by two short diagonal or vertical lines. It was employed on some English creamware.

Bead and reel border. A border relief pattern consisting of a series of beads between each pair of which are two or three diagonal dashes, or 'reels'.

Beaded border. A border pattern made of a continuous row of small painted beads.

Beaded edge. An edge decorated with BEADING.

Beading. A decoration in the form of a continuous row of small relief beads. *See* DIAMOND BEADING.

Beak. A type of projecting lip, usually on a jug; *see* HAWK-BEAK; PARROT-BEAK; SPARROW-BEAK.

Beaker. A drinking vessel, usually with a wide, flaring mouth, sometimes entirely of circular section down to the base, but sometimes supported on a stem and base. It has no handle, although the term as originally used did refer to a vessel with a handle and a spout (beak). *See* MUG; TANKARD.

Bear-jug. A pottery jug made in the form of a seated bear, the detachable head forming a cup. Early examples were made *c.* 1530 at Brixen in the Tyrol, and these probably inspired later versions in England (Nottingham, Derby, Yorkshire and Staffordshire), where some were saltglazed. The body of these is often covered with fragments of clay to represent fur. In some models the bear hugs a dog. *See* OWL-JUG; SUSSEX PIG.

Beau bleu (French). Similar to BLEU CÉLESTE or *bleu de Sèvres.*

Beaucage (French). *See* BOCAGE.

Beckoning Chinaman, The. A decorative subject depicting a moustached Chinaman pointing upwards to a flock of birds, and sometimes with a small boy leaping at his side; employed on Worcester porcelain.

Beckoning Chinaman. Decoration on porcelain teapot, Worcester. Courtesy, Worcester Royal Porcelain Co.

Bedpan. A vessel for bed use by invalids, usually circular or oval with a flattened inverted rim. Some have a spout at the rear for emptying. *See* SLIPPER.

Bedrieger. The Dutch term for PUZZLE-JUG. Early examples were made in Haarlem (Holland).

Beetle trap. Creamware, early 19th century; diam. 9¼ in. Wellcome Museum, London.

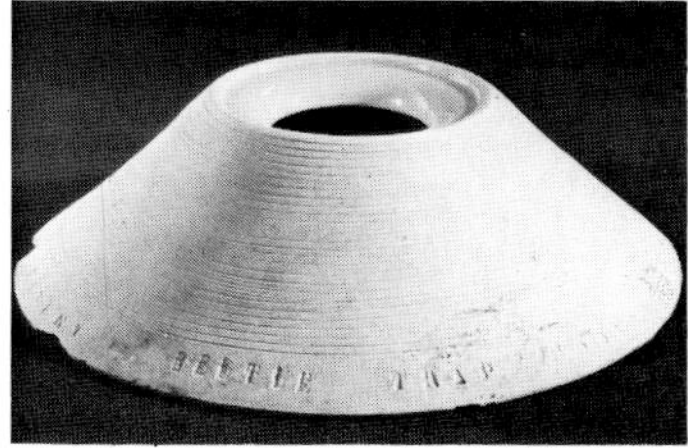

Beetle trap. A trap for beetles and cockroaches, baited with beer. It was in the form of a low truncated cone, the ridged, unglazed

Bell. Saltglazed stoneware; ht 5¾ in., Staffordshire, *c.* 1745. Victoria and Albert Museum, London.

Belleek ware. Sweetmeat dish. *c.* 1865–70. Victoria and Albert Museum, London.

Bell-toy pattern. Soft-paste porcelain saucer decorated in underglaze blue, Caughley, *c.* 1776. Courtesy, Antique Porcelain Co., London.

exterior sloping upwards to a slippery glazed opening in the top, whence the beetles dropped into the interior. Beetle traps were made in creamware in the early years of the 19th century under royal patent by W. H. Fordham & Son, London, whose impressed mark they bear.

Begging bowl. Chinese Buddhist alms bowl (*sa kung*), usually of oblate spheroidal shape. The type existed at least from the T'ang dynasty (618–906).

Bell. A hand-bell with a clapper and a vertical handle, made usually of porcelain. Some were made in England of saltglazed stoneware in the form of a woman.

Bell-ringers' jug. A large ale jug said to be used by bell-ringers, and kept either in the church tower or at the home of one of the bell-ringers.

Bell-toy pattern. A decorative subject depicting a Chinese lady sitting before a large urn of fruit with a child at her side; the child holds up a toy in the form of a stick with crossed arms from which are suspended four bells. It was one of the earliest patterns used at Caughley, *c.* 1776. Another version, used at Caughley and at Worcester, *c.* 1780–90, depicts the child holding a fan in the crook of his elbow; this was called the MOTHER AND CHILD PATTERN.

Bellarmine. A stoneware bottle, globular or pear-shaped, that has a moulded bearded mask on, or just below, the neck, and often a coat of arms below the mask. Bellarmines were originally made in Cologne (Germany) in the 16th century, and the mask was thought in England, to which they were exported in large quantities, to represent Cardinal Bellarmino (1542–1621), one of the leaders of the Counter Reformation. The mask was also sometimes thought to caricature the Spanish Duke d'Alva (Alba), and hence the bellarmine is also called a d'Alva bottle. Bellarmines were copied in England, *c.* 1675, by John Dwight of Fulham, and reproductions of bellarmines continued to be produced in Germany until late in the 19th century. Coats of arms appearing on specimens made for export correspond with those of the country for which the wares were intended. The German term is *Bartmannkrug*. In England they were also termed 'greybeards'. *See* MASK JUGS AND MUGS; TIGERWARE.

Belleek ware. A very thin porcelain, often of almost eggshell thickness, principally made at Belleek (Ireland), but also in the United States at Baltimore (Maryland) and Trenton (New Jersey). Ware of this kind made at East Liverpool (Ohio) was termed Lotus ware. Manufacture was started in Ireland in 1863 and still continues. The glaze has a nacreous lustre derived from bismuth, similar to that of BRIANÇON LUSTRE WARE. Production includes useful wares, and decorative pieces such as figures, openwork baskets, dishes, and pieces of marine form featuring modelled shells and coral branches. *See* EGGSHELL.

Bengal tyger pattern. A decorative pattern of oriental derivation employed on Plymouth and Worcester porcelain. It has barbed, radiating panels with fabulous animals and the EIGHT PRECIOUS THINGS (*Pa-pao*). It depicts a tiger with its body bent around a tree, baskets containing growing flowers, with a red-and-gold border in the KAKIEMON STYLE.

Bénitier (French). A small stoup or font for holy water, often made of faience in Italy, France and Spain, and occasionally in England. The projecting lip is often in the form of a shell.

Bennington ware. Various kinds of pottery made at Bennington (Vermont) between 1846 and 1858. The term usually refers to wares with a rich brown glaze, often mottled with yellow, blue, and orange (termed Rockingham ware in the United States), although the factory made many other kinds of ware. *See* BROWN CHINA.

Bérain motifs. A type of decoration originating with Jean Bérain *père* and followed by his son, Jean Bérain *fils*. Taken from his design books, it was an elaborate pattern of mythological and grotesque figures and half-figures, vases of flowers, drapes, baldachins, balustrades, and urns, all seeming to be floating in mid-air. Motifs based on the work of Bérain occur on the marquetry furniture of Boulle, and as ornament to many other works of art. In ceramics they are most notable as the decoration of certain kinds of mid-18th-century faience from Moustiers, but they can also be found on some French porcelain of the same date. The work of Bérain reflects the transitional stage between baroque and rococo. In modern times Bérain patterns have been employed to decorate porcelain by the Worcester Royal Porcelain Company.

Bellarmine. Brown-glazed earthenware, ht 18 in., with mask on neck and apostle frieze, Raeren, *c.* 1575. Victoria and Albert Museum, London.

Berettino (Italian). A tin-glaze ground colour of light lavender-blue used to decorate Italian maiolica from the early years of the 16th century, having been introduced *c.* 1520 at Faenza, where decoration was carried out in opaque white enamel (BLANC FIXE) on a dark-blue ground. *See* BIANCO SOPRA AZZURRO; BIANCO SOPRA BIANCO; LUMETTO.

Berlin cup. A style of coffee-cup, tall and resting on three feet which were sometimes of paw form, with a handle rising above the rim and usually having relief decoration.

Berlin transparency. Same as LITHOPHANE.

Betrothal jug. A jug with figures depicting a betrothed couple and bearing an appropriate inscription. Faience examples were made at Salzburg (Austria).

Beurrier. The French term for a BUTTER-DISH.

Bianchetto (Italian). A type of Italian earthenware with a buff or whitish body dipped in white slip and fired, after which it was decorated with painted designs and lead-glazed. It has the appearance of tin-glazed maiolica and so is often called MEZZA-MAIOLICA, but this is misleading, since maiolica is always tin-glazed.

Bianco di Faenza (Italian). Maiolica with a white glaze and coloured decoration developed at Faenza about the middle of the 16th century.

Bianco sopra azzurro (Italian). Decoration in opaque white on a lavender-blue tin-glaze ground known as BERETTINO. It was used in Italy, and also at Nevers (France). The French term BLANC FIXE embraces both this decoration and BIANCO SOPRA BIANCO.

Bianco sopra bianco (Italian). Decoration on tin-glazed earthenware in opaque white on a slightly bluish or greyish ground. It was employed on Italian maiolica from the early years of the 16th century, and on English delftware in the 18th century, as well as in Scandinavia and France (especially at Saint-Amand-les-Eaux, *c.* 1745). The French term BLANC FIXE embraces both this decoration and BIANCO SOPRA AZZURRO.

Bénitier. Glazed earthenware, Staffordshire, early 19th century. City Museums, Stoke-on-Trent.

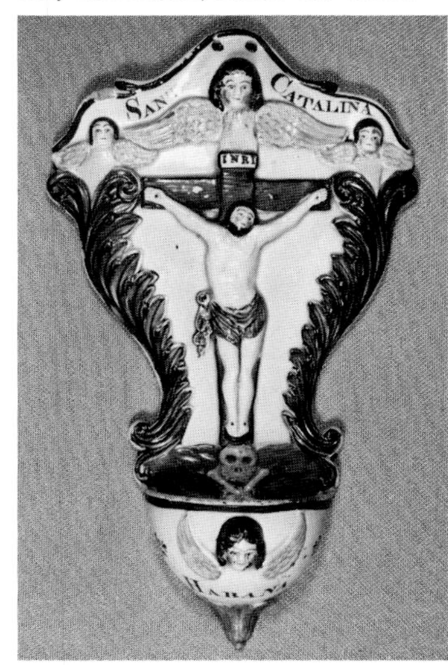

Bier-la-la. Porcelain figure, ht 11½ in., Höchst, *c.* 1760. Dr Siegfried Ducret Collection, Zurich.

Biberon (French). A FEEDING-BOTTLE, usually ovoid in shape, on a stemmed base, with from one to four feeding spouts projecting from around the centre of the body, and an overhead handle. Specimens exist in HENRI DEUX WARE.

Bidet (French). A small shallow bath for female use. The *bidet*, without any plumbing attachment, was introduced into France during the 18th century. Writing of his travels, Arthur Young (1741–1820) stated that it was very rare in England in 1790, and it remained so throughout the 19th and for most of the 20th century; some examples were made by Wedgwood. Examples in faience and porcelain (or ceramic pyriform bowls set in wooden stands) with floral decoration are usually French, and are sometimes used today for flower arrangements. *See* SANITARY WARE.

Biedermeier style. A German style which derived its name from satirical drawings in a Berlin journal featuring two smug bourgeois characters called Biedermann and Bummelmeier, whose taste in decoration was for a plain late EMPIRE STYLE. The term Biedermeier came to be applied to this style, current *c.* 1820–40, which is somewhat similar to the William IV and early Victorian styles in England. Although principally a furniture style, the term is sometimes employed of pottery and porcelain made to harmonize with it.

Bienenmuster (German). Literally, bee pattern. A decorative pattern used at Meissen depicting exotic bees and butterflies perched on HOLZSCHNITTBLUMEN. *See* SCHMETTERLINGMUSTER.

Bier-la-la (German). A figure made of porcelain at Höchst (Germany) in the form of a ragged old man standing with hands across his body, a long coat and falling socks, unshaven face and an ill-fitting wig, and having a sack at his feet. The figure has its origins in Flemish popular songs; it has sometimes been designated 'L'Avare'.

Biggin. A 19th-century English coffee-infuser; it is in the form of a cylindrical holder for the coffee-grounds, and is similar in appearance to a coffee-dripper. Sometimes said to be named after its inventor.

Bird-cage. Dutch delftware; ht 17¼ in., early 18th century. Fitzwilliam Museum, Cambridge.

Billingsley roses. Roses painted by, or in the style of, William Billingsley (1758–1828), who was apprenticed to the Derby factory in 1774, and was later at Pinxton, Mansfield, Worcester, Nantgarw, Swansea, and Coalport. About 1784 he began to paint in a naturalistic style in which the painting of the flower-petals, especially roses, was executed with a heavily loaded brush in full colour, the highlights then being wiped out with a dry brush. This mannerism was later extensively copied in England. *See* FLOWERS.

Bin label. A pottery or porcelain PLAQUE, rectangular (about 6 × 3¾ inches), triangular, or circular, made to be suspended by a string through a pierced hole from a wine-bin. Made from 1751 when the binning of wine was legalized, most examples are, however, of the 19th century. They were inscribed with the name, painted or stencilled, of the contents, such as Port, Hock, Malmsey, Sherry, Madeira, Claret, and Brandy, or were left blank with a mat finish for the name to be written in. In England they were made by Wedgwood, Leeds, Minton, and others. *See* WINE LABEL.

Bird-cage. A cage of conventional form made entirely (except for functional fittings) of ceramic ware. Examples are known in early 18th-century delftware and in porcelain.

Bird-call. Same as BIRD-WHISTLE.

Bird-feeder. A hollow receptacle with one or more apertures around its side to enable birds to feed. They were used in aviaries. Some of English delftware are circular; Rouen made faience examples which were rectangular.

Bird-spout. A type of baroque spout, derived from contemporary silver, the tip of which is in the form of a bird with an open beak. Examples are to be found in Saint-Cloud (France) porcelain of the first quarter of the 18th century. *See* EAGLE SPOUT.

Bird-whistle. A pottery or porcelain bird modelled so that when blown at an aperture in the tail it emits a whistling sound. Sometimes referred to as a bird-call. *See* WHISTLE; MUSICAL WARE.

Bird-whistle. Staffordshire (?) slipware, *c.* 1800–20. Burnap Collection, William Rockhill Nelson Gallery of Art, Kansas City, Mo.

Birds. Naturalistically modelled and painted birds were made, usually of porcelain, at many factories. Birds were also extensively used as painted decoration. *See* EXOTIC BIRDS; FANTASIE VÖGEL; DISHEVELLED BIRDS; DOUGHTY BIRDS; BOEHM BIRDS; BIRDS IN BRANCHIS; ORNITHOID PORCELAIN; QUIZZICAL BIRDS; BIRD-WHISTLE; PHOENIX; SIMURGH.

Birds in branchis. An 18th-century designation of figures of birds perched in the branches of a tree. It was usually employed of figures of this kind made at Bow, *c.* 1760.

Birth of Bacchus. Plaque, blue and white jasper, *c.* 1790. Courtesy, Wedgwood.

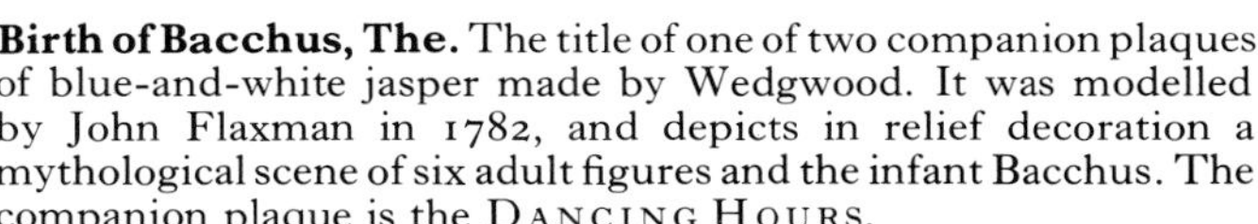

Birth of Bacchus, The. The title of one of two companion plaques of blue-and-white jasper made by Wedgwood. It was modelled by John Flaxman in 1782, and depicts in relief decoration a mythological scene of six adult figures and the infant Bacchus. The companion plaque is the DANCING HOURS.

Birth-tablet. A small plaque painted on one side with flowers in underglaze blue and on the other with an inscription recording the name and date of birth of an infant. Also called a birthday plaque. They were made in porcelain at Lowestoft in the 18th century. One example has been noticed recording the date of birth on one side and of the death on the other. *See* BIRTHDAY PLATE.

Birthday cup. A type of Chinese porcelain cup allegedly made to commemorate the sixtieth birthday of the Emperor K'ang Hsi in 1713. The cups are characterized by fine potting and decoration of exceptional quality, and bear seal characters meaning 'a myriad longevities without ending'. Plates with the same purpose were also made.

Billingsley roses. Bowl with painted decoration in the style of William Billingsley, Swansea, *c.* 1817.

Birthday plate. A plate with an inscription of the name and date of birth, usually employed as a christening gift. Examples are known in English delftware. *See* BIRTH-TABLET; MARRIAGE PLATE.

Bischofschüte (German). Same as BISHOP BOWL.

Biscuit. Unglazed porcelain or earthenware which has been fired only once. Such ware is sometimes erroneously termed 'bisque' in England and the United States. Wares deliberately left unglazed include porcelain originally introduced at Sèvres in the 1750s for modelling figures and groups, perhaps suggested by a resemblance to marble. Biscuit was subsequently made elsewhere on the Continent, and in England at the Derby factory from *c.* 1770. At Sèvres all figures and groups were made of biscuit porcelain (apart from a few exceedingly rare glazed specimens), but at Derby only faultless wares were left unglazed, those with minor defects being glazed and painted and sold more cheaply. The fashion was revived in the 19th century, *c.* 1840, with the introduction of a porcelain body termed PARIAN, and towards the end of the century decoration in enamel colours of pale pastel shades was used on such ware in England and on the Continent. *See* CARRARA PORCELAIN.

The phrase 'on (the) biscuit' is often used to refer to enamel decoration applied direct to biscuit as opposed to a previously applied glaze. *See* ENAMEL ON BISCUIT.

Bishop bowl. Faience bowl, Herrebøe, Norway, *c.* 1760. Kunstindustriemuseet, Oslo.

Biscuit firing. A preliminary firing of pottery and porcelain which transforms the ware into the BISCUIT state. This is followed by glazing and decoration, unless the ware is intended to be left unglazed.

Bishop bowl. A type of faience bowl in the form of a bishop's mitre, made for serving a variety of punch known as 'bishop'. The decoration in relief included a lemon and a bunch of grapes, indicative of the ingredients of the punch. Most come from the Scandinavian and Schleswig-Holstein faience factories and date from the middle of the 18th century.

Bishop Sumner pattern. A decorative subject on Worcester porcelain which combines a central panel of a KYLIN and a PHOENIX surrounded by a border with panels of rocks, plants, and fabulous animals. It is a Worcester version of a Chinese pattern, and first occurs during the Dr Wall period.

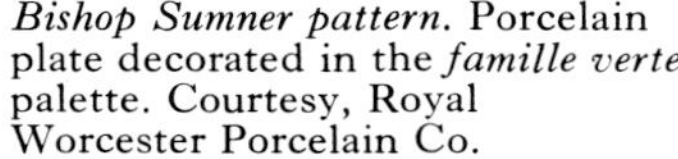

Bishop Sumner pattern. Porcelain plate decorated in the *famille verte* palette. Courtesy, Royal Worcester Porcelain Co.

Bishop's purple. Same as AUBERGINE.

Bison-head handle. A type of handle on porcelain vases made by William Boch at Greenpoint, N.Y. *See* AMERICAN PORCELAIN.

Bisque (French). A term erroneously applied to BISCUIT ware.

Bizen ware. A type of Japanese pottery made at Imbe (Bizen province) from *c.* 1583. A variety of wares was made here in a hard-fired body, either red or bluish brown, the latter being unglazed. The wares of YI-HSING were also copied.

Black. A colour produced by mixing cobalt oxide, iron oxide, and manganese oxide. It was employed in the form of glazes, and, mixed with the body, it formed the basis of some of the black wares. *See* BLACK BASALTES; WHIELDON WARE; MIRROR-BLACK GLAZE.

Black basaltes. A name adopted by Josiah Wedgwood to designate a black stoneware perfected by him *c.* 1768. However, black wares had been made in Staffordshire before this date, the earliest by the Elers brothers at the beginning of the 18th century. Black basaltes is a fine-grained unglazed body stained with cobalt and manganese oxides. It could be cut and polished on a lathe or a lapidary's wheel, and was the first strictly ornamental ware to be developed by Wedgwood, although production also included wares of domestic utility. For the most part it was employed to make busts, vases, plaques, and medallions, often by CASTING, and sometimes with additional ornament formed on the engine-turning lathe. Some early examples, damaged in the kiln, were refurbished with added wooden bases and covers made by the wood-carver, Coward. On the Continent black basaltes ware in imitation of Wedgwood was made at a number of factories, Königsberg being an example. It was also called 'Black Egyptian' and 'Egyptian Black'. *See* BLACK PORCELAIN; EGYPTIAN WARE; ETRUSCAN WARE; BRONZE ETRUSCAN WARE.

Black basaltes. Vases from designs in Wedgwood's 'First Shape Book', 1770, marked Wedgwood and Bentley, 1775. Courtesy, Wedgwood.

Black Egyptian. Same as BLACK BASALTES and 'Egyptian Black'.

Black-figure style. A decorative style on Greek pottery, *c.* 600–300 BC, the distinctive feature of which is decoration in black silhouette painted on a red ground. On some pieces the body is partly covered with a black varnish, leaving panels of red clay into which the figures were incised. The figures usually have incised details with some touches of white. The style is generally archaic and stiff compared with the later RED-FIGURE STYLE. Black figures were also painted on a white ground in the decoration of funerary vases of the LEKYTHOS type. *See* FRANÇOIS VASE.

Black glazed earthenware. Red earthenware with a lustrous black or brownish-black glaze made in the second half of the 18th century in Staffordshire generally, and particularly at Burslem. Similar wares were made at Jackfield (Shropshire); *see* JACKFIELD WARE. Reproductions of black-glazed COW CREAMERS or CREAM-JUGS are now common.

Black pencilled ware. *See* PENCILLED WARE.

Black porcelain. A term applied to BLACK BASALTES by Josiah Wedgwood, although such ware was not generally fired to the point of vitrification necessary for it to be classified as porcelain. *See* JASPER.

Blackamoor. A figure of a blackamoor which has been produced in porcelain principally in three forms: (1) as an allegorical figure of Africa in the set of the FOUR CONTINENTS; (2) as an African Negro in his native surroundings; and (3) as a young serving attendant to 18th-century aristocracy. They were made at Meissen and other Continental factories and in England at Chelsea and Derby. *See* GUERIDON; AESOP.

Blanc de Chine. Figure of Buddha. Reign of K'ang Hsi (1662–1722). Wadsworth Atheneum, Hartford, Conn.

Blanc de Chine (French). An 18th-century French term used to designate a highly translucent Chinese porcelain made at Tê Hua (Fukien province) from the latter part of the Ming dynasty until the present day. Probably all the wares exported during the 17th and 18th centuries were left unpainted, hence the name, although specimens decorated in blue underglaze and in enamels are known in Europe, and may be a later importation. The colour ranges from ivory to chalk-white, the former probably being the earlier. The glaze is thick, rich, and unctuous. Most wares are small figures, finely and crisply modelled, which usually represent deities (KUAN-YIN being the most frequent), dignitaries, persons in European costume (such as the Dutch Governor), cups, bottles, dishes, etc. A frequent decoration of dishes etc. was the prunus blossom in relief. *Blanc de Chine* was copied at Saint-

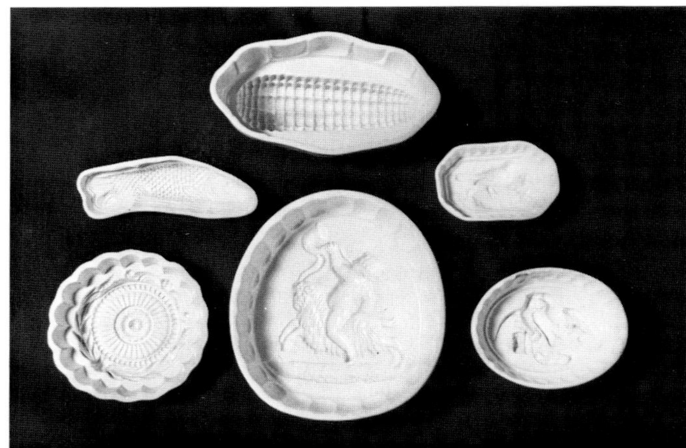

Blancmange mould. Creamware moulds, Wedgwood, late 18th century. Buten Museum of Wedgwood, Merion, Pa.

Cloud and Mennecy, and in England at Bow and Chelsea. A copy of a *blanc de Chine* figure of one of the EIGHT IMMORTALS was among the first productions of Lund's Bristol factory, and is marked in relief '*Bristoll 1750*'. *See* TÊ-HUA YAO.

Blanc de rehaut (French). Same as BLANC FIXE.

Blanc fixe (French). An opaque white enamel used for decoration on a darker tin-glaze ground. The term embraces both BIANCO SOPRA BIANCO and BIANCO SOPRA AZZURRO. The technique was employed at Nevers (France) after *c.* 1632 on the BLEU PERSAN ground. Also called *blanc de rehaut* and 'opaque white'.

Blancmange mould. A mould, made in various shapes with intaglio decoration, to be used for blancmange dessert. Examples were made in creamware by Wedgwood. *See* JELLY MOULD.

Blätterkantenmuster (German). Literally, leaf-border pattern. A blue-and-white border pattern of interlacing leaves, used at Meissen in the 18th century.

Blaublümchenmuster (German). Literally, little blue flower pattern. A decorative pattern of small blue flowers derived from the well-known ASTER PATTERN on Chinese porcelain of the late Ming dynasty. It was popular at Meissen and much copied in Germany. At Copenhagen it was called the Copenhagen pattern. At Worcester it inspired the ROYAL LILY PATTERN. *See* ZWIEBELMUSTER.

Blauwerk (German). Literally, blue work. A term sometimes employed to designate certain stonewares with engraved designs enhanced with cobalt blue (or sometimes manganese), made in the Westerwald by potters who had migrated there from Raeren in the Rhineland. Production has recently been revived in the Westerwald region. *See* RAEREN STONEWARE; WESTERWALD WARE.

Bleeding. A defect which results when a colour 'bleeds' or mingles with a different colour employed in the decoration.

Bleeding-bowl. A shallow bowl from 4 to 6 inches in diameter, with one flat handle usually flush with the rim, employed by the barber-surgeons of the 17th and 18th centuries in bleeding a patient. It is similar in form to the PORRINGER, apart from having one handle and not two, and also resembles the smaller TEA-MEASURE, and the even smaller GODET and ASPARAGUS BUTTER-BOWL. It is sometimes termed a 'cupping-bowl'. *See* BAGYNE CUP; BARBER'S BOWL.

Bleeding bowl. Porcelain bowl, diam. 5¼ in., decorated in underglaze blue, Worcester, 18th century. Victoria and Albert Museum, London.

Blenheim Palace service. A dinner-service of Derby porcelain, each piece painted with named views in circular panels, perhaps decorated by Zachariah Boreman.

Bleu agate (French). A very pale COBALT BLUE used at Sèvres in the 19th century on true porcelain.

Bleu céleste (French). A cerulean blue enamel ground colour employed at Sèvres. It was developed in 1752 by the chemist, Jean Hellot, and was introduced at Vincennes in 1753. Sometimes called *bleu de Sèvres*, as well as *bleu nouveau, beau bleu*, or, erroneously, *bleu turquoise*.

Bleu de roi (French). A rich enamel blue first developed at Vincennes *c.* 1749 and later used at Sèvres. It is also termed *bleu royal*. Eventually it largely superseded GROS BLEU, an underglaze ground popular in the 1750s. *Bleu de roi* was later imitated in England, at Worcester and Chelsea.

Bleu de Sèvres (French). Same as BLEU CÉLESTE (*bleu nouveau*).

Bleu de Vincennes (French). Same as BLEU LAPIS.

Bleu fouetté (French). A type of blue applied by insufflation, and used in France and at Meissen. It was lighter in hue than POWDER-BLUE (*bleu soufflé*).

Bleu lapis (French). A bright copper blue, popular at Vincennes in the early 1750s (termed *bleu de Vincennes*) and introduced by this factory before its removal to Sèvres. It is streaked with veins, similar to lapis lazuli stone, the lines sometimes being touched with gold. *See* LAPIS LAZULI.

Bleu persan. Faience plate decorated in white, orange and yellow over the blue ground, Nevers, *c.* 1660. Victoria and Albert Museum, London.

Bleu nouveau (French). Same as BLEU CÉLESTE (*bleu de Sèvres*).

Bleu nuagé (French). A cobalt-blue ground colour applied by SPONGING; it was employed at Sèvres in the 19th century, and has the appearance of a somewhat mottled BLEU CÉLESTE.

Bleu persan (French). Literally, Persian blue. A brilliant dark-blue ground colour developed at Nevers (France), inspired by Persian sources. It was employed on faience in the second half of the 17th century, in conjunction with opaque white, yellow, and orange applied over the blue ground. The style was copied on delftware in England at Lambeth, and also in Holland.

Bleu royal (French). Same as BLEU DE ROI.

Bleu soufflé (French). A widely used European term for POWDER-BLUE. *See* BLEU FOUETTÉ.

Bleu turc (French). A greyish-blue ground colour employed at Sèvres.

Bleu turquin (French). A brilliant turquoise enamel ground colour introduced at Sèvres in 1752; it later proved extremely popular, being revived *c.* 1870.

Blind basket ware. Moulded basket ware of the OZIER type which is unpierced.

Blind Earl pattern. Dish with moulded and painted decoration, Worcester, *c.* 1760. Courtesy, Sotheby's.

Block mould. Mould for cream jug, with vine-leaf decoration, Wedgwood, *c.* 1810. Courtesy, Wedgwood.

Blind Earl pattern. A decorative pattern of low-relief rosebuds, large leaves, and butterflies which covers the entire surface of plates. It was once thought to have been devised for the blind Earl of Coventry to feel, but as the design seems first to have appeared at Chelsea, *c.* 1755, and his blindness dated only from 1780, it is impossible for it to have been designed expressly for him. The pattern was also employed at Worcester before 1780, and is still used there today. It is sometimes called the 'Earl of Coventry pattern'.

Block (mould). The basic MOULD from which hollow potter's moulds (working moulds) are made. During the first half of the 18th century in Staffordshire they were often made from carved wood or alabaster, but plaster of Paris was commonly employed after *c.* 1745. Some early carved moulds were signed and dated by the block-cutter, Aaron Wood (1717–85) being perhaps the best known.

Block-cutting. The act of carving a BLOCK-MOULD, generally in wood or in alabaster, as a permanent source from which working moulds could be taken. Block-cutting was superseded by the casting of block-moulds in plaster of Paris after *c.* 1745.

Blue. A colour used in the decoration of pottery and porcelain, usually derived from cobalt oxide, but sometimes from copper oxide. The various hues include: BLEU AGATE; BLEU CÉLESTE (*bleu de Sèvres*; *bleu nouveau*; *beau bleu*); BLEU DE ROI (*bleu royal*; ultramarine); BLEU LAPIS (*bleu de Vincennes*); BLEU NUAGÉ; BLEU PERSAN; BLEU TURC; BLEU TURQUIN; POWDER-BLUE (*bleu fouetté*; *bleu soufflé*); CLAIR DE LUNE; DERBY BLUE; DRY BLUE; EGYPTIAN BLUE; GROS BLEU (Mazarine blue); LAPIS LAZULI; LITTLER'S BLUE; MOHAMMEDAN BLUE; ROBIN'S-EGG BLUE; SMITH'S BLUE. *See also* COBALT BLUE; FLOWN BLUE; SMALT; ZAFFER.

Blue-and-white porcelain. White porcelain decorated with COBALT BLUE underglaze, first made in China in the Yüan dynasty (1280–1368), the colour coming from Persian sources. Blue was used from the earliest years of the 18th century to decorate French porcelain made at Saint-Cloud, but it was rarely employed at Meissen, which had some difficulty in firing the colour successfully. It was very commonly used in England from *c.* 1750, especially at Worcester and Bow, although the Chelsea factory made little porcelain thus decorated. Blue was also employed as a ground colour (*see* GROS BLEU; POWDER-BLUE). Cobalt blue employed as an underglaze colour was painted on the unfired ware in China and covered with a feldspathic glaze, the whole being fired in one operation. In the 18th century soft-paste porcelains were fired to BISCUIT first, painted, and then covered with a lead glaze in preparation for firing.

Blue-and-white pottery. The wide range of earthenware painted with blue underglaze, the colour used being COBALT OXIDE. Tin-glazed earthenware has the decoration painted on the raw glaze before firing, and the decoration can therefore be more correctly described as 'in' the glaze rather than 'under' it.

Blue clay. Same as BALL CLAY.

Blue-dash charger. A tin-glazed CHARGER with a decoration of slanting cobalt-blue dashes along the rim, forming a kind of primitive rope-pattern. Although a dashed border of this kind occurs on some Continental wares, the term is particularly used of a specific group of 17th- and early 18th-century chargers of English delftware made in London and at Brislington (Bristol). The central polychrome painting is naïve, and includes Biblical subjects, representations of royalty, fruit, and abstract motifs. *See* OAK-LEAF CHARGER; ADAM AND EVE; PATRIOTIC CHARGER.

Blue-dash charger. English delftware, *c.* 1670–80. Courtesy, Sotheby's.

Blue dragon pattern. *See* BROSELEY BLUE DRAGON.

Blue lily pattern. *See* ROYAL LILY PATTERN.

Blue scale. *See* SCALE GROUND.

Blumen. The German term for flowers. *See* DEUTSCHE BLUMEN; INDIANISCHE BLUMEN; OBRIERTE DEUTSCHE BLUMEN; HOLZSCHNITTBLUMEN; SCHNITTBLUMEN; STREUBLUMEN; STROHBLUMEN; GOTZKOWSKY ERHABENE BLUMEN; MANIERBLUMEN.

Bobêche (French). The drip-pan of a CANDLE-NOZZLE.

Bocage (French). Literally, a grove, thicket, or woodland. Closely clustered modelled porcelain flowers, foliage, and branches, usually in the form of a canopy or arbour, and used as a background to porcelain figures. The custom seems to have been derived from arbours employed in the stage scenery of the 1750s, and some of the figures thus enhanced are of actors and actresses. The fashion is particularly noticeable in England, and is only rarely found abroad, where TRELLISAGE was apt to take the place of the *bocage*, as may be seen in the figures of Frankenthal and Nymphenburg of the early 1760s. The *bocage* was widely employed at Chelsea during the gold-anchor period (1758–70), at Derby about the same time, and to some extent at Plymouth. It belongs to the rococo style, and had largely disappeared by 1770, to return to favour later with some Staffordshire pottery figures in a much cruder form. Figures thus made were for mantelpiece decoration, or for side-tables, since the lack of detailed finish at the back made them unsuitable as a TABLE-DECORATION where the whole of the figure had to be seen. Subjects were very commonly taken from engravings by various hands (Boucher is an example) where only the front was shown. The *bocage* is sometimes called a 'boscage' or 'boskie'. *See* ARBOUR GROUP.

Bocage. Candlestick with pair of jackdaws, ht 10½ in., Chelsea, *c.* 1758–70. Smithsonian Institution, Washington, D.C.

Boccale (Italian). A type of jug made of maiolica in the early period with a large trefoil or pinched lip and a large loop handle. Jugs of this kind came from Orvieto in the 14th century.

Boccaro ware. A term meaning originally a scented, red, unglazed pottery imported into Europe from Mexico by the Portuguese, and later given to a somewhat similar ware made at Talavera (Spain). Subsequently the term was erroneously employed to describe red stoneware made in YI-HSING (China), and imported into Europe during the 17th century in the form of WINE-POTS which were used to brew the new drink of tea. *See* RED PORCELAIN.

Bodhidharma. An Indian Buddhist disciple, one of the eighteen LOHAN, whose name in Chinese is P'u-t'i Ta-mo. He is said to have reached China in AD 520, having crossed the river Yangtze standing on a reed plucked from the bank. He occurs as painted decoration, and in *blanc de Chine* as a figure. A large stoneware figure in the Victoria and Albert Museum (London) bears the date corresponding to 1484. *See* RAKAN.

Bodorf ware. Earthenware made *c.* 720–860 at Bodorf in the Vorgebirge (Germany), and exported down the Rhine.

Body. (1) The composite material from which earthenware, stoneware, or porcelain is made. In the case of porcelain, the word paste is more generally employed with the same meaning. (2) The main portion of a vessel, as distinguished from the base, handle, spout, cover, or applied decoration.

Boehm birds. Contemporary figures of birds naturalistically modelled and coloured by Edward Marshall Boehm at his pottery in Trenton, N.J., *c.* 1955–69. *See* DOUGHTY BIRDS.

Bohemian porcelain. Porcelain made in the 18th and 19th centuries in what is now Czechoslovakia, but which was formerly part of the German territories. The principal factories, with names in German and Czech, are: Pirkenhammer (Brezová), Elbogen (Loket), Schlaggenwald (Slavkov). Klösterle (Klásterec), Alt Rohlau (Stará Role), Dalwitz (Dalovice), Tannawa (Zdanav), Giesshübel (Kysibl), Chodau (Chodov), Budav (Budov), and Prague (Praha). Many Bohemian potteries were situated in the Karlsbad (Karlovy-Vary) district, formerly in the Austrian Empire.

Bois simulé (French). *See* FOND BOIS.

Boîte (French). A small, shallow decorative porcelain BOX employed in the 18th century by aristocratic society for a variety of purposes, including a *tabatière* (SNUFF-BOX), *boîte à fard* (ROUGE-BOX), and *boîte à mouche* (PATCH-BOX).

Boîte à fard. The French term for a ROUGE-BOX.

Boîte à mouche. The French term for a PATCH-BOX.

Bombé (French). Convex; bulged. Strictly, a term employed in the description of furniture, applied to bulging panels, and by analogy to pottery or porcelain of similar shape.

Bombylios (Greek). A small flask, relatively tall and elongated and having a small loop handle and a rounded base. It was used for holding perfume. The name is an obsolete term for an early form of ALABASTRON.

Bonbonnière (French). A small covered receptacle for sweetmeats, often modelled in a variety of ornamental forms, e.g. a shoe, a CHOPINE, or a covered box as at Chelsea. *See* COMFIT BOX.

Bone-ash. The product of calcined animal bones, mainly of cattle, which contains both lime and phosphoric acid. In a small quantity it acts as a flux, promoting the fusion of the ingredients of porcelain. In large quantities, up to 40 per cent, as used in the artificial porcelains of 18th-century England, it helps to stabilize the body and reduces kiln-wastage. First introduced at Bow *c.* 1750, it was later used at Chelsea from *c.* 1755. Lowestoft made a porcelain similar to Bow, and Derby employed bone-ash after 1770. About 1800 it was added to TRUE PORCELAIN to produce the standard English BONE-CHINA body which has been almost exclusively employed by English manufacturers since. Bone-ash has rarely been employed outside England, Continental and American manufacturers preferring the true porcelain of clay and feldspathic rock made on Chinese principles. The Worcester Royal Porcelain Company is now producing true porcelain of this kind as well as the standard bone-china hitherto preferred in

Böttger red stoneware. Flask of polished stoneware, Meissen, *c.* 1715. Victoria and Albert Museum, London.

England. Bone-ash reveals its presence on analysis by a variable proportion (usually about 17 per cent) of phosphoric acid and about 23 per cent of lime. *See* ARTIFICIAL PORCELAIN.

Bone-china. Usually termed 'china', this is a TRUE PORCELAIN of clay and feldspathic rock modified by the addition of BONE-ASH. The introduction of bone-china in England is ascribed to Josiah Spode II, *c.* 1794, and it is now almost exclusively used in England. Bone-china is sometimes termed 'English china'.

Border. The decoration added to the rim of such objects as plates and bowls. Some borders are painted, some are in relief, and some combine both techniques. Among the many varieties are: BEADED; BRÜHLSCHES ALLERLEI-DESSIN; CHAIN; CHEVRON; CIRCLE AND SQUARE; CLOUD AND THUNDER FRET; COIN; CRENELATED; DASH; DOLLAR; EGG AND ANCHOR; EGG AND DART; EGG AND TONGUE; EMBATTLED; FLORETTE; GREEK FRET; GUILLOCHE; HERRING-BONE; HONEYSUCKLE; HUSK; HYACINTH; INTERLOCKING CIRCLES; IVY; IVY WREATH; JAPANESE FRET; JU'I; KEY FRET; LAPPET; LATTICE; LAUREL; LEAF; LILY; LINK; LOTUS; LOTUS BUD; MEANDER; MEANDER AND STAR; MEANDER AND SWASTIKA; MOCK ARABIC; O-X; PALMETTE; PIE-CRUST; RIBBON AND LEAF; ROMANESQUE; ROSETTE; SAW-EDGE; SCEPTRE; SCROLL; SPEARHEAD; TEARDROP; TONGUE; TRELLIS; TRIANGLE; VANDYKE. For some German border-patterns, *see* MUSTER.

Borogove vase. A vase inspired by Tenniel's drawing of the borogove which appeared as an illustration to Lewis Carroll's *Alice through the Looking-glass*. It takes the form of a fabulous animal, half hedgehog and half fish, and was modelled in 1890 for Doulton by Mark V. Marshall. The vase is of saltglazed earthenware, decorated with light- and dark-brown and green slip, and is 5½ inches high.

Borogove vase. Saltglazed earthenware; ht 5½ in. Courtesy, Doulton & Co.

Boscage. Same as BOCAGE.

Boskie. Same as BOCAGE.

Boss. The raised central ornament in the well of a plate or bowl, sometimes referred to tautologically as a 'convex boss'. *See* PHIALE.

***Bossierer*.** The German term for REPAIRER.

Botanical ware. Service ware decorated with painted reproductions of FLOWERS taken from works on botany. The style was introduced at Meissen, and was copied in England during the 1750s by Chelsea, which, *c.* 1753, began to use flowers derived from an English work, *The Gardener's Dictionary*, by Phillip Miller. On some ware the flowers, with their botanical names, were transfer-printed, as at Swansea. Flowers of this kind are found decorating porcelain from most of the major 18th-century factories. *See* HANS SLOANE FLOWERS; FLORA DANICA SERVICE.

Botijo (Spanish). *See* WET-DRUG JAR.

Böttger handle. A loop handle which has its ends curved in opposing directions, like an inverted *S*, the larger, top curve joining the top of the vessel, the small curve attached and turning outwards lower down, as on coffee-pots made of BÖTTGER RED STONEWARE.

Böttger handle. Coffee-pot, Böttger red stoneware decorated with lacquer, Meissen, *c.* 1715. Victoria and Albert Museum, London.

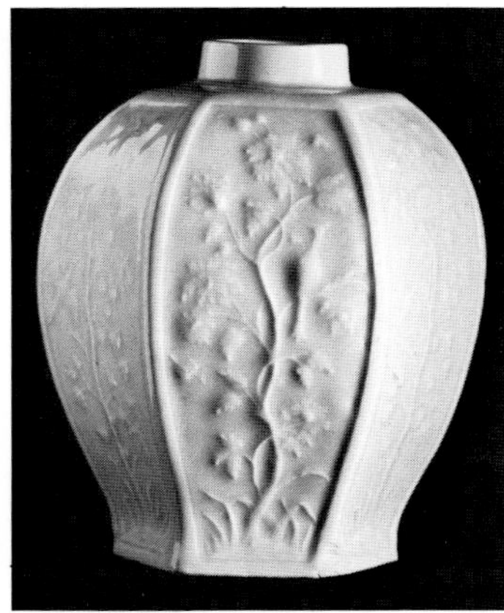

Böttger Porzellan. Tea-jar with moulded decoration based on oriental designs, Meissen, *c.* 1715. Museum of Fine Arts, Boston, Mass.

Böttger Porzellan (German). The first European porcelain developed *c.* 1709 at Meissen by Johann Friedrich Böttger, and based on earlier researches by Ehrenfried Walther von Tschirnhaus. It is not highly translucent, and in colour it has a smoky appearance, or is sometimes a creamy yellow. The glaze is thick and even, and the minute 'bubbles' in suspension are due to the body being first fired to BISCUIT, the glaze being added afterwards. It was decorated characteristically with applied ornament, and a limited range of enamel colours was also employed. Specimens are very rare.

Böttger red stoneware. The RED STONEWARE (*Steinzeug*) made by J. F. Böttger in association with E. W. von Tschirnhaus, *c.* 1708. It was an offshoot of experiments towards the manufacture of porcelain and artificial hardstones. The body ranged in colour from brownish-red to dark brown and almost black, the latter being termed EISENPORZELLAN (iron porcelain). Decoration included incised and engraved designs, relief decoration, pierced work, lacquer or cold painting, and insetting (*see* FACETED WARE). It was discontinued *c.* 1730. It is occasionally termed JASPIS PORZELLAN (jasper porcelain) which records its origin in experiments directed towards the manufacture of artificial hardstone. It was the subject of many imitations, notably those of almost contemporary date from Plaue-an-der-Havel (Germany), but it may be distinguished from them by its extreme hardness; *see* BRANDENBURG PORCELAIN.

Bottle Kiln. Earthenware model of a kiln by C. Shufflebotham. City Museums, Stoke-on-Trent.

Bottle. A vessel for holding liquids, usually with a long neck and a narrow mouth. Bottles are often cylindrical, but may be globular, ovoid, pear-shaped, or of square section, with a great many variations. They may have flat or rounded sides. *See* DOUBLE BOTTLE: PILGRIM-FLASK; BELLARMINE; FLASK; EWER.

Bottle kiln. The older type of KILN, now superseded by the TUNNEL KILN. It is so called from its bottle-shaped appearance; an alternative term is 'beehive kiln'. In kilns of this kind the ware was usually sealed in SAGGERS to keep it from contact with smoke and dust resulting from coal- or wood-firing.

Bottle label. Same as WINE LABEL.

Bottle-stand. A circular, flat-bottomed receptacle with a low, vertical rim made as a rest or stand for a wine-bottle on the dinner-table; a coaster. The term is sometimes applied also to a CRUET-STAND.

Bottle vase. A pear-shaped vase of Chinese porcelain, from the latter part of the T'ang dynasty, that has a contracted neck and a flaring mouth. The Chinese term is *yu-hu-ch'un p'ing.*

Boucher, style (French). *See* ROCOCO.

Bougeoir. The French term for CHAMBER CANDLESTICK.

Bouillon cup. Porcelain, Worcester, *c.* 1770. Courtesy, Christie's.

Bough-pot. A pot or vase in which cut sprays of flowering shrubs or small blossom-bearing branches of trees are placed through holes in the cover. They were intended for use near the hearth or on a mantelpiece. *See* BOUQUETIÈRE; ROOT-POT.

Bouillon cup. A type of shallow cup (somewhat similar to an ÉCUELLE) with two side handles, for serving bouillon; sometimes called a broth bowl. *See* TREMBLEUSE.

Bouquet. Assorted flowers tied together in a bunch. They were made of soft-paste porcelain at Vincennes in the late 1740s. The flowers were mounted by padding the branches with a wadding of soft linen thread bound with a waxed linen tape on a wire foundation. Sometimes leaves of stiffened green-painted fabric were added, cut to match those of the particular flower. On some examples both branches and leaves were made of bronze. The flowers copied either Meissen types or natural specimens.

Bouquetière (French). A vase for cut flowers which has a cover pierced with holes for the stems. Although usually made for standing on a table or mantelpiece, some were pierced for hanging on a wall and appropriately shaped. *See* BOUGH-POT; BOUQUETIÈRE FIGURES.

Bouquetière figures. Figures in pairs, in a sitting position, usually with baskets beside or behind them, or in their laps, pierced with holes to hold cut flowers. They were made at Meissen, Chantilly, and other Continental factories in the 18th century, and in England at Chelsea. *See* SWEETMEAT FIGURE.

Bourdalou (French). A small oval urinary receptacle for female use, made of pottery or porcelain, *c.* 1710–1850, by the leading Continental factories and in England by Bow, Leeds, Wedgwood, Derby, and others. Sometimes confused with a SAUCE-BOAT, it is basically different in form in that the front end has an in-curved rim rather than a pouring lip, and there is usually a simple foot-rim (or none at all) rather than a stemmed base. The single handle, at the end of the long axis, is usually a simple loop, but some have an ornate thumb-rest. A few have an eye painted on the bottom inside or an appropriate *grivois* legend (perhaps added later). Some Chinese export examples, *c.* 1722–95, have a cover. An apocryphal explanation of the name attributes it to Père Louis Bourdaloue (1632–1704), a Jesuit preacher at the court of Louis XIV, whose long discourses detained the ladies of the court so as to necessitate this practical receptacle. However, the first known examples are of Dutch delftware made *c.* 1710, and the handsome porcelain ones from Sèvres, Meissen, and elsewhere, date from *c.* 1725. Terms used in England by Wedgwood and Leeds are COACH-POT, oval chamber-pot, and slipper. *See* URINAL.

Bow dragon. A decorative subject employed on Bow porcelain in the 1750s depicting a DRAGON with an arrow protruding from its mouth in place of a tongue. It should be distinguished from the BROSELEY BLUE DRAGON and the WORCESTER DRAGON.

Bowen style. A style of painting on Bristol delftware, so called from its similarity to that on a bowl, now lost, inscribed 'Bowen', and characterized by washes of contrasting shades of blue. Although now generally referred to as the style of John Bowen, the original bowl was signed without an initial, and both John Bowen and H. Bowen are known to have been decorators at Bristol. The original bowl was in blue and MANGANESE, but most painting described as being in the Bowen style is only in blue.

Bowl. A concave vessel, wider than it is high, but deeper than a SAUCER. It usually, but not invariably, has a foot-ring. Small bowls for table purposes often have two lateral handles, similar to an ÉCUELLE. Some have a cover. The French terms are *bol*, and, when larger, *jatte*; the German term is *Schale*. *See* BASIN; ACCOUCHEMENT BOWL; BARBER'S BOWL; BISHOP BOWL; BLEEDING-BOWL; BREAST BOWL; BRIDAL BOWL; BRINJAL BOWL; COLANDER BOWL; PUNCH-BOWL; SHIP BOWL.

Box. A receptacle with a cover, or with a lid pierced and attached with metal hinges or mounted in a metal frame for the same

Bouquet. Porcelain flowers on padded metal branches, Vincennes, *c.* 1747–50. Courtesy, Sotheby's.

Bouquetière figures. Pair of porcelain figures, ht 8¾ in., with polychrome decoration, Chelsea (red anchor period). Courtesy, Christie's.

Bourdalou. Porcelain, with turquoise floral decoration *en camaïeu*, Chelsea-Derby, *c.* 1770–84. Harold Newman Collection.

Box. Sugar-box (*Zuckerdose*) decorated with *chinoiseries*, Meissen, *c.* 1725. Cecil Higgins Museum, Bedford.

purpose. Ceramic boxes are usually small, e.g. a SNUFF-BOX, and if much larger they are usually termed CASKETS. The French term is *boîte*; the German terms are *Dose* when flattened, and *Böchse* when high. Early flattened, covered sugar-receptacles made at Meissen are usually termed sugar-boxes (*Zuckerdose*) rather than sugar-bowls (*Zuckerschale*). *See* BOÎTE; COMFIT-BOX; PATCH-BOX; PYXIS; ROSE-BOX; ROUGE-BOX; SAND-BOX; SNUFF-BOX; TRIFLE-BOX; TRINKET-BOX.

Boxing figures. Individual figures of boxers in fighting attitudes, or a group of two on a common base. The earliest recorded English examples were made at Bow in the 1750s, but most surviving examples are of Staffordshire earthenware. The most popular of the later figures were of Tom Molyneux, a former American Negro slave, and Tom Cribb, the English champion, whom Molyneux challenged in 1810. Transfer-printed plaques of this subject were made in Staffordshire early in the 19th century; these are very rare.

Boy in a tree. A decorative subject depicting a Chinese boy; the same as the NAKED BOY pattern.

Brack (German). A term sometimes used to designate AUSSCHUSS PORZELLAN.

Boxing figures. Pair of earthenware figures (Molyneux and Cribb), Staffordshire. Courtesy, Christie's.

Bracket. A support to be attached to a wall and having a flat platform on which to rest a vase, figure, clock, etc. Although usually of wood or metal, ceramic examples were made at a number of factories. The French term is *console*.

Bragget-pot. A cylindrical drinking-vessel with two loop handles and sometimes a cover, used in late 17th-century England for drinking bragget (a beverage of ale and honey fermented and flavoured with spices, especially drunk on Bragget Sunday in mid-Lent). They were made in Staffordshire of slipware. *See* POSSET-POT; TYG.

Branch handle. A type of CRABSTOCK handle which has a projecting piece of branch attached to the main stalk.

Brandenburg porcelain. A dark brown stoneware made at Plaue-an-der-Havel which is contemporary with BÖTTGER RED STONEWARE, and often similarly decorated. It is both coarser and softer than Böttger's product.

Brandensteinmuster (German). Literally, Brandenstein pattern. A moulded basketwork border pattern introduced at Meissen by J. G. Höroldt. It has a double OZIER relief pattern, one on the outer border of the plate and the other encroaching on the well. *See* MUSTER; ALTBRANDENSTEINMUSTER; NEUBRANDENSTEINMUSTER.

Bowen style. Decoration on pedestal of food-warmer, Bristol delftware, *c.* 1750. Harold Newman Collection.

Brasero. *See* FOOT-WARMER.

Breakfast can. A large coffee-can made of Derby porcelain, *c.* 1790. It measures about 3¼ inches in both height and diameter. *See* CAN.

Breakfast service. A CABARET SERVICE; sometimes called a déjeuner service.

Breast bowl. A bowl in the form of, and moulded from, a woman's breast, the most famous example being that made for Marie-Antoinette. It is a type of drinking cup, similar to the Greek MASTOS. The French term is *bol sein*.

Brede hedgehog. An ornamental pottery piece in the form of a hedgehog, made in the village of Brede, Sussex. *See* SUSSEX WARE.

Breloque. A small charm for a watch chain. Examples in porcelain were made at Chelsea and Derby and have a small metal suspensory ring.

Brewster teapot. An oval teapot with vertical sides, the cover fitting into an oval vertical neck. Made by Wedgwood and others, inspired by contemporary silver, in the late 18th century.

Briançon lustreware. A nacreous (mother-of-pearl) LUSTREWARE having a metallic opalescence, developed and patented by Gillet et Briançon, rue Lafayette, Paris, *c.* 1755–60. Similar to the nitrate of bismuth lustreware developed at Worcester, and also to BELLEEK WARE. It exhibits pastel hues.

Brick. A rectangular block of fired clay used for building or paving purposes. The modern brick measures about 9 × 4½ × 3 inches, but older bricks vary considerably in dimensions and were usually flatter. Sun-dried mud-bricks have been used since ancient times in the Middle East, and in Central and South America (*see* ADOBE). In ancient Rome bricks, often bearing a maker's mark, were kiln-baked. *See* FLOWER-BRICK.

Bridal bowl. A bowl of Chinese porcelain decorated with two fish (the symbol of wedded bliss), either in relief or incised.

Bridal vase. A vase of jasper ware made by Wedgwood, *c.* 1793, and so called because the main decoration is an encircling series of Hymeneal torches entwined by three horizontal interlacing rope bands.

Bridge spout. A type of spout that is attached to a jug, ewer, coffee-pot, or teapot by a horizontal bar.

Brindille, à la. The French term for CHANTILLY SPRAYS.

Brinjal bowl. A Chinese porcelain bowl of the reign of K'ang Hsi (1662–1722); it has a dark manganese or aubergine (*brinjal*) ground colour, with incised floral sprays and enamels in green and yellow applied on the biscuit.

Briqueté ground. A ground simulating brickwork. First used at Sèvres, in gold over dark blue.

Bristol delftware. Tin-glazed earthenware (English delftware) made at or near Bristol from the second half of the 17th century to the last quarter of the 18th. This term (or sometimes West

Briqueté ground. Porcelain coffee-cup with polychrome and gilt decoration, Sèvres, *c.* 1775. Victoria and Albert Museum, London.

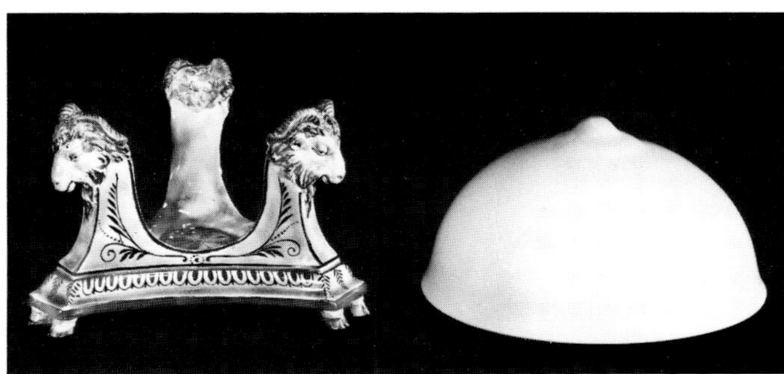

Breast bowl. Bowl and stand made for Marie Antoinette, Sèvres, 1787; ht of bowl 2¾ in. Courtesy, Antique Porcelain Co., London.

Country delftware) includes the wares of five factories in Bristol, and also of factories at Brislington (2 miles away) and at Wincanton (30 miles away). The principal potters at Bristol were Richard Frank and Joseph Flower. The glaze has a slightly greenish-blue tint, and early 18th-century wares are sometimes covered with an additional clear lead glaze. Decoration, usually in indigo-blue, was mostly based on oriental designs. Production was mainly of FLATWARE and HOLLOW-WARE; figures, sometimes birds, are very rare. *See* LONDON DELFTWARE; LAMBETH DELFTWARE; LIVERPOOL DELFTWARE.

Brocade pattern. A decorative pattern on ARITA PORCELAIN of the IMARI type, with red, blue, and gold designs imitative of brocade, sometimes including purple and red dragons among mons and diaper bands. Sometimes called the 'Japan brocade pattern' or 'Old Japan brocade pattern'. Brocade patterns were employed at Meissen, and influenced English factories, such as Worcester and Chelsea. They also occur on Chinese porcelain of the first half of the 18th century. *See* JAPAN PATTERNS; OLD PATTERN.

Brocaded ware. Porcelain of the IMARI type decorated with the BROCADE PATTERN.

Bronze Etruscan ware. A type of BLACK BASALTES ware produced by Wedgwood and 'bronzed' with gold dissolved in aqua regia precipitated with copper filings. Some examples were also painted with red and white mat-surfaced encaustic enamels. *See* ETRUSCAN WARE; BRONZED POTTERY.

Bronzed pottery. Bronze-coloured pottery developed by Josiah Wedgwood, who was experimenting before 1769 with techniques for producing an imitation-bronze surface, and took out a patent in that year for a process for preparing bronze powder and its application to pottery. Imitations of the bronze surface were produced elsewhere in Staffordshire, *c.* 1800, notably by Enoch Wood. *See* BRONZE ETRUSCAN WARE.

Bronzo antico (Italian). Literally, antique bronze. A kind of maiolica vase or ewer of pyriform shape; it has moulded side-handles, and a shaped spout or lip, and was inspired by bronze vessels of this form.

Brocade pattern. Scalloped dish painted with prunus branches, a dragon between mons, and diaper bands, Worcester (first period). Courtesy, Sotheby's.

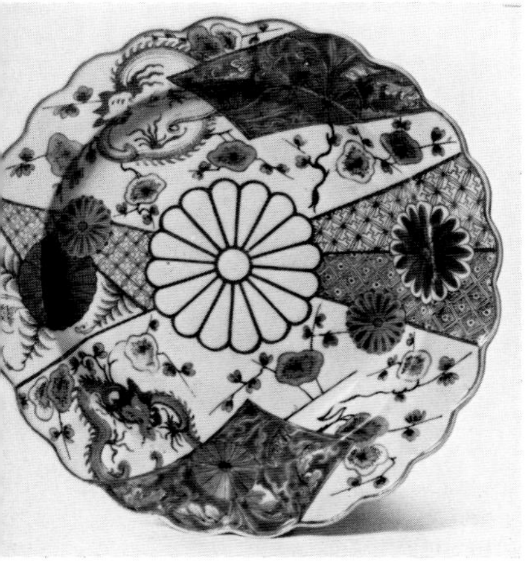

Broseley blue dragon. A transfer-printed decorative subject in blue employed at Caughley, derived from the Chinese DRAGON, and introduced by Thomas Turner, *c.* 1780. It is reputed to have been engraved by Thomas Minton, and is to be distinguished from the BOW DRAGON and WORCESTER DRAGON. It is still used today, and there are several variations. It is sometimes termed the 'Blue Dragon' pattern. *See* SALOPIAN WARE.

Broth bowl. *See* ACCOUCHEMENT BOWL; BOUILLON CUP.

Brown china. Earthenware made *c.* 1796 at Rockingham (Swinton, Yorkshire). The body is a hard, white earthenware covered with a fine brown mottled glaze, the ware having been dipped and fired three times. The glaze probably contained iron as well as manganese. It is also called 'Rockingham ware'. The designation 'china' has led to its being erroneously considered to be porcelain. *See* BENNINGTON WARE.

Brown edge. A term used to describe the contrasting colour of the edge of some TING YAO bowls and other wares, each of the pieces having been inverted in the kiln with the result that the mouth was bare of glaze; the edge was therefore covered by a thin copper band (*see* COPPER BOUND), giving the appearance of having been painted. Some Ting vases and those of later date fired in the same way have the mouth similarly bound with metal. Some European porcelain and delftware is decorated in enamel to simulate this ware. *See* RED EDGE.

Brown stoneware. Stoneware with a deep-brown glaze, which usually covers the top part of the piece to a variable depth, the remainder being light brown or buff. *See* DWIGHT WARE; FULHAM WARE; LAMBETH STONEWARE.

Bruciaprofumo. The Italian term for a PASTILLE-BURNER.

Brühl pattern. *See* BRÜHLSCHES ALLERLEI-DESSIN.

Brühlsches Allerlei-Dessin (German). An elaborate border with a complicated pattern of basketwork, flowers, trellisage, etc. arranged in panels confined by rococo scrolls, no two panels being alike. It was introduced at Meissen in 1742 as decoration for a dinner-service made for Count Heinrich von Brühl, the factory director.

Brûle-parfum. The French term for a PERFUME-BURNER. *See* CASSOLETTE.

Brun de Rouen (French). A type of Rouen pottery, principally useful ware, covered with a brown lead glaze. A similar ware was also made at Tournai (Belgium).

Brush-pot. Same as BRUSH-WASHER.

Brush-rest. A Chinese ornamental rest for brushes, one of the implements found on the scholar's table, usually in the form of the Five Sacred Mountains, with the tallest in the centre.

Brush-washer. A Chinese or Japanese receptacle for holding and washing the brushes used in painting and calligraphy. It was one of the objects to be found on the scholar's table.

Bryony-leaf ground. A ground pattern of bryony leaves and flowers. It occurs as part of the decoration of some HISPANO-MORESQUE WARES.

Bubby-pot. A patent BABY-FEEDER, invented in 1777 by Dr Hugh Smith and known as 'Smith's Bubby Pot', made by Wedgwood in plain or transfer-printed creamware. *See* FEEDING POT.

Búcaro (Spanish). A vessel of porous pottery used for cooling water. The ware was made of red clay in Estremadura (Spain), and is more porous than the ALCARAZZA.

Bucchero ware. The earliest known native Italian pottery of its type, dating from about the 8th century BC. Its colour ranges from grey to glossy black, and the ornament is usually moulded or incised. Sometimes called *bucchero nero*.

Buckwheat celadon. A term sometimes applied to a type of Chinese celadon ware of the Sung dynasty, much prized in Japan; it has a green glaze dappled at intervals with small brown spots due to the presence of ferric oxide. The Japanese term is *tobi seiji*.

Bucranium (Latin). A decorative design depicting an ox-skull adorned with wreaths. Taken from ancient Roman sources, it was employed on Italian maiolica of the 15th and 16th centuries.

Brush-rest. Blue-and-white porcelain, Ming dynasty, reign of Chêng-tê (1506–21). British Museum, London.

Brush-washer. Porcelain, with decoration depicting Lao Tzŭ and the Eight Immortals, 18th century. Victoria and Albert Museum, London.

Bryony-leaf ground. Plate of Hispano-Moresque ware, with decoration in brownish lustre, Valencia, 16th century. British Museum, London.

Buddha's-hand citron. Red stoneware teapot, Yi-hsing, Kuangtung province, 18th century. British Museum, London.

Buddha's-hand citron. An East Asian fruit with finger-like fleshy appendages somewhat resembling a hand. It was used in painted or modelled form in China to symbolize happiness or wealth. It was one of the THREE ABUNDANCES. *See* FITZHUGH PATTERN.

Buddhist lion. *See* LION OF FO.

Buire, sometimes ***buie*** (French). A FLAGON or EWER resembling an AIGUIÈRE, but usually less slender.

Bulb-jar. Same as ROOT-POT.

Bulb-tray. A shallow ceramic receptacle for growing bulbs in wet pebbles.

Bulb-vase. A circular vase with a removable cup-like cover, made for planting bulbs. *See* ROOT-POT; VASE À L'OIGNON.

Bull-baiting group. A pottery group made in Staffordshire depicting a bull being provoked by dogs, sometimes with a dog thrown on to the bull's neck. Some examples include a man in the group. One version was made by Obadiah Sherratt of Burslem, *c.* 1822–35. Similar pieces depict bear-baiting.

Bun finial. A finial in the form of a flattened ball.

Bun foot. A foot in the form of a flattened ball.

Bungay mug. *See* TRIFLE-MUG; TRIFLE-BOX.

Buona notte. Literally, good night. An Italian term for a VEILLEUSE, employed because these words were sometimes inscribed on the piece, indicative of its night-time use.

Burette. The French term for a CRUET, and especially an altar-cruet for sacramental wine.

Burgautée (French). *See* PORCELAINE LAQUÉE BURGAUTÉE.

Burnished. Polished by friction. Gilding when first applied to porcelain has a mat or dull surface which needs to be polished, and this is done with a metal tool or an agate or dog's-tooth burnisher. The French term for this process is *brunissage*, and when the burnishing is done by a metal tool '*au clou*' is added to indicate this fact. *See* MATT-BRILLANT.

Burnt-in. Decoration fired with the glaze, as in the case of high-temperature faience colours, as distinguished from enamelled decoration applied after glazing. The term is, however, often loosely used.

Bust. A full-relief representation (usually a portrait), including the shoulders and breast of the sitter. Ceramic busts of all sizes were commonly made during the 18th and 19th centuries, especially in BISCUIT, PARIAN PORCELAIN, and BLACK BASALTES. The French term is *buste*, and the Italian *busto*.

Bustelli figure. The Postman, Nymphenburg, *c.* 1763; the flattened rococo scroll base is a characteristic feature of such figures. Courtesy, Christie's.

Bustelli figures. Figures modelled at Nymphenburg by Franz Anton Bustelli (1723–64) in the rococo style, many of them being from the Italian Comedy (*see* COMMEDIA DELL'ARTE FIGURES). Bustelli's style was much influenced by the Bavarian sculptor Gunther, and his preliminary models were carved in limewood. The poses of the figures are theatrical and full of life; they usually have open mouths, and are placed on bases which are thin and flat. Some of the groups especially have rococo scrollwork rising from the base. Colouring is relatively slight. Properly marked reproductions of these figures taken from the old moulds are at present being made by the Bavarian State Porcelain Factory. *See* OVIDIAN GODS.

Butter-cooler. A cylindrical or oval dish, in the interior of some of which rests a liner, the space between the inner and outer receptacles being filled with iced water to chill the butter. Some versions have no liner but perforations on the sides and bottom for ventilation. The dish has a cover and sometimes two protruding vertical lug handles. The diameter is about 5 inches. *See* BUTTER-DISH.

Butter-cooler. Oval coolers with covers, Worcester (Dr Wall period). Courtesy, Christie's.

Butter-dish. A shallow dish with vertical sides for serving butter at the table. Rectangular, circular, and hexagonal versions exist. Some have a cover and two protruding vertical lug handles, and some a pierced strainer on which the butter rests. Occasionally there is provision for ice or iced water to chill the butter. Dishes of this kind are usually accompanied by a tray, or stand. *See* BUTTER-COOLER; BUTTER-TUB.

Butter-pot. A coarse lead-glazed cylindrical pottery vessel in which butter was sold to the London market in the late 17th century. They usually held 14 lb of butter.

Butter-spoon. A type of spoon for serving butter, the bowl being given an upward curve and moulded with horizontal ribbing. They were made at Meissen and other German factories.

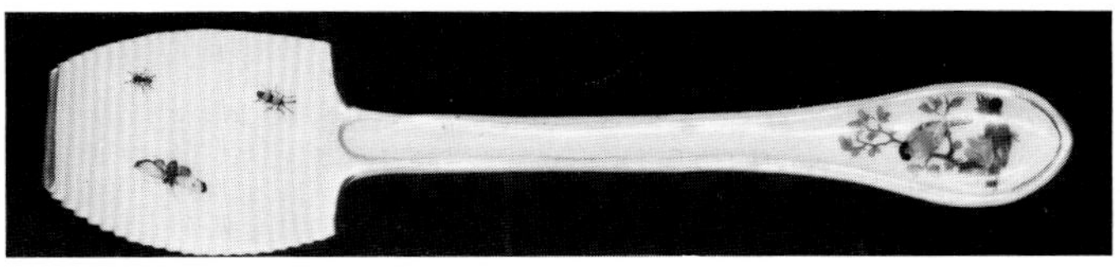

Butter-spoon. Porcelain; length 6¼ in., with curled ribbed bowl, Meissen. Courtesy, Christie's.

Butter-tub. The term is employed of deeper receptacles than those usually called a BUTTER-DISH.

Buttons. First employed in southern Europe in the 13th or 14th century, these were made in porcelain and in Wedgwood's jasper in the 18th century.

C

C-and-S scroll. A form of SCROLLWORK which is found as part of ROCOCO ornament, painted or modelled; it also occurs later during the 19th-century revival of the rococo style.

C.R. jug. A type of COMMEMORATIVE JUG made of saltglazed stoneware, globular in shape, with a relief medallion bearing the initials C.R. for 'Carolus Rex' (Charles II of England). They were made at Grenzhausen, Germany, of WESTERWALD WARE for export to England. *See* A.R. JUG; G.R. JUG; W.R. JUG.

C-scroll. Scrollwork in the form of the letter C (facing in either direction) used as rococo decoration, painted or modelled.

C-shaped handle. A handle in the form of a letter C.

Cabaret service. The term 'cabaret' originally referred to a tea-table, but came to mean a set of porcelain vessels comprising a small breakfast- or tea-service, together with a PLATEAU. A complete service included a teapot (or coffee-pot or chocolate-pot), teapot-stand, milk-jug, cream-jug (creamer), sugar-basin, tea-caddy, jam-pot, cups and saucers, and plateau. A small service for a Continental breakfast was sometimes called a déjeuner service, and if for one person, a *solitaire*, or for two persons, a *tête-à-tête*. *See* TEA-SERVICE.

Cabbage ware. Porcelain sauce-boat with moulded decoration of overlapping leaves, Worcester, *c.* 1760.

Cabbage-leaf jug. An ovoid jug with a cylindrical neck (some examples have a mask below the spout), decorated overall with overlapping cabbage leaves in low relief. Although not originally intended to be decorated in this way, some also have a superimposed painted or printed decoration. The earliest were made at Worcester, *c.* 1757, and later at Lowestoft, Liverpool and Caughley. *See* CABBAGE WARE.

Cabbage ware. Pottery and porcelain naturalistically modelled and coloured in imitation of cabbage leaves in low relief, usually a bowl, tureen, teapot, or jug. The decoration, in its origin, is typically rococo. *See* FEUILLE DE CHOU; CABBAGE-LEAF JUG; CAULIFLOWER WARE.

Cabinet cups and saucers. Cups and saucers with decoration of high quality, primarily for display in a cabinet rather than for use. The cups are often of waisted BEAKER shape, with one handle. In England the Derby factory made cups and COFFEE-CANS of this type at the end of the 18th century, and the Sèvres factory made many specimens of the finest quality. *See* CAN.

Cachepot. Porcelain with polychrome decoration, Chantilly, mid-18th century. Victoria and Albert Museum, London.

Cachemire decoration. A rather crowded decoration of flowers, fantastic birds, figures, and animals within rich borders of LAMBREQUINS and SCROLLS. The palette was mainly red and blue, with some green, yellow, and black. Devised by Samuel van Eenhorn of Delft (Holland), it was popular in the late 17th and early 18th centuries. The subjects were derived from oriental sources, Cachemire being the French form of Cashmere, modern Kashmir.

Cachepot (French). An ornamental pot (the name is derived from *cacher*, to hide) to contain and conceal a utilitarian flower pot. *See* JARDINIÈRE.

Caddy. *See* TEA-CADDY.

Caddy-spoon. A type of spoon with an elongated bowl for use with a TEA-CADDY. When made with a bowl pierced with holes they served as EGG-DRAINERS, SUGAR-SPOONS (sifter spoons), or TEA-STRAINERS. Caddy-spoons were made of porcelain at Worcester.

Cadogan. A type of teapot, closed at the top, which is filled through a conical aperture in the bottom. The pot is peach-shaped, with the usual spout and handle. Originally, like the conventional teapot, a Chinese wine-pot, the cadogan was adapted in England for serving tea; first made at Rockingham (Swinton, Yorks.), *c*. 1795, for the china-dealer, John Mortlock, of Oxford Street, London, and later in Staffordshire by Copeland, Davenport, and others. The type was named after the Hon. Mrs Cadogan who gave a Chinese PEACH WINE-POT (brought to England by her son) to Lady Rockingham. *See* VASO SENZA BOCCA.

Cadogan. Teapot of Rockingham pottery, *c*. 1810. Courtesy, Ceylon Tea Centre, London.

Caesar, Julius, jug. A jug made by Charles Meigh of Hanley (Staffordshire), *c*. 1830–50. It has a RUSTIC HANDLE and is completely covered with a moulded relief decoration depicting Julius Caesar in battle scenes. The same motif was also used at other factories.

Café au lait (French). A high-temperature brown ground colour derived from iron. It is not uncommon on Chinese porcelain of the 18th century, especially BATAVIAN WARE, and was introduced at Meissen (where it was called *Kapuzinerbraun*) by the kilnmaster Samuel Stölzel, *c*. 1720. It occurs on Vienna porcelain, and as a tin-glazed ground on the faience of Milan and Warsaw, as well as a colour for FOND LAQUÉ.

Cailloutages (French). From *caillou*, flint or pebble. (1) A hard, white-coloured earthenware, lead-glazed, containing flint. (2) A type of PEARLWARE. *See* CREAMWARE; TERRE DE PIPE; FAÏENCE FINE.

Cailloutė (French). From *caillou*, pebble. A decorative pattern of meshed oval forms devised at Sèvres, *c*. 1752, and usually employed as a gold network over a dark-blue underglaze ground. It was copied at Worcester, Derby, and Swansea.

Caisse à fleurs (French). A porcelain flower pot, usually square or rectangular, sometimes containing a tree with leaves of *tôle-peinte* (thin sheet-iron, painted) and flowers of porcelain. Some have a cover with holes for placing the flowers. The square pots thus designated at Sèvres are usually in the form of a miniature ORANGE-TUB. *See* JARDINIÈRE.

Calcine. (1) The product of the process of reducing animal bones or such hard stones as flint, by exposing them to intense heat, to a state in which they can easily be crushed for mixing in powder form with clay. (2) The combination of tin oxide and lead oxide used in the glaze of some English delftware.

Callot figures. Porcelain figures, ht $2\frac{3}{4}$ in., with polychrome decoration, Venice. Courtesy, Christie's.

Callot figures. Grotesque figures of dwarfs (MAGOTS) inspired by engravings of the subject by Jacques Callot (1592–1635) of Nancy. They occur in painted form on faience and porcelain made in France and Germany, and as figures made at Meissen, Vienna, Mennecy, Venice, and Capodimonte. The Derby figures known as MANSION HOUSE DWARFS are derived from this source.

Calpis (Greek). *See* KALPIS.

Camaïeu, en (French). Painting in several tones of the same colour. *See* GRISAILLE; CHIAROSCURO; MONOCHROME.

Cambria clay. Same as ARGIL.

Cambrian ware. Pottery made at Swansea (South Wales) from 1765 to 1870 which includes a somewhat underfired creamware, black basaltes, an unglazed buff-coloured ware, Etruscan ware, and opaque (ironstone) china.

Camel. Pottery figure with three-colour glaze; ht 34½ in., T'ang dynasty. Wadsworth Atheneum, Hartford, Conn.

Camel teapot. Saltglazed stoneware, Staffordshire, *c.* 1745.

Camel. A figure of a Bactrian camel made of soft earthenware (unglazed, glazed or partially glazed), originally used in China as a TOMB-FIGURE. Examples were made during the T'ang dynasty (618–906), but some harder fired early specimens date from the Han dynasty (206 BC–AD 220) and earlier. *See* HORSES.

Camel teapot. A saltglazed stoneware teapot in the form of a kneeling camel with its saddle. The loop handle on some examples is in the form of a dolphin. They were made in Staffordshire, *c.* 1740–60. *See* ELEPHANT TEAPOT.

Camellia-leaf green. A bright green used on Chinese porcelain.

Cameo. A term originally applied to a gemstone (often having layers of different colours) carved in low relief to show the design and background in contrasting colours. This effect was imitated by Josiah Wedgwood: first with wares having a white or buff body sometimes with coloured enamels burnt in; later with JASPER and other bodies, the contrasting relief decoration being applied to a coloured background. Rare double cameos have two pieces luted back to back, while others similarly luted consist of a cameo and an INTAGLIO piece. Cameos, some made in more than two colours, were used for many purposes, e.g. as JEWELLERY and furniture decoration. *See* MEDALLION; PATERA.

Campana (Italian). *See* VASO CAMPANA.

Can. A cylindrical cup made in England towards the end of the 18th century, especially at Derby, and used for serving coffee. Most were elaborately decorated and used for cabinet display. *See* COFFEE-CAN; BREAKFAST-CAN; CABINET CUPS AND SAUCERS.

Canary lustre. A term often inaccurately applied to pottery decorated with lustre, especially RESIST WARE, over a yellow body or a yellow glaze. Such ware, usually in the form of jugs, was made at many potteries in England and Wales, *c.* 1790–1820. The lustre itself is usually platinum resist, although rare specimens exist on which the lustre has been applied freehand. Similar ware was made at Creil (France). *See* YELLOW WARE.

Cancellation mark. One or more strokes incised through, or painted across, an original factory mark to indicate that the specimen was regarded as defective or outmoded, and sold as substandard. At Meissen a line was cut across the mark by an engraver's wheel to denote white-ware sold to a HAUSMALER, and two such cuts were made on factory-decorated ware which was rejected for normal sale owing to defects. *See* AUSSCHUSS PORZELLAN.

Candelabrum. A large ornamental candle-holder, with several branches, for table use. The plural, candelabra, is now sometimes used for a single piece. The term TABLE-LUSTRE, sometimes used, should strictly be reserved for table-candlesticks with faceted glass or rock-crystal drops. *See* CHANDELIER; GIRANDOLE.

Candeliere, a (Italian). A style of decoration with grotesque figures symmetrically placed on either side of a vertical axis. It was employed on the maiolica of Castel Durante, Gubbio, Deruta, and Urbino.

Candiana. Maiolica made at, or near, Padua (Italy), so called from a misinterpreted inscription which led to its attribution to Candiana, a village near Padua. The ware imitated ISNIK POTTERY of the 16th and 17th centuries, except that the bright sealing-wax red of the source of its inspiration was replaced by brownish orange sometimes accompanied by blue and green, with dark grey for the outlines. Reproductions of Isnik pottery were also made in Italy in the 19th century by Cantagalli of Florence and others. *See* CANTAGALLI WARE.

Candle-nozzle. The socket for a candle. Usually part of a CANDLESTICK, but also on the cover of FOOD-WARMERS and VASE-CANDLESTICKS. The socket is sometimes completed by the addition of a small tray, known as the DRIP-PAN (*bobêche*), to catch the wax drippings.

Candle-recess. A concave tile, to be set into the rear of a tiled wash-basin recess in a wall, in which a candle was placed; such tiles were made in ENGLISH DELFTWARE, *c.* 1750.

Candle-snuffer. A hollow, conical object with a handle, sometimes made in the form of a figure; when placed over the lighted candle it extinguished the flame by depriving it of oxygen, and prevented the wick from smoking.

Candlestick. A candle-holder, usually with a circular flat base, and having a central socket or nozzle, and a drip-pan. *See* CHAMBER CANDLESTICK; COLUMN CANDLESTICK; FIGURE CANDLESTICK; LISART CANDLESTICK; PRICKET CANDLESTICK; VASE-CANDLESTICK; TAPERSTICK; TRITON CANDLESTICK; CANDELABRUM; CANDLE-NOZZLE; SCONCE; TABLE-LUSTRE.

Candlestick salt. A figure holding a SALT-CELLAR, and having one or two CANDLE-NOZZLES attached.

Cane-handle. A porcelain or maiolica handle for a walking-stick, sometimes in the form of a figure or a head. The Italian term is *bastone*. *See* CHACAN.

Cane-ware. A tan-coloured unglazed stoneware developed by Wedgwood, *c.* 1770, by refining the clay used by peasant potters to make buff-brown wares. Originally it was used for coarse game- and pie-dishes as a form of ovenware, but later it was decorated with enamel and encaustic painting, and with sprigged decoration in the same way as jasper ware. Pieces of useful ware were usually glazed on the interior. *See* BAMBOO WARE; DRY BODY; WEDGWOOD COLOURED BODIES.

Canephoros (Greek). A draped female figure bearing on her head a wicker-basket containing sacred offerings or utensils in religious festivals, and used as part of a frieze, or as a column to support an entablature. Similar in function to a CARYATID. *See* ATLANTES; TELAMON.

Canestrella (Italian). A circular plate of Italian maiolica, usually with pierced decoration around the rim, which was used as a fruit-basket.

Canette (French). Same as SCHNELLE.

Cameo. Portrait of Benjamin Franklin, blue and white jasper; diam. 3⅜ in., Wedgwood. Courtesy, Sotheby's.

Candle-recess. Bristol delftware, *c.* 1750. Courtesy, A. F. Allbrook, London.

Cane-handle. Modelled by Simon Feilner, Fürstenberg, *c.* 1753–66. Dr Hans Syz Collection, Smithsonian Institution, Washington, D.C.

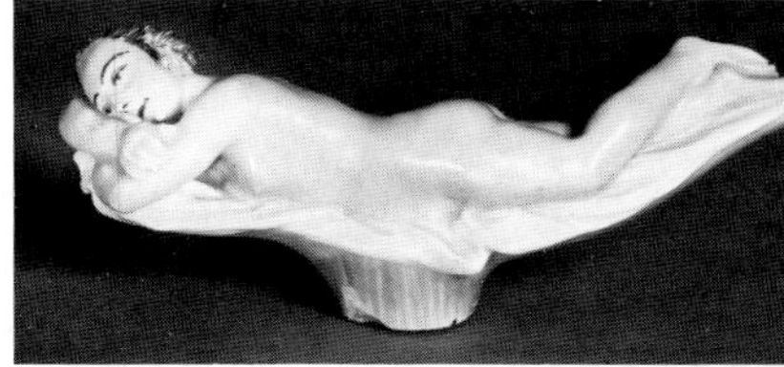

Cannon-ball pattern. Porcelain teapot with painted decoration, Worcester, *c.* 1760. Courtesy, Sotheby's.

Cangiante lustre. An iridescent lustre which changes its appearance when seen from different angles, showing violet, blue and ruby hues.

Canister. A small container for dry tea. *See* TEA-CADDY; TEAPOY.

Cannon-ball pattern. A decorative pattern depicting a pagoda on an island with a smaller island in the background, and three round unidentified blobs which give the name to the pattern. It was used at Worcester.

Cannon spout. A type of spout of tapering cylindrical form, the mouth of which has a slightly raised rim, suggestive of the name.

Canopic jar. One of the set of four such jars in which the ancient Egyptians preserved the embalmed viscera of the deceased, usually for burial with the mummy. They were made at Canopus, a city of Egypt, and their covers are representations of the four Sons of Horus (genii of Amenti). Jars of similar style for use as CINERARY URNS were made of BUCCHERO WARE by the Etruscans, some having the cover in the form of the head of a deity.

Canopic vase. Black basaltes, encaustic painted, Wedgwood, *c.* 1809. Courtesy, Wedgwood.

Canopic vase. A type of Etruscan CINERARY URN made of terracotta with a cover in the form of a human head. The term was used by Wedgwood for an urn in this form made in Ptolemaic style after an illustration in Bernard de Montfaucon's *L'Antiquité Expliquée,* Paris, 1722.

Cantagalli ware. Pottery made at Florence by a 19th-century manufacturer of reproductions of Italian maiolica, Hispano-Moresque ware, lustre ware, Isnik pottery, etc. The mark of a crowing cock is a rebus for the maker's name, Cantagalli.

Canted corner. Same as CHAMFERED CORNER.

***Cantharus*.** Same as KANTHAROS.

Canton porcelain. Porcelain decorated in the enamelling shops of Canton (Kuangtung province), and shipped thence to Europe during the 18th and the early part of the 19th century. It was also at this port that European merchants had their warehouses (*see* HONG). Porcelain was sent in white from the kilns at Ching-tê-Chên to Canton for polychrome enamel painting to the merchant's or customer's order. Since decoration in underglaze blue was a factory operation, ware of this kind intended for the European market usually went by way of Nanking, though no doubt porcelain decorated with both underglaze blue and enamel colours came through Canton. Canton porcelain was for a long time erroneously called ORIENTAL LOWESTOFT. The category includes JESUIT PORCELAIN. Today it is properly called EXPORT CHINA or CHINESE EXPORT PORCELAIN. *See* MANDARIN DECORATION.

Cap cover. A circular cover for a jar. It is low and flat-topped, and fits over an upright collar on the jar. *See* DOME COVER.

Capacity mug. A type of English cylindrical mug formerly used as a measure in taverns and alehouses, as well as shops, the certified content being stamped with an additional excise mark. Early types were first made in the late 17th century of saltglazed stoneware. Towards the end of the 18th century examples in dipped, banded, and MOCHA WARE were made.

Capanna (Italian). *See* HOUSE URN.

Caramanian pattern. A decorative pattern used on a dinner-service of underglaze blue transfer-printed earthenware by Spode, 1810–35, which was inspired by a travel-book by Luigi Mayer, *Views in Egypt, Palestine and the Ottoman Empire.* (Caramania was formerly the name for the southern shore of Anatolia.) *See* MONOPTEROS PATTERN; INDIAN SPORTING PATTERN.

Caramanian pattern. Soup plate with underglaze-blue transfer-printed decoration, Spode, 1810–35. J.K. des Fontaines Collection, London.

Carchesion (Greek). Same as KARCHESION.

Card-rack. A rack for cards, somewhat similar in form to a toast-rack.

Carpet-ball. A large ball used in the Victorian indoor game of carpet-bowls. They were made in England, but especially in Scotland, of agate ware, brown stoneware, and glazed earthenware painted with coloured designs. A complete set consisted of one plain taw and six decorated balls. Also called carpet-bowl.

Carpet-bowl. Same as CARPET-BALL.

Carquois, à la (French). Literally, with quiver. A decorative pattern of quivers, arrows, and flowers developed at Rouen for faience, but imitated elsewhere in France. Also called quiver pattern.

Carrack porcelain. Chinese porcelain which formed part of the cargo of Portuguese carracks captured on the high seas by the Dutch soon after 1600 and taken to Holland for sale. The porcelain was made in the reign of Wan-li (1573–1619), and decorated in underglaze blue. It was later extensively copied in tin-enamelware at Delft (Holland). The Dutch term is *kraak porselein.*

Carrara porcelain. (1) A type of BISCUIT porcelain so called from its resemblance to the white marble from the Carrara quarries in Italy. (2) A name sometimes given to PARIAN PORCELAIN made by Josiah Wedgwood.

Carreau de revêtement (French). Literally, facing tile. Glazed tiles with which the pavement and walls of the ground floors of most residences, palaces and chapels of France were ornamented from the 12th to the 16th century. Tile flooring is still popular in many parts of France and Italy today, although wall-tiles are less often seen.

Cartel (French). Strictly, the case of a type of clock made during the currency of the rococo style and intended to be hung on the wall. Porcelain specimens are known, but are exceedingly rare. By extension the term is applied to the scrolled frame surrounding a painted decoration, usually bordering a reserve, which is similar in form. *See* CARTOUCHE; VIGNETTE; VASE À CARTEL.

Cartouche. Putto holding inscribed rococo cartouche, Meissen, 1757. Courtesy, Antique Porcelain Co., London.

Cartouche. Strictly, a decoration in the form of a scroll of paper with rolled ends on which there is a picture, a design, an ornamental monogram, or a coat of arms. The term is often used loosely to mean an oval frame decorated with scrollwork. *See* VIGNETTE; ESCUTCHEON; CARTEL.

Carved ware. Ware, usually Chinese, decorated with designs carved into the clay before glazing and firing.

Caryatid (Greek). A draped or partially draped female figure serving in place of a column to support an entablature. Caryatids decorate some ceramic ware, either painted or in relief. *See* ATLANTES; CANEPHOROS; TELAMON; GUÉRIDON.

Caryatid handle. A handle in the form of a female figure resembling a caryatid.

Case-mould. The hollow MOULD made first in the process of mould-making and taken from the model or maquette. It is used to make a plaster cast of the model.

Cash. Small circular Chinese coins with a square central hole for stringing. They sometimes occur as part of the decoration of painted porcelain, and as an attribute of the Immortal, Liu Hai. *See* TOAD, THREE-LEGGED.

Casket. An ornamental box of porcelain or faience, normally with metal mounts and hinges for a lid. It is larger than a snuff-box, and was usually intended to hold jewels. The German term is *Böchse*.

Casque ewer. Same as HELMET PITCHER.

Cassolette. One of a pair of celadon cassolettes, Ming dynasty, with French gilt-bronze mounts, *c.* 1745–49. Courtesy, Frank Partridge & Sons Ltd, London.

Cassolette (French). A covered vase to contain perfume for scenting a room, and hence having holes on the shoulder or the cover, or pierced decoration, or being mounted in ormolu or gilt-bronze with openwork decoration. Matthew Boulton, who made many mounts, called the pieces 'essence vases' or 'essence pots'. If a vase with a reversible candlestick cover (sometimes called a 'cassolette') has no such holes, it should preferably be designated a VASE-CANDLESTICK. *See* POT-POURRI VASE.

Cast. The product of pouring into a MOULD a liquid substance which has the property of setting or hardening, and which takes and retains the shape imposed on it by the mould. The process is an important method of producing ceramic wares which cannot be thrown on the POTTER'S WHEEL. The two substances most frequently employed for this purpose in the ceramic industry are SLIP and plaster of Paris. *See* CASTING.

Caster. A receptacle with a pierced cover for sprinkling. Sometimes called a CRUET, and sometimes spelled 'castor'. *See* SUGAR-CASTER; PEPPER-CASTER; POUNCE-POT.

Casting. The process of shaping a ceramic object by pouring SLIP into a dry plaster MOULD. The mould absorbs water from the slip, with the result that a layer of clay is built up on the inner surface of the mould. When the clay has reached a sufficient thickness the surplus slip is poured off, and the object dries to become CHEESE-HARD and shrinks, facilitating removal from the plaster mould. Seams and mould marks are then removed by FETTLING. Slip-cast ware of this kind is generally hollow, and usually of a shape which cannot be produced by throwing on the POTTER'S WHEEL. *See* CAST.

Castleford ware. Teapot with characteristic blue enamel border.

Castleford ware. White stoneware, mainly teapots and jugs, made at Castleford, near Leeds, *c.* 1800–20, and decorated in relief with coloured ornament in a manner reminiscent of Wedgwood's JASPER. Usually a blue-enamel line-border is present. The body, almost translucent, is not unlike a kind of PARIAN PORCELAIN. Most was made by David Dunderdale & Co., but similar ware was also made elsewhere. A popular form was the teapot, the design of which resembles contemporary octagonal silver models.

Castor ware. Pottery made at Castor, near Peterborough, during the Roman period in the 2nd and 3rd centuries AD. It is a grey earthenware with an incised decoration of human and animal figures.

Catherine wheel pattern. A decorative design, derived from Japanese IMARI, in the form of alternating spiral bands, one usually having coloured flowers applied overglaze on a white ground and the other white flowers reserved on a blue or red ground with gilt enrichments. The design occurs principally on Worcester porcelain of the First period; it has sometimes been called the 'wheel pattern', 'whorl pattern', 'spiral pattern', and 'QUEEN'S PATTERN', but must be distinguished from 'Queen Charlotte's pattern' (*see* ROYAL LILY PATTERN).

Catherine wheel pattern. Detail of porcelain teapot, Worcester, *c.* 1770. Courtesy, Worcester Royal Porcelain Co.

Cats. Figures of cats, more or less naturalistically modelled and coloured, were made in many different wares from the late 17th century onwards, including porcelain, earthenware, delftware, stoneware, agate ware and Whieldon ware. Later specimens were mainly intended to serve as chimney-piece ornaments. *See* WHISTLE.

Caudle-cup. A small covered cup with a saucer for drinking caudle (a warm gruel made from wine or ale, with eggs, bread or oatmeal, sugar and spices, usually intended for invalids). Some cups were made with one handle, others with two. *See* CAUDLE-POT; CAUDLE-URN; CHOCOLATE-CUP.

Caudle-flask. A brown stoneware spirit-flask with figures in relief of Mr and Mrs Caudle and Miss Prettyman, inspired by Douglas Jerrold's 'Mrs. Caudle's Curtain Lectures', featured in *Punch* in the 1840s.

Caudle-pot. A type of mug, usually in delftware, with two or more handles and a spout; used for making and drinking caudle. *See* CAUDLE-CUP; CAUDLE-URN.

Caudle-urn. An ornate CAUDLE-POT, usually with feet. *See* CAUDLE-CUP.

Cauliflower ware. Porcelain tureen, Chelsea, *c.* 1755. Courtesy, Antique Porcelain Co., London.

Cauliflower ware. Creamware vessels naturalistically modelled and coloured in imitation of the cauliflower, usually made as a covered bowl or tureen, or as a teapot. The lower part, covered with a green glaze, was modelled to represent the leaves, and the flower-head was white or cream. The cauliflower was usually shown in an upright position, though sometimes lying on its side. Ware of this kind was made by Thomas Whieldon and Josiah Wedgwood (*c.* 1759), and in porcelain at Chelsea and Worcester. Porcelain versions have been reproduced. *See* CABBAGE WARE; PINEAPPLE WARE.

Cavallo's Worcester. Worcester porcelain of the 18th century, redecorated with a fake claret ground and figures in the 1870s by a workman named Cavallo with the purpose of enhancing its value. Genuine examples of this type are very rare. *See* REFIRED WARE.

Cavetto (Italian). The well of a plate, especially the deep well of a TONDINO.

Ceiling ornament. A decorative piece to be affixed to a ceiling. An example in Chelsea porcelain, ornately modelled and painted, was owned by Sir Hans Sloane.

Ceiling ornament. Porcelain, Chelsea; ht 12 in. Courtesy, Sotheby's.

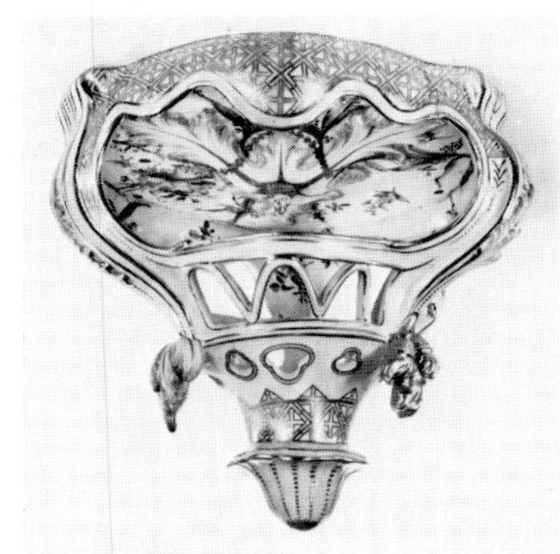

Celadon. A glaze, used on Chinese stoneware, which is derived from iron and ranges in colour from putty to sea-green. It is usually applied before firing in the form of a ferruginous wash. The principal early sources are Yüeh Chou, Lung Ch'üan, and Ch'u Chou in China, but similar ware was made in South Korea, Siam (Thailand) and Japan. The glaze is semi-translucent, and decoration is usually by means of carved or incised designs visible through it. Occasionally parts of the decoration are left unglazed, and are then reddish-brown in colour. Ware of this kind was greatly prized throughout the East, and was copied in Persia in a pottery body. The name is probably a corruption of Salah-ed-din (Saladin), Sultan of Egypt, who sent forty pieces of this ware to Nur-ed-din, Sultan of Damascus, in 1171. Another explanation, that the term was derived from the grey-green costume of Céladon, a character in a 17th-century French romance, *L'Astrée*, is less likely. The colour was not achieved in Europe during the 18th century except at Meissen, where only a few specimens were produced. Wedgwood applied the name to a green-glazed earthenware. *See* NORTHERN CELADON; BUCKWHEAT CELADON; MALLET VASE; MARTABANI WARE; SANGGAM CELADON; SAWANKHALOK WARE; YÜEH YAO.

Chandelier. Porcelain chandelier, ht 28½ in., with six arms decorated with *indianische Blumen*; Vienna, *c.* 1720–25. From the porcelain room of the Palais Dubsky, Brünn; now in the Österreichisches Museum für angewandte Kunst, Vienna.

Celebe (Greek). Same as KELEBE.

Cell ground. A ground pattern in DIAPER form made up of a large number of symmetrical adjoining cells.

Censer. Similar to an INCENSE-BURNER, but solely for ecclesiastical use. *See* HILL CENSER.

Central American pottery. The pottery of Mexico and Central America, which generally includes wares made by the Aztecs, Mayas, Toltecs, and Zapotecs. Geometric patterns are very common, and red, brown, and white slips were frequently employed. They also employed a technique which is probably unique (and which has been likened to the Batik method of patterning textiles), in which the surface of the pot was covered with wax, the pattern then scraped away, and the resulting exposed surface covered with pigment; the wax burned away in firing, leaving the pigment adhering to the unwaxed part. Another decorative technique involved the covering of the surface with a thick slip followed by scraping away part of it to form compartments, which were then filled with slip of a contrasting colour. Ornament was also carved in relief after firing. The Mayas were making good pottery from *c.* 600 BC to AD 1000. The Zapotecs made urns in the form of gods between the 4th and 10th centuries. The Toltecs made an orange-coloured ware with painted decoration, and a glossy dark-coloured ware with incised ornament. No Aztec pottery earlier than *c.* 1325 has been certainly identified; after this date a curvilinear geometric style of decoration was employed in black on an orange-coloured ware. Designs of birds, fishes, and plant forms are much more naturalistically treated in the 15th century, and European motifs begin to occur in the 16th century after the Spanish conquest, as well as such European techniques as tin-enamelling.

Centrepiece. The Temple of Love, from a table-decoration by J. J. Kändler, Meissen, *c.* 1750; ht 3 ft 9 in. Museum für Kunsthandwerk, Frankfurt/Main.

Centrepiece. An ornamental object of pottery or porcelain intended to decorate the centre of the dining-table. It was made in a wide variety of forms, including temples and other buildings, and was usually *en suite* with a TABLE-DECORATION or service. *See* ÉPERGNE; PLAT MÉNAGE; GRAND PLAT MÉNAGE; SURTOUT DE TABLE; SUBTLETY.

Ceramic ware. The broad term for all objects made of fired clay. Principal divisions are earthenware, stoneware and porcelain, each category being distinguished by the fact that it is fired at a temperature higher than the preceding one. The word is derived from the Greek word *keramikos* ('of pottery'), formed on *keramos* ('potter's earth'), and a variant spelling is 'keramik'; it is pronounced, according to the *Oxford English Dictionary*, 'seramic' and, according to the *Webster Dictionary*, 'keramic' only when so spelled. The French term is *céramique*, the German is *Keramik*, and the Italian *ceramica*.

Céramique siliceuse (French). Siliceous pottery, or pottery the body of which has been mixed with a proportion of siliceous glaze material. Certain varieties of blue-painted white Persian pottery of the 16th century were made thus, probably in an attempt to produce a kind of porcelain, and specimens are slightly translucent in places. It is probable that this attempt was known to the Italian potters responsible for the production of MEDICI PORCELAIN, and the experiments towards this end in Persia may have formed the basis of manufacture towards the end of the 16th century in Florence.

Cerquate (Italian). A decoration of oak-leaves and acorns employed to decorate the maiolica of Urbino in the 16th century. The name was derived from the fact that the factory was under the patronage of the della Rovere family, the Dukes of Urbino (1508–1626). In Italian *rovere* and *quercia* both mean 'oak'. The decoration was also employed at Castel Durante.

Cerquate decoration. Maiolica dish, Urbino or Castel Durante, first half of 16th century. Wallace Collection, London.

Chacan. An 18th-century German porcelain CANE-HANDLE in the form of a figure.

Ch'ai ware (Chinese). A type of Chinese porcelain, made *c.* 907–960, which is known only from literary references. The glaze is described as 'blue as heaven after rain'.

Chain border. Similar to CIRCLE AND SQUARE BORDER.

Chalk engraving. A type of engraving used in transfer-printing which has the softness of outline associated with pencil or pastel drawing. *See* FLOWN BLUE.

Chamber candlestick. A type of candlestick mounted in the centre of a saucer with a single handle, sometimes called a hand-candlestick. The French term is *bougeoir*. Candlesticks for this purpose in the 18th century were also made in the form of porcelain figures with a CANDLE-NOZZLE and a carrying handle.

Chamber candlestick. Porcelain, with nozzle resting on a boss, Bow. Courtesy, Christie's.

Chamber-pot. A bed-chamber vessel for urine. Some fine specimens occur in 18th-century porcelain, particularly those of Meissen and Sèvres. The best have enamel painting of exceptional quality. Early in the 19th century English potteries made specimens with ribald verses, and sometimes a portrait of Napoleon in the bottom or, not infrequently, an eye. The French term is *pot de chambre*. *See* BOURDALOU.

Chambrelan (French). Same as HAUSMALER.

Chamfered corner. A corner formed by trimming away the angle made by two adjacent faces; also termed canted corner. *See* INDENTED CORNER.

Champlevé (French). With respect to enamel on metal, having cells scooped into the metal which are then filled with powdered enamel and fired to fuse it. The technique has been infrequently used on a ceramic base. *See* CLOISONNÉ; ÉMAIL OMBRANT; BASSE-TAILLE.

Chandelier. A lighting-fixture made to be suspended from the ceiling and equipped with candle-nozzles and drip-pans. Porcelain versions (especially those made for a PORCELAIN ROOM) were produced at Sèvres, Meissen, and elsewhere, although those of glass or metal are much more common. *See* CANDELABRUM.

Chantilly sprays. Plate with enamel decoration, Chantilly, 18th century. Victoria and Albert Museum, London.

Cha-no-yu. The Japanese TEA CEREMONY.

Chantilly sprays (or **sprig**). A decoration of stylized sprays (somewhat resembling pairs of budding wheat-ears across a main stem) usually painted in blue. Created at Chantilly, the pattern was copied at Mennecy and Tournai, and adapted at several English factories, e.g. Caughley and Derby. The French term is *à la brindille*. *See* ANGOULÊME SPRIG.

Char-pot. A circular dish, from 6 to 10 inches wide, with a flat bottom and a one-inch vertical side-wall, often decorated on the outside of the wall with painted fish. They were used in England for serving potted char (a Lake District trout), and were made of English delftware, pearlware, or Leeds creamware. Specimens are rare. *See* PILCHARD-POT.

Character-mark (six or **four).** The name sometimes given to the reign-marks which appear on some Chinese porcelain, consisting of four or six characters or ideograms. The first two of the six-character mark denote the dynasty, the second two the name of the emperor, and the last two (which are invariable in form) represent *nien hao*, meaning 'in the reign of'. Four-character marks give only the name of the emperor followed by *nien hao*. Marks of this kind should not be accepted as necessarily denoting manufacture in the dynasty or reign referred to. The mark of an earlier reign was often added to porcelain of later date as a mark of commendation when the style of decoration was in the spirit of ware made during the period of the earlier emperor. Especially is this the case with some marks of the Ming dynasty (1368–1643), and most such marks that one sees were added to porcelain of the 18th century and later. A marked specimen of porcelain must have the characteristics of its supposed period before the mark can be accepted at its face value.

Sale-catalogues of Chinese porcelain sometimes list objects as 'Mark of . . .' and others as 'Mark and reign of . . .'; the former is usually intended to convey that the period of manufacture is doubtful, and probably later than the mark would imply. *See* SEAL-MARK; CHINESE REIGN-MARK; NENGO.

Charger. A large PLATTER or PLATE, usually circular or oval, used for serving meat at a table. Some highly decorative examples were made to be hung on the wall as PLAQUES, and have two holes in the foot-ring for a suspensory cord. Holes in the foot-ring were often for the purpose of suspending a piece in the enamelling kiln. *See* BLUE-DASH CHARGER; OAK-LEAF CHARGER; ADAM AND EVE; PATRIOTIC CHARGER.

Charlotte mourning at the tomb of Werther. A decorative subject of the late 18th century, either painted or modelled as a figure in relief. The subject was taken from Goethe's sentimental novel, *The Sorrows of Werther*; it depicts Charlotte standing or kneeling beside a column surmounted by an urn. The subject was especially popular at Leeds and in Staffordshire.

Chased. A silversmith's term meaning decoration indented from the front, as opposed to *repoussé*. It is also loosely applied to decoration cut with chisels and punches, and (by extension) to gilding on porcelain worked with tools into decorative patterns. The French term is *ciselé*. In the application of the technique to porcelain gilding, 'tooled' is a more appropriate word.

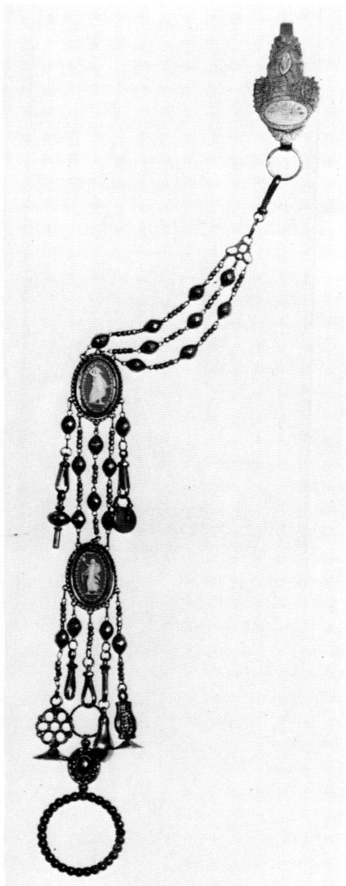

Chatelaine. Wedgwood jasper cameos mounted in chased cut steel, Etruria, 1786. Courtesy, Wedgwood.

Chatelaine. An ornamental clasp worn at a woman's waist with a chain from which were suspended keys, ÉTUIS, watches, and other objects. Wedgwood's JASPER was sometimes employed for some of the ornamental objects.

Chauffe-nourriture. A French term for a FOOD-WARMER.

Ch'a-yeh mo (Chinese). *See* TEA-DUST GLAZE.

Checkerboard ground. A ground pattern of connected squares of alternating colours resembling a draught- or checkerboard. Also called a chessboard ground.

Charlotte mourning at the tomb of Werther. Decoration in relief on a caneware flower-pot, Turner of Lane End (Staffordshire), *c.* 1790. City Museums, Stoke-on-Trent.

Cheese-dish. A utensil for storing and serving cheese. It is usually a flat platter with a high-domed cover. Examples with a cylindrical cover, when large enough, were for serving a whole Stilton cheese, and these occur in Wedgwood's JASPER; those with a sloping, rectangular cover were for serving a wedge of cheese.

Cheese-hard. The consistency of clay after some of the moisture has evaporated, but when it is still soft enough to be worked. *See* LEATHER-HARD.

Cheese-mould. A bowl for making cream cheeses. It has pierced sides to allow the excess moisture to escape, the bowl having been lined with cheesecloth before filling with curds and cream for solidifying into cheese. Cheese-moulds (curd-moulds) were made in creamware by Wedgwood.

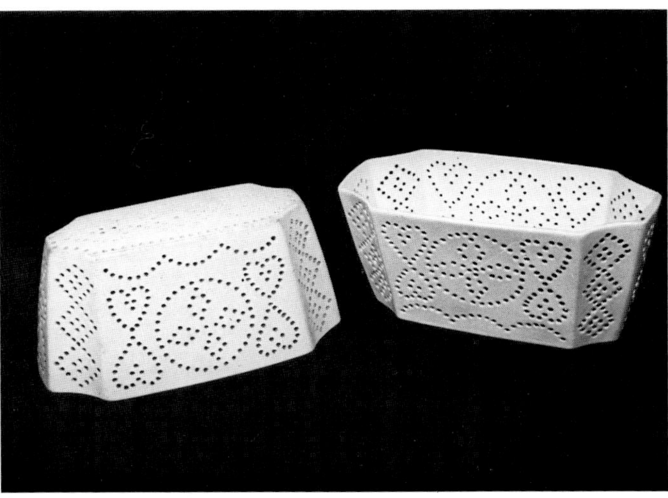

Cheese-mould. Creamware moulds, Wedgwood, *c.* 1790. Buten Museum of Wedgwood, Merion, Pa.

Chelsea toys. Examples of TOYS (scent-bottles, seals, boxes, miniature figures, etc.) made at Chelsea during the red- and gold-anchor periods, *c.* 1750–70.

Chertsey tiles. Tiles made in England in the 13th century, and so called because many have been found at Chertsey Abbey (Surrey). Examples are now at Westminster Abbey and the British Museum. They were made in geometrical shapes and used to make floor mosaics in Cistercian abbeys of the time. The designs, depicting medieval scenes, were made by impressing blocks into the clay, filling with lightly fired white clay ground up and mixed with slip, followed by glazing and firing, thus fusing the glaze and the body. Also perhaps originally from Chertsey Abbey are some wall-tiles, probably 14th century, decorated in a *sgraffito* technique and depicting the Apocryphal Infancy Gospels; these were found at a church at Tring (Hertfordshire) and are known as 'Tring tiles'.

Chessboard ground. Same as CHECKERBOARD GROUND.

Chessmen. Sets of chessmen have been made in pottery and porcelain in many countries and in most periods. Some were made of Chinese export porcelain. Those of Meissen porcelain are especially fine. Wedgwood made chessmen in jasper in the 18th century, and Rockingham and Doulton in porcelain in the 19th. Usually the pieces are very ornate, and in some sets the pawns are all of different form.

Chessmen. Pieces from a set in blue and white jasper modelled in 1784 by John Flaxman, Wedgwood, 1790. Courtesy, Wedgwood.

Chestnut basket. Creamware basket, cover and stand, Leeds 1780. Victoria and Albert Museum, London.

Chestnut basket. A pierced basket with a domed, pierced cover for serving hot chestnuts. A conforming stand was provided. Examples were made of porcelain at Worcester during the 18th century, and in creamware at Leeds and elsewhere. Sometimes called a chestnut bowl.

Chevrette. The French term for a WET-DRUG JAR.

Chevron border. A decorative border composed of a repeating series of motifs of inverted V-shape (chevrons).

Chiang t'ai (Chinese). *See* SOFT PASTE, CHINESE.

Chiaroscuro. Decoration painted in one or more colours with especial emphasis on light and shade, as seen in some early 19th-century topographical landscape painting on vases. The French term is *clair-obscur*. *See* GRISAILLE, EN; CAMAÏEU, EN; MONOCHROME.

Chicken skin. A glaze slightly pitted on the surface and resembling, in the opinion of Chinese commentators, chicken skin. *See* MING DYNASTY. The effect often occurs when a glaze is added to TRUE PORCELAIN and the second firing is at a lower temperature than that used to fire the body itself. Japanese porcelain was thus glazed, and this effect is therefore very commonly seen on Japanese ware. *See* ORANGE SKIN.

Chicken ware. Cups, saucers, dishes, and vases first made during the reign of Ch'êng Hua (1465–87), of the Ming dynasty. In form the cups are like small bowls, and the ware is decorated with chickens painted in a palette termed *tou ts'ai* (contrasting colours), no doubt referring to the contrast between the blue underglaze and the enamel colours applied over underglaze blue outlining. They were repeated in the 18th century.

Chicken ware. Ruby-back dish of eggshell porcelain, with *famille rose* enamel decoration, 18th century. Percival David Foundation of Chinese Art, London.

Chien yao (Chinese). Chien ware. Stoneware made in Chien-an (Fukien province) during the Sung dynasty (960–1280), and much sought in Japan for use in the TEA CEREMONY (*cha-no-yu*). The body is dark in colour. The glaze is thick, dark brown in colour, and ends in a treacly roll near the base. *See* HARE'S FUR; OIL-SPOT GLAZE; TEMMOKU.

Chih-ch'ui p'ing (Chinese). *See* MALLET VASE.

Chi-hung (Chinese). Underglaze copper-red produced by firing in a reducing atmosphere. *See* SACRIFICIAL RED.

Ch'ih lung (Chinese). A dragon (*lung*), which is one of the Four Supernatural Creatures (SSŬ LING). *See* CH'ING LUNG.

Ch'i-lin (Chinese). The correct term for the Chinese mythological creature usually called a KYLIN.

Chimney-piece ornament. Pottery and porcelain made to be displayed on a mantelpiece, and so with a sketchily finished or flat back. Many were made of pottery in Staffordshire during the 19th century. *See* ARBOUR GROUP; BOCAGE; FLATBACK; IMAGE TOY; STAFFORDSHIRE FIGURES.

Chimú pottery. Pottery made by the Chimú, who succeeded the Mochica people in northern Peru (*see* MOCHICA POTTERY). The wares vary from grey to black, or are of a red polished type decorated with white slip. The BRIDGE SPOUT and the STIRRUP SPOUT HANDLE were both employed.

China. A common term for porcelain; it is derived from the fact that, at the beginning of the 18th century, Chinese porcelain was known as 'the China ware' (e.g. by Defoe), which by *c.* 1750 had been contracted to 'China' and was later referred to simply as 'china'. Since *c.* 1800 in England the term has, in industrial circles, been increasingly taken to mean BONE-CHINA. Outside England the term usually employed is porcelain.

Chinaman teapot. Porcelain teapot with serpent spout, Chelsea, *c.* 1747. Courtesy, Tilley & Co., London.

China clay. The English term for the Chinese white clay termed KAOLIN after the district where some of the largest deposits were situated. It is derived from decomposed granitic rocks. The largest English deposits are in Cornwall, while those of France are situated at Saint-Yrieix, near the porcelain manufacturing centre of Limoges.

China glaze. An early English term for a ware similar to pearlware, the white surface of which resembles that of porcelain. It was popular at the end of the 18th century, and much of it was decorated with underglaze blue.

China-stone. The English term for PETUNTSE, itself a French corruption of the Chinese *pai-tun-tzû*. It is also called Cornish stone. *Petuntse* is an essential ingredient of TRUE PORCELAIN, fusing at about 1,450°C. into a hard, white, glass-like substance.

Chinaman teapot. A teapot modelled in the form of a Chinese man seated cross-legged and holding a parrot, which forms the spout. Such teapots were made at Meissen, and (some with a

Chinese export porcelain. Caster based on a French silver shape; reign of K'ang Hsi (1662–1722).

serpent spout) at Chelsea during the early period, 1745–49. *See* MAGOT TEAPOT.

Chine sur commande (French). Same as COMPAGNIE DES INDES WARE.

Chinese export porcelain. Porcelain made and decorated in China to European order, as distinct from porcelain in native taste. The Chinese began to export porcelain to Europe in the 16th century, and a few pieces with European inscriptions are known which were made before 1600. After this date the trade greatly expanded, and during the 17th century the Dutch East India Company was the largest importer. During the 18th century much white ware was enamelled in Canton for export to Europe (*see* CANTON CHINA). Wares in the native taste are usually a more recent import for the purpose of supplying the collectors' market for Chinese works of art. *See* EXPORT CHINA; ORIENTAL LOWESTOFT.

Chinese Imari. Porcelain made in China soon after 1700 in imitation of the IMARI porcelain of Japan. At the end of the 17th century, and for several decades afterwards, Japanese porcelain was more highly valued in the West than Chinese and, like the KAKIEMON wares, Imari patterns were copied for export, and also for home consumption. The porcelain itself is characteristically Chinese, and the decoration, while remaining in the general Imari style, differs noticeably from contemporary Japanese wares. The SPUR-MARKS which characterize Japanese porcelain do not appear on the Chinese versions.

Chinese Lowestoft. The so-called ORIENTAL LOWESTOFT. *See* CANTON CHINA; CHINESE EXPORT PORCELAIN; EXPORT CHINA.

Chinese reign-mark. *See* CHARACTER-MARK. Such marks are not a certain indication of manufacture in the reign of the emperor named, and the mark may merely indicate that the style of the reign has been imitated. The reign-mark of K'ang Hsi (1662–1722) is very rarely found, since the emperor thought it would be sacrilege if a piece bearing his name were to be broken. A pair of circles, one within the other, inside the foot-ring is often an indication of manufacture during this reign. The Japanese equivalent is NENGO.

Chinese reign-mark. Porcelain saucer with painted decoration of nine bats on the rim, mark and reign of Yung Chêng (1723–35). Percival David Foundation of Chinese Art, London.

Chinese seal-mark. The mark of the reigning emperor in a square, conventional form similar to that used for seals. *See* SEAL-MARK; PSEUDO-CHINESE SEAL-MARK; CHARACTER-MARK.

Chinese triad. Three figures to be found as painted decoration on European and Chinese porcelain representing Lao Tzŭ, Confucius (Kung-fu Tzŭ), and Buddha (Fo). *See* THREE FRIENDS, THE.

Ch'ing dynasty. A Manchu ruling dynasty (1644–1912) which followed the native MING DYNASTY. So far as the arts are concerned the Ch'ing dynasty is notable for three emperors, K'ang Hsi (1662–1722), Yung Chêng (1723–35), and Ch'ien Lung (1736–96), and most specimens of porcelain desirable to collectors are referable to one of these three reigns, of which the first two are the most important and the last the most prolific. Much fine quality porcelain was manufactured, and during the reigns of Yung Chêng and Ch'ien Lung especially the export trade with Europe was built up, much ware being both made and painted to European order (*see* CHINESE EXPORT PORCELAIN). It was also at this time that Chinese wares most influenced porcelain in Europe, and Jesuit missionaries, notably Père d'Entrecolles in two letters of September 1712 and January 1722, provided information which was intensively studied by aspiring manufacturers in the West. Ch'ing wares are meticulously potted and decorated, losing much of the individuality which marks most Ming porcelain. The wares of the reign of K'ang Hsi continued Ming styles, and began to be classifiable in such terms as FAMILLE VERTE and FAMILLE JAUNE, and with the introduction of the rose enamel towards the end of his reign, the distinctive class known as FAMILLE ROSE soon emerged. The blue and white of this reign is noted for a pure white and a sapphire blue, and many monochromes were devised, such as the LANG YAO. In the reign of Ch'ien Lung notable experiments were made with FLAMBÉ GLAZES, fired in a reducing atmosphere, while underglaze painting in copper-red, sometimes in conjunction with blue, had already formed part of Yung Chêng production. The reign of Yung Chêng also saw a revival of early Ming and Sung styles; examples made at this time include the STEM-CUPS of the Hsüan-tê period of the Ming dynasty, decorated with three red fruit or fish, and copies of Sung dynasty KUAN and KO ware which are not infrequent. The 19th century has little to show that is either new or valuable. The reign of Chia Ch'ing (1796–1820) is noted for wares which are hardly more than repetitions of Ch'ien Lung styles. Coarse, over-decorated export porcelain in a combination of the *rose* and *verte* palettes was produced, and specimens are comparatively frequent. The reign of Tao Kuang (1821–51) saw a repetition of Yung Chêng styles, and there is very little to commend the period which followed. There was some repetition of earlier types, such as SANG-DE-BŒUF, apple-green, FAMILLE NOIRE, and peach-bloom. Most Chinese porcelain SNUFF-BOTTLES belong to the reign of Chia Ch'ing.

Chinese triad. Porcelain teapot with painted decoration, Worcester (First period). Courtesy, Sotheby's.

Ch'ing lung (Chinese). Literally, blue dragon, which this decorative motif depicts. *See* LUNG; CH'IH LUNG; BROSELEY BLUE DRAGON.

Ch'ing-pai (Chinese). Literally, blue-white. An early variety of Chinese porcelain. *See* YING-CH'ING.

Ching-tê Chên. The site of the Chinese Imperial porcelain kilns in Kiangsi province. There were kilns on this site from very early times. They were largely destroyed by fire in 1853 and rebuilt in 1864; production still continues. The secret of porcelain manufacture is traditionally said to have been taken from here to Japan.

Chinoiserie (French). European decoration inspired by oriental sources, particularly Chinese. *Chinoiseries* are pseudo-Chinese figures, pagodas, monsters, landscapes, and so forth, with imaginative fantasy elements. They occur in polychrome, monochrome, and gold and silver silhouette. The term *Japonaiserie* is sometimes employed for such decoration derived from Japanese sources. *Chinoiseries* were introduced at the end of the 17th century in the designs of such *ornemanistes* as Bérain (*see* BÉRAIN MOTIFS) and others, and the style was developed for porcelain painting at Meissen by J. G. Höroldt soon after 1721. It was widely used in decoration of all kinds until *c.* 1760.

Chinoiseries. Porcelain teapot with scenes on body and cover, Vienna, *c.* 1750–55. Österreichisches Museum für angewandte Kunst, Vienna.

Chocolate-cup. A large cup for drinking hot chocolate, usually with two side handles, a cover, and a saucer. *See* CAUDLE-CUP; COFFEE-CUP; TEACUP.

Chocolate-pot. A covered pot for serving hot chocolate, usually pear-shaped or cylindrical, and often with a handle placed at a right angle to the spout, although this feature is not, as is sometimes supposed, proof that a vessel is a chocolate-pot. A more certain indication is the presence in the cover of a hole for the purpose of inserting a wooden utensil (called a *molionet*) to stir the contents. *See* VERSEUSE; COFFEE-POT.

Chocolate-stand. Creamware stand, Leeds, *c.* 1790. Lady Gollancz Collection, London.

Chocolate-stand. A low circular receptacle affixed to the centre of a saucer, into which a CHOCOLATE-CUP could be placed so as to avoid spilling by a trembling hand; a type of TREMBLEUSE. Some Meissen porcelain examples have three cup-holders on a single tray with a serving handle. Examples in creamware from Leeds are of several styles, some having a notch in the rim of the cup-holder for the handle of the cup. *See* PRÉSENTOIR.

Chopine (French). A decorative faience object in the form of a lady's SHOE, made in Holland, England, and France. The true *chopine* is a platform-shoe with high soles and heels, as used in Asia, in 16th-century Venice, and later in England.

Christening goblet. A type of LOVING-CUP with four handles, and with a whistle to attract attention when a refill was desired.

Christie-Miller service. A dinner-service made at Meissen, *c.* 1740, and acquired about a hundred years later by the Christie-Miller family of Newcastle-under-Lyme (England). The plates and dishes are octagonal, with an inner border of small puce vignettes in alternate panels reserved on a border of gilt trellis diapers, and an outer border of larger polychrome vignettes between palmettes and scrolls. The vignettes are of harbour scenes. In the well are polychrome European landscapes derived from 17th-century engravings of Italian, German, and Austrian scenes painted by several of the factory's leading workmen. The service includes gilt-bronze mounted bowls, the mounts having dolphin feet; the bowls, with lobed and barbed rims, are painted on the outside and inside with scenes and figures. A large part of the service was dispersed at auction in 1970.

Chrome-green. Green from chromium oxide, introduced at Sèvres in 1804. In shade it is similar to APPLE-GREEN (*vert jaune* or *vert pomme*).

Chrysanthemummuster (German). Literally, chrysanthemum pattern. An elaborate blue-and-white floral pattern used in conjunction with a diaper border at Meissen. *See* MUSTER.

Cistern. Faience cistern, Limoges, 1739. Musée National de Céramique Adrien Dubouché, Limoges.

Ch'u Chou yao (Chinese). Celadon ware made at Ch'u Chou (Chekiang province) whither the Sung dynasty kilns at Lung Ch'üan were removed in the early years of the Ming dynasty, or perhaps a little before. It is said that an unglazed reddish-brown ring within the foot-ring of a dish indicates manufacture here rather than at Lung Ch'üan, and this accords reasonably well with observation. The incised and carved underglaze designs are usually characteristically Ming. The painting of designs in white slip under the CELADON glaze, common in the 18th century, may have begun here.

Ch'ui ch'ing (Chinese). Same as POWDER-BLUE. COBALT BLUE, used as an underglaze ground colour, was blown on to the surface of the piece to be decorated through a bamboo tube with a silk screen at the end of it. The technique dates from the reign of K'ang Hsi (1662–1722) of the Ch'ing dynasty; it was imitated in Europe, usually by SPONGING.

Chu-lu Hsien (Chinese). White PORCELLANEOUS WARES made during the SUNG DYNASTY at the city of this name in Chihli province (China). Many specimens are stained brown as the result of burial.

Chün yao (Chinese). Stoneware from Chün Chou (Honan province) first made during the Sung dynasty (960–1280). The body is a hard-fired stoneware covered with a glaze of varying shades centred around lavender-grey, often either splashed or suffused with a colour varying between crimson and purple. The glaze is thick, and contains myriads of tiny bubbles. In the interior of bowls and dishes the glaze sometimes shows small partings of *V* or *Y* form among the bubbles; these are called 'earthworm tracks' by the Chinese, and are regarded as a sign of genuineness. The surface is often minutely pitted at intervals. Wares include bulb-pots, flower pots (with size numbers from 1 to 10 incised into the base), bowls of characteristic shape, dishes, and stands. Chün ware is showy in colour; it is the earliest of the transmutation glazes fired in a reducing atmosphere. *See* FLAMBÉ; SANG-DE-BŒUF; SHU T'AI; MA CHÜN.

Chün yao. Flower-pot with characteristic glaze, Sung dynasty (960–1280). Victoria and Albert Museum, London.

Church Gresley pattern. A decorative pattern having a complicated ground of diamond and octagonal yellow panels alternating with panels of coloured roses and cornflowers. There is no evidence to associate it with the small pottery at Church Gresley, near Burton-on-Trent (England), *c.* 1794–1808, and there is no known explanation of the derivation of the name.

Cider-jug. A large jug for pouring cider, with a loop handle as well as a LIFT HANDLE.

Cinerary urn. A vessel to contain the ashes of the dead, and sometimes also food for his spirit. Some were inscribed with the name of the deceased. Urns of this kind were made in pottery from the earliest times, and they vary in shape. Sometimes called a funerary urn. *See* CANOPIC JAR; CANOPIC VASE; DEINOS.

Cinq bouquets (French). *See* DÉCOR À CINQ BOUQUETS.

Cinquefoil. A decorative shape having five equal lobes, as in the compound leaf of certain plants which are so described.

Cipher. *See* MONOGRAM.

Circle and square border. A border pattern of interlaced circles each enclosing a square with concave sides. The squares sometimes contain a pattern of dots. Also called 'chain border' and 'coin border'. It was used on Wedgwood's JASPER.

Ciselé (French). Literally, chiselled. *See* CHASED.

Cistercian ware. Earthenware vessels (often mugs and tankards) with a red body and a brownish-black glaze, commonly found near the sites of Cistercian monasteries in England. This ware was produced during the early part of the 16th century.

Cistercian ware. Mug, ht 4 in. Courtesy, Sotheby's.

Cistern. A large receptacle for water, sometimes in the form of a deep basin, and sometimes of a vessel with a spigot. Those in two parts, with the spigoted vessel uppermost and the basin below, were part of the household water-supply, being filled from the well as required. Containers of this kind were made of maiolica or faience in Italy, France, and Spain and frequently survive there. They date from the 16th century. *See* WALL-CISTERN; FOUNTAIN.

Clair de lune (French). Literally, moonlight. A pale lavender-blue glaze obtained by adding a little COBALT BLUE to a clear

FELDSPATHIC GLAZE, usually in conjunction with a controlled CRACKLE, coloured black and brownish-red. This glaze was used mostly in China in the 18th century for pieces of restrained form with Sung dynasty affiliations, but it was copied to a very limited extent at Meissen where the pale greyish-blue lacks the crackle of the Chinese varieties. *See* YÜEH-PAI.

Clock-case. Porcelain case decorated with a *putto* on the base and an *amorino* opposite the clock, with French gilt-bronze mounts. Courtesy, Antique Porcelain Co., London.

Clarence, Duke of, pattern. *See* HOPE SERVICE.

Claret. A crimson ground colour in imitation of the ROSE POMPADOUR of Sèvres, introduced at Chelsea in 1760. The colour was successfully used on Worcester porcelain soon afterwards, although it is probable that the London decorator, James Giles, was responsible for ware thus decorated. It was imitated elsewhere with little success, and in the first half of the 19th century it was revived by Coalport and Minton for use on bone-china under the name of 'rose du Barry'.

Classical. Of the first, or highest, class. During the Renaissance the civilization of ancient Greece and Rome was accorded this status, and the term therefore came to have a secondary meaning applicable to works from this period, and those which were derived from them. Pottery in the classical style is characterized by ornament taken from Greek and Roman sources, and by formality, dignity, and simplicity. *See* RENAISSANCE STYLE; NEO-CLASSICAL STYLE.

Classical handle. A vertical loop handle rising above the rim of a vessel, as on a LEKANE.

Claw and ball foot. A decoration consisting of a clawed foot grasping a ball, more familiar on furniture than on ceramics. It is nevertheless derived in both cases from a Chinese porcelain decoration depicting a dragon with clawed foot grasping the SACRED PEARL.

Clay. An earth whose essential constituent is hydrous aluminium silicate. Clay in its natural state is plastic, i.e. it will take and retain any reasonable shape imposed on it. It remains plastic while mixed with water, but when the water evaporates this property disappears, to return when water is again added. When exposed to temperatures above 450°C. it becomes permanently hard. There are many types and colours of clay which are used, and sometimes blended, in making ceramic ware. Most clay contains iron oxide as an impurity, and this causes it to exhibit a colour varying from buff to red after firing; KAOLIN, or china clay, remains white after firing. The French term is *argile*. *See* POTTER'S CLAY; BALL CLAY; MARL; FIRE-CLAY.

Clay-size. The size of a clay model when made, without allowing for shrinkage in drying and firing. *See* MODELLING.

Clobbering. Over-painting in enamels on previously decorated porcelain, first practised by Dutch decorators who used sparsely decorated porcelain, usually in blue underglaze, from China, Japan, and Meissen. One German HAUSMALER, J.F. Ferner, did similar work. Blue-and-white porcelain was thus decorated with red and green enamels and gilding in England early in the 19th century when oriental blue-and-white porcelain had become temporarily unfashionable. The quality of work of this kind is variable, but is rarely very good. *See* REFIRED WARE.

Clock. An ornamental piece, usually of earthenware, in the form of a grandfather clock about 10 inches high, sometimes flanked by figures. Some examples were made of PRATTWARE.

Clock-case. An ornamental piece to accommodate a clock, made of faience or porcelain at Sèvres, Meissen, Strasbourg, and elsewhere, usually in either the rococo or the Louis Seize style. *See* VASE À CARTEL; WATCH-STAND.

Cloisonné (French). A type of decoration using enamel on a metal base, in which the design is outlined by wire fillets (*cloisons*) secured to the metal, the enclosed spaces being filled in with coloured enamels which are then fired. Some porcelain closely imitating such decoration was made in Japan in the second half of the 19th century, and also (with slightly raised and gilded lines simulating wire) occurs in Europe. *See* CHAMPLEVÉ; ÉMAIL OMBRANT; CLUNY ENAMEL WARE; BASSE-TAILLE.

Clou, au (French). Literally, with a nail. The term refers to the CHASING of gilding with a metal implement.

Cloud and thunder fret. A decorative FRET pattern of volute motifs of square form, originally a background to relief ornament on early bronze vessels, but later employed on porcelain in a variety of ways in painted or incised form. In Chinese it is termed the *lei-wên*.

Clouded ware. Ware made by a technique known as 'clouding', by which unfired earthenware was sponged with coloured glazes with a tool called a 'clouder' and then dipped into a clear glaze. *See* TORTOISESHELL WARE; WHIELDON WARE.

Cluny enamel ware. Ware made at Cluny (France) in imitation of *cloisonné* enamel. Also called 'Longwy enamel ware'.

Coach-pot. An English term for a BOURDALOU. Coach-pots were made in England in creamware by Wedgwood and at Leeds, in porcelain at Derby and Caughley, and in earthenware by Spode, and elsewhere in Staffordshire. Also called in England an 'oval chamber-pot' or 'slipper'.

Coalbrookdale ware. Ware made at Coalport (Shropshire) by John Rose and his partners from 1799 to 1814, and heavily encrusted with modelled flowers. The Coalport factory used the word 'Coalbrookdale' (the name of a place nearby) on the base of some of its wares, but present-day collectors have applied the term to the encrusted ware mentioned, and it is often inaccurately extended to wares from other factories in the same style, especially when unmarked.

Cobalt blue. A mineral which is basically cobalt aluminate; it is the widely used colouring agent for blue-and-white porcelain, especially that which is painted underglaze. First used by the Persians, it was introduced into China during the Yüan dynasty (1280–1368), and was extensively used underglaze during the Ming dynasty. Although it was used in Europe as an underglaze colour from the earliest beginnings of ARTIFICIAL PORCELAIN its use on the TRUE PORCELAIN of Meissen did not occur until comparatively late, *c.* 1725, owing to difficulties experienced in firing it properly. It ranges from a greyish or blackish blue to a pure sapphire, the shade and purity of the colour being affected by the presence of impurities in the cobalt ore. *See* BLUE; LITTLER'S BLUE.

Cobbler and wife. A common Staffordshire earthenware group or pair of figures depicting a cobbler at work and his wife holding a jug and a cup. The origin of this group seems to have been Continental; it was probably based on models by Paul-Louis Cyfflé at Niderviller (France).

Clobbering. Meissen blue-and-white porcelain teapot with added decoration by J.F. Ferner *c.* 1750.

Cobbler and wife. Staffordshire glazed earthenware group.

Cock and hen teapots. Porcelain teapots modelled by J. J. Kändler, Meissen, *c.* 1734–45. Courtesy, Christie's.

Cock and hen teapots. Porcelain teapots, made as a pair, in the form of a seated cock and hen with naturalistically coloured plumage and with the open beak acting as the spout. In some examples chicks are added under the wing of the hen, and other variations in modelling and colouring are found. The type was first modelled by J. J. Kändler at Meissen from 1734.

Cock and peony. A decorative subject of 18th-century Chinese porcelain depicting one or two cocks and several peonies.

Cock tureen. A covered tureen in the form of a sitting cock. They were made of Chinese porcelain in the reign of Ch'ien Lung (1736–95).

Cockle-pot. A large receptacle for serving the shellfish known as cockles. The lower half of the vessel is a bowl on a stemmed base on which rest two covers, the inner one plain and low-domed, the outer one high and elaborately moulded. Examples in creamware made at Leeds have pierced decoration, and also relief decoration which includes cockle-shells.

Cockspur. A support for holding ware while in the kiln. It had three legs and one upward point. Sometimes called a stilt. *See* SPUR-MARK; STILT-MARK; KILN FURNITURE.

Coffee-can. A straight-sided cylindrical cup shaped like a mug. It has a slight foot-ring, and is about 2½ inches in both height and width. The shape was introduced at Sèvres, and was widely copied elsewhere. In England it is sometimes called a CAN, the term BREAKFAST-CAN being applied to larger specimens.

Coffee-cup. A cup of several sizes and in many styles, with one or two handles, or with none. The diameter is usually smaller than the height, which is the opposite of the proportions of the TEACUP. The usual size for post-prandial coffee is much smaller, and is often (especially in the United States) termed a 'demi-tasse'. For some of the many styles *see* BERLIN CUP; FONTAINEBLEAU CUP; FRAGONARD CUP; HESSIAN CUP; JASMIN CUP; PEYRE CUP; RAMBOUILLET CUP; REGNIER CUP; SAINT-CLOUD CUP; SEMIOVE CUP; VINCENNES CUP; TASSE À FILET; CAN; COFFEE-CAN; BREAKFAST-CAN.

Coffee-urn. Porcelain, Weesp, Holland, *c.* 1760–70. Bernhard Houthakker Collection, Municipal Museum, Amsterdam.

Coffee-maker. A type of COFFEE-POT adapted for brewing coffee by either percolating or dripping, usually with a pierced liner, or surmounted by a dripper with a perforated bottom, and frequently with a tamper to press the coffee grounds. Coffee-makers may be globular or severely columnar. Some are accompanied by a heating device, such as a GODET. The German term is KAFFEEMASCHINE. *See* COFFEE-WARMER; COFFEE-URN.

Coffee-pot. A covered vessel of varying forms for serving coffee. It has one handle and a long spout, or, as in the case of early Meissen specimens, a pouring lip like a jug. Coffee-pots are usually pear-shaped, or in the form of a truncated cone. The French term is *cafetière*. *See* COFFEE-WARMER; COFFEE-MAKER; COFFEE-URN; CHOCOLATE-POT.

Coffee-service. A set of cups, saucers, etc., for the service of coffee, with a coffee-pot replacing the teapot of the TEA-SERVICE. During the 18th century the tea-service was often provided with coffee-cups *en suite*, but with no additional saucers. *See* MOKA SET.

Coffee-urn. A vessel for dispensing coffee, having a spigot rather than a spout. *See* TEA-URN.

Coffee-warmer. A coffee-pot on a reticulated stand in which rests a GODET or spirit-lamp for keeping the coffee warm. Some examples have a spigot on the pot instead of a spout; *see* COFFEE-URN. Some have an accompanying vessel for brewing coffee; *see* COFFEE-MAKER.

Coggle. A wheel of metal or wood fixed on an axle in a handle. It has an engraved or carved pattern so that, when rolled on soft clay, it leaves an impression; used to form repetitive relief patterns.

Coiling. A primitive method of forming pots by coiling long rolls of clay until the desired shape had been attained, after which inside and outside are smoothed by being scraped and smeared. The method was used to make pots of extremely large size, and it is still sometimes employed today by makers of STUDIO POTTERY.

Coin border. *See* CIRCLE AND SQUARE BORDER.

Coin ground. A ground in the style of the CIRCLE AND SQUARE BORDER pattern.

Colander bowl. A low, circular bowl with a fixed, pierced colander top, and a larger hole to one side, just below the rim, for draining the contents; sometimes referred to as a 'watercress bowl', a 'lettuce-draining dish', or a 'flower-holder'. Such bowls, made of English delftware, usually come from Bristol; specimens are rare. A bowl for a similar purpose but with drainage holes in the wall and bottom was made of brown stoneware. *See* CRESS-DISH.

Cold colours. Lacquer colours or oil-paint applied as decoration to porcelain without firing. Lacquer colours were employed on BÖTTGER RED STONEWARE at Meissen, and on some early Meissen white porcelain. Lacquer colours or oil-paint were used to decorate some early Bow figures. These are now found in white, without decoration, although occasional examples may be noted with a little paint still adhering. The German term is *Kaltmalerei* (cold painting).

Cold printing. A term sometimes employed to describe BAT-PRINTING in which a bat of gelatine or soft glue was used to transfer the engraved design from the copper plate to the surface of the ware. The impression of the copper plate on the glue surface was taken in a thin, colourless oil, and this was dusted with powder colour which adhered to the oil. The technique is used for on-glaze printing. *See* HOT PRINTING.

Colimaçon, à (French). Modelled with spiral swirls in the form of a snail shell, as on some sauce-boats and bourdalous.

Collar. The short, vertical neck of a Chinese porcelain vase or bottle (or a European copy) which is in the form of an upright narrow collar.

Cologne ware. (1) RHENISH STONEWARE of the 16th and 17th centuries made in Cologne (Germany). (2) Certain brown SALT-GLAZED STONEWARE made in England in the 17th century.

Colour. For the various colours used in ceramic decoration, *see* BLUE; GREEN; PINK; RED; PURPLE; YELLOW; BLACK. Colours may be applied over the glaze, or under the glaze, and, in the case of tin-enamel ware, are in the glaze. Transparent glazes are coloured by the addition of metallic oxides, and the bodies of

Coffee-maker (*warmer*). Porcelain, with godet and dripper, Vienna, 1813. Harold Newman Collection.

both pottery and porcelain are sometimes coloured in this way. *See* COLOURED BODY; COLOURED GLAZE; COLOURED SLIP.

Coloured body. A porcelain or pottery BODY into which colouring matter has been introduced, and which may be unglazed, or covered with a transparent glaze. *See* WEDGWOOD COLOURED BODIES.

Coloured glaze. A GLAZE coloured by staining with a metallic oxide, such as copper to produce green, manganese for brown-purple, cobalt for blue, etc.

Commedia dell'Arte figures. Pantaloon and Columbine, by Bustelli, Nymphenburg, *c.* 1755–60. Victoria and Albert Museum, London.

Coloured lustre ware. Pottery decorated with LUSTRE (including resist ware) and then with designs in enamels of various colours.

Coloured Shonsui. A type of Chinese SHONSUI WARE decorated with geometric patterns and with the addition of enamel colours, *c.* 1643–62.

Coloured slip. A SLIP into which colouring matter has been introduced before application to the body, after which the ware is either left unglazed or covered with a transparent glaze.

Column candlestick. A type of candlestick which has its nozzle on a support in the form of a classical column or a CARYATID.

Columnar handle. A handle in the form of a vertical column joined by a horizontal bar to the rim of the vessel, as on a KELEBE.

Comb design. *See* KUSITAKADE.

Combed decoration. A wavy or zig-zag pattern in two or more colours which was produced by combing newly applied wet slip with a comb or a wire brush. The technique was developed in England by John Dwight and John Astbury, and refined by Thomas Whieldon. It was employed on Staffordshire slipware of the late 17th and early 18th centuries. *See* FEATHER PATTERN.

Comfit-box. A type of BOX to hold comfits (a kind of sweetmeat like a crystallized fruit, or a confection for sweetening the breath). *See* COMFIT-HOLDER; BONBONNIÈRE.

Comfit-holder. A small openwork basket, shell, or other container, often held by a porcelain figure, and generally in a pair, for serving comfits (*see* COMFIT-BOX). They were made at a number of English and Continental factories during the 18th century, including Chelsea, *c.* 1752–56.

Commedia dell'Arte figures. A series of figures, up to sixteen in number, depicting characters from the Italian Comedy, or *Commedia dell'Arte.* The series includes Arlecchino (Harlequin), Pantaloon, Brigella, Pulcinella (Punch), Mezzetino, Pedrolini (Pierrot), Scaramuccia (Scaramouche), Doctor Baloardo (Balvorel), and the Lover as the principal male characters, and with Isabella, Columbine, and the *inamorata* taking the parts of serving-maids and soubrettes. The principal characters were often masked. The Comedy was played by travelling troupes, and existed only as a scenario, the dialogue and stage-business being largely improvised. It was at the height of its popularity from the end of the 17th century to *c.* 1760. The subject appeared in painted form on Meissen porcelain, *c.* 1725, and soon after 1730 J. J. Kändler began to model his famous series of HARLEQUIN figures in a variety of poses. Peter Reinicke modelled figures from the Comedy for Meissen *c.* 1743, but the finest, by common consent, are those modelled by Franz Anton Bustelli for Nymphenburg, *c.* 1755–60. Others in the 18th century came from Höchst, Fulda, Frankenthal, Fürstenberg, and Kloster-Veilsdorf. A series in miniature size, 4 inches high, was made of porcelain at Doccia (Italy), and a series of terracotta models was made, 1745–59, for Capodimonte by Giuseppe Gricci. In England they occur in the porcelain of Chelsea and Bow, and copies of porcelain versions occur in enamelled saltglazed stoneware and earthenware. The figures were usually taken from Luigi Riccoboni's *Histoire du Théâtre Italien*, 1728. *See* WEISSENFELS, DUKE OF, SERIES.

Commemorative jug. Any jug which commemorates an event or person in its decoration or in an inscription, for example jugs of saltglazed stoneware made in the Rhineland bearing medallions with the monogram of the reigning English sovereign in commemoration of his reign. *See* A.R. JUG; C.R. JUG; G.R. JUG; W.R. JUG.

Commemorative ware. Plates and other pieces decorated with a scene or an inscription recording some historical person or event. *See* COMMEMORATIVE JUG.

Commendation mark. Characters sometimes found on Chinese porcelain which, on translation, prove to be a commendation of the piece, for example, 'jade', 'artistic', 'precious'.

Compagnie des Indes ware. Porcelain made in China to special order and shipped to France by the Compagnie des Indes. Shapes are often derived from metal and silver models sent to China for the purpose. The decoration is European in style, and was sometimes taken from contemporary engravings. It is also called *Chine sur commande*. *See* CANTON PORCELAIN.

Companion piece. One of a pair, set, or group, in relation to the remainder.

Compendiario dish. A dish of 16th-century Italian maiolica decorated in the STILE COMPENDIARIO.

Comport. A form of dessert dish on a stem base, popular in the 19th century. Examples were made of BELLEEK WARE, and in England at Coalport, Rockingham, and elsewhere.

Composite service. A service that is not complete as originally made by the factory, but which includes pieces of similar form and decoration, perhaps made at a different date and even by a different factory, possibly made as REPLACERS.

Compôtier (French). A bowl or dish, sometimes on a stemmed base, for serving *compôte* (cooked, whole fruit); often loosely called a *compôte*.

Conceit. An object in the form of a round cake for the decoration of the dinner-table. Some examples were made by Wedgwood in jasper ware.

Condiment ledge. *See* LEDGE.

Cone. (1) A support, in the form of a cone, for an object while being fired; *see* COCKSPUR; SEPULCHRAL CONE. (2) A device for measuring the temperature of a kiln. Such cones are made in the form of a pyramid and are given an index number corresponding to a certain melting-point. When the pre-determined temperature is reached the tip of the pyramid sags over until it is level

Comfit-holders. Pair of figures with polychrome decoration, Chelsea, *c.* 1752–56. Courtesy, Christie's.

with the base. Also known as pyrometric cones, Seger cones (Europe), and Orton cones (America). They are principally employed to measure temperatures in those kilns where this factor is not controlled automatically, or for experimental purposes.

Confiturier (French). A JAM-POT or conserve cup.

Conjuring cup. A cup, in which (by means of a concealed siphon) the contents recede from the lips of the drinker and are spilled on him. Examples were made in Chinese porcelain. *See* PUZZLE-JUG.

Conjuring cup. Porcelain cup, diam. 3½ in., decorated with *tou-ts'ai* enamel. Reign of Wan-li (1573–1619). Percival David Foundation of Chinese Art, London.

Conoidal. Paraboloid or sugar-loaf shape.

Conserve cup. Same as *confiturier*; *see* JAM-POT.

Continents, The Four (or **Five**). *See* FOUR CONTINENTS.

Contour-framing. A border surrounding an ornamental design and conforming to its outline. It occurs on English delftware.

Contracted neck. The neck of a vessel which is narrow in proportion to the body.

Conversation pattern. A decorative subject depicting pagoda-type buildings with, in an irregular white reserve, two figures facing each other as though in conversation. It is a rare pattern, employed at Caughley in the 18th century.

Cooks, Bow. A pair of figures made at Bow, 1756, traditionally attributed to John Bacon, the sculptor, and copied from the CRIS DE PARIS after Bouchardon's engravings. They are frequently mentioned as being among the finest figures made at Bow.

Copenhagen blue fluted service. A Danish dinner-service with underglaze blue decoration made by the Royal Copenhagen Manufactory continuously since its establishment in 1775. The ledges of the plates and the sides of the hollow ware are REEDED, although called 'fluted'. The blue floral sprays are from an old Chinese motif, adapted in Europe in the early 18th century. Later versions have added blue decoration on the border (termed 'half-lace') and pierced decoration (termed 'full-lace').

Copenhagen figure. The Goose Girl, by Christian Thomsen, decorated in grey and blue underglaze. Courtesy, Royal Copenhagen Manufactory.

Copenhagen figures. Figures made in porcelain by the Royal Copenhagen Manufactory. (1) The underglaze coloured figures, usually in tones of blue and grey, were made from 1885 under the direction of Arnold Krog, and feature a wide range of subjects from Danish folk life. (2) Figures in more colourful overglaze decoration include 10 children in native costume and holding regional flowers moulded in relief, created by the sculptor Carl Martin Hansen; the original set was a gift of the Danish people to King Christian X and Queen Alexandrine in 1923, and another set was presented to Queen Elizabeth and Prince Philip in 1957.

Copenhagen pattern. Same as BLAUBLÜMCHENMUSTER.

Coperta (Italian). A flashing of transparent glaze applied to Italian maiolica at a second firing to enhance the brilliance of the colours and the sheen of the surface. *See* MARZACOTTO; KWAART.

Coppa amatoria (Italian). Same as AMATORI.

Copper bound. The edge of some Chinese porcelain plates and bowls, especially of the Sung dynasty, covered with a thin copper band; *see* TING YAO; BROWN EDGE.

Copper-green. Slightly bluish GREEN derived from copper oxide, and one of the basic ceramic colours.

Copper lustre. Decoration in LUSTRE utilizing copper. Methods commonly employed were: (1) using copper in a colloidal state (i.e. in particles too small to sink in the liquid of suspension), as in Spain, where the copper often has an iridescent appearance; (2) the process of firing the metallic oxide, as in England. In the English ware the use of copper resulted in a natural copper colour. Gold on a brown-glazed ground gave an effect similar to bronzed copper. *See* COPPER RESIST.

Copper resist. Resist ware of COPPER LUSTRE, the pattern being the colour of the body against a copper lustre ground.

Coquetière (French). (1) An EGG-CUP. (2) A misnomer for a type of VEILLEUSE made at Sèvres, 1757–58, of *pâte tendre*, which is a pastille burner.

Coquetière (2). Porcelain veilleuse with godet, Sèvres, 1758. Wallace Collection, London.

Coral-red. A Chinese glaze colour of the reign of K'ang Hsi (1662–1722), sometimes repeated later; an orange-red derived from iron. *See* IRON-RED.

Coréen (French). Korean. *See* DÉCOR CORÉEN.

Cormorant fisherman. A transfer-printed decorative subject used at Worcester from *c.* 1754 and Caughley. It depicts a Chinese fisherman holding a fish, with a cormorant perched on a nearby bush, ducks in flight, and another fisherman seated on the bank, which is embellished with chrysanthemums with broad leaves. It is said that the Worcester fishing-line is wavy, and the Caughley version straight, but this is not always the case. *See* FISHERMAN.

Cooks. Pair of porcelain figures, Bow, *c.* 1756.

Corn pitcher. A type of jug or pitcher with moulded relief decoration of corn (maize) ears and husks. Examples were made by the United States Pottery Co., Bennington, Vt, and Charles Cartlidge & Co., Greenpoint, N.Y. *See* AMERICAN PORCELAIN. Similar ware occurs in English pottery and porcelain.

Corne, à la (French). Same as CORNUCOPIA PATTERN; a term for this pattern first used at Rouen, and later elsewhere in France.

Corner. The angle where two flat sides meet. *See* CHAMFERED CORNER; INDENTED CORNER.

Cornflower. *See* ANGOULÊME SPRIG.

Cornish stone. Feldspathic rock of a kind known as pegmatite found in Cornwall (England). After being ground it is used in the making of porcelain and some kinds of pottery. *See* FELDSPAR.

Cornucopia. A type of WALL-POCKET in the form of a cornucopia.

Cornucopia pattern. A polychrome pattern first introduced at Rouen as a decoration on faience. It depicts a cornucopia overflowing with flowers, with birds, butterflies, and insects in addition. It was copied elsewhere in France at the time, and forgeries purporting to be Rouen pieces with this pattern are not uncommon. The French terms are *à la corne* and *décor à la corne*.

Costrel. Same as PILGRIM-FLASK.

Cottage. Porcelain pastille-burner in the revived Gothic style, Staffordshire, *c*. 1825.

Cottage. A small pottery or porcelain ornament in the form of a cottage made in many sizes, styles, and degrees of elaboration. Cottages often have an aperture at the back for inserting a scented pastille; *see* PASTILLE-BURNER. They were commonly made in Staffordshire by many of the porcelain and earthenware factories. Models with a slot in the roof were money-boxes; *see* PENNY-BANK.

Cottage Bristol. A term loosely employed to include English porcelain wares made at Bristol or at New Hall (Shropshire) which were of poor quality and decoration in relation to the general production of the Bristol factory and perhaps made to compete with Wedgwood's creamware. True cottage Bristol (i.e. porcelain made at Champion's Bristol factory until 1780) has the normal idiosyncrasies of the factory's productions, viz. the handle of teacups slightly askew and WREATHING in the paste.

Cottage china. Same as COTTAGE BRISTOL.

Cotyliscos (Greek). Same as KOTYLISCOS.

Country of origin mark. A mark designating the country where a piece of ceramic ware was made, added after 1891 to ware exported to the United States in order to comply with the McKinley Tariff Act. Similar marks added to pottery or porcelain for the same purpose, such as 'Made in Japan' on wares exported to England, are all of recent origin.

Coupe (French). A 20th-century plate without a ledge, similar to the Chinese SAUCER-DISH.

Courtship and marriage. A decorative subject used on English creamware transfer-printed in black. One version depicts reversible masks, with a man and woman smiling when held one way up, and scowling when turned upside down.

Couverte. A French term for the glaze on porcelain. See ÉMAIL; VERNIS.

Coventry, Earl of, pattern. *See* BLIND EARL PATTERN.

Cover. An unattached top (as distinguished from a LID, which is usually hinged) for closing the mouth of a jar, vase, pot, bowl, tureen, or other open vessel. It varies in shape – flat, conical, dome-shaped – and is usually surmounted by a decorative handle termed a knop or FINIAL. Screw covers occur on some CASTERS, SNUFF-BOXES, etc. The French term is *couvercle*. *See* DOME COVER; CAP COVER.

Crackle. Pear-shaped water-dropper with crackled glaze, Chinese stoneware, 18th century. Percival David Foundation of Chinese Art, London.

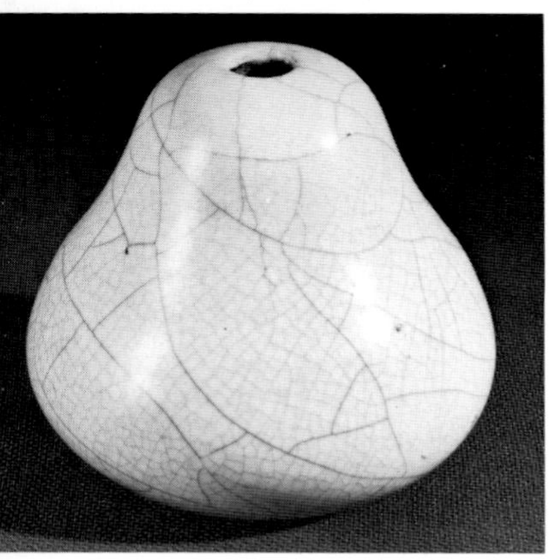

Coverdish. Any tureen, vegetable dish, or other piece of similar shape having a cover.

Cow creamer. A silver-pattern cream-jug in the form of a cow, with an opening in the back for filling, a spout in the form of the mouth, and a curved tail as a handle. In some versions there is a seated milkmaid alongside. The earthenware versions, the earliest of which were made in Staffordshire in the second half of the 18th century, may have been based on contemporary Dutch and English silver jugs of the same kind, but they were also made in tin-glazed ware *c*. 1755 at Delft (Holland). English versions occur in Whieldon ware, Prattware, creamware, and in the earthenware of Obadiah Sherratt (Burslem), *c*. 1822–35. Those of large size are sometimes called 'cow milk-jug'. *See* ST ANTHONY COW CREAMER.

Cozzi porcelain. A type of SOFT-PASTE PORCELAIN made in Venice by Geminiano Cozzi from 1765 to 1812. Most of the wares produced were derivative, and Meissen inspired a good deal of the earlier wares. The factory used a red anchor as a mark, but in a much larger version than that normally employed at Chelsea.

Cozzi porcelain. Teapot decorated with acanthus foliage and rococo scrolls, Venice, *c.* 1770. Courtesy, Newman & Newman Ltd, London.

Crab-claw markings. A name given in the 18th century by Chinese commentators to the appearance of the CRACKLE occurring on Kuan wares (*see* KUAN YAO) of the Sung dynasty (960–1280), and to similar decorative effects appearing on copies made during the reign of Yung Chêng (1722–36).

Crabstock. A type of handle, spout, or foot, moulded in relief to represent a gnarled branch of a crab-apple tree with the side-branches cut off. A pot with such a spout usually has a conforming handle. Also called 'rustic'. *See* BRANCH HANDLE: TREE-TRUNK.

Cracked-ice ground. A ground pattern used on Chinese porcelain from the 17th century onwards. It is blue, of varying intensity, and irregularly divided by dark lines to suggest the cracked ice of Spring. Usually the PRUNUS blossom is shown reserved in white against the blue. It was not often copied in Europe, but a few examples of Bristol delftware thus decorated survive, dating from *c.* 1750, and also some rare specimens of Worcester porcelain.

Crackle. Numerous minute surface cracks in a glaze, deliberately induced as decoration by creating a disagreement in the shrinkage rates of body and glaze during cooling. The French term is *craquelure*. The technique of deliberately inducing such an effect was developed in China as early as the beginning of the Sung dynasty (960–1280) in KUAN and KO ware, and again came into vogue with the revival of Sung styles in the 18th century. The exact method adopted is unknown, but it is believed that steatite was introduced into the glaze material to obtain the necessary disagreement between body and glaze. There are several varieties: the 'giant' (or 'crab-claw') variety has cracks which are few and widely spaced; 'fissured ice' has cracks more closely spaced; and *truité* has cracks so closely spaced as to be reminiscent of fish-scales. Some pieces feature both giant and *truité* crackle. *See* CRAZING; EEL'S-BLOOD CRACKLE; FISH-ROE GLAZE.

Cradle. A miniature infant-cradle, originally made of slipware. Cradles were originally used for wedding-gifts as a fertility symbol, dated pieces from 1673 to 1839 being recorded. Later they were presented on the birth of the first child, and were modified by adding the figure of an infant covered with a blanket and sometimes an inscription recording the child's name and birth-date. These were made from the end of the 18th century in glazed earthenware, saltglazed ware, delftware, and similar types of pottery.

Cradle. Brown-glazed earthenware decorated with trailed slip, by Ralph Shaw, Cobridge, Staffordshire, 1745. City Museums, Stoke-on-Trent.

Craftsmen, The. A series of porcelain figures depicting various contemporary craftsmen, e.g. coppersmith, joiner, etc., modelled by J. J. Kändler at Meissen, *c.* 1750.

Craquelure. The French term for CRACKLE.

Crater. Same as KRATER.

Crayfish salt. A SALT-CELLAR modelled as a shell and supported on rocks on which lie a crayfish, small shells and weeds. It was modelled at Chelsea, *c.* 1745, from a silver prototype by Nicolas Sprimont. The design was taken originally from the design-books of the French silversmith and *ornemaniste*, Juste-Aurèle Meissonnier. A rare version made at Chelsea has a grey crab crawling up the side.

Cream-boat. Silver shape, porcelain, Worcester, *c.* 1755.

Cream-pail. Porcelain, with bail-handle and applied prunus blossom decoration, Bow, *c.* 1752. Courtesy, Newman & Newman Ltd, London.

Crazing. Minute surface cracks in the glaze of porcelain as a result of an unintended disagreement between the shrinkage rate of glaze and body during cooling. Although the effect was used decoratively by the Chinese (*see* CRACKLE), it is a defect on porcelain from elsewhere. It often develops on tableware as a result of reheating in an oven.

Cream-boat. A small boat-shaped dish used for serving cream, usually having a handle at one end and a pouring lip at the other, and often resting on a splayed base; it is similar in general form to a sauce-boat, though smaller.

Cream-jug. A small jug or pitcher for serving cream. It is often pear-shaped, with a cover, and is smaller than a milk-jug. *See* COW CREAMER.

Cream-pail. A small bucket-shaped receptacle for cream, usually in Bow porcelain *c.* 1752, with an applied decoration of PRUNUS blossom and a BAIL HANDLE.

Creamer. *See* CREAM-JUG; COW CREAMER.

Creamware. Cream-coloured earthenware with a transparent lead glaze originally developed by Josiah Wedgwood *c.* 1760 from existing earthenware bodies to compete with porcelain. The body was made of whitish clay from Devon which was mixed with calcined flint. Its success was almost immediate and, as a result of an order for a tea-service from Queen Charlotte, Wedgwood renamed it 'Queen's ware'. Its manufacture was started at Leeds and Derby (Cockpit Hill), and also in Staffordshire generally in the 1760s, and it was much in demand as a substitute not for porcelain, but for delftware. As a result factories making tin-enamel earthenware in England successively closed, and exports to the Continent seriously affected both faience and porcelain production. Manufacture on the Continent started before 1775, although it did not reach a large scale till towards the end of the century. Creamware was decorated by painting under- and overglaze, transfer-printing, moulding, and pierced work. Figures of creamware were made at Leeds. In France it was termed *faïence fine, faïence anglaise, terre de pipe anglaise*, and *cailloutages*; in Germany, *Steingut*; in Italy, *terraglia*; and in Sweden, *flintporslin. See* PONT-AUX-CHOUX WARE.

Crespina. Maiolica, with wavy rim and with a central boss, Faenza (workshop of Virgiliotto Calamelli), *c.* 1543. Courtesy, Sotheby's.

Crenelated. In the form of battlements; to be found, for instance, on the rim of some 19th-century vases or socles under the influence of the Gothic Revival. The French term is *crenelé*.

Crenelated border. A border pattern of the simple fret type, with a continuous line turning at right angles and resembling battlements; also called an embattled border.

Crespina (Italian). From *crespa*, meaning wrinkled or rippled. A plate, dish, or bowl of maiolica characterized by a wavy rim.

Cress-dish. A shallow bowl pierced at the bottom for drainage and accompanied by a matching dish. Cress-dishes occur in Worcester and Lowestoft porcelain, usually decorated in underglaze blue. *See* COLANDER BOWL.

Crich ware. Brown ware, similar to that made at Nottingham, produced at Crich (or Critch) in Derbyshire in the second half of the 18th century, and not to be confused with CROUCH WARE.

Cricket-cage. Chinese porcelain with enamel decoration, 18th century. Gulbenkian Museum of Oriental Art, Durham University.

Cricket-cage. A rectangular BOX of Chinese porcelain closed with a cork at one end and having pierced sides, for keeping fighting crickets used in a popular Chinese sport.

Crinoline figures. A series of porcelain figures modelled at Meissen by J. J. Kändler and Johann Friedrich Eberlein, starting *c.* 1737. They are so called from their skirts – hoop-skirts to which the term 'crinoline' has been loosely applied by erroneous association with the 19th-century skirts worn over stiff crinoline petticoats. Early specimens are rare, but they have been extensively reproduced by, among others, Carl Thieme of Potschappel (Germany).

Crinoline figure. Lady with pug dogs, by J. J. Kändler, Meissen, *c.* 1745. Victoria and Albert Museum, London.

Cris de Londres. A series of porcelain figures modelled at Derby in the 1760s to depict London street-hawkers in the style of the Meissen CRIS DE PARIS. *See* VYSE FIGURES.

Cris de Paris. A series of porcelain figures modelled at Meissen by J. J. Kändler and Peter Reinicke in the 1740s to represent Paris street-hawkers. They were inspired by engravings by the Comte de Caylus after Bouchardon. A second series was made by Kändler and Reinicke in 1753–55 after drawings by Christoph Huet. Another series was modelled at Niderviller by Paul-Louis Cyfflé in TERRE DE LORRAINE, and some were copied in England by Chelsea (which added some original figures modelled by Joseph Willems) and at Bow. The series includes vendors of grapes, pies, oysters, cocoa, cakes, scallops, pancakes, flowers, birds, eggs, rabbits, chickens, absinthe, wine, lemons, and trinkets. Included were a chimney-sweep, peepshow-man, cook, bird-plucker, organ-grinder, drummer, a waiter carrying a laden tray, and a quack doctor.

Cris de Vienne. A series of porcelain figures modelled by J. J. Niedermeyer at Vienna depicting Viennese street-hawkers, more or less contemporary with the CRIS DE PARIS of Meissen. They include a trinket-seller, greengrocer, pastry-cook, tailor, etc.

Cris de Paris. Figures from the Meissen series by Reinicke, *c.* 1740–50. Courtesy, Sotheby's.

Crock. Any crude earthenware vessel; usually a jar, with or without a cover, of cylindrical or globular shape.

Crock handle. A horizontal, ear-shaped handle, hollowed beneath for inserting the fingers to lift the vessel.

Crockery. A general term applied to ceramic articles for daily household use. The term was once used in England to designate fine earthenware, including Wedgwood's 'Queen's ware'.

Crocus-pot. Same as ROOT-POT.

Cross hatch ground. A diaper ground pattern of sets of equidistant parallel lines crossing each other at an oblique angle, or at right angles, the lines being close together to create an effect of shading. *See* HATCHED.

Crouch ware. A ware, the nature of which had for long been uncertain until recently identified by Arnold Mountford as an inexpensive product, made principally in Staffordshire *c.* 1740–60 from local clays mixed with sand and given a ferruginous wash before being fired in a saltglaze oven, from which it emerged as brown saltglazed earthenware. Sometimes termed 'Critch ware', it is not to be confused with CRICH WARE from Derbyshire.

Crown Derby. Porcelain made by the Royal Crown Derby porcelain factory founded in 1876. The term is erroneously applied to some of the wares of the old Derby factory, probably because from 1780 the mark of a crown and crossed batons had been adopted there.

Crown Dresden. Ware made by Helena Wolfsohn of Dresden (Germany), who owned a decorating studio in the 1870s where she decorated porcelain with WATTEAU SUBJECTS alternating with coloured panels painted with flowers, usually vases and quatrefoil cups and saucers. On these she at first employed the royal factory mark of Meissen, 'AR' (*see* AUGUSTUS REX WARE). After a law-suit brought by the Meissen factory she changed her mark to a crown with the word 'Dresden' in script underneath. This ware is often referred to as 'Crown Dresden', especially in provincial auctioneers' catalogues.

Cruet-stand. Creamware, ht 9½ in., Leeds, *c.* 1780. Courtesy, Jellinek & Sampson, London.

Cruet. A bottle or vial, usually with a handle and a stopper, for the service of condiments at table. Some cruets were inscribed with the name of the contents, the usual names being oil, vinegar, mustard, pepper, sugar; sets in Leeds creamware for export to the Continent bore the equivalent names in German, Polish, etc. With a pierced cover the proper term is CASTER. Cruets were usually made in a matching set and accompanied by a CRUET-STAND. The French term is *burette. See* PEPPER-CASTER; SUGAR-CASTER.

Cruet-stand. A receptacle, often part of a dinner-service, for holding two or more CRUETS. Some have space for up to five large cruets and two small ones, as well as for a SALT-CELLAR. Made in England of creamware at Leeds and elsewhere, and sometimes called a bottle-stand. *See* PORTE-HUILIER.

Cucumber green glaze. A dark-green glaze used on Chinese porcelain during the late 17th and 18th centuries. The Chinese term is *kua p'i lü*.

Cuenca (Spanish). A technique of decoration employed in Spain for tiles and other wares which superseded the CUERDA SECA method. It involved impressing the pattern on tiles to form ridges which prevented the coloured glazes used from intermingling. The term means cell.

Cuerda seca (Spanish). A technique adopted from Near Eastern potters, and used in Spain for the decoration of tiles. Outlines were drawn on the surface of the ware with a greasy substance coloured with manganese, and this allowed glazes of several colours to be used without intermingling, the grease acting as a barrier and disappearing during firing. It was superseded by the CUENCA technique. The technique was also used occasionally to decorate plates, dishes, and vases.

Cumberland, Duke of. *See* WILLIAM III.

Cup. A small bowl-shaped vessel employed primarily for drinking, usually deeper than it is wide, and with one or two side handles. Occasionally it also has a cover, and may be on a stem or foot. Generally it is accompanied by a saucer similarly decorated. The French term is *tasse*; the German is *Tasse* or *Becher*; and the Italian is *tazza. See* COFFEE-CUP; TEACUP; CHOCOLATE-CUP; CAUDLE-CUP; TREMBLEUSE; TAZZA; CAN; COFFEE-CAN; RETICULATED CUP; LEG CUP; LIBATION CUP; KANG; CUSTARD-CUP; STEM CUP.

Cup-warmer. Probably French, first half of the 19th century. Harold Newman Collection.

Cup stand. A rare object of Chinese pottery of the Sung dynasty in the form of a small footed tray in the centre of which is a ring for placing a cup. Examples are known in glazed stoneware in CHÜN YAO, CELADON, and JU YAO. *See* TREMBLEUSE.

Cup-warmer. A type of VEILLEUSE, the upper unit of which is a drinking cup instead of a teapot or bowl. The cup usually rests in a BAIN-MARIE or LINER. It was made of porcelain in the middle of the 19th century, mainly in France, and used for milk.

Cupping-bowl. *See* BLEEDING BOWL; PORRINGER; BAGYNE CUP.

Curfew. From the French *couvre feu* (fire-cover). Some examples, similar to a DUTCH OVEN, are made of pottery.

Curl ground. A ground pattern of voluted or curled lines placed close together in a checkerboard pattern.

Cuspidor. *See* SPITTOON.

Custard-cup. A small cup with a cover for serving custard, usually made in a set *en suite* and accompanied by a serving PLATEAU or a TRAY with a stemmed base.

Custard-cups. Plateau and cups with covers, all with acanthus motif in relief, blue and white jasper, Wedgwood, 1784. Courtesy, Wedgwood.

Cut-out rim. A type of RIM with portions cut away, as distinct from one modelled in an irregular shape, in a decorative form.

Cuvette à fleurs (French). Literally, a basin for flowers. A type of flower-stand or vase, made at Sèvres in the 18th century, which was usually oval, the sides rising to a point at either end.

Cyathus (Greek). Same as KYATHOS.

Cylix (Greek). Same as KYLIX.

Cyma. A decoration or shape in the form of a cyma moulding, that is, a curve of ogee shape. It is called 'cyma recta' when the concave curve is in the upper part, and 'cyma reversa' when the concave curve is in the lower part.

D

D-shaped handle. A handle in the form of a capital *D* attached with the loop outwards.

Dallwitzer Nagel (German). A nick near the foot-ring of Meissen tableware which was made from *c.* 1720 before the introduction of a factory mark, *c.* 1723. It was named after the collector who first called attention to it.

Damascus ware. A type of pottery made in the 16th century at Damascus (Syria) which somewhat resembles ISNIK POTTERY. The body was white, with painted decoration of stylized flowers and leaves outlined in black. Manganese was frequently used.

Damask'd. A term used to describe a decorative pattern suggestive of the repetitive designs of damask fabrics.

Dancing Hours, The. The title of one of two companion plaques of blue-and-white jasper ware made by Wedgwood, *c.* 1777. It was modelled by John Flaxman in 1775. The figures are in the form of dancing maidens in low relief, and were originally nude. They were subsequently draped at Etruria in 1777 by William Hackwood in deference to the refined sentiments of neo-classical England. The companion plaque is the BIRTH OF BACCHUS.

The Dancing Hours. Plaque, blue and white jasper, modelled in 1775 by John Flaxman, Wedgwood, *c.* 1777. Courtesy, Wedgwood.

Dancing Lesson, The. *See* FLUTE LESSON, THE.

Darwin, Erasmus, service. Same as the WATER-LILY SERVICE.

Dash border. A border pattern in the form of short (usually diagonal) lines or dashes. *See* BLUE-DASH CHARGER.

Date-letter. A letter included with the FACTORY-MARK of certain porcelains to indicate the date of manufacture. Vincennes-Sèvres used a single letter for this purpose from 1753 to 1777, and a double letter from 1778 to 1793. Wedgwood used a three-letter group from 1860 to 1930, and other factories have devised similar systems. *See* DATE-MARK.

Date-mark. A mark, with numerals or letters, to indicate date of manufacture. *See* DATE-LETTER.

Dead-leaf brown. *See* BATAVIAN WARE.

Dealer's mark. A mark on some wares (especially in Holland and England) in the late 18th and the 19th centuries indicating the dealer for whom they were made.

Decalcomania. *See* LITHOGRAPHIC DECORATION.

Decanter bottle. A type of jug used for bringing wine to the table. They are bulbous in form, with a splayed base, narrow neck, and a single curved handle. They were made of stoneware in England and Germany, and also of English delftware.

Décor à cinq bouquets (French). A decoration for plates, developed at Tournai (Belgium), which employs five sprays of DEUTSCHE BLUMEN, four on the ledge or marli and one in the well. It was usually in blue outlined with gold.

Décor à guirlandes (French). A decorative border style introduced at Moustiers (France) in the form of FESTOONS around a central panel.

Décor à la corne (French). Same as CORNUCOPIA PATTERN.

Décor à la fleur de pomme de terre. Platter with painted decoration, faience, Moustiers, *c.* 1750. Victoria and Albert Museum, London.

Décor à la fleur de pomme de terre (French). Literally, potato-flower decoration. A decorative design, used *c.* 1750 on faience at Moustiers, in which so-called potato flowers (probably in fact nightshade), usually depicted in yellow, were used in conjunction with garlands. Also termed in France *décor à la fleur de solanée.*

Décor à rubans (French). A favourite decorative pattern of interlacing ribbons used at Sèvres during the 1750s and 1760s.

Décor bois (French). *See* FOND BOIS.

Décor carquois (French). Literally, quiver decoration. Same as CARQUOIS, À LA.

Décor coréen (French). A term by which the decorations of Japanese KAKIEMON PORCELAIN were known in the 18th century. They were copied in Europe, and the most characteristic come from Chantilly, *c.* 1725–40. Typical are the SQUIRREL, GOURD VINE, AND BANDED HEDGE PATTERN and the PRINCE HENRI PATTERN. Also known in France during the 18th century as '*première qualité du Japon*', the '*deuxième qualité*' being the IMARI patterns.

Décor sur émail cru (French). Decoration painted on the absorbent surface of unfired tin-enamel earthenware, after which the piece was fired in the GRAND FEU.

Décor sur émail cuit (French). Decoration painted over the glaze in enamel colours after the first firing of tin-enamel ware (faience), and then fired at a low temperature in the PETIT FEU (MUFFLE).

Decoration. The enhancement of the basic form of a piece of ceramic ware by any of many techniques such as painting, enamelling, gilding, burnishing, the application of relief work, transfer-printing, etc. The term 'undecorated' in factory parlance refers to glazed but unpainted ware. In appropriate cases it is said to be 'in the white'. Factories sometimes accumulated stocks of substandard ware 'in the white' which were sold and subsequently enamelled by outside decorators. A case in point is the sale of white, substandard wares by the Sèvres factory in 1810, which were bought by both Paris and London decorators. *See* HAUSMALER; CHAMBRELAN.

Deinos. From Vulci, 6th century BC; ht 9 in. Victoria and Albert Museum, London.

Deinos, sometimes *dinos* (Greek). A vessel of Greek pottery with a wide mouth and no handle; some examples have a somewhat rounded bottom and rest on a stand with a stemmed base, similar to a LEBES.

Déjeuner service. A breakfast-service, or CABARET SERVICE.

Delft dorée. Polychrome tin-glazed earthenware made at Delft (Holland) and gilded after being painted with enamel colours. Only the finest wares were thus decorated.

Delft noire. Tin-glazed earthenware, such as that made in the late 17th century by Adriaen Pijnacker (or Pynacker) at Delft (Holland), with a black ground and polychrome decoration in enamel. Later specimens had polychrome decoration in panels reserved in white on a black ground. The style was suggested by oriental lacquer then being extensively imported into Holland, since the black glazes of Chinese porcelain had not then reached Europe.

Delftware. Tin-glazed earthenware made at Delft (Holland) and also in England where the industry was introduced by immigrant Dutch potters. For the sake of clarity the latter wares are best termed ENGLISH DELFTWARE to separate them from those of Holland. The term is synonymous with MAIOLICA, which is Italian tin-glazed earthenware, and FAIENCE, which is the term used of European tin-glazed earthenware made in countries other than those already mentioned. Early Dutch wares, made from the first half of the 16th century onwards, are sometimes confusingly termed 'Dutch maiolica' because they were much influenced by Italian wares. The rise of the industry at Delft took place towards the middle of the 17th century, when potters took over many of the existing breweries at Delft in consequence of a decline in the brewing industry. Throughout the 17th century the Dutch East India Company was importing large quantities of oriental porcelain, and the potters of Delft turned to this as a source of inspiration, copying much of it with considerable exactness. The finest Dutch wares from Delft were made between 1640 and 1740, and painted decoration of the most ambitious wares was extremely elaborate towards the end of the 17th century. *See* DELFT DORÉE; DELFT NOIRE.

Della Robbia ware. Votive group with the Virgin adoring the Child, by Andrea della Robbia, *c.* 1500. Victoria and Albert Museum, London.

Della Robbia pottery. Pottery with glazes resembling those of maiolica, principally tiles, plaques, and vases, made in England by the Della Robbia Company of Birkenhead, Cheshire, under the ownership of Harold Rathbone, from 1894 to 1901. Decoration was in the ART NOUVEAU style. *See* DELLA ROBBIA WARE.

Della Robbia ware. Terracotta covered with a heavy tin glaze, often in the form of large sculptured medallions in relief depicting *putti* and *amorini*, made in Italy at Florence, *c.* 1438–1520, by Luca della Robbia, his nephew, Andrea, and the latter's four sons, Giovanni, Luca, Ambrogio, and Girolamo. Most della Robbia ware is white on a blue ground, but some examples have passages of green, maroon, and yellow. *See* DELLA ROBBIA POTTERY; TERRA INVETRIATA.

Demi-grand feu (French). A kiln temperature between those of the GRAND FEU and the PETIT FEU.

Demi-tasse. A small COFFEE-CUP, so called principally in the United States. It is usually used for serving post-prandial coffee.

De Morgan ware. A type of STUDIO POTTERY made in England in the 19th century by William de Morgan, who had been associated with William Morris. He copied and adapted Persian and Spanish designs in a coppery-red LUSTRE. Dishes and tiles are the most characteristic of surviving wares, but a few vases are known.

De Morgan ware. Plate decorated in copper lustre in the Persian style, *c.* 1880. City Museums, Stoke-on-Trent.

Dendritic. Decoration in a branching, tree-like pattern. *See* MOCHA WARE.

Dentate. A decorative design having regularly spaced sharp-pointed teeth, or triangles or scallops of tooth-like form, such as often appear in gold as the outer border on 18th-century plates. Sometimes incorrectly called DENTIL.

Dentelle, à (French). A decorative lacework pattern employed on faience of the mid-18th century from Moustiers.

Dentil. A decorative border pattern, usually gilt, in the form of a series of small rectangular blocks in imitation of those found immediately under the pediment in classical architecture. Sometimes incorrectly called DENTATE.

Derby blue. A bright lapis-lazuli blue developed at Derby in imitation of the BLEU DE ROI of Sèvres. *See* DRY BLUE.

Desk set. Same as LIBRARY SET.

Dessert. *See* SUBTLETY.

Dessert-service. A set of plates, compôtiers, tureens, ice-pails, bowls, etc., specially adapted for serving dessert, and usually separate from the dinner-service. Early services were dual-purpose, but the custom arose of setting out a separate table for dessert owing to the complicated nature of the table-decoration. This led to the making of a service complete in itself, often with many ornamental items added. From about 1750 onwards many factories made dessert-services of this kind, but they became unfashionable towards the end of the 19th century. *See* SUBTLETY.

Deutsche Blumen (German). Literally, German flowers. Naturalistically painted flowers, either separately or loosely tied in bouquets, introduced by J. G. Höroldt at Meissen, *c.* 1740, and derived from engravings illustrating the works of the botanist, Johann Wilhelm Weidemann. They followed the INDIANISCHE BLUMEN. Natural flowers appeared somewhat earlier at Vienna, between 1725 and 1730, but the Meissen version was extensively copied at other Continental faience and porcelain factories, and in England at Worcester, Chelsea, Bow, etc., especially between 1750 and 1765. *See* BLUMEN; FLOWERS; OMBRIERTE DEUTSCHE BLUMEN.

Deutsche Blumen. Bouillon cup with painted decoration, Meissen, *c.* 1745–50. Victoria and Albert Museum, London.

Devil's work. *See* LING-LUNG YAO.

Diamond beading. A continuous row of small diamond-shaped beads in relief, with alternate beads having a slight central depression. It is characteristic of creamware made at Melbourne (Derbyshire). Sometimes as many as six rows occur on a piece.

Dice pattern. Decoration on jasper flower-pot, Wedgwood. Buten Museum of Wedgwood, Merion, Pa.

Diamond ground. A diaper ground comprising two sets of parallel lines crossing each other to form diamond or lozenge figures, and sometimes with the addition of dots in the centre of the lozenges.

Diaper. Strictly, an ornamental design of a predominantly diamond or lozenge pattern. Loosely, the term is used of repetitive patterns in a ground or border, the units of the design being similar and usually connected to each other. The motif was popular at Sèvres. *See* OEIL DE PERDRIX; CAILLOUTÉ; SCALE; VERMICULÉ; DIAMOND GROUND; DOT AND STALK; QUADRILLÉ; TRELLIS; MOSAIK PATTERN.

Dice pattern. A decorative pattern of parallel vertical columns, used by Wedgwood on JASPER ware. Alternate columns are decorated with trailing flowers, and between are columns divided horizontally into squares alternately dark coloured and white, with coloured rosettes.

Dinner-service. A set of tableware in pottery or porcelain decorated *en suite* and used for serving a dinner. A full service may include plates, bowls, dishes, chargers, tureens, sauce-boats, salt-cellars, sugar-casters, sugar-basins, as well as (sometimes) ice-pails, cheese-dishes, plateaux, custard-cups, mustard pots, and decorative articles such as vases and épergnes. In the 18th century dinner-services also included (*en suite*) an ornamental CENTREPIECE and figures as table-decoration. Coffee-cups and saucers also form part of some dinner-services. *See* TEA-SERVICE; CABARET SERVICE; JAGD SERVICE; COMPOSITE SERVICE.

Dinos (Greek). Same as DEINOS.

Diota (Greek). A jar of Greek pottery for storing water, wine, or oil; it is somewhat similar to an AMPHORA with a pointed bottom, and is characterized by two side handles which gave rise to the name (meaning 'two-eared') of the vessel.

Disguised numeral mark. Openwork basket of Derby porcelain with mock Chinese reign-mark disguising the date 1778.

Dip-decorated ware. Pottery decorated by dipping in coloured slip. It sometimes has incised decoration that shows the colour of the body.

Dip jasper. Dip-decorated JASPER ware, coloured only on the surface, as distinguished from SOLID JASPER. Some specimens are coloured only on one side, but some are coloured front and back. In later wares the colour may be brushed or sprayed on.

Dipped. Glazed by being immersed in a liquid in which glaze particles are suspended.

Dipylon style. A style of Greek pottery decorated geometrically and typified by specimens excavated near the Dipylon Gate, Athens. *See* GEOMETRIC STYLE.

Directoire style. A decorative style current in France during the Directory, 1795–99, which followed the French Revolution. It represents the transition from the LOUIS SEIZE STYLE to the EMPIRE STYLE. The major influence is neo-classical, but it is much simpler and less ornate than the Louis Seize version. Principally a furniture style, it is reflected in PORCELAINE DE PARIS of the period.

Disguised numeral mark. A mark with numerals concealed by mock Chinese characters. Usually found on 18th-century Derby and Worcester porcelain. *See* PSEUDO-CHINESE SEAL MARKS.

Dish. A shallow ceramic utensil on which food is served, or from which it is eaten. The dish is usually circular or oval, with a MARLI or LEDGE and a WELL. The term is usually reserved for utensils 12 inches or more in diameter, those smaller than this being termed a plate. The Chinese dish, like a large saucer in shape, is termed a saucer-dish. The French term is *plat*. The Germans distinguish between a dish with a broad ledge (*Schüssel*), and one without a ledge (*Schale*). *See* PLATTER; BOWL; COUPE; HANDLED DISH.

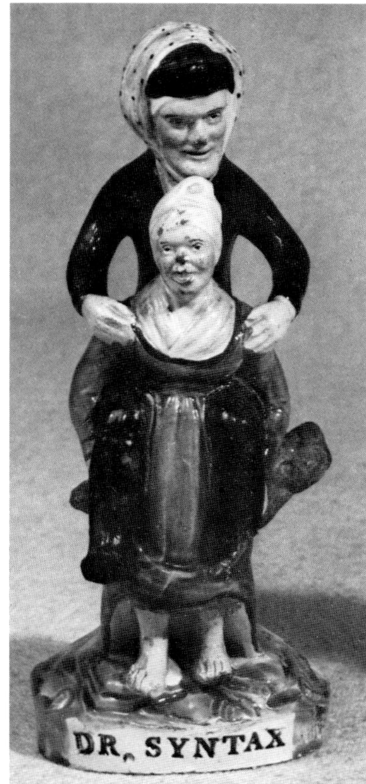

Doctor Syntax. Earthenware figure, probably by Ralph Salt, in the style of John Walton, Staffordshire, *c.* 1820. City Museums, Stoke-on-Trent.

Dishevelled birds. Painted decoration of birds which have a 'dishevelled' or 'agitated' appearance, to be found on English porcelain of the 1760s, principally on Worcester porcelain. The type is attributed to an independent decorator, James Giles, or to one of the assistants in his studio, which was in Clerkenwell, London. *See* EXOTIC BIRDS; ORNITHOID PORCELAIN.

Dismal hound. A small figure of a seated hound made in porcelain at Bow, *c.* 1751, and so called from its lugubrious appearance.

Divine tortoise. Same as MINOGAME.

Doctor Syntax. A popular character depicted in many attitudes in a series of porcelain figures modelled by Edward Keys at Derby, *c.* 1815, and also produced by successors at the Derby factory, as well as by Staffordshire factories which made such figures in earthenware. Dr Syntax was also depicted in transfer-printed scenes in blue underglaze on earthenware made by James and Ralph Clews of Cobridge (Staffordshire), and in enamelled scenes on porcelain jugs by Chamberlain's at Worcester. The subject is derived from a cartoon character, created by Rowlandson in 1809, who appeared first in a magazine series, and later in several books accompanied by verses by William Combe. He is portrayed in adventures on various tours.

Documentary specimens. Examples of ceramic ware which throw light on ceramic history, including pieces: signed by the modeller or decorator; bearing a rare mark or an informative inscription; discovered during a particular factory excavation (*see* WASTER); descended in a family connected with an early pottery; decorated with armorial bearings; referred to in old documents, etc.

Documentary specimen. Detail of decoration on a porcelain plate showing initials and date inscribed on a box, Chelsea, *c.* 1752.

Dod. A die through which a strip of clay is squeezed into a desired form and size, after which the soft clay is cut off into lengths and bent by hand into the requisite shape. The technique is employed for making certain handles which are then LUTED to the vessel.

Dog of Fo. *See* LION OF FO.

Dog orchestra. A series of porcelain figures of dogs dressed as performing musicians. *See* AFFENKAPELLE.

Dog orchestra. Porcelain figures, Chelsea, *c.* 1760. Wadsworth Atheneum, Hartford, Conn.

Dogs. Figures of various types of dog more or less realistically modelled and painted. They were very popular during the second half of the 18th century, both in England and on the Continent. Specimens are to be found in porcelain, stoneware, and earthenware. *See* DISMAL HOUND; PUG DOG; STAFFORDSHIRE SPANIELS; TRUMP; DOG ORCHESTRA.

Dollar pattern. A decorative border used on 17th-century ISNIK POTTERY. It takes the form of a figure drawn like a large *S* lying on its side between ammonite scrolls. It is actually a degenerate version of the rock and wave pattern found on 15th-century Chinese blue-and-white porcelain. *See* ROCK OF AGES BORDER.

Doll's house pattern. A decorative subject of buildings, used on some rare early Lowestoft porcelain, *c.* 1760.

Dolphin jug. A jug (or sauce-boat), the spout of which is modelled in the form of a dolphin's head with open mouth.

Dombari (Japanese). A large porcelain bowl.

Dome cover. A type of circular cover which is low-domed in shape and fits on the upright collar of a vessel. *See* CAP COVER.

Door-furniture. Finger-plates, escutcheon plates, key-hole covers, knobs, and handles of porcelain, usually decorated with enamel colours. Porcelain door-furniture was popular during the Victorian period. *See* FURNITURE ORNAMENT.

Doppelfrieskrug (German). A large jug made in the Rhineland in the last quarter of the 16th century which has a frieze in relief of classical subjects in a broad band around the centre.

Doughty birds. Chiff-chaff on hogweed, from the British birds series. Courtesy, Worcester Royal Porcelain Co.

Dot and stalk ground. A ground pattern of parallel designs resembling stalks intermingled with rows of dots.

Double bottle. A yoked bottle consisting of two containers connected between the bodies and necks, such as bottles used for oil and vinegar at the table. The French term is *bijugué*. *See* DOUBLE VASE; GIMMEL FLASK.

Double cup. *See* RETICULATED CUP.

Double gourd vase. A vase the lower part of which is of globular form and the upper part similar in shape but slightly smaller, the space between being occupied by a short, contracted waist. These vases were made in Chinese porcelain, and in European faience (particularly at Frankfurt) which imitated Chinese porcelain. *See* TRIPLE GOURD VASE.

Double-lipped sauce-boat. A sauce-boat with a lip at each end and a handle on each side.

Double ogee. An ornamentation or shape in the form of an extended OGEE moulding, resembling two connected *S*'s.

Double scroll. A decorative pattern or shape in the form of two connected scrolls, as in the double-scroll handle.

Double tea-caddy. A TEA-CADDY divided into two sections for holding two varieties of dry tea.

Double teapot. A TEAPOT with two spouts. There are three types: (1) A divided pot with two handles, for brewing two kinds of tea simultaneously; examples were made in Chinese redware and also in creamware at Leeds. (2) A pot with no interior division, but two spouts close together and one handle, for pouring two cups simultaneously. (3) A pot with one handle and with a spout near the bottom for pouring tea through a strainer, and another spout near the rim for pouring off floating tea-dust (tea motes).

Double vase. Two vases, the bodies of which are joined. Although the vases are similarly shaped, sometimes the one in the rear is larger. *See* DOUBLE BOTTLE; GIMMEL FLASK.

Double-wall. A term referring to a vessel made with two walls and an intervening space, the outer wall of which has a decoration of pierced work. *See* RETICULATED. To be found in Chinese porcelain and in that of Meissen and one or two other European factories, and also in Leeds creamware.

Doughty birds. Porcelain birds naturalistically modelled and painted against a background of flowers and foliage. There are two series – American Birds and British Birds. They were designed by Dorothy Doughty and made at the Worcester Royal Porcelain factory from 1933 onwards. They are issued in limited editions. *See* BIRDS; ORNITHOID PORCELAIN.

Drab body. Same as DRY BODY.

Dragon. A decorative subject on oriental porcelain which has been freely copied in Europe. In China it is one of the Four Supernatural Creatures (SSŬ LING), and is often depicted among clouds pursuing the SACRED PEARL. It is a harmless, beneficent creature emblematic of fertility, particularly in relation to crops, and a symbol of the Emperor. When it has the latter connotation it is given five claws. Four claws denote a prince, and three claws

Double teapot. Teapot with spouts having brass tips marked 'Bohea' and 'Green', and Shou ideogram on side of pot, Chinese redware, *c*. 1720. Courtesy, David Newbon Ltd, London.

Dragon. Chinese saucer-dish decorated with five-clawed Imperial dragon. Ming dynasty, reign of Hung Chih (1488–1505). Victoria and Albert Museum, London.

Dragon. Paperweight in the form of a European-style dragon, Belleek ware, *c*. 1860. Victoria and Albert Museum, London.

Drum. Jasper, late 18th century. Courtesy, Wedgwood.

an official; the Japanese dragon, *ryu*, always has three claws. The dragon was commonly employed in Europe as part of patterns and motifs copied from the Orient. The European dragon, rarely found as a decoration on ceramic wares, is fierce in nature and appearance, and often has one pair of legs and one pair of wings; it occurs on Italian maiolica as part of the subject of Perseus rescuing Andromeda. *See* BOW DRAGON; BROSELEY BLUE DRAGON; WORCESTER DRAGON; LUNG; CH'ING LUNG; CH'IH LUNG; NAGA; KUEI; RED DRAGON PATTERN; PRINCE HENRI PATTERN.

Dragon lustre. A type of LUSTRE ware devised at Wedgwood by Daisy Makeig-Jones in 1914. The decoration is Chinese in style with scaly dragons chasing SACRED PEARLS in coloured lustre reserved on a lustre ground. *See* FAIRYLAND LUSTRE.

Dragon service. A dinner-service made at Meissen, copied from a KAKIEMON pattern, with a circling phoenix (HO-HO BIRD) in the centre and a border of DRAGONS and foliage.

Drainer. A flat, pierced false bottom resting on a PLATTER.

Draped swag. A decorative pattern in the form of a SWAG embellished with drapery or ribbons.

Dresden china. A name popularly and erroneously applied to Meissen porcelain, perhaps due to the fact that the factory was situated only about 12 miles from Dresden, although in the town of Meissen. Dresden was the capital of the Electors of Saxony, and Meissen porcelain has always been termed 'Saxe' in France. There were numerous small factories in and around the city of Dresden in the 19th century, and wares made at any of these may correctly be designated 'Dresden'. *See* CROWN DRESDEN.

Drillingsbecher (German). A triple-connected drinking-vessel similar in principle to the English FUDDLING-CUP.

Drip-pan. The tray immediately beneath and surrounding the nozzle of a candlestick for the purpose of catching dripping wax or tallow. The French term is *bobêche*.

Dry-drug jar. Maiolica, Savona, early 18th century.

Drug jar. A jar, usually of blue-painted or polychrome tin-glazed earthenware, but also, from the early 19th century, of creamware. They were for holding dry or wet drugs in a pharmacy. The more affluent apothecary's and druggist's shops considered them important for display, so that attractive painted decoration is common, the principal motifs being an angel with spread wings (17th century), cherubs and scallop shell, and birds and basket of fruit (both 18th century). Originally the number of jars in a set *en suite* was perhaps 75 to 100. *See* DRY-DRUG JAR; WET-DRUG JAR; ALBARELLO; STORAGE JAR; PHARMACY WARE; PEACOCK JAR; APOSTLE JAR; ELECTUARY POT; FARMACIA ORSINI COLONNA DRUG-JARS.

Drum. A cylindrical pedestal of pottery or porcelain on which is mounted a lamp, vase, figure, etc. Candelabra with crystal drops and ormolu mounts were set on drums of jasper ware towards the end of the 18th century.

Drunken parson jug. A type of TOBY JUG depicting an inebriated parson with his hat awry and an empty beer-mug turned upside-down. *See* PARSON AND CLERK.

Dry blue. A brilliant enamel blue of lapis-lazuli colour and 'dry' appearance on Worcester porcelain, the use of which is sometimes attributed to the studio of James Giles. A similar blue occurs occasionally on Caughley porcelain. It is related to BLEU DE ROI and DERBY BLUE.

Dry body. Sometimes called 'drab body'. A non-porous stoneware that required no glaze; it was made by adding to local clay various colouring oxides or coloured earths to create the desired effect. Dry bodies made by Wedgwood include cane-ware, bamboo-ware, jasper, black basaltes, and *rosso antico*. The interior of USEFUL WARES made with this body is sometimes glazed.

Dry-drug jar. A DRUG-JAR of tin-glazed pottery (very rarely of creamware), for holding dry drugs and ointments in a pharmacy. One type is the ALBARELLO, and another is an ovoid or baluster-shaped jar with two side handles. *See* WET-DRUG JAR; PHARMACY WARE.

Dry edge. An unglazed edge around the base of certain figures, especially those made at Derby and Cockpit Hill (Derbyshire), *c.* 1751, where this characteristic commonly appears.

Dry mustard-jar. Porcelain jar with screw cover, transfer-printed in black, Caughley, *c.* 1770–80. Courtesy, Newman & Newman Ltd, London.

Dry mustard-jar. A type of MUSTARD-JAR for holding dry unprepared mustard and so having, instead of a removable cover, a screw cover with holes for sprinkling.

Dublin delftware. Delftware made at Dublin (Ireland), *c.* 1737–76. *See* ENGLISH DELFTWARE.

Duck-egg body. A type of ARTIFICIAL PORCELAIN made by William Billingsley at Swansea (South Wales), *c.* 1816–17, which has a greenish translucency.

Duck tureen. A tureen naturalistically modelled and decorated in the form of a duck, often with the head turned to form the handle. They were made in porcelain at several Continental factories.

Dudley, Countess of, service. *See* JEWELLED DECORATION.

Dudley vases. A set of seven porcelain vases made at Chelsea, *c.* 1760, so called because they were formerly in the possession of the Earl of Dudley. They were decorated with voluptuous mythological scenes after Boucher and had elaborate rococo handles.

Dulongmuster (German). Also referred to as the *Dulongrelief-zierat*. A border pattern which has four panels with painted vignettes of flowers or scenes surrounded by rococo scrolls, alternating with four equal panels each divided into three sections having rococo moulded floral motifs which intrude slightly into the well of the plates. It was introduced by J. J. Kändler at Meissen, *c.* 1743, and named after an Amsterdam merchant who dealt with the factory. Tureens and other pieces of the service have similar relief rococo scrolls and painted vignettes.

Dummy ware. Same as PIE-CRUST WARE.

Duplessis vase. Porcelain, Vincennes-Sèvres. Wadsworth Atheneum, Hartford, Conn.

Duplessis vase. A Vincennes-Sèvres porcelain vase with a bulbous body and trumpet neck, a short stem and spreading foot, and two rococo handles. The type was designed by the French Court goldsmith, Claude-Thomas Duplessis.

Dusting. The process of applying glaze to the surface of a vessel by dusting in powder form. *See* GALENA GLAZE.

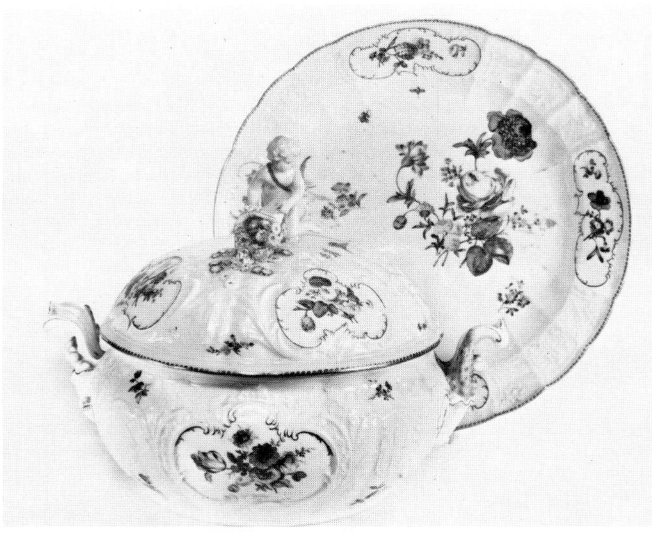

Dulongmuster. Porcelain tureen and stand with moulded decoration and reserved cartouches of *deutsche Blumen*, Meissen, *c.* 1750–60. Courtesy, Sotheby's.

Dutch oven. Glazed stoneware, with slip decoration, Staffordshire, early 18th century. City Museums, Stoke-on-Trent.

Dutch delftware. DELFTWARE made in Holland, as distinct from English delftware.

Dutch jugs. *See* MASK-JUGS.

Dutch maiolica. *See* DELFTWARE; EARTHENWARE.

Dutch oven. A hollow object with two vertical sides and a curved sloping top to which is attached a vertical loop handle. It was placed in front of the grate to utilize the reflected heat. Such pieces were made in Staffordshire of stoneware, *c.* 1690–1760. *See* CURFEW.

Dutch stove. A low circular stand, with an aperture at the side for inserting a GODET, on which plates were placed for the purpose of keeping food hot; examples were made by Wedgwood in Queen's ware and jasper, and also in Holland. The primary inspiration was probably Dutch by way of the Far East, where similar stands for warming plates are commonly used. *See* RÉCHAUD; FOOD-WARMER.

Dutch ware. Probably a corrupt form of 'Deutsch' (German) which was applied to RHENISH STONEWARE. A similar corruption occurs in the case of PENNSYLVANIA DUTCH WARE.

Dwight ware. Stoneware made by John Dwight of Fulham in the last quarter of the 17th century. His fine 'mouse-coloured' stoneware is sometimes slightly translucent. *See* BROWN STONEWARE.

Dysart ware. A type of QUEEN'S WARE made by Wedgwood, *c.* 1870, which was covered with a yellow glaze obtained from vanadium, and was not otherwise decorated. It was developed at the request of Lord Dysart.

Dwight ware. Tankard, saltglazed stoneware, factory of John Dwight, 1740. Burnap Collection, William Rockhill Nelson Gallery of Art, Kansas City, Mo.

Eagle spout. A spout, occurring on teapots, modelled in the form of an eagle with the open beak forming the mouth and the spread wings extending on either side of the pot. The moulded eagle, examples of which occur in BÖTTGER RED STONEWARE and BÖTTGER PORZELLAN, has a mat surface contrasting with the highly polished surface of the body of the pot.

Ear. A small protuberance on a vessel which serves as a handle. The French term is *oreille.*

Earthenware. The English term for pottery that is not vitrified, i.e. all pottery except stoneware. Earthenware is porous if not covered with a glaze. It is grouped, according to the manner of glazing and decoration, into DELFTWARE (maiolica or faience), CREAMWARE (and *faïence fine*), and SLIPWARE. The distinction between FAÏENCE, DELFTWARE, and MAIOLICA is a regional one, or related to the style of decoration, the type of glaze being the same in all three. Delftware comes from Holland and England, maiolica from Italy, and faience from everywhere else, but all have a TIN GLAZE. Usage is made more confusing, however, by the fact that some writers refer to tin-glazed ware coming from Holland and decorated in the Italian style as 'Dutch maiolica'. The Germans mean by *Fayence-Porzellan* tin-glazed earthenware decorated in enamel colours like porcelain. The creamware body, or one approaching it, is often covered with coloured glazes, as in WHIELDON WARE, rather than with a clear glaze. *See* PORCELAIN.

Eagle spout. Teapot of Böttger red stoneware, Meissen *c.* 1715. Courtesy, Stodel and Emden Ltd, London.

Earthworm tracks. *See* CHÜN YAO.

Echinus. A rather flattened Greek version of the quarter-round moulding (OVOLO); found on capitals, it is sometimes ornamented in relief with the EGG-AND-DART, EGG-AND-TONGUE, or EGG-AND-ANCHOR border patterns. It is found as decoration on some ceramic ware in the classical style.

Écritoire (French). A porcelain writing-stand with receptacles for ink, sand, and pens. *See* DESK-SET; LIBRARY-SET; STANDISH.

Écuelle (French). A covered shallow bowl, usually with two flat lateral handles level with the rim, and a conforming stand. It was mainly used for serving soup. *See* PORRINGER.

Edge. A term applied to the narrow band: (1) between upper and lower or inner and outer rims of a plate, vase, or other object (*see* BEADED EDGE; BROWN EDGE; RED EDGE); (2) around the base of a solid or moulded object (*see* DRY EDGE).

Edo period. The Japanese period (1600–1868) which, following the MOMOYAMA PERIOD, saw the rise of the Tokugawa Shoguns. The Dutch trading-settlement on the island of Deshima, near Nagasaki, dates from 1609. The English were allowed a trading-station at Hirado in 1611 which closed in 1623. Porcelain was first made during this period, and new influences were brought to its manufacture by the KAKIEMON family. Pottery assumed smaller importance than in the earlier periods, and Korean influence is less noticeable. In the earliest Japanese porcelain from ARITA Chinese influence is fairly strong, but

Egg-beater. Creamware, Wedgwood. Byron Born Collection, New York.

the styles introduced by Kakiemon and others, because of their success in the European export market, were later adopted and adapted in China.

Eel's blood crackle. A CRACKLE into the lines of which a red pigment has been introduced. The Chinese term is *shou-hsueh wên*.

Eel-skin yellow. Brownish or olive-green glaze sometimes used on 18th-century Chinese porcelain.

Eel tureen. A circular TUREEN and cover in the form of a naturalistically modelled coiled eel. It occurs in Chelsea porcelain during the red-anchor period, *c.* 1755.

Egg. An ornamental ovoid piece, sometimes with painted decoration. Examples were made in Europe of glazed earthenware and of porcelain, notably in Russia, and in China of glazed stoneware.

Egg-and-anchor border. A border pattern consisting of alternate semi-oval and anchor-shaped motifs. *See* ECHINUS.

Egg-and-dart border. A border pattern consisting of ovoid figures and darts pointed at both ends, or of alternating semi-ovals with darts all pointing in the same direction. *See* ECHINUS.

Egg-and-spinach glaze. A yellow and green mottled lead glaze occurring on Chinese porcelain, usually bowls, from the reign of K'ang Hsi onwards. *See* TIGER SKIN. A somewhat similar colour scheme is sometimes found on WHIELDON WARE.

Egg-and-tongue border. A border pattern consisting of alternating ovals and tongue-shaped motifs. *See* ECHINUS.

Egg-beater. A small, circular covered vessel used to beat an egg, having attached to the inner wall a series of spikes pointing towards the centre. Made in creamware by Wedgwood.

Egg border. A border pattern of adjacent ovoid motifs, or of such motifs cut in half horizontally.

Egg-cup. A small semi-ovoid cup on a stemmed base, for serving a boiled egg in the shell. Sometimes it has a base that is an inverted second cup of a slightly different size; this is called a 'double egg-cup'. The French term is *coquetière*. *See* EGG-RING; EGG-STAND.

Egg-cup stand. Creamware, Leeds or Staffordshire, *c.* 1775. Victoria and Albert Museum, London.

Egg-cup stand. A stand for holding egg-cups, usually six, with sometimes a tray *en suite* for spoons.

Egg-drainer. A type of small, low cup or spoon with pierced holes, used for draining poached eggs. It has a flat, leaf-like handle, or a loop handle. They were made of porcelain at Worcester in the 18th century. The same form without the holes was made as a CADDY-SPOON, and with smaller holes as a TEA-STRAINER.

Egg-poacher. A small shallow circular receptacle with small pierced holes in the bottom and with two hooked side handles for suspending the piece over hot water, to poach an egg. They were made of creamware by Wedgwood.

Egg-ring. A small, waisted cylindrical receptacle for serving a boiled egg, the upper part being shaped to hold the egg. They were made in England by Davenport and others. *See* EGG-CUP.

Egg-separator. A shallow dish with a recessed cover, the cover having several holes to permit the white of the egg to pass through

Egyptian service. Two plates and a sugar-bowl from the service now at Stratfield Saye. Courtesy, His Grace the Duke of Wellington.

in separating it from the yolk, which remained above. Some were made by Wedgwood in creamware. *See* EGG-DRAINER.

Egg-stand. A low receptacle with several holes in a horizontal top, used for serving boiled eggs. Examples occur in Staffordshire earthenware.

Eggshell. A type of porcelain so thin as to resemble an eggshell. Wares of this kind were made in China during the Ming and Ch'ing dynasties, and some were so thin that the Chinese termed them T'O T'AI (bodiless). Some examples are decorated in the AN HUA technique. Porcelains of this kind have been made in Europe by a number of factories, such as Minton and Belleek.

Eggshell glaze. (1) A soft cream glaze used on pottery made at Rhages (Persia) into which enamel colours tended to sink. (2) A mat porcelain glaze that resembles the surface of an eggshell.

Egnatian ware. Pottery from Apulia (Italy) made in imitation of ware of the RED-FIGURE STYLE from the 3rd century BC, and found at Egnatia in Apulia. It has a black surface with red painted decoration. Also called Apulian ware.

Egyptian black. Same as BLACK BASALTES, and sometimes in the form 'black Egyptian'.

Egyptian blue. A blue pigment made from silicate of copper and calcium (not COBALT, as was at one time thought) and used in ancient Egypt and Rome.

Egyptian faience. A ware made from sand held together with some kind of cement as a binder and covered with a glassy glaze, usually ranging in colour from green to dark blue. It was made from *c.* 3300 to *c.* 30 BC. The term 'faience' is incorrect – the body is not pottery, and the glaze contains no tin oxide. *See* USHABTI.

Egyptian pottery. *See* FOSTAT WARE.

Egyptian service. A large dinner-service made of true porcelain at Sèvres in 1808 which has Egyptian motifs on the borders, and centres painted with scenes EN GRISAILLE. It was presented by Napoleon I to Tsar Alexander I of Russia. A like service made for the Empress Josephine, but declined by her after her divorce, was given by Louis XVIII to the Duke of Wellington.

Egyptian ware. A name used by Josiah Wedgwood during the early period for BLACK BASALTES.

Egg-poachers. Creamware, Wedgwood, *c.* 1780. Donald C. Towner Collection, London.

Eight horses of Mu Wang. Porcelain plate with painted decoration, 18th century. Victoria and Albert Museum, London.

Eight Immortals. Plate with painted decoration depicting the Eight Immortals paying homage to Lao Tzŭ. Reign of Wan-li (1573–1619). Victoria and Albert Museum, London.

Eichhörnchendekor (German). Literally, squirrel decoration. The term used at Meissen for the FLYING FOX AND SQUIRREL pattern.

Eight Buddhist emblems, The. Symbols (*pa-chi-hsiang*) used decoratively on Chinese porcelain: *Lun*, a flaming wheel; *Lo*, a conch shell; *San*, a state umbrella; *Kai*, a canopy; *Hua*, a lotus, emblem of purity; *P'ing*, a vase; *Yu*, a pair of fish; and *Chang*, the endless knot.

Eight horses of Mu Wang, The. A Chinese decorative pattern of eight horses, some frolicking, some standing alert in a plain with a willow tree, and foothills in the distance where two birds are flying. This was used on blue-and-white porcelain at Worcester. The design, however, is Chinese in origin, representing the horses which drew the chariot of the Emperor Mu Wang (Chou dynasty; 1122–249 BC) on his journey to the Western Gardens in search of the Peach of Immortality. On Chinese porcelain it occurs in a variety of versions, and also in the form of small white figures of horses, many of which have been made in modern times.

Eight Immortals, The. A Taoist decorative subject representing the eight *Pa-hsien*, to which the addition of LAO-TZŬ (Shou Lao) brings the total group to nine. The eight are: Chung-li Chüan, a fat man with a feather fan, holding the peach of longevity; Lü Tung-pin, skilled as a fencer, who carries a sword and fly-whisk; Li T'ieh-kuai, a lame beggar with a crutch, carrying a gourd; Ts'ao Kuo-ch'iu, who usually carries his tablets of admission to the Sung Court, sometimes incorrectly described as castanets; Lan Ts'ai-ho, either a woman or hermaphrodite, represented as a gardener with a flower-basket and spade; Chang Kao, who carries a peach, a feather, and a bamboo tube-drum, and is sometimes represented seated on a mule, occasionally facing the tail; Han Hsiang Tzŭ, who carries a flute; and Ho Hsien Ku, a maiden Immortal, who holds either a peach or a lotus. They are employed as painted decoration, and are sometimes modelled as a set of figures. Often they are accompanied by a figure of Lao Tzŭ (Shou Lao), who is recognizable from an enlarged and protuberant forehead. The *Pa Hsien Kuo Lai* refers to the Immortals on their way to the Isles of the Blest, either riding on the surface of the water or seated on clouds. The figures have been reproduced in Europe; a well-known example is Lü Tung-pin, made at Bristol (England), 1750.

Eight Precious Things, The. Chinese symbols used in the decoration of porcelain, which form part of the PO-KU (or Hundred Antiques), a collection of implements and instruments used in the arts and sciences. The Eight Precious Things (*Pa-pao*) are: a pair of rhinoceros-horn cups, a musical stone of jade, the ARTEMISIA LEAF, a jewel, a coin, a painting, a pair of books or tablets, and a lozenge-shaped symbol of victory.

Eight Trigrams, The. *See* PA-KUA.

Eighteen Lohan, The. *See* LOHAN.

Eisenporzellan (German). Specimens of BÖTTGER RED STONEWARE which have a blackish-grey surface resulting from over-firing.

Eisenrot. The German term for IRON-RED.

Electioneering ware. Plates, jugs, and other ware inscribed with names or slogans of electoral candidates. They were made in England of English delftware, and also in porcelain by Worcester and others.

Electuary-pot. A type of drug-pot of Italian maiolica which has a handle and a spout. It was used to hold an electuary (a mixture of medicinal powder with honey). *See* PHARMACY WARE.

Elements, The Four. *See* FOUR ELEMENTS, THE.

Elephant teapot. A type of teapot modelled and naturalistically painted in the form of a standing elephant, its raised trunk being the spout, the handle occasionally being in the form of a coiled snake on its back. The rim of the pot is sometimes in the form of a howdah. It was made in earthenware by Ralph Wood. *See* CAMEL TEAPOT.

Elers redware. Teapot with moulded panels, Staffordshire, *c.* 1700. Courtesy, Tilley & Co., London.

Elers redware. Red stoneware made in Staffordshire by the brothers John Philip Elers and David Elers at the end of the 17th century and in the early years of the 18th century. The ware was precisely and thinly potted, the colour varying from buff through red to brown as a result of variations in the firing temperature. It was inspired by the red stoneware of YI-HSING, and was the ancestor of Wedgwood's ROSSO ANTICO.

Elevator. *See* FURNITURE SUPPORT.

Elizabethan ware. A term formerly applied to fine English earthenware (erroneously supposed to have been made under the patronage of Elizabeth I) moulded from contemporary silver.

Eloping bride. A decorative subject depicting a galloping horse ridden by an archer and his bride. Derived from a Chinese pattern of the reign of K'ang Hsi (1662–1722), and occurring on English blue-and-white porcelain.

Émail (French). Literally, enamel. The French word is, however, frequently employed to refer to TIN GLAZES, and sometimes to other glazes, such as the transparent coloured glazes of Bernard Palissy. It is also employed to mean overglaze colours employed to decorate pottery and porcelain, and coloured opaque glazes on metal, utilizing either the CLOISONNÉ or CHAMPLEVÉ techniques. The word is used very loosely. *Vernis* (varnish) is also employed to mean a transparent glaze over an earthenware body, as in creamware (*faïence fine*), and *couverte* is commonly used to refer to a porcelain glaze.

Émail ombrant (French). Pottery impressed with a picture or design, and then completely covered with a translucent coloured glaze to form a smooth surface, and thus producing an effect of light and shade due to the varying depths of the glaze. The process, sometimes referred to as a 'counterpart of lithophane' (where the design is likewise in relief), was invented *c.* 1842 by Baron A. du Tremblay at Rubelles, near Melun, France. *See* LITHOPHANE; BASSE-TAILLE; CHAMPLEVÉ; CLOISONNÉ.

Émail sur bisque (or ***biscuit***). The French term for ENAMEL ON BISCUIT.

Embattled border. Same as CRENELATED BORDER.

Empire style. Vase decorated with anthemion borders and Pompeian frieze; ht 17½ in. Naples (Ferdinand IV). Courtesy, Christie's.

Empire style. A version of the NEO-CLASSICAL STYLE, current in France *c.* 1800–20, which followed the DIRECTOIRE STYLE. It is more or less equivalent to the REGENCY STYLE in England which is often called 'English Empire'. It is noted for the use of florid CLASSICAL styles, to which are added Egyptian motifs, and others stemming from the Napoleonic campaigns. Mounting in gilt-bronze was continued, and new

Encrusted. Flower-encrusted vase with cover; ht 19¾ in. Berlin, Wegely's factory (1752–57). Courtesy, Sotheby's.

Enamel on biscuit. Chinese teapot, reign of K'ang Hsi (1662–1722). Victoria and Albert Museum, London.

decorative themes introduced, such as a vogue for topographical landscape painting on English porcelain. The style made little impact on pottery and stoneware, and is mainly confined to the finer-quality porcelains, and to a lesser extent to such wares as Wedgwood's JASPER. Porcelain had, in any case, entered a phase when it had lost its earlier popularity as an art-form, and had not yet achieved the status of a factory-made product catering to popular taste.

Empress Elizabeth of Russia service. A dinner-service of Meissen porcelain said to have been made for the Empress Elizabeth, *c.* 1745. The plates are of rounded cruciform shape, moulded with the GOTZOWSKY ERHABENE BLUMEN and painted around the ledge with four cartouches enclosing quay scenes within blue SCALE GROUND reserves and in the well with INDIANISCHE BLUMEN or HOLZSCHNITTBLUMEN and scattered birds, moths, etc. The service was in the Hermitage Museum, Leningrad, in 1911.

Enamel. An opaque or transparent pigment of a vitreous nature coloured with metallic oxides and applied to ceramic ware as decoration over the glaze by low-temperature firing. Enamel colours often sink deeply into the glaze of artificial porcelains, but are not absorbed into the feldspathic glazes of true porcelain, remaining on the surface and easily palpable to the finger-tips. The French term is *émail*; the Italian, *smalto*; and the German, *Schmelz*. *See* ENAMEL FIRING; TIN ENAMEL.

Enamel colours. Colours derived from metallic oxides and applied over the glaze. The range of overglaze colours is much greater than those used under the glaze, which necessarily have to be fired at a much higher temperature.

Enamel firing. A low-temperature firing to affix permanently enamel decoration to the glaze of ceramic ware. This firing is done in a MUFFLE kiln, or PETIT FEU.

Enamel on biscuit. The application of enamels which are akin to coloured glazes directly on to BISCUIT porcelain without an intervening glaze, the enamels taking its place. The technique is Chinese, and has never been used in Europe in the same way. Firing temperature was above that customary for ordinary enamels, but below the normal firing temperature for glazed porcelain, since the enamels were prepared from lead silicate glass and are not feldspathic. The technique occurs principally on some comparatively rare wares from the reign of K'ang Hsi (1662–1722), but it is also related to the Ming dynasty FA HUA wares. *See* SAN TS'AI.

Encaustic decoration. Painting with colours mixed with wax, and fused to the ware by heat. The technique was used principally in Egypt in Roman times on a base of wood. The term was applied by Josiah Wedgwood to his ETRUSCAN WARE with decoration in red and white in imitation of ancient Etruscan pottery, but the two processes have no connection.

Encrier. The French term for inkstand. Many were made of porcelain or faience, with separate inkwells and provision for pens. *See* STANDISH.

Encrusted. (1) Decoration in low relief, including honey-gold thickly applied to porcelain; *see* RAISED GILDING. (2) Moulded and applied flowers as found on porcelain, e.g. pieces made by Minton, Meissen and other factories. *See* ENCRUSTED WARE; SNOWBALL VASES.

Encrusted ware. (1) In general, ceramic ware with applied relief decoration; *see* SNOWBALL VASES. (2) Pale-coloured CREAMWARE made at Leeds in the early part of the 19th century which has small particles of coloured clays fired on to the body to form a rough surface.

Enfants Boucher, Les (French). A series of figures of children modelled by Blondeau at Vincennes in the early 1750s from designs by François Boucher (1703–70). Children after Boucher were also used in painted form as decoration. Both the figures and the painted versions were widely copied elsewhere.

Enghalskrug (German). Literally, narrow-necked jug. A pottery jug (usually of tin-enamelled ware) of plain globular form with a long narrow neck, and a handle extending from mouth to body. The jug often has a pewter lid, and most examples were intended to have one even when it is now missing. A variant of this form from the early faience factories of Germany has a body which is spirally fluted in conjunction with a handle in a form suggestive of twisted rope. Some of the most desirable specimens were decorated by HAUSMALER like Seuter of Augsburg or Helmhack of Nuremberg.

Engine-turned decoration. Incised decoration done on unfired pottery when LEATHER HARD with the aid of the engine-turning lathe. This lathe has an eccentric motion which enables it to cut a variety of patterns, the more elaborate of which were done with a guide called a 'rosette', hence ROSE-ENGINE TURNED which is applied to such patterns done in this way. The first such lathe in Staffordshire was acquired in 1763 by Josiah Wedgwood, after he had seen one in operation at the factory of Boulton & Fothergill, Soho, Birmingham. This lathe is still in occasional use. The French term is *guillochage*.

English china. Although loosely used to mean almost any kind of English porcelain, the term is more properly employed to refer to BONE-CHINA.

English delftware. Tin-glazed earthenware (delftware) made in England, principally at or near Bristol, and in London and Liverpool. The term is also used to include such wares made in Ireland and Scotland. Tin-enamel ware was first made in England at Norwich (Norfolk) soon after the middle of the 16th century, but the centre of manufacture shifted to London shortly afterwards and was first located at Southwark, and later at the Lambeth potteries that came into existence in the early years of the 17th century. Most English delftware is decorated in blue, but high-temperature colours were also in use, although their incidence is considerably rarer. Enamels over a fired tin-glaze were employed at Liverpool (*see* FAZACKERLEY STYLE) and probably at Bristol. Attribution between the various centres of production is often difficult and uncertain. Like all delftware, the body is fragile and easily chipped, and perfect specimens are unusual. *See* LONDON DELFTWARE; BRISTOL DELFTWARE; LAMBETH DELFTWARE; SOUTHWARK DELFTWARE; STAFFORDSHIRE DELFTWARE; LIVERPOOL DELFTWARE; IRISH DELFTWARE; GLASGOW DELFTWARE.

Engobe. The French term for SLIP.

Engrailed. A decorative border pattern indented on both sides with connected, small, equal concave curves.

Engraved decoration. A technique developed by August Otto Ernst von dem Busch, Canon of Hildesheim (Germany), who

Les Enfants Boucher. Biscuit figures, Vincennes, *c.* 1750–55. Courtesy, Sotheby's.

engraved designs into porcelain glazes with a diamond, the INCISED lines being filled with a black pigment. This pigment, which was not fired, will wash off but can be easily replaced. Another Canon of Hildesheim, J. G. Kratzberg, did similar work. Sporadic and isolated examples of a similar technique have been observed on porcelain from elsewhere. An 18th-century Worcester cup and saucer thus decorated was sold some years ago, and a Chinese plaque decorated in native taste in this way has been observed. The technique has never been a factory operation. *See* ETCHED DECORATION; WHEEL-ENGRAVED.

Engraved decoration. Porcelain bowl and cover, decorated by Canon A. O. E. von dem Busch of Hildesheim, *c.* 1760.

Engraved designs. Engravings of pictorial subjects and decorative patterns employed by ceramic decorators as inspiration for their work. They were extensively used for painted decoration, as well as for figures, in the porcelain factories of England, France, Germany, and Italy, and engravings were sent to Canton as a basis for the decoration of CHINESE EXPORT PORCELAIN. In a few cases, such as JESUIT PORCELAIN and SCHWARZLOT, the engravings were copied fairly closely. *See* HANCOCK ENGRAVINGS; PILLEMENT ENGRAVINGS; LADIES' AMUSEMENT, THE.

Épergne (plat ménage). Creamware, Leeds, *c.* 1780. City Art Gallery, Leeds.

Épergne (French). A centrepiece for the dinner-table, which includes numerous small dishes, CRUETS, and SALT-CELLARS, supported by branching arms; it is sometimes also provided with candle-nozzles. English versions, often of creamware from Leeds, are usually based in design on contemporary silver, and belong to the last quarter of the 18th century. *See* SURTOUT DE TABLE; GRAND PLAT MÉNAGE.

Epichysis (Greek). A type of jug of Greek pottery for pouring oil or wine. The base resembles a PYXIS with a tall neck and a long spout, and it has a high loop handle. They were also made in Apulia (Italy).

Epinetron (Greek). A curved shield in the form of a cylinder cut in half lengthwise and having one end closed. It was used to cover the thigh and knee of a spinner who passed the thread over it. The *epinetron* was made in Greece of terracotta. It was also called an *onos* or IMBREX.

Ermine ground. A diaper pattern in black or brown on a white ground, having the appearance of ermine tails. It was employed on English salt-glazed earthenware, *c.* 1756–60.

Escutcheon. (1) The ornamental form, usually shield-shaped, on which armorial bearings are displayed; *see* CARTOUCHE. (2) An ornamental cover for a key-hole which is similar in form, sometimes in the 19th century made of porcelain.

Etched decoration. A kind of decoration in which the surface of a ceramic object is covered with an acid-resistant varnish which is then scratched through to form the design, and the exposed design etched into the body with hydrofluoric acid.

Epinetron. Terracotta, *c.* 500 BC; length 12¼ in. British Museum, London.

Pigment is then rubbed into the lines, the varnish removed, and the piece refired. *See* ENGRAVED DECORATION.

Etruria. The name given by Josiah Wedgwood to a new factory in Staffordshire started in 1766 and opened in 1769. The name was inspired by ancient Etruscan pottery, which influenced some of the new factory's productions.

Etruscan pottery. Ancient Etruscan pottery, often inspired by imported wares of contemporary Greece (some of the finest examples of which have been found in Etruscan tombs). Collections of vases of Etruscan pottery were made in the 18th century, the most notable of which was that assembled by Sir William Hamilton, Ambassador to the Court of Naples, and subsequently sold to the British Museum.

Some examples of painted terracotta removed from Etruscan tombs have proved to be modern forgeries made from the same clay as the original pre-Roman ware, and cast suspicion on the genuineness of other specimens of supposedly ancient pottery. *See* BUCCHERO WARE; ETRUSCAN WARE.

Etruscan ware. Black basaltes ware made by Josiah Wedgwood with ENCAUSTIC DECORATION of red and white figures in imitation of ancient Etruscan pottery. The painting of this ware was probably done originally by Aaron Steele at Wedgwood's London decorating establishment at Chelsea, which was supervised by Thomas Bentley. The ware has a soft mat finish.

Étui (French). A small case fitted with miniature implements, such as scissors, bodkins, needles, a tiny knife, pencil, ivory writing-tablet, etc. They were variously shaped, delicately decorated with enamels, and richly mounted with gilt hinges and collars. Some were modelled in the form of a maiden's leg, with stocking, shoe, and garter (*see* JUNGFERNBEINCHEN), a lady's arm, with sleeve, cuff, and ringed finger, a stick of asparagus or broccoli, and similar ornamental forms.

Eulenkrug. The German term for an OWL-JUG.

Éventail jardinière (French). A fan-shaped JARDINIÈRE either of Sèvres porcelain or inspired by mid-18th-century Sèvres styles. *See* VASE HOLLANDAIS.

Everted. Turned outwards in shape, such as the lip of a pitcher, jug, or sauce-boat.

Ewer. A tall, wide-mouthed jug or pitcher with one handle, used, in conjunction with a basin decorated *en suite*, for washing the hands. The term is also applied to the long-necked globular BOTTLE (which had an accompanying basin) sent to Europe from China during the 18th century and used for the same purpose. Similar sets were made at Worcester. *See* AIGUIÈRE.

Excise mark. Markings occasionally found on mugs used in taverns in the 19th century to denote the amount of fluid contained.

Exotic birds. *See* FANTASIE VÖGEL.

Export china. *See* CANTON CHINA and CHINESE EXPORT PORCELAIN. All three terms are in common use for the ware still sometimes erroneously called ORIENTAL LOWESTOFT. *See* COMPAGNIE DES INDES WARE.

Eye-bath. A small cup-like utensil with dipped rim to conform to the shape of the eye and resting on a stemmed base.

Enghalskrug. Pottery, with pewter lid, decorated with enamel colours of the *famille verte* palette, Ansbach, *c.* 1735. Germanisches Nationalmuseum, Nuremberg.

Étuis. Porcelain examples, ht 3 in., made at Kelsterbach. Dr Siegfried Ducret Collection, Zurich.

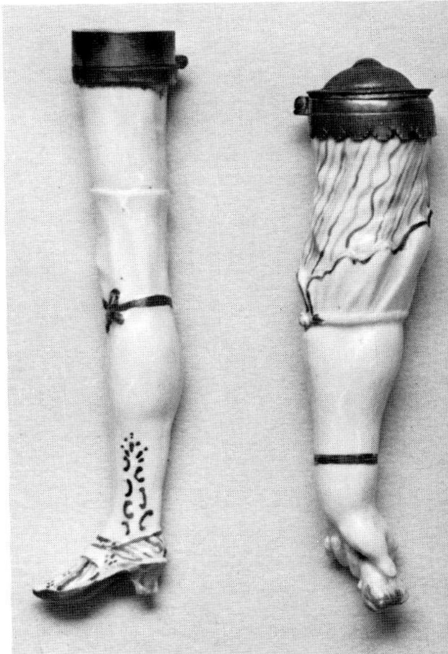

F

Fabeltiere (German). Literally, fable animals. Decoration on German porcelain, usually from Meissen of the first half of the 18th century, which has animal fables (such as those of Aesop) as its theme. The term is often also applied to the porcelain painting of A.F. von Löwenfinck (*see* LÖWENFINCK STYLE), when it denotes his animals inspired by the FABULOUS ANIMALS on oriental porcelain. *See* FABLES, AESOP'S; FABLE DECORATION.

Fable decoration. Porcelain plate painted by Jeffryes Hamett O'Neale with the 'Raven and the Water-jar', Worcester, *c.* 1765.

Fable decoration. Illustrations to the *Fables* of Aesop, La Fontaine, and others, employed as painted decoration on porcelain especially. Animal subjects are the most commonly seen, and those with human figures are distinctly rare. They occur on English and Continental porcelain of the 18th century. *See* FABLES, AESOP'S.

Fables, Aesop's. Decorative painted subjects taken from the *Fables* of AESOP, especially those employed on Chelsea porcelain between 1750 and 1756 which were based on the Francis Barlow edition of 1687. They were also the subject of figure groups. *See* FABELTIERE; FABLE DECORATION; HASTINGS, WARREN, SERVICE.

Fabulous animals. Mythological animals of the Orient, such as those depicted as decoration on ARITA porcelain, including the dragon (RYU); the Chinese KYLIN (sometimes called a 'unicorn' and in Japanese *kirin*); the water-tortoise (MINOGAME); the HO-HO BIRD, the Japanese version of the FÊNG-HUANG, often called a phoenix; the lion (SHI-SHI); and the tiger (HU). The term is also applied to animals derived from oriental sources, particularly those of Japanese inspiration which were painted on Meissen porcelain by A.F. von Löwenfinck (*see* LÖWENFINCK STYLE) and others. Less often the term is applied to European mythological animals such as the GRIFFIN.

Face-jug. Jug moulded with faces of Queen Charlotte and (on reverse) George III, Staffordshire, *c.* 1790–1800. Burnap Collection, William Rockhill Nelson Gallery of Art, Kansas City, Mo.

Face-jug. A type of jug modelled on each side with a face, such as those made in England of MARTINWARE, *c.* 1899, and certain 18th-century jugs in this form. *See* MASK JUGS AND MUGS; FACE-POT.

Face-pot. A globular vessel or urn of coarse Roman pottery with applied decoration in the form of a primitively modelled face. The type dates from the mid-1st century and specimens have been excavated in England at Trent Vale, near Stoke-on-Trent.

Faceted ware. Ware with a number of connected plane surfaces, such as the six- or eight-sided faceted handles on some Cockpit Hill (Derbyshire) teapots or coffee-pots, or pieces with hexagonal or pentagonal facets. The technique was employed to decorate some specimens of BÖTTGER RED STONEWARE, *c.* 1715. At Meissen particularly the decoration was done by glass-workers and is analogous to the faceting of glass. *See* MUSCHELN.

Factory-mark. A mark on ceramic ware to indicate the place of manufacture, and sometimes also the date. Such marks are impressed, incised, painted, or stamped (*see* BACK-STAMP), and appear underglaze or overglaze. The factory-mark is often a symbol, or series of symbols, which vary at different periods.

Among the best-known 18th-century examples are the crossed swords of Meissen (taken from the Electoral arms), the double *L* monogram of Sèvres (for Louis XV), the anchor of Chelsea, and the crescent of Worcester. Many 18th-century factories used no marks at all, and others used marks imitative of one of the principal factories, such as the crossed hayforks of Volkstedt or Rudolstadt (Thuringia) intended to be mistaken for the crossed swords of Meissen. The year of manufacture was sometimes shown by a DATE-MARK, either by itself or integrated into the factory-mark, and this practice has continued at some of the major factories for important wares. Such date-marks are usually numerals or letters (*see* DATE-LETTER) but periods are often indicated by changes in the form of the principal factory-mark which are comparatively slight. It should be emphasized that a mark is not a guarantee of origin. All the principal factories have, at one time or another, suffered from the copying of their marks. *See* CANCELLATION MARK.

For some major European factory-marks, *see* introductory section, pp. 7–18.

Faïence fine. Eye-bath with relief decoration, Pont-aux-Choux (Paris), mid-18th century. Courtesy, Newman & Newman Ltd, London.

Fa-hua (Chinese). Ming dynasty wares decorated with different coloured glazes which are kept apart by slightly elevated lines of clay. The body may be either stoneware or porcelain. *See* SAN-TS'AI.

Fa-lang (Chinese). Porcelain painting in the style of Canton enamel painting on a copper base. The palette includes the rose-pink of the FAMILLE ROSE. *See* JUAN-TS'AI.

Faience. Tin-glazed earthenware, especially that made in France, Germany and Scandinavia. The term is of French derivation, and probably comes from the 16th-century popularity in France of wares made at Faenza (Italy). The technique is exactly the same as that of MAIOLICA and DELFTWARE, the only difference being the place of origin. The German term is *Fayence*. *See* EGYPTIAN FAIENCE; FAÏENCE FINE.

Faïence anglaise (French). A term used in France to describe imported English CREAMWARE, as distinct from tin-glazed earthenware. Same as FAÏENCE FINE D'ANGLETERRE.

Faïence à niellure (French). A fine glazed earthenware with impressed decoration filled with clays of contrasting colour and originally made at Saint-Porchaire (Deux-Sèvres, France) and perhaps at nearby Oiron. This 16th-century ware is not faience, but a kind of FAÏENCE FINE. It has been termed in the past HENRI DEUX WARE and SAINT-PORCHAIRE WARE. *See* FAÏENCE D'OIRON.

Faïence d'Oiron (French). A type of FAÏENCE À NIELLURE said to have been made at Oiron, near Saint-Porchaire, France, and similar to SAINT-PORCHAIRE WARE. In past years all such wares were grouped together as HENRI DEUX WARE.

Faïence fine (French). Earthenware covered with a transparent lead glaze in imitation of English CREAMWARE. The term is a misnomer since the ware, not being tin-glazed, is not faience; in fact, it superseded the manufacture of tin-glazed pottery (FAIENCE) in France, and in Europe generally. *See* STEINGUT.

***Faïence fine d'Angleterre*.** The normal term in French for English CREAMWARE. The term *grès anglais* or *grès d'Angleterre* sometimes used are both inaccurate, *grès* actually referring to STONEWARE, as in *grès de Flandres*, the 19th-century name for reproductions of Westerwald stoneware.

Face-pot. Roman pottery, mid-1st century. City Museums, Stoke-on-Trent.

Fair Hebe. Teapot modelled by Jean Voyez, Staffordshire, *c*. 1788. Burnap Collection, William Rockhill Nelson Gallery of Art, Kansas City, Mo.

Fairings. 'After Marriage' and 'Taking the Cream'. Courtesy, Christie's.

Fairyland lustre. Vase by Daisy Makeig-Jones, *c*. 1920. Courtesy, Wedgwood.

Faïence hollandaise (French). Same as DUTCH DELFTWARE. *See* DELFTWARE.

Faïence parlante French faience decorated with inscriptions or commemorative dates made in the 18th century, and especially at Nevers. Wares thus decorated include plates, jugs, plaques, fountains and *livre-flacons*.

Faïence patriotique (French). Plates and other objects of faience bearing patriotic inscriptions and revolutionary subjects, such as flags or a Phrygian cap. Such ware is usually crude in execution, and was made at the time of the French Revolution, *c*. 1789–94. Genuine specimens, especially those of Auxerre and Nevers, are now rare, but there are in existence many modern forgeries.

Fair Hebe jug. A type of pottery jug probably modelled *c*. 1788 by Jean Voyez in Staffordshire. It is concurrent with the fashion for rustic things, such as furniture in the form of natural tree branches. The jug is modelled in the form of a tree-trunk with a spreading base; on one side a youth seated by the trunk is shown offering a bird's nest to a seated girl, above which scene is a scroll bearing the words 'Fair Hebe'. (The same motif was also used on teapots.) There are several variations in the motifs of the reverse side, such as a man and a dog (or a man holding a glass) above which is inscribed 'A Bumper'. The original model may have been made by Voyez for Richard Meir Astbury, whose initials appear on some examples. Similar jugs were modelled for other potters, including the factory of Ralph Wood I at Burslem. It has been reproduced. *See* TREE-TRUNK.

Fairings. Small porcelain groups made at Pössneck, Saxony, *c*. 1860–90, for sale or as prizes at fairgrounds. The humour of the inscriptions in English is often naïve or intended to be *risqué*. The subject is often a couple in, or about to get into, bed but there are many other less suggestive subjects. In the same category are some small BOXES bearing similar inscriptions.

Fairyland lustre. A type of LUSTRE ware made by Wedgwood from November 1915. The decoration by Daisy Makeig-Jones depicts whimsical creatures in a fairyland setting, the colours having a marked iridescent appearance. *See* DRAGON LUSTRE.

Fake. A piece of genuinely old pottery or porcelain which has been altered or added to for the purpose of enhancing its value, e.g. one which has an added coloured ground, added decoration in a style that is more keenly sought, or added inscriptions and marks; similarly any object from which marks (which might otherwise identify it as being a reproduction or less desirable piece) have been erased. *See* REFIRED WARE; REPRODUCTION; FORGERY.

False flutes. Decoration painted in such a way as to give the impression of FLUTING.

False gadroon. A painted, decorative border pattern simulating a GADROON.

Famille (French). Literally, family, as in FAMILLE VERTE, FAMILLE JAUNE, FAMILLE NOIRE, and FAMILLE ROSE. These 'families' were an arbitrary classification made in the middle of the 19th century by the French ceramic historian, Albert Jacquemart, and based on the occurrence and distribution of green, yellow, black, and rose enamels in the decoration of Chinese porcelain made from the reign of K'ang Hsi (1662–1722) onwards. *Rose-verte* is a combination of these palettes.

Famille jaune (French). Chinese decoration of the reign of K'ang Hsi (1662–1722) of the Ch'ing dynasty, in which the palette of the FAMILLE VERTE is employed in conjunction with extensive passages of yellow in various combinations.

Famille noire (French). Chinese decoration of the reign of K'ang Hsi (1662–1722) of the Ch'ing dynasty which has a black ground washed over with transparent green enamel, and added decoration in the FAMILLE VERTE palette. The type was very popular with the Empress-Dowager and some late 19th-century European collectors. In some cases a black ground was added to what had originally been basically *famille verte* vases for sale or presentation to them. *See* MIRROR-BLACK GLAZE; DELFT NOIRE.

Famille rose (French). The category of Chinese decoration which is characterized by the inclusion of an opaque enamel colour that ranges from pink to a purplish rose. The pigment itself is the European PURPLE OF CASSIUS which was taken to China by Jesuit missionaries, *c.* 1685, appearing first on enamels on copper and then, by *c.* 1700, on porcelain. *Famille rose* porcelain was at its best during the reign of Yung Chêng (1723–35), and thereafter became increasingly commercial, and largely for export to Europe. The colour itself was employed by a number of European factories for wares in the Chinese style, and it also occurs on German faience decorated by HAUSMALER before its arrival in China. The style was copied on English porcelain especially at Worcester. *See* RUBY-BACK WARE; CANTON WARE; COMPAGNIE DES INDES WARE; YANG-TS'AI.

Famille verte (French). The category of Chinese decoration which was so called because of its predominant characteristic, a brilliant, transparent, green enamel. The palette also includes iron-red, blue, yellow, and aubergine-purple. The earliest examples have underglaze blue, but the later versions an enamel blue which causes the surrounding glaze to become slightly mat on 17th- and early 18th-century specimens. The best examples are from the reign of K'ang Hsi (1662–1722). The body of K'ang Hsi porcelain is very white, of fine quality, and with a clear and even glaze. The style and palette were sometimes copied on early European porcelain, and on some rare varieties of faience, such as that made at Ansbach.

Fan-hung (Chinese). Iron-red. A Chinese enamel colour used from the early years of the 16th century onwards; sometimes termed tomato red. This enamel occasionally induces a mat appearance in the glaze of the area immediately surrounding it, somewhat in the manner of the blue enamel of the FAMILLE VERTE.

Fantasie Vögel. Vase with painted decoration, Augustus Rex ware (AR mark in underglaze blue), Meissen. Courtesy, Sotheby's.

Fantasie Vögel (German). A popular painted decoration, termed in English 'exotic birds'. It was introduced at Meissen, and at first featured birds of exotic types from the Moritzburg aviaries, but, under the influence of such oriental motifs as the FÊNG-HUANG (phoenix), they became increasingly fantastic. The style was employed at Sèvres, and in England at Worcester especially. *See* DISHEVELLED BIRDS; ORNITHOID PORCELAIN.

Farmacia Orsini Colonna drug-jars. A series of DRUG JARS and other PHARMACY WARE decorated with portraits of members of the Orsini family. Some jugs have animal-mask spouts. They are attributed to Faenza, early 16th century.

Fatimid ware. Egyptian pottery made at Fostat (Old Cairo) during the Fatimid dynasty (969–1171). *See* FOSTAT WARE.

Fazackerley style. Flower decoration on bowl, Liverpool delftware, mid-18th century. Victoria and Albert Museum, London.

Feather-edged. Detail of creamware platter with moulded eight-barbed border, Melbourne (Derbyshire). Victoria and Albert Museum, London.

Fatshan Chün (Chinese). Stoneware, with a dense turquoise-blue glaze sometimes suffused or splashed with copper-red, which somewhat resembles the earlier CHÜN YAO of the Sung dynasty. It came from the area around Canton, in Kuangtung province.

Fayence. The German term for FAIENCE.

Fayence-Porzellan. The German term for faience decorated with enamel colours in the manner of porcelain.

Fazackerl(e)y flowers. Polychrome painted flowers, used as decoration on Liverpool delftware, characterized by a palette of simple enamel colours in hues of red, blue, yellow, and green, with drawing in black. Various styles of floral painting occur, the introduction of which has been ascribed to Thomas Fazackerl(e)y whose initials, together with those of Catherine Fazackerl(e)y, appear on a specimen of *c.* 1758.

Feather decoration. A decorative motif of painted feathers, in groups or scattered, used notably on Worcester porcelain, *c.* 1807–18, and also at Minton, *c.* 1839–40. *See* FEATHER PATTERN.

Feather-edged. A moulded border decoration on the scalloped rim of plates, consisting of repeated feathery forms with barbs disposed diagonally to the edge. It has slightly different details characteristic of the particular factory, Wedgwood feathers having seven barbs with a space between the third and fourth, Leeds seven to nine barbs, and Melbourne (Derbyshire) eight barbs with some space after the first three and with the last two closely attached. The decoration occurs mainly on creamware, but is also found on 18th-century English porcelain, e.g. Chelsea, and on some saltglazed stoneware presumed to be of Leeds manufacture. *See* SHELL-EDGED.

Feather pattern. (1) COMBED DECORATION on slipware of the late 17th century from Staffordshire. It was made by combing a white and brown slip, which was then covered with a yellowish glaze. (2) A painted feathery border pattern employed at Sèvres and elsewhere on porcelain.

Fécondité, La (French). A relief decoration depicting a reclining woman with five children playing in front of a draped curtain.

La Fécondité. Dish with relief decoration, Palissy ware, second half of 17th century. Victoria and Albert Museum, London.

The subject was first used on PALISSY WARE by Bernard Palissy, or one of his immediate followers, on a platter decorated with coloured glazes, and it was repeated on Lambeth delftware, *c.* 1633–97.

Feeding bottle. A boat-shaped vessel completely enclosed except for a hole in the top for filling and a projecting feeding tube at one end. Such bottles were used for feeding infants and invalids, and were made of porcelain, stoneware, and glazed earthenware. *See* FEEDING CUP; PAP-BOAT; BIBERON.

Feeding bottle. White glazed earthenware with decoration in blue; length 7 in. Wellcome Museum, London.

Feeding cup. A type of cup, partially covered to prevent spillage, for feeding children and invalids. It has a spout (usually straight on early examples, curved on later ones) at the front and generally two loop handles at right angles to the spout. Early examples are cylindrical or bucket-shaped, but later, *c.* 1790, they were hemispherical with a flaring base. The covering segment is flat on early examples, convex on later ones. They were made in England in porcelain, and in delftware and creamware, some of the latter being in white, others with transfer-printed decoration. *See* FEEDING BOTTLE; SICK-POT; PHYSIC CUP.

Feeding cup. Porcelain, Bow, *c.* 1760.

Feeding pot. A type of small covered pot having one handle opposite a nipple spout; a BABY-FEEDER. *See* BUBBY-POT.

Feeding spoon. A type of spoon for feeding infants. It is partially covered and has a curled handle which also serves as a support. Examples occur in English porcelain. *See* PAP-SPOON; MEDICAL SPOON.

Feeding pot. Stoneware, with nipple-spout, Castleford, *c.* 1790. Donald C. Towner Collection, London.

Feldspar (feldspathic rock). An essential constituent of almost all crystalline rocks including aluminium silicates with potassium, sodium, calcium, or barium. Feldspathic rock fuses under a sufficiently high temperature (about 1,450°C.) into a kind of natural glass. It is an essential constituent of most true porcelains, although it was sometimes replaced by SOAPROCK. Feldspathic rock was employed for glazing true porcelains in China and Japan, and it also formed part of some European glazes. In China it is called PAI-TUN-TZŬ, gallicized as *petuntse. See* CORNISH STONE.

Feldspar porcelain. A porcelain including feldspathic rock made by Josiah Spode, *c.* 1820, and so marked.

Feldspathic glaze. A glaze made from feldspar, as distinguished from glazes which are similar in their nature to ordinary glass. It requires a very high temperature to fuse it, and it can only be used on TRUE PORCELAIN. It is fired at the same time as the body.

Fên Ting yao (Chinese). Literally, flour Ting ware. A type of TING YAO inferior in quality to *pai Ting*, descriptions of which occur in the works of Chinese commentators on porcelain. It dates from the Sung dynasty (960–1280), and attribution of specimens is uncertain.

Feeding spoon. Porcelain, with decoration in blue. Wellcome Museum, London.

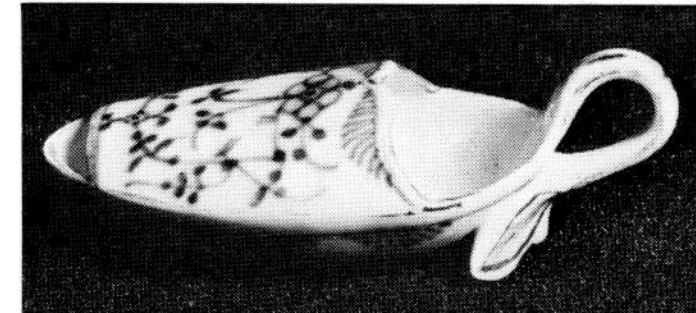

Fên-ts'ai (Chinese). Literally, pale colours. A term applied to the rose enamel of the FAMILLE ROSE palette. *See* YANG-TS'AI.

Fence pattern. Same as ZIG-ZAG FENCE PATTERN.

Fêng-huang (Chinese). A decorative motif depicting a fantastic bird (often called a phoenix) which is a symbol of the Empress. It is also one of the Four Supernatural Creatures (*see* SSŬ LING) and the FOUR QUADRANTS. The same bird in Japanese is termed a HO-HO.

Fern-ash. Wood-ash obtained by burning ferns. It was added, according to the patent specification, to Bow porcelain made experimentally before 1750, of which no surviving examples have been identified. It contains phosphates, and porcelain thus made would yield a slightly phosphatic reaction. The ash acts as a FLUX. *See* BONE-ASH; SEAWEED, ASHES OF.

Fern pot. A type of vase of rectangular section, larger at the mouth and tapering down to a smaller base, standing in a rectangular rimmed receptacle. Usually decorated with floral sprays and swags in relief, sometimes coloured, examples were made in creamware by Leeds and other factories, *c.* 1780.

Fern pottery. *See* MOCHA WARE.

Ferronerie (French). Ornamental decoration, usually painted, resembling wrought-iron work, and consisting of arabesques, volutes, and scrolls. Belonging to the late 17th century, it can be found in the designs of Jean Bérain, and as a decorative motif on faience of the late 17th and early 18th centuries. *See* LAMBREQUINS; LAUB- UND BANDELWERK; BÉRAIN MOTIFS.

Ferruginous. Containing iron, as with certain glazes. Oxide of iron colours many clays which burn from buff to a brownish-red in the kiln. Celadon glazes of an early type were produced by washing the body with a ferruginous slip before glazing. Sometimes iron particles were removed by passing liquid slip near magnets.

Festonenmuster (German). Literally, festoon pattern. A border of festooned leaves developed at Meissen. *See* MUSTER.

Festoon. A decorative pattern in the form of garlands of flowers, leaves, fruit, or drapery hanging in a natural curve and suspended from the two ends. *See* SWAG.

Fettling. The process of finishing a vessel before firing by removing with a metal tool any seam marks, casting marks, and other blemishes. It is especially applied to SLIP-CAST hollow ware.

Feu de moufle (French). The MUFFLE kiln. The same as the PETIT FEU. *See* ENAMEL FIRING.

Feuille de chou (French). Literally, cabbage leaf. Pottery and porcelain naturalistically modelled or moulded, and painted like a cabbage leaf, a style employed in the 1750s for bowls, plates, and tureens. *See* CABBAGE WARE.

Fictile. Made by moulding, or capable of being moulded. The term is used to refer to any vessel made of clay. *See* PLASTIC.

Fiddler jug. A type of TOBY JUG depicting a seated man playing a fiddle.

Figulines rustiques (French). A term applied by Bernard Palissy (Bernard de Tuileries) to his 16th-century pottery decorated with objects in relief, e.g. snakes, lizards, and fish, which were copied from nature, and covered with coloured glazes. Later, the term was more widely applied to wares in this style made by others. *See* PALISSY WARE.

Figure. A ceramic object representing a human being or animal alone or as a group, or as ornament on a vessel, such as a vase. The French term is *statuette*. *See* FIGURINE; IMAGE; FIGURE

Fern pot. Creamware, with green applied relief decoration, Leeds, *c.* 1780. Victoria and Albert Museum, London.

Filter. Stoneware (Pasteur-Chamberland Patent), made by J. Defries & Sons Ltd. Wellcome Museum, London.

GROUP; PERSONNAGE. For figures by well-known modellers, *see* ASTBURY FIGURES; BUSTELLI FIGURES; KÄNDLER FIGURES; LINDNER FIGURES; WOOD, RALPH, FIGURES. For special types, *see* BOXING FIGURES; CALLOT FIGURES; COMMEDIA DELL'ARTE FIGURES; COPENHAGEN FIGURES; CRINOLINE FIGURES; MASONIC FIGURES; MYTHOLOGICAL FIGURES; STAFFORDSHIRE FIGURES; TANAGRA FIGURES; THEATRICAL FIGURES; TOMB-FIGURES; VYSE FIGURES.

Figure candlestick. A candlestick in the form of a figure supporting the candle-nozzle. *See* CHAMBER CANDLESTICK.

Figure group. Two or more figures on a common BASE.

Figure jug. *See* TOBY JUG.

Figure-of-eight garlands. Floral or foliate garlands in the form of a double loop.

Figurine. (1) A small, individual figure, employed especially of ancient pottery examples. *See* TANAGRA FIGURES. (2) A common expression in the United States for any figure. *See* STATUETTE.

Filter. A large water-vessel with a cover and spigot, having inside a porous stone filter. They were made in England in the 19th century, and often have a five-gallon capacity; smaller sizes were made for table use.

Fine stoneware. Fine-grained STONEWARE of sophisticated form, such as Wedgwood's jasper and black basaltes.

Finger-vase. A vase with five flower-holders arranged in a fan shape. They were made of porcelain at Vienna; of tin-glazed earthenware at Delft in Holland, and in England at Bristol; and of creamware at Leeds. Also called a 'quintal flower horn'. *See* TULIP VASE.

Finger-vase. Porcelain, Vienna (du Paquier's factory), 1721. British Museum, London.

Finial. The terminal ornament of any object, but particularly on the cover of a pot, bowl, tureen, vase, or other receptacle, where it also serves as a handle. It is sometimes termed a 'knop'. Finials are made in a great variety of forms, such as a figure (*see* WIDOW FINIAL), animal (dog, dolphin, swan), flower, fruit

Figulines rustiques. Glazed earthenware, by Bernard Palissy, second half of 16th century. Wallace Collection, London.

(apple, peach, pear, pineapple), leaf, loop, mushroom, pine-cone, shell, sphere, sphinx, etc. Certain finials are characteristic of particular periods, such as flowers and fruits of the rococo style, pine-cones and acorns of the neo-classical style, and sphinxes of the Empire period. *See* BUN FINIAL; BARBED FINIAL; PIERCED FINIAL.

Fire-clay. Clay capable of being subjected to a high temperature without fusing, and hence used for KILN FURNITURE. It contains much silica and only small amounts of lime, iron, and alkalis.

Fire-crack. Bust of the Emperor Vitellius, showing fire-crack on the neck, red stoneware, Meissen, *c.* 1715. Museum of Fine Arts, Boston, Mass.

Fire-crack. A crack or split in porcelain or stoneware arising, for a variety of reasons, during the actual firing in the kiln. Fire-cracks are generally to be seen in primitive or early wares, since such faulty pieces are now generally discarded as WASTERS, although they were once decorated and sold. The usual cause is faulty design, since thicker parts take up heat more slowly than thinner parts and likewise give it off more slowly during cooling; this sets up unequal stresses which result in a crack or split. During the 18th century fire-cracks were sometimes partially disguised by enamelling over them. A fire-crack is usually slightly wider at its terminal end, whereas a damage crack leaves the two parts in contact throughout. Fire-cracks are sometimes termed 'age-cracks', but this is a misnomer since no porcelain or stoneware develops cracks as a result of age; the same term is sometimes also applied in the United States to cracks resulting from damage, and is again a misnomer. *See* CRAZING; CRACKLE.

Fire-speckling. Minute pieces of carbon or other material, usually black, embedded in the glaze either during the original firing or (as is sometimes the case) as a result of refiring to add enamel decoration at a later date.

Firing. The process of transforming the body into pottery or porcelain by exposing it to the requisite degree of heat in a KILN. The temperature varies according to the type of ware, and usually ranges from about 800°C. for EARTHENWARE to 1450°C. for oriental TRUE PORCELAIN. According to the type of ware there may be several firings before the manufacturing process is complete. *See* BISCUIT FIRING; ENAMEL FIRING; GLOST FIRING; GRAND FEU; PETIT FEU.

Firing-ring. An object on which ware was stood in the SAGGER, sometimes triangular in section with a flat base, and used instead of COCKSPURS (stilts). *See* KILN-FURNITURE; TRIVET.

First day's vase. Black basaltes, with inscription and on reverse figures in the red-figure style, Wedgwood and Bentley, Etruria, 1769. Courtesy, Wedgwood.

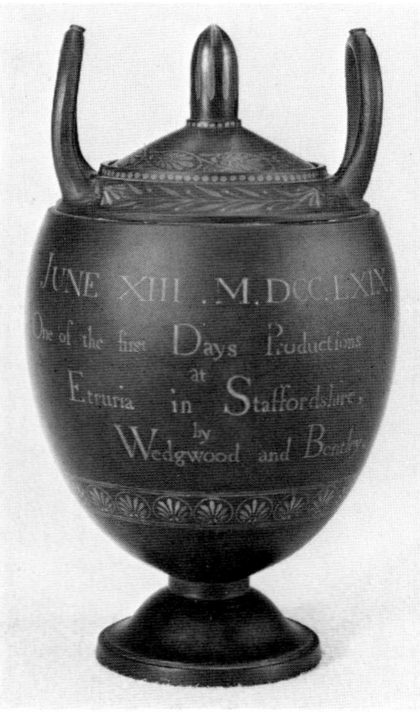

First day's vase. A black basaltes vase, somewhat in the form of a Greek AMPHORA, thrown by Josiah Wedgwood and appropriately inscribed to record the opening of the Wedgwood & Bentley factory for the making of decorative pottery at Etruria (Staffordshire) on 13 June 1769. Six examples were made, decorated with figures in the classical RED-FIGURE STYLE. Fifty replicas, issued in 1930 to mark the bicentenary of Wedgwood's birth, bore inscriptions giving the dates of his birth and death.

Fish. (1) A decorative motif on Chinese porcelain, such as those in underglaze SACRIFICIAL RED on stem-cups of the Ming dynasty. (2) Naturalistically modelled and painted fish made as tureens in faience and porcelain. *See* CHAR-POT.

Fish-roe glaze. A Chinese glaze which is finely crackled, resembling fish-roe. Also called *fond truité*. *See* CRACKLE.

Fish-roe ground. A ground of small, tangent, equal circles without dots in the circles. *See* ŒIL-DE-PERDRIX.

Fish-roe yellow. A greenish-yellow colour with a fine CRACKLE used on Chinese porcelain. Same as mustard yellow.

Fish-scale ground. *See* SCALE GROUND.

Fish-trowel. A flat implement, shaped like a trowel, with a pointed or slightly rounded end and a handle, for serving fish; made of creamware with PIERCED DECORATION.

Fish trowel. Creamware, Leeds, *c.* 1790. Victoria and Albert Museum, London.

Fisherman, The. A decorative pattern used at Worcester and Caughley, called 'The Pleasure Boat' in the 18th century, which was transfer-printed on blue-and-white porcelain. It depicts a fisherman on a rock holding a fishing-line and another in a boat holding a fish. The design at Worcester has a wavy fishing-line, which is usually straight at Caughley. The fish is long and slender on Worcester examples, and short and fat on Caughley specimens. *See* CORMORANT FISHERMAN.

Fitzhugh pattern. Underglaze blue decoration on dish, Chinese export porcelain, *c.* 1775–1800.

Fitzhugh pattern. A border pattern employed on Chinese BLUE-AND-WHITE PORCELAIN of the last quarter of the 18th century. It is extremely elaborate, and features open POMEGRANATES, BUDDHA'S-HAND CITRONS, flowers, and DIAPERS, with occasional butterflies. The origin of the pattern is unknown, but it is generally accepted that it was devised for a Chinese export service made for an English family of this name. Replacers were made by Spode. The pattern was adapted for use on English porcelain at Caughley and Coalport.

The Fisherman. Transfer-printed decoration on mask-jug, Caughley, *c.* 1780. Victoria and Albert Museum, London.

Five Blessings, The. A decorative design on Chinese porcelain depicting five bats (FU); it is a wish for longevity, wealth, serenity, virtue, and an easy death.

Five Continents, The. *See* FOUR CONTINENTS, THE.

Five Senses, The. A group of allegorical figures representing the five Aristotelian senses. Hearing, though made in several versions, was often depicted playing a musical instrument. Smell is suggested by the act of sniffing a bouquet of flowers, Taste by eating, and Feeling by a caged bird pecking a finger, while Seeing is rendered in a variety of less immediately recognizable forms. The subject seems to have been first depicted in porcelain figures by J. J. Kändler at Meissen in the 1740s.

Flagon. A pouring vessel shaped like an AIGUIÈRE, but with a long spout instead of a pouring lip, and with a hinged metal lid. The term is often employed loosely for any vessel intended for pouring or drinking.

Flambé (French). A term employed to describe glazes of reduced copper (i.e. those fired in a REDUCING ATMOSPHERE). Wares of this kind were first developed in China during the Sung dynasty (960–1280), CHÜN YAO being the earliest. Other wares of the same sort include the later FATSHAN CHÜN of the Ming dynasty. Porcelain glazes of this kind became especially popular during the reign of Emperor Ch'ien Lung (1736–96) of the Ch'ing dynasty, and they are usually a deep crimson suffused or streaked with turquoise blue. The effect was unattainable in Europe until late in the 19th century, when a Staffordshire potter named Bernard Moore succeeded in imitating it on a stoneware body. It has since been used to good effect by other European factories, such as Copenhagen. The technique is allied to the use of copper-red for underglaze painting. *See* SANG-DE-BŒUF.

Flaming Pearl. Same as SACRED PEARL.

Flaming tortoise. A KAKIEMON pattern depicting a tortoise with seaweed streaming from its tail. It occurs on some late 17th-century Chinese porcelain, and was copied in the 18th century on Continental and English porcelain. *See* MINOGAME.

Flammiform. Modelled or painted to represent a flame, e.g. as a finial.

Flanged spout. A short stubby spout with a wider flange midway to the mouth, as found on some WET-DRUG JARS.

Flask. Creamware, Leeds, *c.* 1775. Donald C. Towner Collection, London.

Flask. (1) A vessel with a cover for carrying liquids, usually of flattened globular form or pear-shaped, with a short neck and a small mouth; it somewhat resembles a pilgrim-bottle (PILGRIM-FLASK), but has no lugs for a carrying strap. (2) A 19th-century vessel of brown STONEWARE or brown-glazed pottery (BROWN CHINA) made in England in the form of a mermaid, pistol, etc., or decorated in relief with topical motifs – often political. Such flasks were intended for the sale of gin, and often bear the impressed name of a tavern.

The French term is *flacon*, and the German, *Flasche*. *See* CAUDLE-FLASK; WINE-FLASK; GIMMEL FLASK.

Flatback. A pottery figure made in the 19th century for the decoration of cottage mantelpieces, and so called because the back is flat and virtually without modelling to facilitate quantity production in moulds. Most examples were made in Staffordshire, but few can be traced definitely to a particular factory, although the name of Sampson Smith is often mentioned in this connection. Subjects include royalty, military, theatrical, and sporting personalities, notorious criminals, and fictional characters; some were named on the base. They are decorated in both underglaze and enamel colours. Identifiable subjects are rare, but a large number have no special connotation and are of small interest to collectors. Many have been reproduced (using the old moulds) in recent years. *See* STAFFORDSHIRE FIGURES; CHIMNEY-PIECE ORNAMENTS.

Flatware. Tableware that is flat or shallow, such as dishes, plates, platters, saucers, and shallow bowls, as distinguished from HOLLOW WARE.

Flechtmuster (German). Literally, plaited pattern. A border pattern developed at Meissen in the 18th century.

Flemish ware. A Wedgwood coloured body introduced *c.* 1805, similar to DRY BODY but having a grey-green or bluish-sage colour, the variations in hue being due to differences of temperature during the firing of individual batches.

Fleurs des Indes (French). Same as INDIANISCHE BLUMEN.

Fleurs fines (French). Naturalistic flowers painted without any outline and then shaded. They were introduced at Strasbourg, *c.* 1749, and are comparable to DEUTSCHE BLUMEN. *See* STRASBOURG FLOWERS.

Fliegender Hund (German). Literally, flying dog. A decorative design from KAKIEMON sources developed at Meissen in the early 1730s and featuring the flying fox. *See* FLYING FOX AND SQUIRREL.

Flint. A substance consisting of small quartz crystals in conjunction with molecules of water; after being heated to *c.* 400°C., it can be easily crumbled or powdered. It was one of the ingredients of 18th-century English creamware, helping to give lightness of colour, greater hardness, and freedom from warping during firing. In the United States the term is generally employed to refer to any kind of powdered quartz.

Flint enamel ware. An American term for ware with a type of coloured mottled glaze such as that employed at the United States Pottery Co., Bennington, Vt. *See* AMERICAN POTTERY; BENNINGTON WARE.

Flintporslin (Swedish). Creamware in the English manner, such as that made in the 18th century at Marieberg. Same as FAÏENCE FINE or STEINGUT.

Flintware. An 18th-century term for English white saltglazed stoneware which contained FLINT.

Flohbein (German). Literally, flea leg. A porcelain leg, usually female, with a stocking, garter, and shoe, which has a small flea near the knee. Made at Meissen, Kelsterbach, and elsewhere in Germany, some were in the form of an ÉTUI or a PIPE-STOPPER. *See* JUNGFERNBEINCHEN.

Flora Danica service. Plate from the dinner service. Courtesy, Royal Copenhagen Porcelain Manufactory.

Flora Danica service. A dinner-service made by the Royal Copenhagen Porcelain Manufactory. The original service had over 1,800 pieces; it was ordered in 1789 by the Danish king, Christian VII, for, it is said, a gift to Catherine II (Catherine the Great) of Russia, who, however, died before it was completed. The making of the service required twelve years. In 1802 it was delivered to the Danish royal household and used for the first time on Christian VII's birthday in 1803. Today about 1,500 pieces exist, the main part being on exhibit at Rosenborg Castle, Copenhagen. A second service was made in 1863 for the wedding of Princess Alexandra of Denmark to the Prince of Wales (later Edward VII), and is now at Sandringham House. Since then reproductions have been in regular production commercially. The ware has serrated edges and pierced borders, with relief flowers on the covers. The plates are painted with botanical specimens exactly copied from engravings in Danish works devoted to the national flora; much of the painting was done by Johann Christian Bayer. Each piece bears on the reverse the Latin name of the particular flower depicted. *See* BOTANICAL WARE.

Floral meander. A border decoration of flowers in a continuous twisting line. *See* MEANDER BORDER.

Floral swag. A decorative pattern in the form of a SWAG consisting of flowers and leaves.

Floral swag. Porcelain *cachepot* decorated with enamel colours, Sceaux, *c.* 1765. Victoria and Albert Museum, London.

Floramuster (German). *See* GOTZKOWSKY ERHABENE BLUMEN.

Flower-brick. Bristol delftware, *c.* 1750. Courtesy, Jellinek & Sampson, London.

Florette. A small stylized flower used in decoration.

Florette border. A border pattern of a series of florettes.

Flour Ting. Same as FÊN TING YAO.

Flower-basket pattern. Same as HANAKAGO-DE.

Flower-brick. A small, brick-like flower-holder of 18th-century English delftware, the top being pierced with holes for cut-flowers.

Pieces of similar appearance, with a square hole for an inkpot and numerous small holes for quills, are inkstands. *See* STANDISH.

Flower-dish. A dish shaped and coloured naturalistically to represent flowers, or flowers and leaves of various plants, such as peonies, sunflowers, etc. Some rare specimens were made at Chelsea in the 1750s. *See* LEAF-DISH; STRAWBERRY-LEAF DISH; SUNFLOWER DISH.

Flower-pot. Porcelain, Bow, *c.* 1750; ht 7 in. Smithsonian Institution, Washington, D.C.

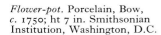

Flower-pot. (1) A utilitarian pottery receptacle in which to grow flowering plants. (2) An ornamental pot, similar in form to a CACHEPOT, but with an integral flowering plant, the leaves of which are often of gilded bronze and the flowers of porcelain; such pots were made at Meissen and at Bow. *See* CAISSE À FLEURS; ORANGE-TUB.

Flowers. Flowers and sprays, either modelled or moulded, or as painted decoration, used to embellish vases, figures, and other ornamental wares. They have always been popular with the principal porcelain factories, and most of the small ones. The fashion for modelled flowers as decoration, usually mounted on bronze stalks and with bronze leaves, was started at Vincennes, *c.* 1750. Flowers of extremely fine quality have been made since the 1930s by the Worcester Royal Porcelain Company, of which those accompanying the series of DOUGHTY BIRDS are the most notable. *See* BLUMEN; BILLINGSLEY ROSES; HANS SLOANE FLOWERS; FAZACKERLEY FLOWERS; FLEURS FINES; VINCENNES FLOWERS; STRASBOURG FLOWERS; MILLEFLEURS PATTERN; BOUQUET; BOTANICAL WARE.

Flown blue. The soft but unattractive colour which results from the diffusion of blue pigment into the glaze as a result of firing in an atmosphere containing volatile chlorides.

Flute Lesson, The. A decorative subject (also known as '*L'agréable leçon*' and 'The Music Lesson') after François Boucher, depicting a man and woman seated on a bench by a fountain, he teaching her to play the flute. Porcelain groups based on this theme were made at a number of factories during the middle years of the 18th century, the most impressive example being the Chelsea version, *c.* 1763, where the figures are almost enveloped in a large flowering maybush. A companion group, 'The Dancing Lesson', depicts a man and woman teaching a monkey to dance; this also is a subject after Boucher. The same subject occurs on Worcester porcelain in transfer-printed form engraved by Robert Hancock, and it also occurs on Chinese export porcelain, *c.* 1760. *See* SINGING LESSON, THE; HANCOCK ENGRAVINGS.

Flowers. Mexican Feijoa, by Dorothy Doughty. Courtesy, Worcester Royal Porcelain Co.

Fluted ground. A ground pattern consisting of a series of lines giving the effect of fluting.

Fluting. A series of parallel moulded grooves, of semi-circular, semi-elliptical, or rectangular section. The grooves may be separated by a common arris (as with Doric columns). The converse is REEDING or ribbing.

Flux. A substance added to glass, glazes, or vitrifiable bodies, such as porcelain, to lower the fusion point during firing. Fluxes are commonly added to ENAMEL COLOURS to lower their fusion point to slightly below that of the GLAZE to which they are applied, although some softening of the glaze is essential to key the enamels to it. Fluxes include borax, potash, soda, and ash (BONE-ASH; FERN-ASH; SEAWEED, ASHES OF).

Flying Fox and squirrel. Porcelain plate with painted decoration showing the flying fox above a gourd vine and banded hedge, Meissen, *c.* 1740. Courtesy, Antique Porcelain Co., London.

Flying fox and squirrel. A decorative subject derived from KAKIEMON porcelain and developed at Meissen in the 1720s. It depicts a red fox in apparent flight above a squirrel and a gourd vine. The same subject was used at Chelsea, *c.* 1755. The German term is *Eichhörnchendekor*. *See* FLIEGENDER HUND.

Flying gallop. A relief ornament of hunting-scenes depicting mounted horsemen. It was a decoration on certain vessels (HU) made in China during the Han dynasty (206 BC–AD 220).

Foliate. Shaped or decorated in a leaf-like pattern.

Foliate cartouche. A cartouche with a foliate border.

Folly pattern. A decorative subject depicting a pyramid and a hermit. It occurs on 18th-century porcelain from English factories, e.g. Longton Hall.

Fond bois. Decoration on plate, Vienna, late 18th century. Victoria and Albert Museum, London.

Fond bois (French). A ground pattern resembling grained wood. In this style of decoration there sometimes appears, apparently pinned to the wood, a representation of an engraving depicting a landscape, often in black, grey, or red. This *trompe l'œil* style was introduced as faience decoration at Niderviller, *c.* 1770, and it is generally associated with that factory, although it was extensively copied elsewhere. The pattern is also known as *décor bois*, *bois simulé*, or *trompe l'œil sur fond bois*. *See* TROMPE L'ŒIL.

Fond écaillé (French). Literally, shell ground. A high-temperature colour introduced at Sèvres in the 1770s as a ground colour. It simulates tortoiseshell. *See* TORTOISESHELL WARE.

Fond Arlequin (French). Same as HARLEQUIN GROUND.

Fond laqué (French). Literally, lacquer ground. A porcelain ground of various colours simulating lacquer.

Fond taillandier (French). A ground pattern of gold dots surrounded by small pale-blue dots, used at Sèvres in the 18th century. *See* ŒIL-DE-PERDRIX.

Fond truité (French). Same as FISH-ROE GROUND.

Food-carrier. Queen's ware, Wedgwood, *c.* 1850. Courtesy, Wedgwood.

Fondporzellan (German). Porcelain decorated with a monochrome ground and panels reserved in white for enamel painting. The technique, imitated from the Chinese, was introduced at Meissen in the 1720s.

Fontainebleau cup. A style of small COFFEE-CUP, goblet-shaped, with a stemmed base, and a handle resembling in shape an inverted figure 5. Introduced at Sèvres, *c.* 1838.

Fontana workshop style. Maiolica decorated in the style of the workshop of Orazio Fontana founded at Urbino, *c.* 1565. The decoration consists of grotesques of a kind derived from Raphael's *loggie* in the Vatican which, in turn, were based on wall-paintings discovered in the ruins of Nero's Golden House, excavated soon after 1500.

Food-carrier. A utensil consisting of several similar shallow, flat-bottomed bowls stacked one above the other so that hot water in the lowest bowl provides heat to keep warm the contents of the upper bowls. Each bowl usually has side-handles. Food-carriers were made of Wedgwood's Queen's ware and in Italian maiolica, but the idea was, no doubt, originally derived from Chinese and Japanese utensils of this kind.

Food-warmer. A type of VEILLEUSE, the upper unit of which is a covered bowl in which the food is warmed over a flame from the GODET housed within the pedestal beneath. The bowl itself is sometimes provided with a liner for hot water, making it a BAIN-MARIE. These are of larger diameter than the type of veilleuse where the upper unit is a teapot. The pedestal usually has two handles (masks, scrolls, or loops) and two hooded vents, or pierced holes, for air circulation. The bowl generally has two lateral handles and a cover. The covers of some early English models have a candle-nozzle instead of a finial, the candle to be lit from the flame of the godet. The earliest examples, of tin-

Food-warmer. Creamware, with sepia transfer-printed decoration, showing bowl, pedestal, liner, cover, and godet. Wedgwood. Harold Newman Collection.

glazed earthenware, date from *c.* 1750, but others, of pottery, stoneware, or porcelain, were made from *c.* 1760 until the middle of the 19th century in almost every European country. Also called a *réchaud*; pap-warmer; *chauffe-nourriture*; *Suppenwärmer*; *scaldavivande*. *See* TEA-WARMER. *See* also ARGYLL; DUTCH STOVE; WARMING URN.

Foot. The part of a vessel on which it stands. The foot itself may rest on a BASE or PLINTH. The term is applied either to the part, usually circular, which broadens out from the stem, or to the bottom part of separate legs. The various forms in the latter category include: BALL FOOT; BUN; CLAW AND BALL; CRAB-STOCK; DENTIL; LION MASK AND PAW; PIED-DE-BICHE; TERRACE; wave-scroll; wedge; dolphin; shell; splayed; branch; paw; skirt; bracket; flared.

Foot-bath. Basin with underglaze blue transfer-printed decoration, Hanley, Staffordshire, *c.* 1800–25; length 20 in. Courtesy, Godden of Worthing Ltd.

Foot-bath. A deep basin, usually with two lateral handles, and varying in length from 10 to 20 inches. Examples made before 1820 had simple vertical sides, but later ones had curving sides; they were made in Yorkshire and Staffordshire. Some were deep, wide receptacles in the form of a boot.

Foot-rim. Same as FOOT-RING or BASAL RIM.

Foot-ring. A slightly projecting ring on the bottom side of a vessel or plate, on which it stands. Certain types of foot-ring are characteristic of some 18th-century porcelain production, and are used to help in identification. The foot-ring serves to raise the body of a piece in the kiln during firing, and sometimes bears only traces of glaze. Sometimes called a foot-rim, a basal rim, or a chime.

Foot-scraper. Persian pottery, mid-17th century; length 5 in. City Museums, Stoke-on-Trent.

Foot-scraper. A small object with a mesh-bottom used for scraping and cleaning the feet; sometimes made to resemble a duck or a wooden shoe, it occurs in Egyptian and Persian pottery. Sometimes called a rasp.

Foot-warmer. A pottery utensil made to rest on the floor, heat being provided by means of charcoal burned in a metal brazier suspended within it. Foot-warmers were made in Flanders and northern France during the latter years of the 18th century and are often baluster-shaped, about 20 inches high, with an aperture to one side, near the bottom, to permit an air-draught. Sometimes termed a 'brasero'.

Foot-warmer. Faience, northern France or Flanders, *c.* 1750; ht 20 in. Museo Duca di Martina, Naples.

Forgery. A close copy of valuable old porcelain, especially figures, made for the purpose of deception and offered for sale at a high price as genuine. Forged pieces often bear the marks of the original factory, but often in the wrong place, and sometimes of the wrong size. Forgers are rarely expert in the history and technique of old porcelain, and frequently the mark is incorrect, as in the case of forged Derby figures bearing the red-anchor mark of Chelsea. Forgeries of figures which have been reproduced from moulds taken from a genuine figure will be about one-sixth smaller than the original, since porcelain shrinks by this amount during firing (*see* SHRINKAGE). Few forgeries are really dangerous to anyone acquainted with genuine examples, but in porcelain the most dangerous are perhaps those of 18th-century Meissen figures, made in Germany during the second half of the 19th century. Nearly all forgeries of 18th-century English SOFT-PASTE PORCELAIN figures have been of Continental manufacture; such forgeries were in practice made of hard-paste porcelain (TRUE PORCELAIN), which makes differentiation comparatively easy. *See* FAKE; REPRODUCTION; REFIRED WARE.

Forget-me-not pattern. A decorative pattern developed at Meissen, *c.* 1740, as a DIAPER of forget-me-not blossoms in a criss-cross of diagonal lines. The German term is *Vergissmeinnichtmuster*.

Forked handle. A handle bifurcated near its top end, the upper 'prong' of the fork being affixed to the rim of a teapot or other vessel, and the lower one curved downwards and affixed to the body. Examples also occur with the handle divided at the lower end.

Fortune Teller. Porcelain group by the Muses Modeller, Bow, *c.* 1752. Victoria and Albert Museum, London.

Form. The shape of an object, as distinguished from the material of which it is made. For instance, geometrical forms (cubical, globular, cylindrical, conical, pyramidal, ovoid, oblate, conoidal); natural forms (pear-, apple-, mushroom-, onion-, gourd-, peach-shaped); architectural forms (ogee, double ogee, baluster); and forms copying a variety of objects (annular, bell-shaped, bullet-shaped, funnel-shaped, helmet-shaped, shell-shaped, tassel-shaped, flammiform, pagoda-shaped, cruciform, barrel-shaped, dumb-bell shaped).

Fortune Teller, The. A decorative subject in the form of a figure group which occurs in Bow porcelain, *c.* 1751, after a Boucher subject entitled *La Bonne Aventure* which depicts a girl standing beside a bearded man who reads her hand. The modelling is by the MUSES MODELLER.

As transfer-printed decoration, fortune telling occurs in two versions taken from HANCOCK ENGRAVINGS: (1) a garden-scene depicting a group of ladies at a table with an old gypsy woman telling their fortune from tea-leaves in a cup; and (2) two ladies standing in a garden, with the fortune teller holding a child on her back and having another child behind her.

Fossil pattern. A zig-zag pattern in imitation of encrinal limestone.

Fountain figure. One of a pair, with attached fountain, mounted in ormolu in Louis XV style; figure decorated in *famille rose* palette, ht 10½ in. Reign of Ch'ien Lung (1736–95). Courtesy, Frank Partridge & Sons Ltd.

Fostat ware. Egyptian pottery made during the Fatimid dynasty (969–1171) at Fostat (Old Cairo), where a great quantity of WASTERS have been found among the rubbish heaps. Among the types thus recovered the most characteristic are bowls with deep sides and a high base, and having a thick and heavy body, some lustre ware, *sgraffito* ware, and pieces with a dark-brown, highly fired glaze. Many specimens bear signatures on the bottom.

Fountain. A type of CISTERN made to be hung on a wall, with a hole near the bottom to take a spigot. It was usually made with a matching basin, and sometimes a matching ewer. Sometimes called a wall-fountain. *See* CISTERN.

Fountain figures. A pair of cylindrical water receptacles, each having a metal spigot, mounted on an ormolu base behind a figure of a Chinese boy. They were made of porcelain in China.

Four Ages of Man, The. A set of four engravings emblematic of the Four Ages of Man (infancy, youth, maturity, old age) from designs by L.P. Boitard and used as transfer-printed decoration in England, especially at Worcester.

Four-character mark. A mark on the bottom of Chinese porcelain comprising four ideograms which include the name of the emperor and the NIEN HAO. *See* CHARACTER MARK.

Four Continents, The. A group of four allegorical figures, occurring either singly or on a common base, representing the historical four continents – Europe, Asia, Africa and America.

Four Continents. Figures by J. F. Eberlein, on gilt-bronze bases, Meissen, *c.* 1740: Europe, Asia, America, Africa. Wadsworth Atheneum, Hartford, Conn.

(Later groups including Australia are called the Five Continents.) Groups of this kind were made in porcelain at many 18th-century factories, notably at Derby in England and at Meissen and Nymphenburg in Germany.

Four Elements, The. A group of allegorical figures (sometimes two figures on one base) representing the four elements of antiquity – earth, air, fire, and water. Porcelain versions were popular in the 18th century in Germany, England, and elsewhere. A group made in biscuit porcelain at Sèvres depicts contemporary persons in this guise. Chelsea, Bow, and Derby made groups with each figure accompanied by its attribute.

The subject was also used as transfer-printed decoration on Bow and Worcester porcelain from a HANCOCK ENGRAVING based on an engraving by P. Aveline after a painting by François Boucher.

Four Monarchs, The. A group of four figures modelled at Meissen by J. J. Kändler, *c.* 1770, representing Alexander the Great, Nimrud of Assyria, Cyrus the Great of Persia, and Julius Caesar. Other versions have been made elsewhere.

Four Quadrants, The. Symbols on Chinese porcelain representing the cardinal points of the compass: the White Tiger or *hu*, west; the Dragon, east; the Phoenix or *fêng-huang*, south; and the Tortoise, north.

Four Elements. Porcelain group, Bristol (Champion's factory), *c.* 1772. Courtesy, Delomosne Ltd.

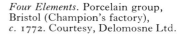

Four Seasons. Porcelain group by F.E. Meyer, Meissen, *c.* 1746–61. Courtesy, Sotheby's.

Four Seasons, The. A group of allegorical figures clothed in ancient or contemporary costume, representing the seasons, each with an identifiable attribute – flowers (Spring), sheaves of corn (Summer), grapes (Autumn), and furs or a brazier (Winter). The subject was popular throughout the 18th century in porcelain. A noted set made at Meissen by J.J. Kändler and J.F. Eberlein was much copied; another Meissen set was made by Friedrich Elias Meyer, 1746–61.

A decorative transfer-printed design on English porcelain, from a HANCOCK ENGRAVING after Boitard, has the same motif. In the case of Chinese porcelain, the seasons are symbolized by flowers, and also by the symbolic animals of the FOUR QUADRANTS: the Dragon (Spring), the Phoenix (Summer), the Tiger (Autumn), and the Tortoise (Winter).

Four Supernatural Creatures, The. *See* SSŬ LING.

Fox-head. A STIRRUP-CUP made in the form of a fox's head. Popular at the end of the 18th century, the type has since been reproduced. *See* RHYTON.

Fragonard cup. A style of small coffee-cup, drum-shaped, with a slightly flaring base and rim, and a tall, curved handle rising above the rim. Introduced at Sèvres, *c.* 1818.

François vase. Greek krater with black-figure decoration, *c.* 570 BC. Archaeological Museum, Florence.

François vase. A Greek KRATER, made *c.* 570 BC, and named after its finder André François (1814–83), a French engraver; it is now in the Archaeological Museum, Florence. It is of the type called VASO A ROTELLE, and is the earliest important example of a vase in the BLACK-FIGURE STYLE, richly decorated with five encircling friezes of mythological subjects.

French chalk. *See* SOAPROCK.

Fret. A decorative border pattern in continuous repetitive form made by short lines of equal length meeting at 90 degrees, or (less often) at a slightly larger or smaller angle. Fret patterns are sometimes incised or in relief. *See* KEY FRET; GREEK FRET; JAPANESE FRET; CLOUD AND THUNDER FRET; MEANDER

BORDER; MEANDER AND STAR BORDER; MEANDER AND SWASTIKA BORDER.

Frill vase. A vase originally designed by J. F. Eberlein at Meissen, *c.* 1748, which was extremely popular with English porcelain factories of ten years or so later, the Bow version being perhaps the most frequent survival. The vase is characterized by a leafy 'frill' about one-third of the way up from the bottom. That it was a POT-POURRI vase is proved by the piercings on the shoulder.

Frit. The vitrifiable, glassy material that is mixed with clay in making ARTIFICIAL PORCELAIN. The substances used to make the frit were first fused (or fritted) together, then ground to powder and mixed with clay to form a body ready to be used in manufacturing operations.

Frit porcelain. A term which is sometimes used in England to describe ARTIFICIAL PORCELAIN or PÂTE TENDRE.

Frog mug. A drinking mug of Sunderland or Staffordshire pottery with a naturalistically modelled and painted frog in the interior which is revealed to the drinker as he finishes his drink; also called a 'toad mug' and 'surprise mug'.

Frog service. A 952-piece DINNER-SERVICE made in 1773–4 by Josiah Wedgwood and Thomas Bentley for Catherine the Great of Russia. The service, the most important ever made in cream-ware (QUEEN'S WARE), owes its name to the fact that it was made for use at the Palace of Chesme – called La Grenouillère because it was built on a site known as the 'frog marsh', south of St Petersburg, on the road to Tsarskoye-Selo – and for this reason each piece bears a crest depicting a green frog. It is sometimes called the Green Frog Service or the Imperial Russian Service; 810 pieces are in the Hermitage, Leningrad. The decoration in purple, by seven individual hands, featured 1,244 different English views. Pieces from another service, similarly decorated but without the frog, are in several collections.

Fröhlich. A figure modelled by J. J. Kändler at Meissen in 1736, representing Joseph Fröhlich, a rich builder from the Salz-kammergut who went as *Hofnarr* (court jester) to the Court of Augustus the Strong of Saxony in 1728, after having served at the Bayreuth Court. He was modelled as a bust and as a figure. The figure, sometimes also referred to as *Hofnarr*, represents Fröhlich standing with his hands tucked into his red braces, and wearing a high conical hat, baggy breeches, and black boots. *See* FRÖHLICH AND SCHMIEDEL.

Fröhlich and Schmiedel. A porcelain group with figures of FRÖHLICH and the postmaster Schmiedel. It was made by J. J. Kändler at Meissen, *c.* 1741.

Fromager (French). A cheese-maker or cheese-mould. A sort of porcelain strainer standing on three feet, and resting on a stand.

Fruttiera (Italian). A plate of Italian maiolica used to present confections to young ladies attending fêtes and balls. The centre was painted with Cupid in various attitudes. *See* AMATORI.

Fu (Chinese). A decorative symbol in the form of a bat, signifying happiness, used on Chinese porcelain. Similar to the Japanese KOMORI. In Chinese, the word *fu* is a homonym signifying both happiness and a bat, and a decoration of five bats is regarded as especially auspicious. *See* SHOU; FU SHOU; FIVE BLESSINGS.

Frill vase. Worcester porcelain, *c.* 1768, based on the original design by J. F. Eberlein.

Fröhlich. Figure modelled by J. J. Kändler, Meissen. Courtesy, Christie's.

Fuddling-cup. Lambeth delftware, 1633; ht 3½ in. Burnap Collection, William Rockhill Nelson Gallery of Art, Kansas City, Mo.

Furniture. Console, maiolica, Nove (Bassano); ht 2 ft 6 in. Victoria and Albert Museum, London.

Fu shou (Chinese). Characters or ideograms representing FU (the bat) and SHOU (longevity) used on Chinese porcelain. The combination of the two characters represents a wish for long life and happiness.

Fuddling-cup. A group of from three to six small cups joined laterally, and connected internally, so that a person drinking from any one could drain them all. They were made in the 17th and 18th centuries in England, Holland, and Germany. The German term is *Drillingsbecher*.

Fukien ware. BLANC DE CHINE porcelain made at Tê Hua (Fukien province).

Fulham stoneware. A type of English BROWN STONEWARE decorated with stamped ornament, made at Fulham from 1671 by John Dwight and later by others. The body is coarse and glazed with salt, the glaze being brown on the upper part and drab below; survivals are principally mugs and tankards. Production continued until the 19th century when Dwight's original factory was sold to Doulton's. *See* LAMBETH STONEWARE.

Funeral urn. A large pottery vessel made for containing the human corpse after death; a kind of coffin. They were made from ancient times, especially in Corsica and Mesopotamia.

Funerary urn. *See* CINERARY URN.

Funnel-mouth. A mouth (of a receptacle) shaped like a funnel. *See* TRICHTENBECHER; SPITTOON.

Furniture. (1) Miniature furniture in pottery or porcelain, either by itself or as part of a figure group. (2) Actual furniture of pottery or porcelain, such as side-tables, as found decorating a PORCELAIN ROOM. Examples are very rare, but there is a small console table of faience made *c.* 1740–50 at Nove (Bassano), Italy, which is now in the Victoria and Albert Museum, London, and one of Meissen porcelain in the Musée des Arts Décoratifs, Paris. A *chaise percée* of Rouen faience is in the Musée National de Céramique, Sèvres.

Furniture ornaments. Decorative accessories on cabinets and other furniture, such as plaques, knobs, key escutcheons, handles, etc. They were made of porcelain at Sèvres and elsewhere, and in jasper by Wedgwood. The use of painted porcelain PLAQUES for ornamenting furniture was introduced in France early in the 1760s, probably as a result of a suggestion by the dealer, Poirier, and, framed in GILT-BRONZE, superbly painted examples from Sèvres decorated furniture made for Mme du Barry and Marie-Antoinette. *See* DOOR-FURNITURE.

Furniture support. A small ceramic stand used to raise the leg of a piece of furniture from the floor, often decorated with a mask. They usually occur in sets of four. Sometimes called an elevator.

Fury group. A porcelain group depicting a man flanked by two scolding women; made at Derby.

Furniture support. English yellow-glazed earthenware, decorated with a relief bust, early 19th century; ht 4¼ in. Leon Collection, Smithsonian Institution, Washington, D.C.

G.R. Jug. A type of COMMEMORATIVE JUG made of saltglazed stoneware, globular in shape, with a relief medallion bearing the initials G.R., referring to George I, or George II, or perhaps George III of England. They were made at Grenzhausen, Germany, of WESTERWALD WARE for export to England. *See* A.R. JUG; C.R. JUG; W.R. JUG.

Gabri ware. A term applied to certain SGRAFFITO ware with a red or buff body covered with white slip and a yellowish lead glaze, made in Persia in the 8th century. Similar ware was made in the 13th century and thereafter in Egypt and elsewhere around the eastern Mediterranean littoral. The name derives from a presumed connection with the Gabri, a pre-Islamic 7th-century sect of Persian fire-worshippers, but this is probably incorrect. *See* PERSIAN POTTERY.

Gadroon. An ornamental border in a continuous pattern of short, repetitive section of REEDING set vertically, diagonally, or twisted. It has the same appearance as a round encircling moulding with continuous regular notching. It was originally inspired by contemporary silverware of the 18th century. The French term is *godron. See* FALSE GADROON.

Gadroon. Vase with gadrooned ornament around the rim and above the stem, Worcester, *c.* 1810.

Gaki ware. Japanese pottery made in the 9th century, the wares being unglazed but with the surfaces smoked to become black and then polished.

Galanteriewaren (German). Various small trinkets given in the 18th century by gentlemen to ladies. They were intended to be carried in the pocket or hand-bag, or displayed in a cabinet. Included are ÉTUIS, BONBONNIÈRES, SNUFF-BOXES, PATCH-BOXES, SCENT-BOTTLES, and *carnets de bal.* Produced by most of the porcelain factories, especially fine examples were made at Meissen and Nymphenburg. *See* TOYS.

Galena. Sulphide of lead which, when dusted on to unfired slipware and subsequently fired in a kiln at a low temperature, forms a vitreous glaze on the surface. Due to impurities in the lead (usually iron) the resultant glaze is a rich yellow, and gives this colour to the underlying slip.

Galleried rim. Veilleuse pedestal with pierced decoration, Sassuolo, Italy, *c.* 1840; ht 7 in. Harold Newman Collection.

Galleried rim. The rim (of a bowl or other receptacle) which extends horizontally outwards for about an inch and vertically upwards by the same amount, the rim thus being greater in diameter than the body of the vessel. It is found on Chinese porcelain and occasionally on European copies and derivations.

Galley tile. A TILE of glazed or ornamented earthenware. *See* AZULEJO.

Gallipot. A term of uncertain origin and having a variety of meanings, first used in the 15th century. At one time it was thought to refer to ceramic ware brought to Europe from the Far East in galleys (*see* CARRACK PORCELAIN), but later it seems to have been used to refer to ware that 'glittered', presumably tin-glazed earthenware, and in particular small containers, basically cylindrical, for unguents and other substances, such as jams, conserves, and sweetmeats. In the later decades of the

19th century common cylindrical stoneware jam-pots were often termed gallipots. The term 'galleyware' was also used in earlier times.

Game-pie dish. A covered bowl, oval or circular, modelled and coloured to resemble pastry-crust, sometimes with relief floral decoration around the bowl and on the flat cover. They were made by Wedgwood of CANE-WARE. *See* PIECRUST WARE.

Game terrine. A covered bowl, naturalistically modelled and coloured, for making and serving *pâté*. A frequent type was in the form of a duck.

Gaming set. Variously shaped and decorated porcelain counters for gaming, with accompanying porcelain BOXES and sometimes a leather carrying-case.

Garden seat. A backless stool, cylindrical or polygonal, about 14 to 16 inches high. Made of Chinese stoneware or porcelain from the Ming dynasty onwards, specimens are decorated in underglaze blue, or in enamels.

Gaming set. Porcelain counters and boxes, Meissen, *c.* 1735–45, with contemporary leather case. Courtesy, Christie's.

Garden seat. Chinese export porcelain with enamel decoration. Reign of Tao Kuang (1821–50). Courtesy, David Newbon Ltd, London.

Gardner figures. Porcelain figures depicting Russian peasants in traditional attire, made at Moscow at the factory of Francis Gardner, an Englishman who went to Russia in 1767. The figures, which are of excellent quality, are painted in a Slavic palette; some examples are glazed, some mat, and some partially glazed.

Gargoyle spout. A type of spout with a modelled gargoyle at the mouth.

Garlic-mouth. A narrow neck, as on a bottle, which swells out near the mouth into a globular form; found on Chinese porcelain bottles, Persian pottery, and European imitations.

Garniture de cheminée (French). A set of porcelain vases to decorate the mantelshelf of the chimney-piece. The number varied, three, five, or seven, but earlier *garnitures* usually comprised five – a central covered vase, two smaller vases of the same kind, usually of BALUSTER shape, and two slender cylindrical or concave-sided, beaker-shaped vases which alternated with them; they were decorated *en suite.* At first made in China in porcelain for the European market towards the end of the 17th century, they were repeated in Holland in blue-and-white delftware, and in porcelain at a number of European factories. Many small vases of the period now found singly originally belonged to a *garniture* of this kind. A *garniture* was sometimes, as at Chelsea, made in the form of three figure groups. The fashion began to decline *c.* 1735. *See* GARNITURE DE TABLE.

Garniture de table (French). A set of porcelain vases made for a side-table in a reception-hall (anteroom) or salon. They are smaller than a GARNITURE DE CHEMINÉE.

Garniture de toilette (French). A set of porcelain objects for a lady's dressing-table, including scent-bottles, powder-boxes, jewel-boxes, and ring-stands. *See* BOX.

Gaudy ware. Earthenware of the 19th century gaudily painted with stylized flower-patterns. It was made in the west of England for the cheapest market and is sometimes called 'Gaudy Welsh'.

Gazebo, The. A decorative subject on Worcester porcelain depicting a gazebo (a summer-house with a view) on an island in a lake, with a man standing on a promontory and another in a boat.

Gen Shonsui. The Japanese term for the earliest type of Chinese SHONSUI ware, the precursor of HON SHONSUI from which it is not always easily distinguished. It is also called *Ko Shonsui* (old Shonsui).

Geometric style. A decorative style of Greek pottery which follows that of the Mycenaean period. It belongs to the period *c.* 900–700 BC. The ornament is characterized by simple geometric designs, such as narrow horizontal bands, by rows of repeated figures and designs, and especially by the MEANDER. Stylized animals and human figures occur on later examples. The decoration was applied in black on a buff ware. *See* PROTO-GEOMETRIC STYLE; DIPYLON STYLE; MYCENAEAN POTTERY; SUB-MYCENAEAN POTTERY.

Geschirr (German). Useful ware, including table-services, e.g. the *Schwanengeschirr* (SWAN SERVICE).

Ghori ware. The name given in India to Chinese CELADON, the term being derived from Afghanistan, the seat of the Ghori kings, which was on that branch of the caravan route to the West which turned southwards to India.

Gibson spoon. A patented type of spoon with a hollow handle; the bowl is covered except at its extremity, which is open for administering medicine. It was usually made of metal, but rare examples are of ceramic ware. *See* PAP-SPOON; MEDICAL SPOON.

Gilder's mark. A mark identifying the decorator who applied the gilding to porcelain, especially to be found on 18th-century Sèvres porcelain.

Gilding. The application of gold to the decoration of porcelain and, to a much lesser extent, fine earthenware. In China, prior to *c.* 1780, gold was applied to porcelain in the form of gold-leaf (which has since largely rubbed off); later, and also in Europe from about the same date, gilding was applied with a brush and took the form of a mercury AMALGAM. In Europe before 1755 gilding was usually applied in the form of gold-leaf secured by means of oil or size, and most has since worn off. Gilding on porcelain in England was employed at Chelsea from *c.* 1756 in the form of HONEY-GOLD; MERCURIC GILDING, popularized at Derby, was lavishly employed at several factories. Gilding in slight relief, often TOOLED with ornamental motifs, was introduced at Sèvres in the 1750s. *See* SIZE-GILDING; LACQUER GILDING; TRANSFER GILDING; ACID GILDING; RAISED GILDING.

Gilt-bronze. Bronze mercurically gilded, employed in France as a mount for porcelain, especially during the currency of the rococo style. The most spectacular examples of mounting in gilt-bronze came from France in the middle of the 18th century, in conjunction with Chinese porcelain and that of Meissen, Vincennes, and Sèvres. It is often loosely called ORMOLU.

Gilt silhouette. Decoration in gold of CHINOISERIES, exotic birds (FANTASIE VÖGEL), etc. as SILHOUETTES. The fashion appeared first at Meissen, perhaps the work of the Augsburg HAUSMALER Johann Aufenwerth, *c.* 1720, when *chinoiseries* were executed in this form. Some faking of this type on porcelain of the period has been noted as coming from Berlin in recent years. Exotic birds in gilt silhouette occur on Vincennes and

Gardner figure. The Milkmaid, porcelain partially glazed, Moscow, *c.* 1780–1830. Courtesy, Wartski Ltd, London.

Gilt silhouette. Sugar-bowl decorated with exotic birds, Vincennes, 1753. Wallace Collection, London.

Sèvres porcelain by Vieillard and others from about 1752 onwards. Examples of both kinds of decoration occur from other factories. *See* GOLDCHINESEN.

Gimmel flask. Two flasks, the bodies of which are joined, and each having a separate spout. Such twin flasks are said to have been used by lovers who plighted their troth by drinking simultaneously from the two spouts. They were made of English stoneware by Doulton and other Lambeth potteries, *c.* 1790–1820. *See* DOUBLE BOTTLE.

Gin bottle. A type of saltglazed brown stoneware bottle, variously shaped and decorated with moulded relief figures (sometimes those appearing on REFORM WARE) and with the name of the tavern for which it was made. Such bottles were made principally at Lambeth, *c.* 1840. *See* FLASK.

Ginger-jar. A globular jar, usually an oblate spheroid with flattened shoulder, having a DOME COVER or CAP COVER fitting over an upright collar. Used for containing preserved ginger, such jars were popular during the reign of K'ang Hsi (1662–1722), decorated with white prunus blossoms on a CRACKED-ICE GROUND which is sometimes described as 'pulsating'. This type of ginger-jar is sometimes termed PRUNUS VASE or HAWTHORN VASE, these terms being misnomers.

Girandole (French). (1) A usually ornamental branched candelabrum or TABLE-LUSTRE; one with pendent drops of glass or rock-crystal. (2) A porcelain candle-sconce, or a small mirror with a porcelain frame and candleholders attached. The term is used very loosely for objects of this nature.

Girl-in-a-swing ware. (Above) Original group, *c.* 1750, from which the name is derived. Victoria and Albert Museum, London. (Below) Figure, probably based on a Vincennes model, *c.* 1750–52. Dudley Delevigne Collection, London.

Girder. A thin slab of earthenware or fired clay placed vertically in a kiln as a prop to support TILES, RAFTERS, or other flat pieces during firing; it is sometimes called a 'slugg'. *See* KILN FURNITURE.

Giretto (Italian). The foot-ring on a BACILE.

Girl-in-a-swing ware. The term refers to a number of early English porcelain figures, groups of figures, and scent-bottles made *c.* 1749–58, and is derived from the first such figure to be identified, a girl in a swing, represented in the Victoria and Albert Museum, London, and the Museum of Fine Arts, Boston, Mass. The body is greyish in colour, and the modelling is sharp and well defined. The source is now believed to be a seceding Chelsea factory, probably under the direction of the former proprietor of the original Lawrence Street factory, Charles Gouyn, and established *c.* 1749 with the aid of some Staffordshire potters. The body is characterized by a very high content (about 17 per cent) of lead oxide.

Gläserwärmer (German). Literally, glass-warmer. A version of the MONTEITH which could be used equally well for warming or cooling glasses.

Glasgow delftware. Delftware made in Glasgow, *c.* 1748–1810. Very few examples now survive. Some depict flowers with whiplash tendrils which are characteristic. *See* ENGLISH DELFTWARE.

Glaze. Chinese and European TRUE PORCELAIN apart, a glaze is a coating of glass applied to a porous body to seal it against the penetration of liquids, and to porcelain and stoneware to give a smooth and brilliant surface. True porcelain has a

FELDSPATHIC GLAZE, which is the product of covering the surface with powdered feldspathic rock and then firing it at a high enough temperature (about 1450°C.) to fuse it into natural glass. The glassy glazes are made by heating the ingredients of glass together until they form an amorphous mass (FRIT), which is then ground to a fine powder. The powder is dusted on to the surface of the ware, or applied by dipping the object into a suspension of the powder in water, and this is followed by GLOST FIRING, i.e. at a lower temperature than that needed to fire the ware to BISCUIT; this melts the powder and allows it to spread over the surface in liquid form. No preliminary biscuit firing is needed with a feldspathic glaze, which is fired in one operation with the body, or sometimes after a very light biscuit firing. As a result, glazes on ARTIFICIAL PORCELAIN are inclined to be thick and soft, easily scratched, and have a tendency for enamel colours to sink into them due to partial remelting in the enamelling kiln. The latter is especially true of early Sèvres porcelain. In the case of the thin, hard, brilliant feldspathic glazes, which are actually incorporated into the surface of the body, the enamels usually appear in slight relief, palpable to the finger-tips. Glazes fall into five main categories: FELDSPATHIC GLAZES; siliceous glazes (akin to soda-glass) which have not generally been used in modern times; LEAD GLAZES; TIN GLAZES, made opaque with tin oxide; and salt glazes, the product of the addition of common salt to the kiln-furnace. *See* OVERGLAZE; UNDERGLAZE; COLOURED GLAZE; CLAIR DE LUNE; COPERTA; DYSART; FLAMBÉ; GALENA; IRON RUST; PEACH-BLOOM; PENNINE; POTATO SOUP; RAVENSTONE; ROBIN'S-EGG; SANG-DE-BŒUF; SMALTINO; SMEAR; SOUFFLÉ; TEA-DUST; TEMMOKU; TIGER'S-EYE; tortoiseshell (FOND ÉCAILLÉ); TREACLE GLAZE.

Duke of Gloucester service. Plate from the service decorated in the workshop of James Giles, Worcester (First period). Courtesy, Sotheby's.

Glazing. The process of applying GLAZE to the BODY, by dipping or spraying, after which it is fixed in the GLOST FIRING. The composition of the glaze must be adjusted to the SHRINKAGE rate of the body, otherwise the glaze will craze or become detached. *See* CRACKLE; CRAZING.

Glost firing. A second firing of ceramic ware for the purpose of fusing the glaze which is applied after the BISCUIT firing. The requisite temperatures are usually about 1100°C. for porcelain and 1050°C. for earthenware, but these temperatures can be modified by the addition of a FLUX to assist fusion. Decoration applied overglaze (ENAMEL FIRING) is fused at a slightly lower temperature which is just sufficient to remelt the surface of the glaze.

Gloucester, Duke of, service. A porcelain dinner-service made at Worcester, supposedly for William Henry, Duke of Gloucester (1743–1805). It was decorated in the London workshop of James Giles with assorted fruits in the well, and with butterflies and insects in panels along the border, edged with green and with gilt feathering. *See* INDEPENDENT DECORATOR.

Goat and bee jug. Porcelain, painted with coloured enamels, Chelsea, *c.* 1745–49. Victoria and Albert Museum, London.

Goat and bee jug. A moulded jug decorated with two recumbent goats, and a small bee applied to a branch just below the pouring lip. The rustic handle is embellished with leaves, and the whole with applied flowers. The design is said to be based on a rococo silver prototype which no longer exists, although forgeries in silver were made late in the 19th century for the purpose of supplying one. Goat and bee jugs were among the earliest productions of the Chelsea factory, and some bear the incised date 1745, as well as the mark of an incised triangle, used from 1745 (or slightly earlier) till 1749. The BODY is very glassy, and is characterized by the appearance of numerous luminous points, termed PINHOLES. Forgeries of these jugs are not uncommon, and are thought to have been made at Coalport, *c.* 1830–40. This, however, seems unlikely, since the collecting of 18th-century porcelain was not then well established. The question must remain open. Goat and bee jugs are frequently white, but some specimens have been enamelled, wholly or partially, either at the factory or at one of the enamelling shops of the time. Some examples omit the bee, and the horns of the goat may be long or short. One or two very rare specimens in SALTGLAZED WARE have been recorded.

Goat. Porcelain figure, ht 2 ft, modelled by J. J. Kändler, Meissen, 1732. Victoria and Albert Museum, London.

Goats. Figures of goats more or less realistically modelled and painted. A large recumbent figure was made *c.* 1732 by J. J. Kändler at Meissen for the Japanische Palais, Dresden, another of the same model being in the Victoria and Albert Museum, London. Small figure groups including goats were also modelled by Kändler, e.g. COUNT BRÜHL'S TAILOR AND WIFE and the Cavalier. An earthenware goat was made by Ralph Wood.

Goblet. A drinking vessel with a FOOT and STEM made to contain more than 4 fluid ounces. This is the standard definition for a glass goblet, but the term is sometimes used loosely in describing pottery and porcelain examples. *See* TAZZA; STEM-CUP.

Godet (French). A small, cup-like ceramic utensil for supplying low heat below a pot by means of a wick floating in oil in the cup. The *godet* is also (but rarely) made with a cover which has a central hole or chimney for a wick, and sometimes another hole to allow the circulation of air. They are used with VEILLEUSES, URNS, and occasionally with KETTLES on a stand. They are usually circular or oval, of ordinary ware, but sometimes they are of the same body as the main piece, and are modelled and decorated *en suite*.

Godron. The French term for GADROON.

Goglet. Variant spellings: gugglet, guglet, and gurglet. (1) A long-necked water-vessel of porous earthenware for cooling water by evaporation. (2) A bottle, of porcelain or glazed earthenware, having a bulbous body, a long narrow neck with a convex ring below the mouth; some examples were made for use with a basin on a wash-stand.

Godet. Food-warmer with godet, English delftware, *c.* 1750–55. Colonial Williamsburg Collection, Williamsburg, Va.

Gold lustre ware. Pottery decorated with LUSTRE derived from gold. When applied by the English method of firing metallic salts the gold gave varying colours. On a brown ground the colour ranged from a coppery tone to golden yellow. On a white, cream, or buff ground it ranged from pale pink to ruby or purple, depending on the thickness of the coating and the firing temperature. The same pigment on REDWARE yielded a copper colour. Although it had been used experimentally before 1800–05, gold lustre was not commercially produced in England before this date. *See* GOLD RESIST; PURPLE LUSTRE; PURPLE RESIST; ROSE LUSTRE; ROSE RESIST; MOONLIGHT LUSTRE.

Gold resist. A type of RESIST WARE made of GOLD LUSTRE, ranging in colour from pink to purple.

Goldchinesen (German). Literally, gold Chinese. A style of CHINOISERIE decoration with figures in CISELÉ gold silhouette. It was initiated at Meissen, *c.* 1720, and developed by the HAUSMALER, Johann Aufenwerth and Bartholomäus Seuter, at Augsburg on pieces sent to them from Meissen for decoration, or bought by them. The porcelain itself belongs to the end of the Böttger period. Recently genuine early Meissen white porcelain has been decorated with gold *chinoiseries* in Berlin, and such examples are fakes. *See* GILT SILHOUETTE.

Golden pottery. HISPANO-MORESQUE WARE decorated with silver oxide which fired to a golden colour; similar ware was later made in Italy at Deruta.

Golfer and caddy pattern. A decorative subject depicting a moustached Chinese striding ahead of a small boy carrying what seems to be a golf-bag in a landscape of shrubs and flowering trees. It occurs on English blue-and-white porcelain.

Gombroon ware. Persian pottery bowl with rice-grain piercing, 17th century. Victoria and Albert Museum, London.

Gombroon ware. Persian pottery made in imitation of Chinese porcelain during the 17th and 18th centuries, and so called because it was shipped from the Persian seaport of Gombroon (now Bandar Abbas). Bowls of this ware are pierced, the openings filled with transparent glaze. The body of some Persian wares of this kind has been mixed with the glaze material, so that specimens are slightly translucent, making it, in fact, a primitive kind of ARTIFICIAL PORCELAIN. Sometimes incorrectly called 'Gombron ware'. *See* RICE-GRAIN PIERCING; PLIQUE-À-JOUR.

Gomm, Ann, plate. A plate made of English delftware, and so called by Professor F.H. Garner from the name appearing in the centre, accompanied by the date 1793. The pattern includes an octagonal design within which is the name and date. There is a border pattern of floral sprays.

Ann Gomm plate. English delftware, 1793. City Museums, Stoke-on-Trent.

Gorgelet. A term used in the 17th century by Dutch importers of a type of porcelain drinking-vessel made in Japan for the Near East and sometimes adapted as a HOOKAH or *narghile*. Similar vessels were also made in China.

Gothic foliage. A decorative motif on Italian maiolica made in the second half of the 15th century, mainly at Faenza. It depicts a broad leaf powerfully curved into a VOLUTE. The pigments were usually dark blue, manganese purple, and orange, laid in bands of varying intensity parallel to the midrib of the leaf.

Gothic style. The form and decoration related to ornament used during the currency of the Gothic style in architecture from the 12th century until a variable date, depending on the country under consideration. It lingered in England, for instance, far longer than in Italy, where it was never widely adopted. It was superseded by the CLASSICAL STYLE of the Renaissance. The Gothic style was revived in England in the middle of the 18th century by Horace Walpole and others, but it made small impact on ceramic design at this time. It was again revived in the 1820s (called 'revived Gothic') when its influence on the porcelain design of the time is somewhat more perceptible, but, in general, it affected furniture and metalwork to a far greater extent.

Gotzkowsky erhabene Blumen. Plate with relief moulding and painted panels, Chelsea (red anchor period). Courtesy, Sotheby's.

Gotzkowsky erhabene Blumen (German). A relief decoration for borders designed by J.F. Eberlein at Meissen, *c.* 1744, developed from a moulded pattern first used in 1741. It has four narrow panels decorated with painted birds, butterflies, a fox, and DEUTSCHE BLUMEN, alternating with four wide panels decorated with uncoloured floral moulding, the moulded flowers also appearing in the well of the plate. The design was named after Johann Ernst Gotzkowsky, a Prussian financier, art-collector, and later (for two years or so) owner of the Berlin Porcelain Manufactory, who bought porcelain from Meissen. The design was copied at Berlin, and there called the *Floramuster* (flower-pattern). It occurs on Chelsea porcelain of the red-anchor period, and on porcelain from elsewhere.

Grace-cup. A type of LOVING-CUP used after the saying of grace at the end of a meal, being passed round among the diners. The custom was started in the 11th century in Scotland by Margaret Atheling, the consort of Malcolm Canmore, to induce her guests to remain at table until grace had been said.

Grace plates. A set of six plates of English delftware each having a different inscription which, together, made up a doggerel verse. *See* MERRY MAN PLATES; SERVANT PLATES.

Graffiato (Italian). Also *graffito*. *See* SGRAFFITO.

Granary jar. An object of Chinese tomb-ware of the Han dynasty (206 BC–AD 220) in the form of an almost cylindrical vessel, tapering towards the bottom, on four feet, and with a cover having a central hole. A model of a grain silo, it was placed in the tomb with models of farm-houses, animals, etc., to provide for the spirit of the deceased.

Grand feu (French). The high-temperature kiln used for firing the body and glaze of porcelain, or tin-enamel ware decorated with high-temperature colours. The temperature ranges from about 1100 to 1450°C.

Grand plat ménage. Creamware, ht 25 in., Leeds, *c*. 1780. Donald C. Towner Collection, London.

Grand plat ménage (French). An ÉPERGNE. The term is sometimes applied to those made of Leeds creamware (designated in *Leeds Pattern Books* 'Grand Platt Ménage'). Those in less ornate form are termed merely *plat ménage*. *See* SURTOUT DE TABLE.

Granite ware. A kind of STONE CHINA with a speckled appearance in imitation of granite. It was made by Wedgwood, and classified among the VARIEGATED WARES.

Grasswork. Decoration in imitation of grass, usually found on the base of a figure.

Grave-slabs. Earthenware slabs employed as a substitute for more conventional grave memorials in 17th- and 18th-century England.

Grease-spot pattern. A decorative pattern of patches of GILDING on a coloured ground. The term grease spot is sometimes employed to refer to MOONS in early porcelain.

Greek curve border. A curvilinear variant of the KEY-FRET border.

Greek fret border. A type of FRET border in which the lines, vertical and horizontal, are all at right angles. A MEANDER BORDER.

Greek vases. Jugs, jars, bowls, cups, and other utensils (the Latin *vasa* broadly meaning utensil) made of pottery in ancient Greece; some were copied from metal vessels, and vice versa. There are various basic forms having accepted names, but these forms are known with many variations. The following categories are based on the intended purpose of the various types: (1) vessels for holding and storing water, oil, or wine – AMPHORA, DIOTA, LEKANE, PELIKE, PITHOS, STAMNOS; (2) vessels for carrying water – HYDRIA, KALPIS; (3) vessels for mixing wine and water – DEINOS, KELEBE, KRATER, KALATHOS, LEBES, NESTORIS; (4) vessels for pouring wine – LAGYNOS, OENOCHOË, OLPE, PROCHOÖS; (5) drinking vessels – HOLCION, KANTHAROS, KARCHESION, KOTYLE, KYLIX, LAKAINA, MASTOS, RHYTON,

SKYPHOS; (6) vessels for oil, ointment, or perfume – ALABASTRON, ARYBALLOS, BOMBYLIOS, LEKYTHOS. Less easily categorized are: ASKOS, KYATHOS, LEBES GAMYKOS, LEKANIS, LOUTROPHOROS, PHIALE, PSYKTER, PYXIS. *See also* BLACK-FIGURE STYLE; RED-FIGURE STYLE.

Greek wave pattern. Same as the VITRUVIAN SCROLL.

Green. A colour used in decorating pottery and porcelain produced by oxides of copper and sometimes protoxide of chrome; CELADON green is a product of iron oxide. Green glazes are very common on earthenware, and green enamels of a number of shades are used both as a ground colour and an enamel in the decoration of porcelain. *See* APPLE GREEN (*vert jaune*; *vert pomme*); CAMELLIA GREEN; COPPER GREEN; CHROME GREEN; MALACHITE; MEADOW GREEN (*vert pré*; *vert anglais*); SARDINIAN GREEN; CUCUMBER GREEN GLAZE.

Green glazed ware. Earthenware vessels completely covered with green glaze and sometimes ornamented with gilded applied decoration. They were made in the form of teapots, *c.* 1760, by Wedgwood and others. Similar green glaze was used in the 19th century by Wedgwood for leaf-moulded dessert-services.

Green glazed ware. Earthenware teapot with gilded applied decoration, Wedgwood, *c.* 1760. Victoria and Albert Museum, London.

Green Kutani (Japanese). The same as AO KUTANI.

Green ware. Potter's term for unfired pottery.

Grès A French term for stoneware, shortened from *grès cérame*. It is usually applied to RHENISH STONEWARE in the misnomer of *grès de Flandres*. English creamware is sometimes called *grès anglais* or *grès d'Angleterre*, but such ware is more correctly designated *faïence fine d'Angleterre*.

Grès d'Angleterre (French). A term used at Tournai to describe English CREAMWARE.

Grès de Beauvais (French). A partially vitrified ware resembling stoneware decorated with an opaque blue enamel made at Beauvais in the 16th and 17th centuries. Also called *grès de Savignies*.

Grès de Flandres (French). A misnomer for RHENISH STONEWARE, especially Westerwald ware, which is also incorrectly called *grès Flamand*.

Grès de Savignies (French). Same as GRÈS DE BEAUVAIS.

Greybeard. A term used in England for a BELLARMINE.

Griffin. Also griffon, gryphon. A decorative subject in the form of a FABULOUS ANIMAL, half-lion and half-eagle. It originated in Greek and Roman art, and it can frequently be observed as part of the decoration of post-Renaissance pottery and porcelain, especially that in the Empire style.

Grinding. The process of thinning pressed ornamentation so that after SPRIGGING the ground colour will be slightly visible. Grinding on the abrasive wheel was also employed in the 18th century to remove unwanted glaze from the foot-ring of a vessel.

Gris d'Angleterre (French). *See* GRÈS D'ANGLETERRE.

Grisaille, en (French). Decorative painting on porcelain in varying shades of grey, originally to imitate relief sculpture. *See* CHIAROSCURO; MONOCHROME; CAMAÏEU, EN.

Grotesques. (Above) Maiolica dish decorated with early grotesques, Caffaggiolo, *c.* 1515. Wallace Collection, London. (Below) Detail of maiolica dish decorated with later, more fanciful forms. Urbino second half of 16th century. Victoria and Albert Museum, London.

Grog. Pulverized broken pottery added to clay to reduce the shrinkage resulting from loss of water during firing. *See* SHARD.

Gros bleu (French). A dark-blue underglaze ground colour applied to wares by SPONGING. It was developed at Sèvres in 1749, but was largely superseded there by BLEU DE ROI. *See* MAZARINE BLUE.

Grotesque Punches. A term used in the Derby catalogue to describe the figures more generally known as MANSION HOUSE DWARFS. *See* CALLOT FIGURES.

Grotesques (from Italian, *Grotteschi*). A decorative motif consisting of fanciful figures and half-figures which are partly human or animal and partly acanthus foliage, used in conjunction with distorted masks based on the old classical theatrical masks, and such mythological figures as satyrs, sphinxes, etc. They were originally inspired by mural decoration in the ruins of Nero's Golden House in Rome, and adapted by Raphael to the decoration of the *loggie* of the Vatican (hence sometimes Raffaelesche); they should not be confused with ARABESQUES. They continued to be popular in various guises and modifications until the beginning of the ROCOCO period, *c.* 1730. *See* BÉRAIN MOTIFS.

Grotto. An object of Chinese porcelain or stoneware made to represent a grotto or mountain village, with rocky cliffs, winding stairways, terraces, and a central pavilion and pagodas, together with figures of sages and others. They occur in stoneware, perhaps from the end of the Ming dynasty onwards, and very occasionally in 18th-century porcelain, including a monochrome RETICULATED version. In Europe Bernard Palissy made decorative ware suitable for ornamenting the grottoes which were a feature in the design of late 16th-century gardens. *See* PALISSY WARE.

Grotto. Glazed earthenware, ht 20½ in., probably from Kuangtung province. British Museum, London.

Ground. A monochrome surface colour on ceramic ware, especially porcelain, to which painted and gilded decoration was often added. Ground colours were first employed in China during the Ming dynasty, and were introduced into Europe at Meissen soon after 1720. They soon became an established method of decoration at almost all porcelain factories, and are common today. The ground itself may be over-decorated with an ornamental pattern of which there are many varieties, such as: BRIQUETÉ; BRYONY-LEAF; CELL; CHECKERBOARD; COIN; CROSS-HATCH; CURL; DIAMOND; DOT AND STALK; ERMINE; FISH-ROE; FLUTED; HONEYCOMB; HOUR-GLASS; LACE-WORK; MOCK ARABIC; NETWORK PATTERN; OCTAGON AND SQUARE; ŒIL-DE-PERDRIX; PLUME; RING; SCALE; SEEDED; SHUTTLE; SPONGED; SPUR; STAR AND CUBE; SWASTIKA AND BAR; SWASTIKA AND SQUARE; TARTAN; TRELLIS; VERMICELLI; VERMICULATED; VINE-LEAF; Y-DIAPER.

Ground-laying. The process of applying a GROUND colour to the body. It is sometimes done by painting a thin coating of oil over the area to be coloured and then padding it with fine silk to produce an even surface. The colour is then dusted on and adheres to the oiled surface.

Group. (1) An assemblage of two or more objects of the same (or similar) form, suited to each other and intended to be used together, but not identical, and not incomplete if separated, such as figures representing the FOUR SEASONS or the FOUR CONTINENTS. (2) A single object that depicts two or more figures on a common base, such as a BULL-BAITING GROUP. *See* SET; PAIR; SERIES; COMPANION-PIECE.

Grubbe plates. Plates of Worcester porcelain of the first period, decorated during the 1760s by James Giles, independent decorator, of Clerkenwell, London, and so called from having been presented to the Victoria and Albert Museum by one of his descendants. Mrs Dora Edgell Grubbe. The ledges are decorated with floral sprays and are edged with gilt, and the wells have scenes with figures *en camaïeu* in carmine. They are regarded as DOCUMENTARY SPECIMENS of the work done by this decorator or in his workshop, but not all the styles attributed to him are represented.

Grubbe plate. Worcester porcelain, decorated in the workshop of James Giles, London, *c.* 1765. Courtesy, Sotheby's.

Gubbio lustre. A brilliant iridescent LUSTRE applied at Gubbio (Italy) to maiolica from nearby Deruta, Faenza, and Castel Durante, and later to maiolica manufactured at Gubbio. This lustre was developed by Maestro Giorgio Andreoli after 1498. The best known is a ruby colour, but lighter varieties were also employed, all probably from gold.

Guelder-rose vase. Same as SNOWBALL VASE.

Guéridon (French). The figure of a kneeling Negro or Moor carved in wood and supporting a flat top on which a candlestick or candelabra was placed. The name is derived from Guéridon, a Moor in a French play of the late 17th century. The motif occurs occasionally in porcelain. Porcelain plaques from Sèvres were employed after *c.* 1760 to ornament small circular tables which became known as *guéridons*, perhaps because most originally carried a bronze candleholder, or were used as stands for candelabra.

Guilloche border. An ornate border pattern in the form of two or three bands twisted over each other in a series in such a way as to leave circular openings which are sometimes filled in with round ornament. It was frequently used in the second half of the 18th century as porcelain decoration, especially at Sèvres.

Guirlandes (French). See DÉCOR À GUIRLANDES.

Guldan (Persian ?). A Persian pottery flower-holder in the form of a jar with a central tube, and several surrounding tubes projecting from the shoulder. It was copied from a Chinese porcelain vase of similar shape which first made its appearance towards the close of the Ming dynasty. *See* TULIP VASE; QUINTAL VASE.

Gunn, Martha, jug. A type of TOBY JUG depicting Martha Gunn, the celebrated 18th-century Brighton bathing-woman, who is said to have dipped the Prince Regent (later George IV) into the sea as an infant. She is shown seated, holding a jug and glass, and wearing a feathered tricorn hat.

Martha Gunn jug. Glazed earthenware, by Ralph Wood II, *c.* 1770. City Museums, Stoke-on-Trent.

Gut (German). Literally, good. The first grade of porcelain at Meissen, as distinguished from MITTEL and AUSSCHUSS.

Guttus (Latin). A small oil-flask of Italian maiolica which was used for filling oil-lamps. It is circular and shallow, with a ring handle set at a right angle to the spout.

Gyoki ware. Japanese pottery made in the latter part of the Heian period (794–1185); it is a type of HAJIKI WARE, mass-produced and simpler in form.

H

Hacilar pottery. Anthropomorphic pot with obsidian eyes. Koçabas Museum, Istanbul. Photo Josephine Powell.

Habaner ware. Peasant ware of HALB-FAYENCE made in the late 16th and throughout the 17th century in Moravia (Czechoslovakia). The decoration is usually of flowers and scrolls in a stylized manner, with vigorously drawn houses, animals, and occasionally figures. Somewhat similar wares were made at Salzburg (Austria) and Winterthur (Switzerland). Typical products are plates with a wide flat ledge, and globular short-necked jugs.

Hachiroemon Kutani (Japanese). Same as SAIKO KUTANI.

Hacilar pottery. Pottery from Anatolia dating from the Neolithic age, *c*. 5600–5200 BC. First discovered in 1956 in the settlement and cemetery of Hacilar in south-west Turkey; the wares include painted bowls, vases, figurines, and rare single-headed anthropomorphic jars, as well as one double-headed specimen. Many pieces previously considered to have been genuine have recently been shown by the technique of THERMO-LUMINESCENCE DATING to be forgeries.

Hadley ware. Porcelain designed and modelled by James Hadley (1837–1903), made at the Royal Worcester Factory from 1875 and at his own factory from 1896 to 1905 when it was purchased by the Worcester factory. Some of his designs are closely based on wood-engravings from an edition of Thomas Moore's *Lallah Rookh*, published in 1868.

Hafner ware. Mainly lead-glazed tiles used in the construction of stoves in Germany and in Alpine regions such as those of Switzerland and Central Europe. Manufacture goes back to *c*. 1350, and the tiles were moulded in relief and at first covered with a green glaze. By 1500 other colours, principally yellow and brown, were in use, and from the middle of the 16th century tin-glazed tiles were gradually substituted for the lead-glazed type, especially at Nuremberg. Silesian Hafner-ware dishes, made by the *Hafner* (or stove) potters, had designs cut with a knife to prevent the intermingling of the tin glazes employed. The subjects were principally biblical, but historical and mythological scenes also occur. Other objects made by the *Hafner* potters in the same or similar techniques include jugs and dishes.

Hafner ware. Stove made up from separate glazed tile panels, Nuremberg, 16th century. City Museums, Stoke-on-Trent.

Hai shou (Chinese). A decorative pattern on CHINESE EXPORT PORCELAIN depicting a sea-monster.

Haji(ki) ware. Japanese pottery made from the 4th century until the Heian period (794–1185). Early pieces are restored, resembling YAYOI WARE but less refined; it was made by COILING or modelled by hand. Some pieces are decorated with coloured pigments.

Hakeme (Japanese). A covering of white or grey slip roughly brushed on to the surface of a vessel. It is to be found on wares from Korea and Japan.

Halb-Fayence (German). Same as MEZZA-MAIOLICA.

Half-palmette. A PALMETTE divided in half vertically. It occurs in particular on Greek pottery of the RED-FIGURE STYLE, and subsequently on Roman pottery.

Han dynasty. The earliest Chinese dynasty (206 BC–AD 220) of which the ceramic wares are well known. The surviving wares fall into several groups, of which perhaps the best known is the HU and the HILL CENSER. Some of the decorative motifs are probably derived from Parthian sources. Lion-mask handles with rings occur on some pieces and suggest a Roman origin. TOMB-FIGURES are fairly numerous, but do not possess the quality of the later T'ang dynasty wares of this kind. The use of the green lead glaze is rather surprising at this time, and it appears to have been learned from the West, perhaps taught by immigrant potters. The earliest experiments towards the production of a hard-fired ware (which eventually developed into translucent porcelain) took place during this period.

Han pottery. Pottery and stoneware made in China during the Han dynasty. The first glazes were used slightly before this period, but by the Han dynasty the technique had been mastered, and a green glaze on wine-jars (HU) seems to have been intended as an imitation of patinated bronze. Pottery figures of servants and retainers, animals, and farm-buildings were buried with the dead, and excavated specimens are to be found in many Western collections.

Hanakago-de (Japanese). A decorative motif used on ARITA PORCELAIN and on Chinese FAMILLE VERTE porcelain during the reign of K'ang Hsi (1662–1722), depicting a wicker flower-basket, usually with a high loop handle, supporting a profusion of flowers, some of which can be seen through the open sides of the basket. Also called Flower Basket pattern.

Hanap. (1) A large 17th-century drinking cup of GOBLET shape. (2) A large EWER, with a curved handle and spout, sometimes modelled with ornament based on human figures or animals. (The silver hanap, however, is a large standing cup, and to apply this term to a vessel shaped as a ewer is an error, although the ewer was also modelled after a 17th-century metal prototype.)

Hancock engraving. The Flute Lesson, transfer-print on porcelain mug, Worcester, *c.* 1756. Courtesy, Worcester Royal Porcelain Co.

Hancock engravings. Engravings by Robert Hancock (1731–1817) which were used for TRANSFER-PRINTING in England from *c.* 1753, first at Bow, and then at Worcester, Caughley, and other factories. Among his best-known subjects are the TEA PARTY, L'AMOUR, and the FORTUNE TELLER. Over one hundred subjects have been recognized, some with several variations. Most are reproduced in Cyril Cook, *Life and Works of Robert Hancock* (1948), with its *Supplement* (1955). Some transfer-printed examples on Worcester porcelain are marked with the initials 'RH' and an anchor. The significance of the initials is not entirely certain, but they probably stand for Robert Hancock. The anchor is the rebus of Richard Holdship, a director of the factory, who seems to have been in charge of the printing-shop. There is evidence that Holdship attempted to claim some of the credit rightly due to Hancock. *See* LADIES' AMUSEMENT, THE.

Hand-warmer. Lambeth delftware, ht $4\frac{3}{4}$ in., dated 1663. Fitzwilliam Museum, Cambridge.

Hand and cup vase. A vase in the form of a naturally modelled hand holding a cup. This, and variations on the same theme, were popular porcelain models during the 1840s and 1850s, often made in PARIAN WARE.

Hand-candlestick. Same as CHAMBER CANDLESTICK.

Hand of Buddha citron. Same as BUDDHA'S-HAND CITRON.

Hand-warmer. A small container of decorative form, intended to be filled with hot water and held in the muff or pocket to warm

Handel vase. Porcelain, Bow, 1759. British Museum, London.

Hare's fur. Tea-bowl with characteristic glaze, Honan province, Sung dynasty (960–1280). Victoria and Albert Museum, London.

Harlequin. The Frightened Harlequin, one of the series modelled by J. J. Kändler, Meissen, *c.* 1740. Courtesy, Newman & Newman Ltd, London.

the hands. Examples are known in 17th-century Dutch and English delftware, in the form of a book or books.

Handel vase. A vase, now in the British Museum, made at Bow to commemorate the death in 1759 of the composer George Frederick Handel. It is of double ogee shape on a triangular base, with a *putto* standing at each corner and representing respectively Music, Drama, and Dancing. The vase is decorated on the front with a musical score headed 'Minuet', and on the sides with moulded scrolls and painted relief flowers, and has applied garlands on the pierced neck and columnar support. Similar vases and clock-cases, but with different decoration, were made at the same factory.

Handle. That part of a cup, jug, mug, vase, or other vessel by which it is held in the hand when used or carried, usually with a space for the fingers or hand to be passed through, as distinguished from a LUG. They are usually single, but double handles are not uncommon, while triple (*see* TYG) and up to eleven (*see* POSSET-POT), have been recorded. They can be horizontal or perpendicular, simple or interlaced, at the side of the vessel, or overhead (*see* BAIL HANDLE), and of many shapes and styles, such as AIGUIÈRE; BARBERINI; BÖTTGER; BRANCH; B-SHAPED; CARYATID; CLASSICAL; COLUMNAR; CRABSTOCK (or rustic); CROCK; C-SHAPED; D-SHAPED; FORKED; GROOVED; harp-shaped; INTERTWINED; ROPE; sea-horse; serpent; S-SHAPED; STRAP; angular; T-SHAPED; VOLUTE; WING; WISHBONE. The French term is *anse*; the German, *Henkel*.

Handle-tag. A small moulded relief decoration, usually heart-shaped or triangular, beneath the lower TERMINAL of some English porcelain handles.

Handled dish. A type of dish or plate with a projecting integrated handle extending about one inch along approximately a quarter of the rim.

Haniwa figures. Japanese terracotta TOMB-FIGURES made *c.* 300–645 AD. They are relatively unusual in Europe, but specimens are to be found in most major museums with collections of Far Eastern art.

Harbour scenes. A decoration introduced on Meissen porcelain *c.* 1724. It remained very popular until the 1730s, and continued into the late 1760s. It depicts a harbour with buildings, boats, and figures often in oriental costume, with bales and cases on the quayside. The subject was used at Nymphenburg by G. S. Lindemann, and it occurs in a variant form at Chelsea, where scenes of this kind were, apparently, painted by William Duvivier.

Hard-fired. Subjected to the GRAND FEU.

Hard-paste porcelain. More correctly called TRUE PORCELAIN. Porcelain made from clay and natural rock. Termed *pâte dure* in France, and *porcelaine royale* at Sèvres.

Hardening-on. Firing underglaze decoration lightly in order to fix it to the BISCUIT and burn out the oils which are the medium for the application of the colour so that the glaze will adhere properly and, if there are any reserves, will not run into them.

Hare plate. A type of pottery plate decorated with a hare outlined in trailed slip, made in Staffordshire and at Wrotham (Kent), *c.* 1670–80.

Hare's fur. A Chinese glaze of the Sung dynasty (960–1280) used on CHIEN YAO made in Honan province. It is black, or near black, streaked with brown. *See* TEMMOKU GLAZE.

Harlequin. A character from the Commedia dell'Arte who was often depicted in porcelain figures, notably the series of figures of Harlequin in various poses modelled by J. J. Kändler at Meissen after 1730. *See* INDISCREET HARLEQUIN, THE; COMMEDIA DELL'ARTE FIGURES.

Harlequin glaze. A spotted glaze of several colours.

Harlequin ground. A ground of parallel bands of several different colours. The French term is *fond arlequin.*

Harlequin set. A mixed set of like objects, such as coffee-cups and saucers, in the same style but with different decoration, in contrast to a set decorated *en suite.* Sets of this kind are usually made up from odd cups and saucers.

Harvest jug. A ring-shaped bottle of stoneware or earthenware, so called because it was allegedly carried around the arm of the harvester while working in the fields. The earliest examples occur in Italian maiolica of the 16th century, and in German stoneware in the 17th century. Some were made in England by Dixon, Austin & Co. of Sunderland.

Hastings, Warren, service. A porcelain dinner-service made at Chelsea, *c.* 1754, and so called because it was once in the possession of Warren Hastings. The pieces have lobed rims, and the border of the plates is decorated with reserved panels enclosing scenes depicting Aesop's *Fables*, which were probably painted by Jeffryes Hamett O'Neale. The same scheme was used for services decorated by another hand. *See* FABLE DECORATION; FABLES, AESOP'S.

Hatched. Decorated with fine lines to give the effect of shading, sometimes two sets of equidistant parallel lines crossing each other at an oblique or right angle (cross-hatching). *See* CROSS-HATCHED GROUND.

Hausmaler (German). Literally, home-painter. A decorator of faience, porcelain, or glass, who bought undecorated ware from the factory and painted it with enamels at home, or in his own studio. The best of the *Hausmaler* were often superior to the factory's own painters, and some maintained studios with a number of assistants and apprentices. After *c.* 1750 the quality of HAUSMALEREI deteriorated, due to the increasing unwillingness of porcelain factories to sell anything but the most defective ware 'in white'. The *Hausmaler* operated chiefly in Germany, but they were also to be found in Austria, France, and England. The French term was *chambrelan,* the Austrian *Winckelmann,* and the English INDEPENDENT (or outside) DECORATOR. *See* CANCELLATION MARK.

Hausmalerei (German). Literally, home-painting. Porcelain or faience decorated by HAUSMALER. The practice started in Germany in the second half of the 17th century, when glass-enamellers began to paint on contemporary faience. It became common in the first half of the 18th century, when porcelain from Meissen and Vienna was decorated with great skill. Later, when the factories became much less willing to supply any but defective ware, sparsely decorated factory-ware was given additional decoration by *Hausmaler.* Chinese and Japanese blue-and-white porcelain thus over-decorated with enamels is termed

Hare plate. Plate with decoration in cream-coloured trailed slip, Wrotham, *c.* 1670–80. Burnap Collection, William Rockhill Nelson Gallery of Art, Kansas City, Mo.

Harvest jug. Maiolica, ht 10 in., Faenza, *c.* 1510. Victoria and Albert Museum, London.

Warren Hastings service. Detail of plate painted by Jeffryes Hamett O'Neale, Chelsea, *c.* 1753.

'clobbered'; this kind of work was principally done in Holland, where decorating studios also painted porcelain in white imported for the purpose from the Far East. *See* CLOBBERING.

Hawk beak. A type of lip in the form of a hawk's beak, arched and curving downward towards the tip.

Hawthorn pattern. A term often used loosely to refer to the PRUNUS PATTERN.

Hawthorn vase. A vase or jar decorated with the hawthorn pattern or PRUNUS PATTERN, usually in blue underglaze but sometimes in enamel colours. To be found on Chinese porcelain, beginning in the reign of K'ang Hsi (1662–1722). *See* GINGER-JAR.

Head vase. *See* KANTHAROS.

Heavily potted. Made with a BODY which is thicker and heavier than average. Usually to be found in early or primitive wares.

Hispano-Moresque ware. Vase of the Alhambra type with wing handles and vine-leaf decoration in lustre; ht 20 in. Valencia, 15th century, Victoria and Albert Museum, London.

Hedgehog crocus-pot. A hollow receptacle naturalistically modelled in the form of a hedgehog, its bristly body pierced by many holes. It was accompanied by a tray to hold water. Bulbs were planted in soil or moss packed inside the hedgehog which was then placed on the tray. Examples were made by Wedgwood in BLACK BASALTES. *See* ROOT-POT.

Helix. A spiral curve moving round a focal point, as a watch-spring or the volute on Ionic and Corinthian capitals; sometimes called VOLUTE. *See* VOLUTE HANDLE.

Helmet pitcher. A tall ewer shaped like a helmet upside down. Sometimes called a casque ewer.

Henri Deux ware. A term loosely applied in past years to SAINT-PORCHAIRE WARE and also to FAÏENCE D'OIRON. Such wares were first made during the reign of François I (1515–47), and afterwards under Henri II (1547–59), the period of manufacture lasting from *c.* 1520 until *c.* 1550. Imitations were made in England by Minton, *c.* 1860. *See* FAÏENCE À NIELLURE.

Heraldic ware. Same as ARMORIAL WARE.

Herculaneum ware. Creamware and pearlware made in England at a factory in Liverpool founded *c.* 1793 by Richard Abbey, and renamed Herculaneum by his successors in imitation of Wedgwood's ETRURIA. It also made other types of ware similar to those of Wedgwood. Some porcelain made at Liverpool from *c.* 1800 is also marked 'Herculaneum'.

Herma (Greek). A quadrangular pedestal or pillar surmounted by a bust, similar to a TERM except that the bust is that of a bearded Hermes, and sometimes halfway up the front there is a phallus. They appear as painted decoration on some Greek vases.

Herringbone. A pattern in the form of a herring's skeleton, being two or more series of diagonal lines, each series sloping the opposite way to the adjacent series.

Hessian cup. A style of small coffee-cup, pot-shaped and tapering towards the bottom, with a small loop handle. Introduced at Sèvres in 1830.

Hexafoil. A shape or ornamentation having six foils or lobes.

High relief. Relief decoration where the projected portion is half, or more than half, the natural circumference of the object. The French term is *haut relief*; the Italian is *alto rilievo*. *See* LOW RELIEF; MEDIUM RELIEF.

High-temperature colours. Colours painted before firing in the high-temperature kiln (GRAND FEU) at temperatures ranging from 1100 to 1450°C. They were used underglaze on porcelain, and painted on to the raw glaze on maiolica, delftware, and faience, being fired in one operation with the glaze. The high-temperature colours are cobalt, copper, manganese, antimony, and iron which, under normal conditions, yield respectively blue, green, purple, yellow, and red. The use of iron for delftware painting is rare; all red pigments gave trouble and were applied in the form of enamels painted on after the first firing. Colours on tin-enamel ware were painted in broad washes rather than in the detail possible with the enamels of the PETIT FEU, since, being painted on the raw glaze, erasures were impossible, and simple designs were preferred.

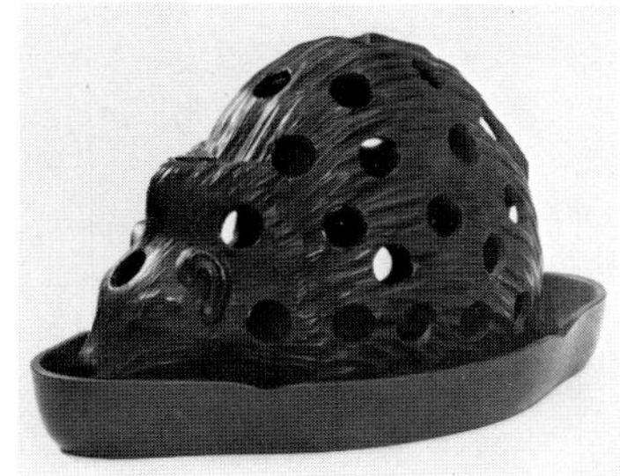

Hedgehog crocus-pot. Black basaltes, length of tray 11 in. Wedgwood, *c.* 1800. Courtesy, Wedgwood.

Hill censer. A Chinese STEM-CUP on a saucer-like base, with a cover similar to that of a HILL JAR; made during the Han dynasty (206 BC–AD 220).

Hill jar. A cylindrical jar covered with a green or greenish-brown lead glaze, and surmounted by a cover modelled in the form of hills or mountains representing the Taoist Isles of the Blest; made during the Han dynasty (206 BC–AD 220). *See* HILL CENSER.

Hill jar. Glazed earthenware, Han dynasty (206 BC–AD 220). Victoria and Albert Museum, London.

Hirado ware. A type of Japanese blue-and-white porcelain made at the Mikawachi kilns for the Prince of Hirado (a small island off the coast of Hizen province). The kilns were not far from ARITA. The wares are usually small and of fine quality, e.g. fish, dragons, and ducks, and a CELADON ware was also made. Only low-grade pieces made after 1843 are marked. The finest were made between 1751 and 1830.

Hispano-Moresque ware. Spanish TIN-GLAZED EARTHENWARE decorated principally with LUSTRE, and made from the 12th century onwards. Nearly all surviving specimens date from between the 15th and 18th centuries. The body is usually a coarse clay which burns to a pinkish buff. It is covered either with slip or enamel which has sometimes flaked off in parts. The design is executed in lustre pigments of a variable hue, from golden to pale straw in colour, and some specimens have the addition of motifs in cobalt blue. The backs of some of the early dishes are remarkable for finely executed heraldic animals done in lustre with a broad brush. Specimens are principally dishes, vases, and drug-jars. The finest wares were made during the Moorish occupation, much coarse ware decorated mainly in a coppery lustre being produced from the beginning of the 17th century onwards. The 19th-century supposition that these later wares were made at Bristol (England) followed the dredging of fragments from Bristol Docks, and is erroneous. Dating and exact attribution of early wares is often difficult and based on documentary specimens such as the well-known ALHAMBRA VASE. Centres of manufacture were located at Málaga and Valencia. *See* MADREPERLA LUSTRE; MOTHER-OF-PEARL GLAZE.

Hob-in-the-well pattern. Octagonal porcelain plate with painted decoration. Meissen, *c.* 1745. Syz Collection, Smithsonian Institution, Washington, D.C.

Hob-in-the-well pattern. A KAKIEMON design based on a legend of the boyhood of a Chinese sage of the Sung dynasty, Ssŭ Ma Kuang (1019–86), whose playmate fell into a large fish-

Ho-ho and Erh-hsien. Figure group, blanc de Chine, Tê-Hua, 17th century. British Museum, London.

bowl and was in danger of drowning; Ssŭ Ma Kuang smashed the bowl with a stone and saved his companion. The pattern was copied at Chelsea, *c.* 1752, from a Japanese ARITA original, and also at Meissen. The Japanese term is *Shiba buko*, known in German as *Shiba Buko Dekor*.

Hogarth's dog. *See* TRUMP; DOGS.

Ho-ho and Erh-hsien. Decorative subjects on Chinese porcelain in which the twin spirits of Mirth and Harmony are depicted seated in loose robes, one sometimes holding a box and the other a vase with a spray of lotus.

Ho-ho bird (Japanese). A decorative subject on Arita porcelain in the Kakiemon style depicting a phoenix. The comparable Chinese motif is the FÊNG-HUANG. It is one of the FABULOUS ANIMALS.

Hohokam pottery. Pottery made by the Hohokam tribes living in the desert region (now southern Arizona) from *c.* AD 300 to 1100. Votive figures consist mainly of crudely modelled naked women. The buff pottery was decorated with IRON-RED.

Holcion (Greek). A vase of Greek pottery used as a drinking cup or goblet. It was like a small KANTHAROS, but without handles.

Holländische Porselein (Dutch). DUTCH DELFTWARE, especially that decorated in the manner of porcelain.

Hollow ware. All ware which is hollow, and usually narrower at the mouth than at the main convexity, as distinguished from FLATWARE. Usually for containing liquids.

Holmos (Greek). A drinking cup of Greek pottery. The name is applied both to a goblet with a stem and foot, and to a drinking cup of horn shape.

Holzschnittblumen (German). A style of DEUTSCHE BLUMEN based on woodcuts illustrating botanical treatises. *See* FLOWERS.

Homeric Vase. Blue jasper with white relief decoration, modelled by John Flaxman, 1786. Courtesy, Wedgwood.

Homeric Vase. A vase modelled by John Flaxman in 1786, and made by Josiah Wedgwood in jasper with white relief decoration; later copies were made in black basaltes. The vase depicts the apotheosis of Homer, and has a cover surmounted by a figure of Pegasus. A companion piece is decorated with the apotheosis of Virgil. The same subjects also appear on Wedgwood PLAQUES, and the figure of Pegasus as a finial on other Wedgwood vases.

Hon Shonsui. The Japanese term for the Chinese SHONSUI ware which followed GEN SHONSUI. It has a pure white body with a glazed rim, a high base, and a carefully scraped foot, not with a MUSHIKUI lip, but rather with a lip known as *kuchihani* ('mouth rouge') which has a brown edge.

Honan ware. A type of Chinese stoneware from Honan province, made during the Sung dynasty (960–1280), which has treacly and lustrous black and brown glazes. *See* HARE'S FUR; TEMMOKU.

Honeycomb ground. A ground consisting of adjacent hexagons, with or without enclosed flower designs.

Honey-gold. Gold-leaf pulverized in honey and fixed to porcelain by a low-temperature firing. In appearance it is dull, with a rich and sumptuous effect. It was often applied thickly and ornamented by tooling with a metal point. Honey-gold was developed at Sèvres, and much used on important pieces at Chelsea from *c.* 1756 onwards (the first mention of gilding at Chelsea occurs in a sale-catalogue of 1756). It was superseded *c.* 1775 by the Derby development of MERCURIC GILDING.

Honey-jar. A small jar of pottery or porcelain for serving honey; it is usually cylindrical and provided with a cover, some examples being made to simulate a beehive. Some jars have a fixed saucer-like stand.

Honeysuckle border. (1) The ANTHEMION border. (2) A border pattern with alternating PALMETTES and honeysuckle flowers.

Hong (Chinese). Factories (or warehouses) on the banks of the Pearl river, Canton, owned by the East India Companies, and used as depots for the reception and storage of goods, including porcelain, for shipment. The Portuguese factory was at Macao. The word 'factory' is here used in the sense of a warehouse belonging to foreign merchants, and not as a place in which goods were manufactured.

Hookah. Persian pottery, mid-17th century. City Museums, Stoke-on-Trent.

Hong. Punch-bowl with decoration depicting the *hongs* of the East India Companies at Canton, Chinese export porcelain, *c.* 1750.

Hookah (hooka). An apparatus used in the Near and Middle East for smoking tobacco. It is in the form of a pottery or porcelain bottle with a long flexible stem or tube (connected to a separate container for tobacco) so that the smoke is cooled by passing it through the water in the bottle. In the case of some Persian specimens with a short protruding aperture on the shoulder, the water receptacle is sometimes referred to as a drinking vessel. The hookah occurs in Islamic pottery and Chinese porcelain. The Persian term is *kalian*, and the Turkish *narghile*. *See* GORGELET; KENDI.

Hop-trellis pattern. A pattern of trellis-work entwined with hop-vines, originally created at Sèvres and adapted by Worcester for the decoration of porcelain made *c.* 1770 and later.

Hop-trellis pattern. Porcelain teapot painted with enamels and gilt, Sèvres, 1765. Victoria and Albert Museum, London.

Hope service. A dinner-service made at Worcester in the Flight period (1792) for the Duke of Clarence, later to become William IV. Painted *en grisaille* by John Pennington, it depicts a figure representing Hope in various postures. The GROS BLEU rim is decorated in gilding with PATERAE and FALSE GADROONS.

Hors d'œuvre dish. A dish divided by partitions into several sections for serving an assortment of hors d'œuvres. It usually has a domed cover. *See* SWEETMEAT DISH.

Horses. Figures of horses in various attitudes, usually on a rectangular base. Horses (popular as displays in saddlers' shops in the early 19th century) were made at Leeds in creamware, sometimes undecorated but occasionally coloured or dappled. Horses were also made in Staffordshire, *c.* 1800, in dappled glazed earthenware. Horses in porcelain, mostly from Continental factories, were, in the 18th century, often based on earlier bronzes, or on the Lipizzaner horses of the Spanish Riding School in Vienna. The terracotta and glazed earthenware horses of the T'ang dynasty, originally TOMB-FIGURES, are well known, and most of them are superbly modelled. T'ang horses have been widely forged. The EIGHT HORSES OF MU WANG are a frequent decoration on early Chinese porcelain. *See* PAI-MA.

Horticultural trophies. *See* TROPHIES.

Ho-tei. The Japanese equivalent of the Buddhist monk PU-TAI HO-SHANG.

Hot printing. The technique of TRANSFER-PRINTING by means of tissue paper, so called because the mixture of oil and colouring-matter was added hot to a heated copper plate before the tissue was placed on to the plate. The whole was covered with flannel and passed through a roller press, after which the printed tissue was placed on the object while in a BISCUIT state. The back of the tissue was rubbed with a boss to transfer the design evenly, and the object was subjected to another firing in a MUFFLE kiln before the final glazing. *See* COLD PRINTING.

Hotteurs. Pair of flower-holder figures, ht 11 in., Chantilly, 18th century. Courtesy, Sotheby's.

Hot-water plate. A double-walled plate with a hollow space between the upper and lower surfaces for containing hot water to keep food warm. The water was poured in through a small hole in the rim. Examples occur in Chinese porcelain, English delftware, and Leeds creamware, as well as in ware from many other potteries. The lower part is sometimes made of pewter with a ceramic plate inserted in the top.

Hotteur (French). Literally, back-basket carrier. A figure carrying a basket (intended to be a flower-holder) on his back. The best known are a pair of 18th-century Chantilly figures with panniers of this kind.

Hound-handle pitcher. A type of earthenware jug or pitcher with the handle in the form of a dog with its forepaws on the rim and its hindpaws attached midway up the body of the piece. It was first made in the Unites States, *c.* 1837, by Daniel Greatbach at the American Pottery Manufacturing Co., Bennington, Vt. Comparable handles had been made earlier in Hungary and in Staffordshire. Such pitchers were later made elsewhere in the United States, often with a moulded decoration of game or a hunting scene.

Hour-glass ground. A ground of lines with opposing curves crossing at right angles so as to form a checkered pattern of hour-glass-like motifs.

House urn. A terracotta burial-urn, shaped like a circular hut with a conical roof, of the prehistoric civilization in Italy known as the Villanovan culture; also called *capanna*.

Howe, Admiral, jug. A type of TOBY JUG depicting Admiral Lord Howe and made to commemorate his victory over the French in 1794.

Hsing ware. White porcelain produced at Hsing-chou (Hopei province) during the T'ang dynasty.

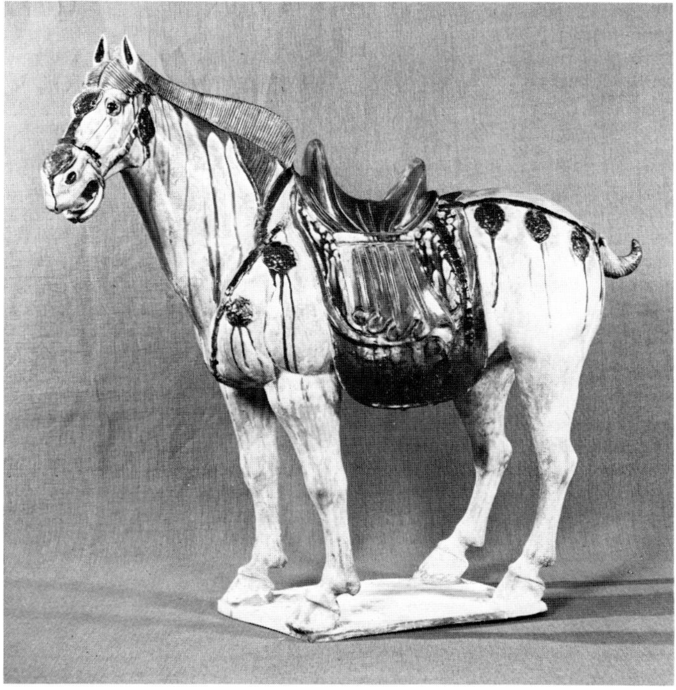

Horse. Glazed earthenware figure, T'ang dynasty (618–906). Victoria and Albert Museum, London.

Hu (Chinese). (1) A tiger, symbolizing, on Chinese porcelain, Autumn in the FOUR SEASONS and West in the FOUR QUADRANTS. (2) A baluster-shaped wine vessel, based on a much earlier bronze vessel, usually covered with green lead glaze, probably in imitation of patinated bronze. It was sometimes decorated with bands of modelled relief ornament depicting hunting scenes (apparently taken from contemporary sculptured reliefs, often of a type called the Flying Gallop), and was made during the Han dynasty (206 BC–AD 220).

Hua shih (Chinese). Literally, slippery stone. A type of stone, perhaps soaprock or pegmatite, called 'slippery stone' in the letters of Père d'Entrecolles, a Jesuit missionary whose letters, 1712–22, furnished much information (some of it erroneous) about Chinese porcelain manufacture.

Hudibras. Glazed earthenware figure, by Ralph Wood I, *c*. 1770. City Museums, Stoke-on-Trent.

Hudibras. A noted equestrian figure in pottery, made by Ralph Wood I (possibly modelled by Jean Voyez, but perhaps by Aaron Wood), based on an engraving by William Hogarth of 1726. The hero of a satirical poem by Samuel Butler, Hudibras was a Presbyterian justice who set out to enforce strict laws for the suppression of sports and amusements in the 17th century, and was a figure of fun. Other versions were made later in Staffordshire, *c*. 1780–1800.

Hui ch'ing The Chinese term for a greyish-blue colour.

Hui hui ch'ing (Chinese). Same as Mohammedan blue. Cobalt blue obtained by the Chinese in the 14th and 15th centuries from Islamic sources, perhaps from the extensive cobalt deposits in Baluchistan. It is said to have been used again in the reign of Chêng Tê (1506–21), when some very fine quality blue-and-white porcelain was produced, and it may have continued in use till the end of the 16th century.

Hundred Antiques, The. Same as PO KU.

Hung (Chinese). Literally, red; the word occurs in many compound phrases: *chi hung* – copper red, SACRIFICIAL RED, perhaps so called because vessels of this colour were used on the Altar of the Sun; *pao-shih hung* – ruby red, SANG-DE-BOEUF; *chiang-tsu hung* – bean red, copper red with small patches of brown and green, the PEACH-BLOOM GLAZE; *fan-hung* – IRON-RED, in enamel painting, or as a monochrome coral red; *mo hung* – IRON-RED used as a monochrome; *yen-chih-hung* – the crimson of the FAMILLE ROSE palette; *fen-hung* – pink, the crimson of the FAMILLF ROSE palette (*fen ts'ai*) lightened with opaque white enamel; *hsien hung* – fresh or bright red.

Husk service. Plate of the Queen's shape with husk border, *c.* 1770. Courtesy, Wedgwood.

Huntley, Marchioness of, service. A porcelain DINNER-SERVICE made at Worcester, decorated with two festoons of garden flowers trailing into the well of the plates and with apple-green borders of rococo outline edged in gilt scrolls from which hang polychrome sprigs.

Husk border. A border pattern of continuous wheat-husks placed vertically. It was a feature of designs by Robert Adam in the NEO-CLASSICAL STYLE. The husks are occasionally festooned, as in the HUSK SERVICE.

Husk service. A large creamware DINNER-SERVICE made by Josiah Wedgwood in 1770 for Catherine the Great of Russia. The pieces feature the lobed rim known as the QUEEN'S SHAPE, and were decorated with the HUSK BORDER in purple, and with floral patterns in the well. The decoration was executed in Wedgwood's Chelsea studio. Some of the existing service in Russia includes REPLACERS made in that country.

Hyacinth border. A border pattern of a series of hyacinth flowers placed horizontally end-to-end and pointing in the same direction. It occurs on Wedgwood's jasper.

Hydria. Black clay with reeded body; ht 17 in., central Italy, 3rd century BC. Copenhagen, Danish National Museum, Antiksamlingen.

Hydria. A jar of Greek pottery for storing or carrying water; it is usually large and urn-shaped and has a flat bottom. It is characterized by two horizontal loop handles (for lifting) and one or two vertical handles (for dipping or pouring). Early examples have a distinct neck set off from the shoulder, and later ones (*see* KALPIS) have a rounded shoulder with the neck forming a continuous curve with the body.

Hydrocérame (French). A term applied to vessels of a porous texture used for cooling water by evaporation. *See* ALCARAZZA; BÚCARO; GOGLET.

Hydrofluoric acid. The only acid which will attack silica and silica products. It is used for etching glass, for SPOT TESTS to determine the nature of soft porcelains, and by fakers to remove sparse decoration in overglaze enamels leaving the porcelain surface ready to be redecorated with more sumptuous and expensive designs. It is also sometimes used to remove inconvenient factory-marks from reproductions when these have been painted overglaze. It is a strong acid which is supplied in non-vitreous containers, and if the vapour escapes from a loosely stoppered bottle stored in an enclosed space it will affect any glassware or ceramic glazes nearby.

I

Ice-cream cup. Same as TASSE À GLACE.

Ice-pail. Same as SEAU À GLACE.

Ichirin zashi (Japanese). A vase for a single flower. *See* PRUNUS VASE; MEI-P'ING; MAE-PYŎNG.

Image. A figure representing an identifiable person. The term is used today mainly in connection with figures having a religious connotation, e.g. those of saints.

Image pattern. A decorative design on Chinese porcelain of the reign of K'ang Hsi (1662–1722) depicting a man holding an axe followed by a boy with a bundle of sticks. It was copied at Bow soon after 1750. The term was also applied to a Worcester version of the MOTHER AND CHILD PATTERN.

Image pattern. Sauce-boat with decoration in underglaze blue, Bow, *c.* 1755.

Image toy. A contemporary term (*c.* 1750) for STAFFORDSHIRE FIGURES made during the 18th century and intended mainly for use as CHIMNEY-PIECE ORNAMENTS.

Imari. Japanese porcelain made at ARITA (Hizen province) from the beginning of the 18th century onwards, and shipped from the port of Imari not far away. The decoration, perhaps influenced by Dutch traders, was overcrowded, and based on native textiles and brocades. Its popularity was such that it was copied, with variations, in China – a ware known as CHINESE IMARI. It is painted in several colours, of which a blackish underglaze blue and a strong dark red predominate. Its forms, decoration, and palette were copied in Europe, although not, in the 18th century, to the extent of the KAKIEMON patterns. Late in the century, and in the 19th century, it formed the inspiration for what came to be termed JAPAN PATTERNS, some of which are still in use today.

Imbrex. A Roman roof-tile of semi-circular section, used to cover a joint between two flat tiles (TEGULAE). *See* EPINETRON.

Imbricated. Arranged to overlap, in the manner of roof-tiles or fish-scales. The term is applied to SCALE-GROUND patterns, and to porcelain such as that of Saint-Cloud, which is moulded in the form of overlapping leaves.

Imari. Porcelain plate decorated in enamel colours and gilt, Arita, *c.* 1725. Victoria and Albert Museum, London.

Immortals. *See* EIGHT IMMORTALS, THE.

Impasto. A technique of applying pigment in such a way as to stand out from the glazed surface in slight but noticeable relief, as with the blue pigment of certain kinds of early Florentine MAIOLICA, or the Armenian red pigment characteristic of ISNIK POTTERY.

Impasto blue. A thickly applied blue pigment used on the 15th-century OAK-LEAF JARS of Italian maiolica, the blue being blackish and rather inky in tone.

Impasto red. A thickly applied brilliant red pigment employed in the decoration of Isnik pottery. It is called ARMENIAN RED, also tomato red and sealing-wax red.

Indian sporting pattern. Earthenware drainer with blue transfer-printed underglaze decoration, Spode, 1810–35. J.K. des Fontaines Collection, London.

Imperial yellow. A lead glaze of deep rich yellow colour, slightly brownish in tone, which is derived from iron or antimony. It had its origin during the Ming dynasty (1368–1644), but was at its best during the reign of K'ang Hsi (1662–1722); specimens are rare.

Impressed. Indented, as distinguished from INCISED or cut-in, by means of a stamp while the clay was still soft. Many factory-marks were impressed. *See* STAMPED.

Inca pottery. Pottery made by the Incas who originally settled in Cuzco, the old capital of Peru, in the 11th century, but by the 15th century had established their ascendancy over the Chimú (*see* CHIMÚ POTTERY). Most of the pottery was a red polished ware painted with geometric designs in red, black, and white, or with relief decoration on black ware. Nothing of importance was made after the Spanish conquest.

Incense-burner. A receptacle for burning incense for the purpose of scenting a room, or (termed a censer) for ecclesiastical use. Oriental incense-burners (KORO) were usually made of porcelain, but Japanese specimens of earthenware, usually from Kyoto, can occasionally be observed. The Italian term is *brucia-profumo*. For related types, *see* PASTILLE-BURNER; PERFUME-BURNER.

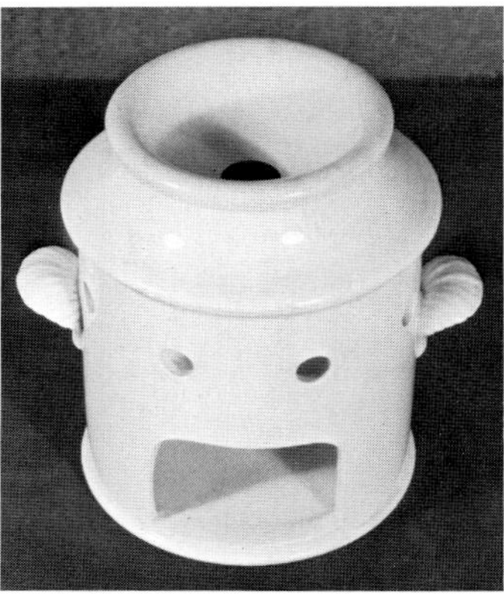

Inhalator. (Above) Veilleuse type, English white-glazed stoneware. Harold Newman Collection. (Below) Dr Nelson's 'Improved Inhaler', English glazed stoneware, *c.* 1865. Wellcome Museum, London.

Incised. Scratched into the body or paste of a vessel with a sharp instrument, such as a metal point, either as decoration or to record a name, date, or inscription. Incised marks have been added to porcelain after firing for a variety of reasons, usually with a diamond point. Incised work is to be distinguished from IMPRESSED. *See* SGRAFFITO.

Indented corner. Similar to a CHAMFERED CORNER, but with the narrow edge having a concave surface.

Independent decorator. A painter of pottery and porcelain who worked, not at the factory in which the ware was made, but at home or in his own studio; also called an 'outside decorator'. The practice was well known in England in the 18th century, the leading exponents being James Giles (who had a workshop with a number of artists at Clerkenwell, north of London, *c.* 1750–80, where much Worcester porcelain was decorated), and Jeffryes Hamett O'Neale (who decorated wares made at Worcester and by Wedgwood, *c.* 1748–1801); it continued into the 19th century, although little professional work of this kind was done after the 1830s. The German term is HAUSMALER, the Austrian *Winckelmann*, and the French *chambrelan*.

Indian sporting pattern. A decorative pattern used on a dinner-service made by Spode, 1810–35, in underglaze blue transfer-printing. It was adapted from engravings by Samuel Howitt in a travel-book by Captain Thomas Williamson, *Oriental Field Sports*, and depicts various field-sports with the title of each print on the underside of the plate. Other potteries used adaptations of this pattern. *See* MONOPTEROS PATTERN; CARAMANIAN PATTERN.

Indian tree pattern. A popular floral pattern, based on oriental sources, introduced by Coalport *c.* 1801.

Indianische Blumen (German). Literally, East Indies flowers. A style of floral decoration introduced by J.G. Höroldt at Meissen soon after 1720. It was principally based on Japanese KAKIEMON styles, with some inspiration from Chinese por-

Indianische Blumen. Painted decoration on porcelain bowl, Vienna (du Paquier's factory), *c*. 1725. Cecil Higgins Museum, Bedford.

celain of the FAMILLE VERTE. The name is derived from the fact that much oriental export porcelain arrived in Europe in ships of the East India Companies. The style was extensively used at Meissen until the introduction of DEUTSCHE BLUMEN, when it was gradually discarded, and it is not often seen on pieces made after 1740. It was also employed by other factories in Europe, including Chelsea. The French term is *fleurs des Indes*. *See* FLOWERS.

Indiscreet Harlequin, The. A porcelain group from the series of HARLEQUIN figures in various guises modelled by J.J. Kändler at Meissen in the 1740s. It depicts lovers seated on a mound embracing, while Harlequin at their feet, his tongue hanging out, lifts the girl's skirts. *See* COMMEDIA DELL'ARTE FIGURES.

Indiscreet Harlequin. Porcelain group by J.J. Kändler, Meissen, *c*. 1740. Courtesy, Newman & Newman Ltd, London.

Inglaze decoration. Decoration carried out on an unfired glaze which becomes merged with the glaze when fired. This technique is characteristic of much tin-enamelled ware.

Inhalator. A ceramic apparatus to facilitate the inhaling of medicated vapours, such as a globular vessel with a projecting tube, or a vessel in the form of a VEILLEUSE which has, above the pot, a concave cover with a hole in it. Inhalators were made in the late 18th century, but were most used in the second half of the 19th century.

Ink-slab. A slab of Chinese porcelain with a recess for holding a cake of ink similar in constitution and appearance to solid water-colour. Ink-slabs were of various decorative forms and occur from the Ming dynasty onwards; they formed part of the equipment for the SCHOLAR'S TABLE, with BRUSH-HOLDERS, WATER-DROPPERS, TABLE SCREEN, etc.

Ink-slab. Porcelain, with underglaze blue and enamel decoration. Reign of Wan-li (1573–1619). Victoria and Albert Museum, London.

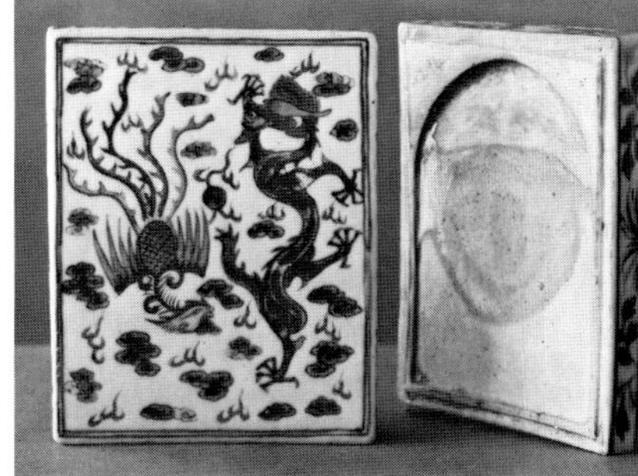

Inkstandish. Same as STANDISH.

Inlaid decoration. A style of decoration done by impressing the body with a stamped design which is then filled with slip of a different colour, as with SAINT-PORCHAIRE WARE. The technique may be noticed in medieval tiles made in England (*see* CHERTSEY TILES) and France, and on peasant pottery from Sussex. *See* ÉMAIL OMBRANT; MISHIMA.

Inro (Japanese). A medicine- or seal-case of several compartments, worn suspended from the sash in company with a netsuke. They were only rarely made of porcelain but commonly of lighter ivory or lacquer.

Inscriptions. Words, names, and dates (other than MARKS) found on some pottery and porcelain to record the name of the owner, the date of manufacture, information about the circumstances in which it was ordered, the purpose for which it was made, or information about the maker or decorator. Inscribed pieces made before 1800 are usually valued more highly than ordinary wares, especially when the inscription relates to manufacture rather than to the original owner. *See* DOCUMENTARY SPECIMENS.

Insects. Small beetles, mosquitoes, and other insects often painted on porcelain, not primarily as decoration but to conceal small flaws in the glaze.

Insufflation. The Chinese process of applying colour to porcelain by blowing the pigment in powder form through a bamboo tube, the end of which is covered by a silk screen. The result was known in France as *bleu soufflé* or *bleu fouetté*, blue being the colour normally used in this way. *See* POWDER-BLUE.

Intaglio. A design created by incising and carving below the surface. It is the opposite of CAMEO or RELIEF, where the design is raised. Wedgwood made rings and seals of this kind in black basaltes and jasper. In LITHOPHANES the design is intaglio rather than relief. It is sometimes called *cavo rilievo*. *See* RELIEF DECORATION.

Interlocking circle border. A border pattern of one or two rows of overlapping circles.

Intertwined handle. Creamware teapot with fluted body and pierced gallery, Leeds, *c.* 1780. Victoria and Albert Museum, London.

Intertwined handle. A handle made of two loops, in rope or strap form, which overlap twice.

Inverted pyriform. *See* PEAR-SHAPED.

Ionian ware. Ancient pottery made at Rhodes, having a buff-coloured body usually covered with white slip. The category includes vases often in the form of heads with helmets. Similar ware was made in many Greek colonies. *See* RHODIAN POTTERY.

Iridescent lustre. Same as STAINED LUSTRE.

Irish delftware. Tin-glazed earthenware (delftware) made from the late 17th to the end of the 18th century at about six factories in Ireland, mainly at Dublin and Belfast. *See* ENGLISH DELFTWARE.

Iron-red. An orange-red colour made from a base of ferric oxide. It is a pigment especially employed for enamel painting on Chinese porcelain, and as a ground colour, the Chinese term being FAN-HUNG. The French term is *rouge de fer*.

Iron rust glaze. A glaze of a brownish-black colour made in China during the reign of Ch'ien Lung (1736–96). It had its origins in the HONAN glazes of the Sung dynasty.

Ironstone china. A type of opaque STONE CHINA made in England, and supposed to contain slag of iron. *See* MASON'S IRONSTONE CHINA.

Islamic pottery. Earthenware made from the 9th century onwards in Persia (now Iran), Mesopotamia (now Iraq), and Egypt by Mohammedan potters and by Christian potters in their employ. Persian wares include MINAI and those from AMOL, KASHAN, GABRI, LAKABI, LAJVARDINA, RAYY, NISHAPUR, and SULTANABAD. Mesopotamian wares include those of RAKKA, and Egyptian, FOSTAT.

Isnik pottery. Pottery from Isnik (ancient Nicaea) in Anatolia (Turkey) not far from, and east of, Istanbul, on the other side of the Bosphorus. It was made from a coarse, sandy body, and is usually covered with a white slip or tin-enamel (it is not always clear which) and then with a clear glaze. The glaze covers the high-temperature colours used, and the painting is therefore technically underglaze decoration. Isnik wares were usually painted with brilliant colours, commonly blue, turquoise, and green, to which is added a thick, impasto red. Early pieces decorated with floral motifs are in dark and light blue, but soon after the middle of the 16th century a polychrome palette was introduced, with a design of stylized flowers. The early blue wares were often based on Chinese porcelain of the Ming dynasty, and the Ming ROCK OF AGES BORDER persists till the middle of the 17th century in an increasingly debased version. Isnik pottery was imported into England in Elizabethan times, where silver mounts were sometimes added. For many years it was erroneously termed 'Rhodian'.

Isnik pottery. Jug with polychrome decoration, second half of 16th century. Victoria and Albert Museum, London.

Istoriato (Italian). Decorated with scenes. A polychrome pictorial decorative style developed on Italian maiolica, especially at Urbino, in the 16th century. At first confined to the well of plates and dishes, the decoration later spread over the whole surface. The subject-matter was often derived from the work of great artists of the time, usually by way of engravings by Marcantonio Raimondi. Subjects are mythological, biblical, and *genre* scenes.

Italian Comedy figures. *See* COMMEDIA DELL'ARTE FIGURES.

Ivy border. A border pattern of a series of ivy leaves, sometimes in double rows. It was originally a Greek pattern used by Wedgwood in the 18th century.

Istoriato. Maiolica plate with polychrome enamel decoration. Urbino, 1533. Wallace Collection, London.

J

Jabberwocky pattern. Porcelain plate with polychrome decoration, Worcester (First period). Courtesy, Christie's.

Jabberwocky pattern. A decorative pattern at Worcester, inspired by Chinese porcelain, showing a fantastic creature amid exotic fruits and flowers. The name (taken from Lewis Carroll's *Through the Looking Glass*) became current in the late 19th century.

Jackfield ware. A type of black glazed pottery made at Jackfield (Shropshire) at a factory started by Maurice Thursfield, *c.* 1750. It has a red body covered with a lustrous black glaze to which decoration in OIL-GILDING was added, although this has often worn off. Some ware was probably decorated with unfired painting, but this also has yielded to time. A few pieces have decoration in relief. Ware of this kind was also made in Staffordshire by Astbury, Whieldon, and Wedgwood, and it is now difficult to separate the various kinds. A Jackfield COW CREAMER has been reproduced recently. This pottery was sometimes known as 'Japanned ware'.

Jacobite ware. English ware with emblems and inscriptions indicating sympathies with the exiled James II (after his abdication in 1688) and with his descendants (James Edward Stuart, the 'Old Pretender', and his son Bonnie Prince Charlie, the 'Young Pretender'); the relevant period lasted until 1807 when the claims of the direct Stuart line ended. Jacobite inscriptions and emblems are known on Jackfield ware and on Staffordshire saltglazed ware. Portraits of the Pretenders also appear on some pieces.

Jacobus kannetje An early type of SCHNELLE of Siegburg stoneware.

Jacqueline. A type of faience jug in the form of a seated female figure whose dress is decorated with coarsely painted flowers; it was so called because it was wrongly supposed to have been made by Countess Jacqueline of Bavaria while imprisoned, *c.* 1425. The jugs were made at Desvres, France. Similar jugs were made of stoneware in Germany, and of delftware in Holland. They are comparable with English TOBY JUGS, especially that depicting Martha Gunn (*see* GUNN, MARTHA, JUG).

Jackfield ware. Black-glazed jug with oil-gilding, *c.* 1760. Hove Museum and Art Gallery.

Jagd service. Literally, hunting service. A DINNER-SERVICE decorated with hunting scenes, and made for a hunting-lodge. Examples are known in Meissen and Vienna porcelain of the early years of the 18th century.

Jaloux, Le (French). A porcelain group depicting a young man kneeling beside a young girl who is seated in front of a pedestal or tree-stump on which leans the rejected suitor. The scene is after a drawing by Boucher, the subject of which was derived from a scene in a comedy by Mme Marie Favart entitled *La Vallée de Montmorency*. Examples occur in BISCUIT porcelain from Vincennes. The subject also appears in painted form at Vienna and Chelsea.

Jam-pot. A small jar of pottery or porcelain for serving preserves or jam, usually with a cover and a fixed saucer-like stand. The cover usually has an indentation on the rim for placing a serving spoon. It often formed part of a CABARET SERVICE. The French term is *confiturier*.

Janus figure. A reversible figure with two faces, usually one side symbolizing gin and holding a bottle, and the other water, holding a fish.

Japan fan pattern. A decorative pattern on Worcester porcelain plates with four fan-shaped ornaments alternating with four gold DIAPER designs, and with a large KIKUMON in the well. The fan-shaped ornaments have seven brocade diaper patterns of alternating colours. It is sometimes called the 'Old Japan Fan Pattern'.

Japan patterns. Patterns on English porcelain inspired by Japanese IMARI ware, and usually of bold floral design in underglaze blue with overglaze green and red enamel ornament. In England this decoration was employed at Chelsea, *c.* 1755, although rarely, and later at Derby and elsewhere, being especially popular towards the end of the 18th century. *See* OLD PATTERN; JAPAN FAN PATTERN; BROCADE PATTERN.

Le Jaloux. Group, ht 9½ in., biscuit porcelain, Vincennes, 1748–56. Courtesy, Sotheby's.

Japanese fret border. A type of FRET border with lines running obliquely in two directions.

Japanese imitation Shonsui. Porcelain made in Japan in imitation of SHONSUI ware which was made in China for export to Japan.

Japanned ware. Pottery decorated with European imitations of Japanese lacquer. *See* JACKFIELD WARE.

Japans. A broad term for JAPAN PATTERNS other than Kakiemon, and also (mistakenly) for certain designs principally inspired by Chinese porcelain.

Japonaiserie (French). European decoration with a fantasy element, analogous to CHINOISERIE, but based on Japanese themes.

Jardinière. Porcelain, with raised gilding, Sèvres, 1763. British Museum London.

Jar. A deep, wide-mouthed vessel for holding a variety of substances, usually without handles, and generally cylindrical, although sometimes of BALUSTER or other shapes. They vary greatly in size. Mainly utilitarian, many jars are of undecorated pottery, but small ones for such purposes as the storage of toilet preparations are often of porcelain, and sometimes well decorated. *See* CROCK; PITHOS; POTICHE; TINAJA; DRUG-JAR.

Jardinière (French). A large ornamental vessel, particularly one of French porcelain or faience, for holding cut flowers or for growing flowering plants. *See* CACHEPOT; CAISSE À FLEURS; VASE HOLLANDAIS.

Jasmin cup. A style of small coffee-cup, cylindrical, but with a flaring mouth and tall handle. Introduced at Sèvres in 1808.

Jasper. Cream-jug, lilac with white relief decoration, Wedgwood, *c.* 1790. Hove Museum and Art Gallery.

Jaspée ware. *See* TERRE JASPÉE.

Jasper. A hard, fine-grained, unglazed, sometimes slightly translucent STONEWARE introduced by Josiah Wedgwood in 1774. It resembles BISCUIT porcelain, and was so regarded by Wedgwood. It was sometimes fired to the point of vitrification and was then slightly translucent; several letters exist from Wedgwood's partner, Thomas Bentley, warning him against allowing this to happen, since Bentley considered that it would be an infringement of Richard Champion's porcelain patent. Jasper differs from 18th-century ARTIFICIAL PORCELAIN (with which it has sometimes been grouped) in containing about 50

Jelly mould. Wedge-shaped mould and cover, creamware, Wedgwood. Courtesy, Christie's.

per cent of barium sulphate, and its general lack of translucency was the result of deliberate slight underfiring. Although it can therefore with justification be regarded as an artificial porcelain, it is generally classified as a fine stoneware. The body was stained with metallic oxides with a number of colours, of which cobalt blue is the most used, and this varies in shade with firing temperature and the amount added to the body. Other colours included lilac, sage-green, yellow, and black (the last to be differentiated from BLACK BASALTES ware). Decoration in relief was usually white and applied to the coloured background. Sometimes three or more colours were used to decorate the same piece; these are rare. The earliest jasper, with colouring matter mixed with the body, was termed SOLID JASPER. A later type, DIP JASPER, was coloured only on the surface. A SMEAR GLAZE occurs on some early examples. From *c.* 1785 jasper was copied at a number of factories in Staffordshire and elsewhere in England. It was copied at Sèvres in BISCUIT porcelain, and at other French and German factories (*see* WEDGWOOD ARBEIT). It was usually fired once only, but some useful ware is glazed on the interior by a second firing. The ware includes vases, plaques, buttons, cameos, portrait medallions, and furniture ornaments. *See* PORTLAND (WEDGWOOD) VASES; JEWELLERY.

Jaspis Porzellan (German). A term employed for BÖTTGER (RED) STONEWARE imitating the hardstone known as jasper. It has no connection with Wedgwood JASPER ware.

Jatte à glace (French). An ice-pail; same as SEAU À GLACE.

Jatte à punch (French). A term sometimes employed to refer to a PUNCH-BOWL.

Jaune jonquille (French). Jonquil yellow; a shade of yellow developed in 1752 at Sèvres by the chemist Jean Hellot, and employed as a ground colour.

Jesuit ware. Teapot, with pencilled decoration depicting the Crucifixion, Canton, *c.* 1750. Victoria and Albert Museum, London.

Jelly mould. A vessel for gelatinous desserts. There are two forms: (1) a hollow mould to form an overall shape, used for jelly or blancmange; (2) a mould in the shape of a cone, pyramid, or wedge with painted decoration, the decoration being visible when a clear jelly (such as calves' foot jelly) is turned out; the mould was accompanied by a conforming cover to be removed before serving. Such moulds were made by Wedgwood of creamware and pearlware, and by others.

Jesuit ware. Porcelain from China made during the Ch'ing dynasty and decorated with Christian subjects taken from European engravings meticulously copied in black, sometimes almost line for line. Some slight gilding, and flesh tones in iron-red, form part of the scheme, which strongly resembles SCHWARZLOT from which it was probably derived. Most such ware was made during the first half of the 18th century, and was probably inspired but not ordered by Jesuit missionaries.

Jewelled decoration. Detail of covered vase in Louis XVI style, Sèvres, 1781. Wallace Collection, London.

Jet-enamelled. An 18th-century term, mainly used at Worcester, for TRANSFER-PRINTED decoration.

Jeu de l'écharpe (French). A series of dancing figures in the ART NOUVEAU style, originally made in BISCUIT at Sèvres for the 1900 Paris Exposition. Some of the figures were inspired by Loïe Fuller, an American artiste who achieved fame at the Folies Bergère in Paris, 1893–94. They were copied in gilt-bronze.

Jewelled decoration. A decoration introduced at Sèvres *c.* 1780, probably by Cotteau, by which drops of coloured translucent

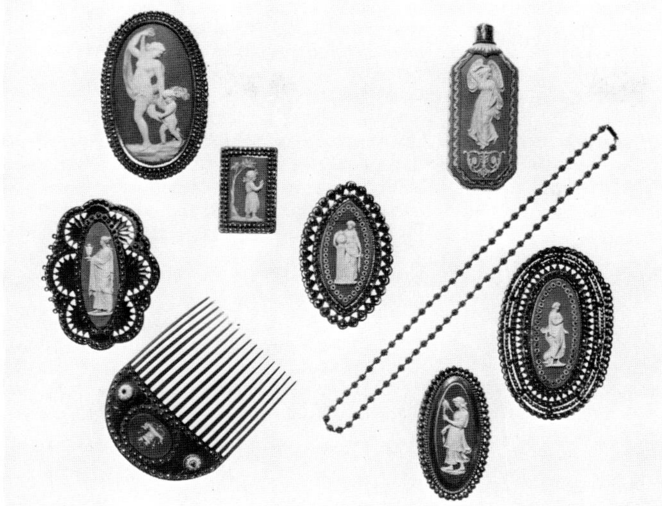

Jewellery. Examples in blue-and-white jasper, Wedgwood, *c.* 1786–90. Courtesy, Wedgwood.

enamel were fused over gold and silver foil to simulate precious stones. A similar technique was used by the Worcester factory to decorate the Countess of Dudley service in the mid-19th century.

Jewellery. Various ornaments, including brooches, clasps, buckles, necklaces, earrings, and chatelaines, that utilized jasper or porcelain pieces set in metal mountings. Wedgwood made jasper cameos that were set in cut steel mounts made by Matthew Boulton of Birmingham, *c.* 1790, and later bone-china flowers set in metal. Modern pieces include cameos set in silver.

Jigger. A machine with a revolving MOULD used in the making of plates and other flatware in conjunction with a PROFILE which is borne down on the bat of clay, pressing it into the mould and cutting away excess material. The mould forms the inside of the plate and the profile cuts the outside and the footring. This method of quantity production is an old one, having been used at porcelain factories in the 18th century. *See* JOLLY; SPREADER.

Johanneum. Marks on a Japanese bowl and (below) a Meissen bowl in imitation of it; the letter N and the numbers below the factory mark are the Johanneum inventory marks. British Museum, London.

Johanneum. The building in Dresden to which the collection of Augustus the Strong of Saxony, patron of the Meissen factory, was transferred from the Japanische Palais in the 18th century. His collection included Chinese and Japanese porcelain, and a large quantity of Meissen wares of all kinds, many especially made for the Japanische Palais. When the collection was transferred it was catalogued, and a special mark was incised into the glaze with a diamond; this mark, by reference to the inventory, showed the date of acquisition, and is often a useful indication of the date of production. Surplus specimens from the Johanneum were sold in the 1920s, and appear on the market from time to time. The inventory mark has been fraudulently added to examples of Meissen and other porcelains not from the collection.

Jolly. A machine with a revolving MOULD used in making ceramic cups in a similar way to the process of making plates with a JIGGER. The mould forms the outside of the cups, the PROFILE the inside. The profile is pressed into the bat of clay within the mould while it revolves on the jolly.

Jomon ware. Black pottery excavated in Japan which features ornament in the form of twisted rope. It was originally thought to belong to the last centuries of the first millennium BC, but the radio-activity of carbon deposits found at the same levels suggests that it may belong to a much earlier period.

Jorum. Same as PUNCH-BOWL.

Joss-stick holder. A Chinese or Japanese receptacle for joss-sticks (reeds covered with a paste made of the dust of odoriferous woods, or slender cylinders of the same paste) which were burned to scent the air. The holders are sometimes in the form of a LION OF FO to which is added a hollow column to contain the sticks.

Jour, à (French). The French term for PIERCED DECORATION. *See* PLIQUE-À-JOUR.

Ju yao (Chinese). A type of porcelain made at the Imperial factory at Ju Chou (Honan province) during the Sung dynasty, between 1107 and 1127. The body is buff-coloured, and the glaze a fine pale lavender, closely crackled. On the underside of the base there is a ring of small oval SPUR-MARKS. *See* CRACKLE.

Juan-ts'ai (Chinese). Soft colours. A palette which includes colours opacified by the inclusion of tin oxide, such as the rose enamel of the FAMILLE ROSE. These colours were of Western origin, and are in contrast to the translucent or semi-translucent Chinese enamels. *See* FA-LANG.

Judge of Hell. Stoneware figure, decorated with coloured glazes, late Ming dynasty. British Museum, London.

Judge of Hell. A Chinese pottery or stoneware figure (specimens of which range in date from the T'ang to the Ming dynasty) of stern and forbidding aspect, assumed to have the function indicated by its name. The name is sometimes erroneously applied to standing figures of demonic appearance made during the T'ang dynasty and decorated with coloured glazes; these, however, are TOMB-GUARDIANS.

Jug. A vessel, made of earthenware, stoneware, or porcelain, for holding or pouring liquids. Jugs are often of large capacity, with a pouring lip or spout, and with a handle on the opposite side. The form in general is globular, baluster-shaped, conical, ovoid, or helmet-shaped. The lip takes various forms, some ornamental. In the 18th century MILK-JUGS or CREAM-JUGS generally had a cover, but this is less often to be seen thereafter. Some so-called jugs are drinking vessels. The French term is *cruche*; the German, *Krug*. *See* PITCHER; AIGUIÈRE; AQUAMANILE; BEAR JUG; BELL-RINGER'S JUG; BETROTHAL JUG; BOCCALE; CIDER-JUG; CORN PITCHER; BEAR-JUG; OWL-JUG; GOAT AND BEE JUG; DECANTER; TOBY JUG; PUZZLE-JUG.

Ju'i. Border decoration on neck of vase, reign of Ch'ien Lung (1736–96). Victoria and Albert Museum, London.

Ju'i (Chinese). A decorative symbol or motif, vaguely heart-shaped, employed on Chinese porcelain. It resembles the head of a mandarin's or Buddhist monk's sceptre, known as a *ju'i*, and signifies 'as you wish'. *See* SCEPTRE BORDER.

Ju'i lappet border. A border pattern of connected LAPPETS in the form of the JU'I motif.

Jumping boy. A decorative subject, employed *c.* 1755 on Bow and Liverpool porcelain, depicting a boy jumping before a woman seated in a Chinese landscape.

Jungfernbeinchen (German). Small articles, such as an ÉTUI or a TOBACCO-STOPPER, modelled in the form of a maiden's leg. *See* FLOHBEIN.

Junket dish. A circular dish, shallow or slightly deep, with moulded rim, for making and serving junket.

K

Kaffeemaschine (German). A utensil for brewing coffee – a dripper or percolator – made of porcelain in Germany and Bohemia (now Czechoslovakia), sometimes in the form of an urn with a spigot, and sometimes of a coffee-pot surmounted by a dripper. *See* COFFEE-MAKER; COFFEE-WARMER; COFFEE-URN.

Kakiemon porcelain. Polychrome enamelled porcelain made at the ARITA kilns (Hizen province, Japan) and decorated by members of the Sakaida Kakiemon family. The term is commonly employed of porcelain decorated in an asymmetrical style with a variety of patterns such as the QUAIL AND MILLET, the BANDED HEDGE, and the FLYING SQUIRREL, and with flowers known in 18th-century Germany as INDIANISCHE BLUMEN. The palette includes iron-red, bluish-green, light blue, and yellow, with, occasionally, slight gilding. Effective use was made of the white porcelain surface, which was balanced very effectively with the carefully judged asymmetry of the painted motifs. Porcelain in this style was first imported by the Dutch towards the end of the 17th century, and soon became extremely popular, being widely copied and adapted at Meissen and elsewhere. Characteristic Arita shapes on which this decorative scheme was used include bowls and vases of octagonal, hexagonal, and square section which were also copied in Europe. Kakiemon-style Arita porcelain of this kind is now very rare. The twelfth-generation member of this family to bear the same name, also a porcelain painter, was born in 1879.

Kakiemon porcelain. Double-gourd vase with characteristic Kakiemon painted decoration, late 17th century. Victoria and Albert Museum, London.

Kakiemon style. Decoration on European porcelain in the style of KAKIEMON PORCELAIN of the end of the 17th century. At the beginning of the 18th century porcelain of this kind was more popular even than that of China, and when Augustus the Strong, Elector of Saxony, bought a palace to house his porcelain collection he renamed it the Japanische Palais. The Meissen factory was much influenced by it during the 1720s and 1730s, and in England some of the earliest Chelsea porcelain was so closely based on it that the two have sometimes been confused. The QUAIL AND MILLET pattern in particular occurs on Bow porcelain, but Kakiemon designs do not appear with the same frequency on Worcester porcelain. For the first two decades of its life the Chantilly factory utilized Kakiemon patterns almost exclusively. A collection of this kind of porcelain, formed by Queen Mary, was brought to England when she and her husband, William III, acceded to the throne in 1689. It was housed at Hampton Court, but much has since apparently disappeared.

Kakiemon style. Worcester porcelain plate decorated with the Bengal tyger pattern. Courtesy, Worcester Royal Porcelain Co.

Kalathos (Greek). A rare type of KRATER, bucket-shaped and without handles, and sometimes having a spout near the base.

Kalian. The Persian term for a HOOKAH.

Kalpis (Greek). Sometimes *calpis.* A late form of vase of Greek pottery of the HYDRIA type, used for carrying oil or water. It has two side loop-handles, and also a vertical handle on the shoulder reaching to the neck that was used when pouring. The neck forms a continuous curve with the body.

Kamares style. A decorative style on Cretan pottery of the

Kang. Cup decorated with enamels of the *famille rose* palette; mark and reign of Ch'ien Lung (1736–95). Percival David Foundation of Chinese Art, London.

Kantharos. Greek drinking-cup (head vase), before 510 BC. Museum of Fine Arts, Boston, Mass. (Pierce Fund).

Middle Minoan period, *c*. 2000–1800 BC. It is usually painted in mat red and white on a mat black ground. It was named after the cave in Crete where much of it was found.

Kändler figures. Porcelain figures, made initially in the BAROQUE style, and from the late 1740s in the ROCOCO style, modelled by Johann Joachim Kändler (1706–75), *Modellmeister* at the Meissen factory from 1733 to his death. Kändler also worked in collaboration with J. F. Eberlein and Peter Reinicke on several series of figures. Although best known for his small figures (*Kleinplastik*) for table decoration, Kändler began by modelling almost life-size animals for the Japanische Palais in Dresden, and was for many years engaged on a life-size equestrian statue of Augustus the Strong, Elector of Saxony, which was never finished. *See* COMMEDIA DELL'ARTE FIGURES; HARLEQUIN FIGURES; AFFENKAPELLE; FRÖHLICH; FIVE SENSES; FOUR MONARCHS; MASONIC FIGURES; MONTHS, THE; GOATS.

Kang (Chinese). A tub-shaped cup of Chinese porcelain; it has vertical sides slightly curving towards the base.

Kantharos (Greek). Sometimes *cantharus*. A drinking-cup of Greek pottery having a tall, footed stem and two loop side-handles each extending from the bottom of the bowl to the rim. Some were made in the form of a head, or with a head front and back; this type is sometimes referred to as a head vase. The *kantharos* was associated with Bacchus. *See* HOLCION; KARCHESION; FACE-JUG; MASK MUGS AND JUGS.

Kaolin. White CHINA CLAY which is an extremely pure aluminium silicate. An essential ingredient of most TRUE PORCELAIN, it is now employed for all types of porcelain. The word means 'high ridge'. Such clay came from deposits near the Imperial kilns at Ching-tê Chên. Deposits exist in Cornwall (England), a number of places on the Continent, such as Saint-Yrieix, near Limoges (France), and in the United States. Kaolin remains white after firing, although Chinese porcelain made with it sometimes shows an inclination to buff (due to traces of iron) on the unglazed part of the foot-ring.

Kapuzinerbraun (German). A ground colour, perhaps so named because it was similar to the colour of the robes of Capuchin monks of the Franciscan Order. It was devised at Meissen, *c*. 1722, by the kilnmaster Samuel Stölzel, and was there sometimes called *Kaffeebraun*. *See* CAFÉ AU LAIT.

Karatsu. A type of pottery made by Korean potters working in Japan at Karatsu, near Arita (Hizen province), in the late 16th century.

Karchesion (Greek). Sometimes *carchesium*. A type of footless KANTHAROS; it is associated with Bacchus.

Kashān ware (Persian). A type of Persian pottery from the Kashān district, south of Teheran, made from 1215 to 1334. The area is well known for wall-tiles painted with lustre, usually in conjunction with relief modelling and a blue glaze, and also for ware with a deep-blue glaze, sometimes over a body on which designs have been painted in black, and occasionally over moulded or engraved decoration. *See* MINAI WARE.

Keep-within-compass plate. A plate decorated by John Aynsley (1752–1829), of Longton (Staffordshire), with a popular black transfer-print of scenes and inscriptions counselling virtue.

Kelebe (Greek). Sometimes *celebe.* A KRATER of the Corinthian type.

Kempthorne pattern. A decorative pattern on a Worcester porcelain dinner-service; it has oriental flowers and shrubs in iron-red and green enamel on underglaze blue, with gilding and a diaper border. The service was named after a Mr Kempthorne of Cornwall, who was presented with one after he refused payment in 1760 for lodging one of the original shareholders of the Worcester factory, John Thornloe, who was in Cornwall searching for soaprock.

Kendi (Persian). A drinking-vessel of globular shape, with a vertical neck for filling and a short spout projecting from the shoulder for drinking. Made in porcelain in China in the 15th and 16th centuries for export to the Middle East. *See* HOOKAH.

Kendi. Porcelain, decorated in underglaze red, second half of 15th century. Victoria and Albert Museum, London.

Kent ware. A kind of coarse earthenware made by several potteries in Kent (England), using local red or pink clay, the only decoration being designs of a simple kind in slip.

Kerbschnitt (German). Carved decoration occurring on RHENISH STONEWARE, e.g. on the TRAUERKRUG, in the form of geometric patterns.

Kertch ware. Greek pottery, probably Athenian, found at Kertch in southern Russia and also in North Africa, which was made from the end of the 4th century BC, after the art had passed its best period. The craftsmanship is poor and the designs overcrowded, with blue, red, green, and gilding added to decoration in the RED-FIGURE STYLE.

Kettle. A pottery or porcelain covered vessel of large size, with an overhead (BAIL) handle and a spout, employed for heating liquids. Kettles may be globular, pear-shaped, or oblate, with either a fixed ceramic handle or a swing handle with metal arms connected at the top by a wood or ceramic hand-grip. The spout is curved in a variety of ways, and some kettles have spouts on either side, occasionally elaborately modelled, e.g. in the form of swans' heads. Some kettles rest on a stand which contains a device for heating. The stands are usually either basin-shaped to contain charcoal, or three-legged, with a GODET or spirit-lamp in the centre. The term 'punch-kettle' is occasionally given to vessels resembling a large TEA-KETTLE in shape and intended for serving punch. *See* PUNCH-POT; RUM-KETTLE.

Key-fret. A border pattern or frieze consisting of straight lines turning at right angles in a continuous repetitive design reminiscent of the wards of a key. Sometimes termed GREEK FRET. *See* MEANDER.

Kiangnan Ting (Chinese). A cream-glazed Chinese ware, somewhat resembling the earlier TING YAO but made during the Ming and Ch'ing dynasties; it was probably made at several places, and cannot be assigned with certainty to any one. The earliest may have been made at Tz'ŭ Chou. *See* TZ'Ŭ CHOU YAO.

Keep-within-compass plate. Transfer-printed decoration, John Aynsley, Staffordshire. Courtesy, Jellinek & Sampson, London.

Kick terminal. A TERMINAL, on the lower end of a handle, which curls away from the body and ends in a small knop, as distinguished from the simple curled extremity such as the one employed on much Wedgwood ware.

Kick-in base. The base of some bowls, bottles, and decanters made before 1760 with a dent in the shape of a cone, imitative of the base of some glass vessels.

Kikumon (Japanese). A MON (or heraldic device) which is the most frequently used Japanese Imperial crest. It resembles an open stylized chrysanthemum with sixteen complete petals. *See* KIRIMON. It was used as a decorative design on Japanese IMARI ware, was imitated on Chinese Imari, and later was widely used at Worcester. On some ARITA PORCELAIN it is moulded in relief with the petals enamelled or gilded.

Kiln. The oven used for firing all ceramic wares. *See* GRAND FEU; PETIT FEU; MUFFLE; BOTTLE-KILN; TUNNEL-KILN; KILN FURNITURE.

Kiln furniture. Objects usually made of fire-clay for use in the kiln to support and protect ceramic ware during firing, e.g. SAGGERS, SAGGER PINS, TRIVETS, COCKSPURS (stilts), FIRING RINGS, GIRDERS (sluggs), RAFTERS, PARTING SHARDS, CONES, and kiln tiles.

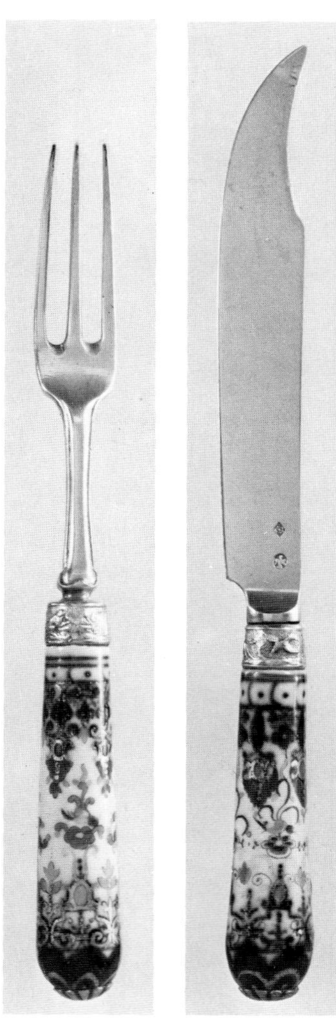

Knife and fork handles. Silver-gilt dessert knife and fork with porcelain handles, Meissen, *c.* 1735. Courtesy, Christie's.

Kiln waster. Same as WASTER.

King of Prussia. A decorative motif featuring Frederick the Great of Prussia, allied to England during the Seven Years' War (1756–63); it was especially popular in England during the years 1756–57. The King's portrait occurs in transfer-printed form on much contemporary Worcester porcelain, principally mugs and jugs. There are three different engravings, in each of which the King is shown in armour: (1) seated on a prancing charger, riding on the battlefield, with a dead soldier on the ground; (2) half-length; (3) full-length. Usually an allegorical figure of Fame is shown, together with trophies, flags, and the date 1757. Plates with a moulded border have relevant inscriptions, trophies, and a portrait. Portraits on Worcester porcelain are from HANCOCK ENGRAVINGS. The close connection which existed at the time between England and Prussia was due to the fact that the English kings were also Electors of Hanover, which territory adjoined Prussia.

Kingfisher glaze. The same as KORYO PI-SAEK. The Chinese term is *fei-ts'ui*.

Kinrande (Japanese). Gilt decoration on a red ground, found on Chinese porcelain made during and after the reign of Chia Ching (1522–66) and much favoured in Japan.

Kinuta seiji (Japanese). A term for the greenish-blue celadon glaze to be found on Chinese MALLET VASES made during the Sung dynasty (960–1280).

Kirimon (Japanese). A MON (or heraldic device) which is an alternative to the more customary Japanese Imperial device, the KIKUMON. It consists of spikes of blossom of the *kiri* tree (*Paulownia*) towering above a trefoil leaf. It was employed on ARITA porcelain.

Kirin. The Japanese version of the Chinese KYLIN (one of the Four Supernatural Creatures; SSŬ LING), used as a decorative motif on ARITA PORCELAIN.

Knife and fork handles. Porcelain and stoneware handles, often shaped in the form of a pistol-butt (*see* PISTOL HANDLE) into which were inserted a steel or silver knife or fork.

Knife-rest. A small, low utensil for supporting a knife at the dinner-table and sometimes part of a dinner-service; *see* ASPARAGUS SHELL.

Knop. Same as FINIAL.

Ko Kutani (Japanese). Old Kutani, as distinguished from AO KUTANI and also SAIKO KUTANI. *See* KUTANI PORCELAIN.

Ko Shonsui (Japanese). The same as GEN SHONSUI.

Ko sometsuke. The Japanese term for Chinese blue-and-white porcelain made *c.* 1578–1643 for export to Japan. It is coarse, with a thick, often misshapen body, and spontaneously drawn decoration, all made to conform to contemporary Japanese taste. *See* RANZOHAN WARE.

Ko yao (Chinese). Literally, the ware of the elder brother, so called because it was, by tradition, made by the elder of two brothers named Chang, although this explanation may be apocryphal. It was stoneware probably made at Lung-ch'üan (Chekiang province) during the Sung dynasty (960–1280). The body is dark brown where exposed, and the glaze is greyish white and covered with a closely meshed CRACKLE, the lines of the crackle being emphasized by reddish-brown or black pigment. It was much valued in old China, and was copied during the early years of the 18th century. *See* KUAN YAO.

King of Prussia. Mask jug with transfer-printed decoration, Worcester, 1757. Victoria and Albert Museum, London.

Kochi ware. A type of pottery from southern China that was exported to Japan, the term *kochi* being derived from Cochin-China. The ware is decorated with lead glazes in three colours, green, yellow, and aubergine. It ranges from soft pottery, light in weight, to stoneware and coarse porcelain. Small boxes, called KOGO, have survived in Japan.

Kogo (Japanese). A small, round BOX with a cover in the form of an animal, bird, fruit, or flower in relief. They were adapted to hold incense for the Tea Ceremony, and were widely copied in the 19th century. Early specimens were made of KOCHI WARE.

Komori (Japanese). The bat, to be found as a decorative motif on some Japanese porcelain. It is the same as the Chinese FU.

Königliche Hof-Konditorei (or **Conditorei**; German). Royal Court Confectionery. This is the meaning of the initials KHK or KHC on some early Meissen porcelain, especially figures as part of a TABLE-DECORATION. 'Königliche Hof-Konditorei Warschau' refers to the Warsaw Confectionery, since Augustus III, patron of the Meissen factory, was also King of Poland. *See* OWNERSHIP MARK.

Korean tyger pattern. Same as TYGER AND WHEATSHEAF PATTERN.

Korean ware. Ware made in Korea, including the pottery of the Silla dynasty (*c.* 57 BC – AD 935), the Koryu or Koryŏ dynasty (918–1392), and the Yi dynasty (1392–1910). *See* PUNCH-ŎNG WARE; MISHIMA; SANGGAM CELADON.

Koro (Japanese). An incense-burner made of either porcelain or pottery. Chinese incense-burners based on the old bronze TING, of globular shape on three feet and surmounted by a cover, are also often referred to by this Japanese term.

Koroplastae (Greek). Literally, plastic figures. The Greek term for terracotta figures made at Tanagra and elsewhere. *See* TANAGRA FIGURES.

Kretschmar ware. Tureen and cover with underglaze blue decoration, Meissen, *c.* 1730. Courtesy, Antique Porcelain Co., London.

Krater. Corinthian or columnar type (*kelebe*), ht 18⅜ in., Agrigentum, *c*. 440 BC. British Museum, London.

Krater. Calyx type, decorated in the red-figure style, *c*. 480 BC. British Museum, London.

Krater. Bell krater, decorated in the red-figure style, 4th century BC. Victoria and Albert Museum, London.

Koryŏ (Koryu or Korai) **dynasty**. Korean wares made during this period (918–1392) include a porcelain with a creamy glaze analogous to Chinese *Ting* wares (*see* TING YAO); a porcelain of the YING CH'ING type; and celadons with a green or bluish-green glaze. The inlaid MISHIMA decoration belongs to this period. During the latter part of the dynasty some notable wares, especially some not very precisely potted vases of a coarse, greyish porcelain, were decorated in a sensitive style with birds (both aquatic and flying amid clouds), trees, grasses, and floral scrolls, the technique of painting in brownish-black slip being akin to that of TZ'Ŭ CHOU YAO. *See* PAEK-KORYŎ; KORYŎ PI-SAEK.

Koryŏ pi-saek (Korean). A fine bluish-green glaze to be found on CELADON wares made in south Korea from the 11th century, during the Koryŏ dynasty (918–1392). It is also known as 'king-fisher glaze'.

Kotyle (Greek). Sometimes *cotula*. A drinking-cup of Greek pottery; the term is sometimes applied to a SKYPHOS.

Kotyliskos (Greek). Sometimes *cotyliscos*. A small toilet vase of Greek pottery of elongated form tapering to a small, flat base. It was used for ointments or perfumes.

Kraak porselein (Dutch). Same as CARRACK PORCELAIN.

Krater**.** Often *crater*. A vase of Greek pottery for mixing wine and water; large, with a wide body and mouth, it has two side handles and a small circular base. There are several variations: (1) Corinthian or columnar-handled (called a KELEBE or *vaso a colonette*); (2) volute-handled (p. 242), with vertical handles rising from loops on the shoulder to a point above the rim and ending in a volute (called a *vaso a rotelle*); (3) calyx-shaped – like a chalice or the calyx of a flower – with two horizontal uplifted loop handles attached at the lower part of the body (called a *vaso a calice*); and (4) in the shape of an inverted bell with two horizontal uplifted handles just below the rim (called a *vaso campana*). The Lucanian *krater* has four handles, two vertical and two horizontal. *See* FRANÇOIS VASE; KALATHOS.

Kretschmar ware. Very rare Meissen porcelain decorated in underglaze blue *c*. 1725 or soon afterwards, so called because the technique of employing this colour was discovered by David Kretschmar.

Kriegvasen (German). Literally, war vases. A series of vases modelled at Meissen by J. J. Kändler and J. F. Eberlein, and decorated with figures of warriors and reliefs depicting battle scenes. The vases were made in 1741–42 for presentation to Louis XV.

Ku (Chinese). A Chinese porcelain vase of beaker shape based on an ancient bronze form, cylindrical, with a bulge midway, and a trumpet mouth. They are similar to but smaller than the TSUN, and were copied in England at Worcester.

Ku yüeh hsüan (Chinese). Literally, ancient moon pavilion. A rare type of Chinese porcelain, belonging to the early decades of the 18th century, in the decoration of which the painter attempted to imitate the European style in brushwork. It is thought to have been made by T'ang Ying (director of the Imperial Factory at Ching-tê Chên from the accession of Ch'ien Lung in 1736 to *c*. 1750), who was also noted for his clever reproductions of earlier wares. *See* CH'ING DYNASTY.

Kua p'i lū (Chinese). Same as CUCUMBER GREEN GLAZE.

Kuan-ti. The Chinese god of war who is represented as a figure made in BLANC DE CHINE porcelain from Tê Hua during the closing years of the Ming dynasty.

Kuan yao (Chinese). Fine stoneware made in the Sung dynasty (960–1280), first at Kai-fêng Fu (Honan province) and later (after 1127) at Hangchou (Chekiang province). It was said to have a 'brown mouth and iron foot', which refers to the colours exhibited by the body at the rim and foot-ring. The glaze varies between lavender and grey, with an inclination to blue or green. Specimens of likely attribution have either a widely or a closely meshed crackled glaze, often emphasized by the application of brown or black pigment. The glaze is almost opaque, and very rich. The Chinese sometimes refer to it as resembling 'massed lard'. The term means 'official ware', and it was made for the Court. *See* KO YAO.

Kuan-yin. A Buddhist deity, the goddess of mercy, often depicted as a figure in BLANC DE CHINE from Tê Hua, or, less often, in painted form. She is usually shown seated on a lotus throne in the Lalitsana pose with an ambrosia bottle in her left hand, a bowl beside her elbow, and her right hand entwined in a pearl rosary resting on her knee. In later versions she holds an infant on her lap. A standing pose is also not uncommon. Kuan-yin developed from the male Bodhisattva, Avalokiteshvara, appearing in female form by the Sung dynasty (960–1280).

Kuan-yin. Figure in blanc de Chine, Tê-Hua, 17th century. Victoria and Albert Museum, London.

Kuangtung ware (Chinese). Ware from Kuangtung province, the body of which is porcellaneous and fires to a dark reddish-brown. Glazes range from a Chün type (*see* CHÜN YAO), through celadon, to a dark brown. FATSHAN CHÜN comes from this region, as well as figures (in shrines) with flesh areas left unglazed and consequently reddish-brown in colour. Specimens are crudely finished. Early examples are not likely to be before the Ming dynasty, and most are quite modern. *See* SWATOW WARE.

Kuchihani (Japanese). *See* HON SHONSUI.

Kuei (Chinese). An early form of DRAGON used as a decorative design on Chinese porcelain. It is usually simpler in drawing, and much less detailed, than later dragons.

Kufic script. A kind of angular and formal Arabic calligraphy used as decoration on ISLAMIC POTTERY. *See* NESKHI; MOCK ARABIC.

Kurawanka (Japanese). A term used in Japan for everyday pottery utensils. It is sometimes applied to a low-grade form of blue-and-white ARITA PORCELAIN decorated with free and simple designs.

Kusitakade (Japanese). A style of decoration that was common on NABESHIMA WARE, but is also to be found on ARITA and KUTANI porcelain. It was probably of Chinese origin. It occurs on the outside of a high foot-ring in the form of a serrated comb-like design in underglaze blue.

Kütahya ware. Pottery from Kütahya (central Anatolia), Turkey, dating from the 17th century. It has some affinities with ISNIK POTTERY, but the decoration frequently contains a yellow pigment not to be found on wares from Isnik. Some pieces are painted with the thick red obtained from ARMENIAN BOLE known as Armenian red.

Kuan-ti. Figure in blanc de Chine, Tê-Hua, 17th century. Courtesy, Bluett and Sons, London.

Kyathos. Red earthenware, with black and red painted decoration, Cerveteri, 550–530 BC. Victoria and Albert Museum, London.

Kylin pattern. Porcelain plate with four panels, Worcester.

Kylix. Eye kylix, diam. 11¾ in., from Vulci, *c.* 520 BC. British Museum, London.

Kutani porcelain. Japanese porcelain attributed to kilns at Kutani (Kaga province), although there is an element of uncertainty as to its origin. It was made from *c.* 1639 to 1692–94. Genuine examples of KO KUTANI (old Kutani) are of fine quality as to decoration, although both body and glaze show defects. The best examples are noted for brilliant enamel colouring in reserved panels on a red-patterned ground. Ko Kutani is to be distinguished from AO KUTANI (green Kutani) and also from SAIKO KUTANI (revived Kutani) made in the 19th century in Kaga and elsewhere. Some examples decorated with gold and silver with a Ko Kutani attribution have been questioned. The surviving wares include large and small dishes, potiches, and bottles.

Kwaart (Dutch). A lead glaze added after the decoration and firing of the tin-glaze of Dutch delftware to enhance the appearance. It gave the ware a smooth and glassy finish. The absence of *kwaart* helps to distinguish some English and German wares from Dutch, although in England the practice of adding a lead overglaze was employed at Bristol during the first part of the 18th century. *See* COPERTA.

Kyathos (Greek). Sometimes *cyathus*. A Greek ladle with a long, upright, looped handle. Used for transferring wine from a KRATER into an OENOCHOË or a cup.

Kylin (Chinese). Properly, *lin* or *ch'i-lin*. A mythical fabulous animal compounded from the head of a dragon, with a scaly body, deer-hooves, a bushy tail, and a single horn. From this last feature it is sometimes termed the 'Chinese unicorn'. It is an extremely auspicious creature in Chinese mythology, but it is rarely used as painted decoration, and only occasionally as a figure in the BLANC DE CHINE of Tê Hua. The LION (or Dog) OF FO is often miscalled a *kylin*, especially in provincial auctioneers' catalogues. The comparable Japanese term is *kirin*. The *kylin* is one of the Four Supernatural Creatures (SSŬ LING).

Kylin pattern. A decorative pattern, derived from oriental sources, employed on Worcester porcelain. It has, encircling a central motif, barbed radiating panels enclosing alternately a KYLIN and a table with plants, the whole being surrounded by a border of red, green, and gold. Chamberlain called the pattern 'dragon in compartments'.

Kylix (Greek). Sometimes *cylix*. A wide, shallow drinking-cup on a footed stem, with two large upcurved handles; its shape is one of the most graceful among Greek pottery types. There are three forms: (1) with the lip set off from the body of the bowl; (2) with a deep and continuously curved bowl; and (3) with a continuous curve from the lip to the rim of the foot. Some wide two-handled cups have no stem between the bowl and base and are referred to as stemless cups. The *kylix* was used at banquets in both Greece and Rome; examples are often finely decorated, especially inside. A variant form known as an eye kylix, found in Sicily and at Vulci (Etruria), is so called from the fact that specimens are often painted with two large pairs of eyes. The term was latinized as *calicis*. *See* LEPASTE.

Kyoto ware (Japanese). A type of buff-glazed crackled stoneware usually of inferior quality and extensively exported to Europe in the second half of the 19th century under the misnomer of 'Satsuma'. Most of it was made at Awata, a suburb of Kyoto, Japan.

L

Label. *See* BIN-LABEL; WINE-LABEL.

Lac burgauté (French). *See* PORCELAINE LAQUÉE BURGAUTÉE.

Lace bowl. A Chinese bowl with RICE-GRAIN PIERCING made during the reign of Ch'ien Lung (1736–96).

Lacework ground. A ground pattern of non-tangent equal circles in a checkered pattern with numerous small dots in the spaces between the circles.

Lacework porcelain. A decoration to figures made by dipping lace into porcelain slip. The threads burned away during firing, leaving a replica of the mesh in porcelain. The technique was probably first introduced at Meissen, *c.* 1770, and is to be seen on figures by Michel-Victor Acier, who may have developed the idea. About the same time it was being used at Strasbourg by J. A. Hannong. First employed as a fussy addition to the dress of some figures, the technique was developed in the 19th century and employed to make figures in elaborately flounced lace-skirts. It was also used at Sèvres and Derby in the 19th century for minor additions to costume.

Lag and feather pattern. Parapet teapot and stand with painted decoration, creamware, Staffordshire, *c.* 1805. Victoria and Albert Museum, London.

Lacquer. Coloured varnishes employed to decorate early porcelain, and occasionally pottery. Unlike enamel it did not require firing, and so it has mostly worn off. Lacquer decoration by Martin Schnell at Meissen occurs on red stoneware made soon after 1710 and is highly valued. Early porcelain from the same source sometimes shows slight remaining traces of lacquer colour. The German term is *Kaltmalerei. See* COLD COLOURS; LACQUER DECORATION.

Lacquer decoration. The decoration of pottery and porcelain by the application of unfired lacquer colours, or in the manner of oriental lacquer panels imported into Europe from the 17th century onwards. Chinese lacquer was an occasional source of inspiration at Vienna, whereas Meissen was much more inclined to copy oriental porcelain.

Lacquer gilding. An early method of gilding porcelain by which gold leaf was powdered, mixed with varnish, and applied to the ware with a brush. The gold has mostly worn off. It was also termed 'varnish gilding'.

Ladies' Amusement, The. A book of engravings by Jean Pillement and others 'to assist those engaged in the art of japanning'. It was published by Robert Sayer, London, *c.* 1760, and contains 200 copperplate illustrations showing 1,500 designs, many of them engraved and signed by Robert Hancock. These, and some of Pillement's designs, were the source of much transfer-printed decoration on English porcelain, especially at Worcester. A later, similar, source book was *The Ladies' Amusement and Designers' Assistant*, *c.* 1821. *See* HANCOCK ENGRAVINGS.

Lambeth delftware. Blue-dash charger with equestrian portrait of William III, *c.* 1695. City Museums, Stoke-on-Trent.

Ladle. A cup-like spoon, usually with a long handle which is sometimes curved, employed for transferring liquids from one utensil to another. Some examples were made of porcelain either as part of a dinner-service, or were *en suite* with a tureen. *See* KYATHOS.

Lady-and-squirrel pattern. A decorative subject on Lowestoft porcelain depicting a Chinese woman seated in a trellised arbour with a squirrel crawling along the top.

Lady-in-a-pavilion pattern. A KAKIEMON pattern, popular at Chelsea during the raised-anchor period (1750–53), which depicts a lady in a pavilion with draped curtains and tassels, a bird-cage to one side, and two escaped birds in flight.

Lag and feather pattern. A painted pattern consisting of a fluted ribbon decorated with a continuous feathery motif. It was developed by Wedgwood, *c.* 1790, and is still used.

Lagynos. Pottery, width 7 in., Salamis, *c.* 150–50 BC. British Museum, London.

Lagynos (Greek). A type of OENOCHOË with a low wide body, angular shoulder, high neck, circular mouth, and a single loop handle extending from the top of the neck to the shoulder.

Lajvardina ware. A type of Persian pottery made in the 13th and 14th centuries, with alkaline glazes of deep blue and turquoise over a coarse, greyish and inferior body. It was gilded over the glaze.

Lakabi ware. A type of Persian pottery from Rayy (Rhages), near Teheran, glazed in various colours in conjunction with a SGRAFFITO technique, the engraved lines limiting the flow of glaze (a CLOISONNÉ technique). The designs are usually animals and birds done in a simple style which was imposed by the difficulty of the technique. *See* RAYY WARE.

Lakaina (Greek). A Laconian drinking-cup, the sides of which are slightly tapered; the lower part of the body has a bulge from which two horizontal loop handles extend.

Lambrequins. Porcelain jar and cover decorated in underglaze blue, Saint-Cloud, *c.* 1700. Victoria and Albert Museum, London.

Lambeth delftware. Tin-glazed earthenware (ENGLISH DELFTWARE) made from *c.* 1601 at various potteries situated in Lambeth, south London. The body is pale buff where unglazed, and the ware differs somewhat from other English delftware in its tone, glaze, and decoration. The lettering on inscribed pieces is fairly characteristic. Where the glaze is thin the pale buff body is inclined to show through it and exhibit a pinkish tinge in consequence. Usually the blue is paler than on most other English delftware. Wine-bottles were a speciality, and a spatter design in purple or blue is occasionally to be seen. The early ware, *c.* 1601–20, was influenced by Italian maiolica from Urbino, and has been called 'English maiolica'. *See* SOUTHWARK DELFTWARE; LONDON DELFTWARE.

Lambeth stoneware. A type of BROWN STONEWARE made at Lambeth, south London, from the middle of the 18th century. The saltglaze is inclined to be more brilliant than that of the wares of nearby Fulham, and the brown on the upper part of a richer colour. Wares include mugs decorated with applied reliefs of hunting and drinking scenes.

Lambrequin (French). A baroque, scalloped border pattern of pendent drapery, lacework, leaves, and scrollwork adapted from design-books of the period, and possibly influenced by the bed-drapes of Daniel Marot (1650–1700). Usually there are alternating large and small motifs. A variety in which the *lambrequins* radiate from the centre of a plate or dish is known as the *style rayonnant*. *Lambrequins* were introduced at Rouen as a faience decoration by Louis Poterat, and were much used there from *c.* 1700 till the middle of the century; they also occur as decoration on Saint-Cloud porcelain. *See* LAUB- UND BANDELWERK; RAYONNANT, STYLE; LAPPET PATTERN.

Lamp. A utensil for producing artificial light. Originally this was by means of a lighted wick floating on oil, or protruding from a small spout left for the purpose (as with Roman terracotta lamps). Occasionally they were employed to produce a low heat (*see* GODET). Some lamps stand on a base; others are intended for suspension by a chain. The variety of shapes of ceramic lamps is very great; they range from the early Greek and Roman types (like an Aladdin's lamp) to modern porcelain lamps, many of which are vases converted for use with electric bulbs.

Lamp. Terracotta oil-lamp, Roman, 3rd–4th century.

Lang yao (Chinese). Wares glazed with a type of SANG-DE-BŒUF, or copper transmutation glaze. Copper-red in colour, they are said to have been made in the 18th century under the direction of Lang T'ing-chi, Governor of Kiangsi province, who owned a private kiln.

Lange Lijzen (Dutch). *See* LONG ELIZA PATTERN.

Lantern. A portable enclosure for a light. Lanterns in the form of lamp-shades of highly translucent porcelain, sometimes pierced with elaborate patterns, were made in China during the reign of Ch'ien Lung (1736–96). Most were intended for suspension from carved wood stands, and decoration was in the *famille rose* palette. Lanterns were also made in Italy and elsewhere in Europe.

Lantern. Chinese porcelain lantern with pierced decoration and enamels of the *famille rose* palette; reign of Ch'ien Lung (1736–95). Courtesy, Frank Partridge & Sons Ltd, London.

Lao Tzŭ. The Chinese philosopher of the 6th century BC who founded Taoism (The Way), and is often represented on porcelain, usually with the EIGHT IMMORTALS. He is also called Shou (Old) Lao. *See* CHINESE TRIAD.

Lapidary-polished. As applied to hard ceramic substances – polished by the same techniques as those used to polish precious stones with the object of imparting a high gloss. Lapidaries also engraved decoration on certain early wares, notably BÖTTGER RED STONEWARE at Meissen.

Lapis lazuli. A dark crackled blue derived from cobalt, used on Chinese porcelain during the reign of Ch'ien Lung (1736–96). The colour is not the same as the copper blue of lapis lazuli stone. The term was employed by Wedgwood for a type of variegated ware which was blue and pebbled with gold veining. *See* BLEU LAPIS.

Lappet pattern. A border pattern of pendent motifs. When the motifs are in the form of a JU'I, it is referred to as a Ju'i lappet border. *See* LAMBREQUIN.

Laquée burgautée, porcelaine (French). *See* PORCELAINE LAQUÉE BURGAUTÉE.

Lathe. A machine-tool in which the ware is held between rotating centres on a horizontal axis, and various stationary cutting tools are brought into contact with it for the purpose of paring it down, or incising ornament. The simple lathe was probably introduced into Staffordshire by the Elers brothers, *c.* 1700, and was much used thereafter, leading to greater precision in the finishing of the ware. The engine-turning lathe was introduced by Josiah Wedgwood in 1763 and used for the decoration of such wares as black basaltes with repetitive incised patterns. *See* ENGINE-TURNED DECORATION: ROSE-ENGINE TURNED.

Laub- und Bandelwerk. Detail showing frame surrounding painted landscape, Meissen, *c.* 1740. Hastings Museum and Art Gallery.

Lattice border. Same as TRELLIS BORDER.

Laub- und Bandelwerk (German). Literally, leaf- and strap-work. Late baroque ornament of this kind was used at Meissen and Vienna especially, and usually framed a decorative painting on porcelain, either in gold silhouette or in enamel colours. Its origin is to be found in baroque metalwork, and it owes something to the designs of Jean Bérain *père* in France.

Laubengruppe (German). Same as ARBOUR GROUP.

Laurel border. A border pattern of a series of laurel leaves placed horizontally, and separated by flowers and berries. It was used quite commonly on pottery and on Wedgwood's jasper during the period of the neo-classical (or Adam) style in England.

Lava ware. (1) A coarse STONEWARE made in England and Germany by mixing clay with slag from iron-smelting. It has a hard glaze fused at great heat. In England in the 19th century it was used as a kind of cottage china. (2) An American term for SCRODLED WARE.

Lavabo. A wash-basin; *see* LAVER.

Lavender-jar. A jar or vase with a pierced cover to allow the scent of dried lavender to diffuse. It is similar to a POT-POURRI VASE. The German term is *Lavendelkrug*.

Lavender ware. A lavender-coloured earthenware introduced by Wedgwood, *c.* 1840, the body similar to that of CANE-WARE.

Laver. A large wash-basin with a flat bottom and flaring sides. Some were made of pottery in Spain. The French term is *lavabo*.

Lazulite. A type of PARIAN PORCELAIN coloured blue, similar in hue to the mineral lazulite.

Lead glaze. A transparent glaze containing lead oxide. It probably dates from Ptolemaic times, and was occasionally used by some Roman potters. Its distribution is very wide. Lead glazes are apt to become stained and discoloured, but they allow the decorative use of a wide range of metallic pigments. Lead glazes were originally applied in powder form (*see* GALENA), but later in the form of a suspension in water. *See* CREAMWARE; QUEEN'S WARE.

Leadless glaze. A glaze without a lead content, such as the feldspathic glaze. In the 18th century the poisonous effect of lead compounds on workers in the pottery industry was recognized, and in the early years of the 19th century a variety of glazes utilizing other fluxes (notably borax) were introduced by John Rose at Coalport. Lead glazes are now rarely used in advanced industrial countries except for special purposes.

Leaf-border. A border pattern consisting of a series of identical stylized leaves placed diagonally in a zig-zag pattern.

Lebes gamykos. Attic, ht 11 in., with black-figure decoration, *c.* 520 BC. British Museum, London.

Leaf-dish. A dish naturalistically modelled in leaf form, or as a series of overlapping leaves, and coloured to represent the veining. The rims were often shaded in yellow and green, and a handle was added in the form of a curved stem. Leaves employed include those of the vine, strawberry, geranium, cabbage, and mulberry. The motif belongs typically to the ROCOCO period, and to the rococo revival. *See* STRAWBERRY-LEAF DISH; FLOWER DISH; PICKLE-TRAY.

Leather-hard. The state of the body of pottery and porcelain after it has partially hardened in consequence of the evaporation of the moisture content; it is harder than the state termed CHEESE-HARD, and it is not unlike leather. In this state the body can be turned on a lathe, and ornament incised by engine-turning (*see* ENGINE-TURNED DECORATION). It is also in this state that SLIP is applied to the body to make MARBLED WARE.

Lebes (Greek). A type of bowl of Greek pottery used for mixing wine and water. It is ovoid in form and has a high shoulder, a low neck, and two vertical handles; it usually has a rounded bottom and rests on a stand, like a DEINOS.

Lebes gamykos (Greek). A type of LEBES used as a wedding gift. There are two types: (1) with an integrated bowl and stand; and (2) with the bowl having a simple circular base. Both have two vertical loop handles and a conical cover with a pomegranate finial.

Ledge, or condiment ledge. The flattened, raised part of the plate which surrounds the well; it was originally found on European pewter dishes which were copied in pottery. The presence of a ledge in plates of Chinese porcelain is an indication that they were made for export to Europe, even though the decoration be in Chinese taste, since the Chinese use the saucer-dish and the bowl for serving food. *See* MARLI; SAUCER.

Leech-jar. A jar usually inscribed 'Leeches', with a pierced cover. These jars were made for use in apothecary-shops; *see* PHARMACY WARE.

Leech-jar. Creamware jar, Leeds, *c*. 1780. Courtesy, Royal Pharmaceutical Society, London.

Leeds ware. Glazed earthenware made at potteries in and near Leeds (Yorkshire) from *c*. 1760 to 1820. The term is especially identified with a thinly potted creamware of fine quality, often decorated with pierced-work, relief decoration, transfer-printing, and polychrome painted decoration. Leeds ware also includes blue-and-white earthenware, a type of black basaltes ware, redware, agate ware, pearlware, tortoiseshell ware, marbled ware, drab ware, saltglazed ware, figures, and resist ware. Much early polychrome decoration was done by David Rhodes, *c*. 1760–68, and a quantity of Leeds creamware, especially that with religious subjects, was decorated in Dutch studios. From 1820 to 1878 successors to the original factory-owners used the old models and moulds to produce inferior ware with the impressed mark 'Leeds pottery'.

Leg-cup. A drinking-cup made in the form of a human leg, with a small handle at the back of the calf. They were made of pottery in the 5th century BC and specimens have been found at Vulci (Italy). A comparable cup in the form of a military boot was made of earthenware in France in the 19th century.

Lei-wên (Chinese). Same as the CLOUD AND THUNDER FRET.

Lekane (Greek). A vase of Greek pottery resembling a STAMNOS, but with two vertical loop handles rising above the rim, and a cover with an elaborate finial.

Lekanis (Greek). A small, shallow bowl of Greek pottery, with two horizontal handles, a small foot, and a ridge to receive a cover; the cover has a finial in the form of a flat or concave disk. The type has been called a *lepaste*.

Lekanis. Pottery, diam. 9¾ in., from Apulia, *c*. 460 BC. British Museum, London.

Lekythos (Greek). Sometimes *lecythus*. A type of small jug of Greek pottery, for perfume, oil, or ointment; it is tall and slender,

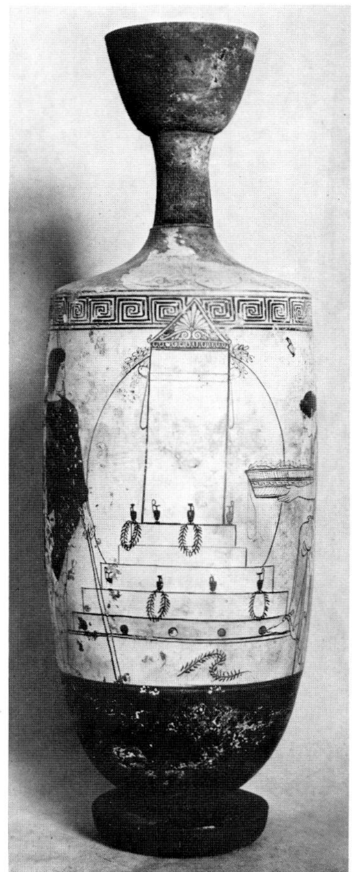

Lekythos. Vase with decoration including key-fret borders on a white ground, 4th century BC. National Museum, Athens.

Lessore ware. Plate with designs painted by Lessore, Queen's ware, Wedgwood, *c*. 1865. Courtesy, Wedgwood.

with a small loop handle attached at the shoulder and neck, a narrow neck for slow, controlled pouring, a cup-like mouth, and a flat base. Older forms have a cylindrical body, later ones a squat, round body. Examples with monochrome or polychrome decoration on a white ground were used from the 6th century BC as funeral offerings. Some *lekythoi* have a small elongated receptacle (inside and attached to the lower part of the neck) to hold a small quantity of oil when the piece was used as a tomb offering, and such pieces have a VENT-HOLE. The body of some examples is in the form of a head, like the RHYTON.

Lemon-box. A small covered bowl or box naturalistically modelled and coloured in imitation of a lemon. Some examples have a knobby roughened surface. They were made in the middle of the 18th century at Chelsea, Derby, Meissen, and elsewhere. Sometimes two or three lemons are affixed to a single leaf-shaped stand.

Lemon-yellow. A pale yellow ground colour on 18th-century porcelain, including Chinese.

Lepaste (Greek). *See* LEKANIS.

Lessore ware. Creamware made by Wedgwood and decorated by Emil Lessore, from 1858 to 1863 at the factory, and later in France till 1875. He painted in a very distinctive style, depicting children and romantic couples, using soft pale colours and usually without either a ground or border. Some of his work is done on bone-china.

Letter snuff-box. A type of porcelain snuff-box decorated on the cover or lid as an envelope inscribed with the name of the owner. They were made in Russia at St Petersburg (Leningrad), *c*. 1760.

Levant, Les Différentes Nations du. A series of figures in the form of candlesticks, each representing a person of a nation in the Levant dressed in the costume of the relevant country. They were inspired by engravings in a book of the same title by the Comte de Ferriol, published in Paris in 1714. One series was modelled at Meissen, *c*. 1745, by J. J. Kändler and P. Reinicke.

Levigation. A method of refining clay by carrying it in a current of water so that the finer particles are held in suspension while the coarser and heavier ones sink and are removed. The muddy liquid is then drawn off and the finer particles allowed to settle. The process is sometimes repeated to produce a greater refinement.

Li (Chinese). A circular pottery vessel of the Neolithic period with three hollow legs. It is sometimes called a hollow-legged TING, from its resemblance to the bronze vessel of this name. It was probably derived from three amphora-like vessels with a pointed bottom leaning against each other over a fire; these were combined together to make a single vessel with a common mouth.

Li T'ieh-kuai (Chinese). One of the EIGHT IMMORTALS, a lame beggar with a stick or crutch carrying a gourd.

Libation cup. A ceremonial cup for pouring wine as a libation. One Chinese porcelain version (*chüeh*) is derived from an early bronze vessel used for this purpose, and is boat-shaped with three legs.

Liberty and Matrimony. A pair of allegorical figures made originally at Meissen, and copied or adapted by Bow and other English porcelain factories, *c.* 1755–60. The man is often seated on a tree-trunk with a bird-cage on one knee and a bird perched on his wrist; in another version, he is shown standing and holding a nest of birds. The girl sometimes holds a closed bird-cage and has sheep at her feet. In the English versions BOCAGE supports are customary. Variations were made at Derby and elsewhere.

Library set. A porcelain tray, usually with a STANDISH with taper-stick, pounce-pot, pen-tray, and a spill-vase. Also called a desk-set. *See* ÉCRITOIRE.

Lid. A covering for closing the mouth of a mug, tankard, snuff-box, or other object, usually attached to the body by a metal hinge, or mounted in a hinged frame. *See* COVER; POT-LID.

Lift-handle. A projection at the shoulder of a large jug or pitcher, opposite the handle proper, as an aid to lifting.

Lily border. A pattern of a series of stylized lilies with four petals and pairs of side-leaves, the flowers set in a series of adjacent pointed arches. It is found on Wedgwood's jasper.

Lily pattern. *See* ROYAL LILY PATTERN.

Lindner figures. Modern porcelain figures of animals, usually cattle and horses naturalistically modelled and coloured, designed by Doris Lindner for the Worcester Royal Porcelain Company, and issued in limited editions. Among the most popular subjects are equestrian figures of Queen Elizabeth II on Tommy (1947), Prince Philip on Inez playing polo (1968), and the Irish steeplechaser Arkle (1967).

Liner. A vessel which fits snugly within another, such as the inner bowl of a BAIN-MARIE. The term, in the case of a FOOD-WARMER, is used in England to correspond to the French BAIN-MARIE, and refers to the hot-water pan in which the food-bowl rests, like the lower pot of a double-boiler.

Ling-chih (Chinese). A decorative symbol on Chinese porcelain signifying longevity, and probably intended to represent the fungus, *Fomes japonicus*.

Ling-lung yao (Chinese). Chinese porcelain, especially of the later part of the Ming dynasty (1368–1644), with pierced decoration which the Chinese termed 'devil's work', probably an allusion to the superhuman skill supposedly involved. This work inspired similar ware in Europe, for instance, some WHIELDON WARE in England.

Link border. A border pattern of a series of connecting links in the form of a chain.

Lion, Florentine. A porcelain figure of a lion standing with its left fore-paw placed on a ball, copied from a late-16th-century bronze lion in Florence by Pietro Tacca. Several examples are known from the Bow Factory during the early period, *c.* 1750–52, and another of about the same date from Chelsea.

Lion of Buddha. *See* LION OF FO.

Lion of Fo. A Chinese lion. The lions were originally temple-guardians, often miscalled 'dogs'; the male is represented playing with a ball, and the female with a cub or cubs. *Fo* means Buddha.

Liberty and Matrimony. Porcelain group decorated in enamel colours by Ralph or Enoch Wood, Staffordshire, *c.* 1790. Victoria and Albert Museum, London.

Ling-lung yao. Porcelain double-walled bottle, with celadon glaze, the outer wall having pierced decoration, 14th–15th century. Victoria and Albert Museum, London.

These lions are often represented in painted decoration or modelled as figures, usually as a facing pair. The Japanese term is *shi-shi*. *See* JOSS-STICK HOLDER.

Lion's mask and paw. A relief decoration of columnar form with a lion's mask at the top and a lion's paw at the foot. It is used as the foot of an object, usually of porcelain, such as the LISART CANDLESTICK.

Lip. The pouring projection at the front edge of the mouth of a jug, pitcher, or sauce-boat. Some are in pinched, or trefoil, shape. *See* BEAK.

Lip-spout. A type of spout which has a pouring lip rather than a cut-off end as on a SNIP-SPOUT.

Lisart candlestick. A type of candlestick made at Bow with three LION'S MASK-AND-PAW feet supporting a short columnar stem entwined by a dragon, once thought to be a lizard, hence the name 'lisard' or 'lisart'. On some examples the dragon's tail supports the DRIP-PAN, above which is a tulip-shaped CANDLE-NOZZLE and metal flowers and leaves.

Lithocérame. The French term for STONEWARE.

Lithographic decoration. Now the most widely employed kind of printing for overglaze decoration, and it can also be used underglaze. Patterns, made by the lithographic process as opposed to TRANSFER-PRINTING, are supplied in the form of paper-backed sheets to be cut up as required and pressed on to the vessel to be decorated, the surface of which is first covered with a layer of varnish and allowed to become slightly tacky. The backing paper is then sponged off. More recently an improved technique has done away with the necessity for varnishing. The process in the United States is known as decalcomania.

Lion of Fo. One of a pair of joss-stick holders, enamel on biscuit; reign of K'ang Hsi (1662–1722). Victoria and Albert Museum, London.

Lithophane. A thin TRANSLUCENT plaque, usually flat but often curved, made of HARD-PASTE PORCELAIN and generally of white unglazed (BISCUIT) body, having a recessed decorative motif intended to be viewed by transmitted light, i.e., when illuminated from behind. The varying depths of the porcelain (which has an indistinct surface, unlike the usual intaglio that is the exact reverse of a cameo) result in gradations of the transmitted light, and consequently the design, when lit from behind, takes on a three-dimensional appearance, resembling decoration painted EN GRISAILLE.

First, the design model is carved in wax expressly to provide the appropriate variation in depth, and from it a plaster of Paris mould is made for casting the plaque. The subjects of the decorative motifs are often copies of paintings, views of buildings, or *genre* scenes. Such plaques have been incorporated into lampshades, lanterns, and VEILLEUSES, as well as being used as the bottom of mugs and as panels to be hung in windows and viewed against sunlight.

The process was invented in France by Baron Paul de Bourgoing (1791–1861) at his ceramic factory on the estate of his friend, Baron Alexis du Tremblay, at Rubelles, near Melun. It was patented in France in 1827 by its inventor, who, being in the diplomatic corps, did not want his name to be used, and hence the pieces made at Rubelles bear instead the initials 'AdT' (for du Tremblay) in cursive script. The process was used only experimentally at Sèvres. Many lithophanes were made in Germany, principally under licence at the Royal Porcelain Manufactory (mark: 'KPM') in Berlin, hence the name 'Berlin transparency' often applied to such ware. Lithophanes have also been made at

Lithophane. Lamp with shade and base incorporating lithophane panels. Blair Museum of Lithophanes, Toledo, Ohio.

several other Continental potteries. A licence was granted to Robert Griffith Jones, of London, who took out an English patent in 1828 and sublicensed several potteries, including Minton and Copelands in Stoke-on-Trent and Lee & Grainger of Worcester. *See* ÉMAIL OMBRANT.

Littler-Wedgwood blue ware. Blue STONEWARE made first by William Littler and Aaron Wedgwood, from *c.* 1749 to *c.* 1763, at Brownhills (north of Stoke-on-Trent), by dipping GREEN WARE into a very fusible mixture containing cobalt and firing it in a saltglaze oven. The resulting surface was dark blue, but without the characteristic pitted effect of saltglazed ware. *See* LITTLER'S BLUE.

Littler's blue. A cobalt-blue ground developed by William Littler, who founded the porcelain factory at Longton Hall, *c.* 1750–58. It is vivid and streaky, and thinner on the raised parts of the surface. It ran into the glaze, and hence is inclined to be blurred and indistinct. It was employed by Littler on some Longton Hall plates and on saltglazed ware. *See* LITTLER-WEDGWOOD BLUE WARE.

Liverpool delftware. Tin-glazed earthenware (ENGLISH DELFTWARE) made at about twenty factories in or near Liverpool from *c.* 1710. A characteristic feature on some plates is a RED EDGE, inspired by a similar edge on some Chinese and Japanese porcelain. *See* SUNKEN BLUE; FAZACKERL(E)Y FLOWERS.

Livre flacon (French). A flask in the form of a standing book, often with an inscription. *See* FAÏENCE PARLANTE.

Lizard-skin glaze. A type of glaze, so called from its appearance, employed by Korean potters who settled at Satsuma, on the Japanese island of Kyushu. *See* SATSUMA WARE.

Lobed. Shaped with projections of rounded form.

Lohan. A saintly disciple (*arhat*) of Buddha. Lohans are usually arranged in groups of sixteen or eighteen; they are to be found in Chinese porcelain either as figures or as painted decoration. A ceramic seated figure, life-size, is in the British Museum, London. *See* BODHIDHARMA; RAKAN.

Lohan. Figure, ht 6½ in., blanc de Chine, Tê-Hua, late 17th century. Victoria and Albert Museum, London.

London delftware. Tin-glazed earthenware (ENGLISH DELFTWARE) made at several factories in London on both sides of the Thames, but mainly in Lambeth and Southwark. *See* LAMBETH DELFTWARE; SOUTHWARK DELFTWARE.

London slipware. Same as METROPOLITAN SLIPWARE.

Long Eliza pattern. A pattern of curiously elongated Chinese women. The Chinese term is *mei jên*. Chinese porcelain painting was adapted by the Dutch in the 17th century for the decoration of delftware. They called some of the female figures of this kind *Lange Lijzen*, from which the name has been anglicized. The pattern occurs on Dutch and English delftware, and on Worcester porcelain.

Long Eliza. Porcelain vase, in the form of the bronze *tsun*, with painted decoration. Worcester, *c.* 1758.

Longwy enamel ware. Same as CLUNY ENAMEL WARE.

Lotus border. A border pattern of heart-shaped lotus petals all pointing up or down. It was employed by Wedgwood.

Lotus-bud border. A border pattern of continuous circles slightly interlaced, with lotus buds covering the interlaced segments, and with a dot between each bud.

Lotus ware. *See* BELLEEK WARE.

Loubak (Russian). A jug in the form of a human head with a loop handle at the rear. Specimens used as tobacco-jars have a cover. *See* TOBY JUG; MASK JUGS AND MUGS.

Loutrophoros. Pottery, decorated in the red-figure style, 5th century BC. Louvre, Paris.

Louis-Philippe style. The main decorative style in France during the reign of Louis-Philippe (1830–48). It is characterized by a reaction from the severity of the EMPIRE STYLE, and by the use of ornate forms and vivid colours and gilding, as exemplified by the porcelain of Jacob Petit. The principal feature was a ROCOCO revival which had begun in the reign of Charles X (1824–30).

Louis Quinze style. The ROCOCO style, current principally between 1735 and 1765 during the reign of Louis XV (1715–74). Also known as ROCAILLE and *style Pompadour*.

Louis XVI service. A dinner-service of Sèvres soft-paste porcelain ordered by Louis XVI and started in 1783. It is decorated with mythological and historical scenes in reserved panels on a *bleu de roi* ground. Part of the service, bought by George IV, is in the English royal collections.

Louis Seize style. The NEO-CLASSICAL STYLE, current in France from about the end of the Seven Years' War in 1763 – long before the accession of Louis XVI in 1774 – till the Revolution in 1789, after which a much plainer style, termed DIRECTOIRE, supervened between it and the EMPIRE STYLE. Early specimens of the Louis Seize style in porcelain retain some elements of the preceding ROCOCO style, but these were progressively discarded in favour of the type of classical ornament in general use for furniture, etc. *See* ADAM STYLE.

Loutrophoros (Greek). A tall, long-necked vase (a type of AMPHORA), usually with two vertical loop-handles, a large mouth, and sometimes open at the bottom. A variant form has three handles (similar to a HYDRIA). It was used as a funerary vase, as a funnel, or for pouring libations on the grave of an unmarried youth or maiden. Those with a bottom were employed for bringing water for the ceremonial bath on the eve of a marriage, and hence were often buried in the grave of one dying in betrothal.

Loving-cup. A large ornamental drinking-vessel with two or more handles to be passed round at a banquet or similar gathering. *See* TYG; GRACE-CUP; CHRISTENING GOBLET.

Low relief. Relief decoration where the projecting part is only slightly raised, as on a coin, no part being entirely detached. The French term is *bas relief*, and the Italian *basso rilievo*. *See* HIGH RELIEF; MEDIUM RELIEF.

Lowdin's Bristol. Porcelain made at Bristol (England) from *c.* 1748 onwards in a glasshouse owned by William Lowdin. It is now more commonly known as Lund's Bristol porcelain, after Benjamin Lund who was much more closely concerned with the actual manufacture. The body employed was principally clay and soaprock, and was the precursor of Worcester porcelain similarly constituted. The Bristol enterprise was sold to the Worcester Company, founded for the purpose of buying it, in 1751. Most of the painted ware was decorated at Worcester after it acquired the Bristol factory.

Löwenfinck style. Decoration, in the form of CHINOISERIES and JAPONAISERIES, painted in the manner of Adam Friedrich von Löwenfinck at Meissen. Löwenfinck was apprenticed to the factory in 1726 at the age of thirteen. He was subsequently at a number of other factories, but his characteristic FABULOUS ANIMALS in the oriental style appear only on Meissen wares.

Lozenge. A decorative form in the shape of a diamond having four equal sides making two acute and two obtuse angles. The corners are sometimes rounded.

Lug. An ear, knob, solid scroll, or other attachment for lifting or holding a piece of ceramic ware, but not including a handle which has space for the fingers or hand to be passed through.

Lumetto (Italian). Tin-enamel white tracery on Italian maiolica which has a BERETTINO ground.

Lund's Bristol. *See* LOWDIN'S BRISTOL.

Lung. The Chinese term for a DRAGON.

Lung-ch'üan yao (Chinese). Celadon stoneware made in the Sung dynasty (960–1280), at Lung-ch'üan (Chekiang province). The body is greyish in colour, and some of the thinner specimens are faintly translucent. The foot-ring where unglazed is usually dark red owing to oxidation of the iron in the highly ferruginous clay, producing ferric oxide, and an inclination to brown can be seen at the rim where the glaze is thin, the two features being described by the Chinese as 'a brown mouth and iron foot'. The glaze is transparent but hazy, and the body is often decorated with carved and incised designs which are visible through it. Other specimens have moulded decoration, left unglazed, which burns to the same dark brownish-red as the foot-ring, providing an effective contrast to the green glaze.

Lustration vase. A vessel used at Buddhist purification ceremonies.

Lustre. (1) A technique of decoration giving a metallic (sometimes iridescent) appearance, either as a ground completely covering the piece, or as a design or pattern; largely used on pottery, it was also used occasionally on porcelain. Two processes were employed: STAINED (iridescent) LUSTRE and METALLIC LUSTRE. *See* SILVER LUSTRE; PLATINUM LUSTRE; GOLD LUSTRE; COPPER LUSTRE; PINK LUSTRE; PURPLE LUSTRE; CANARY LUSTRE; RUBY LUSTRE; MADREPERLA LUSTRE; MOONLIGHT LUSTRE; PERLMUTTER LUSTRE; SPLASHED LUSTRE; SUNDERLAND LUSTRE; COLOURED LUSTRE; BRIANÇON LUSTRE; GUBBIO LUSTRE; FAIRY-LAND LUSTRE; DRAGON LUSTRE; CANGIANTE LUSTRE; STENCILLED LUSTRE; SILVERING; RESIST WARE; SPORTING LUSTRE-WARE. (2) A chandelier or vase with prismatic pendent drops of glass or rock-crystal. Best known are those of jasper, mounted in ormolu with added drops, made towards the end of the 18th century.

Lustrous glaze. A thin glaze used on certain kinds of Greek and Roman pottery to make it impermeable.

Luting. The process of cementing together parts of a ceramic object with fluid clay slip; thus, a vase, the neck of which is too small to admit the potter's hand, is made in two parts which are then joined by luting. Joints are usually perceptible, but this is minimized by the process of FETTLING. In the making of figures the various components are luted to the torso and base. *See* SPRIGGING; ORNAMENTING.

Loving cup. Saltglazed stoneware, ht 8¼ in., Nottingham (or Crich?), 1739. Fitzwilliam Museum, Cambridge.

Löwenfinck style. Plate decorated with characteristic fabulous animal, Meissen, *c.* 1735. Metropolitan Museum of Art, New York.

Lustre. Maiolica *fruttiera* with lustre decoration of Cupid and border of grotesques, Gubbio, first half of 16th century. Wallace Collection, London.

M

Ma-chang pottery. *See* PANSHAN POTTERY.

Ma Chün (Chinese). A variety of CHÜN YAO named after a potter called Ma, who is reputed to have originated this particular version of the Chün glaze. The body is a buff stoneware. The glaze is similar in colour to that of the true Chün ware, but is denser, more opaque, and minutely crackled. The colour is often a marked turquoise, unusual in the classic Sung dynasty type. Most known specimens of Ma Chün were made during the Ming dynasty, and few can be regarded as earlier in date. This ware is sometimes termed *Shu t'ai* or 'soft Chün'.

Magot teapot. Teapot, probably based on a silver prototype, Meissen, *c.* 1720. Cecil Higgins Museum, Bedford.

Mallet vase. Celadon vase of Lung ch'üan yao, Sung dynasty (960–1280). Victoria and Albert Museum, London.

Madreperla lustre. Lustre decoration appearing on Italian MAIOLICA and some HISPANO-MORESQUE WARE. The colour was determined by the presence of oxides of silver, copper, and gold in pigments yielding yellow, a coppery-red, and a ruby-red respectively. This was painted on to the surface of the ware and fired in a REDUCING ATMOSPHERE, giving a metallic iridescent film resembling mother-of-pearl. *See* BRIANÇON LUSTRE-WARE; PERLMUTTER LUSTRE.

Mae-pyŏng (Korean). A type of PRUNUS VASE, similar to the Chinese MEI-P'ING but bulging more at the shoulder and tapering towards the foot in a graceful curve with a single return at the bottom. Those of the late 14th century had a contracted waist towards the bottom. They were made of KORYŎ CELADON and PUNCH'ONG WARE. *See* ICHIRIN ZASHI.

Magot (French). Literally, a dwarf. (1) A figure of a seated Chinese with a smiling face and long pendulous ears, made in several versions at Chantilly, Mennecy, and Meissen, and based on Chinese figures of the monk PU-TAI HO-SHANG. *See* PAGOD. (2) A figure or painted decoration inspired by the work of Jacques Callot (1593–1635). *See* CALLOT FIGURES.

Magot teapot. A teapot in the form of a grotesque dwarf. Usually a serpent forms the spout, the handle being in the form of a figure or entwined branches spreading round the pot. First made at Meissen in the 1720s, probably modelled by Georg Fritzsche, the type was repeated at Chelsea during the period of the incised triangle mark, 1745–50. *See* CHINAMAN TEAPOT.

Maiden's leg. *See* JUNGFERNBEINCHEN; FLOHBEIN.

Maiolica. Tin-glazed earthenware made in Italy, or, more loosely, made in the Italian style. The name is derived from a term employed in Italy for the lustre ware of Valencia which was sent there via the island of Maiolica, now Majorca. The term should preferably be limited to wares of Italian origin. The technique, however, is exactly the same as that of DELFTWARE or FAIENCE. *See* MAJOLICA; MEZZA-MAIOLICA; RAFFAELE WARE.

Majolica. Sometimes employed as an anglicized version of MAIOLICA, but, more correctly, a trade-name used by Minton for a type of earthenware covered with coloured lead glazes, introduced *c.* 1850. Other English potters, such as George Jones & Sons, Stoke-on-Trent, and Wedgwood, made ware decorated with semi-transparent glazes during the 19th century which was also thus called.

Malabar figures. A series of porcelain figures of Chinese playing musical instruments, modelled at Meissen by Friedrich Elias Meyer, *c.* 1745–61. *See* MUSIKOLI FIGURES.

Malachite. A dark green colour resembling that of malachite, which is an ore of copper. PARIAN PORCELAIN was sometimes thus coloured.

Mallet vase. A type of Chinese vase so called from its mallet shape. One well-known type in porcelain features a bluish-green celadon glaze which is frequently called in Japanese *kinuta seiji* (meaning 'mallet celadon'). Vases of this shape were made during the Sung dynasty (960–1280) and are called in Chinese *chih-ch'ui pi'ng.*

Malling jug. A type of 16th-century English tin-enamelled jug with a cylindrical neck, the shape inspired by those of RHENISH STONEWARE, usually with a mottled glaze (predominantly blue or brown). It was so called because the first specimen to be discovered was excavated in the churchyard at West Malling, Kent; there is no evidence that such jugs were made there. London is the more likely place of origin. Some are mounted in silver and can be dated from the hall-mark. *See* TIGER WARE.

Mambrino's helmet. A barber's bowl; the name given by Don Quixote to the barber's bowl which he appropriated and wore in place of a helmet.

Mandarin decoration. A decoration of figure-subjects, sometimes alternating with flowers in panels, which were usually framed in underglaze blue. The palette is mainly rose-pink (sometimes inclining to a purplish shade), iron-red, green, and gilding. It was employed on CHINESE EXPORT PORCELAIN towards the end of the 18th century and in the early years of the 19th century. The style became very popular with a number of English factories, notably those making porcelain and ironstone china. The overglaze painting of the Chinese ware was executed at Canton. *See* CANTON PORCELAIN; MANDARIN STYLE.

Mandarin porcelain. *See* MANDARIN DECORATION.

Mandarin service. A porcelain dinner-service made at Swansea (South Wales), transfer-printed in black outline and brightly coloured; the design, a scene on a riverside terrace, features a Chinese holding a flower, and four companions.

Mandarin style. Mandarin decoration on English porcelain in imitation of the Chinese ware.

Manfredi peacock-feather decoration. An IMBRICATED diaper pattern formed of rows of peacock-feathers in blue, ochre, and manganese high-temperature colours, used on maiolica made at Faenza in the 15th century. It is said to have been introduced as a complimentary allusion (*pavón* meaning peacock in Italian) to Cassandra Pavona, mistress of the Lord of Faenza, Galeotto Manfredi (d. 1488). The same decoration was used at Caffaggiolo in the 16th century.

Manganese. Manganese oxide employed to decorate pottery and porcelain. It yields a variable colour, from purple to a rich brown, but usually resembles in shade a solution of permanganate of potash. Used with a lead glaze it becomes purple-brown;

Malabar figures. Pair of figures, ht 12½ in., by F.E. Meyer, Meissen, *c.* 1750–55. Wadsworth Atheneum, Hartford, Conn.

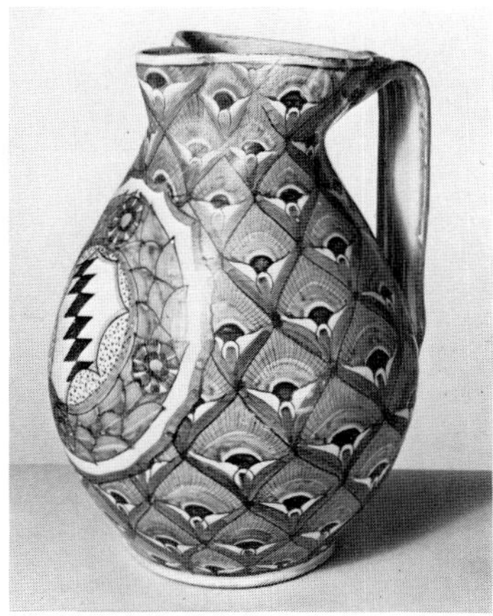

Manfredi peacock-feather pattern. Decoration on maiolica jug, Caffaggiolo, *c.* 1515. Victoria and Albert Museum, London.

Majolica. Beer-jug with decoration depicting 'The Hop Story', Minton, *c.* 1860. Victoria and Albert Museum, London.

with an alkaline glaze, purple-violet; and in combination with iron, almost black. Employed by potters in ancient Egypt, it has since been used extensively, especially to decorate tin-glazed earthenware.

Manierblumen (German). Literally, mannered flowers. Flowers painted in a well-marked manner or style. Occasionally employed to describe 18th-century flower-painting on Meissen porcelain.

Manises ware. Pottery made at a factory at Manises, a suburb of Valencia (Spain) in the 15th century and later, mainly HISPANO-MORESQUE WARE and tiles.

Mansion House dwarf. Porcelain figure, ht 7¼ in., with auction sale announcement on hat, Derby, *c.* 1790. Courtesy, Christie's.

Mansion House dwarfs. Figures based on designs by Jacques Callot (*see* CALLOT FIGURES) produced by the Derby porcelain factory from 1784 onwards, and called after two dwarfs who from 1780 stood outside the Mansion House, London, displaying advertisements. There are two types – one with a conical hat and one with a wide-brimmed hat. Advertisements for sales and theatrical performances (of which at least twenty-five are known) appear on their hats. They have protuberant bellies, and are elaborately decorated with a profusion of enamel colours and gilding. They have been reproduced by Edmé Samson et Cie of Paris, and others. *See* GROTESQUE PUNCHES; SAMSON COPIES.

Mantelshelf garniture. *See* GARNITURE DE CHEMINÉE.

Mantling. Arrangement of drapery around and behind a coat of arms.

Manvers, Earl, service. A dinner-service made at Worcester in the first period with a pink diaper border of pendent branches of hops behind puce scrolls curving towards the central gilt medallion, and forming a radiating pattern from it.

Maquette. A preliminary model or study in clay or wax.

Marbled ware. Pottery made in imitation of the surface appearance of coloured marble by means of WEDGING tinted or coloured clays, or by employing coloured SLIPS or GLAZES. Glazed ware was made in the 18th century by Josiah Wedgwood to resemble marble, porphyry, malachite, lapis lazuli, and onyx. With narrow streaks it is known as 'fine marbling', with wide streaks, 'open marbling'. A small quantity of marbled ware was made in China during the T'ang dynasty. *See* AGATE WARE; COMBED WARE; VARIEGATED WARE.

Marks. Names, letters, numbers, or symbols placed over or under the glaze on ceramic wares to indicate facts relevant to origin, and to the workman engaged in its manufacture. Marks may be impressed, incised, painted, printed, moulded (sometimes raised from the surface), scratched, or stencilled. Although usually on the base, the mark sometimes forms part of the decoration, notably on some Nymphenburg wares. During the 18th century instances of important FACTORY-MARKS (*see* illustrations on pp. 7–18) being copied by minor factories were common, and later forgeries make such marks very unreliable evidence of origin. *See* DATE-LETTER; CANCELLATION MARK; MODELLER'S MARK; GILDER'S MARK; POTTER'S MARK; PAINTER'S MARK; WORKMAN'S MARK. In some instances marks indicate data relevant to the piece itself, such as catalogue-number, price, pattern-number, or original ownership; *see* DEALER'S MARK; SCRATCHED MARK; OWNERSHIP MARK. *See also* CHARACTER

MARK; SEAL-MARK; NIEN HAO; CHINESE SEAL-MARK; PSEUDO-CHINESE SEAL-MARK; CHINESE REIGN-MARK; COUNTRY OF ORIGIN MARK; REGISTRY MARK; EXCISE MARK; DISGUISED NUMERAL MARK; COMMENDATION MARK; SHOP MARK; BACK-STAMP.

Japanese marks. A variety of marks occur on later specimens of Japanese porcelain, although these are rarely to be seen before the second half of the 18th century. Seal-marks are often the name of the potter, although these cannot be regarded as trustworthy. Copies of Chinese reign-marks of the Ming dynasty are not infrequent, and can usually be detected from the excessively angular and stilted way in which they have been drawn. Japanese date-marks and period names are unusual. *See* NENGO.

Marl. A type of coarse clay which contains a high proportion of lime.

Marli (or **marly**). The raised border of a plate or dish which surrounds the WELL, and is often almost parallel with the bottom of the well. *See* LEDGE.

Marriage plate. One of a pair of plates, decorated respectively with a representation of the bride and groom and inscribed with their names and the date of the marriage. Some examples were made of Leeds creamware, *c.* 1777.

Marriage plates. Pair of plates with decoration in blue and feather-edged border, creamware, Leeds, 1777. Courtesy, Christie's.

Marrow tureen. A naturalistically modelled and coloured TUREEN in the form of a vegetable marrow or squash, principally fashionable during the currency of the ROCOCO style, but reproduced since.

Marseillemuster (German). A decorative moulded border pattern for plates, introduced at Meissen, *c.* 1743. It has six plain panels, surrounded by narrow bands of rococo scrolls which encroach on the centre of the plate, and dotted trellis ornament. The plain panels were used for painted decoration, principally DEUTSCHE BLUMEN and birds.

Martabani ware. A Persian term for Chinese celadon ware shipped from the port of Moulmein on the Gulf of Martaban, and for Persian pottery copies of such ware.

Martial trophies. A decorative motif depicting a group of weapons. *See* TROPHIES; WAPPENGESCHIRR.

Martinware. Saltglazed stoneware, made by the Martin brothers at Fulham, London, and at Southall, from *c.* 1873 to 1914. The glazes are usually mottled, including grey, brown, blue, and yellow, in muted tones. Forms are often grotesque, and include QUIZZICAL BIRDS, comical fish, frogs, owls, armadillos, salamanders, hedgehogs, and goblins, serving as tobacco-jars, spoon-warmers, jugs, etc. Some vases were also made. All pieces are signed and dated. *See* MUSICAL IMPS.

Martinware. Jug in the form of a grotesque head, late 19th century. Victoria and Albert Museum, London.

Marzacotto (Italian). A silicate of potash made by mixing and fusing sand with calcined wine-lees. When combined with oxides of tin it formed the enamel termed *bianco*, which was applied as a glaze on early Italian maiolica. When applied over the fired tin-glaze of some maiolica to enhance its brilliance, it was termed COPERTA.

Mask. A representation, usually in relief, of a face as decorative ornament. Masks were originally derived from ancient Greek and Roman sources; often grotesque, they depict human beings, satyrs, and animals. Masks occur in two forms; in full relief, as

Mask-jug. (Above) English yellow-glazed earthenware (2), *c.* 1820. Leon Collection, Smithsonian Institution, Washington, D.C. (Below) Staffordshire pottery in the form of a satyr's head (3), *c.* 1770. City Museums, Stoke-on-Trent.

ornamental ware; and as decorative ornament in low relief on mugs, jugs, and other objects. Used on the pedestal of a food-warmer, they serve as handles and conceal ventilation holes. *See* MASK MUGS AND JUGS; T'AO T'IEH.

Mask mugs and jugs. Pottery and porcelain mugs and jugs modelled in various forms. (1) Jugs with a relief mask as part of the pouring lip. Porcelain jugs of this type, known at the factory as Dutch jugs, were made in the 18th century at Worcester, Caughley, and Liverpool; examples in earthenware were produced by Ralph Wood, father and son, from original models by Jean Voyez, and later by other potteries in Staffordshire. Jugs in this form also occur in German porcelain. (2) Mugs and jugs with a relief mask opposite the handle, or with three masks around the body (one opposite the handle and one on each side); the latter type was made in white or yellow earthenware. (3) Mugs and jugs modelled in the form of a head. *See* BACCHUS JUG; BELLARMINE; FACE JUG; KANTHAROS; LOUBAK; RODNEY WARE; SATYR MUG; TOBY JUG.

Masonic figures. Figures of Freemasons modelled by J.J. Kändler at Meissen just before the middle of the 18th century. *See* MASONIC WARE.

Masonic ware. Porcelain or pottery decorated with Masonic emblems or insignia. In English pottery, especially from Liverpool, transfer-printed decoration depicts the arms of the Freemasons, flanked by two Masons, and pyramids surmounted by a celestial and a terrestrial globe. Masonic insignia appear on lustre pottery from Sunderland, with an appropriate verse, and Masonic motifs occur on Italian maiolica.

Mason's Ironstone China. A type of fine STONE CHINA imitating porcelain introduced in England in 1813 by Charles James Mason of Lane Delph (Staffordshire), son of Miles Mason. It is often decorated in MANDARIN STYLE. Also called Patent Ironstone China, it was supposed to contain iron slag, but in appearance it is very similar to more or less contemporary stone-china made at several other factories. Blue printed decoration was also common. *See* LAVA WARE.

Massed lard. The translation of a Chinese description of the glaze of KUAN YAO. *See* SUNG DYNASTY.

Masso bastardo (Italian). A type of hard-paste porcelain made in the 18th century at Doccia (Italy), more distinctly grey than most other Italian porcelains.

Mastos. Drinking-cup, *c.* 530 BC. British Museum, London.

Mastos (Greek). Literally, breast. A Greek pottery drinking-cup in the form of a woman's breast, pointed downwards so that it cannot be stood on a table except when empty (*see* BREAST CUP). Some have two loop handles, one vertical and one horizontal.

Mat or **Matt.** Having a dull finish; not glossy. For example, mat gilding, or a mat glaze. *See* MATT-BRILLANT.

Mat-markings. Decoration on unglazed pottery impressed in more or less irregular patterns consisting of lines which form a vague and indistinct ornament. So called because they were thought to have been caused by pressure from coarse textiles, but this is often doubtful. They occur, for instance, on unglazed Chinese pottery of the Chou dynasty (1122–249 BC).

Matt-brillant (French). Decoration in gold where the design is mat against a burnished ground.

May day. A decorative subject from a HANCOCK ENGRAVING transfer-printed on English Worcester porcelain, *c.* 1760. It depicts three girls dancing to the music of a one-legged fiddler, with another man behind carrying a bundle on his head.

Mayan pottery. *See* CENTRAL AMERICAN POTTERY

Mayblossom. Hawthorn blossom used as a decorative motif either painted or in relief on porcelain, each of the small white flowers usually having a yellow centre. Some vases, completely covered by such flowers in high relief, are called 'snowball' or 'may-blossom' vases; *see* SNOWBALL VASE.

Mazarine blue. An English version of the dark-blue underglaze ground colour termed GROS BLEU at Sèvres. It was first employed by the Chelsea porcelain factory, *c.* 1755. The overglaze blue ground at Sèvres was termed BLEU DE ROI. The use of the term 'Mazarine blue' for the colour goes back to at least 1686, but it seems to have no traceable connection with Cardinal Mazarin, who died in 1661.

Meadow-green. A ground colour employed in the 18th century at Sèvres, and there known as *vert pré* or *vert anglais.*

Meander-and-star border. A type of GREEK FRET BORDER pattern in which a single meander form alternates with a star-like rosette.

Meander-and-swastika border. A type of GREEK FRET BORDER in which two continuous lines form swastikas as they cross each other.

Meander border. A type of GREEK FRET BORDER in which one or two continuous lines, turning at right angles, make a repetitive labyrinthine pattern. *See* FLORAL MEANDER.

Mecklenburg-Strelitz service. A porcelain dinner-service completed at Chelsea in 1763 for the Duke of Mecklenburg-Strelitz to the order of George III and Queen Charlotte. The Duke was the Queen's brother. The principal decoration is of birds, perhaps painted by Zachariah Boreman. Around the border are five MAZARINE BLUE panels alternating with floral sprays. The curves over the panels are convex. The service is now at Buckingham Palace, London. A duplicate service was made at the same time, but it may be distinguished by the curves over the panels, which are concave instead of convex.

Medallion. (1) A flat, thin tablet of ceramic ware, usually oval or circular, bearing a portrait or design either painted or in relief (sometimes in intaglio). They were used principally for personal wear or for cabinet display, as distinct from a PLAQUE used mainly for wall or furniture decoration. Many portrait medallions in relief were made by Josiah Wedgwood in JASPER or BLACK BASALTES, and were often framed in metal. Wedgwood also made medallions in creamware for use as factory pattern models. (2) A painted decoration within a border, usually circular or oval, suggestive of a relief medallion. *See* TASSIE MEDALLION; WATTLE MEDALLION; CAMEO; TONDO.

Medical spoon. A spoon having, instead of the usual elongated handle, a loop handle whose terminal curls under the bowl of the spoon and serves as a foot. Some examples, made from *c.* 1875, have graduated markings on the interior. They were made of creamware. Rare examples have a hinged lid. *See* PAP-SPOON; FEEDING SPOON.

May day. Porcelain mask-jug with transfer-printed decoration, Worcester, *c.* 1760. Courtesy, Worcester Royal Porcelain Co.

Medallion. Black basaltes, with portrait of General Lafayette, diam. 4¼ in., Wedgwood. Courtesy, Sotheby's.

Medical spoon. English porcelain with gilding. Wellcome Museum, London.

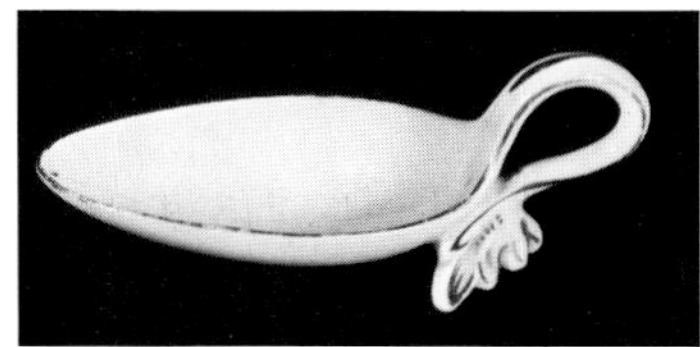

Medici porcelain. Lobed bottle painted in underglaze blue, *c.* 1580. Victoria and Albert Museum, London.

Medici porcelain. An artificial, or soft-paste, porcelain made *c.* 1575–83 at kilns in the Boboli Gardens, Florence (Italy). It was the first of its type to be made in Europe, probably by maiolica potters, and it largely imitated Chinese porcelain, then a very rare import coming by way of Venice. Medici porcelain is made with a white clay and a FRIT the composition of which is hardly distinguishable from powdered glass. The decoration is in underglaze blue, except for one polychrome example of uncertain attribution. Specimens are extremely rare; 59 extant pieces have been recorded. Some pieces are marked.

Medici vase. A large vase decorated with relief ornament in Renaissance style, made at Sèvres, *c.* 1783.

Medium relief. Relief decoration of a height from the surface intermediate between HIGH RELIEF and LOW RELIEF. The Italian term is *mezzo rilievo*; the French is *demi-relief.*

Megarian ware. Pottery from Megara, in ancient Greece, made during the Hellenistic period, *c.* 323–25 BC. Specimens are usually vases formed in a mould and decorated with figures in relief imitating *repoussé* decoration on metal.

Mei (Chinese). Prunus blossom. For instance, *mei-hua p'an* – prunus-flower dish – which has five lobes.

Mei-jên (Chinese). A decoration originating during the later years of the Ming dynasty consisting of elongated female figures. These were termed by the Dutch *Lange Lijzen*, a phrase which emerged in English as LONG ELIZAS.

Mei-p'ing (Chinese). A vase shape dating perhaps from the late Sung dynasty, which has a short, narrow neck and is intended to hold a single spray of prunus blossom. The earliest are of TZ'Ŭ CHOU ware, but those of the Ming dynasty are of porcelain, usually decorated in blue underglaze. A truncated version, consisting only of the upper half, was made at Tz'ŭ Chou. *See* PRUNUS VASE; MAE-PYŎNG; ICHIRIN ZASHI.

Meissner Porzellan. The German term for the porcelain of Meissen. *See* DRESDEN CHINA; SAXE.

Meissner Streublümchen (German). A term for a decoration of strewn flowers as used at the Meissen factory. *See* STREUBLUMEN.

Melon ware. Covered BOWLS and TUREENS naturalistically modelled and painted in imitation of a melon. On some the cover has a handle in the form of a tendril. Wares of this kind were made on the Continent by several faience and porcelain factories, and in England at Chelsea and Coalport. They also occur in creamware from Leeds and elsewhere.

Menagerie group. A pottery group made in Staffordshire, originally by Obadiah Sherratt of Hot Lane, Burslem, *c.* 1822–35, which depicts a carnival side-show with various animals. It rests on a rectangular base supported by paw feet and scrolls. *See* POLITO'S MENAGERIE; WOMBWELL'S MENAGERIE.

Menu-holder. A small decorative object, part of a dinner-service, with a slot for holding a menu or place-card.

Menu-stand. A wedge-shaped rectangular stand, raised at one end and sloping down to table level, with its top surface having a mat finish on which to write the menu.

Mercuric gilding. The process of applying gold to porcelain by means of an amalgam of gold and mercury. Low-temperature firing caused the mercury to vaporize, leaving a gold deposit which was then burnished to brightness. Mercuric gold has a thin, metallic, slightly brassy appearance, quite unlike the dull rich colour of HONEY GOLD; it was much cheaper and easier to apply and fix, and therefore suited to the large-scale production of the latter part of the 18th century and the 19th century. The process was perhaps originated at, and certainly popularized by, the Derby factory, *c.* 1780.

Merry man plates. A set of six plates of English (usually Lambeth) delftware, each bearing a different line of a doggerel verse, beginning 'What is a merry man'. They were inspired by a Dutch potter, John Ariens van Hamme, who took out a patent in 1676. Sets with matching decoration are very rare; those with the verse in sequence but with different decoration are more common. Similar sets of plates, each with a line from a verse, are known as SERVANT PLATES or GRACE PLATES.

Merry man plate. The last of a set of six, English delftware, 1687. City Museums, Stoke-on-Trent.

Metallic lustre. The application of a thin film of metal to the glaze as decoration. *See* LUSTRE. The technique was discovered in Persia about the 8th century AD and spread by way of Egypt along the North African coast, being imported into Spain probably during the 13th century, and there used to decorate the pottery termed HISPANO-MORESQUE WARE. By the early years of the 16th century it was known in Italy, and employed to decorate some of the MAIOLICA of Deruta and of Maestro Giorgio Andreoli at Gubbio. In England its introduction is attributed to John Hancock, *c.* 1790–99, and it was first employed in Staffordshire by Wedgwood in 1805. It was principally used in Staffordshire, at Leeds, and at Sunderland.

Oxides of gold, platinum, or silver were dissolved in acid, and after being mixed with an oily medium they were painted on to the glazed ware. Firing caused the metal to fuse into a thin film, producing a very thin and even metallic flashing. Gold yielded a ruby colour, silver a straw colour, and platinum, silver. Copper when employed for this purpose gave a copper colour. The final effect depended on the colour of the body, the thickness of the film, and the kind of FIRING. A much-sought variety was decorated by the resist process; *see* RESIST WARE.

Tea-ware decorated with an all-over film of platinum lustre was termed 'poor man's silver'. Figures were decorated in lustre by Wedgwood and others. Lustre was also employed in conjunction with transfer-prints (especially at Sunderland), or with designs painted in enamel. *See* BRONZED POTTERY.

Mei-p'ing. Vase decorated in underglaze blue, Ming dynasty, second half of 14th century. Victoria and Albert Museum, London.

Metallic oxide. The oxide of a metal employed as a pigment in the decoration of pottery and porcelain, either over or under the glaze. Oxides were suspended in an oily medium to make them suitable for application with a brush, and the actual colours were developed by the subsequent FIRING. The oxides most commonly used for this purpose were those of copper, iron, manganese, antimony, and cobalt.

Metropolitan slipware. A lead-glazed red earthenware decorated with white trailed slip found, and probably made, in the London area between 1630 and 1730. The ware included bowls, chamber-pots, jugs, mugs, and dishes. The glaze is less brilliant, and the inscriptions in lower relief, than is usual on Staffordshire and Kent slipware. Also called London slipware.

Mexican maiolica. Tin-glazed pottery made in Mexico after the Spanish conquest in 1521. Early decoration was influenced by Spanish wares, especially those of Talavera, and Chinese influence

Midnight Modern Conversation (2). Decoration on glazed earthenware plate, Staffordshire, *c.* 1770. City Museums, Stoke-on-Trent.

occurs during the 18th century, perhaps by way of Holland. Deterioration was marked in the 19th century and mainly tourist souvenirs are now made.

Mezza-maiolica (Italian). An earthenware body which has been dipped in slip and covered with a transparent glaze so that it resembles faience or maiolica. Painted decoration was done before glazing. Slip-covered ware of this kind was also decorated with incised lines (in the *sgraffito* technique) in conjunction with coloured glazes. The technique is an early one, and for the most part preceded the use of the tin-enamel glaze. In Germany it was termed *Halb-fayence*. *See* BIANCHETTO.

Midnight Modern Conversation. (1) An English stoneware jug made in the mid-18th century at Fulham; it bore applied relief decoration after Hogarth's *Midnight Modern Conversation*. (2) The same motif employed, e.g. on Staffordshire ware, as painted decoration, also in the mid-18th century.

Milde, Arij de, stoneware. A type of red stoneware, similar to the red stoneware of YI-HSING and of Böttger at Meissen, but softer than either, made by Arij (or Ary) de Milde at Delft in the 17th century. He worked in association with Samuel van Eenhoorn. His redware is decorated in relief in the manner of Yi-hsing.

Milk-jug. A jug or pitcher of medium size, larger than a cream-jug, for serving milk.

Milk-skimmer. *See* SKIMMER.

Milking group, The. An 18th-century figure group depicting a cow standing under a tree and being milked by a girl seated on a stool; at the side of the milkmaid a young girl watches, and a wolfhound gnaws a bone. Examples were made in Staffordshire in ASTBURY-WHIELDON WARE.

Milking scene, The. A decorative subject on Worcester transfer-printed porcelain, depicting a milkmaid watched by a companion who leans on a tree. The subject was adapted by Robert Hancock from an engraving by Luke Sullivan published in 1759. *See* HANCOCK ENGRAVINGS.

The Milkmaids. Covered porcelain vase with transfer-printed decoration (one of many variations), Worcester, *c.* 1760. Courtesy, Worcester Royal Porcelain Co.

Milkmaids, The. A frequent decorative subject on Worcester transfer-printed porcelain. It usually depicts two milkmaids carrying pails, with a man helping, and a barn and cattle in the background. Another version shows one milkmaid carrying a pail on her head, and another having hers removed by the man. Variations also include a third milkmaid and a dog. The subject was adapted by Robert Hancock from an engraving by Robert Sayer in 1766. *See* HANCOCK ENGRAVINGS.

Millefleurs pattern. (1) A decorative motif on Chinese porcelain of the reign of K'ang Hsi (1662–1722) and later, consisting of painted flowers covering the surface. (2) The same motif in relief, used at Meissen and elsewhere. *See* SNOWBALL VASE.

Minai ware. A type of Persian pottery from Rayy (Rhages), near Teheran, decorated in polychrome enamel colours over a cream glaze. The addition of gold-leaf was not unusual. Similar ware also came from Kashān and Saveh. The vessel was often painted in pale blue, green, or light purple under the glaze. Designs in black outline and a wide range of enamel colours were then added over the glaze. Some of the colours tended to sink into the soft glaze during the subsequent firing. *See* KASHĀN WARE; RAYY WARE.

Miners, The. A series of porcelain figures, modelled *c.* 1748–50 by J.J. Kändler at Meissen, after engravings by Christoph Weigel of Nuremberg. They depict members of the Saxon Court attired in miners' dress for a festive occasion.

Miners. Figures from the series modelled by J.J. Kändler, Meissen, *c.* 1750. Wadsworth Atheneum, Hartford, Conn.

Ming dynasty. The Chinese dynasty, from 1368 to 1644, whose reigning house was founded by Hung-wu (1368–98), after a successful nationalist revolt against the alien Mongol régime. It was during this period especially that white porcelain decorated either in blue underglaze or with enamel colours was developed. Early glazes are comparatively thick, with an appearance, as described by a Chinese commentator, of 'massed lard'. 'Pinholes' in the glaze are common, and some glazes show what the Chinese refer to as a CHICKEN-SKIN effect, because the surface, when held at an angle to the light, looks a little like the skin of a chicken in its slightly pitted unevenness. Unlike the later CH'ING DYNASTY wares, Ming wares are not as a rule precisely finished, but sufficient survive to prove that porcelain which was both thin and neatly finished was also successfully produced. Since there was a considerable export trade it is to be assumed that the more heavily potted wares were made for export.

The reign of Hsüan-tê (1426–35) is particularly noted for blue-and-white porcelain, and for underglaze copper-red, of which few specimens have survived; STEM-CUPS decorated with three red fish or three fruit are probably the most frequent, although many are 18th-century copies. Enamel colours seem first to have been used during this reign, but few specimens can be regarded as likely to have been made at this time. The employment of OIL-GILDING is mentioned by Chinese sources.

Enamelled porcelain of the reign of Chêng-Hua (1465–87) is much sought, and at this time the art of applying enamel directly to the BISCUIT (*émail sur biscuit*) without an intervening glaze was first practised. The reign of Hung Chih (1488–1505) is notable for yellow glazes, and that of Chêng-tê (1506–21) for blue-and-white wares of fine quality, some of which bear inscriptions in Arabic. The reign (1522–66) of Chia Ching (to be distinguished from the 19th-century Ch'ing dynasty Emperor, Chia Ch'ing) is noted for porcelain painted with a violet-blue, and much porcelain for export to the West was made in the reign of Wan-li (1573–1619). The porcelain is thin, hard, brilliant, crisp, and resonant, but the blue inclines to be pale.

From *c.* 1620 to the beginning of the following dynasty the wares are usually termed 'Transition Ming', and in style are the obvious precursors of the late 17th-century wares. YI-HSING stoneware and the BLANC DE CHINE of Tê Hua were first made during this period. *See* YÜAN DYNASTY.

Milking group. Figure group, ht 8 in., Astbury-Whieldon ware, Staffordshire, *c.* 1750–55. Courtesy, Sotheby's.

Miniature. A tiny replica of an object. Ceramic examples include dinner- and tea-services, plates, tureens, jugs, mugs, veilleuses, and bourdalous. *See* TOYS.

Minogame (Japanese). The water tortoise, a decorative Kakiemon design used on ARITA PORCELAIN, and copied in the 18th century on Continental ware, and in England, as at Chelsea. The tortoise is said to have lived for a thousand years and to have received the names 'raincoat tortoise' and 'flaming tortoise' because at the end of five centuries it acquired on its shell a plantation of seaweed (mistaken for a flame), which is seen streaming out behind it. The Chinese version of the subject is called the 'Divine Tortoise', and is one of the Four Supernatural Creatures (SSŬ LING).

Minogame. Octagonal beaker with painted decoration in the Arita style, Chelsea, *c.* 1750–52. Courtesy, Christie's.

Minuet, The. A decorative subject on Worcester transfer-printed porcelain depicting a lady and gentleman dancing in a landscape, with a violinist standing in front of a nearby tree. The engraving is by Robert Hancock after Francis Hayman. *See* HANCOCK ENGRAVINGS.

Mirror-black glaze. A lustrous, brilliant black glaze produced by a mixture of manganese and iron, employed in China during the Ch'ing dynasty (1666–1912), as a monochrome, usually in conjunction with a slight decoration in OIL-GILDING. It is distinct from FAMILLE NOIRE which is a black ground colour washed over with a translucent green enamel. The Chinese term is *wu-chin*, black gold.

Mirror-black glaze. Vase with oil gilding, reign of K'ang Hsi (1662–1722). Victoria and Albert Museum, London.

Mirror-shaped. Oval, or sometimes round, with a decorative frame of the type often employed for hand-mirrors; the frame is often outlined by several scrolls, asymmetrical in form.

Mishima (Japanese). The Japanese term for a type of decoration found on porcelain from Korea in which the piece is inlaid with black and white clays and covered with a CELADON glaze. The design was first incised into the surface of the plastic clay, the coloured clays afterwards being rubbed into the incisions. The whole was then glazed and fired. The term is said to be derived from the radiating characters of certain almanacs made at Mishima in Japan, but this is very uncertain; it may have been acquired by association with the island of Mishima, through which the wares were transshipped. The decoration has been copied in Japan in recent times. *See* ROPE CURTAIN PATTERN; CHAMPLEVÉ.

Mitsusashi (Japanese). A Japanese porcelain water-container made in the form of a baluster-shaped bowl with a flat cover.

Mittel (German). The term used to describe the middle (or second) grade of porcelain (i.e. the best imperfect ware) at Meissen and other 18th-century German factories. It was usually sold undecorated to private purchasers until *c.* 1740, when, to prevent its use by HAUSMALER, it was slightly decorated. At Meissen after 1760 the factory mark was defaced by one or more incised lines across it. *See* AUSSCHUSS PORZELLAN; GUT; CANCELLATION MARK.

Mocha ware. Coffee-pot with dendritic decoration, Staffordshire, early 19th century. City Museums, Stoke-on-Trent.

Mocha ware. Pottery made principally in England, beginning before 1785, which is ornamented with moss-like designs made by dabbing the body (as GREEN WARE, or after covering with slip) with a brush charged with a liquid pigment (said to contain tobacco) which spread out in branching tree-like traceries. The body varied, the earliest specimens being of creamware and later ones of white earthenware or pearlware. Before application of the mocha decoration, some pieces were painted with horizontal bands of various colours. The name is derived from mocha stone, an ornamental quartz with dendritic markings from Arabia. Specimens are usually of inexpensive domestic wares, especially jugs, mugs, and measuring vessels. Also called moss pottery, fern pottery, and tree pottery. *See* BANDED CREAMWARE.

Mochica pottery. Pottery made by the Mochica peoples around the north Peruvian coast about the 7th century AD. Notable are jars in the form of human heads which are naturally treated and superbly modelled. Subjects of decoration of vessels are nearly always votive, and the motifs stylized.

Mock Arabic. A border pattern, or ground pattern, suggestive of an Arabic inscription, but actually consisting of meaningless conventional linear designs, as seen on certain later specimens of HISPANO-MORESQUE WARE painted by European potters. *See* NESKHI; KUFIC SCRIPT.

Mockery of Age, The. A porcelain figure group modelled by J. J. Kändler at Meissen, *c.* 1745, depicting an aged man flirting with a young lady and, behind them, two mocking Harlequin figures. The group was copied at Vienna, and inspired a group made at Derby, *c.* 1755.

Mockery of Age. Group by J. J. Kändler, Meissen, *c.* 1745. Wadsworth Atheneum, Hartford, Conn.

Model. *See* MODELLING.

Modeller's mark. A mark on ceramic ware to indicate the identity of the modeller. Such marks were rarely employed, but occasionally a modeller added his initials or his signature. *See* POTTER'S MARK.

Modelling. The process of shaping an original piece of ceramic ware (or the model or maquette from which is made a MOULD to be used in producing reproductions for sale). Usually the original model of clay or wax is made from a drawing, the modeller seeking to preserve the spirit and details of the designer. The modeller must allow for shrinkage when the clay dries, and again when it is fired; the model is said to be in 'clay-size', and the fired piece is about one-sixth smaller. Some ceramic designers, notably Bustelli at Nymphenburg, produced original models in carved lime-wood instead of in modelled clay, and the moulds were made from these.

Mogollon pottery. Pottery of the Mogollon culture of the mountain regions of present-day Arizona and New Mexico, the most important of which was made during the 11th and 12th centuries. It is noted for a vigorous decoration of human, animal, and insect forms.

Mohammedan blue. A cobalt-blue pigment from Persia. *See* HUI HUI CH'ING.

Moka set. A tray with a set of four small coffee-cups without saucers.

Möllendorf service. A porcelain dinner-service made at Meissen in 1761 to the order of Frederick the Great as a gift to General Möllendorf. It has on the border the PREUSSISCH-MUSIKALISCHE PATTERN, together with MOSAIK PATTERNS and INDIANISCHE BLUMEN. The plastic decoration is by J. J. Kändler.

Momoyama period. The period (1576–1700) of the Japanese ruler Hideyoshi and of the country's first contacts with the West. It followed the MUROMACHI PERIOD and preceded the EDO PERIOD. Pottery design was still under the influence of the TEA CEREMONY at this time, but new glazes were introduced. Roof-tiles formed part of the production of the period, and these are often elaborate and of excellent quality.

Mon (Japanese). The badge of a family, particularly of the ancient feudal nobility, comparable with European armorial bearings. That of the Japanese Emperor is the KIKUMON (chrysanthemum). The most frequent form is circular, enclosing a stylized flower, insect, bird, or some other natural object. Badges of this kind were employed as porcelain decoration. *See* KIRIMON.

Money-box. Sussex ware, early 19th century. City Museums, Stoke-on-Trent.

Money-box. A popular form of peasant pottery in a variety of forms intended for small savings, and having a slot for the insertion of coins. Money-boxes were made in the form of cottages, chests of drawers, dovecots, hens, pigs, and other objects. They date from the end of the 17th century, one or two rare examples of London delftware having survived from this period. Early money-boxes are comparatively rare, since most were broken in order to extract the contents. Also called a penny-bank. *See* COTTAGE.

Monkey band. *See* AFFENKAPELLE.

Monkey teapot. A teapot naturalistically modelled and painted in the form of a seated female monkey with – forming the handle – a young monkey clinging to her back and holding a bowl, and – forming the spout – another young monkey playing in her arms. Typically a baroque concept, these teapots were modelled *c.* 1735 at Meissen.

Monk's-cap jug. A Chinese porcelain jug made from the Ming dynasty onwards, and usually covered with a reduced copper glaze. The outline of the top resembles a cap often worn by Buddhist monks. The Chinese term is *seng-mao-hu.*

Monochrome. Painted or other decoration employing a single colour, or a glaze of this kind. *See* CAMAÏEU, EN; GRISAILLE, EN; POLYCHROME.

Monogram. A character composed of two or more initial letters interwoven, usually representing a name, and employed as an identifying ornament. Monograms thus employed on ceramic wares are often the initials of the original owner. They were also sometimes used as a FACTORY-MARK, e.g. the double *L* monogram of Louis XV employed for this purpose at Sèvres. Monograms are sometimes termed ciphers.

Monopteros pattern. Earthenware plate with underglaze blue transfer-printed decoration, Staffordshire, *c.* 1815. J.K. des Fontaines Collection, London.

Monopteros pattern. A decorative pattern depicting circular temple buildings in a wooded landscape. The name 'monopteros', apparently first used by E. Morton Nance, is derived from the Greek word for a circular pillared and domed shrine. The pattern was adapted from engravings in a travel book, *Oriental Scenery, 1795–1810*, by Thomas and William Daniell. Used on glazed earthenware with transfer-printed decoration made by Spode, *c.* 1810–35, it was adapted at Swansea, 1817–24. *See* INDIAN SPORTING PATTERN; CARAMANIAN PATTERN.

Death of Monro. Group modelled by Obadiah Sherratt, early 19th century. Courtesy, Christie's.

Monro, Death of. An earthenware group made by Obadiah Sherratt in the early 19th century depicting the prostrate figure of Lieutenant Hector Monro, his head in the mouth of a tiger standing over him. He was killed in this way on 22 December 1792 while shooting on the island of Saugor, near Calcutta. Another Staffordshire version depicts him being carried off by a lion.

Lady Mary Wortley Montagu service. Porcelain plate, Worcester, *c.* 1768, decorated in the London workshop of James Giles. Courtesy, Worcester Royal Porcelain Co.

Montagu, Lady Mary Wortley, service. A porcelain dinner-service made at Worcester and decorated in the London workshop of the independent decorator, James Giles; the plates have a border of dishevelled birds in reserved cartouches flanked by gilt trellisage and flower-sprays on a blue-scale ground.

Monteith. A large circular or oval bowl to contain iced water; the rim has a series of scallops, alternately bent outward, for the purpose of suspending wine-glasses by the foot so that they can be cooled by immersion before use. Originally of silver, monteiths were later made in porcelain and glazed earthenware, and in glass. In France the monteith was termed *seau à verre, seau crenelé, verrière*, and *rafraîchissoir*. The term is said to have been derived from a Scotsman named Monteith who, at Oxford in the reign of Charles II, wore a cloak or coat scalloped at the bottom. *See* GLÄSERWÄRMER.

Month plate. One of a set of twelve pottery ISTORIATO plates, each having on the reverse the name of a month and an inscription, and on the front painted scenes and figures with attributes allegorical of a particular month. Made in the second half of the 16th century.

Months, The. A group of figures emblematic of the twelve months, first introduced by J. J. Kändler at Meissen, *c.* 1732–40, which became popular during the 18th century.

Moon. A circular spot of greater translucency than the remainder of a porcelain piece when viewed by transmitted light. It results from the imperfect mixture (*see* WEDGING; PUGGING) of ingredients, and the expansion of the resulting air-bubbles in the paste during the process of firing. It is noteworthy that moons occur most frequently in plates made with a JIGGER. Some broken Chelsea plates exhibiting moons have been found to have small flattened cavities at the site of the fracture. Moons are known in Chelsea porcelain especially, but they also occur in porcelain from Sèvres and Tournai, in early Meissen production, and in early porcelain from Vienna, Frankenthal, Ludwigsburg, and Nymphenburg. They are not, therefore, confined to soft-paste porcelains, although they are here the more frequent.

Monk's-cap jug. Porcelain, probably Tz'ŭ Chou yao, Ming dynasty. British Museum, London.

Moonlight lustre. A type of splashed or marbled pink or purple GOLD LUSTRE with tinges of yellow and green, developed by Wedgwood between 1805 and 1815.

Moonstone. A mat white glaze developed by Wedgwood in 1933.

Moresques. A term sometimes used in the 19th century for decorative motifs similar to ARABESQUES, especially those derived from Spain and Sicily, both of which were, at one time, under Saracen domination. Similar motifs based on Roman decorative motifs are more usually termed GROTESQUES.

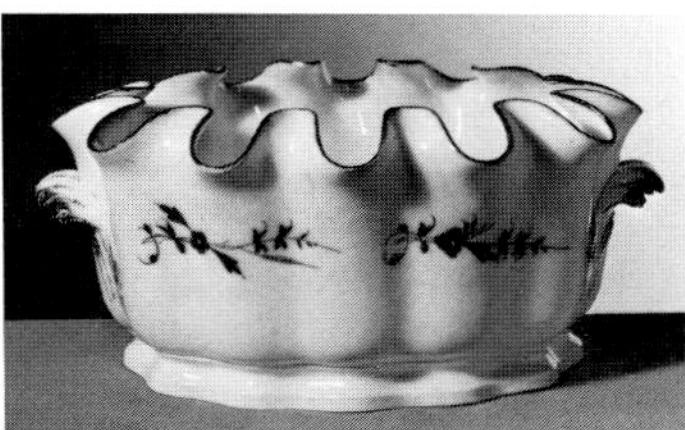

Monteith. Porcelain, with painted decoration of modified Chantilly sprays, Caughley, *c.* 1772–99. Victoria and Albert Museum, London.

Morgan, de, ware. *See* DE MORGAN WARE.

Mortar. A round vessel of heavy and substantial pottery, usually stoneware, in which various materials are triturated with a pestle.

Mortarium. A vessel of Roman pottery similar to a mortar, made with pebbles embedded into the bottom to facilitate triturating and having a lip for pouring.

Mosaik pattern. A border pattern in which areas of ground colour are overpainted with DIAPER patterns and IMBRICATED designs. These patterns were introduced at Meissen soon after 1750, and were much used at Berlin after 1763. *See* OLD MOSAIK PATTERN.

Moss pottery. *See* MOCHA WARE.

Mother and child pattern. A decorative subject similar to the BELL-TOY PATTERN, except that the child holds a fan in the crook of his elbow instead of holding a toy. It was employed at Worcester, from *c.* 1770.

Mother and child pattern. Tea-bowl with decoration in underglaze blue, Worcester, *c.* 1770. Courtesy, Worcester Royal Porcelain Co.

Mother-of-pearl glaze. A glaze having a nacreous appearance. French terms are *lustre nacré* and *reflets métalliques*. *See* PERLMUTTER LUSTRE; MADREPERLA LUSTRE; BRIANÇON LUSTREWARE; HISPANO-MORESQUE WARE.

Moonlight lustre. Pot-pourri vase, pearlware with purple gold-lustre decoration, Wedgwood *c.* 1810. Buten Museum of Wedgwood, Merion, Pa.

Mould. A form used in making, from an original model, various ceramic vessels, figures, etc. Hollow moulds are taken from an original model, from another piece of ceramic ware, from an object in wood, silver, or some other material, or even from a natural object; they are usually of clay or plaster of Paris.

There are three steps in the making of moulds for quantity production of ceramic wares: (1) a hollow case-mould is made from the original model; (2) a block-mould is made from the case-mould, taking the form of the original model; (3) the hollow potter's mould or working mould is made from the block-mould, and it is in this that the ware (in a state ready for glazing and firing) is made.

Moulds were sometimes made in INTAGLIO form by cutting. In Staffordshire in the 18th century those who cut moulds were called 'block-cutters'; in this period carved wooden and alabaster moulds were often employed, especially before the introduction in England of the plaster of Paris mould, *c.* 1745, reputedly by Ralph Daniels of Cobridge. *See* MOULDING; CASE-MOULD; PITCHER-MOULD; PRESS-MOULD; BLOCK-MOULD; POTTER'S MOULD: PIECE-MOULD; WASTE-MOULD.

Moulding. The process of shaping ceramic objects by pressing soft clay into moulds (or pitchers) made from a hand-modelled prototype. As objects made in moulds were often of several parts, the separate parts were joined by a REPAIRER to make the whole by LUTING. *See* CASTING; SLIP-CAST.

Mount. A decorative metal ornament attached to porcelain wares of superior quality. In the 18th century such mounts were made of GILT-BRONZE, ORMOLU (a kind of brass), silver, and pewter. Mugs were commonly given pewter or silver lids, and Wedgwood mounted his jasper PLAQUES and CAMEOS in cut-steel as jewellery. The most spectacular examples of mounting came from France in the middle of the 18th century, when gilt-bronze was employed in conjunction with porcelain from Vincennes and Sèvres, as well as with pieces from Meissen and the Orient.

Mourning jug. A type of stoneware jug with lid; examples were made in Germany in the 17th and 18th centuries. *See* TRAUERKRUG.

Moustache cup. Bone-china cup with painted decoration, Wedgwood, *c.* 1900. Buten Museum of Wedgwood, Merion, Pa.

Moustache cup. A cup having a guard behind the rim to protect the moustache while drinking; a 19th-century innovation.

Moutardier. The French term for a MUSTARD-JAR.

Mouth. (1) The orifice of a jar, jug, or pitcher from which the contents are poured. The mouth may or may not be given a lip. Some are of special form, such as the GARLIC MOUTH, COLLAR or FUNNEL-MOUTH. (2) Any one of several furnaces which are connected to a central opening in the oven of a kiln.

Muffin. A plate from 6 to 7 inches wide, variously shaped.

Muffin-dish. A medium-sized round dish with a domed cover, for the service of warm muffins. It is also sometimes referred to as a muffineer.

Muffle. An inner chamber or box in which objects were enclosed to keep them away from flames or smoke while being subjected to firing in the PETIT FEU, especially in the process of applying enamel colours to glazed ware. PETIT FEU COLOURS or 'muffle colours' are those developed in the *petit feu*, in which the temperature is normally in the range 700 to 900°C.

Mug. A drinking-vessel with a handle, and a plain, circular rim without a lip. Some have a lid, usually of metal, such as silver or pewter. Mugs were made in various forms, usually cylindrical, but sometimes waisted, barrel-shaped, inverted bell-shaped, and occasionally 'square' (i.e. cylindrical, but having the same diameter as the height, so as to have a 'square' silhouette). *See* STEIN; TANKARD; SCHNELLE; THURNDENDEL; BEAKER; APOSTLE MUG; CAPACITY MUG; TRIFLE-MUG.

Muscheln. Teapot of faceted, polished Böttger red stoneware, Meissen, *c.* 1715. Victoria and Albert Museum, London.

Müller service. A breakfast-service made by the Royal Copenhagen Manufactory in 1785 for its founder, Frantz Heinrich Müller. The decoration is in several different styles, but all pieces have a similar *bleu de roi* border.

Mummy cone. Same as a SEPULCHRAL CONE.

Muromachi period. The period (1398–1573) of the Ashikaga Shoguns in Japan, preceding the MOMOYAMA PERIOD. Much TEMMOKU ware was produced at Seto, and shows the influence of Chinese ware of this kind made during the Sung dynasty. TEA CEREMONY wares, now much sought in Japan, were, during this period, influenced by Korean ware. The general style is that of the cult of imprecisely finished wares, and the seeking of fortuitous glaze effects, these being much in demand for the Tea Ceremony.

Murrhine ware. A type of ware imported into Imperial Rome during the 1st century AD. The statement of Propertius that it was 'fired in Parthian kilns' has led to the speculation that Murrhine vases were of some kind of pottery, perhaps Chinese, but surviving descriptions suggest that they were a hardstone. Despite their many trading connections with China, no traces of Chinese objects have been discovered on sites occupied by the Romans, although Roman coins and glass have been found in the Far East. Murrhine vases were copied in Alexandria in opalescent glass; most probably the originals were of jade or agate.

Muscheln (German). A type of decoration, probably suggested by the mussel shell, used on BÖTTGER STONEWARE made at Meissen before 1720. It was executed by cutting the surface into connecting concave facets which are highly polished. The technique was probably introduced by the goldsmith, Johann Jakob Irminger. *See* FACETED WARE.

Muses Modeller. An unidentified modeller working for the Bow porcelain factory, *c.* 1750–55. He was so called because his hand was first recognized from the likeness in style to be observed among figures of the NINE MUSES and Apollo made *c.* 1752, and a number of other models with similar characteristics later grouped with them. The principal features to be observed are crude but lively modelling and faces which are *petite* and oval, with receding chin.

Muses Modeller. Porcelain figure with typical facial characteristics, Bow, *c.* 1750–55.

Mushikui (Japanese). The word means worm-eaten or moth-eaten, and it is applied to RANZOHAN WARE where defects in the composition of the glaze cause it to shrink, revealing bare patches. *See* HON SHONSUI.

Music Lesson, The. *See* FLUTE LESSON, THE.

Music plates. Dessert plates of blue Dutch delftware decorated with the score and verse of a song, presumably to be sung by diners at the end of a meal. Sets are now rare, but were common in 17th-century Holland. They were made at Delft, and have been reproduced at Rouen and Milan.

Musical imps. Martinware figures, late 19th century. City Museums, Stoke-on-Trent.

Musical imps. A series of figures of MARTINWARE, usually seated cross-legged with Puckish faces tilted backwards, and playing various musical instruments. There are at least ten different models. They were made in glazed or biscuit ware.

Musical trophies. *See* TROPHIES; PREUSSISCH-MUSIKALISCHE PATTERN.

Musical ware. (1) Musical instruments made of porcelain, such as the flute, ocarina, whistle, BIRD-WHISTLE, and bells. (2) Ornamental pieces in the form of musical instruments, such as the VIOLIN. Violins were made at Delft, Holland, in tin-glazed earthenware (delftware), and they have been reproduced by Edmé Samson et Cie of Paris (*see* SAMSON COPIES).

Musikoli figures. A series of porcelain figures depicting musical soloists (including those playing the guitar, spinet, violin, etc.) modelled by Johann Christian Wilhelm Beyer at Ludwigsburg, *c.* 1764–67. *See* MALABAR FIGURES.

Mustard-jar. A small jar for the service of prepared mustard, usually with a stand, or saucer, and a cover having an indentation for the spoon. They exist in faience and porcelain, the latter including those made in China for export during the 18th century. Some have a spoon decorated *en suite*, but silver spoons were also employed. The French term is *moutardier*. *See* DRY MUSTARD JAR.

Mustard-yellow. Same as FISH-ROE YELLOW.

Muster (German). Pattern or design; often used in conjunction with terms designating a border (*-rand*) pattern.

Mycenaean pottery. Pottery from the Mediterranean area in the prehistoric time of Mycenaean ascendancy, *c.* 1400–1100 BC, and related in style to that found at Mycenae. It was followed by SUB-MYCENAEAN POTTERY, *c.* 1100–1000, and then the distinctively Greek PROTOGEOMETRIC STYLE, *c.* 1000–900, and GEOMETRIC STYLE, *c.* 900–700. Such ware is sometimes termed 'Late Helladic'.

Myrtle pan. A shallow earthenware container, made in England in the late 18th and early 19th century, for holding growing evergreens. It was made in graduated sizes.

Mysterious basket, The. *See* PANIER MYSTÉRIEUX.

Mythological figures. A series of figures of the gods and goddesses of Greek and Roman mythology. The vogue seems to have started with a series modelled at Meissen by J. F. Eberlein, *c.* 1741. The subject had earlier been much used for painted decoration on tin-glazed earthenware. *See* OVIDIAN GODS.

Mustard-jar. Porcelain, with hinged lid, Mennecy, mid-18th century. Courtesy, Newman & Newman Ltd, London.

N

Nabeshima ware. Japanese porcelain made at Okawachi, not far from Arita (Hizen province), the kilns being founded in the mid-17th century by Nabeshima, Prince of Kaga, with the aid of Korean potters. Early decoration was in a style notably influenced by Sakaida Kakiemon at Arita, but productions also include decoration in a pale underglaze blue, and a combination of red and blue with celadon on a red stoneware body. The body varies from stoneware to a fine porcelain. Principal survivals include dishes with a high foot-ring, small cups, and small dishes with petal-shaped rims. *See* KAKIEMON PORCELAIN.

Naga. The Japanese term for a glazed jar on which is traced the figure of a dragon (*naga*). Of unknown origin, they were found in Borneo, where they were employed to impart certain qualities to water stored in them, and hence were venerated and costly.

Naked Boy, The. A decorative subject in relief depicting a naked Chinese boy crouching in a tree amid luxuriant foliage. Copied from a Chinese design, it occurs on objects in red stoneware, saltglazed stoneware, and Whieldon-Wedgwood ware, especially on the spouts of teapots. Also called 'Boy in a tree' pattern.

Named views. *See* TOPOGRAPHICAL WARE.

Nanking ware. Blue-and-white Chinese porcelain made during the 18th and the early part of the 19th centuries at CHING-TÊ CHÊN and shipped from the port of Nanking. The decoration is usually of Chinese subjects, most frequently landscapes with buildings, although border patterns, such as the FITZHUGH PATTERN, are sometimes inspired by European sources. Enamelled porcelain for export was made at Ching-tê Chên, but was painted in polychrome in the enamelling shops of Canton and shipped from there. *See* CANTON CHINA.

Nanking yellow. A yellowish-brown glaze derived from iron, usually associated with underglaze blue decoration on porcelain decorated at Nanking. The Chinese term is *tzu chin*.

Nappy. (1) A small shallow bowl placed on the table into which a glass of nappy (a strong, foaming ale) was placed, so that the foam spilled into it. Some, with a scalloped rim, were made of Leeds creamware. (2) A small oval or circular dish with a flat bottom and sloping sides; used for baking.

Narghile (or **nargile**). The Turkish term for a HOOKAH.

Narrow-boat teapot. Brown earthenware, ht 13 in., *c*. 1887.

Narrow-boat teapot. An earthenware teapot made in England for use on the barges, or narrow boats, operating on canals. They are usually large, brown, and circled with a floral decoration in colour, sometimes with lustre added. The cover on some of the largest examples often has, as a handle, a finial in the form of a miniature teapot of similar form. Also known as 'Bargee ware', the teapots date from the late 19th century.

Nassau ware. Stoneware made in Westerwald (Germany) in the second half of the 19th century in the style of the old WESTERWALD WARE. It has a grey body with added blue decoration.

Some specimens are original designs, but many were cast from moulds taken from old wares, or even from old moulds. They are of a quality inferior to the earlier ware. This stoneware is so called because in 1803 the district of Westerwald was incorporated into the Duchy of Nassau.

Nautilus service. A dinner-service made in Queen's ware (creamware) by Wedgwood, in which all the pieces were moulded and coloured in the form of sea-shells. The service was named after the CENTREPIECE, which was modelled as a large nautilus shell. Some of the larger tureens and dishes were ornamented with pecten shells, and shells of the cockle and of other small bivalves.

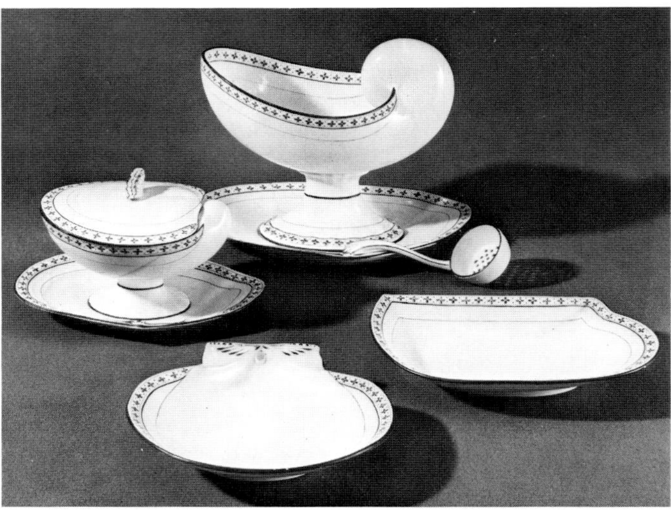

Nautilus service. Pieces from a service made in 1798. Courtesy, Wedgwood.

Nazca pottery. Pottery made by peoples living on the southern coast of Peru, *c.* AD 500–800. The pottery is noted for excellent polychrome painting, and for curiously spouted vessels, the spout being an overhead arched tubular bridge. The motifs of painted decoration are geometric, or stylized birds, human heads, etc., to be found also with vessels made in the form of figures. The centipede god is peculiar to the Nazca, and puma heads are sometimes made in relief, the body added by painting. The wares of peoples of Tiahuanaco, Lake Titicaca, were much influenced by Nazca pottery. *See* BRIDGE SPOUT; STIRRUP SPOUT HANDLE.

Lord Nelson ware. Creamware plate with brown enamel decoration, probably Staffordshire, *c.* 1810. Victoria and Albert Museum, London.

Neck. That part of a bottle, vase, or other vessel between the mouth and the shoulder, or body. It may be long or short, and parallel-sided or with sides sloping inwards or outwards. The French term is *col. See* TRUMPET-NECK; CONTRACTED NECK.

Nelson, Lord, service. An armorial dinner-service decorated with the arms of Vice-Admiral Horatio Nelson, and depicting him wearing the sash of the Order of the Bath and other Orders. It was begun at Chamberlain's Worcester porcelain factory in 1802, but at the time of Lord Nelson's death in 1805 only the breakfast-service had been completed. *See* NELSON, LORD, WARE.

Nelson, Lord, ware. Earthenware, mainly mugs and jugs, commemorating Lord Nelson. Specimens are usually of creamware, transfer-printed in black with portraits or memorabilia. *See* NELSON, LORD, SERVICE.

Nelson vase. A type of tall circular vase of PARIAN PORCELAIN having a handle in the form of a figure of Neptune, and on each side a relief decoration with a scene commemorating Lord Nelson. The vases were made by S. Alcock & Co., 1851.

Nelson vase. Parian porcelain, S. Alcock & Co., 1851. Victoria and Albert Museum, London.

Nengo (Japanese). A reign-mark (called in Chinese, NIEN HAO) used on some ARITA PORCELAIN in the 17th and 18th centuries. Marks of this kind are usually enclosed with a single underglaze blue ring, in contrast to the Chinese double ring.

Neo-classical style. The revival of classical decoration, based on that of Greece and Rome, which followed the ROCOCO style. Neo-classicism was to some extent a product of the excavation of Pompeii in the 1750s, and the term, in its early phases, is more or less interchangeable with what is meant by the ADAM STYLE in England. In France it is quite commonly called the LOUIS SEIZE STYLE, and in reference to porcelain it is notable not only for the employment of swags, husk borders, rams' heads, and similar classical motifs, but also for a mawkish sentimentality which was influenced by the work of such contemporary painters as Greuze. In England the principal exponent of the style in pottery was Josiah Wedgwood, who was much influenced by Robert Adam and 'Athenian' Stuart. After the Revolution of 1789 in France the earlier neo-classical style developed first into the DIRECTOIRE STYLE (which is principally a furniture style), and then into the EMPIRE STYLE; the latter is contemporary with the English REGENCY STYLE, which owes much to it.

Neskhi (Arabic). A type of Arabic calligraphy, a running script, used as decoration on Near Eastern pottery. *See* KUFIC SCRIPT; MOCK ARABIC.

Nestoris (Greek). A globular jar of Greek pottery with two vertical handles attached at the shoulder and at the rim of the mouth; the handles are characterized by two knobs, one at the junction with the body, and the other at the apex. It is also called a *torzella*.

Nestoris. Pottery, with black-figure decoration; ht 9¼ in., southern Italy, 5th century BC. Victoria and Albert Museum, London.

Netherlands maiolica. A term of doubtful value, somewhat confusing, which is sometimes applied to Dutch tin-glazed ware (delftware) influenced by the maiolica of Italy.

Network pattern. A DIAPER pattern of intersecting diagonal parallel lines forming lozenges, sometimes with small crosses at the intersections; mainly used as a border ornament.

Neubrandensteinmuster (German). Literally, new Brandenstein pattern. A moulded basketwork (OZIER) border pattern introduced by J.G. Höroldt at Meissen in 1744. It was similar in some ways to the ALTBRANDENSTEINMUSTER in having the same plain narrow panel, and the panel with dotted squares, but in other respects it resembled the NEUOZIERRAND. *See* ORDINAIR-OZIER; ALTOZIERRAND.

Neuozierrand (German). Literally, new osier border. A moulded basketwork (Ozier) pattern introduced by J. G. Höroldt at Meissen in 1742. It had an outer border of basketwork moulding, and a plain inner border confined by a moulded line of scroll form which encroached on the well of the plate. In addition there were four sets of spiralling ribs which gave twelve narrow panels and four wide ones. *See* ORDINAIR-OZIER; ALTOZIERRAND: ALTBRANDENSTEINMUSTER; NEUBRANDENSTEINMUSTER.

New Canton. A name contemporaneously applied to the Bow factory (*c.* 1747–76), which was situated at Stratford Langthorn, Essex, across the River Lea from Stratford-le-Bow, near London.

Night watchman. Toby jug with pouring lip at the back, probably by Enoch Wood, *c.* 1800. City Museums, Stoke-on-Trent.

La Nourrice. Porcelain figure, ht 7 in., Chelsea, *c.* 1755. Victoria and Albert Museum, London.

New china. Same as STONE CHINA.

New stone ware. Same as STONE CHINA.

Nien hao (Chinese). 'In the reign of'. The meaning of the last two ideograms in a four- or six-character CHINESE REIGN-MARK (reading from the right downwards), the preceding two being the name of the emperor, and the first two in a six-character mark the name of the dynasty. *See* NENGO.

Night watchman. (1) A type of TOBY JUG depicting a man holding a lantern and a hat. (2) The subject of earthenware figures made in Staffordshire towards the end of the 18th century by Enoch Wood.

Nine Muses, The. A group of porcelain figures depicting the Muses, the best-known example being a set of nine, with Apollo additional, made by the so-called MUSES MODELLER for the Bow factory between 1750 and 1755. The subject also occurs elsewhere about the same time.

Nipple spout. A spout to a FEEDING POT which is closed at the end and pierced with holes.

Nishapur ware. Glazed earthenware made at Nishapur (central Persia) in the 9th and 10th centuries. Several types are thus designated, including ware with a red or buff body and designs in several colours under a clear glaze; another has black decoration on a white ground. Similar styles were current at Samarkand.

Nishiki-de ware. Japanese porcelain with an elaborate overall decoration in underglaze blue in conjunction with overglaze coloured enamel designs which often feature a BROCADE PATTERN. It was made at Arita (Hizen province), and is a type of IMARI porcelain.

Northern celadon. Celadon ware that originated in the northern provinces of China. It has a dark olive-green glaze and is characterized by handsome floral decoration, either carved or moulded. It has characteristics which distinguish it from YÜEH YAO, but it is in some respects similar.

Nottingham stoneware. A type of brown saltglazed stoneware made at Nottingham (England) from *c.* 1690 to the end of the 18th century. The glaze has a peculiar metallic appearance which makes it comparatively easy to recognize. Many specimens are decorated with incised work, and wares include mugs, jugs, and BEAR-JUGS.

Nourrice, La. The Nurse, a well-known figure of a seated woman nursing an infant. She is sometimes termed the 'Palissy nurse', but the model appears to have originated at the Avon pottery, near Fontainebleau, and to have been modelled by Bartélémy de Blénod, one of Palissy's followers, in the early 17th century (*see* PALISSY WARE). The subject was modelled by Joseph Willems at Chelsea, *c.* 1752, and was occasionally copied at Worcester and elsewhere subsequent to that date.

Nozzle. *See* CANDLE-NOZZLE.

Nuptial plates. Plates decorated in slip to depict a knife, fork, and spoon. They were given to wedding-guests who had neglected to bring their own implements. They were made in Hungary, and perhaps Silesia.

O-X border. An ornate border pattern resembling a series of alternating letters O and X with floral and foliate embellishments. The letters in a crude form occur on the reverse of some delftware plates.

Oak-leaf charger. A type of BLUE-DASH CHARGER decorated with stylized oak-leaves reserved on a blue ground in radiating panels divided by bands. Bristol delftware examples exist.

Oak-leaf charger. Blue-dash charger, with brown stylized leaves reserved on a blue ground, Bristol delftware, 18th century.

Oak-leaf jar. A very rare early Italian maiolica DRUG-JAR decorated with stylized oak-leaves in the Gothic style, often with the blue pigment heavily applied (impasto). They are of uncertain origin, but most are probably from Florence or some other Tuscan city, and date from the middle of the 15th century. The body is generally pale buff in colour, with a stanniferous glaze ranging in tone from white to ivory. The form is variable, and, like the ornament, probably derived from the HISPANO-MORESQUE WARES of Valencia. Decoration is usually drawn in a purplish-manganese colour, then painted impasto in a blackish-blue. It includes, besides the oak-leaves, heraldic lions, birds, and human profiles. Similar decoration occurs on some early ALBARELLI, BOCCALI, and BACILI.

Oak-leaf pattern. A decorative motif of stylized oak leaves and acorns, with intertwined branches; it was employed on maiolica in the 16th century. *See* CERQUATE.

Oblate. A spheroidal form, depressed or flattened at top or bottom.

Obsidian. A colour, very dark, usually reddish or brownish, which is like the colour of the natural volcanic glass known as obsidian. PARIAN PORCELAIN was sometimes so coloured.

Obverse. The side of a vase or other vessel bearing the principal decoration. *See* REVERSE.

Octagon-and-square ground. A DIAPER ground composed of adjacent octagons, with resultant interstitial small squares. The octagons and squares sometimes have interior decoration of flowers or some similar motif. Principally used on Chinese porcelain.

Octofoil. A shape, or ornamentation, having eight equal foils or lobes.

Œil-de-perdrix (French). Literally, partridge eye. A pattern developed and principally used at Vincennes-Sèvres, *c.* 1752–57, in enamel colours or gilding, often for the purpose of softening the vivid colours of some of the Sèvres ground colours then in use, particularly BLEU DE ROI. The pattern is of dotted circles – hence the name. It was sometimes employed at Meissen and occasionally elsewhere, particularly on porcelain copying Sèvres originals. *See* FISH-ROE GROUND; FOND TAILLANDIER.

Oeil de perdrix. Decoration on clock-case, Sèvres, *c.* 1752–57. Wallace Collection, London.

Oenochoë (Greek). Sometimes *oinochoë*. A type of Greek pottery wine-jug with a vertical loop handle and usually a trefoil (pinched) lip. Examples occur in many shapes and sizes, some having a circular mouth, a beaked lip, or a spout. There are two types: (1) with the neck set off from the shoulder; and (2) with a continuous curve from the neck to the body (the OLPE is a form of this type). They were used to transfer wine from a KRATER to drinking-cups. *See* PROCHOÖS; LAGYNOS.

Oenochoë. Neck type, ht 14 in., with trefoil mouth, Vulci, 3rd century BC. British Museum, London.

Ogee. A shape or ornamentation in the form of a double curve, as in the letter *S*. It is sometimes continued to form a double ogee. *See* CYMA.

Oil-bottle. A small jug with a pouring lip for serving oil at table. The type occurs from classical times onwards, and specimens in Chinese export porcelain exist. Oil-bottles made at Lowestoft in porcelain are characterized by two small holes pierced in the handle for a string to suspend the stopper, thus preventing it from soiling the table.

Oil-dropper. A small receptacle with a short spout having a tiny hole at the tip to release drops of oil.

Oil-gilding. *See* GILDING.

Oil-spot glaze. Silvery spots, often spaced out with a certain recognizable regularity, appearing on the dark-brown glaze of some CHIEN YAO and HONAN WARE made during the Sung dynasty (960–1280). They were the result of the precipitation of particles of iron.

Ointment-pot. A small shallow bowl used principally to store ointments and unguents (some were for cosmetics and dentifrices). They are usually of tin-glazed earthenware, and occur in English delftware. Early specimens were cylindrical, then gradually they became shaped and waisted until *c.* 1735 when they usually had a stemmed and spreading base. They are often decorated with a painted motif of stylized foliage. They date from the 16th century, but it has been suggested that some of the inscribed names of the contents may have been added in the 19th century. Sometimes called a dispensing pot. *See* PHARMACY WARE.

Olpe. Wine-jug, ht 10 in., Attic, *c.* 550 BC. British Museum, London.

Oiron faience. *See* FAÏENCE D'OIRON; HENRI DEUX WARE.

Old Japan brocade pattern. *See* BROCADE PATTERN; OLD PATTERN.

Old Japan fan pattern. *See* JAPAN FAN PATTERN; OLD PATTERN.

Old Mosaik pattern. A decorative pattern used on Worcester and other 18th-century English porcelain; it was based on contemporary Imari patterns from Japan. *See* MOSAIK PATTERN.

Old pattern. A decorative pattern derived from Japanese porcelain. The word 'old' was so used at Chelsea, and refers to an existing JAPAN PATTERN.

Old Wedgwood. Strictly, WEDGWOOD WARE made at Etruria, Staffordshire, during the lifetime of the first Josiah Wedgwood, i.e. before 1795.

Olla (Latin). (1) A type of wide-mouthed vase of Roman pottery which was commonly used for cooking; it was sometimes supported over the fire by a tripod. It was also sometimes used to expose an unwanted infant. (2) A large bulbous cooking-pot with a wide mouth, used in Spain for preparing a stew.

Ollio-pot. A covered bowl with two vertical handles and a flaring rim. It rests on three feet, and was used to serve a kind of stew. Bowls of this kind were made in Dutch delftware, and of porcelain at Vienna. The German term is *Ollientopf*.

Olpe (Greek). A type of wine-jug resembling an OENOCHOË, having a pear-shaped body and a vertical loop handle extending from the shoulder to the rim; it has a large circular or trefoil mouth.

Ombrierte deutsche Blumen (German). Painted decoration of DEUTSCHE BLUMEN with shadows around them; small insects are also shadowed in the same way. The style was introduced just before the middle of the 18th century by the painter, Klinger, and was copied at Chelsea, *c.* 1755. *See* FLOWERS.

On-glaze. Same as OVERGLAZE. Enamel colours thus applied are termed 'on-glaze colours'.

Ongarescha (Italian). A cup or bowl of Italian maiolica mounted on a stemmed foot. It was a unit of the VASO PUERPERALE. Also called a *piadene*.

Oil-spot glaze. Interior of bowl, Sung dynasty (960–1280). Victoria and Albert Museum, London.

Onion pattern. A popular decorative pattern in blue underglaze employed at Meissen and some other Continental factories. It is still in use. *See* ZWIEBELMUSTER.

Onos (Greek). Same as EPINETRON.

Opaque china. A type of fine white porcellaneous stoneware made by the Cambrian Pottery at Swansea from 1815 to 1840. Some of it was painted by William Weston Young. Sometimes used as an alternative term for STONE CHINA.

Opaque porcelain. The same as OPAQUE CHINA or STONE CHINA.

Opaque white. The same as BLANC FIXE.

Orange skin. The slightly pitted surface of some saltglazed stoneware, and also of some Chinese and Japanese porcelain. In China this effect was termed CHICKEN SKIN.

Orange tub. A square (occasionally rectangular) flower pot resting on four small feet, the feet sometimes being extensions of the sides in the form of right-angle corners. *See* CAISSE À FLEURS.

Orca (Greek). A type of vase of Greek pottery, similar to, but smaller than, the AMPHORA, and more spherical. It was employed for holding dried fruit.

Ordinair-Ozier (German). A moulded basketwork border pattern with osiers in sets of four crossing each other diagonally, and divided at frequent intervals by a radial rib in relief. It was confined to the ledge or marli of the plate, and was developed by J.G. Höroldt at Meissen in the early 1730s. *See* OZIER; ALTOZIERRAND; NEUOZIERRAND; ALTBRANDENSTEINMUSTER; NEUBRANDENSTEINMUSTER.

Oriental export porcelain. Chinese and Japanese porcelain made especially for export to Europe which, in form or decoration (or both), was specially adapted to the needs of the European market. CHINESE EXPORT PORCELAIN is sometimes inaccurately termed ORIENTAL LOWESTOFT.

Orange tub. Porcelain, Sèvres, *c.* 1760. Wadsworth Atheneum, Hartford, Conn.

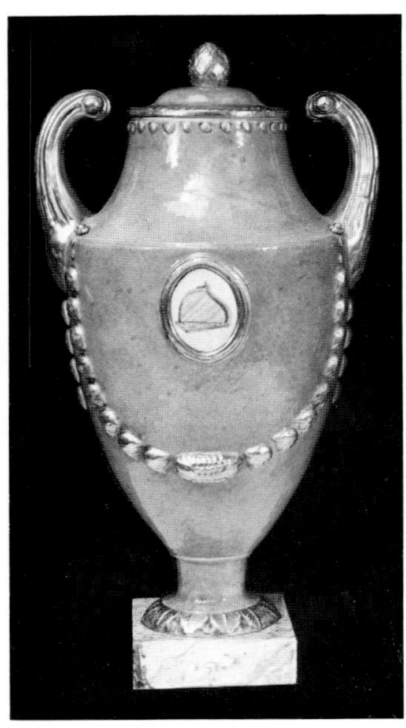

Oriental export porcelain. Neo-classical urn made in China for export to Ireland, *c.* 1775. Courtesy, Christie's.

Oriental Lowestoft. An erroneous term, first given currency by W. Chaffers in *Marks and Monograms on Pottery and Porcelain*, for the enormous quantity of porcelain made in the 18th century in China for export to Europe. This was usually decorated at Canton, and armorial bearings occur frequently. At first this porcelain was attributed by Chaffers to Lowestoft, in East Anglia, but it was later thought that white Chinese porcelain had been imported from Holland (the principal importing country) and decorated at Lowestoft. The ware thus described is undoubtedly Chinese TRUE PORCELAIN, whereas Lowestoft did not at any time depart from an ARTIFICIAL PORCELAIN containing bone-ash. The decoration is obviously by a Chinese and not a European hand, to which errors in copying coats of arms, inscriptions, and European decorative motifs amply testify. Wares of this kind have been extensively reproduced by Edmé Samson et Cie of Paris (*see* SAMSON COPIES), and Herend in Hungary. *See* CHINESE EXPORT PORCELAIN; CANTON CHINA.

Ormolu. A term dating from the middle of the 18th century for an alloy very similar to brass. It was used in England as a mount or an embellishment to objects of porcelain and such fine stonewares as Wedgwood's jasper, but never to the same extent as gilt bronze in France. Many ormolu mounts for a wide variety of purposes were made by Matthew Boulton of Birmingham in imitation of French work. Mounts of this kind in France were usually made of bronze gilded by the mercuric process (*dorure d'or moulu*, gilding with gold paste), and it is from this that the English term 'ormolu' for brass imitating gilded bronze is derived. *See* AMALGAM; MERCURIC GILDING; GILT BRONZE.

Ornamenting. The process of applying relief decoration to the body of a pottery or porcelain vessel before firing. Ornamental pieces, sometimes made in a PITCHER-MOULD, are attached to the body by hand-pressure by the REPAIRER, using great care not to deform it. *See* SPRIGGING; LUTING.

Ornithoid porcelain. Porcelain representations of BIRDS of all kinds, usually naturalistically modelled and painted. Brilliantly coloured birds were made by Chinese potters from the middle of the 17th to the end of the 18th centuries. They were made at Meissen from the earliest years, either copied from exotic specimens in aviaries, or imitated from Chinese sources. Many excellent models were made at Chelsea between 1751 and 1755, based on illustrations from Edwardes's *History of Uncommon Birds*. In modern times American bird-models, and latterly a series of English birds, have been made by the Worcester modeller Dorothy Doughty.

Orton cone. *See* CONE.

Osier. A willow twig used in basketry. *See* OZIER.

Outside decorator. A term frequently used in England to describe an INDEPENDENT DECORATOR.

Oven. The chamber in a furnace or kiln in which ceramic ware is fired, originally with wood as fuel, from towards the end of the 18th century with coal, and now heated by gas or electricity. *See* BOTTLE-KILN; TUNNEL-KILN.

Overglaze. Decoration or marking, either painted or transfer-printed, on the surface of ceramic ware after it has been glazed; also called 'on-glaze'. Such decoration is by means of colours termed enamels, which are fixed in an enamelling or MUFFLE kiln.

Ovidian gods. A series of at least twenty-three small figures modelled by F. A. Bustelli at Nymphenburg in the form of AMORINI representing Apollo, Pluto, and other Greek and Roman gods and goddesses. *See* MYTHOLOGICAL FIGURES.

Oviform. Ovoid, or egg-shaped.

Ovolo (Latin). A decoration in the form of a quarter-round oval moulding (Roman). It occurs as relief decoration, principally to the edges of vases and other vessels in the classical or neo-classical styles. The somewhat flattened Greek version is termed an ECHINUS. *See* RED GLOST POTTERY.

Owl-jug. A jug made in the form of an owl, the head being detached to form a cup. Jugs of this kind were made principally at Brixen, in the Tyrol, of tin-glazed earthenware. Elsewhere they occur in stoneware. Similar vessels were made in Staffordshire in slipware and in saltglazed stoneware. The German term is *Eulenkrug*. *See* BEAR-JUG.

Ownership mark. A mark to indicate the original owner of a purpose-made piece, such as a hospital or pharmacy (on drug-jars), a *château*, or a royal palace. A mark occasionally found on Meissen porcelain, KHC (or KHK), which stands for *Königliche Hof-Conditorei* (Royal Court Confectionery), belongs to this class. Sometimes initials on English delftware are those of the owner for whom the piece was specially made, not the potter or decorator.

Ox-blood glaze. Same as SANG-DE-BŒUF.

Oxherd pattern. A decorative subject on English porcelain, depicting a landscape with an ox ridden by a Chinese. It was sometimes employed as an outline transfer-print filled in with colours; Worcester examples occur from 1758 to 1765. It is sometimes called the red-bull pattern.

Oxide. *See* METALLIC OXIDE.

Oxidized silver. Silver which has become tarnished, i.e. blackened as a result of oxidation. When this metal is applied to porcelain by the SILVERING process it eventually becomes oxidized and it then resembles tarnished silver. True silver lustre decoration (i.e. employing silver, rather than platinum, which fires to a straw colour), remains unaffected. *See* SILVER-LUSTRE WARE.

Oxybaphon (Greek). A utensil the shape of which is not known, but which some consider may have corresponded to the Roman ACETABULUM; it has sometimes been described as resembling an inverted bell-shaped KRATER.

Ozier (German). Literally osier, a willow-twig used in basketry, from which craft a number of patterns have been adapted for use as moulded or painted decoration on ceramic wares. First introduced at Meissen where several versions were used to decorate tableware (an important example being the SULKOWSKY SERVICE) between 1730 and 1742. *Ozier* patterns were later copied extensively elsewhere. *See* ORDINAIR-OZIER; OZIERRAND; ALTOZIERRAND; NEUOZIERRAND; ALTBRANDENSTEINMUSTER; NEUBRANDENSTEINMUSTER.

Ozierrand (German). Literally, osier border. An early type of OZIER border pattern with a diagonal weave, introduced at Meissen, *c.* 1732. *See* SULKOWSKY SERVICE.

Ornithoid porcelain. Pair of porcelain parrots modelled by J. J. Kändler, Meissen, *c.* 1740. Stadtmuseum, Cologne.

Oxherd pattern. Porcelain teapot with pencilled decoration, Worcester, *c.* 1755.

Ozier. Detail of plate with ozier border, Meissen, *c.* 1730–35. Syz Collection, Smithsonian Institution, Washington, D.C.

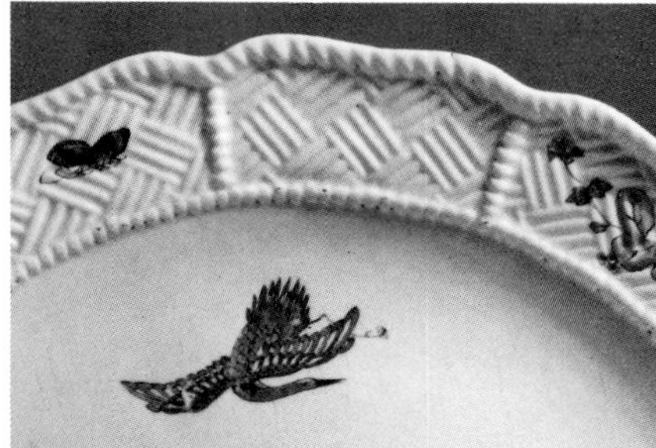

P

Pa-chi-hsiang (Chinese). The EIGHT BUDDHIST EMBLEMS (of happy augury) employed as porcelain decoration.

Pa-hsien (Chinese). The EIGHT IMMORTALS.

Pa-kua (Chinese). A Chinese symbol of ancient origin used as decoration on porcelain. Otherwise referred to as the Eight Trigrams, it consists of eight groups of short horizontal lines, some broken, arranged in different combinations in three parallel rows of equal length; they usually form an octagon (often with the YANG-YIN symbol in the centre), or encircle a vase (*see* PRUNUS). The eight groups represent natural forces – sky, earth, wind, water, fire, thunder, vapour, and mountains. These groups have their origin in the *Book of Changes*, which dates back to the period of the Warring States, *c.* 481–205 BC.

Pa-pao (Chinese). The EIGHT PRECIOUS THINGS, decorative symbols on porcelain.

Paek-Koryŏ (Korean). White porcelain of the KORYŎ DYNASTY made in Korea; a type of Koryŏ ware. It exhibits either the bluish tone of Chinese YING CH'ING ware, or the ivory tone of TING YAO.

Paesi (Italian). Literally, landscapes. Landscapes decorating Italian maiolica, especially in the 16th century.

Pagod. A porcelain figure of a seated Chinese, made in several versions at Meissen. *c.* 1715. The figures usually imitate those of the Chinese Buddhist monk PU-TAI HO-SHANG, but figures of ordinary Chinese men, even women, depicted in the same cross-legged seated position, such as the pair made by J. F. Eberlein in 1735, were probably also called pagods. Some early Meissen figures were hollow and the mouth and ears were pierced; these were probably intended as incense-burners. Similar figures were made elsewhere during the 18th century. *See* MAGOT.

Pagod ware. Porcelain, usually BLANC DE CHINE, from Fukien province, south China, imported into Europe during the 17th century. Apparently a term of disparagement.

Pagoda vase. A type of tall TULIP-VASE with a high finial somewhat resembling a pagoda in form, and having up to eleven separate tiers of spouts added to a plinth.

Pai-ma (Chinese). The white horse of Hsüan Chang, a central figure in a popular Buddhist romance translated into English by Arthur Waley with the title of *Monkey*. The horse was presented to Hsüan Chang by a Han emperor to carry him to India in search of Buddhist scriptures. It was the subject of painted decoration in China.

Pai Ting (Chinese). The finest variety of white TING YAO, one of the classic wares of the Sung dynasty (960–1279).

Pagoda vase. Dutch delftware, ht 3 ft 9 in., early 18th century. Victoria and Albert Museum, London.

Pai-tun-tzŭ (Chinese). The feldspathic rock used as an essential ingredient in the manufacture of most TRUE PORCELAIN. The rock was pulverized at the quarry and compressed into small bricks, whence the name is derived. The name was gallicized in the 18th century to PETUNTSE. *See* FELDSPAR; SOAPROCK.

Pai-tzŭ (Chinese). The term for *tzŭ* (porcelain or stoneware) which is white as well as resonant.

Paint box. A covered container with several small removable receptacles for an artist's paints. They were made of creamware by Swansea, *c.* 1780.

Painted decoration. Decoration on ceramic ware applied with a brush. It may be executed on BISCUIT ware before application of the glaze (UNDERGLAZE COLOURS), or on the surface of the glaze after firing (OVERGLAZE, or ENAMEL COLOURS). Very rarely it was executed in COLD COLOURS (*Kaltmalerei*), either oil or lacquer colours, and left without firing. In the case of tin-glazed earthenware, the painting is executed on the raw glaze before firing (when HIGH-TEMPERATURE COLOURS are used), and the decoration is therefore 'in' the glaze, rather than 'under' or 'over' it.

Pagod. Seated Chinese holding a monkey, one of a pair of figures to be used as incense burners, J. F. Eberlein, Meissen, 1735. Courtesy, Sotheby's.

Painted Etruscan. Black basaltes ware produced by Wedgwood and painted with his encaustic enamels in imitation of the RED-FIGURE STYLE on Greek and Italian pottery. *See* ETRUSCAN WARE.

Painter's mark. A mark on ceramic ware (usually on the base) to indicate the name of the painter. Generally it was a numeral or a letter, sometimes identifiable from a surviving factory-list of workmen, especially at Sèvres. It was added for the use of the factory's management, and not for the convenience of collectors.

Pair. Two objects of the same kind and form, suited to each other, and intended to be used together as a unit, or to stand together, as in the case of figures. Pairs are not necessarily identical, but related. Figures of a man and woman, for instance, may be related by subject, such as LIBERTY AND MATRIMONY. Although symmetry of this kind has always been customary, during the currency of the rococo style single pieces were more frequent, in accordance with the general lack of symmetry which characterized the style. *See* COMPANION PIECE; SET; GROUP.

Palace ware. Chinese porcelain, finely decorated and of especially good quality, made at the Imperial kilns at Ching-tê Chên and once thought (on evidence varying from conjecture to reasonable certainty) to have been in the Imperial collection at the Summer Palace, Peking. The most usual form is a bowl with curving sides and everted rim, known to dealers as a palace bowl.

Palace ware. Blue-and-white porcelain bowl; mark of the Emperor Ch'eng Hua (1465–87). Courtesy, Sotheby's.

Palette. A group of colours used by a particular decorator or factory, or characteristic of a particular style of decoration.

Palissy ware. Pottery ware made by Bernard Palissy (Bernard de Tuileries) at Saintes, France, 1542–62, and thereafter in a workshop situated in the grounds of the Palais des Tuileries, Paris. It is characterized by figures and ornament in relief covered with coloured glazes, mainly yellow, blue, and grey, together with brown and manganese. Although vases, ewers, basins, and similar vessels have survived, the best-known wares are dishes and plates with leaves, lizards, snakes, insects, shells, and other natural objects in high relief, often with a stream as a background. The lead glazes used often approximate fairly closely to the originals in colour, while the reverse of the ware is covered with a mottled glaze in brown, blue, and manganese. *See* FIGULINES RUSTIQUES. The ware was copied by Palissy's successors at the Avon pottery at Fontainebleau, and extensively

Palmettes. Detail of maiolica plate with palmette decoration on the ledge, Faenza, *c.* 1530. Victoria and Albert Museum, London.

during the 19th century in France, Germany, England (Minton), and Portugal (Caldas da Rainha). The Caldas copies, by Manuel Mafra and his son Eduardo, date from 1853 to 1887; they are usually crude, and quite commonly found. *See* FÉCONDITÉ, LA.

Palmette. A decorative ornament in the form of a stylized palm-leaf resembling a spread fan. In appearance it is not unlike the Greek ANTHEMION and the Egyptian lotus. When divided down the centre, it is termed 'half-palmette'.

Palmette border. A border pattern consisting of a series of palmettes. *See* HONEYSUCKLE BORDER.

Pan. A domestic pottery receptacle, shallow and with a flat bottom, usually circular, but sometimes square or rectangular. *See* SETTLING PAN; PANCHEON; PATTY-PAN; POÊLON.

Panathenaic amphora. A large AMPHORA of the 'neck' type that was given, filled with olive oil, as a prize at the Panathenaic Games, *c.* 575–390 BC. Each was painted with a figure of Athene in black-figure style on one side, and on the reverse side were scenes from the contest for which the prize was given, and an inscription with the name of the current *archon* (chief magistrate). Some miniature examples were made as souvenirs.

Pancheon. A large, flaring, shallow earthenware pan used to settle milk before skimming the cream. *See* SETTLING PAN.

Le Panier Mystérieux. Porcelain group, Fulda, *c.* 1770. The Metropolitan Museum of Art, New York.

Panier mystérieux, Le. A porcelain group depicting a boy offering a filled basket to a seated damsel, after a painting of this title by Boucher, which was engraved by René Gaillard. A version was made at Fulda, *c.* 1770.

Panshan pottery. Pottery discovered in the 1920s in a cemetery at Panshan (Kansu province, China) and probably made about 2000 BC. The body is reddish in colour, and the jars, often large, are decorated with swirling geometric patterns in black or purplish-brown. Ma-chang wares, found not far away and of approximately the same date, are fairly similar in appearance. The type is widely distributed, and is found as far away as the Ukraine, in southern Russia.

Pao-shan hai-shui (Chinese). *See* ROCK OF AGES BORDER.

Pap-boat. A small boat-shaped bowl for feeding pap to infants and invalids. The feeding end has an extended lip for placing to the feeder's mouth, and the holding end is rounded without a handle. Later examples in the 19th century have a half-cover over the front, forming a spout instead of a lip. They were made in porcelain at Bow, *c.* 1752, and elsewhere, often after models in silver, Sheffield plate, and pewter, and also occur in creamware and glazed earthenware, often transfer-printed. *See* FEEDING BOTTLE.

Pap-spoon. A spoon for serving pap to infants; it has a hinged lid over the bowl and the handle is hollow to enable the feeding to be controlled by the pressure of a finger over the hole at its end, or (as has been said) to be accelerated by blowing. *See* MEDICAL SPOON; GIBSON SPOON.

Pap-warmer. A term sometimes used in England for a FOOD-WARMER.

Paperweight. Small decorative pieces, usually solid and therefore heavy for their size, made for the purpose of holding down papers on a desk. Some were in the form of figures or groups. The finest were given gilt-bronze mounts. The French term is *presse-papiers*. The Chinese made similar ornamental pieces to weigh down scrolls while in use.

Parapet teapot. A teapot, usually oval, the rim of which curves upwards and slightly outwards towards the spout so as to form a sort of shield. They were made by Wedgwood and others in the early decades of the 19th century.

Parasol pattern. A decorative subject on Arita porcelain, and on Chinese porcelain influenced by Arita designs, depicting two women standing under a parasol and looking down at some marsh-birds against a background of reeds. The birds include a ruff and a spoonbill, both native to Holland; the design is of Dutch origin, perhaps taken from an engraving by Cornelis Pronck (1691–1759).

Parian porcelain. An unglazed BISCUIT porcelain introduced by Copeland's at Stoke-on-Trent in 1846, and later made extensively by other English and American manufacturers. In appearance it superficially resembles marble, and its name was inspired by Parian marble, i.e. marble quarried on the island of Paros. The usual colour is white, but some later specimens are tinted (*see* MALACHITE; OBSIDIAN; LAZULITE; PORPHYRY). Wares, commonly figures, were produced by casting, and the shrinkage after firing exceeded one-quarter of the unfired size. Although most examples were unglazed, a few have a SMEAR GLAZE. Wedgwood introduced an improved Parian body in 1860. An early name was 'statuary porcelain'. *See* CARRARA PORCELAIN.

Parian porcelain (American). A type of PARIAN PORCELAIN made at Bennington, Vt, soon after its introduction in England; early Bennington examples are very scarce. It was subsequently made elsewhere in the United States in considerable quantities. Small figures, vases, pitchers, cow-creamers, Toby jugs, and many other objects were made in this medium, and a variety of pitcher was introduced which was decorated with figures in relief on a blue ground, probably having been inspired by Wedgwood's jasper.

Parlante, faïence (French). *See* FAÏENCE PARLANTE.

Parrot and vine. A decorative subject engraved by Robert Hancock and used on Worcester porcelain. It depicts a parrot perched on a vine eating grapes. It later appears at Caughley, *c.* 1775. *See* PECKING PARROT, THE; HANCOCK ENGRAVINGS.

Parrot-beak. A type of lip on some French and Italian polychrome jugs of the 14th century, moulded in the form of a parrot's beak. *See* SPARROW-BEAK; HAWK-BEAK.

Parson and Clerk. A popular pottery group, derived from the VICAR AND MOSES; it depicts an inebriated parson (holding a mug and a glass of beer), being supported on his way home by his clerk who holds a lantern. It was made by Enoch Wood, *c.* 1790, and the subject was employed on transfer-printed creamware in Leeds and Staffordshire. *See* DRUNKEN PARSON JUG.

Parthian ware. Pre-Islamic earthenware made *c.* 249 BC–AD 226 in the Syro-Mesopotamian area by subjects of the Parthian Empire. The body is coarse and sandy, and the glaze extremely thick and of a blue-green colour. Relief decoration is rare, and bosses and random slices are the usual ornament. The Roman

Pap-boat. Earthenware, with blue transfer-printed decoration. Wellcome Museum, London.

Parian porcelain. Figure of Emily, from Wordsworth's 'White Doe of Rylstone', W.T. Copeland & Son, Stoke-on-Trent. Victoria and Albert Museum, London.

vases of the 1st century AD, termed MURRHINE WARE by some, were said to come from Parthian sources.

Parting shards. Thin SHARDS employed to separate newly glazed wares in the kiln and prevent them from touching. *See* KILN FURNITURE.

Partridge eye. Same as ŒIL-DE-PERDRIX.

Partridge pattern. Same as QUAIL AND MILLET PATTERN.

Partridge tureen. A tureen naturalistically modelled, and often appropriately coloured, in the form of a nesting partridge. Examples come from Bow, Worcester, and Fürstenberg in the 18th century.

Paste. The composite material from which porcelain is made. The French term is *pâte*. *See* BODY; ARTIFICIAL PORCELAIN; TRUE PORCELAIN.

Pastillage (French). (1) Slip applied by TRAILING through a quill, or poured from a spouted vessel; *see* TRAILED DECORATION. (2) The imitation of an object in a paste made of sugar, a feature of confectionery which inspired some porcelain figures.

Pastille-burner. An ornamental object in which may be placed a smouldering, scented pastille. They were employed for scenting a room, and in the 18th century sometimes disguised the smell of defective drains. (The pastille, often pyramidal in shape, was powdered charcoal compressed with an aromatic substance.) Many pastille-burners were made in the 19th century in the form of cottages or churches, with an aperture at the rear, or with a removable roof, or having a separate base, to permit the insertion of the pastille. *See* COTTAGE; INCENSE-BURNER; PERFUME-BURNER.

Pastry-mould. A pottery mould for making pastry or confectionery with the decoration in intaglio; probably first made in Germany in the 15th century.

Pastry-moulded. Ornamented with moulded decoration in the form of a piecrust. *See* PIECRUST WARE.

Patch-box. A small, shallow, decorative porcelain box in which were kept the black patches which were fashionable cosmetic accessories in the 18th century. The French term is *boîte à mouche*. *See* PATCH-STAND.

Patch-boxes. Porcelain: Girl-in-a-swing ware, ht 1⅜ in., *c.* 1749–54; (below) Sprimont's Chelsea factory, ht 2⅞ in., *c.* 1755. Victoria and Albert Museum, London.

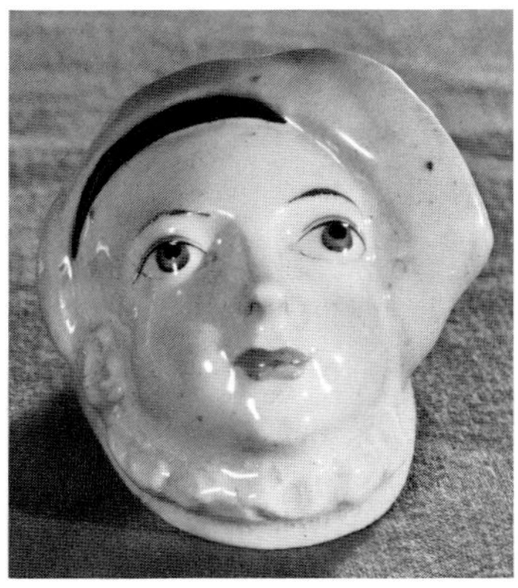

Patch family. Porcelain figures which have patches (*see* PATCH-MARK) bare of glaze on the underside of the base, or rare examples of tableware showing the same feature. Most figures of this class are from Derby, but a few were made at Chelsea.

Patch-mark. A patch bare of glaze on the underside of the base of some figures (*see* PATCH FAMILY) due to the object having been stood on clay pads in the kiln during the GLOST FIRING. The presence of such marks is usually a good indication that the piece is of 18th-century Derby manufacture. They are sometimes called 'thumb marks'. *See* STILT-MARK; SPUR-MARK.

Patch-marks. Base of Derby porcelain figure showing distinctive marks. Victoria and Albert Museum, London.

Patch-stand. A small circular low stand, about 2½ inches in diameter and 1 inch in height, with a flat top and a pedestal base, sometimes having pierced holes. Examples are known in creamware. They were apparently used on the dressing-table instead of a PATCH-BOX.

Pâte d'application (French). Same as PÂTE-SUR-PÂTE.

Pâte de marbre (French). Hard-paste biscuit porcelain made at Lunéville (France) and permitted under a relaxation of the Sèvres monopoly to be sold by the name of *terre cuite*. It was used in the 18th century as a fine-grained true porcelain of warm tone for figures and groups by Paul-Louis Cyfflé. *See* TERRE DE LORRAINE.

Pâte dure. The French term for hard-paste porcelain or TRUE PORCELAIN. Sometimes called *porcelaine royale* at Sèvres.

Pâte-sur-pâte (French). Painting on porcelain in a semi-fluid white SLIP; also known as *pâte d'application*. Successive applications are made to build up the design in slight relief in white on a tinted ground, and the details are then carved before firing. The technique was employed in China during the 18th century, and was introduced at Sèvres by Robert, head of the painting department, soon after 1851. It was employed at Meissen in 1878 by Dr Heintze, who perfected it and added colours in 1880. It was brought to England by Marc-Louis Solon, who left the Sèvres factory during the Franco-Prussian War to work at Minton's.

Patch-stand. Creamware, *c.* 1780. Donald C. Towner Collection, London.

Pâte tendre. The French term for SOFT-PASTE PORCELAIN or ARTIFICIAL PORCELAIN. Called at Vincennes and Sèvres *porcelaine de France* and in England, 'frit porcelain'.

Patent Ironstone China. Same as MASON'S IRONSTONE CHINA.

Patera (Latin). (1) A Roman pottery vessel, similar to the Greek PHIALE. (2) Some circular jasper medallions or cameos by Wedgwood (occasionally only ½ in. to 1½ in. in diameter), decorated in relief with stylized floral patterns, have been so designated. *See* PLAQUE; ROUNDEL.

Paterna ware. Pottery from Paterna, near Valencia (Spain), made in the 14th century and usually painted in green and MANGANESE purple, the latter pigment frequently of a blackish hue. The decoration shows both Moorish and Near Eastern influence. It was later copied in Italy.

Patina (Latin). A broad, shallow pottery dish used by the Romans for cooking or serving food; it sometimes had a cover.

Patriotic charger. A CHARGER with painted decoration depicting royalty (usually Charles II, William III, or Queen Anne), made of English delftware in the late 17th century and early 18th century.

Pattern plate. A plate decorated with samples of several stock designs, with border patterns on the rim and a choice of motifs in the well. Examples were made in China in the late 18th century.

Patty-pan. A low pan of variable size used for baking patties (pasties) or tarts. They were made at Worcester, Caughley, and Lowestoft. Formerly called a tart-pan.

Pax. An osculatory, or early Catholic ecclesiastical tablet bearing a religious representation, which was kissed first by the priest and then by the congregation. Some were made of Italian maiolica in the early part of the 16th century.

Pea green. The term used at Worcester for a ground colour similar to APPLE GREEN. As gilt decoration would not, for chemical reasons, satisfactorily adhere to a pea-green ground, it was applied on the reserve adjacent to the coloured ground.

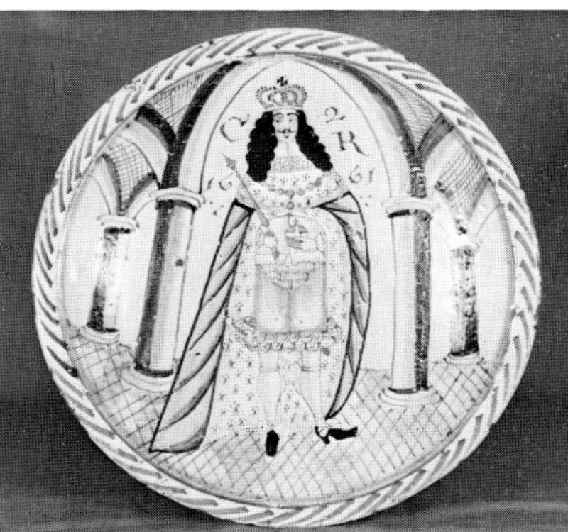

Patriotic charger. Coronation dish, depicting Charles II in Westminster Abbey, Lambeth delftware, 1661. Burnap Collection, William Rockhill Nelson Gallery of Art, Kansas City, Mo.

Peach. A decoration on Chinese porcelain symbolizing longevity; it was one of the THREE ABUNDANCES. *See* SHOU; PEACH-SHAPED.

Peach-bloom glaze. A glaze developed in China during the reign of K'ang Hsi (1662–1722), of the Ch'ing dynasty. It is a reduced copper glaze of pink mottled with deeper red, as well as with slight markings in green and brown. The glaze is highly prized, and was used mostly for small pieces, such as water-pots. The French term is *peau de pêche*.

Peach-shaped. (1) In the form of a peach, as in the case of a CADOGAN teapot. (2) A term applied to a plate, box or dish of slightly irregular form, mainly circular, having at one point a small projection in the rim, which simulates the outline of a peach. Small pieces so shaped were made in the 18th century in China and Europe.

Peepshow group. Porcelain, ht 8 in., Frankenthal, *c*. 1766–67. Courtesy, Sotheby's.

Peach wine-pot. A type of Chinese wine-pot shaped like a peach and having a spout and a loop handle. It had no opening in the top, and was intended to be filled through a conical aperture in the bottom. *See* CADOGAN; VASO SENZA BOCCA.

Peacock-feather decoration. Same as MANFREDI PEACOCK-FEATHER DECORATION.

Peacock jar. A type of DRUG-JAR of Dutch delftware decorated with a cartouche (enclosing the name of the contents of the jar) flanked by two peacocks. Reproductions of such jars are not uncommon.

Peapod. A representation in porcelain of a peapod realistically modelled and coloured, usually with the pod open to reveal several peas inside. Very rare specimens have been uncertainly attributed to Chelsea, but the greater number were undoubtedly made at Coalport, or some other English factory doing similar work in the 19th century.

Pear-shaped. (1) Pyriform, as in the case of a vase or teapot made in the form of a pear; the term 'inverted pyriform' is used when the greatest diameter of the piece is at the top. *See* BALUSTER. (2) A term applied to a dish the outline of which conforms to the vertical section of a pear.

Pear teapot. A pear-shaped teapot, with crabstock spout and handle, and with applied leaves on the body and cover. Such teapots were made of earthenware, with mottled coloured glaze, by William Greatbatch at Wedgwood, *c*. 1755–60. *See* APPLE TEAPOT.

Pearlware. Shell-edged sauceboat and stand decorated in underglaze blue, Wedgwood, late 18th century. Victoria and Albert Museum, London.

Pearlware. A type of earthenware introduced by Josiah Wedgwood in 1779 as an improvement on his QUEEN'S WARE (creamware). By comparison, the body included a greater percentage of flint and white clay, and the glaze contained a trace of cobalt oxide which gave the body a bluish-white cast. It is often recognizable from the bluish glaze that accumulates near the base, and sometimes by the letter *P* (for 'pearl') employed from 1840 to 1868. It was especially effective for ware with underglaze blue decoration, since it avoided the greenish colour which resulted from the use of this pigment in conjunction with a yellowish glaze or body. As it became possible to whiten the body of the ware the bluish glaze was progressively discontinued. Some ware of this kind is decorated with yellow or other coloured glazes. Pearlware was also made elsewhere in Staffordshire, and at other English factories. *See* SHELL-EDGED; FEATHER-EDGED.

Pearl-white. The term originally applied by Josiah Wedgwood, *c.* 1779, to the earthenware which eventually became known as PEARLWARE.

Peasant-dance jug. A drinking-jug with an encircling frieze depicting dancing figures, sometimes with an inscription. Such jugs were made in Germany of reddish-brown saltglazed stoneware at Raeren, and of grey stoneware at Grenzhausen. The German term was *Bauerntanzkrug*. *See* WESTERWALD WARE.

Peasant pottery. The wares of people living in contact with, but on the fringe of, urban civilization, such as those of small rural communities, made for sale at local markets. Wares of this kind are usually artlessly decorated, but often with considerable sensitivity and skill. *See* PRIMITIVE POTTERY.

Peau de pêche (French). Same as PEACH-BLOOM GLAZE.

Pebble-dashed. A term applied to some English saltglazed pottery the surface of which resembles that of some walls rendered in pebble-dash.

Pecking parrot, The. A decorative subject depicting a parrot on a branch stooping to peck at currants, or, in another version, at assorted fruit. A third version substitutes a macaw pecking at assorted fruit. The subject was taken from an engraving by Robert Hancock, and was employed in transfer-printed form at Worcester and Caughley during the 18th century. *See* PARROT AND VINE, THE; HANCOCK ENGRAVINGS.

Pecten shell. The scallop shell; a moulded rococo decoration used extensively on pottery and porcelain during the middle years of the 18th century.

Pedestal. A stand, of pottery or porcelain, higher than it is wide, to support a figure, a bust, or an urn.

Peepshow group. A porcelain group depicting a man with a magic lantern or peepshow, a girl stooping to look through the hole, and a boy waiting his turn. A Sèvres *biscuit* example, *La Curiosité, ou la Foire par le Savoyard*, was modelled soon after 1750 by Falconet after Boucher. The subject also occurs in porcelain made at Frankenthal and Derby.

Peever. A disk of pottery, often coloured and bearing the owner's name, used in lieu of the more usual stone or piece of slate in the game of hopscotch. Peevers were made in Scotland in the 19th century.

Pegasus. A figure of Pegasus, the winged horse of Greek mythology, occurs in the form of a FINIAL on various Wedgwood vases, including the HOMERIC VASE.

Pelike **(*pelice*;** Greek). A type of AMPHORA with a pear-shaped body, a wide mouth, and a neck forming a continuous curve with the body. It was used for holding oil or water; examples range from 4 to 24 in. in height.

Pembroke vase. A tall urn-shaped vase having a spreading circular foot joining a square plinth, with sometimes a circular pedestal between the foot and the plinth. The neck is narrow and the mouth wide, and there are two loop handles. Highly decorated with painted floral ornament and gilding, it was made in porcelain by Minton and Worcester.

Pear teapot. Teapot with crabstock handle and spout, Wedgwood-Whieldon ware, William Greatbatch, Wedgwood, *c.* 1755–60. Colonial Williamsburg Collection, Williamsburg, Va.

Pembroke vase. Porcelain, ht 10 in., Mintons. Courtesy, Sotheby's.

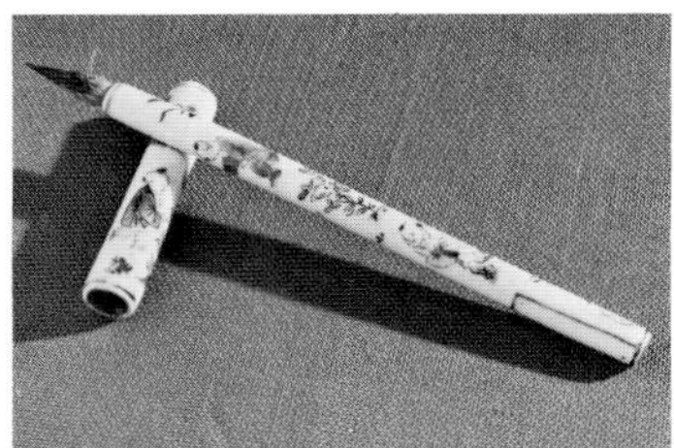

Pencil. Porcelain, length 7½ in., Ming dynasty (16th century). Percival David Foundation of Chinese Art, London.

Personnage. Two French examples in the same form, one showing the separate parts, both *c.* 1840. Harold Newman Collection.

Pen-and-ink stand. *See* FLOWER-BRICK; STANDISH.

Pen-tray. A tray for pens, often a constituent part of a LIBRARY SET.

Pencil. A very fine brush used for making extremely thin lines, such as in designs known as PENCILLED DECORATION.

Pencilled decoration. Decoration on porcelain which is meticulously drawn in black with a fine brush (pencil). It is to be differentiated from transfer-printed ware, for which it can at first glance be mistaken. The technique was first developed in China in the 18th century as a result of the copying there of European engravings which were employed in the decoration of porcelain intended for export. It was used at Worcester soon after 1755 for decoration with Chinese subjects; the best-known example depicts a Chinese seated on a buffalo. It was also employed by HAUSMALER such as J.F. Metzsch of Bayreuth, *c.* 1750. It has affinities with SCHWARZLOT.

Pendent ribbon swag. A decorative pattern in the form of a SWAG of ribbons, or of ribbons suspended from a floral swag.

Pennine glaze. A rich chestnut-coloured glaze developed by Wedgwood.

Pennsylvania Dutch ware (a corruption of *deutsch*, German). Earthenware made by German settlers in Pennsylvania from 1683 onwards, the earliest known dated specimen being made in 1733. The styles were influenced by German SGRAFFITO peasant ware, but the TRAILED SLIP wares were strongly influenced by Staffordshire pottery. *See* TULIP WARE.

Penny bank. Same as MONEY-BOX.

Pepper-caster. A small container, usually of baluster shape or cylindrical, and having a dome cover (sometimes a screw cover) with finely pierced holes for sprinkling ground pepper. *See* CASTER; SUGAR-CASTER; CRUET.

Pepper ware. Creamware made at Leeds early in the 19th century which is covered with a putty-coloured slip 'peppered' with minute particles of black.

Perdifume. An earthenware apparatus conforming to a patented metal object called 'Debaufer's Perdifume, 1824', which was made to be suspended over a gas-burner for the purpose of receiving and eliminating the smoke and vapours arising from the combustion of coal-gas. Known examples occur in gold, copper, and silver lustre, made by Bailey & Batkin, 1824–29, sole patentees, at Lane End, Staffordshire. They occur in two forms: (1) a hollow globe standing on a small hollow cylinder which is mounted on a circular base (diameter 3½ in.), the globe having a lion *couchant* finial pierced with a hole to take a suspending iron ring. It was made to stand on a conical or trumpet-mouthed chimney, 9 in. high and ½-in. in diameter at the top, through which the smoke was drawn into the globe to be burned by the heat of the flame. (2) Similar, but made in one piece with (in lieu of the base and chimney) a hollow cone attached below the globe; one such example bears the arms of George IV. Pieces of this type have been erroneously called a showpiece, a witch's ball, and a wig-stand. The name of the maker appears on the cone of type 1, and encircling the globe of type 2.

Perfume-bottle. *See* SCENT-BOTTLE.

Perfume-burner. An ornamental vessel which holds perfume and has, under the container, a heating device, either a GODET or a small spirit-lamp, for use in scenting a room; the cover is pierced to allow the escape of the scented fumes. The French term is *brûle-parfum.* and the Italian *bruciaprofumo. See* PASTILLE-BURNER; COTTAGE.

Pennsylvania Dutch. Earthenware dish covered with slip and incised to represent a peacock and foliage. Signed and dated 1793. Metropolitan Museum of Art, New York.

Perfume-sprinkler. A small bottle, often pear-shaped, having a long neck with a hole at the top for sprinkling perfumed water. Examples occur in Chinese porcelain. They should be distinguished from the English baby-feeder (BUBBY-POT), which has a nipple spout.

Perlmutter lustre (German). Literally, mother-of-pearl lustre. A lustre developed by J. F. Böttger at Meissen, *c.* 1715, which was made with a preparation of gold. It has a purplish, nacreous appearance. *See* MADREPERLA LUSTRE.

Perlservice (German). A porcelain dinner-service made at Nymphenburg, *c.* 1795, designed by Dominikus Auliczek. Each piece is dodecagonal in form, with moulded pearls along the rim, and painted pearls along the edge of the well. In the well of the plates are pastoral scenes *en camaïeu* in black. The service is in the Residenz, Munich.

Persian pottery. Pottery made in Persia (Iran) from about the 8th century AD onwards. Early wares, until the 12th century, had considerable influence on Chinese porcelain, and Chinese wares were later much copied in Persia, especially the early BLUE-AND-WHITE PORCELAIN of the Ming dynasty. Persian pottery, and its techniques, also had considerable influence on Turkish and European wares, and Persian potters rediscovered the tin-glaze, first employed by the Assyrians around 1000 BC. Surviving Persian pottery consists mainly of dishes, bowls, ewers, vases, and wall-tiles. An important feature was the development of METALLIC LUSTRE decoration. *See* AMOL WARE; GABRI WARE; KASHĀN WARE; LAJVARDINA WARE; LAKABI WARE; NISHAPUR WARE; MINAI WARE; RAYY WARE; SULTANABAD POTTERY; AFTABA.

Personnage (French). A porcelain VEILLEUSE in the form of a figure, usually 10 to 15 inches in height. The piece is divided midway, the lower part being the pedestal in which the GODET rests, and the upper part the teapot. The teapot is usually modelled so that the spout is an upraised arm, or contained in an object held by the figure, such as a fan, pitcher, etc. The handle is also usually an arm, although sometimes a normal handle is at the back. The form was created by Jacob Petit, *c.* 1830, and many specimens bear his mark. Others were made from his moulds, or copied. There are over a hundred different models known, and many are made with slight variations. They are variously decorated. Some 'hybrid' *personnages* have the figure in one piece, and the separate teapot resting on a pedestal alongside, in front of, or behind, the figure. Some represent animals (elephants, camels), and others are in the form of mythological figures, such as Amphitrite or Cupid riding on a dolphin. Most *personnages* are ornately coloured and gilded, but a few are known in white-glazed porcelain. Most are of French origin, but some were made of BOHEMIAN PORCELAIN.

Perdifume (1). Earthenware, Staffordshire, *c.* 1824–29. Courtesy, Godden of Worthing Ltd.

Peruvian pottery. *See* MOCHICA POTTERY; NAZCA POTTERY; CHIMÚ POTTERY; INCA POTTERY.

Petit feu (French). The low-temperature or MUFFLE kiln used to fix enamel colours to the glaze of porcelain, and some kinds of

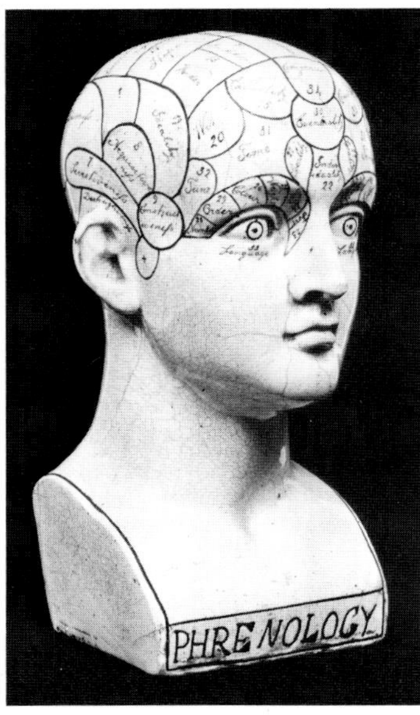

Phrenology head. White earthenware, ht 8 in., with divisions etc. marked in underglaze black, 1821. Wellcome Museum, London.

pottery, at a temperature ranging from 700 to 900°C. Objects so fired were enclosed in a muffle (or fire-clay box) to protect them from the flames and smoke. *See* ENAMEL FIRING.

Petit feu colours. The colours applied at a low temperature in the PETIT FEU. Enamel colours were metallic oxides suspended in an oily medium for ease of application with a brush, the medium burning out during firing; the actual colour for the most part developed in the kiln. Generally, enamel painting tends to be tighter and more detailed than the broad washes of painting in high-temperature colours – those of the GRAND FEU.

Petuntse. The gallicized form of the Chinese PAI-TUN-TZŬ, first employed by Jesuit missionaries in the 18th century to describe the rock which forms an essential part of TRUE PORCELAIN manufacture. It is a silicate of potassium and aluminium, normally referred to as a feldspathic rock (*see* FELDSPAR). It was first used, about the 3rd century BC, in China for glazing PROTOPORCELAIN and later, about the 9th century AD, was mixed with KAOLIN (white china clay) to form the body of the first translucent porcelain. *Petuntse* is a fusible rock which, fired at a sufficiently high temperature, becomes a natural glass, like obsidian. It gives porcelain both its hardness and translucency. The discovery of *petuntse* in Germany, France, and England in the 18th century led to the manufacture of true porcelain in those countries. In France it is sometimes termed *caillou* (pebble or flint), and in England, Cornish stone or china stone. *See* SOAPROCK.

Pew group. A Staffordshire saltglazed stoneware group (also occasionally found in glazed earthenware) made *c.* 1730–45. It depicts a woman with one or two men, often seated on a high-backed oak settle or pew, hence the name. Often the men at either end are playing musical instruments. These groups, primitively modelled and decorated, have been attributed to Thomas Astbury, but it has been suggested that they originated with Aaron Wood.

Peyre cup. A style of small coffee-cup, cylindrical, but tapering slightly towards the bottom to facilitate stacking. It has a loop handle but no foot-ring. Created by Peyre at Sèvres in 1845.

Pharmacy jar. *See* DRUG JAR.

Pharmacy ware. Ceramic ware, usually tin-glazed earthenware but sometimes creamware, for use in a pharmacy. The various types include the ALBARELLO; DRY-DRUG JAR; WET-DRUG JAR (syrup jar); PILL-SLAB; LEECH-JAR; OINTMENT-POT; ELECTUARY-POT; STORAGE JAR; and BOTTLE; FLASK.

Pew group. Saltglazed stoneware, Staffordshire, *c.* 1740–45. Burnap Collection, William Rockhill Nelson Gallery of Art, Kansas City, Mo.

Phiale (Greek). A shallow bowl of Greek pottery, without handles, used as a wall ornament or for libations. The type with a central boss (forming a hollow on the underside) is called a *phiale mesomphalos*. Similar to the Roman PATERA.

Phoenix. A decorative subject on Chinese and Japanese porcelain depicting a richly plumed, long-tailed bird. The Chinese term is FÊNG-HUANG, and in Japan it is the HO-HO BIRD. In China, as the symbol of the Empress, it was sometimes called the Vermilion Bird, representing Summer in the FOUR SEASONS, or south in the FOUR QUADRANTS. *See* BIRDS.

Phosphatic porcelain. A type of ARTIFICIAL PORCELAIN containing a variable percentage of phosphoric acid in the body due to the addition of BONE-ASH or FERN-ASH.

Photographic ware. Pottery with decoration based on a photographic process. Used by Wedgwood, *c.* 1870, and elsewhere.

Phrenology head. A porcelain male head with a bald skull divided by lines into titled compartments. It was used in phrenological analysis.

Physic cup. A type of FEEDING CUP made and so called by Wedgwood; it sometimes had two side handles and a third dog's-head handle opposite the spout. Sometimes called a PAP-BOAT.

Pi (Siamese). Porcelain tokens of various shapes, colours, and values used in Siam as money, *c.* 1850–71.

Piadene (Italian). Same as ONGARESCHA.

Piatto da pompa (Italian). Literally, a ceremonial plate. A plate similar to a BACILE, but highly decorated, and used as an ornament on a buffet, or suspended on a wall. Examples vary as to the depth of the well (*cavetto*), and range in size from 3 inches to 2 feet in diameter. *See* BACINO; SCODELLA; TONDINO.

Picked out. A style of decoration using small flecks of colour to emphasize relief decoration, or to contrast with a ground colour.

Pickle-tray. A small dish, often of leaf-shape or in the form of a scallop or pecten shell, and generally with three small feet or a slight foot-ring. They were popular soon after 1750, and were made for many years thereafter by such English factories as Bow, Worcester, and Caughley. They are nearly always decorated in underglaze blue, but occasionally with an overglaze transfer-print. *See* LEAF-DISH.

Piece-mould. A plaster MOULD made of several interlocking pieces (each one of which will draw from the surface of a cast in plaster), so that the mould can be reassembled and used again.

Piecrust border. A border pattern of a moulded and scalloped form based on a silver pattern similar to the English Chippendale 'piecrust' tip-up tables of the middle of the 18th century.

Piecrust ware. Dishes, bowls, and other pieces with a decorative scalloped rim; also those with a cover simulating a piecrust. Due to the scarcity of flour in England in the early years of the 19th century Wedgwood made objects of the latter kind in unglazed CANEWARE, which was sometimes called 'dummy ware'.

Pied-de-biche (French). Literally, hind's foot. A type of foot usually found on French furniture of the first half of the 18th century, but occasionally on some ceramic ware. More frequently it occurs on gilt-bronze MOUNTS to certain kinds of French porcelain, notably that of Chantilly. As the name suggests, it resembles the cloven hoof of a deer.

Piédouche (French). Literally, pedestal. A term for a base or foot attached to an object, such as a fixed saucer-like stand under some sauce-boats, jam-pots, or *bourdalous* which are then said to be *à piédouche*.

Pien hu (Chinese). *See* PILGRIM-FLASK.

Pien yao (Chinese). Porcelain with a FLAMBÉ GLAZE.

Pierced decoration. Decoration made by piercing the walls of a vessel by hand while the clay is LEATHER HARD, thus creating

Phoenix. Ruby-back porcelain dish with enamelled decoration in the *famille rose* palette, including a phoenix among flowers. Ch'ing dynasty (18th century). Percival David Foundation of Chinese Art, London.

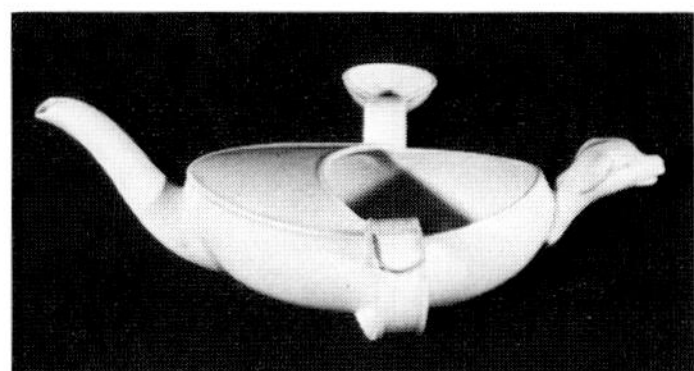

Physic cup. Queen's ware, length 7½ in., Wedgwood, 19th century. Buten Museum of Wedgwood, Merion, Pa.

Piecrust ware. Caneware pie-dish, Wedgwood, mid-19th century (reproduced from an early 19th-century model). Courtesy, Wedgwood.

Piggin. Red stoneware, ht 2½ in., with engine-turned decoration, Staffordshire, *c.* 1700. Victoria and Albert Museum, London.

designs in many different patterns. In pottery the fashion for piercing was derived from the silversmith. Piercing occurs as decoration in England on creamware made by Wedgwood and at Leeds. It occurs also as part of the decoration of certain kinds of porcelain. In Italy several potteries, especially those of Este and Treviso, employed extravagant piercings for ornamental purposes. In China pierced work (known as LING LUNG, or devil's work) was done during the Ming dynasty, but perhaps the most elaborate work of this kind, based on oriental ivory carvings, was done at the turn of the present century at Worcester by George Owen. Piercing was both functional and decorative in the case of POT-POURRI VASES, BOUQUETIÈRES, SUGAR-CASTERS, and POUNCE-POTS. It was especially effective with VEILLEUSES, where light from the flame produced an illuminated design, the holes also producing a current of air. *See* RETICULATED; RICE-GRAIN PIERCING; PLIQUE-À-JOUR.

Pierced finial. A finial, on the cover of a teapot or coffee-pot, having a small hole or vertical slit to allow steam to escape.

Pigeon tureen. An oval tureen in the form of a nesting pigeon, the nest being the bowl and the pigeon, naturalistically coloured, the cover. The Chelsea factory made a tureen in the form of two pigeons on a nest.

Piggin. A small, pail-like receptacle with a handle, used as a dipper for milk or cream. Early specimens in white porcelain from Bow are known and were probably made soon after 1750.

Pigna, a (Italian). A style of decoration on 16th-century Italian maiolica depicting stylized pine-cones in an overall pattern. *See* PINE-CONE PATTERN.

Pilchard pot. An earthenware receptacle made in various sizes for serving pilchards (salt-water fish). Such pots were made in south-west England. *See* CHAR-POT.

Pilgrim-flask. A flattened, gourd-shaped bottle with one or two pairs of lugs at each side through which passed a strap whereby it was slung from the shoulder. Of Roman origin, the pilgrim-flask is also found in Chinese porcelain, where it is termed *pien hu.* As the name suggests, it was used by pilgrims to carry drinking-water. Alternative names are pilgrim-bottle and costrel. The French term is *bouteille de voyage*; the German is *Pilgerflasche*; the Italian *fiaschino. See* FLASK; WINE-FLASK.

Pill-slab. Tile decorated with arms of the Society of Apothecaries, Liverpool delftware, *c.* 1750. Courtesy, Sotheby's.

Pill-slab. Sometimes called a 'pill-tile'. A flat piece of English delftware of various shapes (octagonal, shield, heart, oval) and from 8 to 10 inches in diameter. They were used by pharmacists in England from *c.* 1660–70 until *c.* 1760, as a window display rather than for the purpose suggested by the name (i.e. mixing pharmaceutical pastes and powders), having two glazed holes for a suspensory cord. Pill-slabs were usually decorated in blue (some in polychrome) with the arms of the Society of Apothecaries of London, and (on about 25 per cent of slabs) those of the City of London. After *c.* 1750 the decorated slabs became less popular and were superseded by plain white tiles with graduated markings which were used for actual pill-making until *c.* 1800. *See* PHARMACY WARE.

Pillement engravings. Engravings by the 18th-century French artist, Jean Pillement (1728–1803), which were a source of inspiration for painting on faience, for instance, at Marseilles. They were later used by English porcelain-makers, including Worcester. *See* LADIES' AMUSEMENT, THE.

Pillow. A head-rest of ceramic ware. Pillows were made in numerous forms in stoneware by the Chinese, especially in Tz'ŭ Chou ware, one of which, a kneeling boy, has been reproduced in modern times.

Pinax (Greek). (1) A plate of Greek pottery of varying shape. (2) A plaque of a votive character.

Pinched lip. The lip (of a jug) of trefoil shape made by a pinch of the potter's finger and thumb. First to be seen on the Greek OENOCHOË, it occurs also on Italian maiolica jugs and ewers, and on later pottery and porcelain jugs based on classical prototypes.

Pine-cone pattern. A decorative transfer-printed subject taken from a Chinese original which features a pine-cone amid flowers and leaves. Used at Worcester, Caughley, and Lowestoft in the 18th century. A modelled pine-cone was also employed as a FINIAL during the currency of the NEO-CLASSICAL STYLE. *See* PIGNA, A.

Pineapple stand. A type of dish with relief decoration of pineapple leaves, the painted tips of which extend from the centre to beyond the rim. Made at Chelsea during the red-anchor period, 1752–55, as a stand for a small pineapple tureen.

Pineapple teapot. A type of teapot naturalistically modelled and coloured in imitation of a pineapple. They were made of porcelain, Wedgwood-Whieldon ware, etc.

Pineapple tureen. A tureen modelled in the form of a pineapple and naturalistically coloured. Made at Chelsea and elsewhere.

Pineapple ware. Creamware naturalistically modelled and coloured in imitation of the pineapple, usually in the form of a covered bowl. It was made by Thomas Whieldon and Josiah Wedgwood after 1759, the white body being covered with green and yellow glazes. *See* WHIELDON-WEDGWOOD WARE.

Pingsdorf ware. A type of hard-fired pottery with a buff body and decoration in red, made *c.* 850–1190 in Germany and often exported.

Pinholes. Tiny points of high translucency to be observed in Chelsea porcelain of the triangle period, 1745–49. (*See* GOAT AND BEE JUG.) The cause is not exactly known. The term also refers to minute holes in the glaze of some pottery and porcelain, especially Chinese porcelain (*see* MING DYNASTY) and Dutch delftware.

Pink. *See* FAMILLE ROSE; ROSE POMPADOUR.

Pink lustre. Pottery decorated with LUSTRE on a glazed body of white, cream, or buff colour. The pink or rose colour is due to the use of gold. Pink lustre ware was made at Sunderland and in Staffordshire, often in the form of jugs. Plaques so decorated and inscribed with religious texts or with transfer-prints of ships came from Sunderland. Some ware made by Wedgwood was decorated with pink splashed lustre characteristically flecked with gold. The period of manufacture of old specimens dates from 1800, and it continued to be popular during the first few decades of the 19th century. SUNDERLAND WARE jugs especially have been reproduced recently. *See* PINK RESIST; GOLD LUSTRE.

Pillow. Stoneware, Tz'ŭ Chou yao, 14th century. Victoria and Albert Museum, London.

Pilgrim-flask. Flask with *pâte-sur-pâte* decoration by Marc-Louis Solon, Minton, late 19th century. City Museums, Stoke-on-Trent.

Pillement engravings. Octagonal faience plate with *chinoiserie* decoration after Pillement, by Joseph Hannong, Strasbourg, *c.* 1760–80. Victoria and Albert Museum, London.

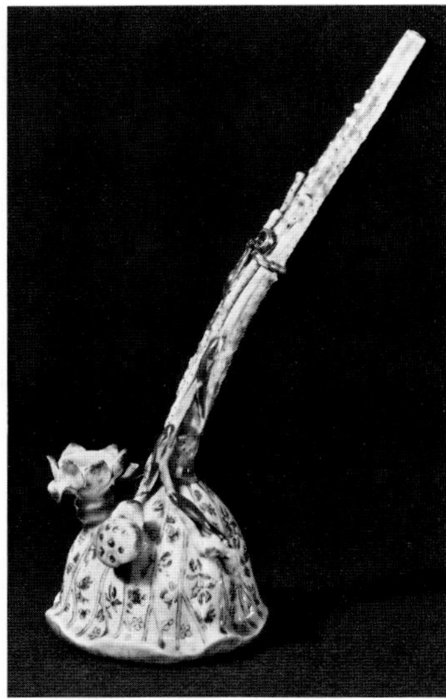

Pipe. Porcelain tobacco pipe, length 8¾ in., with bowl in form of a lotus flower, decorated in *famille verte* enamels; reign of Chia Ch'ing (late 18th century). Percival David Foundation of Chinese Art, London.

Pipe-sleigh. Porcelain, with painted landscape in red, length 2½ in., Loosdrecht, 1774–82. Rijksmuseum, Amsterdam.

Pink resist. RESIST WARE made of pink lustre, the pattern being produced by the white, cream, or buff-coloured glazed body against a pink-coloured lustre ground.

Pipe, tobacco. Tobacco pipes are of various forms and come from many sources. English pipes, of pipe-clay, were first made with a special machine and then, *c.* 1670–90, with a two-piece mould. Later a few hand-made examples were produced. Dutch pipes were made after 1620. All these clay pipes had a long thin stem with a narrow bowl set diagonally to the stem. Few have a factory-mark or date-mark, but characteristics of form and decoration help towards a fairly accurate attribution. The decoration on the mouth of the bowl, and sometimes on the stem, was made by a roulette wheel. There are some tiny 3-inch pipes from the late Elizabethan period, when tobacco was scarce and costly. *See* SNAKE PIPE; HOOKAH; GORGELET; TABAKSKOPF; PIPE-STOPPER; TERRE DE PIPE.

Pipe-bowl. *See* TABAKSKOPF.

Pipe-clay. A type of fine white clay used to make tobacco pipes, and fine earthenwares. *See* TERRE DE PIPE.

Pipe-sleigh. A small, almost rectangular receptacle in which to rest a tobacco-pipe; it has a notch at one end for the stem of the pipe. Examples were made in Holland, *c.* 1774–82.

Pipe-stopper. A tamper for a tobacco-pipe, sometimes in the form of a FLOHBEIN or JUNGFERNBEINCHEN. In Germany they were termed *Tabaksstopfer*. Rare specimens in English porcelain include those made at Chelsea and Worcester, sometimes called a tobacco-stopper.

Pipkin. A small pot, usually circular and with a straight horizontal handle; used for warming brandy. *See* TEA-MEASURE.

Pisa vase. A documentary Italian maiolica vase, *c.* 1590, of ovoid shape, with double mask handles joined to the mouth of the trumpet-neck by entwined serpents, decorated overall in Raphaelesque style with figures, insects, scrolls, and grotesques, and bearing the name 'Pisa'. The type was much reproduced in the 19th century.

Pistol handle. A handle for a knife or fork made in the form of an 18th-century pistol-grip. They occur in porcelain and stoneware. *See* KNIFE AND FORK HANDLES.

Pitcher. A term in general use in the United States for a jug. The French term is *cruche*, and the German, *Krug*.

Pitcher-mould. An absorbent mould made of lightly fired clay rather than plaster of Paris, and used for making relief decoration to be applied to the body of the vessel by SPRIGGING. Moulds of this kind were used in Staffordshire after 1740. The modern term is PRESS-MOULD.

Pithos (Greek). A large cask-like earthenware vessel found throughout the Greek world, some examples dating from the Minoan period. Many had no base for standing, since they were intended to be set into the earth, and some had elaborate relief decoration. They had a wide mouth, and were used for the storage of oil, water, or wine. *See* STORAGE JAR.

Plaque. A flat, thin tablet of ceramic ware decorated with painting or in relief, the latter sometimes painted. They were used as a wall-decoration, or for the decoration of furniture, clock-cases, etc. The shape varies, and includes round, oval, square, rectangular, shield-shaped, and heart-shaped examples. Some plaques were made with a surround simulating a picture-frame. The term has sometimes been applied to a TABLEAU. *See* ROUNDEL; MEDALLION.

Plastic. Capable of being readily modelled or shaped, and retaining the shape imposed, as in the case of wax, or natural clay before being fired. *See* FICTILE.

Plastic ware. Ceramic pieces which have been made by MODELLING, such as figures, as distinguished from ware made by MOULDING, such as tableware.

Plastische Periode. A period at the Meissen factory, 1735–56, during which great emphasis was placed on the production of PLASTIC WARE, such as the porcelain figures modelled by J. J. Kändler and others. Plastic decoration was also a feature of most of the important dinner-services and dessert-services.

Plat ménage (French). Same as ÉPERGNE. *See* GRAND PLAT MÉNAGE.

Plate. A shallow table utensil from which food is eaten, usually circular, and with a ledge (or marli) and a well. The size ranges from about 6 to 11 inches in diameter. The French term is *assiette*, the German *Teller*, and the Italian *piatto* (a circular plate) or *fiamminga* (an oval plate). *See* DISH; PLATTER; MUFFIN; TWIFFLER; PRÉSENTOIR; SALAD PLATE.

Pisa vase. Maiolica, ht 17¾ in., 19th century. Courtesy, Sotheby's.

Plateau (French). A flat porcelain serving-tray with a low vertical rim, often part of a CABARET SERVICE, or for use with CUSTARD CUPS or TASSES À GLACE.

Platinum lustre. A decoration in LUSTRE involving the use of platinum, a metal first isolated in 1750. When fired by the English method platinum salts gave a silvery appearance, hence the frequent misnomer of silver lustre and also silver resist which is applied to RESIST WARE made with platinum salts. Some objects, somewhat resembling contemporary silver and Sheffield plate, were covered wholly with 'silver lustre', and were called 'poor-man's silver'. *See* SILVER-LUSTRE WARE.

Platinum resist. Resist ware made of PLATINUM LUSTRE, the pattern being the colour of the body against the silver ground.

Platter. A large, shallow dish, usually oval, for serving food. It usually has a LEDGE (or MARLI) and a WELL. *See* CHARGER; BLUE-DASH CHARGER; PLATE; TREE-PLATTER; WELL-PLATTER.

Platter tilter. A rectangular slab, slanted to one side, to be placed under one end of a platter so that the gravy would flow to the opposite end. Creamware specimens were made by Wedgwood.

Pleasure-boat pattern. A decorative subject transfer-printed on blue-and-white porcelain made at Worcester and Caughley. It was so called in the 18th century, and it later became known as the FISHERMAN pattern.

Plinth. The lower, usually square, part of the base of a column; correspondingly, the base of a figure or vase when it is similarly designed.

Plaque. Ivory-coloured jasper, width 8 in., Wedgwood & Bentley, *c.* 1770–80. Courtesy, Sotheby's.

Plique-à-jour. Porcelain bowl showing translucent enamel decoration, Limoges. Courtesy, Sotheby's.

Plique-à-jour (French). Decoration consisting of a pierced design filled in with variously coloured translucent enamels. The term is usually applied to jewellery or metal objects, and by extension has been used to describe porcelain decorated by this technique at Limoges in the 19th century. It differs from GOMBROON WARE in that the rice-grain piercing is differently shaped and more closely spaced. *See* ÉMAIL OMBRANT; BASSE-TAILLE.

Plumbiferous. Containing lead; a term used to describe certain glazes.

Plume ground. A ground of plume-like scrolls in a checkered pattern. It occurs on Chinese porcelain.

Po ku (Chinese). The Hundred Antiques, a series of objects used in the decoration of Chinese porcelain. They are various instruments and implements, mostly employed in the arts and sciences, such as musical instruments, brushes and water pots for writing, coins, jewels, books, and ornaments. The series includes the *Pa pao*, or EIGHT PRECIOUS THINGS, and the word 'hundred' in this context can be taken to mean 'many'. These objects were often employed as decorative motifs by Continental and English (e.g. Worcester) decorators in the 18th century, but in their hands often became almost unrecognizable.

Poêlon (French). A saucepan in the form of a shallow bowl with one long handle, usually made in France of hard-fired earthenware. Examples were made in porcelain (undoubtedly for serving food) at Sèvres in the 18th century.

Pokal (German). A tall GOBLET, sometimes with a cover and usually of Bohemian glass, but early German porcelain versions were also made.

Polito's Menagerie. A pottery group modelled by Obadiah Sherratt of Hot Lane, Burslem, *c.* 1808, showing the exterior of a circus booth, with figures and animals. A companion piece depicts WOMBWELL'S MENAGERIE.

Porcelain room. Sconce with *chinoiserie* decoration, Vienna, *c.* 1720–25 (cf. *Chandelier*). From the porcelain room, Palais Dubsky, Brünn; now in the Österreichisches Museum für angewandte Kunst, Vienna.

Polychrome. Strictly, decoration in more than two colours, but with respect to ceramic ware the term is often also applied to ware with two colours, in contrast to MONOCHROME.

Pomade pot. A small covered container for pomade, a perfumed cosmetic ointment originally made with apples. *See* POT-LID.

Pomander. A small container for fragrant spices or perfumes, originally intended to be carried to ward off infections. They are perforated and usually globular or apple-shaped.

Pomegranate. A symbolic decoration on Chinese porcelain, usually represented open and showing its seeds, which signify a numerous progeny. It was one of the THREE ABUNDANCES. *See* JABBERWOCKY PATTERN.

Pompadour, rose. *See* ROSE POMPADOUR.

Pompadour, style. *See* ROCOCO.

Pompeian scroll. A neo-classical decoration with scrolls, *putti*, and grotesques in the style of Pompeian frescoes.

Pont-aux-Choux ware. A type of FAÏENCE FINE made in Paris in the 18th century in imitation of English creamware (*terre de pipe anglaise*).

Pope and Devil cup. A bell-shaped pottery cup made in England in the late 18th century which depicts on one side the Pope and, on the other, the devil.

Po ku. Porcelain vase with sprigged relief decoration representing some of the 'hundred antiques', reign of K'ang Hsi (1662–1722) British Museum, London.

Porcelain. In Europe, a type of hard-fired ceramic ware which is translucent when viewed by transmitted light. In China, any ware sufficiently highly fired to give a ringing note when struck. In practice there is little difference between the two definitions, since any ware which is sufficiently resonant to meet the Chinese test will, if thin enough, also be translucent. The essential constituents of true porcelain, as distinct from artificial porcelain, are a mixture of a refractory white clay (KAOLIN) and a feldspathic rock (PAI-TUN-TZŬ or PETUNTSE). The clay, being refractory, holds the piece in shape while being fired, when the feldspathic rock fuses into a kind of natural glass. Porcelain, unless specially coloured, is usually white. The process of shaping varies, and includes throwing on the wheel, moulding, and modelling. Methods of decoration include glazing, painting, transfer-printing, and sprigging. The three main kinds of porcelain are TRUE PORCELAIN, ARTIFICIAL (or soft) PORCELAIN, and BONE-CHINA. The French term is *porcelaine*; the German, *Porzellan.*

Origin of the term. The usual explanation is that the term is derived from *porcella*, a word applied by the Portuguese to the cowrie shell, because the appearance of the inside of the shell is not unlike that of Chinese porcelain, of which the Portuguese were, in the 16th century, the principal importers. However, the term *pierre de pourcelaine* (porcelain stone) occurs in a French inventory of 1360, although the nature of the substance referred to is not certainly known. Perhaps it was some kind of semi-precious hardstone which Chinese porcelain, the first examples of which must have been imported soon after this date, was thought to resemble.

Porcelain room. A room in certain palaces, especially in Germany and Italy, in which porcelain forms the predominant motif of decoration. Porcelain objects include chandeliers, cornices, plaques, mirror-frames, chimney-pieces, brackets, vases, and figures. A porcelain table made at Meissen was presented to Louis XV, but has since disappeared. The vogue for decorating with porcelain began in the later years of the 17th century, when oriental wares were employed, and ended with the coming of the neo-classical style. Most such rooms belong to the 18th century. A few still survive, including one in the Capodimonte Palace, Naples, and another in the Osterreichisches Museum für angewandte Kunst, Vienna.

Polito's Menagerie. Pottery group, Staffordshire, *c.* 1840. City Museums, Stoke-on-Trent.

Porcelaine de France (French). A French term for ARTIFICIAL PORCELAIN; the same as *pâte tendre*. Principally used of porcelain manufactured at Vincennes, and later at Sèvres.

Porcelaine de la Reine (French). Porcelain made in Paris, 1778–90, by André-Marie Lebœuf at a factory in the rue Thiroux which was under the protection of Marie-Antoinette.

Porcelaine de Paris (French). Porcelain made at any one of a number of factories located in or near Paris, *c.* 1770–1830, several of which were under the protection of the aristocracy and members of the royal family. In this way they were able to defy the monopoly granted to Sèvres by Louis XV. Factories include those of: Pierre Deruelle, rue Clignancourt, under the protection of the Comte de Provence, later Louis XVIII; Pierre-Antoine Hannong, Faubourg St-Denis, under the protection of the Comte d'Artois; André-Marie Lebœuf, rue Thiroux, under the protection of Marie-Antoinette; Dihl et Guérhard, rue de Bondy, under

Portland (Wedgwood) vase. Replica in jasper, Wedgwood, Etruria, *c.* 1790. Victoria and Albert Museum, London.

the protection of the Duc d'Angoulême; Jean-Baptiste Locré de Rossy, rue Fontaine-au-Roy and rue de la Courtille; Jean Nast, rue Amandiers-Popincourt; several proprietors in the rue de la Roquette; also Jacob Petit of Fontainebleau, and a factory at Boisettes, near Melun. *See* VIEUX PARIS.

Porcelaine de santé (French). A type of inferior porcelain made inexpensively with the intention of superseding lead-glazed earthenware which, it was alleged, was injurious to health due to the solubility of the lead in the glaze. *Porcelaine de santé* was made by M. Prässel at Charlottenburg, Germany, where it was called *Sanitätsporzellan* or *Gesundheitsgeschirr* (wholesome ware). Another French term was *Hygiocérame*.

Porcelaine laquée burgautée (French). Imported Chinese porcelain made in the 18th century decorated all over with black lacquer and with a partial inlay of mother-of-pearl. Some work of this kind imitates CLOISONNÉ enamel on a porcelain base. The style was copied by Johann Martin Heinrici at Frankenthal.

Porcelaine royale (French). A term used at Sèvres for TRUE PORCELAIN.

Porcellana, alla (Italian). An early Italian term for slightly painted monochrome blue decoration on maiolica (chiefly Venetian). It takes the form of winding stems and coiled foliage, and it resembles similar decoration on Chinese porcelain of the 15th and 16th centuries.

Porcellaneous ware. Sometimes porcel(l)anous. A hard-fired fine STONE-CHINA having some of the qualities of porcelain, but lacking its translucency. Some Chinese stonewares of the Sung dynasty (960–1279) are sometimes thus described. *See* IRONSTONE CHINA.

Porphyry. A purple or reddish-purple colour resembling that of the stone porphyry. PARIAN PORCELAIN was sometimes thus coloured, and some earthenware was glazed over a light body so as to imitate this stone.

Porringer. A shallow bowl with one flat, horizontal handle, based on silver and pewter prototypes. They are usually in English delftware of the second half of the 17th century. A similar but smaller vessel was termed a 'cupping-bowl' or BLEEDING-BOWL. *See* ÉCUELLE.

Portastecchini (Italian). A toothpick holder, usually in Italian maiolica.

Porte-huilier (French). A type of CRUET-STAND. A small receptacle for several salad-dressing cruets, with holes for large and small cruets. Sometimes called a *porte-vinaigrette*.

Porte-perruque (French). A WIG-STAND.

Porte-vinaigrette (French). *See* PORTE-HUILIER.

Portland (Barberini) Vase. Generally known as the Portland Vase, now in the British Museum. It was originally known as the Barberini Vase because it was owned by Maffeo Barberini, Pope Urban VIII (1623–44), and was in the Palazzo Barberini in Rome. The vase, once thought to be of onyx or chalcedony, is actually of cased, carved glass, the urn-shaped body and handles being of deep-blue (almost black) glass, and the relief frieze of opaque milky-white glass. The frieze is thought to depict the myth of the marriage of Peleus and Thetis. At one time it was believed that the vase was a cinerary urn, that it portrayed the Roman Emperor Alexander Severus and his mother, Mamaea, and that it had been discovered in a marble sarcophagus excavated in 1582; these beliefs are no longer accepted. Its origin and early history are unknown. The vase was sold *c.* 1780 by the last of the Barberini line, the Princess of Palestrina, to a Scottish antiquary resident in Rome, James Byres. He, before 1783, sold it to Sir William Hamilton, British Ambassador to the Court of Naples, who brought it to London and in 1784 sold it to the Dowager Duchess of Portland (from which time it became known as the 'Portland Vase'). After her death in 1785 it was sold to a Mr Tomlinson, who was, presumably, acting for the Duchess's son, the third Duke of Portland. In 1810 it was lent to the British Museum (which purchased it in 1945), where it has since remained. It was smashed in 1845 by a madman named William Lloyd; it has since been expertly reconstructed on two occasions. It was lent in 1786 to Josiah Wedgwood (it is said, under an agreement to make such a loan in consideration of Wedgwood's forgoing a bid for it at auction) for the purpose of his reproducing it. *See* PORTLAND (WEDGWOOD) VASES.

Plaster of Paris reproductions were made before 1783 by James Tassie for James Byres, the mould being made by Giovanni Pichler, the noted gem-engraver. Byres sold 60 replicas of the vase (one is in the British Museum, London) at 10 guineas each. In 1876 John Northwood engraved a glass copy.

Portrait ware (2). Jasper medallion portraying Lord Nelson, Wedgwood, 1797. Courtesy, Wedgwood.

Portland (Wedgwood) Vases. Replicas of the PORTLAND (Barberini) VASE made by Josiah Wedgwood in jasper. After four years of experiment he produced in 1790 perhaps 50 examples, of which 16 are still known to exist. A cheap edition, cast in one piece and with the background painted in enamel colour, was made in 1838. The 1839 edition has the nude figures draped. A number of jasper editions have since been issued with either blue or black ground, including a new colour (Portland blue) in 1972–3.

Portobello ware (2). Teapot with relief decoration, Staffordshire, *c.* 1770. Victoria and Albert Museum, London.

Portobello ware. (1) Pottery made at Portobello, Scotland, *c.* 1786–1845, and ware made at Tunstall, Staffordshire, in imitation. (2) Pottery with applied or moulded decoration depicting ships and figures of Admiral Vernon in commemoration of the English naval victory at Portobello, in South America, in 1739.

Portrait ware. (1) Plates, chargers, *albarelli*, and other ware decorated with a painted or transfer-printed portrait. (2) Medallions, such as those of Wedgwood's jasper, decorated with portraits in relief.

Portuguese ware. A term applied by Horace Walpole to ware said to have been made of a red earth from Iberia.

Positure. An 18th-century term for a FIGURE.

Posset-bowl. *See* ACCOUCHEMENT BOWL.

Posset-pot. A multi-handled vessel used for making and drinking posset (a beverage formerly popular in England, made from hot milk curdled by an infusion of wine or ale, and often spiced). The number of handles varies from two to eleven. Some have a cover with an elaborate knop. Early examples (1628–88) were bucket-shaped, then (1651–1705) cylindrical, later (1653–61) rounded with shoulders, and even later (1680–1749) ogee-shaped. Comparable vessels with spouts are termed SPOUT-POTS or spout-cups. They belong to the late 17th and early 18th centuries and were made of English delftware, slipware, and stoneware. *See* BRAGGET-POT; TYG.

Posset-pot. Slipware, Staffordshire, *c.* 1690.

Posy-holder. A small cornucopia-shaped container for holding a flower or a nosegay, sometimes intended to be worn attached to the dress. Porcelain posy-holders were made at Berlin and elsewhere.

Pot. A vessel of many shapes and sizes, generally of circular section, and employed for a variety of domestic purposes. It usually has a handle and a cover. In popular ceramic parlance pot is a generic term for any vessel of pottery, especially one of some antiquity. The French use specialized terms; the German term is *Topf*. *See* TEAPOT; CHOCOLATE-POT; COFFEE-POT; JAM-POT; OINTMENT-POT; BRAGGET-POT; POSSET-POT; POUNCE-POT; SPOUT-POT; CHAR-POT; VERSEUSE.

Pot à surprise (French). Same as PUZZLE-JUG.

Pot-lid. Colour-printed lid with labelled container, F. & R. Pratt, Fenton, Staffordshire, *c.* 1850. Collection of Geoffrey Godden, Worthing.

Pot-lid. A pottery cover for a circular shallow container of bear's grease, formerly used as a dressing for men's hair, or of pomade. Later, similar pots were employed for fish-pastes and potted shrimps. Pot-lids came principally from F. & R. Pratt of Fenton, Staffordshire, and were made by them between 1846 and 1880. Jesse Austin, an engraver employed by Pratt, developed the process of transfer-printing in polychrome to decorate the lids. Most are decorated with pictures, the subjects of which fall into a number of groups. One popular example depicts a performing bear; others show landscapes, buildings, portraits, and reproductions of paintings. Early examples are flat-topped, often crazed, and of two colours. Later ones are slightly domed, with up to five colours, and were made by several factories until after 1900. A few covers bore the name of the seller, but in general covers were of the so-called 'neutral' type; in some cases the name appeared on the underside of the cover or on the bottom of the pot itself, but in most cases the name was printed on a paper band used to seal the cover to the pot. *See* PRATTWARE; POMADE POT.

Pot-pourri bowl. A circular bowl with a domed, pierced cover, and, in appropriate cases, with piercing on the shoulder, similar to a POT-POURRI VASE. *See* CASSOLETTE.

Pot-pourri vase. Faience vase with cover, Joseph Hannong, Strasbourg, *c.* 1760–80. Victoria and Albert Museum, London.

Pot-pourri vase. A vase, sometimes richly mounted in gilt-bronze, which is characterized by pierced decoration on the shoulder or cover, or both. It was used for holding *pot-pourri* (a liquid deriving its scent from decomposed flower petals and herbs, as the word, *pourri*, meaning rotten, suggests). In England mixtures of dried flowers and herbs were used, and placed in open bowls which were indistinguishable from PUNCH-BOWLS. *See* CASSOLETTE; POT-POURRI BOWL.

Potato-flower pattern. *See* DÉCOR À LA FLEUR DE POMME DE TERRE.

Potato-ring. A stand in the form of a ring on which to rest a dish. They were first made in Irish silver in the 18th century. The name is derived from an erroneous impression that they were used to hold a heap of potatoes. Examples also occur in both Sheffield plate and ceramic ware.

Potato-soup glaze. A defective glaze on large pieces of CHINESE EXPORT PORCELAIN made towards the end of the 18th century. These were too heavily coated, so that the glaze 'crawled' and bubbled during firing.

Potbank. A local term used in Staffordshire for a small factory, of the type usually called a pottery, for the manufacture of fired-clay products.

Poterie (French). A term applied to common varieties of lead-glazed earthenware, but not to FAIENCE, FAÏENCE FINE, and GRÈS.

Pothook pattern. A decorative pattern in the form of a series of horizontal *S*-like lines, sometimes with interlocking ends.

Potiche (French). A covered Chinese or Japanese porcelain jar. The shape is variable, but it has no handles. It originally evolved from a bronze wine-vessel of the Chou dynasty (1122–249 BC), but underwent many modifications during the centuries. Chinese vessels thus called may be approximately dated from their profiles. The section is usually circular, but occasionally polygonal, the latter being nearly always of Japanese origin.

Potiche. Northern celadon, with carved decoration, Sung dynasty (960–1280). Victoria and Albert Museum, London.

Potsherd. Same as SHARD.

Potter's clay. A type of clay suitable for making ceramic ware. Clays for this purpose must be as free as possible of impurities, especially iron, which give rise to discoloration.

Potter's mark. A mark on ceramic ware, usually under the base, to indicate the name of the thrower or repairer. The mark is generally incised, and is now rarely identifiable. *See* MODELLER'S MARK.

Potter's mould. The hollow working mould made from the block mould and from which the ware is made in quantity production, in a state ready for glazing and firing. *See* MOULD.

Potter's wheel. A horizontal disk which revolves on a vertical spindle. A ball (bat) of clay is put on the disk, centred, and then, as it revolves, is shaped by the pressure of the hands or with tools. Only ware with symmetrical spheroidal shapes of circular section can be so produced, and other shapes must be achieved by moulding. The act of making a pot on the wheel is termed throwing. Formerly driven by a foot-pedal, or manually by a young boy employed for the purpose, the wheel is today usually operated by an electric motor. The potter's wheel for use in making domestic wares is an ancient invention, and was known to the Egyptians perhaps as early as 1500 BC; it is mentioned in Homer's *Iliad*. The lathe is a later adaptation. *See* SLOW WHEEL; JIGGER; JOLLY; THROWING.

Pottery. A generic term for all ceramic wares without exception, but in normal use it is employed to designate all wares which are not porcelain. It therefore includes both earthenware and stoneware. Earthenware is pottery which has been comparatively lightly fired, and in which the clay particles have a point-to-point attachment; it is porous until glazed. Stoneware is clay mixed with a proportion of fusible material, and it is therefore impervious, even when unglazed. The process of shaping pottery varies, and it includes throwing, modelling, moulding, and casting. Methods of decoration include glazing, painting, transfer-printing, and sprigging.

Pounced. Stencilled by means of dusting powdered charcoal through a pricked paper pattern to provide outlines for the painter. The process was common in the 18th century.

Pounce-pot. A pot with a perforated cover for sprinkling pounce, a fine powder of gum sandarac formerly used on parchment to prepare it for writing, or to restore the smooth surface after erasure to prevent ink from spreading; pounce is to be distinguished from pumice or other powders used in place of blotting paper to dry ink after writing. The pounce-pot sometimes forms part of an inkstandish or a library set. *See* SANDBOX; STANDISH.

Powder-blue. Cobalt blue applied underglaze as a ground colour, usually in the form of powdered SMALT. In China powder-blue, known as *ch'ui ch'ing*, was applied by INSUFFLATION. Powder-blue was copied at Meissen in the first half of the 18th century by J. G. Höroldt, and at Sèvres, where it was known as *bleu soufflé*. In England it was used at Bow, especially in conjunction with small reserved panels containing *chinoiserie* landscapes in blue underglaze. The same scheme was used at Worcester, Lowestoft, and Caughley. The Wedgwood factory imitated it on bone-china by first painting it on as wet colour and then stippling it with a fine-grained sponge. *See* BLEU FOUETTÉ; COBALT OXIDE; ZAFFER.

Pricket candlestick. Figure modelled by G. Bruschi, Doccia, after 1735; it depicts one of the 'Différentes Nations du Levant'. Courtesy, Sotheby's.

Powder horn. A small receptacle for the storage of gunpowder and for measuring the charge. Usually of metal or leather, a few rare examples of 18th-century porcelain with metal fittings have survived, notably one from Sèvres in the Metropolitan Museum of Art, New York.

Powdered manganese. Manganese purple applied in powder form. *See* POWDER-BLUE. This colour was not used as a ground in China. It occurs on some rare examples of Bow porcelain, and on certain types of 18th-century English delftware, notably from Wincanton (Somerset).

Prattware. Lead-glazed earthenware made at Lane Delph (later Middle Fenton), Staffordshire, at the factory founded *c.* 1775 by William Pratt, and taken over by his elder son Felix in 1810. Later the ware was copied by other local potters. It has a lightweight cream-coloured body, and is characterized by relief decoration in conjunction with underglaze colours, mainly a brownish ochre, dull blue, and green; the principal wares are jugs, oval plaques, and figures.

In the mid-19th century the Pratt factory also produced ware decorated with polychrome transfer-prints, of which POT-LIDS were an example, and terracotta ware with transfer-prints or relief decoration; these wares are, however, not generally included among the earlier products which are designated Prattware.

Pre-Columbian pottery. Pottery made in the Americas before the arrival of Columbus and the spread of European influence there. There are some fundamental differences between this and European and oriental pottery. Until the arrival of Europeans the POTTER'S WHEEL was unknown in the ordinary sense, although the SLOW (or hand-turned) WHEEL may have been used. Vessels were made in moulds by block modelling, and by COILING. The body of vessels was decorated with slips, and free-hand decoration was usually of the geometric type. The use of a glaze is very rare, but polished surfaces are common. A REDUCING ATMOSPHERE was employed to change red and brown clays to grey or black. The most important North American pottery was made in the territory now forming the states of New Mexico and Arizona. *See* PUEBLO INDIAN POTTERY; HOHOKAM POTTERY; MOGOLLON POTTERY; CENTRAL AMERICAN POTTERY; CHIMÚ POTTERY; INCA POTTERY; MOCHICA POTTERY; NAZCA POTTERY.

Présentoir (French). (1) A plate of small size with a central well, used by waiters to serve a glass of wine. *See* CHOCOLATE-STAND. (2) A conforming stand for, e.g., a sauce-boat.

Press-mould. An absorbent mould made of lightly fired clay or plaster of Paris, and into which clay is pressed by hand to make such objects as small ornaments for relief or sprigged decoration. Flowers are commonly made in press-moulds. *See* PRESSING; PITCHER-MOULD.

Pressing. The process of shaping clay by pressing it into a PRESS-MOULD and removing it after it shrinks and becomes cheese-hard. Flowers or small relief ornaments are thus made and then attached to objects by SPRIGGING.

Preussisch-musikalische pattern. A decorative border pattern featuring musical trophies in rococo cartouches in conjunction with floral bouquets. Introduced at Meissen in 1761 for the MÖLLENDORF SERVICE.

Pricket candlestick. A candlestick with a vertical metal point on which to impale a candle.

Primitive pottery. The wares of unsophisticated people out of touch with the mainstream of civilization. They range from certain of the Neolithic wares to the cruder pots of present-day African tribes. *See* PEASANT POTTERY.

Prince Henri pattern. An adaptation of the Meissen RED-DRAGON PATTERN (derived from the Kakiemon wares of Arita, Japan) made at Chantilly. *See* DÉCOR CORÉEN.

Printed. *See* TRANSFER-PRINTING.

Prochoös (Greek). A slender form of OENOCHOË; a small jug with a tapering globular body, a thin neck, small mouth, high arched handle, and a stemmed foot. It was used for pouring wine, and for water for washing the hands before a meal. It was also made in a low, compressed form.

Prattware. Jug in the manner of Felix Pratt, with a portrait of Lord Nelson, Staffordshire, *c.* 1800. Hove Museum and Art Gallery.

Profile. (1) A tool or template used in shaping such vessels as dishes, cups, and shallow bowls. It is cut in the shape of the profile of the piece to be formed. A flat disk (bat) of clay is placed on a revolving mould (*see* JIGGER; JOLLY) and the profile is pressed into the clay; the process, used for quantity production, was well known in the 18th century. (2) A tool used for shaping the outer surface of the body of a vessel while on the POTTER'S WHEEL.

Protogeometric style. A decorative style of Greek pottery of the period *c.* 1000–900 BC, characterized by crude geometric schemes. It followed SUB-MYCENAEAN POTTERY, and preceded pottery in the GEOMETRIC STYLE, *c.* 900–700 BC. *See* MYCENAEAN POTTERY.

Protogeometric style. Vase with characteristic decoration, 10th century BC.

Protoporcelain. An early type of ceramic ware of a porcellaneous nature made in China during the Han dynasty, in the 2nd century BC. It is greyish in colour, and has a glaze derived from feldspathic rock.

Provenance. The origin or source of an important specimen; strictly, the source as applied to prior ownership rather than the place of production.

Provender for the Monastery. A figure of a Franciscan friar carrying a basket and a bottle, and with a girl concealed in a sheaf of wheat on his back. It is the subject of a print published *c.* 1760 by John Bowles after an earlier engraving. The figure was made as a SCENT-BOTTLE at Meissen before 1758 (and was reproduced there later), and at Chelsea.

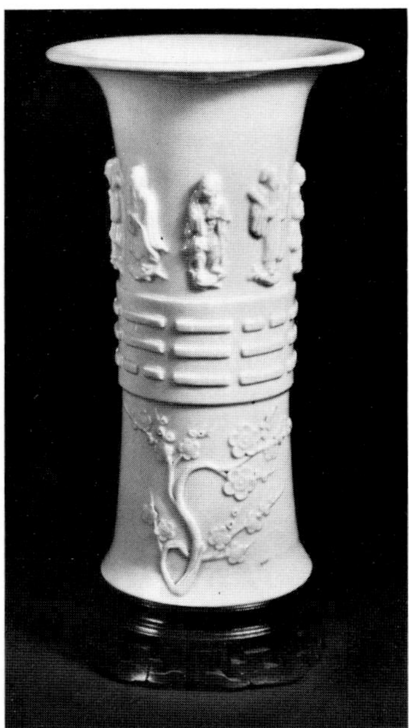

Prunus. Beaker in blanc de Chine with relief decoration showing (top) the Eight Immortals, (centre) the Eight Trigrams (Pa kua) and (bottom) a branch of flowering prunus; 18th century. Courtesy, Spink & Son Ltd, London.

Prunus. The white plum-blossom used as decoration on Chinese porcelain, sometimes against a CRACKED-ICE GROUND, and especially popular on wares of the reign of K'ang Hsi (1662–1722). The prunus blossom also occurs in Japan, sometimes in the form of a MON. In a relief form it decorates some of the *blanc de Chine* wares of Fukien province, made in the Tê Hua kilns, and this type was copied in Europe at, for example, Meissen, Saint-Cloud, Bow, and Chelsea. In Chinese flower-symbolism the prunus blossom signifies the coming of Spring. *See* PRUNUS PATTERN.

Prunus pattern. A Chinese decorative pattern of prunus (or plum) blossom, first used in the reign of K'ang Hsi (1662–1722). It was principally employed on BLUE-AND-WHITE PORCELAIN and occurs in various forms. It is sometimes loosely called the hawthorn pattern.

Prunus vase. A type of vase having an almost baluster-shaped body, broad shoulders, and a very short, narrow neck terminating in a small mouth. It was made in China, Korea, and Japan, to hold a single spray of prunus blossom. *See* MEI-P'ING; MAE PYŎNG; ICHIRIN ZASHI.

Prussian service. A dinner-service originally of about 420 pieces made of Berlin porcelain, *c.* 1816–19, and presented to the first Duke of Wellington by Frederick William III of Prussia. The plates have a burnished gilt rim of varying patterns, enclosing polychrome topographical scenes associated with the Duke's battles. The massive CENTREPIECE includes an inscribed green obelisk surrounded by biscuit figures depicting river gods which were modelled by J. G. Schadow. Now at Apsley House, London.

Pseudo-Chinese seal-mark. A mark on the bottom of both porcelain and pottery simulating a CHINESE REIGN-MARK in the square seal form. Such marks are sometimes called 'seal-marks'. Marks of this kind appear on redware made by the Elers, on porcelain made at Bow, Caughley, and Worcester (square mark), sometimes on Meissen porcelain, and, in general, on many European wares imitative of the Chinese.

Psykter. Greek, *c.* 450 BC, decorated in the red-figure style. British Museum, London.

Psykter (Greek). A type of pottery jug used as a wine-cooler, being filled with snow or ice. There are two types: (1) a squat globular form (to be lowered into a KRATER, some examples having side handles to permit lowering by means of a cord), resting on a base with a high stem; and (2) an ovoid form with double wall and spout.

Puce. A colour especially common on English and German porcelain. A purplish-red in hue, it was derived from manganese oxide. *See* PURPLE OF CASSIUS.

Pueblo Indian pottery. The Pueblo Indians of the plateau region of the present-day south-west United States were preceded by the Anasazi whose pottery dates back to before AD 700. They made pottery in basketwork moulds, and by COILING; decorated ware painted in black and white with geometric designs came later. Polychrome wares made by the Pueblos are decorated with stylized birds, animals, and human figures, principally in red and yellow; these belong to the 12th century and after.

Pug-dog A figure in the form of a pug-dog (on a base or free-standing), or as part of a group, or as ornament on an object such as a snuff-box. Many different porcelain pug-dogs, called MOPS in German, were modelled at Meissen by J. J. Kändler, *c.* 1740–48 for members of the Order of the Pug (Der Mopsorden), a secret society formed by German Catholics (male and female) excluded from the Freemasons after 1736. These have been copied by many German and English factories. Pug-dogs have also been made at English and Continental factories in porcelain and pottery. *See* DOGS.

Pugging. The process of mixing and homogenizing the ingredients of a ceramic body by a kneading operation in a pug-mill, which also disperses air-bubbles. It was done originally by kneading with the feet, but mechanical devices are now used for the purpose. *See* WEDGING.

Pug-dog. Mops, by J. J. Kändler, Meissen, *c.* 1750. Courtesy, Newman & Newman Ltd, London.

Punch-bowl. A large, uncovered circular bowl for serving punch. They were made of saltglazed stoneware, tin-glazed earthenware, and porcelain. Large punch-bowls were decorated with hunting-scenes at Canton and exported to England during the second half of the 18th century. The punch-bowl is sometimes called a jorum. *See* PUNCH-POT.

Punch-ŏng ware (Korean). A development of KORYŎ CELADON made in south Korea during the Yi dynasty, from the early 15th century to the end of the 16th century. It was made of the same greyish clay as the Koryŏ celadons, but was coarser in texture. The surface was wholly or partially covered with slip to distract attention from a poor body and glaze. Some designs were painted on with a brush; others were stamped or incised and filled with slip (inlaid ware).

Punch-pot. A large vessel resembling an outsize teapot or kettle similar to the water-kettle of a tea-service. Usually of oblate shape, it had a curved spout, and sometimes a BAIL HANDLE, although early examples had a handle in the same side position as on the contemporary teapot. Vessels of this kind usually lack the interior strainer at the base of the spout which is invariably present in a teapot. Some examples of Leeds creamware were made with a painted inscription, 'Punch'. Punch-pots are also termed punch-kettles. They were made from *c.* 1750 onwards for brewing and serving hot punch (spirits blended with milk or water and flavoured with sugar, lemon, and spices).

Punch-pot. Porcelain, Liverpool, *c.* 1780. Courtesy, Tilley & Co., London.

Purple. A colour employed to decorate porcelain. It includes: PUCE; PURPLE OF CASSIUS (rose-pink; *rouge d'or*); and the *rose* enamel of the Chinese FAMILLE ROSE which became distinctly purple when fired at a higher temperature than that needed to develop the earlier pink. *See* PORPHYRY.

Purple lustre. Pottery decorated with gold lustre applied thickly to give, after firing, a dark-purple colour. It occurs with resist decoration on a glazed body of white, cream, or buff earthenware. Jugs thus decorated are fairly common, and were made between 1790 and 1830 in Staffordshire and Sunderland. Some examples are decorated with a mottled lustre. *See* GOLD-LUSTRE WARE.

Purple of Cassius. A crimson-purple pigment precipitated from chloride of gold and mixed with chloride of tin to make it opaque. The process, discovered by Andreas Cassius of Leyden, Holland, before 1673, was used by German HAUSMALER in the 17th century to decorate faience. The pigment was also employed in the later years of the 17th century in the manufacture of coloured glass. The process was taken to China by Jesuit missionaries, and there used to produce the principal colour of the palette of the FAMILLE ROSE. It was developed at Meissen and other German and French factories, and especially at Strasbourg, for the decoration of faience and porcelain. The colour varied, depending on the kiln-temperature, from pink to purple. It was also known as *rouge d'or* and rose-pink. *See* PUCE; YANG TS'AI.

Purple resist lustre. RESIST WARE of purple lustre, the pattern being formed by the colour of the white, cream, or buff body against the lustre ground.

Pu-tai Ho-shang (Chinese). A Buddhist monk usually represented seated cross-legged on a cushion, with a protruding belly and a grinning open mouth, his right hand resting on his raised right knee, his left hand holding a peach. Sometimes he is waving a bag of wind. He was depicted on Chinese porcelain, and sometimes as a porcelain figure. In Japan he is synonymous with Ho-tei, god of Contentment. Figures of the monk Pu-tai inspired some of the earliest Meissen porcelain figures. *See* PAGOD.

Pu-tai Ho-shang. Porcelain figure on an oval base painted with lotus leaves in black, ht 6½ in.; reign of K'ang Hsi (1662–1722). Courtesy, Spink & Son Ltd, London.

Putto (Italian). The figure, painted or modelled, of a young boy, usually nude or nearly so. Since the word *putto* (pl., *putti*) is the Italian for a young child, the term, although often used loosely and interchangeably with *amorino*, should preferably be applied only to a wingless figure, as distinguished from a winged AMORINO (a word which has affiliations with Cupid).

Puzzle-jug. A jug with a globular body and a cylindrical neck pierced with openwork in such a way that ordinary pouring or drinking is impossible. It has from three to seven spouts in the rim which surmounts the neck, one of them being connected with a concealed tube or siphon which runs through the rim and handle to the bottom of the jug. There are also holes which need to be closed by the fingers before the contents can be sucked up. Some are inscribed with challenging legends. Earthenware, stoneware, and slipware examples exist; they were common from the 17th to the 19th century in Europe, and especially in England where many were made of English delftware. The French term is *pot à surprise*, and reproductions of early jugs have been made in faience. The Dutch term is *bedrieger*. *See* SURPRISE CUP.

Puzzle-jug. Bristol delftware, ht 9½ in., mid-18th century. Victoria and Albert Museum, London.

Pyrometric cone. *See* CONE.

Pyxis (Greek). A covered box-like receptacle of Greek pottery, usually cylindrical and having a finial in the form of a knob, bronze ring, or figure on the cover. Some examples have a group of figures on the cover. It was used on the toilet table as a container for jewels or trinkets.

Pyxis. Attic, with geometric-style decoration, 8th century BC. Wadsworth Atheneum, Hartford, Conn.

Q

Quadrillé (French). A diaper pattern with squares and QUATREFOILS in blue. It was popular at Chantilly, and was derived from the TRELLIS ground of Rouen.

Quail and millet pattern. A decorative subject derived from the designs of KAKIEMON at Arita (Hizen province) Japan, of the end of the 17th century. There are a number of variants, but basically it depicts a pair of quail with rocks and foliage. Its popularity was such that it was copied on Chinese porcelain during the reign of K'ang Hsi (1662–1722). It was popular at Meissen during the early decades of that factory's existence (where it was termed *Rebhuhnpaar*) in common with other Kakiemon designs, and the palette employed was very similar to that of the Japanese originals. It occurs later at Chelsea and Bow in England (where it was sometimes called the partridge pattern), and it is also to be found on Worcester porcelain, although there is some doubt whether specimens were painted at the factory or by the independent decorator, James Giles of London. In France this and other Kakiemon patterns were extensively employed as a source of inspiration at Chantilly. Of all the 18th-century copies, those of Chelsea most nearly approach the originals, even to the stilt-marks within the foot-ring of plates.

Quartieri, a (Italian). Literally, in quarters. A term applied to borders or patterns in which the design has been divided into four or more repetitive compartments radiating from the centre. Especially employed in describing Italian maiolica so decorated.

Quatrefoil. A shape or ornament having four equal foils or lobes.

Queen Charlotte's pattern. Same as ROYAL LILY PATTERN.

Queen's Beasts, The. A set of ten heraldic figures made by Minton in 1953 from models by James Woodford, each animal seated on a gilded socle and holding a shield charged with a coat of arms. The animals are the Lion of England, the White Horse of Hanover, the Yale of Beaufort, the Plantagenet Falcon, the Black Bull of Clarence, the Red Dragon of Wales, the White Greyhound of Richmond, the Unicorn of Scotland, the Griffin of Edward III, and the White Lion of Mortimer. They were reproduced in niches on the QUEEN'S VASE.

Queen's pattern. A decorative pattern used at Worcester, and now so-called by the Worcester Royal Porcelain Co.; it has two series of spiral lines in gold separated by a scalloped line, with the spirals above and below running in opposite directions. It must be distinguished from the CATHERINE WHEEL PATTERN, which was called the 'Queen's pattern' in a Worcester catalogue of 1769, and from the ROYAL LILY PATTERN (sometimes called the 'Queen Charlotte pattern' after 1788).

Queen's shape. The shape of certain tableware made by Wedgwood. It has a hexafoil lobed rim, and first acquired its name from Queen Charlotte, for whom the original dinner-service of this kind was made. *See* HUSK SERVICE.

Queen's Vase, The. A large ten-sided vase made by Minton, with the collaboration of Wedgwood and other potteries, to

Queen's pattern. Covered bowl with gilt decoration. Courtesy, Worcester Royal Porcelain Co.

Queen's Shape. Creamware plate with hexafoil lobed rim, Wedgwood, *c.* 1775. Courtesy, Wedgwood.

Queen's Vase, with figures of the *Queen's beasts*, made by Minton and other potteries to commemorate the coronation of Queen Elizabeth II in 1953.

commemorate the coronation of Queen Elizabeth II on 2 June 1953; it was presented on 14 July 1954 by the British Pottery Manufacturers' Federation. Surmounted by a crown, it is decorated with floral emblems of the countries of the United Kingdom, and has in niches on each side replicas of the QUEEN'S BEASTS.

Queen's ware. A cream-coloured lead-glazed earthenware developed *c.* 1763 by Josiah Wedgwood at Burslem, and named after Queen Charlotte, whose favour it found after she had been presented with a breakfast-service of the new ware. To eliminate objections to the lead glaze on earlier creamware Wedgwood used a glaze made of white clay and flint, somewhat similar to the composition of the body, and with a smaller quantity of lead than was customary. This glaze, after a second firing, had a transparent lustrous finish. The ware had the commercial advantages of being light, durable, and readily decorated, and it led eventually to the disappearance of the tin-glazed earthenware industry in England, and virtually on the Continent also. It was, towards the end of the 18th century, extensively copied in France, where it was termed *faïence fine*, and in Germany under the name of *Steingut*. In addition to coloured enamels, relief decoration, and pierced work, many pieces were transfer-printed, first by Sadler and Green of Liverpool, and later by the Wedgwood factory. Printing was usually in black, but examples in sepia, blue, and other colours exist. It was employed for the FROG SERVICE. Much tableware was produced in the 18th century and later, as well as commercial and industrial ware. The 18th-century examples are less prone to crazing of the glaze than those of the 19th century. *See* LESSORE WARE.

Quill-box. Same as SLIP-CUP.

Quill-holder. Same as SPILL-VASE.

Quintal flower horn. Same as FINGER-VASE.

Quiver pattern. *See* CARQUOIS, À LA.

Quizzical birds. Bird figures made of MARTINWARE, and sometimes called 'Martin birds', usually standing, with wings folded, and having a long beak and wrinkled eyes. In some examples the head is detachable. *See* BIRDS.

Quodlibet. From Latin *quod libet*, what pleases. A decorative design of playing-cards or addressed envelopes arranged haphazardly, and rendered in *trompe l'œil* as though casting shadows. Used at Copenhagen towards the end of the 18th century, after a somewhat similar design at Meissen fifty years previously.

Quizzical birds. Group of birds in Martinware, *c.* 1900. Courtesy, Godden of Worthing Ltd.

R

Rabbit vase. A type of TERRACE-VASE having a rabbit (or in some cases a different animal, e.g. a squirrel, dog, or cow) at the foot of a stairway which forms part of the base.

Rabeschi (Italian). An old term for ARABESQUES, especially those used on maiolica made in Venice in the middle of the 16th century, the designs being borrowed from damascened metalwork.

Raeren stoneware. Stoneware made at Raeren, near Aachen, in the Rhineland, from the middle of the 16th century. It was an elaborately decorated brown ware in the style of COLOGNE WARE. The most notable potter here was Jan Emens (*fl.* 1566–94), who employed applied moulding, and carved and pierced decoration. Raeren potters migrated *c.* 1600 to the villages of Grenzau and Grenzhausen in the Westerwald. *See* WESTERWALD WARE; BLAUWERK.

Raffaele ware. Italian maiolica of the 16th century once thought to have been painted by, or under the direction of, the artist Raphael (Raffaello Santi; 1483–1520) of Urbino. In fact, the designs were taken from engravings by Marcantonio Raimondi after paintings by Raphael. The finest specimens date from not earlier than 1540, twenty years after the death of Raphael. Examples in the collection of Horace Walpole at Strawberry Hill were catalogued as 'Raphael fayence' or 'Raffaelle ware'.

Rafraichissoir (French). Same as a MONTEITH. Also called in France a *seau à verre, seau crenelé* and *verrière*.

Rafter. A slab of earthenware or fired clay placed horizontally on girders in the kiln to support ware during firing. *See* KILN FURNITURE.

Raised gilding. Gilding thickly applied. A fashion for raised gilding, usually tooled, is to be noticed at Sèvres from *c.* 1756 onwards, and it was imitated at Chelsea during the gold-anchor period, 1758 onwards. Raised gilding in conjunction with decoration in translucent enamels occurs on early German porcelain, *c.* 1715, decorated by Christoph Konrad Hunger, an arcanist who also executed enamelling on copper. *See* ENCRUSTED.

Rabbit vase. One of a pair, faience with transfer-printed decoration, Marieberg, 1773. Courtesy, Sotheby's.

Rakan. The Japanese equivalent of the Chinese LOHAN, or Buddhist disciple. The *Rakan* is used as the subject of both figures and painted decoration.

Rakka (Raqqa) ware. A type of Mesopotamian pottery made at Rakka in Syria, on the Upper Euphrates, *c.* 831–1259. It has a white body with a greenish transparent glaze, and cobalt blue was commonly used. The wares include *sgraffito* decoration under a monochrome glaze, and underglaze painted ornament. Lustre was used from 1171 (date of earliest known specimen).

Raku ware. A type of Japanese pottery originally from near Kyoto (Yamashiro province) which is covered with a lead glaze and fired at, relatively, a very low temperature. For this reason the body is very soft and porous. It was first made by an immigrant Korean potter, *c.* 1525, and continued by his son. The glaze is thick and treacly, and the colour ranges from dark-brown to light-red, and on later examples includes a straw colour, green, and cream. Raku ware is primitive in appearance at first sight, but is, in fact, extremely sophisticated. It is much valued in Japan, and the technique is still in use. *See* TEA CEREMONY.

Rambouillet cup. A style of small coffee-cup shaped somewhat like a Greek SKYPHOS, with two small lateral loop handles. Introduced at Sèvres, 1787.

Ranelagh figures. Porcelain, ht approx. 12 in., Derby, *c.* 1760. Victoria and Albert Museum, London.

Ranelagh figures. Two large Derby porcelain standing figures, *c.* 1765, of a gallant and a lady, the man holding a ticket of admission to Ranelagh Gardens, a popular place of entertainment in south London during the 18th century, and the lady holding a posy.

Ranzohan ware. A type of KO SOMETSUKE ('things made haphazardly'), cherished in Japan for what would be regarded in the West as blemishes. *See* MUSHIKUI.

Raphaelesque style. *See* GROTESQUES; PISA VASE.

Rasp. *See* FOOT-SCRAPER.

Rat-tail handle. A type of handle which, as in the case of a rat's tail, is round, slender and tapering.

Ravenstone. A mat black glaze developed by Wedgwood in 1958.

Rayonnant, style (French). A decorative pattern adapted from the LAMBREQUIN which has a central, radial arrangement of symmetrical motifs. It was popular, *c.* 1720–40, at a number of French factories, especially those making faience. It was originally introduced by the faience makers of Rouen.

Rayy (Rhages) ware. A type of Persian pottery made at Rayy, near Teheran, *c.* 1037–1256. The body is medium-hard and coarse. Many pieces have a blue ground, and the backs of some dishes have a deep-blue glaze. Production included the types known as LAKABI WARE and MINAI WARE. *See* KASHĀN WARE.

Rebhuhnpaar. The German term for the QUAIL AND MILLET PATTERN.

Réchaud (French). (1) A term used, mainly in Germany, to describe a FOOD-WARMER (*see* VEILLEUSE). (2) A low ceramic stand on which is placed a dish with food to be kept warm by means of a godet or a taper set in the stand. *See* DUTCH STOVE.

Red. One of the colours used in decorating ceramic ware. It is produced by various metallic compounds, such as iron nitrate, lead chromate, muriate of magnesium, copper oxide, etc. Apart from iron-red, much used on Chinese enamelled porcelain, the reds have always been difficult colours to use, especially on a tin glaze where they are particularly prone to defects, and were added at a separate firing. *See* ASHES OF ROSES; CORAL RED; IRON-RED (*rouge-de-fer*); SANG-DE-BŒUF (ox-blood); ARMENIAN RED (sealing-wax red; tomato red); ROSSO DI FAENZA (*rosso di Virgiliotto*); SACRIFICIAL RED (*chi hung*).

Red Barn, The. A pottery group commemorating the murder of Maria Marten by William Corder in 1828. He buried her corpse in the Red Barn at Polstead, Suffolk. The group, by Obadiah Sherratt, depicts the man tempting the woman into the open door of a red barn flanked by flowering trees. The figures also exist singly, made in Staffordshire at a later date.

Red bull pattern. A decorative subject from a Chinese prototype employed at Worcester as a coloured transfer-print in the 18th century. It depicts an oriental lady in a field under a red sun pointing to a red bull, with a grey bull and an oxherd in the scene also.

Red china. The same as RED STONEWARE.

Red dragon pattern. A decorative pattern employed at Meissen, *c.* 1730–35, and adapted from Japanese porcelain in the manner of KAKIEMON. It has two dragons and two phoenixes painted in red monochrome. The German term is *rote Drache*. *See* PRINCE HENRI PATTERN; DÉCOR CORÉEN.

Style rayonnant. Faience dish, with decoration in blue and yellow, Rouen, *c.* 1720. Victoria and Albert Museum, London.

Red edge. The edge of some porcelain and delftware plates coloured a brownish-red in imitation of similarly painted edges on Chinese and Japanese porcelain. It was frequent on Liverpool delftware. *See* BROWN EDGE.

Red-figure style. A decorative style on Greek pottery, *c.* 530–400 BC, the distinctive feature of which is red figures reserved on a black ground, the black being a kind of varnish prepared from slip mixed with wine-lees or urine. On some specimens the black was painted on around the figures, but on rare specimens it covered the entire vase and the red figures were over-painted. The style is characterized by greater delicacy and more varied subject-matter than the earlier BLACK-FIGURE STYLE. There were also some pieces with a white ground, mainly for funeral and religious ceremonies. The style was copied in Italy.

Red dragon pattern. Saucer-dish and covered sugar-bowl with red monochrome decoration, Meissen, *c.* 1735. Courtesy, Christie's.

Red glost pottery. A term applied to Roman SAMIAN WARE having a sealing-wax red colour and a fine gloss, undecorated or with relief decoration, and sometimes ornamented with OVOLO moulding.

Red jasper. A term sometimes employed to denote Wedgwood's ROSSO ANTICO.

Red porcelain. Unglazed red stoneware made in China at YI-HSING (Kuangtung province) in the 17th and 18th centuries. Many vessels, strictly wine-pots, were exported with shipments of tea for use as teapots. The body varied from red to dark brown, and was so hard that it could be cut and polished on a lapidary's wheel. The Chinese ware was extensively imitated in Europe, and was sometimes erroneously termed BOCCARO WARE. *See* RED STONEWARE.

Red stoneware. Unglazed stoneware with a red body made in imitation of the so-called RED PORCELAIN of YI-HSING. In Holland manufacture was developed by Lambertus Kleffius in 1672, but the best-known Dutch examples were made a little later by Arij de Milde. In England red stoneware may have been first made by John Dwight, but no recognizable specimens have survived. It was certainly made by the Elers brothers, who came from Cologne, Germany, and founded a pottery at Hammersmith, *c.* 1690, later removing to Bradwell Wood in Staffordshire. It continued to be made in Staffordshire throughout the 18th century, and was refined by Josiah Wedgwood and manufactured by him under the name of ROSSO ANTICO. Red stoneware of fine quality was made at Meissen by J. F. Böttger, and introduced *c.* 1708; manufacture was discontinued *c.* 1730. *See* BÖTTGER RED STONEWARE; ELERS WARE; ARIJ DE MILDE WARE.

Red-figure style. Volute *krater* with painted decoration and anthemion border, *c*. 460 BC. Archaeological Museum, Ferrara.

Redgrave pattern. A decorative pattern employed on Lowestoft porcelain which was copied from a well-known Chinese motif of rocks and peonies. It is painted in a combination of iron-red and underglaze blue, and was the first Lowestoft attempt to use polychrome decoration. The pattern was named after the artist.

Reducing atmosphere. A kiln atmosphere that is rich in carbon monoxide. Copper used as a colouring agent for glazes, or as an underglaze pigment, will yield a crimson-purple or bluish-red if it is fired in a reducing atmosphere. Various methods are employed to attain this, but the Chinese commonly employed wet wood which, when used as fuel for the furnace, yielded the required conditions in the kiln.

Redware. A general term for RED STONEWARE and red earthenware of all kinds, including ROSSO ANTICO.

Reed and tie border. A decorative border pattern in the form of REEDING, but with crossed straps that simulate ribbons and tie the reeding together in bunches.

Reeding. Relief ornamentation in the form of a series of parallel convex reeds. The converse of FLUTING. Also called ribbing. *See* REED AND TIE BORDER.

Refired ware. Porcelain of the 18th and early 19th centuries, either white and undecorated or sparsely decorated, which has, at a later date, had a more elaborate decoration executed in enamel colours, usually in conjunction with a coloured ground, fired on in the enamelling kiln for the purpose of enhancing the market value. Strictly, this can be described as faking, rather than forgery, since the porcelain itself is genuinely old. *See* CLOBBERING. Signs of refiring include black specks in the glaze (sometimes present on genuine early wares), and often an irregularity of the glaze surface due to partial remelting. Much soft-paste Sèvres porcelain sold in white soon after 1800 was re-decorated in this way; its value is nominal. Many VEILLEUSES made in the 19th century in white porcelain for household use have recently been thus decorated. *See* FAKE; REPRODUCTION; FORGERY.

Reform ware. Jugs, flasks, and punch-bowls made at the time of the passage, in England, of the Reform Bill, enacted in 1832. They were made of Staffordshire pottery or saltglazed stoneware, decorated with transfer-printed or moulded portraits of William IV and Queen Adelaide or of the champions of parliamentary reform, Earl Grey, Lords Brougham and Althorp, and Lord John Russell, sometimes with added inscriptions.

Refractory. A term used to describe a clay which will not fuse except at a temperature higher than those customarily used for firing ceramic wares.

Régence style. A French decorative style, transitional between the BAROQUE and ROCOCO styles, which prevailed in France during the Regency of the Duc d'Orléans, 1715–23. Not much evident in pottery and porcelain, it can be seen in the lighter and more graceful decorations of some French faience which exhibit an increasing element of fantasy. In Germany and Austria the same period shows a late baroque style with some of the same elements, but the Meissen porcelain factory especially was much preoccupied with *chinoiseries* at this time. Generally, the Régence style is much more to be found in furniture and interior decoration. *See* LAMBREQUIN; RAYONNANT, STYLE.

Regency style. An English decorative style which prevailed, strictly speaking, from 1811 to 1820, during that part of the reign of George III when the affairs of the country were in the hands of the Prince Regent, afterwards George IV. In common parlance the term is extended both before and after these dates to an indeterminate extent. Regency style in England is a version of the French EMPIRE STYLE, with some modifications. In porcelain the style of classical pottery was still the most common, but emphasis was laid on fine painting, especially painting with a topographical subject. *Chinoiseries* were perhaps inspired by the Prince Regent's taste for the subject, to be seen at the Pavilion, Brighton (Sussex). Generally, the rendering of classical subjects lacks the lightness of the earlier neo-classical and Adam styles, and is inclined to be pompous and heavy. Egyptian motifs belong to this period, and mark the revival of interest in ancient Egypt which followed Napoleon's campaign there of 1798.

Regent body. A porcelain body, hard and with a glossy glaze, introduced at Chamberlain's Worcester factory in 1811 to mark the patronage of the Prince Regent. It was of much better quality than the porcelain hitherto produced by this factory.

Registry mark. A mark required by the British Patent Office from 1842 to 1883 on English manufactured goods using a registered design. The mark shows the year, month, and date of the design registration, but not necessarily that of the manufacture of the object. Such marks were used by Wedgwood and others on ceramic ware, often in moulded form.

Reeding. Teapot with reeded body, creamware, Leeds. Courtesy, Jellinek & Sampson, Ltd.

Regnier cup. A style of small coffee-cup curving markedly inwards towards the bottom, and having a loop handle projecting above the rim. The handle has a mask TERMINAL. Introduced at Sèvres in 1813.

Reign-mark. *See* CHARACTER MARK; CHINESE REIGN-MARK; NIEN HAO; NENGO.

Relief decoration. Decoration which projects from the surface to a varying degree. *See* HIGH RELIEF, MEDIUM RELIEF, and LOW RELIEF. Relief work was produced in varying ways – by moulding, casting, stamping, and sprigging. *See* ORNAMENTING; CAMEO; INTAGLIO.

Renaissance style. The revival of the classical style of Greece and Rome which took place in Italy as early as the 13th century, although its impact on pottery did not become strong until the 16th century. The most notable classical style of ornament adopted as decoration on pottery, chiefly tin-glazed wares, was the GROTESQUE. The classical style of the Renaissance was followed by variants, such as BAROQUE and ROCOCO, and then by the NEO-CLASSICAL STYLE.

Repairer. A workman who joined the various separately cast or moulded parts of a figure or other ceramic object into a completed form. Some repairers were also modellers, responsible for the prototype. They were highly skilled and were occasionally allowed to mark their work. The German term is *Bossierer*.

Replacer (or **replacement**). A dealers' term for a piece of a service made to replace a broken or lost original. The well-known Paris firm, Edmé Samson et Cie, began by making such copies in the 1840s. Derby made replacements for Meissen ware, adding the Meissen mark. Other examples are common, and every piece of an antique service needs to be examined for the presence of replacements. *See* REPRODUCTION; SAMSON COPIES.

Repoussé (French). A silversmiths' term for ornament formed by hammering with punches from the back, and therefore raised from the surface in relief. The term is occasionally employed in describing pottery and porcelain when the relief decoration is in imitation of this technique on silverware. For this purpose moulds were sometimes taken from actual objects of silver thus ornamented.

Reproduction. A close copy of genuinely old porcelain or pottery made at a more recent date, but with identifying marks which allow the date of manufacture and the maker to be ascertained. One of the principal manufacturers of objects of this kind, Edmé Samson et Cie, Paris, uses the mark of a letter *S* to identify its wares, sometimes also adding the original factory-mark. In Germany, the Bayerisches Porzellanmanufaktur, which uses old moulds to reproduce 18th-century wares of Nymphenburg and Frankenthal, fully marks its products, and alters the bases so that confusion is unlikely. Nevertheless, painted marks can be removed with hydrofluoric acid, or ground off. Patches bare of glaze on the underside of plates and dishes in a position where a mark would normally be found need careful examination, since a mark undesirable to the seller may have been removed. Almost every kind of pottery and porcelain which has attracted the attention of collectors has also been reproduced. *See* SAMSON COPIES; FAKE; FORGERY; REFIRED WARE; REPLACER.

Republican ware. Porcelain made at Sèvres during the period of the First Republic, 1792–95.

Rhinoceros vase. One of a pair, porcelain with painted decoration by Edward Steele, Rockingham, *c.* 1830. Victoria and Albert Museum, London.

Reserve. The portion of the surface of an object of pottery or porcelain left without the application of a ground colour, but surrounded by it. Such reserved areas or panels were usually decorated with enamel colours, but occasionally they were decorated in blue underglaze, especially in conjunction with a cobalt blue ground colour. The ragged edges where the ground colour ended were covered with gilding for the sake of neatness, as well as to accentuate and frame the reserve. Occasionally porcelain with the ground already laid, but with the reserved panels unpainted, was sold to INDEPENDENT DECORATORS. Worcester sold blue SCALE-GROUND ware in this state to James Giles, a London independent decorator, and a few unpainted specimens have survived to testify to this practice.

Resist ware. Ware with a decorative pattern of the same colour as the body set against a differently coloured LUSTRE ground. The pattern was normally white, but with some pieces, depending on the colour of the glazed body, it was buff, yellow, or blue. One process involved painting the glaze with a water-resistant substance, such as wax, or partly covering it with a paper cut-out, followed by application of the lustre. Subsequent firing burned away the 'resist', leaving the pattern free of lustre. By another process the design was painted or stencilled with a shellac varnish which resisted the lustre. *See* GOLD RESIST; PLATINUM RESIST; SILVER RESIST; COPPER RESIST; CANARY LUSTRE.

Reticulated. Having a pattern of interlacing lines or pierced work which forms a net or web. On ware with a double wall, such as some teapots, the outer wall was often reticulated by piercing. Teapots of this kind were made in China during the reign of K'ang Hsi (1662–1722), and in Europe at Meissen and elsewhere. *See* LING-LUNG YAO; PIERCED DECORATION.

Reticulated cup. A double-wall cup without a handle, the pierced outer wall of which served to protect the fingers from the heat. Examples exist in Chinese and European porcelain.

Reverse. The side of a vase or other vessel opposite to the one with the principal decoration (obverse).

Revived Gothic. *See* GOTHIC STYLE.

Revived Kutani. Same as SAIKO KUTANI.

Revived rococo. *See* ROCOCO.

Reynolds, Sir Joshua, pattern. A pattern on Worcester porcelain derived from a Kakiemon decoration on porcelain from Arita (Hizen province). It features a phoenix or HO-HO BIRD seated on a rock amidst scattered peonies. It was used at Worcester, with or without a deep border of cobalt blue. The name has also been given to a pattern used at Chelsea depicting two pheasants, one perched on a prunus tree near a BANDED HEDGE.

Sir Joshua Reynolds pattern. Lobed plate with polychrome decoration, Worcester (Dr Wall period). Courtesy, Christie's.

Rhages ware. *See* RAYY WARE.

Rhenish stoneware. Saltglazed stoneware made in the Rhineland from the latter part of the Middle Ages, but principally in the 16th and 17th centuries, at a number of centres, the largest of which was Cologne. It was exported in great quantities at the time, and imitated extensively in the 19th century. It is especially noted for relief work. Rhenish stoneware was sometimes erroneously called 'Dutch ware', perhaps because it was shipped to England from Germany through Dutch ports, or perhaps as a corruption of 'Deutsch'. *See* WESTERWALD WARE; RAEREN WARE; SIEGBURG WARE.

Rhineland stoneware. *See* RHENISH STONEWARE.

Rhinoceros vases. Two huge elaborately decorated Rockingham vases with domed covers, the FINIAL on each of which is a figure of a rhinoceros. There are rhinoceros' feet on the base. The vases have much PIERCED DECORATION and CRABSTOCK handles. They were painted by Edward Steele, *c.* 1830.

Rhodian pottery. An erroneous term for ISNIK POTTERY current in the 19th century, originally due to the fact that fragments of Isnik ware were excavated at Lindos, on the island of Rhodes. *See* IONIAN WARE.

Rhyton (Greek). A pottery drinking-cup in the form of a head. Early examples exist in Mycenaean, Persian, and Chinese pottery. In Greek and Roman models the head was that of a woman, or of an animal such as a dog, fox, bull, horse, stag, boar, ram, eagle, or cock, or of a mythological creature such as a griffin. As the rhyton (like the MASTOS) could stand only when inverted, it was necessary for the drinker to drain it before he could put it down. These early drinking-cups are the ancestors of the 18th-century English MASK JUGS AND MUGS, as well as TOBY JUGS and stirrup-cups. The fox-head STIRRUP-CUP, familiar in English pottery, is often termed a rhyton. *See* LEKYTHOS.

Ribbing. Same as REEDING.

Ribbon and leaf border. A border pattern consisting of a continuous twisting ribbon with a leaf in each curve.

Reticulated. Teapot with reticulated outer wall and handle with moulded terminals, creamware, Leeds, *c.* 1785. City Art Gallery, Leeds.

Rice-grain piercing. A term applied to Chinese porcelain bowls (and Persian pottery bowls made in imitation) in which the walls of the vessel are pierced in a shape and size closely resembling the rice grain, the holes being filled with clear glaze. *See* GOMBROON WARE.

Ridge tile. Glazed earthenware, Chinese, early 19th century; ht 15 in. Victoria and Albert Museum, London.

Ridge tile. A semi-cylindrical tile of stoneware to be set along the ridge of a pitched roof. Early examples made in China from the Han dynasty to the Ming dynasty are decorated with coloured lead glazes. The tiles are often surmounted with a mythological figure, or an animal such as a lion or a leaping carp. Ridge tiles were also made in Normandy of faience from the 15th to the 17th century.

Rim. The narrow area adjacent to the EDGE of a vessel; usually applied to such objects as a vase, plate, or cup. Rims may be decorated with moulding or painting. Moulded rims include CRENELATED, CUT-OUT, DENTATE, BEADED, SERRATED, LOBED, SCALLOPED, BARBED, and PIE-CRUST types.

Ring ground. A ground covered with circles, with or without enclosed dots, the circles being somewhat larger than in the ŒIL-DE-PERDRIX or FISH-ROE ground patterns.

Ring-jug. A type of jug of brown saltglazed RHENISH STONEWARE with a wide mouth, a waisted neck, and rings suspended from loop handles, made at Dreihausen and Siegburg. Late examples from Raeren had a lion-mask at the mouth.

Ring-stand. A columnar holder for ladies' rings, rising from a circular dish. Some were made by Wedgwood in creamware.

Robin's-egg glaze. A glaze of robin's-egg blue marked with a fine network of dark blue. It occurs in Chinese porcelain made during the reign of Yung Chêng (1722–36).

Ring-jug. Brown saltglazed stoneware, ht 10 in., Dreihausen, 16th century. Victoria and Albert Museum, London.

Rocaille (French). A common French term (along with *style Louis Quinze* and *style Pompadour*) to designate the style called in England and Italy ROCOCO.

Rocailleries (French). Ornamentation featuring rockwork, as in the ROCOCO style.

Rock of ages border. A border pattern of waves and rocks used on some early blue-and-white porcelain made in China during the Ming dynasty. It occurs on copies of such wares made in Persian pottery during the 16th century and in a debased form on ISNIK POTTERY, where it is termed the ammonite scroll border. Also called the 'Rock and Wave pattern', apparently a dealers' term for the Chinese motif *pao-shan hai-shui* (precious mountains and the sea). *See* DOLLAR PATTERN.

Rockingham ware. Same as BROWN CHINA. This is not to be confused with Rockingham porcelain. *See* BENNINGTON WARE.

Rockwork. Relief or painted decoration representing rocks, often a form used for bases supporting figures during the currency of the ROCOCO style. The depiction of rocks of fantastic shapes (adapted from those used in garden design) is common on Chinese porcelain. They usually become virtually unrecognizable (as shapeless patches of colour) in European copies of Chinese designs.

Rococo. A style of decoration which followed the BAROQUE style in France, the development of which was mainly influenced by Jean Bérain I and Juste-Aurèle Meissonnier, the latter a silversmith. The principal features of rococo are asymmetricality in ornament and a repertoire consisting to a considerable extent of rockwork, shells, flowers, foliage, and scrollwork (often termed C-AND-S SCROLL, from the typical forms adopted). The rococo style was developed in France under Louis XV (1715–74), and it was much imitated in Italy, Germany, and to a lesser extent in England. In south Germany a well-marked variant of the French style is exemplified in the figures of Bustelli, the Nymphenburg *Modellmeister* (*see* BUSTELLI FIGURES).

Rococo was followed by the NEO-CLASSICAL STYLE, also termed the Adam style or Louis Seize style. A revival of 18th-century rococo (revived rococo) took place in the 19th century during the reign of Louis-Philippe in France, and it is evident also in English decoration of the 1830s. In France rococo is variously termed *rocaille*, *style Boucher*, *style Louis Quinze*, and *style Pompadour*. The term rococo seems to have been of Italian origin, and was first applied to some exaggerated examples of late baroque.

Rodney ware. A mug or jug made in the form of the head of Admiral George Rodney, with his braided hair forming the handle. Also a mask-jug with the head below the lip, and a mug or bowl with an applied profile bust portrait. They were made to commemorate Rodney's victory over the French in 1782. *See* TOBY JUG; MASK JUGS AND MUGS.

Rogers group. A 19th-century group of figures, usually depicting a narrative scene, made by John Rogers in the United States. Generally of plaster of Paris, a few examples were made of BISCUIT porcelain or white PARIAN PORCELAIN. They originally revolved on an ebony pedestal.

Rolwagen (Dutch). *See* ROULEAU VASE.

Roman Charity, The. (1) A pottery or porcelain group inspired by the legend of Climon, who was imprisoned without food or water, and who was fed at her breast by his daughter, Pera, during fleeting daily visits, thus saving his life. A Chelsea porcelain group adapted from a painting by Rubens in the Rijksmuseum, Amsterdam, was made by Joseph Willems, *c.* 1758–59. (2) A Ralph Wood pottery version, *c.* 1770, depicts the woman with a baby at her breast, and a small child clinging to her right arm, with an aged man beside her feeding from a cup. This, perhaps, might well be called simply 'Charity' rather than 'The Roman Charity', since the connection between it and the legend of Climon is somewhat tenuous. It marks the increasing delicacy with which neo-classical modellers treated their subject-matter.

Roman Charity (1). Porcelain, modelled by Joseph Willems, Chelsea, *c.* 1759. British Museum, London.

Roman Charity (2). Glazed earthenware, Ralph Wood, *c.* 1770. City Museums, Stoke-on-Trent.

Roman pottery. The types of pottery included are so diverse that this term can hardly be regarded as more than a description of any pottery manufactured within the boundaries of the Roman Empire. Italian wares include copies of, and derivations from, Greek pottery at all periods from *c.* 500 BC onwards. TERRACOTTA was used for a wide variety of purposes, especially architectural, but the ware which is most closely associated with the Romans is the red polished SAMIAN POTTERY, the principal centre for the manufacture of which was Arretino, although it was undoubtedly made elsewhere in the Empire. The lead glaze first occurs on Syrian pottery of the 1st century BC made during the Roman occupation, but specimens are exceedingly rare. Pottery manufacture under the Romans was well organized on a factory system, and specimens of Samian ware especially sometimes bear a potter's name or mark.

Romanesque border. A border pattern in the form of a continuous scrolled curved line with leaves in each curve.

Roof tile. A thin slab of fired clay in various forms for covering the roofs of buildings, usually undecorated except in the case of the ornamental RIDGE TILE. *See* IMBREX; TEGULA.

Rookwood pottery. Earthenware made at the Rookwood factory, at Cincinnati, Ohio, founded in 1880 by Mrs Maria Longworth Nichols; in 1886 she became Mrs Bellamy Storer and in 1889 transferred ownership to William Watts Taylor, who had managed the company from 1883. He died in 1913, after which the company drifted until it closed in 1941. The factory developed many unusual and decorative glazes. The early wares included pieces with coloured slip painting under the glaze on a dark ground; it became known as 'Standard Rookwood'. In 1884 it developed an AVENTURINE GLAZE, and during the 1890s used mostly floral themes. Mat glazes had been used since 1896, but in 1901 they became a major form of decoration in several styles. Until 1910 all pieces were individually decorated, signed and dated, and none duplicated.

Root pattern. Porcelain teabowls and saucer decorated in underglaze blue, with (left) an unglazed waster to show complete pattern, Worcester, *c.* 1755. Courtesy, Worcester Royal Porcelain Co.

Root pattern. A decorative pattern depicting a flowering prunus tree with gnarled and twisted roots. It was used on blue-and-white porcelain at Worcester.

Root-pot. A pot or vase with a flat back and semi-circular front, having a removable cover often made with three or more removable bottomless cups for planting bulbs, and sometimes with holes for cut flowers. Some were made in animal forms, such as one by Wedgwood in the form of a hedgehog (porcupine) with many holes in its back. Also called a bulb-jar, a crocus-pot, and a bough-pot. *See* BULB-VASE; HEDGEHOG CROCUS-POT.

Rope curtain pattern. A diaper pattern used on wares made in Korea. *See* MISHIMA.

Rope handle. A handle in the form of a rope, consisting of a single strand or of two intertwined.

Rose-box. A naturalistically modelled BOX, in the form of a rose, and decorated with rows of overlapping painted relief petals; the cover is surmounted by a green stalk-handle with a finial in the form of leaf and bud.

Rose du Barry. A term employed by 19th-century Coalport and other English porcelain factories for an imitation of ROSE POMPADOUR.

Rose-engine turned. Tea-kettle, with incised body, and warming-stand, red stoneware, Leeds, *c.* 1770. Victoria and Albert Museum, London.

Rose-engine turned. Curved, symmetrical, geometric patterns incised into the body of stonewares, usually English, of the end of the 18th century and after; the designs were incised with the aid of the engine-turning lathe equipped with a guide-tool known as a rosette. *See* ENGINE-TURNED DECORATION.

Rose marbré (French). A rose ground colour with dark markings resembling marble, developed at Sèvres; known pieces with this ground bear the date-letter for 1761. *See* ROSE POMPADOUR.

Rose-pink. The Chinese rose enamel. *See* ROUGE D'OR.

Rose Pompadour (French). A rose-pink ground colour developed at Sèvres probably by the chemist Hellot, or perhaps by the painter Xhrouet or Chrouet, *c.* 1757, and discontinued after the death of Mme de Pompadour in 1764. It was imitated at Chelsea soon after 1760 and there called claret. It occurs on Worcester porcelain under the same name. Neither closely resembles the French version in appearance. Imitations from Coalport and other English factories in the 19th century were misleadingly termed 'rose du Barry'. The colour was discontinued at Sèvres five years before Mme du Barry became mistress of Louis XV, and no colour was ever named after her by a French factory.

Rose-water bowl (ewer or **bottle).** A porcelain bowl without handles (sometimes a small ewer or long-necked bottle), usually with an accompanying stand; it was filled with perfumed water for use at the dining-table.

Rose-water sprinkler. A small porcelain sprinkler usually in the form of a miniature watering-can, made at Coalport and elsewhere in the early decades of the 19th century. *See* WATERING PAIL.

Rosette. (1) A decorative ornament with its elements disposed on a circular plan as a stylized rose in full bloom; the equally spaced petals were sometimes surrounded by leaves. (2) A tool used in making a ROSE-ENGINE TURNED pattern.

Rosso antico (Italian). Literally, antique red. The name given by Josiah Wedgwood to his unglazed red pottery which was an improvement on ware of this kind introduced at the end of the 17th century by the Elers brothers. Decorative ware based on Greek and Roman pottery (then called antique) formed part of Wedgwood's production, hence the name. A few pieces have ENGINE-TURNED DECORATION, and a PSEUDO-CHINESE SEAL-MARK may have been used on some appropriately formed specimens. By far the greater part of the ornamental production was in the NEO-CLASSICAL STYLE; some domestic ware was also made.

Rosso di Faenza (Italian). A deep Indian red found in small passages on some ISTORIATO ware and other pieces of maiolica attributed to Maestro Virgiliotto Calamelli, a potter from Faenza, *c.* 1543. Sometimes called *rosso Virgiliotto*.

Rote Drache (German). The RED DRAGON PATTERN.

Rouge-box. A small shallow decorative porcelain box used by ladies in the 18th century for carrying rouge. The French term is *boîte à fard*.

Rouge-de-fer (French). Same as IRON-RED.

Rouge d'or (French). Literally, red from gold. A Chinese colour belonging to the FAMILLE ROSE, the same as rose-pink. A variant of the PURPLE OF CASSIUS. The reference to 'gold' arises from the use of gold chloride.

Rouleau vase. A type of vase, almost cylindrical and slightly tapering towards the base, which has a short vertical narrow neck. Vases of this shape were made in China during the reign of K'ang Hsi (1662–1722) and extensively imported from China and Japan by the Dutch, who copied it and called it a *Rolwagen*. It was later made by Continental potteries copying Dutch wares. The Chinese term is *yu-ch'ui p'ing*, although the term *chih-ch'ui p'ing* is sometimes used to designate this shape.

Round game, The. A decorative subject on English porcelain depicting a group of children in a woodland scene playing a 'corner' or 'round' game. It was taken from a HANCOCK ENGRAVING dated 1754, itself adapted from an original engraving by Nicholas Larmessin after a painting by Lancret.

Roundel. A circular decorated PLAQUE.

Royal armorial ware. Porcelain, usually Chinese export porcelain, bearing the heraldic arms and emblems of a Royal House or of a member of the family. *See* ARMORIAL WARE.

Rouleau vase. Vase with enamel decoration in the *famille verte* palette, reign of K'ang Hsi (1662–1722). Victoria and Albert Museum, London.

Royal French service. Platter from the service, with view of the Palace of Versailles, Sèvres, 1821–22. Wellington Museum, Apsley House, London.

Royal Lily pattern. Porcelain mug with underglaze blue decoration, and unglazed fragment excavated at the factory site, Worcester, *c.* 1785. Courtesy, Worcester Royal Porcelain Co.

Royal French service. A porcelain dessert-service originally consisting of 48 pieces made by the Sèvres factory, 1821–22, and presented to the first Duke of Wellington by Louis XVIII. It has a *gros bleu* ground with a gilt double-scroll foliate border, with painting in reserves depicting notable places in France. Now at Apsley House, London.

Royal Lily pattern. A European decorative pattern inspired by the Chinese ASTER PATTERN from the later years of the Ming dynasty. It is in the form of radiating blue vertical panels of stylized lilies enriched, in the European version, with gilding. It was used at Meissen (called *Blaublümchenmuster*) with 6 panels, at Worcester, from *c.* 1780, with 8 panels, and at Caughley with 10 panels. At Worcester it was originally called the Blue Lily pattern, but after being selected by Queen Charlotte during a visit to the factory in 1788, it was called the Royal Lily pattern, and has been thus known ever since. It is still produced there.

Rubans, à (French). Literally, with ribbons. A decoration employed at Sèvres in which different colours were combined in a distinctive way in interlacing ribbon patterns.

Ruby-back porcelain. A type of Chinese porcelain, chiefly made during the reign of Yung Chêng (1723–35), the underside of which, except for the inside of the foot-ring, is covered by a dark rose opaque enamel of the same kind as the predominating pigment of the FAMILLE ROSE palette. Much of it came from Canton. Specimens are always meticulously painted and of fine quality.

Ruby lustre. A LUSTRE developed at Gubbio by Maestro Giorgio Andreoli in the early decades of the 16th century, and used on maiolica made there, and also on wares sent to him to be over-decorated by Castel Durante, Faenza, and Deruta. It was derived from gold.

Rustic Seasons. Group of porcelain figures, Bristol (Champion's factory), *c.* 1772. Courtesy, Christie's.

Rum kettle. A type of KETTLE for serving heated rum drinks; it was usually smaller than a tea-kettle or punch-pot, and often had a beak-shaped pouring lip instead of a spout. Examples were made by Wedgwood in black basaltes.

Runner. A pointed tool used to decorate the body of a piece of pottery while it is CHEESE-HARD and revolving on the POTTER'S WHEEL.

Rural Lovers, The. A transfer-printed decorative subject frequently found on Worcester porcelain; it depicts a milkmaid in conversation with a boy under a tree in a pasture with cows. The subject was adapted by Robert Hancock from an engraving, published in 1760 by Francis Vivares, after *The Rural Lovers* by Gainsborough; *see* HANCOCK ENGRAVINGS. It was also the subject of a group modelled by Joseph Willems and produced at Chelsea *c.* 1749.

Rustic handle. Same as CRABSTOCK HANDLE. *See* BRANCH HANDLE.

Rustic Seasons, The. A group of the FOUR SEASONS in which the figures are distinguished from those in the usual classical attire by their contemporary rustic (or pseudo-rustic) dress. Examples come from Champion's Bristol factory, *c.* 1770.

Ryu (Japanese). The dragon with three claws, depicted as one of the FABULOUS ANIMALS on Arita porcelain.

S

S-scroll. A decorative pattern basically in the form of the letter *S* but variously proportioned. Especially to be seen on porcelain in the rococo style.

S-shaped handle. A handle in the form of a letter *S*. *See* BÖTTGER HANDLE.

Sack-bottle. A globular bottle or jug with a narrow neck, a small mouth and one large loop handle. Made of London delftware it has the word 'Sack' (sherry) inscribed on it in blue, usually with a mid-17th-century date, the earliest known example being dated 1628.

Sacred Pearl. The same as the Flaming Pearl. It occurs as part of a Chinese porcelain design which depicts two opposing dragons with, between them, a circular object with flame-like appendages, which may, in fact, be intended as the sun. The circular object is usually termed the Sacred Pearl.

Sacred Pearl. Porcelain plate with decoration showing dragons chasing the Sacred Pearl amid clouds; reign of Chêng-tê (1506–21). British Museum, London.

Sacrificial red. Underglaze copper red. Probably so called because of the legend that the colour was unattainable, despite numerous experiments to that end, until a potter sacrificed himself by throwing himself into the furnace of the kiln. This might have some foundation in fact, since the combustion of the body would provide the additional carbon monoxide necessary to develop this colour. The Chinese term is *chi-hung*. *See* REDUCING ATMOSPHERE.

Saffer-pot. Same as SAFFRON-POT.

Saffron-pot. A small, spittoon-shaped vessel about 4 inches high, perhaps used to grow saffron (crocus) bulbs. The pots were made at Caughley, where they were sometimes called saffer-pots.

Sagger. Sometimes saggar or seggar. A protective case of fire-clay used to surround objects during firing. Some have the wall pierced at irregular intervals by triangular peg-holes, into which are placed SAGGER PINS to support the ware being fired. They are universally used. *See* KILN FURNITURE.

Sagger. Sagger containing bowl of Chün yao, ht $4\frac{7}{8}$ in., Sung dynasty (960–1280). Victoria and Albert Museum, London.

Sagger pins. Triangular, tapering pieces of fire-clay which are inserted through triangular peg-holes in the walls of the SAGGER, and on which the pieces being fired rest. The length of the pins varies from 1 to 3 inches, depending on the thickness of the sagger wall and the size of the piece to be supported. *See* KILN FURNITURE.

Sagging. The softening of a piece of ceramic ware in the kiln due to excessive heating, resulting in malformation. Before the invention of accurate methods of temperature-control it was a not infrequent accident for part of the contents of a kiln to sag in this way, and those grossly overheated sometimes melted. In England BONE-ASH was added to porcelain, probably from the 1750s onwards, in an attempt to provide a more stable body and thus prevent sagging.

Saiko Kutani (Japanese). A type of KUTANI PORCELAIN, also called 'revived Kutani' or 'Hachiroemon Kutani', made at

St George and the Dragon. Pottery group by Ralph Wood, Staffordshire, *c.* 1760–70. Burnap Collection, William Rockhill Nelson Gallery of Art, Kansas City, Mo.

the site of the old Kutani kiln during the 19th century (when manufacture was revived there in 1811 by Yoshidaya Denemon), and elsewhere in Kaga province. The products, decorated in red and gold, are sometimes known in Japan as Wakasugi ware.

Saint Anthony cow-creamer. A type of cow-creamer made at the St Anthony pottery at Newcastle-upon-Tyne, 1780–1804; it was characterized by the cow's wide, blue-ringed eyes.

Saint-Cloud cup. A style of small coffee-cup, the upper part being cylindrical, then tapering towards the foot-ring; the lower two-thirds of the sides are reeded. It was introduced at Sèvres.

Saint George and the Dragon. A well-known equestrian group in pottery made by Ralph Wood, *c.* 1760, and decorated in coloured glazes. It was later copied by Enoch Wood and other Staffordshire potters.

Saint-Porchaire ware. White earthenware with an inlaid decoration made at Saint-Porchaire, France. It is similar to *faïence d'Oiron* and both have been termed 'Henri Deux ware'. It was first made during the reign of François I and continued under Henri II, the period of manufacture lasting from *c.* 1520 to *c.* 1550. The body is fine in texture, and the thin, overlying lead glaze has the appearance of a varnish and gives the ware a cream colour. Before firing, designs were impressed into the clay with metal stamps of the kind which bookbinders used for tooling leather. These impressed designs were filled with coloured slip, especially yellow ochre and brown. The inlaid designs were scrolls, coats of arms, and a variety of abstract motifs current at the time, especially those employed for ornamenting book-covers. Relief-work in the form of masks and similar details was often added. Less than a hundred pieces have survived, and nearly all of these are in public museums. The ware was imitated in England in the 19th century, *c.* 1860, by Minton especially. *See* FAÏENCE À NIELLURE.

Saké bottle. A Japanese pottery or porcelain bottle, often of square section, for holding *saké* (Japanese rice wine). Copies were made at Meissen.

Salad-plate. A lozenge- or crescent-shaped plate for salad, made to be placed alongside a dinner-plate.

Saliera (Italian). A salt-cellar of Italian maiolica. It formed a unit of the VASO PUERPERALE.

Salière. The French term for SALT-CELLAR. *See* SALT.

Saint-Porchaire ware. Salt with inlaid decoration, *c.* 1550. Victoria and Albert Museum, London.

Salopian ware. Porcelain made at Caughley, near Broseley, Shropshire (the Roman Salopia), by Thomas Turner. The factory, started in 1772, was sold to John Rose of Coalport in 1799. Both body and glaze are very similar to those of Worcester, and much of the ware was decorated in underglaze blue, either painted or transfer-printed. The rare polychrome specimens were probably painted by the outside decorator, Humphrey Chamberlain, who was a partner with his brother, Robert, in the founding of the Chamberlain factory at Worcester.

Salt. A SALT-CELLAR; the addition of the word 'cellar' came about as a result of the corruption of the French *salière*.

Salt-cellar. A small shallow bowl, usually circular, for holding table-salt. Some examples have a moulded base and others with three or four short legs are not unusual. French salt-cellars in faience are sometimes square, or rectangular with two wells. Occasionally a cover is provided. Many Italian examples in maiolica are relatively large, some having a figure mounted on the rim at each end. *See* SALT; CRAYFISH SALT; SCROLL SALT; TRENCHER SALT.

Salt-cellar. Porcelain with polychrome enamel decoration, Frankenthal, *c.* 1770. Victoria and Albert Museum, London.

Salt-kit. A dome-topped jar, usually of brown saltglazed earthenware, with a cylindrical body, loop handle, and a circular aperture in the side for filling and emptying. It was used for storing salt. Examples are also to be found in slipware, and were among the products of the Sussex potteries. *See* BALLOT BOX; BARM POT.

Saltglazed ware. Stoneware glazed with salt, of which there are a number of varieties. The stoneware of the Rhineland is the earliest European example of this type of ware, and it occurs in both a brown and a grey form. Brown stoneware was first made towards the end of the 17th century in England and has continued in use till the present day, although it is now principally employed for such utility wares as drain-pipes. During the 18th century a thin, lightweight and durable stoneware was developed in England, and was extremely popular till it was superseded by porcelain and creamware.

Most stoneware was glazed by throwing common salt into the kiln when the furnace had reached its maximum temperature of about 1000°C. The salt split into its component elements: chlorine, which passed out of the kiln-chimney, and sodium, which combined with the silicates in the body of the ware to form a thin, glass-like glaze. Sometimes a shovelful of red lead was added at the same time as the salt, a practice which had the effect of making the glaze thicker and glassier. John Dwight patented the process in 1693, and it was exploited soon afterwards by Nottingham potters, who produced a brown-glazed ware. By 1720, using a white clay combined with fusible rock, the potters of Staffordshire had succeeded in producing ware white enough to compete to some extent with imports of Chinese porcelain, and excellent tableware was produced which was decorated with low relief and piercing. Dwight also made a light buff (mouse-coloured) stoneware which was perhaps porcellaneous, since some of the few surviving specimens are very slightly translucent. He produced some notable figures in this ware, but they seem to have been hand-modelled and not reproduced.

Salt-kit. Brown-glazed earthenware with slip decoration, English, early 17th century. Victoria and Albert Museum, London.

The later saltglazed ware of the 1750s is a very light buff in colour, usually with a thin, hard glaze of a texture resembling the skin of an orange. Soon after 1750 ware of this kind was decorated with enamel colours, some notable work, especially figures, being done by William Duesbury, later of Derby, who had an enamelling studio in London at this time. A good deal of such ware was transfer-printed by Sadler and Green of Liverpool. Little ware of this kind was produced after 1770, its place being taken by creamware, but brown saltglazed ware continued to be produced until well into the 19th century, gin-bottles in a variety of forms by Doulton and Stephen Green of Lambeth forming one example of an interesting group.

Samarkand ware. Pottery made in the Transoxiana region of Central Asia, near its chief city of Samarkand, in the 9th and 10th centuries AD. The body was of red or pink clay usually covered with a white slip, and decoration was of a formal kind.

Samian pottery. A red glossy pottery made between *c.* 100 BC and the 3rd century AD. According to Pliny the Elder it was so called because of its resemblance to pottery made on the island of Samos, but the term, in fact, covers wares made in many places in the Roman provinces, including: Arretium (Arezzo), Italy; Saguntum (Spain); and several centres in southern France (e.g.

Samian pottery. Bowl (Dragendorff shape 37) with relief ornament, Central Gaul, Trajanic date. British Museum, London.

Millau). It has even been suggested that it was made in Britain, but there seems little doubt that most of the specimens recovered were imported. Samian ware is decorated, as a rule, with relief ornament, and it was made in moulds, some of which have survived. On some examples the name of the potter is stamped on the base. The colour (a sealing-wax red) of this ware is derived from red ochre mixed with the clay. *See* ARRETINE WARE; TERRA SIGILLATA.

Samovar. An urn-shaped container for water for making tea, with a spigot at the base for drawing off the contents. Literally, the word means self-boiler, and the samovar usually has an interior tube heated from the bottom for the purpose of boiling the water. For this reason the term is more correctly applied to metal containers, and pottery and porcelain pieces of this character are preferably termed TEA-URNS.

Samson copies. Figures and other objects, usually in hard-paste porcelain, made by Edmé Samson et Cie of Paris; they are copies of Chinese, Continental, and English porcelain. The reproductions are very close to the originals, but the colours are usually inaccurate; hence the wares can be fairly readily detected as copies. The firm has claimed that all copies made by it are marked with the letter *S* (in addition to the mark of the factory which produced the original), but this mark can be removed with hydrofluoric acid without leaving any very noticeable trace. *See* REPRODUCTION.

San Bernardino rays. Maiolica roundel with rays around the ledge, Faenza, 1491. Victoria and Albert Museum, London.

San Bernardino rays. A decorative pattern in the form of a series of snake-like curved lines derived from the badge of St Bernardino of Siena. It was used from the 15th century in the decoration of maiolica from Faenza and Gubbio. Also called the 'wavy ray border'.

San-ts'ai (Chinese). 'Three-coloured'. This term is used in two senses. (1) The streaked and dappled pottery in three principal colours made during the T'ang dynasty (618–906). (2) A variety of pottery, popular during the Ming and Ch'ing dynasties, covered with coloured glazes (usually manganese-purple, yellow, and green) which are kept apart from each other by the incisions which delineate the design. *See* ENAMEL ON BISCUIT; FA-HUA.

Sand-box. A container with a pierced top, formerly used for sprinkling sand on ink to absorb the moisture. *See* POUNCE-POT.

Sandwich service. Same as SUPPER-SET.

Sang-de-boeuf (French). Literally, ox-blood. A brilliant red glaze which exhibits patches resembling the coagulation of ox-blood, principally on the shoulders of vases and near the base. The colouring agent was copper oxide fired in a reducing atmosphere, and it was developed in China during the Ch'ing dynasty. The best specimens have been attributed to a particular family of potters (*see* LANG YAO). At first the effects of copper oxide used in this way were fortuitous. Later, towards the end of the 18th century, they were to some extent brought under control. Transmutations of this kind came to be called FLAMBÉ glazes; the Chinese term for such ware is *pien yao*. *See* CHÜN YAO.

Sang-de-pigeon (French). Literally, pigeon's blood. A reduced copper-red glaze used in China during the 18th and 19th centuries.

Sanggam celadon. A type of inlaid CELADON developed in south Korea in the 13th century. The design was first incised and then filled in with white or black slip under a celadon glaze. Additional decoration in iron or copper oxide sometimes occurs. *See* MISHIMA.

Sanitary ware. Ceramic ware intended for hygienic purposes, such as W.C. pedestals, wash-basins, bidets, chamber-pots, bed-pans, *bourdalous*, urinals, and spittoons. In the 19th century W.C. pedestals, bidets, and wash-basins were often decorated, usually with floral motifs, and are now sometimes employed for decorative purposes.

Sardinian green. A ground colour introduced in the 19th century by the Staffordshire firm of Spode.

Sassonia, alla. The Italian term for ware in the style of Meissen, the phrase being derived from Saxonia (Saxony); the Meissen factory was situated some 12 miles from Dresden, the capital of Saxony. The French equivalent is SAXE.

Satsuma ware. A type of Japanese pottery made, from the early years of the 17th century, by Korean potters who had settled at Satsuma, on the island of Kyushu (Japan). Until the end of the 18th century it was usually unpainted, but it then included a cream-coloured ware with a finely crackled glaze, decorated with enamel colours and gilding. The painting became increasingly elaborate, covering the entire surface, but done with painstaking care and considerable skill. Crude versions (erroneously described as Satsuma) were exported in the 19th century to the European market; these were made elsewhere, probably at Kyoto, especially for this purpose (*see* KYOTO WARE). True Satsuma is comparatively rare outside Japan.

Satyr mug. Mug, ht 8 in., by Ralph Wood, *c.* 1780–90. Burnap Collection, William Rockhill Nelson Gallery of Art, Kansas City, Mo.

Satyr mug. A mug moulded in the form of a satyr head, with curly beard, prominent nose, and a crown of vine leaves. Some are made as jugs with a lip in the form of a mask representing a laughing face and a handle in the form of a figure of a man. Pieces of this kind were made by the Ralph Woods from models by Jean Voyez. *See* TOBY JUG; MASK JUGS AND MUGS; BACCHUS JUG.

Sauce-boat. A boat-shaped vessel, usually with a handle at one end and a pouring lip at the other, for serving sauce or gravy. The vessel usually rests on a spreading base or on short legs, and often has a cover. Some have a lip at both ends and two side-handles. A few are in the form of an animal, such as a duck or a dolphin, with the head as the spout and the tail as the handle. Some rest on a small conforming dish known in France as a *présentoir*. In design 18th-century sauce-boats are very commonly based on that of contemporary silver. The French term is *saucière*. *See* CREAM-BOAT; ASPARAGUS BUTTER-BOAT; DOUBLE-LIPPED SAUCE-BOAT; PIÉDOUCHE; BOURDALOU.

Sauce-boat. Irish delftware, with double handles and lips, *c.* 1750. Burnap Collection, William Rockhill Nelson Gallery of Art, Kansas City, Mo.

Sauce-tureen. A small covered tureen, sometimes with a conforming stand, for serving sauce.

Saucer. A small dish of concave form, usually circular, either for serving food or as a stand for a cup. Generally, those for use with a cup have a slight depression in the centre in which to place the cup. *See* TREMBLEUSE. Shallow dishes of saucer shape were commonly used in China to contain food, instead of dishes with a well and ledge which are purely a European shape; the Chinese type is termed a saucer-dish. In England a teacup and matching coffee-cup were often sold with a single saucer *en suite*, as an economy. The French term for saucer is *soucoupe*; the German is *Schale*. *See* TEA-SAUCER.

Saucer-dish. *See* SAUCER; DISH; COUPE.

Saucière (French). The French term for SAUCE-BOAT.

Saupoudrière (French). The French term for SUGAR-CASTER.

Saw-edged border. A border pattern with a serrated edge.

Sawankhalok ware (Siamese). Ware made at Sawankhalok, the old capital of Siam. The body is greyish-white, burning brown in exposed places. Some dishes have a ring underneath which is bare of glaze, an indication of the method of support in the kiln. Celadon wares are sometimes painted in black or brownish underglaze pigment. The glaze, usually with an accidental CRACKLE, is pale green inclining to brown. Wares are contemporary with the Yüan dynasty (1280–1368) in China. *See* ANNAMESE WARE.

Saxon service. Plate with view of Apsley House, London; Meissen, *c.* 1818. Wellington Museum, Apsley House.

Saxe. A term used in France to refer to the porcelain of Meissen. The Meissen factory is situated near Dresden, the capital of the former Electorate of Saxony. *Saxe au point* is the German *Punktzeit* ('dot' period), 1763–74, during which a dot was placed between the hilts of the crossed swords mark. *Saxe à l'étoile* refers to the period of the directorate of Count Camillo Marcolini (1774–1814), when an asterisk was similarly used. *See* DRESDEN CHINA.

Saxon service. A porcelain dessert-service originally of 134 pieces made at Meissen, *c.* 1818, and painted under the direction of G. F Kersting; it was presented to the first Duke of Wellington by Frederick Augustus IV of Saxony. The pieces are decorated with encircling gilt laurel wreaths banded with green and white ribbon. The wells of the plates depict battle-scenes, but two of them show contemporary views of Apsley House, London. The service is now at Apsley House.

Sbiancheggiato (Italian). A type of decoration on Italian maiolica of the early 16th century which was done by heightening the lights of the pattern with a very white pigment (*bianchetto*), and by executing white designs on a white ground. The technique was often employed around the centre of a plate where the well joins the ledge, forming a zone of white enamel in a diaper pattern.

Scent-bottles. Porcelain, ht approx. 3 in., Chelsea, *c.* 1760. Victoria and Albert Museum, London.

Scaldavivande (Italian). (1) A vessel in which food was kept warm (*see* FOOD-WARMER); when used for beverages, a vessel of this kind is termed a *scaldabevande.* (2) A type of soup-tureen which rests on another bowl containing hot water. Inside the second bowl there is, occasionally, a third bowl (which contains meat or other food) suspended in the hot water.

Scale-ground. An IMBRICATED ground pattern composed of overlapping scales, especially popular as a decoration of Worcester porcelain from about 1760 to 1785. The pattern was produced by painting each scale separately, or by applying a ground and then wiping out the individual scales. Much ware thus decorated is of the underglaze blue scale variety, but examples are known in overglaze (or enamel) yellow, brick-red, pink, puce, and light blue. Wares decorated with underglaze blue scale-grounds and panels left unpainted were supplied by the Worcester factory to the independent decorator, James Giles, who added painting in reserves, often of exotic birds. It is possible that some of the enamel scale-grounds were done by him on white Worcester porcelain. Although often referred to as 'fish-scale', a fishy origin is very doubtful. Scale-patterns of this kind may have come originally from peacock's feather ornament on ISNIK

POTTERY which inspired similar patterns on Italian maiolica. Such patterns occurred at Meissen, Vienna, and Berlin long before they were used at Worcester, but mainly as a border pattern, and they did not reach the same degree of elaboration as at the English factory.

Scale-moulded. Moulded with an IMBRICATED pattern in low-relief. *See* SCALE-GROUND. Wares of this kind, imitating the globe artichoke, were made at the French porcelain factory of Saint-Cloud at the beginning of the 18th century.

Scalloped. Having a continuous series of segments of a circle, resembling the edge of a scallop shell. Often a rim was so shaped, sometimes with barbs alternating with the scallops.

Scannellato (Italian). A type of GADROONED or FLUTED maiolica dish, made particularly at Faenza from *c.* 1520, and a little later at Castel Durante. It has a central medallion painted with a single figure.

Scent-barrel. A small barrel-shaped receptacle for perfume; about 4–5 inches high, it has a bung-hole in the centre of the side. Examples were made of Bristol and Irish delftware, *c.* 1722–40.

Scent-bottle. A small perfume-bottle made in a wide variety of forms, often those of figures or animals. Scent-bottles were made of terracotta by the Egyptians, Greeks, and Romans. Porcelain scent-bottles were very popular during the 18th century, and those made at Chelsea are especially sought today. They were also made at Meissen and other German factories, and in France and Italy. Double and triple specimens are known.

Scented pottery. A type of pottery made in Portugal and Spain in imitation of scented BOCCARO WARE.

Sceptre border. A Chinese border pattern (often copied on European wares made in imitation) in the form of a series of adjacent JU'I (sceptre) heads in profile. *See* JU'I BORDER.

Schlachtenszenen. The German term for BATTLE-SCENES.

Schmetterlingmuster (German). Literally, butterfly pattern. A decorative design used at Meissen depicting, in the centre, a butterfly on a flowering branch with sprays of INDIANISCHE BLUMEN. *See* BIENENMUSTER.

Schnabelkanne (German). Literally, beak jug. A type of salt-glazed jug of RHENISH STONEWARE, made especially during the late 16th and the early part of the 17th century. It had a tall cylindrical neck, globular body, a loop handle, and a long beak-shaped BRIDGE-SPOUT. It was fitted with a lid and metal mounts. Some were decorated with relief ornament.

Schneeballenvase. The German term for a SNOWBALL VASE.

Schnelle (German). A type of stoneware tankard made in the 16th century at Siegburg in the Rhineland. It is tall and tapering and usually has three vertical panels with biblical or mythological subjects in relief; it has a hinged pewter or silver lid and thumb-piece. It is known in French as a *canette*.

Schnittblumen (German). Literally, cut flowers. An early form of DEUTSCHE BLUMEN which depicted the flowers as individual cut blooms.

Schnabelkanne. Rhenish stoneware, with bridge-spout and silver mounts; ht 10¾ in. Siegburg, 1590. Victoria and Albert Museum, London.

Schnelle. Rhenish stoneware, ht 16 in., Siegburg, 1574. Victoria and Albert Museum, London.

Schwarzlot. Bowl and cover with characteristic decoration, Vienna (du Paquier's factory), *c.* 1730. British Museum, London.

Scholar's table, equipment for. Objects employed in Chinese calligraphy and painting, which were made in porcelain, ivory, jade, and other materials, e.g. PENCIL (brush; *pi*), BRUSH-REST (*pi chia* or *pi shen*), BRUSH-WASHER (*pi hsi*), wrist-rest (*pi ko*), INK-SLAB (*mo yen*), WATER-POT (*shui ch'êng*), WATER-DROPPER (*shui ti*), PAPER-WEIGHT (*chên chih*), TABLE-SCREEN (*yen p'ing*), and the box for seal colour (*yin sê chih*).

Schraubflasche (German). Literally, screw-flask. A type of stoneware flask having a screw cover. The flask is of globular shape with sides flattened into four or six panels decorated with religious inscriptions and relief ornament. They were made at Kreussen in the 17th century, and similar flasks in MAIOLICA came from Savona (Italy).

Schwarzlot (German). Decoration in a black, linear style inspired by engravings, principally used by German HAUSMALER during the last quarter of the 17th century and the first half of the 18th. It occurs on both faience and porcelain, as well as glass. In many cases iron-red is employed as a flesh colour, and a little gilding has often been added. JESUIT PORCELAIN from China, which is decorated in this way, was undoubtedly inspired by European *Schwarzlot* as well as by engravings.

Scolopendrium pattern. Decoration on coffee-cup and saucer, Worcester, First period. Courtesy, Sotheby's.

Scodella (Italian). Sometimes *scudella* or *scodello*. A dish of maiolica with a deep central well and sloping sides. The word was originally applied to the table of a POTTER'S WHEEL but was later employed for dishes of this kind formed on the wheel. *See* PIATTO DA POMPA.

Scodella da donna di parto (Italian). Same as VASO PUERPERALE.

Scolopendrium pattern. A moulded and painted decorative pattern on some Chelsea and Worcester porcelain in the form of the leaves of the hart's-tongue fern.

Sconce. A bracket with a projecting CANDLEHOLDER for attachment to a wall. Some ornate types include a mirror or a plaque or figures which act as candleholders, and some have several candleholders. The candle-nozzle, into which the candle is inserted, usually has a drip-pan affixed to it. Sometimes called a wall sconce or *bras de cheminée*.

Scratch blue. Loving cup, salt-glazed stoneware, Staffordshire, 1748. City Museums, Stoke-on-Trent.

Scratch blue. White saltglazed stoneware with incised inscriptions, stylized flowers, birds, or rouletted patterns filled in with ZAFFER before firing. It was made between 1724 and 1776 in Staffordshire, and possibly at Liverpool and elsewhere in England. The technique was revived by Doulton in the 1870s, using black and brown pigments instead of blue. *See* SCRATCH BROWN.

Scratch brown. Saltglazed stoneware with incised decoration, the incisions being filled with brown (manganese) pigment. *See* SCRATCH BLUE.

Scratched cross ware. Porcelain ware, mainly jugs and mugs, marked with incised lines, usually a cross, within the foot-ring. These lines seem to have been WORKMEN'S MARKS, and most porcelain of this kind has its origin in the west of England during the period 1750–60.

Scratched marks. Marks scratched into the paste of porcelain ware as a guide to the kilnmaster to indicate the composition, or as the modeller's mark of approval of a REPAIRER'S work. Sometimes painted marks were used for the same purpose, such as the blue dot on some fine Sèvres ware to indicate to the kiln workmen that special care should be exercised in firing such pieces.

Scrodled ware. Objects made from WEDGED pieces of clay of different colours. *See* SOLID AGATE WARE; LAVA WARE.

Scroll. A decorative pattern in the form of a spiral or convoluted curve, re-entrant or continuous, including relief ornament in this form which is based on the curve made by a parchment scroll. *See* DOUBLE SCROLL.

Scroll border. *See* WAVE BORDER; VITRUVIAN SCROLL.

Scroll salt. A type of SALT-CELLAR made of Lambeth delftware after a silver model. It has three projecting arms, said to be supports for a napkin or bowl.

Seal. A device bearing a monogram or design in INTAGLIO for imparting an impression on wax. Seals have been mounted in porcelain shanks or shafts, usually about 1 inch in height, by many factories, notably the fine examples from Chelsea in the form of figures, Cupids, birds, and animals. *See* TOYS.

Seal. Porcelain mounted in gold, Chelsea, *c.* 1755; ht $1\frac{3}{8}$ in. Victoria and Albert Museum, London.

Seal-mark. A mark on Chinese porcelain, usually in square form, which indicates the dynasty and the name of one of the emperors. Marks such as these are so called because they were normally made by seals. *See* CHINESE SEAL-MARK; PSEUDO-CHINESE SEAL-MARK.

Sealing-wax red. The same as ARMENIAN RED or tomato red. *See* IMPASTO RED.

Seam mark. A slight, narrow ridge on pottery or porcelain ware which marks the place where the joints of the mould have allowed clay to enter during the process of formation. A well-marked seam often goes hand in hand with blunted relief decoration, and is indicative of a well-worn mould. On the finest wares seam marks were usually smoothed away by FETTLING before firing.

Seasons, The. *See* FOUR SEASONS, THE; RUSTIC SEASONS.

Seau à bouteille (French). A wine-cooler. A bucket-shaped receptacle for holding ice to chill a single bottle of wine. It may be with or without handles, but has no cover; it is similar in shape to a SEAU À GLACE, but larger. Examples of smaller size are intended for half-bottles; this type is called *seau à demi-bouteille.*

Seau à glace (French). An ice-pail. It is bucket-shaped, and occurs with or without side-handles. The flat cover is recessed, and usually has a ring-shaped vertical handle. Also called a *jatte à glace.*

Seau à liqueur (French). A cooler for a liqueur glass, comparable to a SEAU À BOUTEILLE, but smaller and sometimes oval and divided into two compartments.

Seau à verre (French). The same as the English MONTEITH; also termed a *verrière*, *rafraîchissoir*, or *seau crenelé*.

Seau à bouteille. One of a pair, bombé shape, Meissen, *c.* 1750. Courtesy, Sotheby's.

Seaweed, ashes of. Ash obtained from burning seaweed for use as a flux. *See* ALKALINE GLAZE; BONE-ASH; FERN-ASH.

Seau à glace. One of a pair, ht 13¼ in., the cover having a ring handle, Spode. Courtesy, Christie's.

Secret decoration. *See* AN HUA.

Section. The outline of an object as it would appear if dissected by a plane, either horizontally or vertically.

Seeded ground. A ground or border pattern made up of numerous small dots, giving a seeded effect. The French term is *semé*.

Seger cone. *See* CONE.

Seggar. Same as SAGGER.

Semiove cup. A style of small coffee-cup of semi-ovoid shape with a foot-ring and a Q-shaped handle; the lower half of the cup is reeded. Introduced at Sèvres in 1837.

Senses. *See* FIVE SENSES, THE.

Sepulchral cone. An Egyptian conical receptacle with a flat bottom made of pottery in which have been found the mummies of birds and animals. Also termed a mummy-cone.

Series. A number of objects or figures related in form and style, and suited to each other, but not incomplete if used separately; unlike a pair, set, or group, a series does not consist of a definite number of pieces, examples being the CRIS DE PARIS or the AFFENKAPELLE, so that further items may be added.

Serrated. Notched, or resembling the teeth of a saw. *See* SAW-EDGED BORDER.

Servant plates. A set of six English delftware plates having different, but related, inscriptions, each a line from a doggerel verse. *See* MERRY MAN PLATES; GRACE PLATES.

Service. A set of tableware, including both hollow-ware and flatware, made *en suite*. *See* BREAKFAST-SERVICE; DÉJEUNER SERVICE; CABARET SERVICE; DESSERT-SERVICE; DINNER-SERVICE; SOLITAIRE SERVICE; TEA-SERVICE; COFFEE-SERVICE; TÊTE-À-TÊTE SERVICE; SUPPER SET; COMPOSITE SERVICE.

Set. More than two objects of the same or similar form, suited to each other and intended to be used together as a complete unit, but not essentially identical, such as the pieces of a chess-set. An extension of a PAIR. *See* SERIES; GROUP; SERVICE; HARLEQUIN SET; COMPANION-PIECE.

Seto ware. Pottery made at Seto (Owari province), the classical pottery centre of Japan. Apart from a great deal of pottery of a kind highly valued in Japan for aesthetic qualities which are not easily appreciated by Europeans, Seto was the 19th-century source of very large vases decorated, probably in Tokyo, for export to the West. The designs are debased and overcrowded.

Settling-pan. A shallow oval pan in which milk was allowed to stand so that the cream would rise to the surface for skimming. Some were made by Wedgwood in creamware, *c.* 1790. *See* PANCHEON.

Seven-border plate. A Chinese porcelain dish decorated in the FAMILLE ROSE palette, often with a RUBY-BACK, and having a broad border of seven different concentric-patterns. The best examples were made in the reign of Yung Chêng (1722–36).

Sèvres blue. Same as BLEU CÉLESTE. The term is sometimes erroneously employed to describe the darker enamel blue ground colour known as BLEU DE ROI.

Sèvres ground colours. Ground colours introduced by Vincennes-Sèvres from 1738 onwards, and often developed by experts at the factory. The principal colours identified with Sèvres, but frequently copied elsewhere, include: BLEU CÉLESTE; BLEU DE ROI (*bleu royal, beau bleu, bleu nouveau*); BLEU LAPIS; BLEU TURC; BLEU TURQUIN; GROS BLEU; BLEU NUAGÉ; ROSE POMPADOUR; JAUNE JONQUILLE; VERT PRÉ (*vert anglais*); VERT POMME (*vert jaune*). The effect of ground colours was often softened by a contrasting overglaze diaper pattern, e.g. *œil-de-perdrix, caillouté.*

Sgraffito (Italian). Also *graffiato* and *sgraffiato.* Decoration made by scratching or incising the design through slip applied to the body before glazing so as to reveal the body beneath, or by incising through glaze to produce a like effect, sometimes called *a stecco.* The technique is extremely widespread, and was used both in the East and West. In very rare instances it was used on English delftware, where it had to be done with extreme care so that the incised decoration pierced only the surface of the painted area, exposing the white of the tin glaze and not the colour of the body below.

Shabti. *See* USHABTI.

Shadowy blue ware. *See* YING CH'ING.

Shagreen. A decoration on some porcelain resembling the surface of the leather called shagreen, which was produced by pressing small seeds into a moist hide, then scraping them off, followed by soaking the hide to cause the indented portions to swell into a relief sharkskin effect. *See* SHARKSKIN SURFACE.

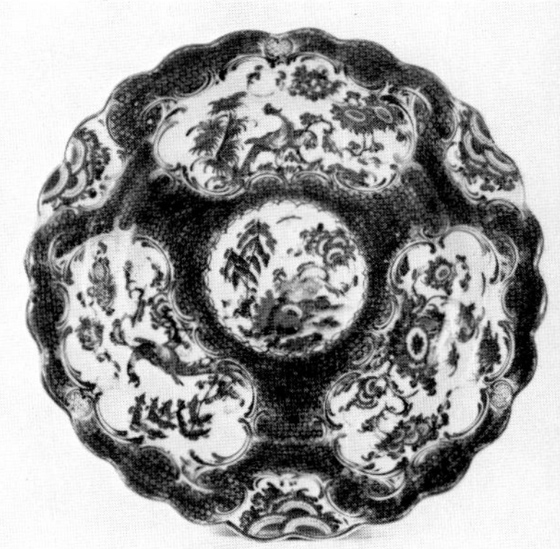

Shagreen. Plate with reserved cartouches on a shagreen ground, Worcester (First period). Courtesy, Sotheby's.

Shakespeare service. A dessert-service made at Worcester in 1853 on the theme of *A Midsummer Night's Dream*, with figures modelled in PARIAN PORCELAIN by W.B. Kirk, and with painted decoration by Thomas Bott.

Shan shui (Chinese). Literally, rocky landscape. The Chinese highly valued rocks of eccentric and unusual shapes (often of volcanic or water-worn origin) which they employed to decorate their gardens, a highly developed aspect of art in China. European potters copying Chinese designs found these forms impossible to interpret, and many curious versions of them occur, on delftware in particular.

Shard (or **sherd**). A fragment of pottery or porcelain, such as those found on excavated kiln-sites and waster-dumps. These usually serve as a reliable means of identifying similar surviving wares, but it is important to distinguish between shards found at a kiln-site, which are likely (but not necessarily) to be pieces from that factory (*see* WASTER), and those discovered on dumps which may be from other sources, not even nearby. Shards were sometimes ground up and used instead of GROG when mixing a body; this minimized subsequent shrinkage while preserving a similarity of composition. Also called a potsherd; the French term is *tesson.*

Sharkskin surface. The surface on some oriental porcelain which exhibits small raised dots close together in a manner which resembles sharkskin. *See* SHAGREEN. The opposite effect is termed a THIMBLE SURFACE.

Shaving bowl. Same as BARBER'S BOWL. *See* MAMBRINO'S HELMET.

Shaving-cup. A small oval receptacle with one half higher than the other. The upper part has a pierced floor for soap, and the lower part has a horizontal opening at the top so that a brush may be inserted into the water that fills the bottom. Shaving-cups were very commonly made in Staffordshire of earthenware in the 19th and 20th centuries.

Shell-dish. Porcelain dish, width $7\frac{7}{8}$ in., Worcester, *c*. 1770. Smithsonian Institution, Washington, D.C.

Shell centrepiece. An ornamental porcelain centrepiece for the dinner-table, with a number of scallop-shell receptacles, and decorated with seashells of several kinds, modelled in porcelain. Made at Bow and Derby soon after the middle of the 18th century.

Shell decoration. A decorative motif of painted seashells, used notably on Worcester porcelain, *c*. 1808–17, and at Coalport, *c*. 1830–45.

Shell-dish. A dish, sometimes with several receptacles, profusely decorated with modelled shells of various molluscs. *See* COCKLE-POT.

Shell-edged. A moulded border decoration on the scalloped rim of certain plates, principally of pearlware, but first used on Bow porcelain and creamware. It was popular with Wedgwood and at other Staffordshire potteries, *c*. 1779–1830. The rims were often painted with blue to harmonize with the grooved modelling of the shell edge, the brush strokes being carried towards the centre to create a feathery effect (but *see* FEATHER-EDGED). Later, a blue stripe was substituted. Some shell-edged ware has a green rim, and painted decoration in polychrome in the well.

Shi shi (Japanese). A decorative subject used on Arita ware depicting the Buddhist lion, one of the FABULOUS ANIMALS. *See* LION OF FO.

Shiba buko (Japanese). The HOB-IN-THE-WELL PATTERN.

Shigaraki-taki (Japanese). A primitive-looking pottery made at the village of Nagawo-Mura, Japan. It is a greyish-buff stoneware with a variety of streaked and spotted glazes, and includes objects intended for the TEA CEREMONY.

Ship bowl. Bristol delftware, 18th century. Ashmolean Museum, Oxford.

Ship bowl. A punch-bowl, sometimes of very large size, decorated on the bottom of the interior with the detailed depiction of a sailing ship, usually inscribed with the name of the ship, and in some cases with that of its master and home port. The bowls were made in delftware at Liverpool and Bristol, and the ships depicted were those entering these ports from Sweden and elsewhere. They were usually made for the ship's master, and date from the period 1760–70.

Shoe. A decorative faience object in the form of a lady's shoe or a sabot. Examples were made in Holland, England, and France (*see* CHOPINE). They were also made of Persian pottery. Porcelain examples were made in China, and the Chinese word *hsai* is a homonym for shoe and understanding, and hence two such objects indicating harmony were used as wedding gifts.

Shonsui (Japanese). The knowledge of porcelain-making is supposed to have been brought from China to Japan early in the 16th century by Gorodayu-go Shonsui, who settled near Arita (Hizen province), where there were deposits of the necessary raw materials. By tradition early wares in the Ming dynasty style, with added repetitive patterns in Japanese taste, are supposed to be his work. The name is also given to porcelain made in China for export to Japan. *See* GEN SHONSUI (*Ko Shonsui*); HON SHONSUI; SHONSUITEI; COLOURED SHONSUI; JAPANESE IMITATION SHONSUI; KO SOMETSUKE.

Shonsuitei The Japanese term for porcelain made in China for export to Japan in imitation of SHONSUI but of a later period, being made in the 18th, 19th, or even 20th centuries. It is also called *Ato Shonsui.*

Shop-mark. Characters on Chinese porcelain which, on translation, prove to refer to the shop or studio where it was made or painted, for example, 'Made at the Abundant Prosperity Hall of Beautiful Jade'. Marks in seal form occasionally record the name of the potter, such as 'Made by the Hsieh-chu Master', but these are uncommon. Shop-marks are usually found on Chinese export ware, and date from the end of the Ming dynasty (1368–1644).

Shou (Chinese). An ideogram which occurs in a large number of ornamental forms. It means longevity, and also peach, which symbolizes longevity; in conjunction with the bat (*fu*), it becomes FU SHOU – happiness and long life.

Shou. Double-gourd vase, decorated with various forms of the ideogram; reign of Wan-li (1573–1619). Victoria and Albert Museum, London.

Shoulder. The bulge just below the neck of a vase, bottle, or similar vessel.

Showpiece. A term erroneously applied to the PERDIFUME in the mistaken belief that such pieces, bearing the name of the maker, were intended to be placed or suspended in a dealer's shop-window for purposes of display.

Shrinkage. The contraction of pottery or porcelain during the process of firing, which varies from 2 to 20 per cent according to the composition of the body. Sometimes a copy moulded from an existing piece is revealed as such by its smaller size, which is due to shrinkage. This is the case with some of the reproductions by Edmé Samson et Cie, of Paris, of Bow figures, which are up to about one-sixth smaller than the originals. Shrinkage is reduced by mixing the clay with either grog or shards suitably ground up, but this is possible only with earthenware or stoneware. The French term for shrinkage is *retraite de la pâte.*

Shu-fu. The Chinese characters marking certain specimens of white porcelain made during the Yüan dynasty (1280–1368) which appear in low relief or in incised form. They mean 'Imperial Palace'.

Shu t'ai (Chinese). A term meaning 'soft Chün'. *See* CHÜN YAO; MA CHÜN.

Shuttle ground. A ground pattern of parallel, shuttle-like figures disposed in a checkered pattern. It is used on Japanese porcelain.

Shi shi. Decagonal bowl with characteristic Kakiemon decoration, *c.* 1700. Courtesy, Sotheby's.

Sick-pot. A term used in the *Drawing Books of the Leeds Pottery* for an invalid's FEEDING CUP.

Siegburg ware. Stoneware made at Siegburg in the Rhineland, north-east of Bonn. It was first made in the 15th century, and was originally a grey or white ware. The best-known examples are handsome *Schnellen.* Potters from Siegburg migrated to the Westerwald, *c.* 1590, settling in the village of Höhr. *See* WESTERWALD WARE; TRICHTERBECHER.

Sifter-spoon. *See* SUGAR-SPOON.

Silenus jug. A jug with sileni and, usually, garlands of grapes in relief. *See* BACCHUS JUG; SATYR MUG.

Silhouette ware. Ceramic ware decorated with silhouettes. CHINOISERIES in gold and silver silhouette were done at Meissen, Bayreuth, and elsewhere early in the 18th century. *See* ANGERSTEIN SERVICE; GILT SILHOUETTE; GOLDCHINESEN; BAYREUTH WARE.

Silver pattern. Sauce-boat moulded in a contemporary silver pattern, Worcester, *c.* 1755.

Silk-screen transfers. Designs transferred to pottery and porcelain by means of finely powdered colour sifted through a silk screen of varying density placed in contact with the surface of the ware. The pattern or design is woven into the silk in such a way that the colour passes through it only where required.

Silla dynasty (Korean). The period, *c.* 57 BC–AD 935, during which pottery and a grey stoneware were made.

Silver-lustre ware. A term often used incorrectly for LUSTRE ware having a silvery appearance due to the use of platinum salts. *See* PLATINUM LUSTRE; PLATINUM RESIST; SILVER RESIST. True silver lustre, made with silver, has a straw colour; it was first made in England, *c.* 1800–05, but had its origin much earlier in the Near East and Spain. *See* HISPANO-MORESQUE WARE.

Silver shape. Porcelain dish, based on a silver prototype, with Kakiemon-style decoration, Chelsea, *c.* 1750–58. Courtesy, Sotheby's.

Silver pattern. Pottery or porcelain the moulding of which is adapted from a silver prototype, or decorated with a pattern first used on silverware. Much 18th-century porcelain was inspired or designed by silversmiths. *See* SILVER SHAPE.

Silver resist. A misnomer for resist ware of PLATINUM LUSTRE, so called due to the silvery appearance of the object.

Silver shape. Pottery or porcelain the form of which is copied or adapted from silverware. Silversmiths were employed by some ceramic factories as designers. *See* SILVER PATTERN.

Silvering. A decorative process whereby silver was applied to pottery and porcelain glazes in the same manner as GILDING. Unlike silver used as a lustre decoration, it retained its natural colour, except that, with the passage of time, it oxidized to black.

Simple yet perfect teapot. Same as SYP TEAPOT.

Simurgh (Persian). A mythical, gigantic, long-tailed bird, probably the roc, depicted on some Near Eastern pottery. *See* PHOENIX.

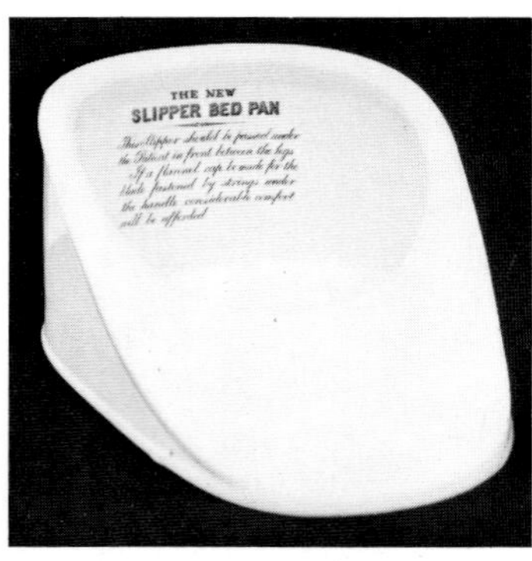

Slipper (2). Bed-pan with directions for use, English, late 19th century. Wellcome Museum, London.

Singerie (French). A painted decoration or figure depicting a monkey (French, *singe*) in costume playing a human rôle. The best-known examples are the famous *Singeries* (a series of mural paintings) by Christoph Huet at Chantilly, *c.* 1730, and – in porcelain – the very popular Meissen AFFENKAPELLE (Monkey Band) which was copied at a number of other factories.

Singing Lesson, The. A decorative subject for a transfer-print engraved by Robert Hancock, after Boitard, and used at Bow and Worcester (*see* HANCOCK ENGRAVINGS). It depicts a couple seated in a garden, the woman holding a song-book and the man playing a flute.

Siren vase. An ARYBALLOS made in the form of an Odyssean siren (a bird with the head of a woman). It occurs in pottery from Greece, made in the 6th century BC. On each side of the neck, or on the back, there is a hole for suspension, and at the top of the head is a hole for filling the vessel.

Situla (Latin). A deep receptacle for carrying water, having a wide mouth, a flat base, and two loops near the rim for attaching an overhead handle. Roman examples occur in bronze and in terracotta.

Six-character mark. A mark on the base of Chinese porcelain comprising six ideograms which record the dynasty and the name of an emperor. *See* CHARACTER MARK.

Size gilding. A primitive method of gilding by which a preparation of linseed oil was applied to the glaze with a brush, after which gold-leaf was affixed and allowed to dry without firing; as a result it subsequently rubbed off easily. The method was used on early porcelain and other wares.

Skimmer. A shallow perforated utensil for removing cream from the surface of milk. Examples were made in creamware by Wedgwood and Leeds.

Skimmer. Creamware, Wedgwood, *c.* 1780. Miss Margaret Thomas Collection, London.

Skyphos. A large drinking-cup of Greek pottery, deep and flat-bottomed, and with tapering sides. It has two loop handles, usually horizontal (but one is sometimes placed vertically), just below the rim. It is sometimes called a *kotyle*.

Skyphos. Buff-coloured earthenware, Attic, 8th century BC. Victoria and Albert Museum, London.

Sleeve vase. A type of tall cylindrical vase, the neck being only slightly waisted; it was made of Chinese porcelain during the Ming dynasty.

Slip. Potter's clay mixed with water to a semi-liquid, creamy state; used to decorate pottery, and for CASTING, SPRIGGING, and LUTING. As decoration it was washed over the entire surface to provide a contrasting colour to that of the body, or applied by TRAILING an ornamental pattern of lines and dots. Some wares are decorated with slips of several colours. The French term is *engobe*. *See* TRAILED DECORATION; SLIPWARE.

Slip-cast ware. Pottery and porcelain made by pouring slip into plaster of Paris moulds. The plaster absorbs water from the slip in contact with it, causing a firm layer to form. The surplus is then poured off, and after the remaining slip has become CHEESE-HARD the moulds are removed. Intricately modelled ware can be cast in this way. The process was introduced in England, *c.* 1745, when plaster moulds were developed, reputedly by Ralph Daniels of Cobridge.

Slip-cup. A cup with a quill spout through which slip is poured to produce TRAILED DECORATION. Also called quill-box.

Slipper. (1) A term sometimes used by Wedgwood for a BOURDALOU, which in England was usually called a coach-pot or oval chamber-pot. (2) More correctly the term refers to a type of wedge-shaped bed-pan, the front section of which is covered and slopes downwards to facilitate use; some examples have a spout at the rear for emptying.

Slipware. A general term for pottery decorated predominantly with slip. *See* COMBED DECORATION; TOFT WARE; WROTHAM WARE.

Sloane, Hans, flowers. A floral decoration employed at Chelsea, *c.* 1752–56, in the tradition of DEUTSCHE BLUMEN,

Hans Sloane flowers. Plate with painted decoration, Chelsea, *c.* 1754.

but much more naturalistically treated. The flowers were inspired by drawings in several source books, including principally Philip Miller's *Figures of the Most Beautiful, Useful, and Uncommon Plants* (often referred to as *The Gardeners' Dictionary*) published in 1752. Miller was gardener to the Worshipful Society of Apothecaries at their Botanick Garden in Chelsea, under the patronage of Sir Hans Sloane. An advertisement in *Faulkner's Dublin Journal*, 1st–4th July 1758, refers to ware 'enamelled from Sir Hans Sloan's plants', and this may have been the source of a misnomer for the style which probably had little or no connection with Sloane himself. *See* BOTANICAL WARE.

Slop-bowl. A small bowl (often referred to as a basin), usually part of a tea-service, for receiving the dregs or rinsings of tea-cups at the table.

Slow wheel. A POTTER'S WHEEL which is rotated by the potter's hand or foot at a slow speed. It is the earliest and most simple kind.

Smalt. A deep-blue pigment prepared by fusing together ZAFFER (an impure cobalt oxide), potassium carbonate, and silica in one form or another. The resulting coloured glass, when ground to a fine powder, formed a blue pigment. This was imported into England from Saxony until native deposits of cobalt oxide were found. Smalt was used in the form of an enamel, as an underglaze colour, for underglaze grounds, and for tinting certain bodies.

Smaltino (Italian). A pale lavender-blue tin glaze used on early 16th-century maiolica from Venice.

Snake-pipe. Prattware type, *c.* 1795. City Museums, Stoke-on-Trent.

Smear glaze. A very thin glaze which is hardly more than a faint gloss, sometimes to be found on biscuit porcelain and Wedgwood's jasper ware. It may have been due to the presence in the kiln of volatile substances acting in the same way as salt imparts a glaze to stoneware. *See* SALTGLAZED WARE.

Smith's blue. An overglaze blue enamel the discovery of which is attributed to William Smith, an apprentice to William Duesbury, *c.* 1779–90. It is found on Derby and Worcester porcelain.

Snake-pipe. A tobacco-pipe of glazed earthenware, the stem of which is in the form of a coiled snake. Made in Staffordshire from *c.* 1750.

Snip-spout. A straight spout with an opening cut horizontally and no everted lip.

Snowball vase. A type of porcelain vase made at Meissen in the mid-18th century which is almost entirely covered with a pattern of small applied white mayblossom flowers (MILLEFLEURS PATTERN). In England the style was copied at Chelsea in the 18th century, and by Spode in the 19th. It is also called a may-blossom vase and a guelder-rose vase; the German term is *Schneeballenvase*. Bowls etc. were similarly decorated.

Snowman figures. English porcelain figures primitively modelled, white, and undecorated, covered with an unusually thick, generally semi-transparent glaze, hence the name. They were made at Longton Hall, *c.* 1750. Nearly all the models known have their counterparts in saltglazed earthenware or Whieldon ware, and in some cases both.

Snuff-bottle. A small cylindrical or flat vial for holding snuff. They were made of porcelain in China, especially in the reign of

Chia Ch'ing (1796–1820), and the best are remarkable for excellent miniature decoration.

Snuff-box. A small box, usually with a hinged lid, for snuff; the bottom part is usually made in one piece, the lid being attached by means of a hinged metal frame fitted to both parts. Examples having two compartments, with a hinged lid at top and bottom, are rare. The frame is frequently of pinchbeck, but in the case of the finest specimens it may be of gold or silver-gilt. Another type was made in the form of a female head with high powdered wig, and had a screw cover which closed the opening at the bottom. Snuff-boxes were objects of considerable luxury during the 18th century, and many were painted by artists of note at the principal factories.

Snuff-box. Shell-shaped box, with painted miniature on the interior of the lid, Capodimonte (Naples), *c.* 1750. Courtesy, Newman & Newman Ltd, London.

Snuff-taker, The. A type of TOBY JUG in which the standing figure has a hunched back and is taking a pinch of snuff. It occurs in a variety of forms, including a brown-glazed earthenware example from Rockingham and Staffordshire.

Soaprock (soapstone). A kind of steatite, a soft mineral which is soapy to the touch, and, when powdered, is commonly called French chalk. It was used in the manufacture of porcelain (*see* SOAPROCK PORCELAIN) instead of the feldspathic rock of the Chinese. The principal deposits in England are in Cornwall, whence supplies were drawn during the 18th century. Its properties in porcelain-making may have been discovered by William Cookworthy of Plymouth, founder of the Plymouth porcelain factory, and communicated by him to Benjamin Lund, who founded the first Bristol factory. Its presence in porcelain is, on analysis, shown by a variable percentage of magnesium oxide, usually in the region of 17 per cent. Soaprock was, at one time, thought to have been used by the Chinese in the 18th century in the manufacture of a variety of porcelain decorated with underglaze blue. Analysis shows this to have been incorrect, since magnesium oxide has not been identified in appreciable quantities. *See* SOFT PASTE, CHINESE.

Soaprock porcelain. A type of porcelain made in the west of England, *c.* 1748–1820, in which the feldspathic rock of true porcelain is replaced by SOAPROCK. In principle it is a TRUE PORCELAIN rather than an ARTIFICIAL (soft-paste) PORCELAIN, since it is made by adding to clay a fusible rock instead of a glassy frit. The soaprock body was first used at Lund's Bristol factory which was transferred to Worcester in 1751. It was also used at Caughley and Liverpool. Soaprock porcelain had many advantages over the artificial porcelains of Bow, Chelsea, and Derby, since it would bear hot water without cracking, and objects could be formed with greater precision and neatness.

Sock-boot. A hollow utensil in the form of, and decorated as, a boot, made in creamware by Wedgwood, *c.* 1890, and in stoneware by Doulton, 1884–89. Its length varied between 8½ and 11½ inches. It was intended to be filled with hot water and used for drying and warming a sock drawn over its foot.

Socle. (1) A low block, rectangular, square, or circular, used as a base below the plinth (if any), for a bust or statue. (2) As part of a VEILLEUSE it is the section on which the warming bowl or teapot rests, and within which the GODET is placed.

Snowman figure. Porcelain, Longton Hall, *c.* 1750. Dr Bernard Watney Collection, London.

Soft-paste, Chinese. A type of finely potted, 18th-century Chinese porcelain (*chiang t'ai*, or paste bodied). It is opaque, with a crazed glaze, and the decoration is usually painted in a soft blue. This ware was formerly thought to contain SOAPROCK, but the supposition is erroneous and the name misleading; it is a TRUE PORCELAIN made with feldspathic rock.

Soft-paste porcelain. The term is sometimes thought to mean that this porcelain body is softer than the hard-paste (TRUE PORCELAIN) body, especially since it can be cut with a file, which the latter cannot, but it actually refers to the soft firing (about 1200°C.) which this kind of porcelain is given, as opposed to the hard firing of true porcelain (about 1450°C.). Also known as artificial porcelain and, in France, as *pâte tendre*. In England it is sometimes called frit porcelain, and at Vincennes and Sèvres, *porcelaine de France*. *See* ARTIFICIAL PORCELAIN.

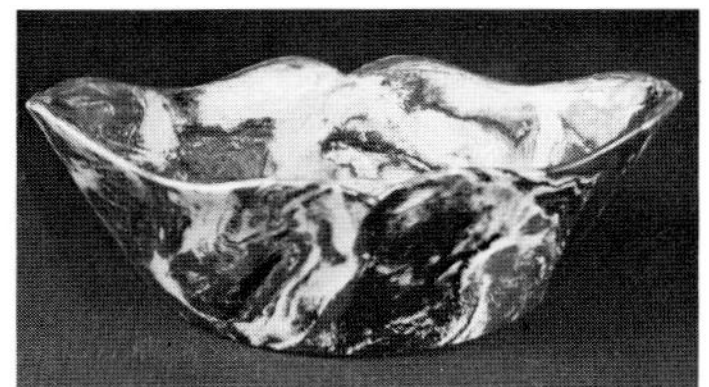

Solid agate ware. Compôtier, Wedgwood, mid-18th century. Buten Museum of Wedgwood, Merion, Pa.

Solid agate ware. Pottery made in imitation of the hardstone agate, the veined and mottled effect being created by pressing slabs of tinted clays together, and then kneading, or WEDGING, slices cut transversely from the mass. It is called 'solid agate' since the variegated effect extends throughout the body, as distinguished from 'surface agate', where the effect is only superficial, just beneath the glaze. Sometimes seams show in the veining where different pieces of clay have been brought together during the wedging process, and there tends to be a muddiness of surface colour in wares which have been worked on the potter's wheel. The process was developed by Thomas Astbury, who is well known for figures, and by Thomas Whieldon who employed it for tableware. It was also used by Josiah Wedgwood. *See* SCRODLED WARE; VARIEGATED WARE.

Solid jasper. A type of JASPER, the body of which is of a uniform colour throughout. It is to be distinguished from DIP JASPER, which is coloured only on the surface.

Solitaire service. A CABARET SERVICE for one person, often with a contemporary fitted travelling-case; it was a Berlin speciality in the later years of the 18th century. *See* TÊTE-À-TÊTE SERVICE; DÉJEUNER SERVICE; TEA-SERVICE.

Sometsuke ware. A type of Chinese blue-and-white porcelain decorated with greyish underglaze blue made at the end of the Ming dynasty and exported to Japan. *See* KO SOMETSUKE.

Soufflé blue. A blue ground colour, the same as BLEU SOUFFLÉ, or powder-blue. *See* BLEU FOUETTÉ.

Soupière. The French term for TUREEN.

Southwark delftware. English delftware made *c.* 1625–65, formerly attributed to Lambeth. The ware was made principally by Christian Wilhelm at Southwark in the period 1628–45.

Sphinx. Porcelain figure, with head of Peg Woffington, on a rococo base, Bow, *c.* 1752. Victoria and Albert Museum, London.

Sovereignty, Twelve emblems of. Symbols that occur principally on Chinese embroidered silk, and very rarely on porcelain, especially all twelve. The complete set symbolized the Universe and was closely associated with the Emperor, who was the only person permitted to display all of them. They are (1) the sun, a circle enclosing the three-legged crow; (2) the moon, a circle enclosing the hare pounding the Elixir of Immortality; (3) a constellation, three circles joined by a line; (4) mountains, symbolizing the Five Elements; (5) opposed dragons; (6) a pheasant, symbol of literary refinement; (7) a pair of bronze sacrificial beakers; (8) waterweed, symbolizing purity; (9) grain seeds in a circle symbolizing the food of the people; (10) fire, in the form of flames; (11) an axe-head, symbol of the Emperor's power; and (12) a *fu* ideogram, two fret-like objects on end and back to back, symbolizing judgment.

Soy pot. A small vessel with a loop handle and cylindrical neck, used for serving soy sauce. Some were made of Lambeth delftware; others of porcelain, but of European delftware shape, were imported in white from Japan and painted in Holland with the name. They were popular in the second half of the 17th century.

Spa cups. Porcelain cups made in Bohemia for use at spas and decorated with painted local scenes and names.

Spanish ware. Pottery made in Spain, including HISPANO-MORESQUE WARE, MANISES WARE, and PATERNA WARE.

Sparrow-beak. A pouring lip resembling the pointed beak of a sparrow. The type occurs on Worcester cream-jugs, and on those made in China for export during the 18th century. *See* PARROT-BEAK; HAWK-BEAK.

Spice-box. Blue-and-white porcelain, ht 3 in., Saint-Cloud, first half of 18th century. Victoria and Albert Museum, London.

Spatter ware. Glazed earthenware made in England, *c.* 1825–50, crudely decorated with splashed or spattered colours, including red, blue, green, and puce.

Spearhead border. A border pattern of a series of motifs resembling spearheads.

Speckled agate ware. A type of variegated ware made in England, especially by Wedgwood, in which the colour is sprayed on instead of using the technique of COMBED DECORATION. *See* SURFACE AGATE WARE.

Spezieria vase. A maiolica DRUG-JAR of a series commissioned by Duke Guidobaldo II of Urbino for the Spezieria, or medical dispensary, attached to the Ducal palace. The designs were by Battista Franco and Raffaello da Colle, and they were painted by Orazio Fontana and others, *c.* 1540–60. The series was subsequently presented to the Casa Santa at Loreto. The Italian term is *Vaso di Spezieria.*

Sphinx. A mythological figure with human head and breasts and the body of a lioness. The fashion for well-known actresses in particular to be portrayed as a sphinx seems to have started in France with the designs of Jean Bérain *père* in which a sphinx frequently occurs; *see* BÉRAIN MOTIFS. Porcelain examples representing Peg Woffington and Kitty Clive were made at Chelsea and Bow, *c.* 1750, and others came from Germany about ten years later.

Spirit-barrel. Porcelain barrel and stand, Meissen, *c.* 1730–35. Wadsworth Atheneum, Hartford, Conn.

Spice-box. A porcelain receptacle for spices, usually with three compartments and a conforming cover, made in France at Saint-Cloud, *c.* 1725, and at Mennecy.

Spice-stand. *See* SPOON-STAND.

Spill-vase. A cylindrical vase with flaring mouth, used for holding spills (wood splinters or paper tapers for obtaining a light from the fire). In the 19th century spill-vases were often made as part of a figure or group. They vary in height from about 3 inches upwards. Also called a quill-holder, match-pot or luminary.

Spinning-wheel, The. A blue-and-white pattern used at Worcester depicting a Chinese girl seated at a spinning-wheel.

Spiral pattern. Same as the CATHERINE WHEEL PATTERN.

Spirit-barrel and stand. A conventionally shaped WINE-BARREL of Continental porcelain, lying on its side and supported

Spittoon. Creamware, with polychrome *chinoiserie* decoration and interlaced strap handle, Leeds, *c.* 1770. Courtesy, Newman & Newman Ltd, London.

by figures (sometimes satyrs), or on a base embellished with small figures, foliage, etc. Sometimes there is an ornate cover on the barrel.

Spittoon. A cuspidor, usually globular-shaped, with a wide flaring rim or a high funnel-shaped mouth, and generally with one handle. Some have a spout for emptying when being cleaned, especially the type that is cylindrical with a concave cover having a central hole. They were made at many factories, of porcelain, creamware, and glazed earthenware, and have painted or transfer-printed decoration.

Splashed lustre. A type of LUSTRE ware made by splashing drops of oil on the lustre. *See* SUNDERLAND WARE.

Splashed ware. Pottery with small streaks of colour applied to the body before glazing, or with decoration made by using coloured glazes, the result being a streaky effect. The process was used by Thomas Whieldon on cream-coloured earthenware in various forms; it preceded the development of TORTOISESHELL WARE.

Splayed base. The base of a vessel that flares outwards towards the bottom.

Sponged ground. A mottled ground made by sponging the colour.

Sponged ware. Staffordshire pottery, made for the cheapest market, decorated with crude painting and by dabbing the ware with a sponge impregnated with colour. Manufacture dates from about the beginning of the 19th century. It is sometimes called 'spatterware' in the United States.

Sponging. The technique of applying a colour or a glaze by dabbing it on to the body with a sponge so as to create a mottled effect after firing. It was done with a single colour, or with several, as in TORTOISESHELL WARE.

Spoon. A household implement for serving, stirring, or eating, consisting of a shallow bowl and a handle of variable length; the bowl is nearly always circular or oval. One of tea-spoon size was usually included in a cabaret-service. *See* BUTTER-SPOON; CADDY-SPOON; EGG-DRAINER; SIFTER-SPOON; SUGAR-SPOON; LADLE.

Spoon-stand. A footed bowl in the centre of which is a column with a pierced gallery for the suspension of spoons; porcelain examples were made at Meissen. It is sometimes called a spice-stand.

Spoon-tray. A narrow tray on which to place a hot or wet spoon. It formed part of a dinner-service, tea-service, or cabaret-service.

Spoon-warmer. A receptacle for hot water in which to warm a spoon at table. Some were made in porcelain, or earthenware decorated with coloured glazes, in the form of open-mouthed animals, e.g. a fish, by Minton, or of various forms in Martinware.

Sporting lustreware. Resist lustreware decorated with a background of a country landscape and sportsmen in pursuit of game, huntsmen with hounds, or game birds.

Sporting subjects. Various decorative subjects depicting contemporary English sports, usually painted or transfer-printed. Popular subjects were archery, bear-baiting, bull-baiting, cock-fighting, coursing, cricket, fishing, fox-hunting, horse-racing, prize-fighting, stag-hunting, and wrestling. *See* BOXING FIGURES; BULL-BAITING GROUP.

Spot test. A test for the nature of SOFT-PASTE PORCELAIN to ascertain whether phosphoric acid is present, thus revealing BONE-ASH as a constituent of the body. A spot of hydrofluoric acid is put on an unglazed part, and after a few minutes is washed with water into a test-tube containing ammonium molybdate in nitric acid which, if phosphoric acid is present, will turn a cloudy yellow. This result proves the specimen to be a porcelain containing bone-ash, which means that it is English, most probably from Bow, Chelsea after 1756, Lowestoft, or late Derby; BONE-CHINA will also give the same reaction. A slight yellowing of the test-solution can be disregarded; a number of soft-paste porcelains exhibit traces of phosphoric acid present accidentally.

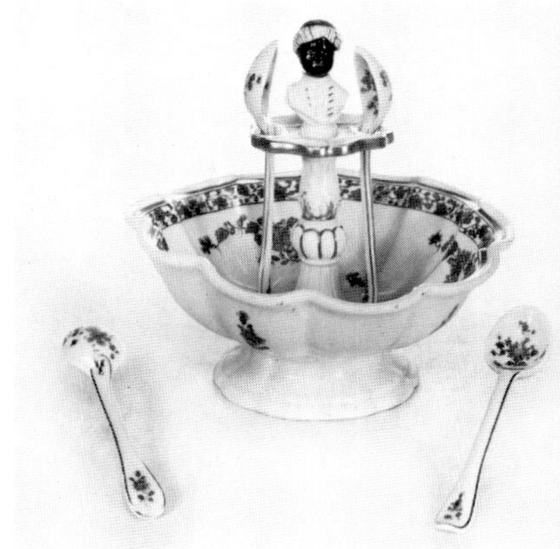

Spoon-stand. Porcelain; ht 5½ in., Meissen. Dr A. Torré Collection, Zurich.

Spout. The tubular protuberance through which the liquid contents of a pot are poured. Sometimes the term is loosely applied to a PINCHED or beak-shaped pouring lip of a jug. Spouts occur in many forms, modelled or moulded, usually the latter, and including the following: straight, curved, FLANGED, fluted, *S*-shaped, cabbage-leaf, CANNON, CRABSTOCK, GARGOYLE, SWAN-NECK, BIRD-SPOUT, BRIDGE-SPOUT, EAGLE-SPOUT, LIP-SPOUT, SNIP-SPOUT, TROUGH-SPOUT; BANDED; TUBULAR.

Spout-cup. *See* SPOUT-POT.

Spout-pot. A type of POSSET-POT having one or more spouts to enable the drinker to avoid the curdled milk on the surface of the posset. Some of these vessels had the spouts removed *c.* 1900 by collectors who thought them to be later additions to an ordinary porringer. Sometimes called a spout-cup.

Spreader. A tool, nowadays electrically operated, for flattening a ball of clay into a bat before it is placed on the JIGGER or JOLLY to be shaped by the PROFILE. Used in the quantity production of plates and similar flatware.

Sprigged ware. Porcelain bottle for toilet water, with applied flower decoration, Coalport, *c.* 1820. Victoria and Albert Museum, London.

Sprigged ware. Pottery decorated in low relief with ornament moulded or stamped separately and then attached (sprigged) to the body with slip (*see* SPRIGGING). The process was used by the Elers brothers and developed by Thomas Whieldon. It was used extensively in the Staffordshire potteries by, among others, Josiah Wedgwood.

Sprigging. The process of attaching parts or ornaments (separately made by moulding or stamping) to the body of an object or vessel with the aid of thin slip, as with JASPER ware. The separate parts or ornaments become permanently attached when fired. When of a different colour each piece retains its own colour. A firm joint can be secured only if the clays used are of exactly the same consistency. *See* ORNAMENTING; LUTING.

Spur. Same as COCKSPUR.

Spur-ground. A ground pattern consisting of parallel bands of interlocking three-pronged motifs resembling spurs, used on HISPANO-MORESQUE WARE.

Spur-mark. A small defect in the glaze on the underside of some pottery and porcelain; such marks are made by the pointed supports (*see* COCKSPUR) on which the piece rested in the kiln. They occur on Arita porcelain from Hizen province, Japan, and almost identical marks are found on Chelsea porcelain in England. They also occur on some celadon wares, and on Chinese JU YAO. The Chinese referred to spur-marks on the latter as 'small supporting nails'. *See* STILT-MARK; PATCH-MARK.

Squirrel, gourd-vine, and banded hedge pattern. A decorative pattern featuring these objects which originated with Kakiemon decoration on ARITA PORCELAIN, and was later used at factories, imitating this ware, such as Meissen, Chantilly, and Chelsea. *See* DÉCOR CORÉEN; BANDED HEDGE.

***Ssŭ ling*.** Symbols employed to decorate Chinese porcelain. They comprise the Four Supernatural Creatures, viz. the *lung* (DRAGON), the *fêng-huang* (PHOENIX), the *ch'i-lin* (KYLIN), and the TORTOISE.

Staffordshire blue-printed ware. Earthenware, usually pearlware, made from the end of the 18th century onwards by most of the large manufacturers in the region of Stoke-on-Trent (Staffordshire), which is the largest of the Five Towns known for their potteries in a group comprising Stoke, Tunstall, Hanley, Burslem, and Longton. The ware was transfer-printed in blue with a large variety of subjects; it was sometimes additionally decorated with enamels. Much is unmarked and of uncertain factory attribution. Large quantities were manufactured by Spode, and William Adams of Tunstall and John Rogers of Longport were among those who produced such wares especially decorated for the American market.

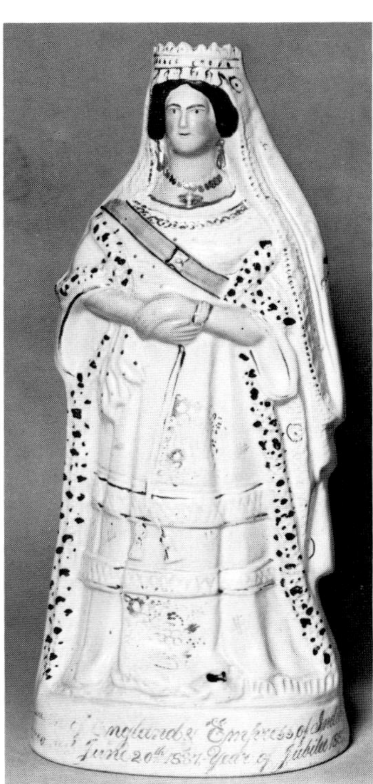

Staffordshire figure. Queen Victoria; ht of figure 16⅜ in., 1887. Smithsonian Institution, Washington, D.C.

Staffordshire delftware. Delftware made at various potteries in Staffordshire. It is coarser in glaze and decoration than other English delftware. The backs of plates are usually covered with a yellowish lead glaze to conceal small imperfections. The glaze has a yellowish cast.

Staffordshire figures. Figures for ornamental purposes, made in the Potteries district of Staffordshire from the early part of the 18th century onwards. The term is limited to figures of earthenware and stoneware in unsophisticated styles common to the region at any given time, porcelain figures from the Potteries being more or less in the styles generally current elsewhere. Examples average about 10 inches in height, but may range from 3 inches to 2 feet. The earliest examples are those attributed to John Astbury, some being glazed in the Whieldon manner (ASTBURY-WHIELDON FIGURES). The actual makers are not certainly known, since other contemporary potters undoubtedly worked in these techniques and styles. Some rare figures and groups occur in the SALT-GLAZED STONEWARE of the middle of the 18th century, among them PEW GROUPS. More sophisticated figures were made by Ralph Wood I after *c.* 1760 and decorated with coloured glazes. His son, Ralph Wood II, produced many figures in earthenware after 1770; these were decorated in enamel colours, and one or two porcelain figures in similar style have been attributed to his hand. The most prolific of the Wood family was undoubtedly Enoch (son of Aaron, the brother of the elder Ralph), who from *c.* 1781 made large numbers of figures decorated with enamel colours, and who was himself a modeller of some distinction. *See* WOOD-FAMILY WARE.

Towards the end of the 18th century Felix Pratt of Lane Delph (Middle Fenton) began to make figures decorated in underglaze HIGH-TEMPERATURE COLOURS, principally cobalt-blue, green, brown, and a rich orange, apparently suggested by tin-enamel ware similarly decorated. Other manufacturers, e.g. Ralph Salt, Obadiah Sherratt, and John Walton, mainly continued the 18th-century tradition with modifications.

Towards the middle of the 19th century a type of figure known as a FLATBACK made its appearance, so called because of the absence of modelling at the back which made possible production in press-moulds. This type is now generally referred to under the heading of Victorian Staffordshire figures. They were produced in large quantities and with a great variety of subjects in the Potteries (e.g. by Sampson Smith of Longton after 1855), although they also came from factories elsewhere. Some are merely ornamental, though many are intended as portraits (usually crude) of historical and fictional characters; among later examples are figures of notorious criminals and theatrical personalities, as well as famous contemporary characters such as Napoleon III, Garibaldi, Dr W. G. Grace, etc. Many have been reproduced in recent years from old moulds, and these are to be detected principally by differences in colouring.

Staffordshire pottery. Wares made at potteries located in Staffordshire (*see* STAFFORDSHIRE BLUE-PRINTED WARE). Among well-known wares made in this region in the 18th and early 19th centuries are ELERS WARE, ASTBURY WARE, WHIELDON WARE, PRATTWARE, and wares identified with Josiah Wedgwood, the two Ralph Woods, Enoch Wood, and Obadiah Sherratt. TOFT WARE is a late-17th-century slipware.

Staffordshire spaniels. Figures in the form of seated spaniels in a variety of colours, and usually made as a facing pair. Many were made in Staffordshire during the early decades of the 19th century, but some were made elsewhere. *See* DOGS.

Stained (iridescent) lustre. A term sometimes employed to describe such lustres as the MADREPERLA.

Stamnos (Greek). A type of storage jar used in ancient Greece; it is ovoid in form, with a high shoulder, short neck, wide mouth, and two horizontal loop handles attached at the shoulder, and is sometimes provided with a cover. It is similar to an AMPHORA of the neck type.

Stamnos. Earthenware, with red-figure decoration, Attic, *c.* 450 BC; ht 10⅜ in. Victoria and Albert Museum, London.

Stamped. (1) Impressed (as in the case of a mark on unfired porcelain) with a stamp or stamps. The method was fairly common in the 18th century, and it was especially adopted by Wedgwood, almost all of whose wares are marked in this manner to indicate the factory and, after 1859, the date. (2) Made by the process of STAMPING, e.g. in the case of small flat relief ornament which is afterwards attached to the body by SPRIGGING.

Stamping. (1) A decorative technique by which the surface of an unfired object is ornamented by impressing the soft clay with stamps of metal or other materials. (2) The process of making a small ornament by pressing soft clay into an intaglio mould.

Stampino, a (Italian). Decorated with designs drawn with the aid of a stencil, as on some early Doccia ware.

Standish (or inkstandish). A desk stand for writing materials, usually including an ink-well, and a drawer or recessed tray for quills. *See* LIBRARY SET; ENCRIER; FLOWER-BRICK.

Standish. Porcelain, with pierced decoration, Vienna (du Paquier's factory), *c.* 1730. Cecil Higgins Museum, Bedford.

Stanniferous. Containing tin oxide as in tin-glazed earthenware, otherwise known as faience, maiolica, and delftware. Some glazes on 18th-century artificial porcelain also contain a proportion of tin oxide, which has an opacifying effect. The most important of these is the early Chantilly glaze, but certain English glazes, notably those of some Liverpool porcelain, contain an appreciable percentage of tin.

Star and cube ground. A diaper ground of straight lines meeting at several angles to make a complex pattern seen as six-pointed stars enclosed in hexagons, and at times (the result of an optical illusion) as a pattern of cubes.

Statuary porcelain. An early term for PARIAN PORCELAIN.

Statuette. A small figure, usually from 1 inch to 2½ inches high, made in porcelain, e.g. at Chelsea, as a SEAL, BRELOQUE, or PIPE-STOPPER. *See* FIGURINE; TOYS.

Steatite. Hydrated silicate of magnesium. *See* SOAPROCK.

Stecco, a (Italian). *See* SGRAFFITO.

Stein (German). Literally, stone. A STONEWARE beer or ale mug, usually cylindrical, with one handle and a hinged lid. They are usually ornamented with relief decoration. *See* MUG; CANETTE; SCHNELLE; TANKARD. In Germany, when the lid is allowed to remain raised, it is a sign that the drinker is prepared to buy drinks for the assembled company.

Steingut. The German term for lead-glazed earthenware similar to English CREAMWARE and French FAÏENCE FINE.

Steinzeug. The German term for STONEWARE.

Stem. That part of a vessel which unites the body to the foot or base, as in the case of a wine-glass; it may be long or short, and of various styles. The French term is *culot. See* STEM BASE; STEM CUP.

Stem base. A base of a vessel that is attached to the body by a stem.

Stem-cup. Porcelain, with decoration of three fish in underglaze copper-red; Ming dynasty, reign of Hsüan-te (1426–35). Victoria and Albert Museum, London.

Stem cup. A shallow cup of Chinese porcelain which has a stem broadening slightly towards the bottom. In the case of the early HILL CENSER the stem is integral with a saucer-like base. Stem-cups painted with three fruit or fish in underglaze copper-red during the early years of the Ming dynasty are very rare. Copies from the early years of the 18th century, however, are far less uncommon. Sometimes erroneously called an altar cup. *See* KYLIX.

Stencilled lustre ware. A type of lustre ware with silhouette decoration made by cutting out paper silhouette patterns, pasting them on the glazed ware, and covering the surface with wax. When the paper was removed, the design was left unwaxed. The piece was then coated with lustre and fired, the wax burning away in the kiln and leaving the silhouette in lustre. The process was introduced in England *c.* 1806 by John Davenport, but a similar technique may have been used elsewhere early in the 18th century for gold and silver silhouette decoration. *See* SILHOUETTE WARE.

Stencilling. The process of applying pigment through a cut-out sheet of card or metal as a method of decorating ceramic ware using relatively unskilled labour. It was infrequently used before the middle of the 19th century. *See* POUNCED.

Sternschüssel (German). Literally, star dish. A circular faience dish with a five-pointed star in the centre, made at Nuremberg.

Stile compendiario (Italian). A decorative style used on mid-16th-century Italian maiolica, featuring a coat of arms within a cartouche, or a single figure (either a saint or a *putto*) drawn in a free, rather sketchy, manner in a palette often limited to greyish-blue and shades of yellow and orange, leaving the white tin-enamel of the ground to a large extent exposed. It remained popular well into the 17th century.

Still. A still (lacking the middle bowl), so called in an early Wedgwood Shape Book, was made in creamware, *c.* 1770; 17½ in. high, it may have been intended for laboratory demonstration purposes.

Still. Creamware, ht 17½ in., Wedgwood, *c.* 1770. Colonial Williamsburg Collection, Williamsburg, Va.

Stilt. Same as COCKSPUR. *See* KILN FURNITURE; FIRING-RING.

Stilt-mark. A small defect in the glaze inside the foot-ring of some plates and dishes, caused by the piece having stood on three or four cone-shaped stilts during firing. The presence of stilt-marks is indicative of origin to a limited extent; they are to be found, for example, on both Chelsea and Arita porcelain. *See* PATCH-MARK; SPUR-MARK.

Stippled. A type of engraving used in transfer-printing by the BAT process in which the design is made up not of lines, but of many small dots or stipples, somewhat analogous to the appearance of the half-tone printing block. The leading exponent of the technique was the Italian engraver Francesco Bartolozzi in the last quarter of the 18th century.

Stirrup-cup. An English drinking vessel which is an adaptation of the ancient RHYTON. It is usually made in the shape of the head of a fox or a hound, but some are in the form of a stag, hare, rabbit, cock, bear, trout, other dogs, and (rarely) of a potato or a clenched fist. The head of Bacchus or of a satyr also occurs in this form. It is without either handle or foot, and is held inverted while in use. Strictly, the term refers to the final drink taken by a mounted rider or huntsman about to depart, but it has come to apply also to this special type of cup which was sometimes used on such occasions. They occur in Whieldon ware, and many were made of earthenware in Staffordshire after *c.* 1765. Porcelain examples were made at Chelsea (after 1770), at Derby, and elsewhere. *See* STURZBECHER.

Stirrup spout handle. An overhead arched handle formed by a tube with a short spout at the mid-point for filling or pouring.

Stone china. A type of fine, white porcellaneous stoneware, hard and compact, and sometimes slightly translucent. It was first developed by John Turner of Lane End, Staffordshire, *c.* 1800, and originally called TURNER'S STONEWARE. In 1805 the patent was reputedly sold to Josiah Spode, who named the new ware 'Stone China' or 'New China', and employed it at his Stoke-on-Trent factory for many services and ornamental wares, usually decorated with oriental patterns transfer-printed in blue and sometimes touched with red. It was intended to supplant the coarse contemporary Chinese export porcelain, and led, in 1813, to the introduction of MASON'S IRONSTONE CHINA, also called New Stone Ware. *See* OPAQUE CHINA; OPAQUE PORCELAIN.

Stoneware. A type of pottery midway between earthenware and porcelain, being made of clay and a fusible stone. It is fired to a point where partial vitrification renders it impervious to liquids, but, unlike porcelain, it is very seldom more than faintly translucent. The vitrification makes it unnecessary to add a glaze, but for reasons of utility and appearance decorative glazes are sometimes used, such as salt glaze and lead glaze. Stoneware was first introduced in England by John Dwight in the late 17th century, and developed by the Elers brothers, who appear to have brought the technique from Cologne (Germany). In 17th-century England saltglazed brown stoneware was often termed 'Cologne ware'. The French term is *lithocérame*, and the German *Steinzeug*. Special varieties of stoneware include STONE CHINA (ironstone china), JASPER, BLACK BASALTES, and BROWN STONEWARE. *See* ELERS REDWARE; DWIGHT WARE; FULHAM WARE; NOTTINGHAM STONEWARE; MARTINWARE; SALT-GLAZED WARE; TURNER'S STONEWARE; CASTLEFORD WARE.

Storage jar. Pottery jar (*pithos*); ht 4 ft, from Knossos, Crete, *c.* 1450–1400 BC. British Museum, London.

Storage jar. (1) A jar for the bulk storage of either dry substances such as corn, or liquids such as wine or oil. Early storage jars of very large size were made in Minoan Crete. *See* PITHOS. (2) A vessel of pharmacy ware usually of baluster shape and with a cover, and larger than the normal DRUG-JAR.

Stoup. Same as BÉNITIER.

Stove. *See* HAFNER WARE.

Strap-handle. A loop handle which is flat, like a narrow strap. The lower extremity is sometimes curled outwards from the body of the vessel. It occurs singly or in the form of two straps intertwined.

Strapwork. A decorative motif of interlacing bands resembling straps usually employed in conjunction with other motifs such as foliage and grotesques, as with the German LAUB- UND BANDELWERK (leaf- and strapwork). Its origin is probably in wrought ironwork used decoratively as part of chests and coffers. Similar to the Italian TIRATE.

Strasbourg flowers. A type of floral decoration based on the DEUTSCHE BLUMEN of Meissen and introduced at Strasbourg by Adam Friedrich von Löwenfinck for the decoration of faience. It is notable for a characteristic deep crimson-purple or carmine, a rich yellow, and a dark blue. This style influenced many French faience factories, particularly those in the central region and the Midi. Strasbourg faience with this decoration has recently been reproduced, but the distinctive crimson-purple has not yet been successfully imitated. *See* FLOWERS; FLEURS FINES; PURPLE OF CASSIUS.

Strawberry-leaf bowl. Porcelain bowl with stand, width 9 in., Longton Hall, *c.* 1750–60. Courtesy, Christie's.

Strawberry-leaf bowl. A small porcelain bowl, sometimes with a stand *en suite*, with painted and relief decoration of strawberry leaves.

Strawberry-leaf dish. A type of dish in the shape of a strawberry leaf, with moulded veins and flowers, and the handle formed as a twig. Chelsea examples of *c.* 1755, based on contemporary silver patterns, are the best known.

Strawberry moulding. A relief decoration on English porcelain of the mid-18th century moulded in the form of strawberry leaves and berries.

Streublumen (German). Literally, strewn flowers. A decorative pattern introduced at Meissen consisting of many scattered and strewn small flowers, some conveniently covering glaze defects. Also termed *Streumuster* and *Meissner Streublümchen. See* FLOWERS.

Striations. Irregular lines in slip or enamel, usually vertical, approximately parallel, and of varying shades of colour, caused by the accidental or intentional running of the material employed, e.g. on Whieldon ware.

String-marks. A series of closely spaced markings in the form of spiralling arcs, appearing on the underside of a vessel; the marks are produced when a ceramic piece is cut off the rotating POTTER'S WHEEL by looping a string or wire around the object and pulling the ends.

Strohblumenmuster (German). A decorative pattern of stylized plum-blossom developed at Meissen from Japanese sources. *See* PRUNUS.

Studio pottery. A class of pottery made by artist-craftsmen rather than by workmen in factories, the ware being modelled or thrown, glazed, decorated, and fired by the designer, or under his immediate supervision. Those making pottery in factories nearly always work to a design provided, and in most cases are responsible only for one operation among many.

Sturzbecher (German). Literally, somersault cup. A type of stoneware (especially SIEGBURG WARE) cup made in the Rhineland during the latter part of the 16th century. When empty the cup must be inverted like a RHYTON or a STIRRUP-CUP, the stem being a figure of a man which is upright in this position.

Style rayonnant (French). *See* RAYONNANT, STYLE; LAMBREQUIN.

Stylized. Modified, as a decoration, from the natural appearance of an object to a more abstract pattern or conventionalized style of expression.

Sub-Mycenaean pottery. Pottery made in the Mediterranean area just after the ascendancy of Mycenae, *c.* 1100–1000 BC, and related in style to that found there. The wares were in the tradition of MYCENAEAN POTTERY, and preceded those of the distinctively Greek PROTOGEOMETRIC STYLE, *c.* 1000–900 BC, and GEOMETRIC STYLE, *c.* 900–700 BC.

Subtlety. An imposing ornament used as a decoration for a dessert-table at a banquet and comprising figures, animals, and other decorative objects made originally, in the 16th and 17th centuries of sugar, wax, or almond paste, but often, in the 18th century, of porcelain, for which purpose small figures were developed. At Meissen especially these sets of figures, designed to conform to a single theme, were accompanied by a CENTREPIECE in the form of a temple or other building, or a large and elaborate floral ornament, often in many parts. Some of the components still survive, with the ownership mark KHC (*Königliche Hof-Conditorei*, or Royal Court Confectionery). Dessert table ornaments of this kind were first made at Meissen in the late 1730s, and later in England at Chelsea, Bow, and Derby. Some of them appear in the Chelsea auction sale catalogues of 1755 and 1756 as 'for dessart'. They also occur in 19th-century PARIAN PORCELAIN. *See* TABLE-DECORATION.

Sucrier. The French term for a SUGAR-BOWL.

Sue(ki) ware. Pottery made in Japan from *c.* AD 400, employing advanced techniques (the POTTER'S WHEEL and kilns built into the hillside) imported from Korea. The ware is hard and grey; it was fired at a high temperature and some pieces have a resonant quality. Copying contemporary Korean forms, the ware included bowls, jars, and other vessels.

Sugar-bowl. A covered bowl for serving sugar, usually part of a service; formerly called a sugar box.

Sugar-bowl. Cauliflower ware bowl, ht 3½ in., Whieldon ware, *c.* 1770–80. Burnap Collection, William Rockhill Nelson Gallery of Art, Kansas City, Mo.

Sugar-caster. Baluster-shaped porcelain caster with screw-cover, decorated in the style of A. F. von Löwenfinck, Chantilly, *c.* 1730–40. Courtesy, Newman & Newman Ltd, London.

Sugar-spoon. Various forms made at Mennecy, Tournai and Meissen; lengths 6¾–8¼ in. Courtesy, Christie's.

Sugar-caster. A small container, usually of baluster or cylindrical shape, with a domed cover (which was sometimes screwed to the container) pierced for the sprinkling of sugar. Sometimes termed a sugar-dredger. The French terms are *saupoudrière* and *saupoudroir.*

Sugar-dredger. Same as SUGAR-CASTER.

Sugar-spoon. A type of spoon for serving sugar. The bowl is pierced with holes of various sizes and patterns, like those made of silver. Such spoons were made at many Continental factories in porcelain and pottery. Also termed a sifter spoon. The French term is *cuiller à sucre en poudre.*

Suite, en. Modelled and decorated in like fashion to form a set, as a dinner-service or tea-service.

Sulkowsky service. An important dinner-service made at Meissen by J. J. Kändler, *c.* 1735–37, for Count Alexander Joseph von Sulkowsky. This, the first of the great Meissen services (of which the best-known is the SWAN SERVICE), has a border decorated with an early OZIER pattern using a diagonal weave, and the tureens are elaborately decorated with moulded ornament. The pieces bear the coat of arms of the Count and of his wife, Maria Anna Franziska von Stein zu Jettingen, which are surrounded by scattered floral sprigs in Kakiemon style.

Sultanabad pottery. Islamic pottery made at Sultanabad, about half-way between Kum and Hamadan in Persia. Since the town did not exist before AD 1200, wares attributed to its kilns were made after this date. The ware is decorated with relief or incised ornament, or painted in black slip under a turquoise, dark blue, or green glaze. *See* PERSIAN POTTERY.

Sunderland lustre. *See* SUNDERLAND WARE.

Sunderland ware. Pottery made at Sunderland, England, *c.* 1800–50, by Dixon, Austin & Co. It is decorated with black transfer-prints, some of which have been coloured, framed by pink lustre, usually in irregular splashes. The prints were generally of sailing vessels, the famous Iron Bridge over the river Wear, or of emblematic subjects, all accompanied by sentimental inscriptions and verses. Jugs are a frequent survival, and chamber-pots with slightly bawdy inscriptions are not uncommon. Plaques inscribed with religious sentiments ('Thou God seest me') were also made in considerable quantities. *See* TYNESIDE POTTERY.

Sunflower dish. A naturalistically modelled and painted dish representing a sunflower. It is formed of overlapping dark green leaves, tending to yellow at the tip, with puce veining. It sometimes has a stalk handle.

Sunflower tureen. A naturalistically modelled and painted tureen formed by overlapping dark green leaves yellowing at the tip, with a seeded cover and a stalk handle; made at Chelsea and Meissen. A dish decorated *en suite* serves as a stand for the tureen.

Sung dynasty. The period in Chinese history which began AD 960 and terminated with a Mongol invasion in 1280. Most of the wares made during this period are of fine stoneware covered with a thick glaze which ends in a roll near the base. Shapes are simple but of great subtlety, and the glazes employed are notable for their colours. This was the period of the classic wares – Ju, Kuan, Ko, Lung-ch'üan, Ting, and Chün. Wares decorated with painting in slip came from TZ'Ŭ CHOU (Chihli province). The period is notable for the first use of underglaze blue, a technique derived from Persia, and of enamel colours. A few specimens of ware from Tz'ŭ Chou, painted simply with primitive red and green enamels, have survived. The translucent ware first developed during the T'ANG DYNASTY (618–906) was continued with Ting wares (*see* TING YAO). The few specimens of YING CH'ING ware which can be reasonably attributed to the later years of this period are also translucent. *See* YÜAN DYNASTY.

Sung glaze. A term used by Doulton of Burslem (England) to designate a glaze used by them which is similar to some Chinese FLAMBÉ GLAZES of the Sung dynasty (960–1280).

Sung yao (Chinese). Literally, Sung ware. Stoneware and porcelain made during the Sung dynasty.

Su-ni-po (Chinese). Cobalt blue traditionally supposed to have come from Sumatra and employed in the decoration of early Ming blue-and-white porcelain. Other terms for imported cobalt blue include *su-ma-ni* and *su-po-ni*. *See* HUI-HUI CH'ING.

Sunken blue. Decoration in cobalt blue on a tin-glaze which has sunk slightly below the level of the surrounding undecorated glaze. The blue is extremely dense, and it is probable that it sank into the glaze during firing, or was absorbed into the glaze, which receded in consequence. The effect is especially to be noticed on Liverpool delftware, and on some Dublin specimens.

Suppenwärmer. A German term for a FOOD-WARMER. Also called a *réchaud*.

Supper-set. Creamware, Wedgwood, *c.* 1785. Courtesy, Wedgwood.

Supper-set. A service for sideboard use consisting of serving dishes that are fan-shaped so that, when placed together, they form a circle or an oval. The centre space is sometimes filled by a deep dish or a tureen. Where there is no recess in the rim for a cover it is safe to assume that no cover was originally provided. Similar sets were also made occasionally in China in porcelain and enamel, apparently not for export, and these may have inspired the supper-sets made in Europe. Sometimes called a sandwich-service or breakfast set. *See* SWEETMEAT-SET.

Surface agate ware. Pottery made in imitation of the hardstone agate, the variegated effect being produced by the blending and combing of variously coloured slips on the surface of the ware. It is often called marbled ware, from its resemblance to marbled end-papers of books. The technique was developed by Thomas Astbury and Thomas Whieldon, and further refined by Wedgwood and Bentley, *c.* 1770–80. *See* SOLID AGATE WARE; VARIEGATED WARE.

Surprise cup. Cup, diam. 4 in., Chün yao, Sung dynasty (960–1280). Percival David Foundation of Chinese Art, London.

Surprise cup. A small bowl of Chinese porcelain, in the centre of which is an upright lotus flower which conceals a tiny figure of a man; when the cup is filled this figure rises through the opening of the lotus. Examples were made in the Sung dynasty of CHÜN YAO.

Surprise mug. Same as FROG-MUG.

Surround. A border or edging.

Surtout-de-table (French). A large, flat, raised tray of ceramic ware for the centre of the dining-table on which a tureen, cruets, and other small vessels could be placed. Some were made with corner holes for candlesticks or ornamental figures, as well as a large central depressed area for an obelisk or other large ornament. *See* ÉPERGNE.

Sussex pig. Drinking-cup, Brede pottery, *c.* 1800. Courtesy, David Newbon Ltd, London.

Sussex pig. A drinking flask of peasant pottery made during the 19th century in Sussex, England, in the form of a pig with a detachable head for use as a drinking-cup. *See* BEAR JUG.

Sussex ware. A type of lead-glazed PEASANT POTTERY made at Brede and various other potteries in Sussex, England. The body is usually a deep red, the local clay being rich in iron, and the glaze is lustrous in quality, varying between mustard yellow and dark brown. Decoration was principally in trailed slip and an inlay of stars, and dated inscriptions impressed in bookbinder's type and filled with slip are fairly common. Most articles are utilitarian, but those of decorative intent include the BREDE HEDGEHOG and the SUSSEX PIG.

Swag. A decorative pattern in the form of a FESTOON, often in relief. *See* DRAPED SWAG; FLORAL SWAG; PENDENT RIBBON SWAG.

Swan cup. Cup and saucer with gilded interior, Sèvres, *c.* 1804–09. Courtesy, Newman & Newman Ltd, London.

Swan cup. A type of coffee-cup made at Sèvres, *c.* 1804–09, in the form of a swan, with the curved-down neck forming the handle, and accompanied by an oval saucer. The interior of the cup and the well of the saucer are completely gilded.

Swan-neck spout. A type of spout, long and thin, with an *S*-shaped curve in the form of a swan's neck.

Swan service. A dinner-service made by J.J. Kändler at Meissen, 1737–41, to the order of Augustus III, Elector of Saxony, for presentation to the factory's director, Count von Brühl and his wife the Countess Kolowrat-Krakowski. It is highly modelled with swans, dolphins, nereids, and *putti*, with a predominating theme of water. The relief-decoration on plates and dishes was so extensive that it left little room for painted decoration, apart from embellishments to the modelling. Each piece bears the arms of the Count (and some the arms of his wife). The motif was derived from an engraving in a travel work published in 1700 by Leonard Buggels of Nuremberg. It was Meissen's first important production in the rococo style which influenced and inspired the development of this style elsewhere. The service comprised over 1,400 pieces. In German it is called the *Schwanengeschirr*.

Swastika. A symbol (gammadion) used from ancient times; a Greek cross with the ends of the arms bent sideways at right angles, usually clockwise (*see* MEANDER-AND-SWASTIKA BORDER). In China a swastika drawn anti-clockwise symbolized 'ten thousand' and signified longevity; it occurs on BLANC-DE-CHINE

Swan service. Plates, monteiths, sauce-boat, etc. from the service by J.J. Kändler, Meissen, 1737–41. Courtesy, Antique Porcelain Co., London.

Sweetmeat set. Creamware, Herculaneum (Liverpool), early 19th century. City of Liverpool Museum.

figures, e.g. of Buddha, and when combined with *shou* denotes a wish for a 'myriad years of life'.

Swastika-and-bar ground. A diaper ground of *I*-shaped bars at right angles, forming a series of swastika-like patterns.

Swastika-and-square ground. A diaper ground of checker-board form with diagonal lines, making a swastika-like pattern.

Swatow ware. Roughly potted Chinese porcelain wares having a thick glaze, and characterized by a gritty bottom and vigorous decoration in blue, red, and green enamels. It was exported in the late Ming dynasty, probably from Swatow (Kuangtung province), especially to the East Indies and Japan. Decoration in underglaze blue is also found. The ware was frequently copied in Japan. *See* KUANGTUNG WARE.

Sweetmeat dish. A dish with several divided compartments for serving an assortment of sweetmeats. *See* HORS-D'ŒUVRE DISH.

Sweetmeat figures. One of a pair of gardeners on rococo bases, Chelsea, *c.* 1760. Courtesy, Antique Porcelain Co., London.

Sweetmeat figures. Figures in pairs, usually seated, to each of which is added a small bowl, often covered, for sweetmeats; they formed part of a dessert-service, and examples occur from Meissen and Chelsea. *See* BOUQUETIÈRE FIGURES.

Sweetmeat set. A set of dishes forming a composite unit, sometimes around a central dish and sometimes resting on a tray or plateau. The dishes are of various shapes (fan-shaped, hexagonal, etc.) and were used to hold assorted sweetmeats. *See* SUPPER-SET.

Swimming ducks pattern. A decorative subject depicting two swimming ducks and two islands connected by an arched bridge, copied from a Chinese original and used on English blue-and-white porcelain.

SYP teapot. Wedgwood, 1907. Buten Museum of Wedgwood, Merion, Pa.

SYP teapot. The acronymic name for a type of teapot introduced by Wedgwood in 1895 and designated 'Simple Yet Perfect'. A covered opening towards the front of the pot enabled hot water to be poured below a horizontal perforated divider on which the dry tea-leaves had been placed. When the pot was tilted backwards it rested on two short legs at the back and on the curved overhead handle, so that water passed through the perforations into the tea-leaves. After the tea was brewed the pot was tilted forward on to its flat base, and the liquid settled below the divider, ready to be poured out through the spout at the front.

Syrup jar. *See* WET-DRUG JAR.

T

T-pattern border. A type of fret border with one continuous line forming a series of Ts, either simple capital letters or with serif-like embellishments.

T-shaped handle. *See* TAU HANDLE.

Tabakskopf (German). A tobacco pipe bowl made of porcelain at Meissen, Nymphenburg, and other German factories, shaped as a head or decorated with various painted subjects.

***Tabaksstopfer*.** The German term for a PIPE-STOPPER.

***Tabatière*.** The French term for a SNUFF-BOX.

Table-decoration. In the 17th century the fashion for decorating the table with figures and ornamental pieces made of wax or confectionery was widespread. After *c.* 1730 porcelain was increasingly used for this purpose, and most of the small figures now treasured in cabinets were originally part of a large table-decoration, usually with a single theme, and often with appropriate accompaniments. For instance, Chelsea doves were obviously made to accompany a large porcelain dovecot, of which an example is preserved at Woburn Abbey. In a Meissen inventory of 1753 temples, town-houses, cottages, grottoes and fountains are mentioned. The larger pieces were made in sections and joined together on the table. In somewhat similar vein was the Shakespeare service made at Worcester in 1853, but in general elaborate table-decorations of this kind disappeared with the 18th century. *See* SUBTLETY; CENTREPIECE.

Table-screen. White porcelain screen, reign of K'ang Hsi (1662–1722). Victoria and Albert Museum, London.

Tanagra figure. Terracotta figure of a seated nude, ht 9 in., 4th century BC.

Table-lustre. A table CANDLESTICK or CANDELABRUM decorated with prismatically cut rock-crystal or glass drops. Mounted in ormolu, they were made by Wedgwood of jasper towards the end of the 18th century. *See* GIRANDOLE.

Table-ornament. A highly ornamental piece, usually a porcelain figure or group set in a porcelain arbour, or with a background of trees in TÔLE PEINTE (painted sheet iron).

Table-screen. A small rectangular porcelain plaque or tile, usually decorated on both sides, mounted vertically on a stand, and intended to be placed on the scholar's table, probably to protect his work from unwanted sunlight. Examples may be up to 18 in. in height.

Tableau. A picture painted on porcelain, often with a rococo frame integrally moulded. They were especially made at Fürstenberg, *c.* 1767–68, the usual subjects being mythological or pastoral. *See* PLAQUE.

Tablet. A term used by Wedgwood and others to refer to a PLAQUE.

Tacchiolo (Italian). A decorative pattern of an oriental flowering-shrub, the spindly branches having feathery leaves, and the yellow, aubergine, and blue flowers being arranged in groups of three. It was used by Pasquale Antonibon of Nove (near Bassano), Italy.

Tagliere (Italian). A shallow plate of maiolica which formed a unit of a VASO PUERPERALE. Usually decorated with a childbirth scene.

Tailor and wife, Count Brühl's. A popular pair of figures first made at Meissen, said to caricature Count Heinrich von Brühl's tailor and his wife. As modelled by J. J. Kändler, *c.* 1740, the tailor, with his shears and other implements, is riding a goat. The wife, modelled about the same time by J. F. Eberlein, is also riding a goat, and holding a baby in swaddling clothes. The model is said to have originated in a rash promise made by Count Brühl to his tailor that, in return for certain services, he should be present at a state banquet. Realizing too late the rashness of his promise, the Count redeemed it by having the porcelain model made and put on the table.

The subject was copied as a group in Derby porcelain and Staffordshire pottery, being called in England the 'Welsh Tailor and his Family'.

Count Brühl's tailor and wife. Porcelain figures, Meissen, *c.* 1740. Wadsworth Atheneum, Hartford, Conn.

Takatori ware (Japanese). Yellow and brown glazed stonewares made in the 16th and 17th centuries at Takatori (Chikuzen province), Japan.

Tambourine pattern. A decorative transfer-printed subject on English porcelain, depicting a woman playing a side-drum and a man playing a tambourine in a landscape or garden, with two distant mountains.

Tanagra figures. Moulded Greek figures of terracotta which were made at several centres in Greece, and at colonies in Italy and Asia Minor, the examples of the highest quality being those discovered in 1874 in the Tanagra district of Boeotia. They date from the latter part of the 4th century BC onwards, and represent men and women, and gods and goddesses, the former usually in costumes of the period. Those made in the Hellenic style represent an idealization of human characteristics, although some grotesque-like distortion can be observed in some examples. Many are delicately modelled due to extensive retouching having taken place after moulding. The normal height is about 7 to 8 inches. The Greek term is *Koroplastae*.

T'ang dynasty. The Chinese dynasty (618–906) particularly noted for the quality of its glazed earthenwares. It was a time of considerable expansion, the borders of China reaching out as far as Persia. An important excavation – from the viewpoint of dating certain wares to the T'ang dynasty – was carried out in 1909 at Samarra on the Tigris on the site of a palace built in 838 for the Caliph Mu'tasim and abandoned in 883; here some undoubted fragments of porcelain were recovered.

A renaissance of the arts in China took place during this dynasty, but little was known of its pottery till the early years of

Table-decoration. Detail showing porcelain groups and figures on a conforming stand (consisting of nine parts, 14 ft by 1 ft 8 in. overall), Vienna, 1767. Österreichisches Museum für angewandte Kunst, Vienna.

the 20th century, when railway-cuttings driven through T'ang graveyards exposed wares buried with the dead. The burying of figures of retainers and domestic animals was extensively practised, and these, variable in quality, include some superb figures of men, women, and such animals as the HORSE and CAMEL, examples of which were first brought to the West in the early 1920s by George Eumorfopolous and others. Some of these are of soft unglazed earthenware and others are decorated with coloured glazes of fine quality which are thin, and often end above the base to a variable extent. Pots and jars are usually covered with glaze to about two-thirds of their surface, the remainder being unglazed earthenware body. Influences from outside were not only from the Near East; traces of Greek and Roman inspiration can also be observed, the result of delayed influence from the conquests of Alexander the Great in Central Asia, and of Roman penetration into the same region. T'ang figures are noted for a lively naturalism and vigorous poses, especially in the depiction of animals and dancers. The body is comparatively lightly fired and absorbs moisture freely. Forgeries, which are fairly numerous, are usually in a harder, less absorbent body. High-fired wares are comparatively rare. The earliest porcelain is the ancestor of YING CH'ING ware, probably from kilns located in Kiangsi province. A fine stoneware, Yüeh celadon, came from Shensi province, and this is the earliest of the CELADON group, first mentioned in the 8th century. Generally, the bases of T'ang pots are flat, and the presence of a FOOT-RING suggests a date in the Sung dynasty (960–1280) or later. *See* TOMB FIGURES.

Tazza. Maiolica, Deruta, *c.* 1510. Victoria and Albert Museum, London.

Tankard. A one-handled drinking vessel, usually with a hinged pewter lid. The prescribed capacity of an old tankard was about a quart; anything smaller is better called a mug. *See* STEIN; SCHNELLE; CANETTE; APOSTLE TANKARD; WALZENKRUG.

T'ao t'ieh (Chinese). A decorative design of very ancient origin, in the form of an animal mask. The head of the animal is split from the back as far as the nose and then opened out in a schematic representation. It is found frequently on bronzes, but rarely on porcelain, although it occurs in painted form.

Taperstick. A holder for a taper or thin candle usually with a flat, circular base and a candle-socket or nozzle of narrow diameter. It was often accompanied by a snuffer. The taper was used mainly to light candles, pipes, etc. *See* CANDLESTICK.

Tart-pan. An early name for a PATTY-PAN.

Tartan ground. A ground pattern in a tartan design, as found, for example, on English Jacobite saltglazed teapots made in Staffordshire, *c.* 1750–60.

Tasse. The French term for CUP. *See* DEMI-TASSE.

Tasse à filet (French). A style of small coffee-cup, tall and slightly conical, with two loop handles extending above the rim. It was introduced at Sèvres, *c.* 1800.

Tasse à glace (French). A cup for serving ice-cream, usually with one vertical loop handle, and a stem base.

Tasse à surprise hydraulique The French term for a CONJURING CUP.

Tassie medallion. Medallions made in glass paste from moulds by James Tassie (a Scottish sculptor, resident of Dublin and

Tasse à glace. Porcelain, with polychrome decoration, Sèvres, 1775. Courtesy, Antique Porcelain Co., London.

later of London), and his nephew, William, from 1768 onwards, some derived from wax-portraits made from life by Tassie. Casts from Tassie's moulds were used by Wedgwood for some of his CAMEOS and INTAGLIOS, *c.* 1769–91.

Tau handle. A handle to teapots, coffee-pots, etc. made in the form of the Greek letter *tau* (T). Sometimes called a T-shaped handle.

Tazza. (1) The Italian term for CUP. (2) A type of ornamental cup having a large flat or shallow bowl which rests on a stem base or a low foot; it may be with or without handles.

Tê Hua yao. Chinese porcelain made at Tê Hua (Fukien province) from the later years of the Ming dynasty (1368–1643) onwards to the present day. It is often termed BLANC DE CHINE, and early specimens are usually of very fine quality, the body being unusually translucent. In colour it ranges from cream-white to chalk-white, and the glaze is thick and unctuous. Many of the wares are small figures finely modelled. These often depict Buddhist deities and persons connected with the Taoist and Confucian religions. Some have detachable heads and hands, and holes are sometimes pierced for the attachment of human hair to form the moustache and beard. Cups and bowls of this ware are usually decorated by SPRIGGING with representations in relief of the prunus and the tea-plant. They were copied in the 18th century by many European porcelain factories, e.g. Saint-Cloud in France, Meissen in Germany, and Bow in England.

Tea-bowl. A small cup without a handle made and used in the Far East for drinking tea, and commonly made by many European factories during the 18th century. Special importance was attached to the heat-retaining qualities of those made in China and Japan. Some European versions are accompanied by a saucer *en suite*.

Tea-caddy. A covered or stoppered container for dry tea used on the tea-table in conjunction with a teapot and a kettle. It is often of rectangular section with sloping, curved shoulders and a short cylindrical neck. Some were elaborately shaped, especially during the currency of the rococo style. They were made of porcelain, delftware, creamware, and stoneware. In England the tea-caddy (or tea-jar) was sometimes erroneously called a teapoy. The tea-caddy was part of the TEA-SERVICE or CABARET-SERVICE. It is the same as a tea-canister or tea-bottle. *See* DOUBLE TEA-CADDY; TEA-VASE.

Tea Ceremony. Called in Japan the *cha-no-yu.* A traditional ceremony related to the drinking of tea for which tea-bowls, tea-jars, trays, charcoal braziers, and other utensils were specially made; the wares were kept, often in special padded boxes, by the Tea Master who selected those to be used. Tea Ceremony ware is of pottery, and its selection is based both on tradition and subtle aesthetic considerations. The latter especially are difficult for Europeans properly to comprehend.

Teacup. A cup, usually of semi-spheroidal form, with one handle, and accompanied by a saucer, used for drinking tea; it holds about 4 fluid ounces. The French term is *tasse. See* TEA-SAUCER.

Tea-dust glaze (Chinese). A dark brown glaze which inclines to green, most specimens of which were made during the reign of Ch'ien Lung (1736–96). The glaze is known in China as *ch'a-yeh mo.*

Tea-caddy. Bristol delftware, *c.* 1760. Victoria and Albert Museum, London.

Tea-bowl. Bowl and saucer with pencilled decoration of harbour scenes, Meissen, *c.* 1750. British Museum, London.

Tea-kettle. Porcelain kettle with bail handle, on warming-stand, Meissen, *c.* 1770. Národní Galerie, Prague.

Temple vase. Blue-and-white porcelain, Yüan dynasty, dated 1351. Percival David Foundation of Chinese Art, London.

Tea-kettle. A kettle for hot water used in the brewing of tea; usually smaller than a kettle used for heating of water. *See* TEA-POT; PUNCH-POT.

Tea-measure. A small shallow bowl, shell-moulded, with one flat side handle. It measures about $3\frac{3}{8}$ inches in width. Examples are to be found in English delftware, and in Worcester and Derby porcelain. *See* WINE-TASTER.

Tea Party, The. A decorative subject on transfer-printed English porcelain of the 18th century depicting a couple seated on a bench before a tea-table. In some versions they are served by an attendant with a kettle, and in others they are seated on chairs on opposite sides of the table. The subject was engraved by Robert Hancock. *See* HANCOCK ENGRAVINGS.

Teapot. A covered vessel in a variety of shapes intended for the brewing and serving of tea, usually with one spout, and, on the opposite side of the vessel, one handle. The spout is usually attached near the bottom so as to drain the tea without disturbing floating tea-leaves. The pot also has a strainer pierced with small holes at the junction of the spout and the body to prevent tea-leaves from being poured into the cup with the liquid. Caution should be exercised in describing oriental vessels of this shape as teapots. They are, unless specially made for the European market, usually WINE-POTS, and the teapot was developed from them. Many teapots are in fanciful forms. *See* CHINAMAN TEAPOT; CAMEL TEAPOT; MONKEY TEAPOT; MAGOT TEAPOT; ELEPHANT TEAPOT; CAULIFLOWER TEAPOT; PINEAPPLE TEAPOT; BREWSTER TEAPOT; CADOGAN; DOUBLE TEAPOT; NARROW-BOAT TEAPOT; SYP TEAPOT; TREE-TRUNK. Some teapots rest on a hollow pedestal above a warming device; *see* VEILLEUSE-THÉIÈRE. For related forms, *see* COFFEE-POT; CHOCOLATE-POT; WINE-EWER; PUNCH-POT.

Teapot warmer. Same as VEILLEUSE-THÉIÈRE.

Teapoy. A term sometimes erroneously employed in England for a TEA-CADDY, tea-canister, or tea-jar. A teapoy is a wooden container, with several compartments for tea and mixing bowls, which rests on a stem ending in a triple- or quadruple-footed support. The term was originally derived from the Indian word *tipai*, meaning a table, which has no connection, other than by association, with tea.

Tea-saucer. A saucer on which a teacup was placed while the user drank the tea from the deeper saucer which was *en suite* with the teacup. Also called a cup-plate. Many were made in STAFFORDSHIRE BLUE-PRINTED WARE.

Tea-service. A service comprising teapot and stand, cream-jug, sugar-bowl, spoon-tray, slop-bowl, and cups and saucers for serving tea. In the case of a combined tea- and coffee-service, only additional coffee-cups (not saucers) were supplied during the 18th century and well into the 19th century. The service originally included two large plates (for bread and butter or cake) for the table, but no small individual plates, these being first introduced *c.* 1840 *See* CABARET SERVICE; DÉJEUNER SERVICE; SOLITAIRE SERVICE; TÊTE-À-TÊTE SERVICE.

Tea-strainer. A small low cup or spoon with patterned holes for straining tea. *See* EGG-DRAINER; CADDY-SPOON.

Tea-urn. An urn for hot water, sometimes part of a tea-service. It may be globular, pyriform, or columnar, with a spigot for dispensing the water. Some rest on a stand which has an aperture into which is placed a GODET to keep the water warm. They were made of porcelain at Meissen, Fürstenberg, Ludwigsburg, Vienna, and Weesp (Holland). *See* COFFEE-URN; SAMOVAR.

Tea-vase. A type of covered TEA-CADDY or tea-jar which is ovoid in shape, and has a small mouth intended for pouring out dry tea-leaves rather than spooning them.

Teardrop pattern. A border or ground pattern of a series of shapes resembling teardrops.

Teardrops. An effect resulting from the tendency of the glaze of some Chinese porcelain of the Sung dynasty (especially the type termed TING YAO) to run and collect in globules, particularly on the exterior of bowls. Sometimes regarded as a sign of genuineness, they are not invariably present. The same effect occurs on some T'ang dynasty porcelain.

Tegula (Latin). A flat Roman roof-tile. *See* IMBREX.

Telamon (Greek). A draped male figure serving as a column to support an entablature. The telamon was employed to decorate some ceramic ware, either in relief or painted. *See* CARYATID; CANEPHOROS; ATLANTES.

Tea Party. Transfer-print on cup and saucer, Worcester, *c.* 1760.

Temmoku. Black-glazed stoneware cups and bowls made during the Sung dynasty (960–1280), at Chien-an (Honan province), China, and so called by the Japanese who sought them for use in the TEA CEREMONY. They also greatly influenced Japanese pottery design. The term is now commonly used by European commentators. *See* CHIEN YAO.

Temmoku glaze. The Japanese term for the type of glaze found on the TEMMOKU wares from Honan province. The glaze is a treacly brown colour, or a lustrous black sometimes shading to a brownish rust where the glaze is thin. *See* HARE'S FUR.

Temple pattern. A popular transfer-printed decorative subject used on blue-and-white porcelain at Caughley, and sometimes in painted form at Worcester. It depicts two pagoda-like temples, and a figure on horseback crossing a bridge accompanied by an umbrella-holding attendant.

Temple vase. A tall ornamental vase made for a temple and often having a dedicatory inscription. Examples were made in China from the Yüan dynasty (1280–1368).

Tenacity. The property possessed by pottery and porcelain by which it resists fracture, whether from a blow, by change in temperature, or from pressure. Coarse pottery will resist a blow, but not pressure. Hard-paste porcelain will resist pressure, and a change of temperature, but fractures and chips comparatively easily. Soft-paste porcelain resists a blow but is very vulnerable to changes in temperature.

Teniers subject. Vase with decoration after Teniers, painted by John Donaldson, Worcester, *c.* 1765. British Museum, London.

Teniers subjects. Peasant scenes painted on porcelain based on French prints of paintings by David Teniers *père* (1582–1649), and David Teniers *fils* (1610–90). They occur on the porcelain of Meissen and Sèvres. *See* WATTEAU SUBJECTS.

Term. Strictly, in architectural usage, a tall quadrangular pedestal, usually one which is surmounted by a bust or figure of classical derivation. The word is a shortened form of the expression 'terminal figure'. The pedestal is about twice the height of the figure surmounting it. The figure is usually head and shoulders only, but sometimes is considerably more, gradually merging with the formal pedestal. Some ceramic pieces or handles were made in this form. *See* HERMA.

Terminal. A sprigged ornament at the end of part of a vessel, such as at the lower end of a handle at the point where it joins the body, or begins to curve away from it. It usually takes the form of an ornamental relief detail, often floral, but sometimes a human mask or a bird's head. Sometimes called an antefix. *See* HANDLE-TAG; KICK TERMINAL.

Terra invetriata (Italian). A term meaning vitrified earth, applied to the glaze of DELLA ROBBIA WARE.

Terra sigillata (Latin). Originally ware made from allegedly medicinal clay from Samos and Lemnos and stamped with a seal (*sigillum*) of authenticity. Later, the term was applied to some Arretine ware and Samian ware, and more recently to a grey Maltese pottery and to Silesian redware.

Theatrical figure. Porcelain figure of Kitty Clive as the Fine Lady in Garrick's *Lethe*, Bow, *c.* 1752. Fitzwilliam Museum, Cambridge.

Terrace vase. A type of vase, urn-shaped or double-ogee shaped, with a high domed cover and sometimes with applied flowers and leaves, the base of the vase being in the form of a winding stairway and balustrade, sometimes with a rabbit (occasionally a squirrel, dog, or cow) at the foot. The vase sometimes has transfer-printed decoration. They were made at Marieberg (Sweden), *c.* 1760–80. *See* RABBIT VASE.

Terraced foot. A style of foot or base the lower half of which is wider than the upper half.

Terracotta. An earthenware body, usually one without a glaze, made of reddish clay and lightly fired. Figures and vessels of terracotta were usually the work of sculptors rather than potters, who normally made useful wares. Terracottas are often single pieces made in a WASTE-MOULD and subsequently fired, or reproduced in strictly limited quantities by means of a PIECE-MOULD. Pottery wares were usually made to be reproduced by less exact methods. The term is often used loosely to mean unglazed ware made of a reddish clay. *See* DELLA ROBBIA WARE; ETRUSCAN POTTERY; ROMAN POTTERY.

Terraglia. The Italian term for CREAMWARE, which in French is called FAÏENCE FINE. *Terraglia fine* is a somewhat vague term often used for tin-glazed earthenware decorated with enamel or overglaze colours.

Terre cuite. The French term for TERRACOTTA.

Terre de Lorraine (French). Literally, earth of Lorraine. A type of soft FAÏENCE FINE which is similar to TERRE DE PIPE, but whitened by the addition of lime phosphate. It was used unglazed as a kind of biscuit earthenware at Lunéville (Lorraine) principally for figures and groups by Paul-Louis Cyfflé. The material was intended as a less expensive substitute for the BISCUIT porcelain made at Sèvres, the manufacture of which was, by royal decree, forbidden to other French factories. *See* PÂTE DE MARBRE.

Terre de pipe (French). Literally, pipe-clay. A white lead-glazed FAÏENCE FINE introduced by Jacques Chambrette at Lunéville (Lorraine) in 1748 and there also used unglazed for BISCUIT figures and groups by Paul-Louis Cyfflé and others. *See* CREAMWARE; CAILLOUTAGES; TERRE DE LORRAINE.

Terre de pipe anglaise. A term for French ware similar to English lead-glazed creamware, such as that made at Douai by the brothers Leigh, *c.* 1781–84. *See* CAILLOUTAGES; FAÏENCE FINE; PONT-AUX-CHOUX WARE; TERRE DE PIPE.

Terre jaspée (French). Literally, jasper earth. This has nothing whatever to do with Wedgwood's JASPER which was popular in France, but is a type of pottery developed *c.* 1545 at Saintes by Bernard Palissy. It refers to his use of mingled lead glazes coloured with various metallic oxides. A similar technique was employed in the 18th century by Thomas Whieldon and other Staffordshire potters. *See* VARIEGATED WARE; WHIELDON WARE; PALISSY WARE.

Terre vernissée (French). The usual French term for GLAZED EARTHENWARE.

Test-piece. An object of Chinese porcelain made as a preliminary to regular production, the prototype being inscribed with the approval of the kiln official who supervised its glazing and firing.

Tête-à-tête service. A CABARET SERVICE for two persons. *See* SOLITAIRE; DÉJEUNER SERVICE; TEA-SERVICE.

Theatrical figures. Portrayals of theatrical characters and actors, usually in the form of figures made of porcelain or earthenware. The most famous are the COMMEDIA DELL'ARTE series made at Meissen, especially the HARLEQUIN series. In France leading stage personalities were the subjects of figures made at Vincennes and Sèvres in the 1750s. In England porcelain figures were made of such prominent actors as David Garrick, Henry Woodward, Peg Woffington, and Kitty Clive (*see* SPHINX), and numerous figures in 19th-century Derby porcelain and Staffordshire earthenware depicted contemporary actors in costume.

Thermo-luminescence dating. A process for establishing the authenticity of allegedly old pottery, in which a tiny sample of the body of the piece to be tested is crushed and heated to a point at which, if genuine, it becomes luminescent. The process has been used to test, for example, terracotta panels from Etruscan tombs, and several, previously accepted as genuine, have thus been established as modern forgeries. *See* HACILAR POTTERY.

Thermometer stand. An arched stand to contain a thermometer; such stands were made by Minton.

Thimble surface. A pitted surface on some PARIAN PORCELAIN resembling the tiny indentations on a thimble. The pitting is produced by the mould. The opposite is SHARKSKIN SURFACE. *See* SHAGREEN.

Three Abundances, The. A symbolic decoration on Chinese porcelain which includes the POMEGRANATE (a large progeny), the PEACH (longevity), and the BUDDHA'S-HAND CITRON (happiness). Also called 'The Threefold Blessing'. *See* FITZHUGH PATTERN.

Three-colour decoration. A type of decoration in coloured lead glazes on Chinese stoneware and porcelain. *See* FA HUA; SAN TS'AI.

Three Fishermen, The. A transfer-printed decorative subject on English porcelain. It depicts a boy crossing a bridge and holding a large net high in the air, a girl with a fishing-rod, and another boy watching.

Terracotta. Nymph and Satyr, figure group by or after Clodion (Claude Michel; 1738–1814); ht 23½ in. Courtesy, Frank Partridge & Sons Ltd, London.

Tête-à-tête service. Porcelain service in mahogany case, *c.* 1785. Courtesy, Royal Copenhagen Porcelain Manufactory.

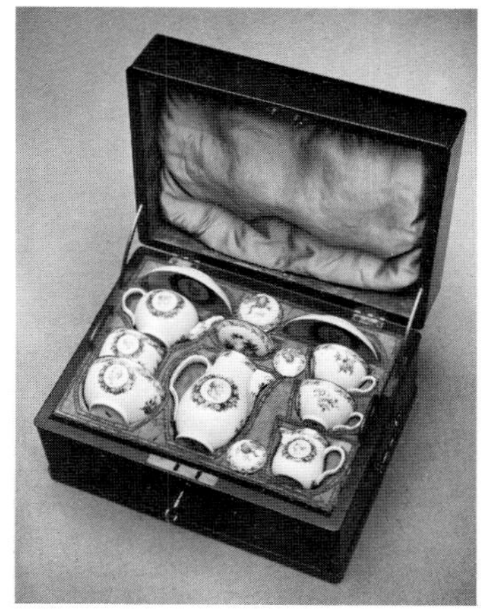

Three Friends. Pine, prunus and bamboo, decoration on blue-and-white bowl, diam. 8¼ in., mark and reign of Hsüan-tê (1426–35). Percival David Foundation of Chinese Art, London.

Three Friends, The. A decorative symbolic subject on Chinese porcelain. It represents the pine, prunus, and bamboo, emblematic of Buddha, Lao Tzŭ, and Confucius, who are sometimes depicted together. It was copied at Derby. *See* CHINESE TRIAD.

Threefold Blessing, The. *See* THREE ABUNDANCES.

Throwing. The act of shaping ceramic ware on a rotating POTTER'S WHEEL by placing a ball (bat) of clay in the centre of the wheel and then, by pressure of the hands and tools, forming it into the desired shape. Large vessels are sometimes thrown in several parts and joined by LUTING. *See* JIGGER; JOLLY.

Thumb-mark. *See* PATCH-MARK.

Thumb-piece. (1) A flat area on the top of a handle, or sometimes on the rim of a plate. to provide a place to rest the thumb for better support. Also called a thumb rest. (2) A projecting piece attached to the metal lid of a tankard by which the lid is raised by pressure of the thumb.

Thuringian ware. Hard-paste porcelain of varying quality, consisting mainly of tableware and figures, was made at the many potteries in Thuringia (now in East Germany) from the mid-18th century. Most of the factories continue production today, including those at Limbach, Ilmenau, Grossbreitenbach, Rauenstein, Volkstedt, Kloster-Veilsdorf, Gotha, Wallendorf, and Gera. Faience in baroque style was made at Dorotheenthal and Abtsbessingen in the 18th and early 19th centuries.

Tiger ware. Jug of Rhenish stoneware, with English silver mounts, 16th century. British Museum, London.

Thurndendel. A tall, cylindrical mug for beer with an encircling exterior band three-quarters of the way up to indicate the height for filling in order to leave space above the band for froth. Its capacity was about 1½ pints. This and the half-thurndendel were made in Staffordshire brown stoneware, *c.* 1684–1710.

Thymiaterion (Greek). A type of CENSER of Greek pottery.

Thynne, Lord Henry, service. A dinner-service made at Worcester with fluted body decorated with circular landscape panels enclosed by a turquoise HUSK BORDER and with sprigs of flowers.

Tichborne trial, The. A pottery group made in Staffordshire depicting the trial at the Old Bailey in 1872–74 of Arthur Orton, the Tichborne claimant. The three judges on the top bench are portrayed as owls, the two counsel on the second bench as a hawk and a cock, and the claimant below as a turtle. The group was modelled by Randolph Caldecott. A figure of Orton was made *c.* 1874 by Sampson Smith of Longton, Staffordshire, depicting him holding a gun and with a bird perched on his arm.

Tiffany pottery. Pottery, nearly always lamp-bases, made in the ART NOUVEAU style by the American glass-maker Louis Comfort Tiffany (1848–1933) after 1906. The initials LCT were incised under the base. Many of his lamp-bases were unique models.

Tiger. A decorative subject on oriental porcelain that has been employed on European ware. The HU (white tiger) symbolized the west in the FOUR QUADRANTS, and Autumn in the FOUR SEASONS. The tiger was also made as a figure, as at Longton Hall where it was sometimes decorated as a leopard.

Tiger-skin decoration. A decorative pattern on some Chinese porcelain of the reign of K'ang Hsi (1662–1722), dappled with patches of green, yellow, and purple, somewhat in the same manner as the pottery of the earlier T'ang dynasty (618–906).

Tiger ware. Or tyger ware. A term used in Elizabethan England for RHENISH STONEWARE, especially jugs with a mottled brown glaze over a greyish body. Jugs of this kind were often mounted with silver, being given a neckband and lid, foot, and handle mounts. Similar ware was made by John Dwight of Fulham who started a factory for the purpose towards the end of the 17th century. *See* MALLING JUG; DWIGHT WARE.

Tiger's-eye glaze. An AVENTURINE GLAZE with markings which resemble the brilliant eye of the tiger.

Tile. A thin slab of fired clay, usually square, and generally used for lining floors and walls, and for a weather-proof covering for roofs. Tiles have been made of pottery of all kinds, but the type most to attract the collector are those of tin-glazed earthenware (delftware, faience, and maiolica). They were a speciality of Delft (Holland), where tile-pictures comprising a number of separate tiles were made to cover relatively large areas of wall-space. Some European palaces and large houses retain tile-panels of this kind, such as the Amalienburg (Schloss Nymphenburg), Munich. The themes of decoration are numerous, but among the best are shipping scenes and landscapes. In England tiles of creamware were transfer-printed at Liverpool by Sadler and Green, including examples representing characters from the English stage of the time. Tiles were extensively used architecturally in Spain, where the house of a poor man was proverbially 'a house without tiles'. In the Near and Middle East, where tiles were also commonly used for the same purpose, they are found in cruciform, hexagonal, and star-shaped form, made to join up with each other into large decorative panels. Tiles, both decorated and undecorated, were also employed in Germany and other central European countries for the making of stoves; these, and vessels made by the stove-potters, are termed HAFNER WARE. *See* AZULEJO; CARREAU DE REVÊTEMENT; ROOF TILE; RIDGE TILE; IMBREX; TEGULA; GALLEY TILE; PILL-SLAB; CHERTSEY TILES; CANDLE RECESS.

Tiles. Tin-enamel tile-panel from the Château d'Écouen, Rouen, 1542. Victoria and Albert Museum, London.

Tin enamel. *See* TIN GLAZE.

Tin glaze. A glaze rendered white and opaque by the addition of tin oxide. A common formula includes 3 parts of sand to 1 part of potash, with 3 parts of lead oxide to 1 part of tin oxide; sometimes a small quantity of cobalt is added to counteract a tendency to yellow, or to confer a bluish tone, and also some alumina to prevent the glaze from running. The tin glaze can also be coloured by the addition of suitable metallic oxides to the glaze material. The tin glaze resembles a fine white enamel paint, and where it has been chipped a differently coloured body can be seen beneath it. Pottery thus glazed must be distinguished from that covered with a white or coloured slip which sometimes closely resembles it. The tin glaze was known to the Assyrians, *c.* 1000 BC, and used by them to colour the well-known brick reliefs. It was revived on Persian pottery in the 8th century AD. Islamic potters adopted it in the 9th century, and it was introduced into Spain by the Moors in the 11th century. It was being used at Paterna and Valencia before the 14th century, and from there it was brought to Italy. By the early years of the 16th century it had arrived in France, Germany, and Holland, being first used in England soon after 1550. Wares glazed in this way are of considerable importance, and are normally termed maiolica, faience, or delftware according to the country of origin. Tin glaze used as a pigment is often termed tin enamel. It yields an opaque white which

Thurndendel. Brown stoneware, Staffordshire, *c.* 1710. Courtesy, Sotheby's.

is often employed for painting on coloured grounds (*see* BIANCO SOPRA BIANCO). With the addition of metallic oxides tin enamel is used as a base for the preparation of a variety of opaque enamel colours employed to decorate both pottery and porcelain. The tin glaze is normally employed only on earthenware, but before *c.* 1750 the Chantilly factory made much porcelain covered with a glaze of this kind.

Tin-glazed earthenware. Jug with decoration depicting an aerial bull-fight; the opaque nature of the glaze can be seen at the base and on the shoulder. Talavera, Spain, late 18th century. Courtesy, Newman & Newman Ltd, London.

Tin-glazed earthenware. Otherwise known as maiolica, faience, or delftware (*see* TIN GLAZE). It was made by dipping a lightly fired object in a very porous state into a liquid glaze suspension to which tin oxide had been added. This was left to dry, leaving a deposit of glaze on the surface in powder form. On this painting was done in high-temperature colours. A final firing both vitrified the glaze and developed the colours. Some pieces were covered by a thin transparent lead glaze (*see* COPERTA and KWAART) in addition to the tin glaze, which had the effect of both protecting and enhancing the surface appearance. The use of enamel colours on the tin glaze, painted on after it had been fired, began in Germany with the HAUSMALER in the second half of the 17th century. As a factory operation it was first developed at Strasbourg soon after 1730 with the object of imitating porcelain. Enamelled tin-glazed ware is often termed *Fayence-Porzellan* in Germany. Tin-glazed ware, when made in Italy, is termed maiolica because the tin glaze was first seen on Spanish wares imported by way of the island of Maiolica (now Majorca). When referring to tin-glazed pottery made in France, Germany, or Scandinavia. the term FAIENCE is normally used, while English and Dutch wares are referred to as DELFTWARE.

Tinaja (Spanish). A large globular or pyriform jar used for the storage of oil, wine, or water. Examples usually have impressed decoration, often with a heraldic motif. Most came from Toledo or Seville.

Ting (Chinese). A bronze form which is very ancient. It is a deep bowl formed with three solid, cylindrical legs, and handles projecting above the rim. They were made in pottery in China in the Neolithic period, and porcelain examples may range in date up to the 18th century, although they are unusual. A similar form made in Japan is termed a KORO, and it was used as an incense-burner. *See* LI.

Ting yao. Jar with incised lotus-flower decoration, Sung dynasty (960–1280). Victoria and Albert Museum, London.

Ting yao (Chinese). A porcelain of variable translucency made at Ting Chou (Chihli province) from the T'ang dynasty (618–906), and throughout the Sung dynasty (960–1280). The translucency, when present, is usually orange in colour. The glaze of the finer variety, called *pai Ting* (white Ting), is inclined to collect, on the exterior of bowls especially, into drops known as 'teardrops'. The colour of the ware is a fine ivory-white, and a particular feature of bowls is a raw (or unglazed) rim which is often bound by a copper or silver band, since they were fired mouth downwards in the kiln. Ting decorative motifs are usually floral. The decoration on the finest specimens is carved or incised, that of lesser examples being moulded. *See* FÊN TING YAO; T'U TING YAO; KIANGNAN TING; COPPER BOUND.

Tirate (Italian). Decoration on Italian maiolica in the form of interlaced bands and foliage, usually in blue on a white ground. *See* STRAPWORK.

Tischchenmuster (German). Literally, little table pattern. A decorative pattern employed at Meissen depicting oriental flowers growing behind a square table.

Tithe pig group. A Derby porcelain group, the earliest version dating from *c.* 1770, portraying a parson standing with a pig in each hand, and a farmer and his wife on either side. The farmer's wife is refusing to part with the tenth (or tithe) pig unless the parson takes the tenth child also. This was a popular subject which sometimes appears in Staffordshire pottery, and also as decoration on porcelain and pottery vessels, especially a jug by Ralph Wood of about the same date. The subject was also used on Longton Hall porcelain as transfer-printed decoration by John Sadler of Liverpool.

Tithe-pig group. Porcelain, Derby, *c.* 1770.

T'o t'ai (Chinese). Literally, bodiless. The Chinese term for EGGSHELL PORCELAIN, the finest of which is little more than two layers of glaze kept apart by a very thin layer of porcelain body. The best work of this kind belongs to the reign of Yung Chêng (1723–35).

Toad, three-legged. A Chinese legendary creature (*ch'ün ch'u*) with only one hind leg. In some rare 17th-century porcelain groups it accompanies an Immortal, Liu Hai, who carries a string of cash (perforated coins). It has been adapted in 19th-century English earthenware, sometimes open-mouthed, as a SPOON-WARMER.

Toad-mug. Same as FROG-MUG.

Toast-rack. A dish with vertical parallel partitions for serving slices of toast. Examples were made, e.g. by Spode, in glazed earthenware in the mid 19th century.

Tobacco-jar. A covered jar for holding tobacco, sometimes made in the form of a head, the top of which forms a cover. *See* LOUBAK. A saltglazed version in the form of a house is sometimes seen, and in its complete form contains a flat piece of stoneware with a central handle for pressing down the tobacco.

Tobacco-leaf pattern. A floral pattern decorating FAMILLE ROSE dinner-services made in China during the reign of Ch'ien Lung (1736–96). It includes large tobacco-leaves and a small barb on the rim of the plates to simulate the leaf-shape.

Tobacco stopper. *See* PIPE-STOPPER; JUNGFERNBEINCHEN; FLOHBEIN.

Tobi seiji (Japanese). *See* BUCKWHEAT CELADON.

Toby jug. A popular pottery drinking jug in the form of a seated man holding a mug and a pipe and wearing a tricorn hat the brim of which was sometimes the pouring lip and the crown a cover which also formed a cup. The Toby jug seems first to have been made by Ralph Wood I, and later by his son Ralph Wood II, in the period 1748–95 in several versions (actually over 25 are recognized), and they were copied in innumerable variations at almost every English pottery factory. They have since been copied on the Continent in both pottery and porcelain, and some have been made in recent times in Japan. Later pottery examples from Staffordshire intended to deceive are also fairly common. It has been suggested that the name derives from Toby Philpot, the subject of a song called *The Brown Jug* which was published in 1761, and this suggestion seems to be well founded. It helps to date the earliest specimens. Toby Philpot was the nickname of Harry Elwes, a celebrated toper who is said to have been the model for the original. Somewhat similar jugs occur in Dutch delftware, however, before they were made in England. A few Toby jugs are of female figures; *see* GUNN, MARTHA, JUG. More recently, a set of World War I Toby jugs portraying 11

Toby jugs. A selection of the many variations. Courtesy, Jellinek & Sampson Ltd, London.

contemporary British and American statesmen and military leaders was designed by Sir F. Carruthers Gould; and one depicting (Sir) Winston Churchill was modelled by L. Jarvis. *See* MASK MUGS AND JUGS; SNUFF-TAKER; RODNEY WARE; SATYR MUG; BACCHUS JUG; DRUNKEN PARSON JUG; NIGHT WATCHMAN; FIDDLER JUG.

Toddy-jug. A barrel-shaped jug with a cover, and one intertwined handle; it also has a lip, inside which is a strainer.

Toft ware. Dish with trailed decoration on a yellow slip ground, *c.* 1690. Burnap Collection, William Rockhill Nelson Gallery of Art, Kansas City, Mo.

Toft ware. Staffordshire lead-glazed ware decorated with trailed slip and made in the second half of the 17th century. The name of the ware derives from dishes conspicuously bearing the name Thomas Toft in trailed slip, and it has been assumed that he was the maker, but other names on similar dishes include Ralph Toft, William Talor (Taylor), and Ralph Simpson, and none of these names, including that of Toft, appear as potters in contemporary lists. It is by no means certain, therefore, that the usual assumption is correct.

Toilet-pot. A covered cylindrical jar, usually an accessory for a toilet-table, to contain cosmetics.

Toilet-set. (1) A set of small boxes, usually of porcelain, for holding toilet preparations. (2) A washing-set, including a ewer, a basin, a jug, and a soap-dish with cover and drainer.

Tôle peinte (French). Sheet-iron covered with several coats of a special varnish, and sometimes with painted decoration of excellent quality. It was used in France in conjunction with porcelain in various ways, e.g. as part of a TABLE-ORNAMENT.

Toltec pottery. *See* CENTRAL AMERICAN POTTERY.

Tomato red. The same as ARMENIAN RED or sealing-wax red. *See* FAN HUNG; IMPASTO RED.

Tondino. Maiolica, with decoration of grotesques and amorini, Fontana workshop, Urbino, *c.* 1555. Courtesy, Sotheby's.

Tomb-figures. Pottery figures buried in tombs. The practice of burying pottery figures with the deceased was very widespread in the ancient world, and in China the custom persisted until the T'ang dynasty (618–906). The making of tomb figures of fired clay superseded the ancient custom of slaying retainers and cattle to provide the deceased with attendants and sustenance in the after-world. In ancient Egypt such figures (*see* USHABTI) were placed in tombs and were thought to come to life when required to do menial tasks. Although pottery figures were being buried in Chinese tombs before the Han dynasty (206 BC–AD 220), those of the T'ang dynasty, often superbly modelled, are the most sought today. Figures intended for a similar purpose in Japan, the HANIWA FIGURES made *c.* 300–645, are not so well known in the West, but they are of considerable interest and importance. *See* CAMEL; HORSE.

Tomb guardian. A figure, usually of a mythological animal or a warrior of fierce aspect, placed at the entrance to a Chinese tomb to protect the spirit of the deceased. Similar figures were also employed as temple guardians. Most surviving specimens date from the T'ang dynasty (618–906); they are made of soft earthenware covered with coloured glazes.

Tomb tablet. A small ceramic memorial to a deceased person. Some Chinese porcelain examples are in the form of a rectangular box with a cover, the box being inscribed with the name, dates of birth and death, and of original burial, together with an epitaph and eulogy and the record of the re-interment of the body.

Tombeau, à (French). Literally, in tomb form. Of a shape somewhat resembling an antique sarcophagus; a term employed for a variety of objects during the 18th century, including furniture and ceramic ware.

Tondino (Italian). A plate of maiolica with a deep well (*cavetto*) and a wide ledge. Such plates do not seem to have been used as tableware, but to serve fruit and confections at fêtes and balls. *See* PIATTO DA POMPA; BACILE; BACINO; SCODELLA.

Tondo (Italian). A large circular MEDALLION with relief decoration; made in Italian maiolica.

Tongue border. A border decoration of adjacent vertical tongue-shaped motifs, all pointing up or down.

Tonquin porcelain. A name used, *c.* 1751, by the Worcester porcelain factory for its wares.

Tooled. A term applied to gilding which implies that it has been worked on with gilders' tools after initial application. *See* CHASED.

Topographical ware. Vases, plates, and other objects of pottery or porcelain painted with a carefully detailed representation of an existing scene, usually a landscape with buildings. The name of the scene is usually added. Paintings of this kind are termed named views.

Tortoise. A decorative motif used on oriental porcelain. In Chinese ornament the tortoise is one of the SSŬ LING, or Four Supernatural Creatures. It is sometimes termed the Divine Tortoise (which is also applied to the Korean dragon-headed tortoise occurring on Koryŏ ware), or the Black Warrior of the North. In Japanese ornament, the tortoise (MINOGAME) is a decorative design which occurs most frequently on Arita porcelain. It sometimes has what seems to be a long, hairy tail which is actually seaweed growing from the shell; this feature has suggested the phrase 'flaming tortoise', which is sometimes used.

Tortoiseshell glaze. *See* FOND ÉCAILLÉ.

Tortoiseshell ware. Creamware, the surface of which somewhat resembles tortoiseshell, made by mingling coloured glazes. The process involved dusting areas of the surface of the unglazed body with manganese to create a brownish-purple effect, with copper for green, and cobalt for blue, then covering the whole with a clear lead glaze and firing it. The simplest of such wares have a brown mottling on a cream-coloured ground, but later examples have several vivid colours applied in a manner which suggests greater control. The process was developed by Thomas Whieldon, and used by Wedgwood for his early wares. *See* VARIEGATED WARE; SPLASHED WARE; WHIELDON WARE.

Torzella. Same as NESTORIS.

Tou ts'ai (Chinese). Literally, contrasting colours. A style of decoration in enamel colours first adopted during the reign of Ch'êng Hua (1465–87). The motifs are outlined in soft underglaze blue, and the painting is completed by adding soft-red, yellow, apple-green and other enamels. The contrast is between the underglaze blue and the overglaze colours. Perhaps the best known is the CHICKEN WARE of this period, so called from the subject of decoration. The style was revived during the reign of Yung Chêng (1723–35), and again in the reign of Tao Kuang (1821–50). *See* WU TS'AI.

Tomb-figure. Grey pottery figure of a duck, with white slip decoration; Chinese, Six Dynasties (220–589). Victoria and Albert Museum, London.

Tomb guardian. Mythological animal figure, glazed earthenware, T'ang dynasty (618–906). Wadsworth Atheneum, Hartford, Conn.

Towing. The process of cleaning and smoothing the edges of dried FLATWARE after removal from the moulds and before the first firing. The materials used were coarse hemp, flax, or jute, and fine sandpaper.

Toys. An 18th-century term used in England for small objects or trifles, e.g. a SCENT-BOTTLE, ÉTUI, PATCH-BOX, BRELOQUE, or BONBONNIÈRE, and other objects such as knife-handles, needle-cases, SEALS, thimbles, and figures; fine-quality porcelain examples were made at Chelsea. *See* MINIATURES; STATUETTES; GALANTERIEWAREN.

Trailed decoration. Decoration on pottery with slip applied to a piece by the process of TRAILING. The French term is *pastillage*.

Trailing. The process of applying slip as a decoration by pouring it through a quill or from a spouted vessel, called a 'slip-cup' or a 'quill-box', where the flow was controlled by a finger closing an air-hole. *See* PASTILLAGE.

Transfer-gilding. A process of transfer-printing in gold which was used in England in the early 19th century by several potters.

Transfer-printing. Outline print filled in with enamel colours, Bow, *c.* 1756.

Transfer-printing. The process of decorating ceramic ware by inking an engraved copper plate (*see* ENGRAVED DESIGNS) with an ink prepared from one of the metallic oxides, and then transferring the design to paper which, while the pigment was still wet, was pressed on to the ware, leaving the desired imprint. This was subsequently fixed by firing. The process was probably invented by an Irish engraver, John Brooks, *c.* 1753, while he was employed at the Battersea Enamel Works which made extensive use of the process. At first the printing was in MONOCHROME – underglaze blue, or black, red, lilac, or sepia overglaze. Printing in POLYCHROME was attempted at Liverpool in the 18th century and a few specimens have survived. Colour-printing was developed during the 19th century, and employed by Felix Pratt (*see* PRATTWARE) for POT-LIDS. Transfer-printing generally is of two kinds: (1) complete in itself, with all the usual hatchings and shadings of a line-engraving; and (2) outlines intended for later colouring by semi-skilled workers in enamel colours. The latter type of print was used at Bow, Worcester, and at Wedgwood's Chelsea decorating establishment. The former type was sometimes coloured over with enamels by INDEPENDENT DECORATORS, principally by James Giles of Clerkenwell (London).

Early Wedgwood creamware and Leeds creamware were often decorated with transfer-printing by Sadler and Green of Liverpool, independent discoverers of the process. The most notable engraver in this field was Robert Hancock, who was at Battersea and Bow before he went to Worcester in 1756 (*see* HANCOCK ENGRAVINGS). Bow examples are in red, lilac, and sepia overglaze; very rarely in blue underglaze. Underglaze blue printing was done at Worcester, Derby (rarely), Lowestoft, and Caughley. The process was hardly used on the Continent before the beginning of the 19th century, when it was employed fairly extensively at Creil in the decoration of FAÏENCE FINE. *See* BAT PRINTING; SILK-SCREEN TRANSFERS; COLD PRINTING; HOT PRINTING; LITHOGRAPHIC DECORATION.

Transition Ming. Chinese porcelain of the MING DYNASTY, made between 1620 and 1644 at Ching-tê Chên; in style it is the precursor of the early wares of the following CH'ING DYNASTY from 1644 until towards the end of the century. The wares thus described are usually VASES and POTICHES decorated in underglaze blue, and extremely well painted with sensitive line and broad washes of colour. The bases are flat and unglazed. Wares of this kind often bear inscriptions, part of which is sometimes a date, enabling the year of manufacture to be precisely placed.

Translucent. Permitting the passage of light in a diffused form, as distinct from transparent. Translucency is the usual European test for porcelain, and this differs from the Chinese test, which is whether or not the ware is resonant when struck. The degree of translucency depends on the degree of vitrification and the thickness of the body. There is, usually, very little to be learned from the colour exhibited by porcelain under transmitted light, since additions were often made to the paste for the purpose of modifying its colour. The Worcester green, for instance, is probably the result of adding a little cobalt blue to a porcelain body which was naturally of an orange cast.

Transmutation glaze. *See* FLAMBÉ.

Transparency, Berlin. Same as LITHOPHANE.

Trauerkrug (German). Literally, mourning jug. A type of grey saltglazed stoneware jug made in Germany in the third quarter of the 17th century. They were of pyriform shape, fitted with a lid and pewter mounts, and decorated with carved patterns (KERBSCHNITT) overpainted with black and white enamels, hence the name.

Trauerkrug. Grey stoneware jug, ht 7 in., decorated in black and white, Freiburg, *c.* 1675. Victoria and Albert Museum, London.

Tray. A flat receptacle, varying in size and shape, with a low vertical, sloping, or curved rim, usually *en suite* with a service. Some examples have a stem base. *See* PLATEAU; VASSOIO.

Tray. Porcelain tray, width 16½ in., with painted view of Vienna seen from the Belvedere; Vienna, *c.* 1780. Österreichisches Museum für angewandte Kunst, Vienna.

Treacle glaze. A thickly applied pottery glaze that gives the impression of being treacly and has often run down the side of the ware in much the same way as treacle would. The effect is particularly noticeable on certain Chinese wares of the Sung dynasty.

Treacle ware. Pottery with a brown treacle glaze. It was developed at Rockingham (Yorkshire) in the early years of the 19th century, and was later made by many Staffordshire factories, as well as at Bennington, Vermont. The wares are usually mugs, jugs, and similar vessels. *See* BROWN CHINA; BENNINGTON WARE.

Tree-platter. A type of platter with lateral grooves extending from a long central groove, giving it somewhat the appearance of a tree, for the purpose of draining gravy into a well at one end. *See* WELL-PLATTER.

Tree pottery. *See* MOCHA WARE.

Tree-trunk. A type of moulded decoration simulating the appearance of a gnarled tree-trunk overgrown with moss and vine. A teapot with the body in this style was modelled by Jean Voyez and made by Whieldon in mottled colours with a crabstock handle and spout. Other examples are known in saltglaze, black basaltes, etc. Rare examples of 17th-century Arita porcelain are in this form. *See* FAIR HEBE JUG.

Tree-trunk. Teapot modelled by Jean Voyez and made by Thomas Whieldon, *c.* 1780–90. British Museum, London.

Trefoil. A form or an ornament which has three equal foils or lobes. *See* PINCHED LIP.

Trek (Dutch). The outline of figures, foliage, etc., on Dutch delftware which was filled in with washes of colour, either blue or polychrome. The outline was usually in dark blue, manganese, or black. The technique, which is akin to a preliminary drawing, was used by other factories, apart from those of Holland.

Trellis border. A border pattern embodying a trellis ground, called *trellisage*.

Trembleuse. Cup and saucer with deep well, Sèvres, *c*. 1765. Wallace Collection, London.

Trellis ground. A diaper ground of diagonal lines which, in crossing, form a series of lozenge shapes the centre of which often contains additional ornament. *See* QUADRILLÉ.

Trellis pattern. A decorative pattern sometimes of diapers (*see* TRELLIS GROUND), but sometimes of the kind of trellis used to support vines, e.g. the HOP TRELLIS PATTERN popular at Worcester, and copied from Sèvres.

Trellisage. *See* TRELLIS BORDER; BOCAGE.

Trembleuse (French). A cup and saucer, of which the saucer has a projecting ring into which the cup fits; the ring may be of considerable height and occasionally pierced with ornamental designs. Sometimes a deep well was used instead of the vertical ring, at Sèvres, and especially at the Chelsea-Derby factory. The *trembleuse* was made in this form to prevent spillage of the contents caused by a shaky hand. Usually saucers of this type were made to accompany a coffee-cup, but were also employed with a bouillon-cup, chocolate-cup, or teacup. *See* CHOCOLATE-STAND.

Trencher. An early term for a large plate, dish, or platter on which to serve or carve food. *See* CHARGER. Trenchers were at first made of wood.

Trencher salt. A type of salt-cellar of SILVER PATTERN which is without feet and rests flat on the table. Trencher salts were circular, oval, or rectangular, and were made with one, two, or three wells.

Triad. *See* CHINESE TRIAD.

Trifle-box. Porcelain, Lowestoft, *c*. 1760. Victoria and Albert Museum, London.

Triangle border. A border pattern comprising a series of connecting equilateral triangles, each enclosing a hatching of parallel diagonal lines, in which those in the triangles with the apex pointing downwards run in the opposite direction from those in the triangles with the apex pointing upwards.

Trichterbecher (German). An early form of baluster-shaped beaker with a funnel-mouth made of SIEGBURG WARE in the 16th century. It is sometimes called a baluster jug. The form also occurs in early faience.

Trifle-box. A small box made of Lowestoft porcelain in the 18th century and inscribed 'A Trifle from . . .' (often 'Lowestoft' or 'Bungay') – an early example of catering specifically for the souvenir trade.

Trifle-mug. A mug made of Lowestoft porcelain in the 18th century inscribed 'A Trifle from . . .'. *See* TRIFLE-BOX.

Trigrams, Eight. *See* PA-KUA.

Tring tiles. *See* CHERTSEY TILES.

Trinket box. A small covered bowl or box, usually circular, used for keeping small trinkets. English delftware specimens were made *c*. 1750.

Trinket stand. A circular flat-topped stand on a stemmed and splayed base for keeping small trinkets on a dressing-table.

Triple gourd vase. A vase similar in section to a DOUBLE GOURD VASE, but with three globular parts, becoming smaller in ascending order.

Triton candlestick. A candlestick in the form of a bearded naked Triton with seaweed clinging to his thighs, who is shown in a kneeling position supporting a cornucopia. The original was designed by John Flaxman for Wedgwood, who made the candlesticks in pairs both in jasper and in black basaltes. The model was copied elsewhere in Staffordshire in earthenware.

Trivet. A triangular slab of earthenware or fired clay with concave sides and three small feet used to support flatware in a kiln by placing it between pieces in stacks. As a result the three feet resting on the lower plate (or other ware) left SPUR-MARKS on its upper surface; these sometimes mar the decoration, as is often seen on delftware.

Trofei. The Italian term for TROPHIES.

Trompe l'œil. Faience plate with high-relief decoration, probably Talavera, Spain, 18th century. Courtesy, Newman & Newman Ltd, London.

Trompe l'œil (French). Literally, deceive the eye. Painted or high-relief decoration executed in a manner so life-like that the eye is deceived into mistaking the apparent for the real. Typical of such painted ware is *trompe l'œil sur fond bois*, a ground (*see* FOND BOIS) representing the grain of wood with an engraving apparently pinned to its surface; it is to be found in faience from Niderviller, and in porcelain from Vienna and some of the German factories. The term is sometimes employed in relation to the naturalism of Palissy's rustic plates and platters which include in their decoration fish and reptiles in high relief, the modelling being so realistic that some have concluded that they were cast from life. *See* FIGULINES RUSTIQUES; PALISSY WARE. The term also refers to some plates with extremely realistic decoration in high relief of fruits, vegetables, nuts, etc.

Trophies. The trophy was, in the first place, the arms of a beaten enemy hung by the Greeks in an oak tree to commemorate a victory. This became a decorative motif depicting martial trophies, including helmets, shields, axes, and drums, either in relief or in painted form. Eventually the martial trophies developed into other motifs emblematic of a particular subject and arranged in ornamental form. Amatory trophies included doves, bows and arrows, and quivers; musical trophies, violins and flutes; and horticultural trophies, beehives, watering-cans, and wheelbarrows. The Italian term is *trofei*. *See* WAPPENGESCHIRR.

Trophies. Porcelain orange tub, painted with trophies and *amorini* in reserves, Vincennes or Sèvres, *c.* 1752–60. Victoria and Albert Museum, London.

Trough spout. A type of spout extended so that the lip of the vessel forms a narrow trough, or is modelled as a half-tube cut horizontally.

True porcelain. The same as hard-paste porcelain. Chinese porcelain made of white china clay (KAOLIN) and *petuntse* (PAI-TUN-TZŬ), a natural fusible rock. The secret of its manufacture was eagerly sought, but it was not discovered in Europe until soon after 1700 by E.W. von Tschirnhausen and J.F. Böttger at Meissen. In France true porcelain is called *pâte dure*, and at Sèvres, *porcelaine royale*. In England it was made in the 18th century only at Bristol, New Hall, and Plymouth. *See* SOAPROCK PORCELAIN.

Truité (French). *See* CRACKLE.

Trump. The dog of William Hogarth (1697–1764), the English painter and engraver, of which a porcelain figure in a seated position was made at Chelsea *c.* 1747–50. Wedgwood made similar pieces in black basaltes, *c.* 1774–77. *See* DOGS.

Trumpet-neck. The neck of a vase or other vessel which is flared towards the mouth.

Trumpet vase. A vase with a trumpet-neck. Although porcelain vases of this type were first made in the 17th century, during the late Ming dynasty, the actual shape is very ancient, being copied from altar-vases in bronze of the first millennium BC. *See* TSUN.

Ts'ai (Chinese). Literally, colour; frequently used in descriptive phases, such as *ying ts'ai*, strong colours, referring to the FAMILLE VERTE palette. *See* FEN TS'AI; SAN TS'AI; TOU TS'AI; WU TS'AI; YANG TS'AI.

Ts'ui (Chinese). The colour of kingfisher's feathers, said by a T'ang poet to be the colour of some YÜEH celadon bowls. It is an example of the poetic imagery with which translators of early Chinese treatises on ceramics have to contend.

Tsun (Chinese). A large bronze vase of ancient origin; it is of beaker shape, with a high, wide trumpet-neck and a globular body incurving towards the base. This is also a characteristic vase-shape in porcelain inspired by the bronze vases, and made especially during the TRANSITION MING period and in the reign of K'ang Hsi (1662–1722). The vases are usually decorated in underglaze blue, and occasionally in enamels of the FAMILLE VERTE. The term is also loosely used for bronze and porcelain vessels of other shapes used to hold wine. *See* KU.

Ts'ung (Chinese). A vase which is cylindrical in the interior and square on the exterior. Originally an ancient jade astronomical instrument, the form was adapted in the 18th century to vases usually covered with a celadon glaze and decorated with the Eight Trigrams (PA-KUA) on the four edges or sides.

T'u Ting yao (Chinese). A type of TING YAO, referred to as earthen Ting, which has a yellowish glaze and a coarse body. It is, by common consent, inferior to *pai-Ting*.

Tubular spout. A type of straight spout, usually tapering towards the mouth, and usually attached to a teapot near the bottom.

Tulip-vase. Dutch delftware, ht 11 in., 17th century. Victoria and Albert Museum, London.

Tudor ware. Pottery made in England between 1485 and 1603, during the reigns of the Tudor sovereigns; it usually has a buff or reddish body covered with a transparent green glaze.

Tulipano. The Italian term for a TULIP-VASE.

Tulipière. The French term for a TULIP-VASE.

Tulip-vase. A vase with multiple spouts in the form of tubes each to hold a single tulip. The simplest form has five large spouts outspread like a fan, sometimes paralleled on each side by fan-like groups of four smaller spouts. Other, more elaborate specimens, often called PAGODA VASES, are in the form of a tall pagoda with a high finial; this type has up to eleven separate tiers of spouts and stands on a plinth. Tulip-vases were made of tin-glazed earthenware at Delft in Holland, and in England, France, Germany, and Italy. They occur in the porcelain of Vienna and China. The French term is *tulipière* and the Italian *tulipano*. *See* FINGER VASE; QUINTAL FLOWER HORN.

Tulip ware. Earthenware made in Pennsylvania towards the end of the 18th century; it is decorated in an unsophisticated style with tulips incised through slip. *See* PENNSYLVANIA DUTCH WARE.

Tung ware. Northern SUNG YAO which has not been certainly identified, but is believed to have been a celadon of grey-green colour over a greyish buff body with carved decoration. It is related to NORTHERN CELADON.

Tunnel-kiln. The modern kiln which replaces the old oven kiln. It is about 275 feet long and electrically heated for the firing of ware carried through on low trucks. As the trucks pass through the kiln the temperature first increases to reach its maximum point, and then gradually diminishes as the tunnel exit is approached.

Tureen. A large circular or oval serving bowl, usually with a cover, for soup or vegetables. Tureens are made in a wide variety of forms, the finest being of porcelain, although those of faience are often well modelled and decorated. During the rococo period tureens were modelled in the form of a variety of birds, animals, fish, vegetables, and fruit. Bird-tureens were especially popular, the forms including cockerel, duck, swan, turkey, partridge, and woodcock. Animal models include the rabbit, while the boar's head (among others) occurs in Chinese export porcelain as well. Tureens in the form of fish include the carp and the coiled eel. Vegetables such as the marrow, a bundle of asparagus, the cabbage, and the cauliflower were popular rococo models. A rare Derby model is in the form of a bunch of grapes. In porcelain Chelsea tureens are especially sought. Faience models of fine quality were made at Brussels, Strasbourg, and Holitsch. Rococo tureens in these forms have been reproduced. The French term is *soupière*. *See* SAUCE-TUREEN; PIGEON TUREEN; COCK TUREEN; ASPARAGUS TUREEN; MARROW TUREEN; CABBAGE WARE; CAULIFLOWER WARE.

Türkenköpge (German). A type of coffee-cup, tall and without a handle, made for the Turkish market by Meissen, Nymphenburg, and other German factories. An order for 3,000 dozen was filled by Meissen in 1734 for Mannases Athanas of Istanbul. They bore the mark of the caduceus instead of the normal factory-mark of crossed swords since the latter was regarded as a Christian symbol.

Turner's stoneware. A type of white stoneware made principally by John Turner of Lane End, Staffordshire, but also by other potters in the vicinity, *c.* 1785–1810. It was principally used for mugs, tankards, and jugs ornamented with drinking or hunting scenes in relief, and often with the addition of silver or plated mounts. From about 1800 the term was also applied to Turner's Patented Earthenware, a hard body sometimes slightly translucent. The patent was reputedly bought by Josiah Spode and renamed Stone China. *See* STONE CHINA.

Turning. A method of finishing ceramic ware, after preliminary shaping on the potter's wheel and drying to leather hardness, by which it is rotated and, while rotating, is brought into contact with tools of various kinds which either pare the walls to make them thinner (giving the surface mechanical precision), or incise rings or other decoration (as more or less elaborate ornamentation). Turning is done on a lathe; incised geometric decoration is done on an engine-turning lathe first employed by Josiah Wedgwood. *See* ENGINE-TURNED DECORATION; ROSE-ENGINE TURNED.

Trump. Porcelain figure, Chelsea, *c.* 1747–50. Victoria and Albert Museum, London.

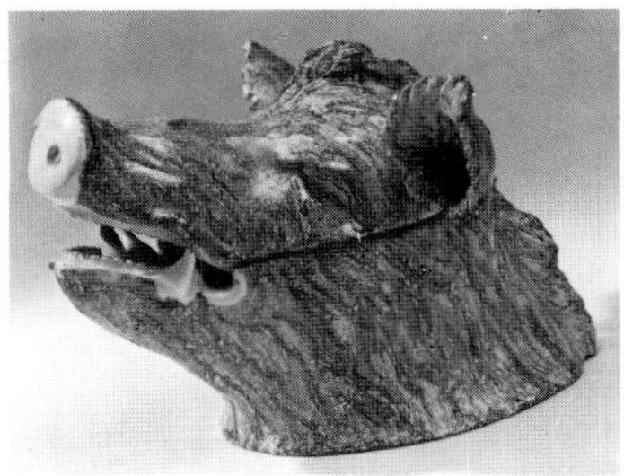

Tureen. Boar's head tureen, faience, Strasbourg, *c.* 1740–60. Courtesy, Antique Porcelain Co., London.

Turning. Vase of red stoneware, thrown and turned on the wheel, Meissen, *c.* 1715. Museum of Fine Arts, Boston, Mass.

Twiffler. An eight-inch plate, variously shaped; so called from 1790 onwards. It is in size between a dinner plate and a muffin plate.

Twig-basket. A bowl-like receptacle the walls of which are built up of separate ceramic twigs of curved form which are bound together round the middle with simulated wickerwork. There is usually a pierced stand with moulded wickerwork (or OZIER) decoration. Twig-baskets are found in Leeds creamware, sometimes with added decoration in blue. *See* BASKET WARE.

Tyg. Red clay body, with applied slipware pads and trailed decoration, Wrotham, 1651. Burnap Collection, William Rockhill Nelson Gallery of Art, Kansas City, Mo.

Tyg. A type of large drinking mug usually with 2 or 4 handles, but it may have up to 11 arranged equidistantly around the exterior. Sometimes it was given several spouts which were intended to provide for a number of drinkers. Tygs were made in England during the 17th and 18th centuries. The earliest dated examples are in WROTHAM WARE. Specimens with many handles were intended as LOVING-CUPS for festive occasions. Early handles were often in the shape of the capital letter B, and some have triple instead of double loops. Examples are known of tygs inscribed with names, initials, and dates. *See* BRAGGET-POT; POSSET-POT.

Tyger and wheatsheaf pattern. Originally a pattern depicting a tiger among wheatsheaves, used on Japanese porcelain made at Arita (Hizen province) and associated with Sakaida Kakiemon. Imported from Japan by the Dutch late in the 17th century, it was frequently copied by Continental and English porcelain factories, especially at Meissen and Chelsea. Also known as the 'Korean tyger'. *See* WHEATSHEAF PATTERN.

Tyneside pottery. Earthenware made in England near Newcastle-on-Tyne, at over a hundred small potteries (including several owned by members of the Maling family) from *c.* 1730 to *c.* 1875. It was made from materials not of local origin, and consisted of low-quality wares, mainly tableware of CREAMWARE, MOCHA WARE, LUSTRE WARE, and blue transfer-printed ware, and figures of celebrities and dogs, usually copied from Staffordshire examples. They were made principally for export. *See* SUNDERLAND WARE.

Tzŭ (Chinese). Any ceramic material which is fired sufficiently to give a resonant note when struck. This classification includes both porcelain and fine stoneware. *See* PAI-TZŬ.

Tzŭ Chou yao. Stoneware pillow with painted decoration of a tethered bear, Sung dynasty (960–1280). British Museum, London.

Tz'ŭ Chou yao (Chinese). Stoneware produced at Tz'ŭ Chou (southern Chihli province). The kilns here have been operating at least since the Sung dynasty (960–1280), and still make wares in the traditional style. The body is usually comparatively coarse and greyish-white in colour, and it was frequently given a preliminary coating of white slip over which was placed a clear transparent glaze. Decoration is often painted in black or brown slip. These kilns were the first to make use of painted decoration. Towards the end of the Sung dynasty primitive red and green enamels occur on some wares from here, and these are the first to be used as ceramic decoration in China. A group of wares is decorated with the *sgraffito* technique, the decoration being incised through a white slip to reveal the body underneath. The same technique is employed more rarely to decorate brown glazed wares. Some large pieces of monumental form were made during the Sung dynasty, and forms unusual to the West include PILLOWS. There are literary references to the use of underglaze blue at Tz'ŭ Chou late in the Sung dynasty, but no confirmatory evidence is available. The attribution of many surviving specimens to the Sung dynasty is neither easy nor certain.

Ultra-violet radiation. When subjected to ultra-violet radiation some ceramic wares fluoresce with a colour which is fairly characteristic. This reaction depends on the presence of fluorescent trace-elements in the body, and the method is sometimes employed as a test for differentiating porcelain made at Chelsea from that of other factories, and from forgeries. It is also used to detect restoration to pottery and porcelain, since the materials employed in work of this kind nearly always fluoresce with a colour markedly different from that of the original glaze.

Ultramarine. Blue made from powdered lapis lazuli. In ceramic parlance the name was applied to an enamel blue used at Chelsea and elsewhere in England which imitated the BLEU DE ROI of Sèvres.

Umbrian ware. A general term formerly used for maiolica, especially that produced in the 15th and early 16th centuries at Urbino, Pesaro and Gubbio, and the somewhat later ware from Castel Durante, Faenza, and other places in the region.

Unaker. An American Indian term for the china clay (KAOLIN) found in Virginia and North Carolina and imported into England during the 18th century. It was first brought to England from Virginia in 1744 by a colonist of Huguenot extraction named Andrew Duché, and reference to it is to be found in patent specifications registered by Thomas Frye of Bow in 1744 and 1749. Duché was, without doubt, the man referred to in 1745 by William Cookworthy as having found the Chinese earth in Virginia, but little or none was imported at the time, due to Cookworthy's discovery of china clay in Cornwall. A small quantity was imported at Bristol in 1765, some of which was retained by Richard Champion, later of the Bristol porcelain factory, and a further quantity was sent to Worcester for experimental purposes. *Unaker* was well known to Josiah Wedgwood who imported some clay of this kind found in North Carolina. He thought it very superior and, at considerable expense, sent an expedition which procured five tons. This was used very sparingly as part of the JASPER body. According to Wedgwood some of this clay was exported to France, probably to Sèvres, but no record of it appears to exist in that country. Nevertheless, in view of the search being made for clay of this kind in France during the 1760s, and the existence of the French colony of Louisiana not far away, relatively speaking, from its source, the possibility is a strong one. The discovery of French sources of china clay at Saint-Yrieix in 1770 made imports unnecessary.

Underglaze. Decoration or marking of any kind applied to the body of ceramic ware before glazing.

Underglaze. Worcester porcelain plate with underglaze blue transfer-printed decoration, and unglazed cup, bowl, and mug, showing the zig-zag fence pattern. Courtesy, Worcester Royal Porcelain Co.

Underglaze colours. Colours employed in the decoration of ceramic ware which, because they develop at about the same temperature as that needed to fuse the glaze material, can be applied before glazing, i.e. under the glaze. Cobalt blue, which is exceptionally tolerant in this way, is the commonest underglaze colour. It was applied to Chinese porcelain before either body or glaze was fired, and it therefore had to withstand an approximate firing temperature of 1450°C. Manganese was also used as an underglaze colour in the West, and copper was so used in

China. Both in the Ming dynasty and the 18th century copper red and cobalt blue were fired together, but the result is usually far from satisfactory, either the copper red or the blue failing to develop properly. HIGH-TEMPERATURE COLOURS are those employed in the decoration of delftware and of earthenware generally; these develop at a somewhat lower temperature than the underglaze colours used to decorate porcelain.

Unguentarium (Latin). The Latin term for a Greek pottery vessel used for holding unguents. *See* AMPULLA; ARYBALLOS; ALABASTRON; LEKYTHOS.

Urinal. A vessel of pottery or porcelain, appropriately shaped for male or female use, to hold urine. It is impossible to say where or at what date urinals originated, but those of the 18th century or earlier are often decorative as well as utilitarian. *See* BOURDALOU; CHAMBER-POT.

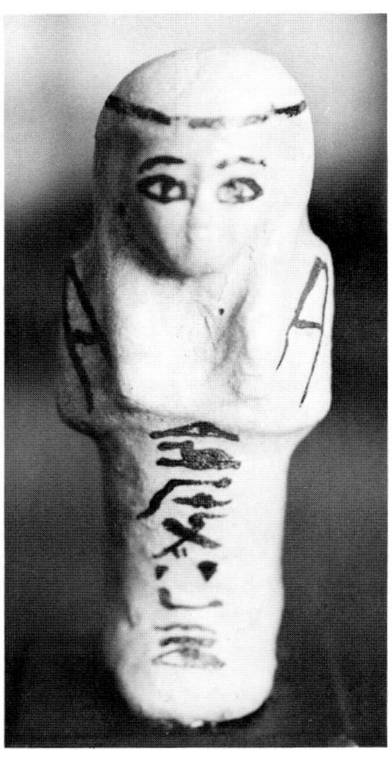

Ushabti. Figure of a priest of Amun, blue faience with ink inscriptions, XXIst Dynasty, *c.* 1000 BC; actual size. Private collection. Photo Peter Clayton.

Urn. (1) A classical vase-form of various shapes, but usually curved inwards to a stemmed base or plinth, and having a mouth which is smaller in diameter than the body. The urn often has two side handles. In classical times it had many uses, for holding liquids, for ornamental purposes, for holding lots to be drawn, and for containing the ashes of the dead, but all vessels for the last purpose are not to be classified as urns, despite popular usage. (2) A closed receptacle of the same general form which has a spigot or tap, and often a heating device for warming the contents; some examples were made of English delftware, *c.* 1765. *See* TEA-URN; COFFEE-URN.

Useful ware. Pottery and porcelain of domestic utility made for preparing, serving, or storing food or beverages, as distinguished from ornamental ware which is primarily decorative.

Ushabti (also *shabti, shawabti*). An ancient Egyptian mummy-form tomb-figure, generally of 'faience' but occurring in wood, stone, glass, and bronze, which was deposited in the tomb with the mummy of the deceased. Such figures were intended to serve the deceased's spirit in the after-world. They were made in large quantities from the XVIIIth Dynasty onwards, but fine quality specimens in faience are unusual before the XXVIth Dynasty. The body of the figure is of a sandy composition, over which a layer of blue or green frit was fired to form a glaze. This has, as a result of decomposition, often turned to white or brown. The material of which they are made can hardly be termed a ceramic ware at all, and it is certainly not true faience, which is tin-glazed ware. Most *ushabtis* bear inscriptions in hieroglyphs. Vases, such figures as the hippopotamus, and scarabs were also made of the same material; the vases nearly always belong to the Ptolemaic or Roman periods. *Ushabtis* are usually about 4 in. in height, but range from 1 inch to over 3 ft. *See* EGYPTIAN FAIENCE.

V

Vaisseau à mât (French). A type of POT-POURRI VASE, in the form of a sailing-ship, made at Vincennes, *c.* 1755. It is made in two parts, the lower being a boat-shaped vessel on four scroll feet with a lion mask at each end; the upper part is the pierced cover in the form of a ship's rigging, with a banner at the mast-head. The banner is dotted with the fleur-de-lys. The form seems to have been derived from the single-masted ship which forms part of the coat of arms of the city of Paris. Copies were made in the 19th century by Minton and others.

Vaisseau à mât. Porcelain, Vincennes, *c.* 1755. Wallace Collection, London.

Valentine pattern. A decorative pattern of billing doves perched on a quiver of arrows beside pine-trees, near which stands an altar of love with two pierced hearts. The pattern was used at Worcester. There are several variants.

Valentine teapot. A teapot decorated with a design of billing doves standing on a quiver; *see* VALENTINE PATTERN.

Vandyke border. A decorative border with a sharply pointed indented edge.

Variegated ware. Glazed pottery the surface of which exhibits a mingling of colours, usually intended to resemble a natural stone. Pottery thus designated includes ware made by mingling (wedging) differently coloured clays (SOLID AGATE WARE), and wares with a surface coating of differently coloured slips (SURFACE AGATE WARE, MARBLED WARE) or glazes (TORTOISESHELL WARE). *See* GRANITE WARE; SPECKLED AGATE WARE.

Varnish gilding. Same as LACQUER GILDING.

Vase. A vessel made in many forms, sections, and styles, but usually rounded and taller than it is wide, which is used mainly for ornamental purposes. Some have an ornamental cover. *See* GARNITURE; DOUBLE VASE; GREEK VASES.

Vase à anses torsés (French). A type of vase made at Sèvres which has two twisted handles extending from the shoulder to the mouth of the tall neck.

Vase à cartel (French). A clock-case in the form of a vase, such as those made at Sèvres.

Vase à compartements (French). A flower vase or CAISSE À FLEURS divided by a vertical partition so as to have two compartments.

Vase à dauphins (French). A type of vase made at Sèvres, and so called from its two side handles which were in the form of dolphins.

Vase à l'oignon (French). A type of vase made at Sèvres which has a cupped mouth for holding a flower-bulb. *See* BULB-VASE; ROOT-POT.

Vaso campana. Porcelain vase, ht 13 in., Derby, early 19th century. Courtesy, Christie's.

Vase à oreilles (French). A type of vase, introduced at Sèvres in the 1750s, of baluster shape supported by a stemmed and spreading base. It has a short, foliate neck, and two scroll handles arising from the sides of the mouth and curving downwards to

Vase candlestick. Black basaltes, with reversible cover to be used as a candle-holder at night, Wedgwood and Bentley, *c.* 1770. Courtesy, David Newbon Ltd, London.

Vase hollandais. Porcelain, Sèvres, 1758. Wallace Collection, London.

the shoulder. These handles have a profile closely resembling the human ear, hence the name.

Vase à panneaux (French). A vase with reserved panels for painted decoration.

Vase antique ferré (French). A type of large ovoid vase with gilded relief decoration in the form of iron chains of links and bars. Made at Sèvres, it was part of a GARNITURE.

Vase candelabra. A candelabrum in the form of a vase with candle-nozzles and drip-pans. *See* VASE FLAMBEAU.

Vase-candlestick. An urn-shaped vase with a reversible cover, one side of which is provided with a candle-nozzle. Originally from the Continent, English examples are known in Chelsea-Derby porcelain, in Leeds creamware, and Wedgwood black basaltes. Sometimes called a CASSOLETTE, but incorrectly so when no pierced holes (to allow perfume to escape) are present.

Vase cassolette à festons (French). A CASSOLETTE in the form of a vase decorated with festooned drapery. Examples were made at Sèvres.

Vase drapé (French). A type of vase made at Sèvres decorated with painted festoons of draped fabric.

Vase flambeau (French). A vase, sometimes baluster-shaped, with a candle-nozzle on either side. *See* VASE CANDELABRA.

Vase hollandais (French). A flared, fan-shaped vase on a plinth, the vase having holes in the bottom to receive water from the plinth, and the plinth having pierced shoulders so that water may be poured in. This type of flower-vase is also called a *jardinière éventail*. The *vase hollandais nouveau* is more elaborate. The type was first introduced at Sèvres in the 1750s.

Vase strié (French). A vase decorated with a series of close vertical stripes.

Vase tourterelle (French). A type of large vase made at Sèvres, so called from a pair of moulded doves on either side.

Vase tulipe (French). A type of large vase made at Sèvres, *c.* 1758, of inverted pear-shape on a stemmed base. The mouth is in the form of an open tulip whose petals form two handles.

Vase Vaisseau à mât (French). Same as VAISSEAU À MÂT.

Vaso a calice (Italian). A vase of the Greek KRATER type, of calyx or chalice shape with two low upright side handles.

Vaso a colonnette (Italian). A vase of the KRATER type with columnar handles, known as a *kelebe*.

Vaso a rotelle (Italian). A vase of the Greek KRATER type with two VOLUTE HANDLES. It dates from the period of the BLACK-FIGURE STYLE. *See* FRANÇOIS VASE.

Vaso campana (Italian). A vase of the Greek KRATER type, of inverted bell-shape and having two side handles on the shoulder. Vases of this type, originally made in classical times, were produced in the early part of the 19th century at many factories.

Vaso di Spezieria (Italian). Same as SPEZIERIA VASE.

Vaso puerperale (Italian). A set of pottery utensils that, in ancient Rome, was given to a woman during confinement. Later accouchement sets consisted of several (usually five) utensils nested together vertically so as to resemble a baluster-shaped vase, being (from bottom upwards): a broth-basin (*scodella*) on a raised foot; its cover in the form of a plate (*tagliere*) in an inverted position; a bowl or cup (*ongarescha*); a salt-cellar (*saliera*); and its domed and pierced cover (*coperchio*). The decoration often depicted the birth of gods or heroes, or Leda and her twins. *See* ACCOUCHEMENT BOWL.

Vaso senza bocca (Italian). A type of coffee-pot with a spout and handle in the usual form, the cover of which is integral with the body. It is filled from the bottom through a funnel inside the pot; when the vessel is turned right side up the liquid descends around the inverted funnel. Pots in this form were made in Italy of maiolica. *See* CADOGAN; WINE-POT.

Vassoio (Italian). A large serving platter, sometimes with sectional partitions.

Veilleuse (French). A ceramic utensil in several parts, for keeping warm the contents of a bowl, teapot, or cup which rests on a hollow pedestal containing a GODET (lamp). Originally made to be used at the bedside to heat food for an invalid or an infant, the *veilleuse* was (after *c.* 1800) similarly used in the bedroom for heating beverages for one person. The name is derived from the verb *veiller*, to keep a night vigil. The characteristic feature is that the bowl or teapot is made with a projecting bottom part which fits into the pedestal, bringing the contents nearer to the warming flame of the *godet*. There are three basic forms: (1) the FOOD-WARMER; (2) the tea-warmer (*see* VEILLEUSE-THÉIÈRE), which includes the PERSONNAGE; (3) the CUP-WARMER. *Veilleuses* were made throughout Europe from *c.* 1750 until after 1860, and copies of early types are still made, as also are modern versions, in France, Italy, Spain, Portugal, and Japan. The *veilleuse* is known in pottery (including creamware and tin-glazed earthenware), porcelain, and stoneware. Some examples have LITHOPHANE panels. The German terms are *Réchaud* and *Suppenwärmer*, and the Italian, *scaldavivande* and *scaldabevende*. *See* COQUETIÈRE; REFIRED WARE.

Veilleuse-théière (French). A type of VEILLEUSE the upper part of which is a teapot. It is the same as the VEILLEUSE-TISANIÈRE, and includes the type known as the PERSONNAGE. The pedestal usually has an aperture for the insertion of the GODET, but some pedestals are without an aperture, and must be lifted from a low base and returned when the *godet* has been placed in position.

Veilleuse-tisanière (French). Same as the VEILLEUSE-THÉIÈRE but so called in France because it was used to make various infusions (*tisanes*) of, for example, camomile, mint, or linden tea.

Venetian Fair group. A porcelain group made at Ludwigsburg depicting booths and related figures appearing at the so-called Venetian Fair held locally. These are said to have been modelled by Jean Louis, *Modellmeister* from 1762 to 1777, in association with the designer, G.F. Riedel. The original Fair was held after Duke Carl Eugen of Württemberg returned from Venice in 1768 and reproduced the Venetian Fair in the market place at Ludwigsburg as a winter pastime for his court.

Vent-hole. A hole in the base of a figure through which occluded

Vase cassolette à festons. Porcelain, Sèvres, *c.* 1760. Wallace Collection, London.

Vaso puerperale. Accouchement set in five parts, ht 8 in., Faenza (Ferniani factory), *c.* 1775–1800. Museo Internationale delle Ceramiche, Faenza.

Veilleuse-théière. Tea-warmer, Minton, *c.* 1817. Victoria and Albert Museum, London.

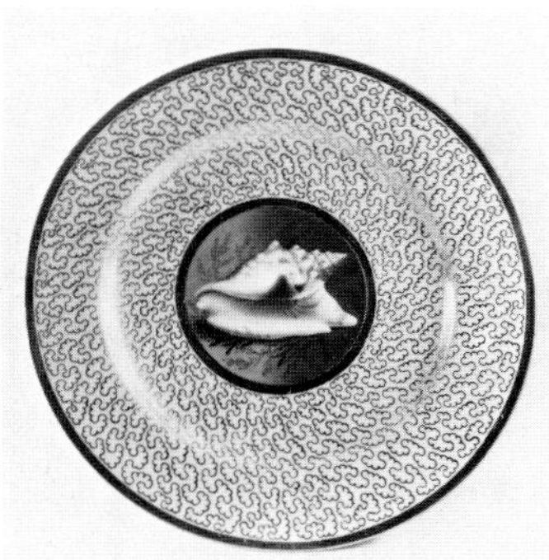

Vermiculated ground. Porcelain plate, Worcester (Barr, Flight and Barr period). Courtesy, Sotheby's.

gases are voided into the atmosphere while the piece is being fired in the kiln. Similar holes occur at the rear of mask handles on vases and some food-warmers. On early DRY-EDGE ware from Derby it frequently has the appearance of a screw-hole, instead of the clean-cut round holes of later date.

Vermicelli ground. A ground pattern, usually in gold on blue, of long, irregular lines. *See* VERMICULATED GROUND.

Vermiculated ground. A ground pattern of curving lines suggesting the appearance of having been eaten by worms, or of having been covered by their tracks. It was developed at Sèvres in the 1750s, where it was sometimes executed in blue on a pink ground, creating the effect of marbling.

Vernis (French). Literally, varnish. The term is employed of glazes, usually those on transparent-glazed earthenware (*faïence fine*). A faience glaze is termed *émail*, and *couverte* is generally employed in connection with porcelain.

Verrière (French). A MONTEITH. Also termed a *seau à verre*, *seau crenelé*, or *rafraîchissoir*.

Verseuse (French). A small baluster-shaped pot with a hinged lid and a single handle protruding at right angles to the pouring lip, often miscalled a CHOCOLATE-POT.

Vert anglais (French). Same as meadow-green. A ground colour used at Sèvres in the 18th century. Also known as *vert pré*.

Vert jaune (French). Same as APPLE-GREEN. *See* CHROME GREEN.

Vert pomme (French). Same as APPLE-GREEN. *See* CHROME GREEN.

Vert pré (French). Same as meadow-green. A ground colour used at Sèvres in the 18th century. Also known as *vert anglais*.

Vezzi porcelain. True porcelain made from 1720 to 1727 by Giuseppe and Francesco Vezzi with the assistance of C.K. Hunger from Vienna, at a factory in Venice. It resembles the porcelain of J.F. Böttger made at Meissen, and the form and decoration owe something to contemporary designs used at Vienna and Meissen. The decoration is often in relief, and some examples have enamelled *chinoiseries*. The Venice factory was the third (following Meissen and Vienna) to be started in Europe for the manufacture of TRUE PORCELAIN.

Twelve Cardinal Virtues. Porcelain figure of Hope, from the series modelled by Simon Feilner, Fürstenberg, *c.* 1760–62. Dr Hans Syz Collection, Smithsonian Institution, Washington, D.C.

Vicar and Moses. A popular pottery group first made by Ralph Wood I, *c.* 1770, from a model perhaps by Aaron Wood, although Jean Voyez is sometimes suggested. Two figures, one above the other, are seated in a pulpit, the Vicar (above) asleep, with his head resting on his hand, and (below) his clerk, Moses, preaching the sermon in his stead. The group was also made later by Enoch Wood. *See* PARSON AND CLERK.

Victorian Staffordshire figures. *See* STAFFORDSHIRE FIGURES.

Vieux Paris (French). A vague dealer's term for hard-paste porcelain ware attributable to any of the many factories active in and around Paris during the late 18th and early 19th centuries. *See* PORCELAINE DE PARIS.

Vignette. A picture or design which shades off into the surrounding area without a fixed or well-defined border. *See* CARTOUCHE; CARTEL.

Vincennes cup. A style of small coffee-cup which is cylindrical and has no foot-ring; its height is equal to its diameter, so that its profile is square. It has an angular loop handle. Introduced at Sèvres, and also called *tasse carrée* (square cup). *See* CAN.

Vincennes flowers. (1) Painted flowers in the manner of those popular at Vincennes before the removal of the factory to Sèvres in 1756. (2) Modelled flowers made to be attached to branches, with leaves added, popular as decoration soon after 1750 and a staple production of the early Vincennes factory. *See* BOUQUET.

Vine-leaf ground. A diaper ground of rows of vine leaves connected by curving tendrils. It is found on Hispano-Moresque ware.

Violet d'évêque (French). Bishop's purple; an alternative name for AUBERGINE.

Violin. A decorative ornament in the form of a violin made in both pottery and porcelain. Early examples in delftware are from Delft, and faience and porcelain specimens exist from potteries in France. *See* MUSICAL WARE.

Virtues, The Twelve Cardinal. A set of figures or figure-groups on rococo bases, depicting the Virtues (Faith, Hope, Charity, Humility, etc.) with their attributes. They were modelled by Simon Feilner at Fürstenberg, *c.* 1760–70.

Vitreous. Having a glassy appearance and character as a result of fusion at a high temperature, i.e. as a result of some of the ingredients of the body having been vitrified.

Vitruvian scroll. A classical ornament of convoluted scrolls resembling stylized waves. Also known as the Greek wave pattern. *See* WAVE BORDER.

Vögleinkrug (German). Literally, little bird jug. A faience jug decorated with a motif of painted birds, made at Hanau, Ansbach, and Nuremberg.

Volute. A spiral curve, sometimes called a helix. *See* VOLUTE HANDLE.

Volute handle. A handle terminating in a HELIX scroll above the rim of the vessel; the type is sometimes to be found, for example, on a KRATER. *See* VASO A ROTELLE.

Von Hennicke service. A dinner-service made at Meissen for Count Johann von Hennicke (1681–1752), who was, from 1739 onwards, deputy director of the Meissen factory. The decoration includes a coat of arms within a blue and gilt scrolled mantling, with scattered flowers in the Kakiemon style (INDIANISCHE BLUMEN). The plates have a central landscape and a chocolate-coloured rim.

Vyse figures. Pottery figures made by the studio potters Charles and Nell Vyse in Cheyne Row, London, 1919–40, principally depicting gipsies and London hawkers. *See* CRIS DE LONDRES.

Vicar and Moses. Group, ht $9\frac{3}{4}$ in., probably modelled by Aaron Wood, Staffordshire, *c.* 1770. Burnap Collection, William Rockhill Nelson Gallery of Art, Kansas City, Mo.

Vyse figure. Flower-seller, 1927; ht $10\frac{3}{4}$ in. Courtesy, Sotheby's, Belgravia.

W

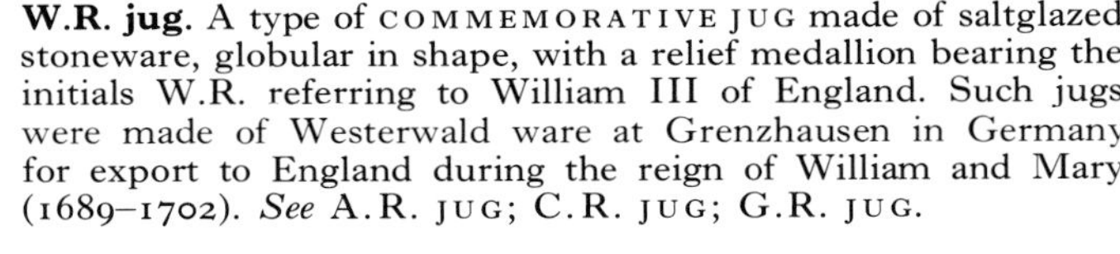

W.R. jug. A type of COMMEMORATIVE JUG made of saltglazed stoneware, globular in shape, with a relief medallion bearing the initials W.R. referring to William III of England. Such jugs were made of Westerwald ware at Grenzhausen in Germany for export to England during the reign of William and Mary (1689–1702). *See* A.R. JUG; C.R. JUG; G.R. JUG.

Wa wa. Decoration on Chinese porcelain bowl, Ming dynasty. Victoria and Albert Museum, London.

Wa wa (Chinese). Literally, playing boys. A Ming dynasty decorative subject, sometimes repeated later. The name is perhaps onomatopœic.

Waisted. Of smaller diameter in the middle than at the top or bottom.

Wakasugi ware. Japanese porcelain in the Arita style made at Wakasugi, *c.* 1810–20.

Wall-cistern. A type of CISTERN suspended from the wall by pierced holes, with a hole for a spigot. An example made of Southwark delftware is inscribed 1641.

Wall-pocket. A flower-vase made to be attached to a wall, often loosely called a cornucopia because most wall-pockets were of this shape. They occur in English creamware, agate ware, delftware, Whieldon ware, and saltglazed ware. They are sometimes in the form of a nautilus shell, especially in lustre ware, and of a human head. Also sometimes termed a wall-vase, but *see* WALL-VASE.

Wall-pocket. Cornucopia, Prattware, *c.* 1810–28. Burnap Collection, William Rockhill Nelson Gallery of Art, Kansas City, Mo.

Wall-sconce. *See* SCONCE.

Wall-vase. A Chinese vase, flat on one side, for hanging on a wall. Specimens do not seem to be earlier than the 17th century. *See* WALL-POCKET.

Walzenkrug (German). From *Walze*, a cylinder. A cylindrical mug or tankard, such as those made at Meissen during the Böttger period, *c.* 1710–19, and later.

Wappengeschirr (German). Literally, armorial service. A service decorated with painted trophies of weapons, armorial bearings, or heraldic devices. *See* MARTIAL TROPHIES.

Warbler pattern. A decorative subject depicting a long-tailed bird perched on a rush, and scattered flying insects. Used on English blue-and-white porcelain, it was copied from a Chinese prototype.

Wärmeglocke (German). Literally, warming-bell. A dome-shaped cover used for keeping hot dishes warm. Also known as a *Bratenglocke*, especially when intended for covering roast meat. They were made at Meissen, and one was included in the SWAN SERVICE.

Warming-urn. A porcelain urn with a spigot near the bottom and resting on a plinth or stand in which is a GODET for heating the contents of the vessel. They are occasionally in the form of a tall cylindrical column.

Warwick vase. A type of vase made at Worcester, *c.* 1810, and elsewhere in the form of a two-handled urn which rests on a stemmed base terminating in a square plinth. Specimens are often finely painted with topographical scenes.

Washington, Martha, service. A dinner-service of CHINESE EXPORT PORCELAIN presented in 1796 to Martha Washington. Her monogram, MW, is encircled by a gold sunburst, and there is a border of fifteen links, each link inscribed with the name of one of the (then) States of the Union. Many reproductions have been made.

Martha Washington service. Saucer from the service, Chinese export porcelain, presented in 1796. Smithsonian Institution, Washington, D.C.

Waste-mould. A plaster mould so made that it has to be destroyed in order to remove the cast. Used for the rapid casting in plaster of Paris of a clay model.

Waster. An embryo pot usually deformed in the kiln by excessive heat above the vitrification point, or ware which is defective to the point of being unsaleable and has been discarded, usually in a particular place known as a waster-heap. When found on kiln-sites wasters are valuable and often conclusive evidence for the identification and dating of wares, but some caution is necessary because wares from elsewhere which had been broken were often discarded with the rest. Chinese porcelain fragments, for instance, have been found on a Worcester waster-heap. *See* DOCUMENTARY SPECIMENS; SHARD.

Watch-stand. An ornamental object of porcelain or pottery with a circular aperture for holding and displaying a watch during the night. They were made at Sèvres, Meissen, Strasbourg, and elsewhere, usually in rococo style, as well as in English PRATTWARE and by other English factories. *See* CLOCK-CASE.

Water-dropper. An oriental vessel for the scholar's table employed in the art of painting and calligraphy for the purpose of providing water to add to the ink. Specimens are sometimes in the form of small jars or vases, and occasionally of human or animal figures. They occur in Chinese and Japanese porcelain, and also in Koryŏ celadon and Annamese ware. *See* WATER-POT.

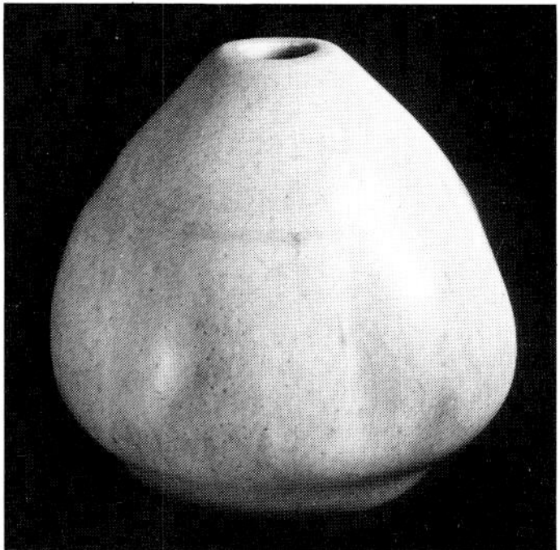

Water-dropper. Stoneware, in the form of a persimmon, with a lavender-blue glaze; Chün yao, Sung dynasty (960–1280). Courtesy, Spink & Son Ltd.

Water filter. *See* FILTER.

Water-lily service. A dinner-service of creamware for twenty-four people (over 150 pieces) made by Wedgwood at Etruria, 1806–07. It has a central design of three water-lilies, with leaves and flowers printed and painted in sepia, the flowers enamelled in pink, and the leaves veined with gold. It was perhaps inspired by a poem by Erasmus Darwin (d. 1802) extolling the water-lily, but was a commercial production and not, as has been said, made as a gift for him. One set was bought in 1807 by his son, Dr Robert Darwin. It is sometimes inaccurately called the Erasmus Darwin, the Nelumbium, or the Lotus service.

Water-lily service. Plate from the service made by Josiah Wedgwood in 1807. Courtesy, Wedgwood.

Water-pot. A type of Chinese pot for holding the water used to dissolve ink for writing or painting. *See* WATER-DROPPER.

Water-smoothed. Unglazed pottery the body of which has been smoothed by water and a sponge.

Water-tortoise. *See* MINOGAME.

Watering pail. A utensil, frequently of porcelain, usually about 10 inches in height, for watering flowers, especially those grown in JARDINIÈRES or in hot-houses. The French term is *arrosoir.* *See* ROSE-WATER SPRINKLER.

Watteau subjects. Vase and cover of *Fond Porzellan*, with decoration after Watteau, Meissen, *c.* 1745. Stadtmuseum, Cologne.

Waters, Billy. A pottery figure made *c.* 1836, depicting a Negro fiddler with a wooden leg – a well-known London character in the early 19th century. It was copied in porcelain at Derby, *c.* 1870.

Watteau subjects. Pastoral scenes occurring as painted decoration on porcelain, and taken from French engravings of paintings by Antoine Watteau (1684–1721). They occur sporadically on Meissen porcelain from *c.* 1740 onwards, but did not become really popular till after 1745. Similar subjects taken from paintings by Nicolas Lancret (1690–1743), and scarcely distinguishable from the work of Watteau, are usually included in this category. *See* TENIERS SUBJECTS.

Wattle medallion. A medallion in the form of a network of interlaced twigs.

Wave border. A border pattern in undulating form made by a continuous centre line forming two rows of scrolls, the upper row being made to contrast with the lower row by use of different colours or shadings. Similar to a VITRUVIAN SCROLL.

Wavy ray border. Same as SAN BERNARDINO RAYS.

Wedging. (1) The method of freeing potter's clay of air pockets and making it into a homogeneous mass ready for THROWING, by cutting it into slices and forcibly throwing it on to a table to re-incorporate it into a mass. The process is repeated until it is of suitable consistency. *See* PUGGING. (2) The process of intermingling clays of different colours in the making of SOLID AGATE WARE.

Wedgwood-Arbeit (German). Literally, Wedgwood-work. Wares in imitation of Wedgwood JASPER made at Meissen during the Marcolini period, 1774–1814. They were made of porcelain, with white reliefs usually against a blue ground.

Wedgwood coloured bodies. Several types of coloured bodies created by the Wedgwood factory by staining creamware (Queen's ware) with metallic oxides. The factory introduced a sage-green Flemish ware, *c.* 1805, which was called Celadon, one of lavender, *c.* 1850, and one of a champagne colour (like its cane-ware), *c.* 1930. Many such wares are undecorated, but a variety of designs have also been used. *See* DRY BODY.

Wet-drug jar. Maiolica, with banded spout, Tuscany, c. 1530. Victoria and Albert Museum, London.

Wedgwood lustre. LUSTRE WARE made by Josiah Wedgwood, who was among the earliest to employ this technique in Staffordshire. He took out his first patent for an Encaustic Gold Bronze in 1769. There are notes by his partner, Thomas Bentley, in 1772, suggesting that a copper lustre was then the subject of experiment, and metallic lustring was perhaps being employed experimentally as early as 1776. Nevertheless, the first commercial production does not seem to have taken place till after 1787, and the first dated examples were not made till 1805. These are decorated with gold lustre. Pink, purple, or moonlight lustre wares were made in a limited quantity, the lustre applied so that it appears to have been splashed on. Shell-shaped dishes and vessels thus decorated are the most frequent. Wares decorated with a gold and silver coloured lustre are rare. About 1862 attempts were made, with the aid of an Italian workman, to reproduce GUBBIO LUSTRE and the lustre of HISPANO-MORESQUE WARES. *See* DRAGON LUSTRE; FAIRYLAND LUSTRE.

Wedgwood ware. A term frequently applied only to JASPER ware developed by Josiah Wedgwood, but which properly includes many other wares made by this factory, including

Queen's ware. tortoiseshell ware, agate ware, black basaltes, Etruscan ware, *rosso antico*, Parian porcelain, variegated ware, cauliflower ware, Wedgwood coloured bodies, and Wedgwood lustre, all of which are closely identified with Wedgwood although they were also made elsewhere. Porcelain (bone-china) was made by Josiah Wedgwood II from 1812 to 1829 in limited amounts, but since 1878 it has become an important part of the factory's production. *See* OLD WEDGWOOD WARE; LESSORE WARE; WHIELDON-WEDGWOOD WARE.

Weidenmuster (German). Literally, willow pattern. The term in relation to Meissen porcelain has nothing to do with the later WILLOW PATTERN of the Staffordshire potters. It refers to the subject of decoration.

Weissenfels, Duke of, series. A set of COMMEDIA DELL' ARTE FIGURES, made by P. Reinicke at Meissen between 1743 and 1745 for the Duke of Weissenfels, partly from engravings by Joullain and partly from those by Callot in Riccoboni's *Histoire du Théâtre Italien*, 1728.

Well. The depressed central portion of a plate or dish within the LEDGE or MARLI. *See* CAVETTO.

Well-platter. A platter having a depressed well at one end for holding gravy. *See* TREE-PLATTER.

Wellington, Duke of, services. Services made for presentation to the first Duke of Wellington, and now preserved at Apsley House, London. *See* PRUSSIAN SERVICE; ROYAL FRENCH SERVICE; EGYPTIAN SERVICE; SAXON SERVICE.

Wellington vase. A type of tall, urn-shaped vase made by Minton; it has a spreading circular foot on a circular pedestal above a square plinth, with a narrow neck, wide collared mouth, and two animal masks at the shoulder in place of handles. It is richly ornamented with floral painting and gilding.

Welsh tailor and his family. *See* TAILOR AND WIFE, COUNT BRÜHL'S.

Westerwald ware. Stoneware made at Grenzau, Grenzhausen, and Höhr, in the district near Koblenz known as the Westerwald, by potters who migrated there from Siegburg and Raeren in the Rhineland after 1590. Wares consisted mainly of jugs, mugs, and chamber-pots, in a grey body with the addition of cobalt blue or manganese to stamped and incised designs. Similar wares are still being produced in this area. *See* NASSAU WARE; BLAUWERK; RAEREN STONEWARE; SIEGBURG WARE; COMMEMORATIVE MUGS; PEASANT DANCE JUG; WORKS OF MERCY JUG.

Wet-drug jar. A bulbous or ovoid jar, usually of tin-glazed earthenware, for syrups and electuaries. It has a handle and a spout. English 17th-century jars of this kind are usually globular, on a spreading foot. All varieties are frequently lettered with the name of a drug. It is the same as the Spanish *botijo* and the French *chevrette*, and is sometimes called a syrup jar. *See* DRY-DRUG JAR; ALBARELLO; PHARMACY WARE; FARMACIA ORSINI COLONNA DRUG-JARS.

Wheatsheaf pattern. A version of the Kakiemon TYGER AND WHEATSHEAF PATTERN in which the tiger has been omitted.

Wheel. *See* POTTER'S WHEEL; SLOW WHEEL.

Westerwald ware. Typical saltglazed stoneware jug, *c.* 1600. Victoria and Albert Museum, London.

Whieldon ware. Moulded plate decorated with polychrome glazes, Staffordshire, *c.* 1758.

Wheel-engraved. Decoration executed by cutting through the glaze into the body underneath by means of the glass-engraver's wheel. Ware thus treated commonly has a brown glaze, and is either of oriental origin (the type known as BATAVIAN WARE) or from Meissen (made during the 1720s). The work was done in Bohemia by glass-workers, or in Dutch glass-engraving studios. Meissen RED STONEWARE was also thus decorated during the early period, by glass-engravers and those working in semi-precious stones. *See* ENGRAVED DECORATION.

Wheel pattern. Same as the CATHERINE WHEEL PATTERN.

Whieldon ware. English pottery made in the middle of the 18th century by Thomas Whieldon and others. It has a cream-coloured earthenware body covered with coloured glazes derived from manganese, copper, cobalt, iron, and antimony. The colours were sponged on to the body and then covered with a clear lead glaze. The subsequent firing caused an intermingling of the colours. Also called CLOUDED WARE or TORTOISE-SHELL WARE.

White House service. Bone-china plate from the service, Wedgwood, 1903. Courtesy, Wedgwood.

Whieldon-Wedgwood ware. Earthenware made during the partnership of Josiah Wedgwood and Thomas Whieldon, much of it being experimental ware. A strong green glaze was developed that led to the production of CAULIFLOWER WARE, CABBAGE WARE, and PINEAPPLE WARE. Their pottery was located at Fenton Vivien, near Stoke-on-Trent, and operated in the period 1754–59. *See* WHIELDON WARE; WEDGWOOD WARE.

Whistle. A pottery whistle, often made in the form of a bird (*see* BIRD WHISTLE), but sometimes a cat with a whistle in the tail.

White House service. A dinner-service of bone-china made by Wedgwood for the White House during the presidency of Theodore Roosevelt in 1903. It is decorated with a colonnade border, into which is set the Great Seal of the United States in polychrome.

Whiteware. (1) White saltglazed stone ware of the 18th century. (2) Any white porcelain that has been glazed but not yet decorated. (3) White-glazed heavily potted earthenware for domestic use.

Wig-stand. Dutch delftware, with decoration in late Ming style, second half of 17th century. Victoria and Albert Museum, London.

Whorl pattern. Same as the CATHERINE WHEEL PATTERN.

Widow finial. A finial in the form of a seated woman wearing widow's attire – a bonnet and shawl, a flat-brimmed hat, a shawl over a cowl, or some such head-dress. The posture varies in different examples. One such finial was used by Josiah Wedgwood, *c.* 1775, and called a 'sibyl finial'; it has been said that it depicted a widow named Sneyd.

Widow of Zarephath. *See* ZAREPHATH, WIDOW OF.

Wig-stand. A globular stand for a wig, supported by a stem and a base. Examples were made of Dutch delftware and of faience from Rouen, Nevers, and Marseilles in the 18th century.

Wigornia. The Roman name for the settlement on the site of which the city of Worcester now stands. The word appears in moulded form on some rare early examples of Worcester porcelain, *c.* 1752. Wares resembling these early pieces are termed 'Wigornia type'.

William III. (1) An equestrian earthenware figure of William III in the guise of a Roman emperor, his charger in a rearing attitude with its forelegs supported on ROCKWORK. It was modelled by Ralph Wood I, *c.* 1765. It is sometimes thought to depict the Duke of Cumberland. (2) A portrait painted on English delftware. (3) A bust in Chelsea white porcelain.

Williams, Hanbury, service. A dinner-service made at Meissen and presented by Augustus III, Elector of Saxony, to the British ambassador to the Court of Dresden, Sir Charles Hanbury Williams, *c.* 1748. It includes figures and replicas of rustic buildings. It was later copied at Chelsea.

William III. Earthenware figure, ht 15 in., modelled by Ralph Wood I, *c.* 1765. Smithsonian Institution, Washington, D.C.

Willow pattern. A decorative subject engraved by Thomas Minton for Thomas Turner and introduced at Caughley, *c.* 1780. There are many different versions of the pattern, the more familiar of which were introduced only in the early years of the 19th century. The Chinese scene that it represents is an English invention, and the legend now attached to it was written by an English author, Ernest Bramah, *c.* 1900. The pattern has been reproduced in underglaze blue transfer-printing on English pottery and porcelain. It was used extensively from 1800 onwards by Josiah Spode, Wedgwood, Davenport, and other English factories. Chinese examples on porcelain are later than, and copied from, English prototypes. The principal variations on the later wares are to be found in the position of the pagoda and the bridge, the number of figures on the bridge, the number of apples on the tree, and the features of the fence.

Winckelmann. The Viennese term for HAUSMALER.

Windmill, The. A decorative subject on transfer-printed English porcelain which depicts a rural scene with a post windmill and formal buildings by a river. It is taken from an engraving by Robert Hancock. *See* HANCOCK ENGRAVINGS.

Wine and water vases. A pair of vases shaped as ewers on square bases and made in black basaltes by Wedgwood and Bentley at Etruria, 1778. The vases have relief figures and decoration indicating that one is for wine and the other for water; the figures are seated on the shoulder within the handle and embrace the neck, and masks are on the shoulder under the pouring lip. The wine vase, called 'Sacred to Bacchus', has a figure of Bacchus, a goat mask, and swags of vines around the body. The water vase, 'Sacred to Neptune', has a figure of Neptune and a dolphin mask, with swags of seaweed. The designs are by John Flaxman.

Wine and water vases. Black basaltes, respectively 'Sacred to Bacchus' and 'Sacred to Neptune', Wedgwood & Bentley, Etruria, 1778. Courtesy, Wedgwood.

Wine-barrel. An earthenware or porcelain barrel with a tap-hole, made by a number of factories. Some large barrels were made with a figure of a PUTTO astride, e.g. in Holland of tin-glazed earthenware. Even larger ornamental barrels of earthenware and stoneware made in England in the 19th century were spirit-barrels intended for use in taverns, and are often appropriately lettered with the name of a spirit. *See* SPIRIT-BARREL AND STAND.

Wine-bottle. A globular tin-glazed earthenware bottle usually inscribed with the name of the contents and the date, and sometimes with initials. Most specimens were made of London delftware between 1640 and 1670. They preceded glass bottles used for this purpose. *See* WINE-POT.

Wine-cistern. A type of CISTERN for serving wine.

Wine-cooler. Same as SEAU À BOUTEILLE.

Wine-cradle. A basket-like receptacle with one handle for

Wine-bottle. London delftware, ht 6 in., Burnap Collection, William Rockhill Nelson Gallery of Art, Kansas City, Mo.

holding a bottle of red wine while pouring. It was sometimes made in porcelain as part of an elaborate dinner service, such as the SWAN SERVICE. The German term is *Flaschenhalter*.

Wine-ewer. An oriental vessel for warming and serving wine, often similar in form to a globular teapot except that the spout is attached near the top of the body. They were made in China and Japan, especially in the 17th century, and some were perhaps copied from metal *saké* pots. The handle usually arches over the top in the form known as a BAIL-HANDLE. Another later type, which is PEAR-SHAPED, was originally inspired by a Middle Eastern spouted ewer used for the same purposes.

Wine-flask. A flask usually of tin-enamel earthenware, for carrying small quantities of wine. It often had two lugs for a carrying strap (as on a PILGRIM-FLASK) and at the top a small drinking orifice.

Wine-glass cooler. Same as a MONTEITH.

Wine-label. A small plaque suspended by a chain around the neck of a wine-bottle or decanter, and lettered with the name of the contents, or left blank, for a name to be inscribed. Known in silver from *c.* 1740, and in Battersea enamel on copper from 1753, examples in pottery and porcelain were made from later in the 18th century, mainly in Staffordshire. Also known as a wine-ticket or bottle-label. *See* BIN-LABEL.

Wine-pot. A type of white jug, globular in form, with a narrow base and a narrower neck, which has a small loop handle. They were made of English delftware, *c.* 1640–70, and are usually inscribed Claret, Sack (sherry), or Whit (white wine). *See* WINE-BOTTLE. The oriental WINE-EWER can be designated a wine-pot with equal accuracy when it is in the form commonly employed in the West for a teapot, which was derived from it. *See* VASO SENZA BOCCA.

Wine-taster. A small shallow cup, about 3 inches wide, with one handle, like the French *tastevin*. They were made at Worcester, Caughley, and Derby. *See* TEA-MEASURE.

Wine-ticket. Same as WINE-LABEL.

Wing-handle. A flat, vertical wing-shaped handle set at a right angle to the body of a vase as on some rare examples of HISPANO-MORESQUE WARE. *See* ALHAMBRA VASE.

Wishbone handle. A handle in the form of a wishbone, with the point at the top.

Witch-bottle. A term for the BELLARMINE derived from the fact that some examples have been excavated containing objects used in the practice of witchcraft.

Wochenterrine (German). Literally, week's tureen. A large oval tureen with side handles and a domed cover. Porcelain examples are known with cover and stand, some made at Meissen. They also occur in faience and *faïence fine*.

Wombwell's Menagerie. *See* POLITO'S MENAGERIE.

Wood-family ware. Earthenware made by members of the Wood family of Burslem, Staffordshire, from the middle of the 18th century. Aaron Wood (1717–85) was a skilled modeller and mould-maker, and his brother Ralph (1715–72) is equally highly regarded for his finely modelled figures. High-temperature colours, derived from metallic oxides, like those used by Thomas Whieldon (*see* WHIELDON WARE), were still used by the Woods but, instead of the haphazard placing of colours to be taken up by the glaze, Ralph Wood I appears to have coloured his glazes and applied them where they were best suited, using an effective pale manganese-purple to produce flesh tints. His son, Ralph Wood II (1748–95), at first continued this manner of colouring, but adopted enamels for his figures and TOBY JUGS. Enoch Wood (1759–1840), a son of Aaron Wood, was an extremely fine modeller, and was probably responsible for some of the Wood figures while in partnership with Ralph Wood II. Many of the later figures are painted with enamel colours in the manner of contemporary porcelain. *See* STAFFORDSHIRE FIGURES.

Wood forms. Pottery objects imitating or moulded from wooden originals, e.g. SCHNELLEN of Rhenish stoneware. *See* TREE-TRUNK.

Wine-flask. Faience, width 12 in., Talavera, Spain, late 17th century. Courtesy, Newman & Newman Ltd, London.

Worcester dragon. A decorative design, based on the Chinese dragon, employed at Worcester as porcelain decoration, to be distinguished from the BROSELEY BLUE DRAGON and the BOW DRAGON.

Workman's mark. A mark on ceramic ware indicating the identity of the workman who potted or decorated it. They were primarily for factory use, and except for such factories as Sèvres, where the names of some of the workmen are known, they are not usually identifiable. At Sèvres, *c.* 1755, a dark-blue dot mark on the base warned the workmen at the kiln to exercise special care when firing a piece so marked. *See* PAINTER'S MARK; POTTER'S MARK; MODELLER'S MARK; SCRATCHED CROSS WARE.

Works of mercy jug. A drinking jug with a central encircling frieze depicting works of mercy. Such jugs were made of brown stoneware at Raeren, and of grey stoneware at Grenzhausen in the 16th and 17th centuries. *See* WESTERWALD WARE.

Wine-taster. Porcelain cup with moulded decoration, Worcester (First period). Courtesy, Sotheby's.

Wreathing. Spiral rings, slightly indented, around the inside of some hollow pottery forms made by the fingers of the potter as he shaped the piece on the potter's wheel. Wreathing is commonly seen on some delftware. It is also a distinguishing mark of certain Plymouth and Bristol porcelain of the 18th century, where it is often found in conjunction with a handle which is slightly askew.

Wrotham ware. Pottery made in England at Wrotham, Kent, from 1612 to 1710. The body was coarse reddish clay decorated with slip and then covered with a transparent lead glaze which gave it a rich yellow tone. The ware included jugs, posset-pots, tygs, dishes, cups, and cradles.

Wu-chin. The Chinese term for MIRROR-BLACK GLAZE.

Wu-ts'ai (Chinese). Five-colour decoration used during the Ming dynasty (1368–1642). Especially popular during the reign of Wan Li (1573–1619), this decorative scheme originated earlier in the Ming dynasty. The characteristic colours are underglaze cobalt blue, in conjunction with iron-red, turquoise, yellow, and green enamels. *See* TOU-TS'AI.

Wurstkrug (German). Literally, sausage jug. A type of jug in the form of two rings which cross each other at right angles, made of Rhenish stoneware in the 17th century.

Y

Yang-yin. One of a pair of blue-and-white porcelain vases decorated with *yang-yin* symbols below a band with *t'ao t'ieh* decoration; reign of K'ang Hsi (1662–1722). Courtesy, Spink & Son Ltd.

Yellow tiger pattern. Porcelain plate and covered sugar-bowl with painted decoration, Meissen, KHC mark, *c.* 1740–50. Courtesy, Christie's.

Y-diaper ground. A diaper ground made up of repeating figures shaped like a letter *Y*. Used on Chinese porcelain.

Yaki (Japanese). A term meaning ware, equivalent to the Chinese *yao*.

Yang-ts'ai (Chinese). Literally, foreign colour. A term applied by the Chinese to the rose enamel of the FAMILLE ROSE palette which was introduced into China by Jesuit missionaries late in the 17th century. *See* PURPLE OF CASSIUS.

Yang-yin (Chinese). A symbol referring to the male-female principle and the duality of nature, sometimes used in the decoration of Chinese porcelain. It was often employed in conjunction with the PA-KUA. It is in the form of a circle crossed by a line with a double curve, giving it somewhat the appearance of two tadpoles, head to tail, of contrasting colours.

Yao (Chinese). A term meaning ware, as in *Chün yao.* It can also mean the kiln in which the ware was fired. The Japanese equivalent is *yaki*.

Yao-pien (Chinese). A FLAMBÉ or transmutation glaze, due to firing in a reducing atmosphere.

Yayoi ware. Pottery made in Japan, *c.* 300 BC–AD 300. In contrast to JOMON WARE, it features flowing shapes, bright colours, and a greater variety of forms, mostly with sparse surface ornament.

Yellow. A colour used in the decoration of pottery and porcelain produced, for the most part, from antimony oxide. There are various shades and hues: burnt Siena; FISH-ROE YELLOW (mustard yellow); IMPERIAL YELLOW; JAUNE JONQUILLE; NANKING YELLOW; and lemon-yellow. *See* YELLOW WARE; CANARY LUSTRE.

Yellow tiger pattern. A Kakiemon pattern depicting a yellow tiger partly encircling a bamboo shoot and facing a flowering prunus. The Meissen version includes *indianische Blumen* strewn on the ground; it was first used there in 1738 and was called the *gelber Löwe* (yellow lion) pattern.

Yellow ware. Earthenware (creamware or pearlware) dipped in a yellow glaze so that the surface, inside and outside (except for any reserved areas), is entirely yellow. Some hollow-ware examples were not dipped with the yellow glaze but coloured by hand on the outside only. The hues of the colour vary considerably due to differences in the amount of each ingredient of the glaze used at various potteries. The decoration of the ware is in lustre (usually by the resist process but sometimes applied freehand) or by transfer-printing, stencilling, enamel hand painting, and applied relief ornament, or a combination of these processes. The best examples were made *c.* 1780–1835 by many potteries in England and Wales; some similar ware was made at Creil, France. Examples are usually jugs, but the ware is found in many forms. It is often called 'canary yellow' and 'canary lustre'; these terms are doubly inaccurate, as the colour varies from a canary hue, and also the lustre (platinum resist) is 'silver', not yellow.

Yen-yen (Chinese). A baluster vase with a long neck and a trumpet mouth and sometimes two side handles midway up the neck. Some copies were made in delftware.

Yi dynasty (Korean). Wares made during this period (1392–1910) include a continuation of the MISHIMA technique, and a heavy, clumsily potted porcelain with a greyish or greenish-blue glaze, well painted in a free style with a blackish underglaze blue. The MEI-PING form is fairly common, and is sometimes decorated with incised and carved ornament under the glaze. Small covered boxes in a porcelain recalling the YING CH'ING types are decorated in the same way. Korean wares usually show spur-marks on the base.

Yi-hsing. A Chinese kiln-site in Kuangtung province at which red stoneware was made. This stoneware, exported to Europe in the 17th century, was the inspiration for certain European wares of considerable importance, such as that of Meissen, the Elers brothers, Arij de Milde, etc. *See* ELERS REDWARE; MILDE, ARIJ DE, STONEWARE; RED PORCELAIN; RED STONEWARE; BOCCARO WARE.

Yi-hsing. Stoneware wine-pot with reeded body and bamboo handle and spout, 18th century.

Ying-ch'ing (Chinese). Literally, shadowy blue. A type of early porcelain derived from a ware made originally in the T'ang dynasty. It is translucent, with a brilliant glaze which is bluish-grey or bluish-green on the early examples, and a purer blue later, although the colour is always very pale. The paste is of a faint reddish-biscuit colour, and fractures show a sugary texture. The decoration is usually of floral motifs, carved or incised. Most surviving specimens belong to the Sung dynasty. The kilns were located at a number of sites in Kiangsi province. The term itself is a recent invention of Chinese dealers, the traditional term being CH'ING-PAI.

Ying-pau. The Chinese term for pure white.

Yu. The Chinese term for glaze.

Yu-ch'ui p'ing. The Chinese term for a ROULEAU VASE.

Yüan dynasty. The Mongol dynasty (1280–1368) in China which followed the Sung dynasty. The most widely known of the emperors of this period is Kublai Khan who held court at Shang-tu (the Xanadu of Coleridge). His court was visited by Marco Polo. The period produced wares in Sung styles, especially celadons, and saw the development of porcelain decorated in underglaze blue, one or two dated specimens of which survive. Underglaze copper red was also first used during this period, and Persian influence is often to be seen. *See* MING DYNASTY.

Yüeh yao. Water-pot in the form of a lion, stoneware with celadon glaze, 3rd–6th century. Victoria and Albert Museum, London.

Yüeh-pai (Chinese). Literally, moon white. Greyish- or bluish-white glaze of the 18th century. *See* CLAIR DE LUNE.

Yüeh yao (Chinese). A fine stoneware covered with a celadon glaze of variable colour made at Yüeh Chou (Shensi province) during the T'ang dynasty, but first occurring at an earlier date. It has affinities with NORTHERN CELADON.

Z

Widow of Zarephath. Glazed earthenware figure modelled by Ralph Wood II, *c.* 1790. Fitzwilliam Museum, Cambridge.

Zaffer (sometimes **zaffre**). A word of Arabic origin referring to an impure cobalt oxide obtained by fusing the mineral ore with sand. It was used in the manufacture of SMALT, and as an underglaze colouring agent for some blue-and-white porcelain, producing a dark, impure blue.

Zapotec pottery. *See* CENTRAL AMERICAN POTTERY.

Zarephath, Widow of. A figure, modelled by Enoch Wood and others, depicting this biblical character (1 Kings xvii, 9–24), usually seated in front of a tree and holding a bundle of faggots, with her son by her side and a barrel of meal and cruse of oil at her feet. Sometimes she is one of a pair, or features in a figure group, with Elijah being fed by ravens. Examples were also made, with variations, in the early 19th century of earthenware in Staffordshire and of PRATTWARE. In some cases the base is inscribed 'Wid(d)o(w)'.

Zig-zag fence pattern. A decorative transfer-printed pattern depicting a five-section zig-zag fence among trees and flowers in an oriental garden, with two ducks flying above. Adapted in the 18th century from a Chinese pattern, versions are found on English blue-and-white porcelain, especially at Worcester and Lowestoft, and also at Caughley and Derby. It is sometimes termed the Fence pattern.

Zwiebelmuster (German). Literally, onion pattern. A decorative underglaze blue pattern introduced at Meissen by J.G. Höroldt, *c.* 1735, and later modified by J.J. Kändler. It depicts a central motif of asters and peonies, around which are several stylized peaches which have been mistaken for onions. It was originally adapted from a Chinese ASTER PATTERN, and has been extensively copied elsewhere. *See* MUSTER; BLAUBLÜMCHENMUSTER.

Zwiebelmuster. Porcelain plate with underglaze blue decoration, Meissen, *c.* 1740. Private Collection. Courtesy, Dr Siegfried Ducret, Zürich.